# THE BILL JAMES BASEBALL ABSTRACT 1983

# THE BILL JAMES BASEBALL ABSTRACT 1983

**Bill James**

BALLANTINE BOOKS NEW YORK

 Published in the United States by Ballantine Books, a division of Random House, Inc., New York, and simultaneously in Canada by Random House of Canada Limited, Toronto.

Library of Congress Catalog Card Number: 82-90833

ISBN 0-345-30367-9

Book design by Gene Siegel

Cover design by James R. Harris

Cover photograph by David Spindell

Manufactured in the United States of America

First Edition: April 1983

10 9 8 7 6 5 4 3 2 1

The 1983 *Baseball Abstract* is dedicated to all of the early readers of the book, to all of the people who helped in one way or another to bring it along to where it was profitable in the ordinary sense, including but not limited to:

Dallas Adams
Roger Angell
Barry Bernstein
John Billheimer
Michael Boyce
Robert Bucknam
Walt Campbell
Jim Carothers
Neal Conan
D.L. Craw
Bob Creamer
John Davenport
Bob Davids
Ted deVries
William Elander
Jack Etkin
Tom Evans
Dave Feldman
Mike Fitzgerald
Rob Fleder
Ted Fontenot
Joel Fritz
Warner Fusselle
Cappy Gagnon
Michael Garvey
Jerry Gibbons
Thomas Gill
Janet Gold
William Goldman
Warren Goldstein
Laurie Graham
Gary Groelle
Rob Harris
Lawrence Hayden
Alan Hendricks
Randy Hendricks
Art Hill
Ron Howard
Charles Huisken
Mark Isaacs
Bryan Johnson
Warren Johnson
Bob Jones
Dave Jones
Stan Jones
Howard Katz
Chris Ketzel
Merl Kleinknecht
Rob Klugman
David Lander
Ward Larkin
David Longhurst
John Lungstrum
Norman Mailer
Dan Marlowe
Marc Maturo
Thomas May
Tom Messner
Vic Meyer
Mike Myers
Tom Nahigan
Sam Narotsky
John Nordin
Richard O'Brien
Dan Okrent
Pete Palmer
Mark Pankin
Bill Parks
Jon Prince
Barry Rubinowitz
Bob Salatino
Mary Jane Schaefer
Philip Schaefer
Mark Schewe
Eli Schleifer
Howard Schwartz
Paul Schwarzenbart
Larry Smith
Randy Spence
Jeff Spivak
Lewis Stadlen
Arthur Susskind
Dennis Telgemeier
Stats Tiebout
Lambros Touris
Kenny Trainor
John Vrabel
Glen Waggoner
Mark Wilensky
Craig Wright
and
Susie

# CONTENTS

# Acknowledgments


| Pos | Player (Type of Assistance Acknowledged) |
| --- | --- |
| 1B | Randy Lakeman (Statistician) |
| 2B | Peter Gethers (Editor) |
| 3B | Craig Wright (Sabermetrician) |
| SS | Dan Okrent (Editor) |
| LF | Pete Palmer (Research) |
| CF | Walt Campbell (Statistician) |
| RF | Liz Darhansoff (Agent) |
| C | Bob Jones (Research) |
| | |
| P | Susie McCarthy (Multi-faceted) |
| RP | D, T, I, the S and LF (Same) |

# NOTICE

I am thinking of starting a newsletter. Such details of the project as length, frequency, exact contents, price, and title have yet to be nailed down. What can safely be said about it, if it does come about, is that it will cover the same sorts of subjects and that part of it (my part) will use the same general approach as is used in this book, only it would be rather more topical. If the San Diego Padres are in first place at the All-Star break, a late July issue might include a look at the phenomena, an attempt to understand how they are winning, an evaluation of their chances of staying up.

If you would be interested in subscribing to such a newsletter please fill in your name and address below and send it to Ballantine. The address is:

Bill James Newsletter
c/o Ballantine Books
201 East 50th St.
New York, N.Y. 10022

NAME: ______________________________

ADDRESS: ______________________________

CITY ______________________________

STATE: ______________ ZIP ______________

# INTRODUCTION

Hi. My name is Bill James, and I'm an eccentric. If you don't believe I'm an eccentric, just go to the library and look me up. The reason that I am eccentric is that I spend all of my time analyzing baseball games. Well, not *all* of my time—I have a wife to neglect—but most all of my time. I count all kinds of stuff that lots of people are sort of interested in, but nobody in his right mind would actually bother to count. I devise theories to explain how things in baseball are connected one to another. Once a year I gather all of my notebooks together, translate the work that I have done into English, lash it into some semblance of an organized pattern (I require the help of two editors to accomplish this), and give it to my wife. She types it up or something and sends it off to my publisher. This is called the *Baseball Abstract*.

The subject of the book is sabermetrics; SABR for the Society for American Baseball Research, Metrics for measurement, with an extra "e" thrown in so you can pronounce it. Most of the time, anyway; sometimes I take off on a tangent and start writing about Princess Margaret, call-in shows or shark jokes. But what the hell, sportswriters will stop writing about baseball at the drop of a hat and start writing about economics, drugs or lawsuits, and they don't feel bad about it. Indeed, what is eccentric about my writing about baseball is that *I write so much about baseball* and sometimes will examine the tiniest parts of the game in exhaustive detail without seeming to feel any compulsion to leave the subject and start writing about leadership or character or personality conflicts or go do an interview somewhere.

Sabermetrics is the mathematical and statistical analysis of baseball records. Suppose, if you will—fantasize to get the full effect—that you have just been named the general manager of your local baseball team. The team is at a critical moment in its history, possessing obvious talent but plagued by mysterious ills that keep slapping it back into the second division. You've been hired to solve those problems. The team employs scouts, coaches, administrators, secretaries, salary negotiators, players, statisticians, PR people, trainers and film analysts. Every one of those people thinks that they know exactly what you should do. And no two of them agree.

The team doesn't turn many double plays, so one of them thinks you should trade the second baseman to get somebody else, and another guy says that instead you should give a shot to the fellow who is playing second base for you in AAA. The first guy says that if you do that you won't be able to trade the incumbent second sacker for a sack of beans after he has lost his job to a minor leaguer, and the second guy says that you need to keep him for backup insurance. Then a third guy tells you that you shouldn't be worrying about the second baseman because he's a good hitter for the position, but a fourth says that baseball is 90% pitching and defense so it doesn't matter that much what he hits. The film analyst chimes in that what you should do is try to correct the second baseman's mechanics on the DP; a coach replies that that should have been done years ago, at the AA level, and that the guy's getting $400,000 a year and he's not going to go out and take extra infield practice. Then somebody else says that it's not really his fault; it's the shortstop. Another opinion is that the team would turn more double plays if somebody would just cheat toward second more with a runner on.

One opinion is that the reason you don't turn many double plays is that you have a lot of high-ball pitchers on the team and so you shouldn't worry about it. Another is that you're losing double plays because the ground crew keeps the grass too long, but another guy says that our team grounds into more double plays than our opponents, so if we cut the grass any shorter we'll just make the problem worse. A scout says that you should trade the second baseman because he's 31 years old and his trade value is going to drop like a rock in a couple of years anyway, but another one says that's a myth.

And remember, when you get this problem sorted out, you've got 45 more just like it.

So what do you do? You don't want to know what people say; you are, in fact, sick to death of hearing what people say. You want to know what the facts are, and once in awhile you can even dream of moving beyond what the facts are and learning what the truth is. You want to be able to evaluate the chance that the AAA player is going to make it. You want to be able to compare the risks involved in trading the incumbent and benching him. You want to know exactly what would happen if you really did cut the damned grass. And if one more person says that baseball is 90% pitching, you want to shoot him.

What you want, Mr. General Manager, is sabermetrics. Sabermetrics is the field of knowledge which has grown from many hundreds of studies that have been made in an attempt to evaluate objectively all of these things which people say. This book is about *my* research, about my work in sabermetrics, with a few selections included discussing the work of my friends and colleagues, men like Pete Palmer, Craig Wright and Dallas Adams.

Like baseball itself, this book is just here for you to enjoy. This is a book for those who can abandon themselves to the game, for those to whom the hurried and casual summaries of journalism are a daily affront. It is not for people who already know all about baseball, but for those who want to learn.

This edition of the *Abstract* is the seventh in a series dating back to 1977. The book is divided into four parts, which are profoundly labeled Part I, Part II, Part III and Part IV. Each of these four parts is divided into many other parts, most of which are also labeled, and many of these are subdivided into smaller parts and still smaller parts and . . . face it, this book has more subdivisions than Houston. The first part, for example, is about the methods that I use to analyze baseball. It's called *Methods.* This is divided into two parts, *Old Business* and *New Business*, for the convenience of the people who read the book last year and don't necessarily want to sit through another explanation of the value approximation method. The old business section is divided into subsections with titles like *Methods That Are Used to Analyze and Evaluate Offense*. There are eight methods introduced in that section, each given its own little heading.

The *Methods* section is much smaller this year, and the sections on the teams and the players are much larger. Having introduced the methods, explained them and defended them a year ago, I was free to spend more time this year applying them, looking at the teams and the players in specific terms. Sections II, *The Teams,* and III, *The Players,* are subdivided into tiny bits, too, but I'm not going to explain all that, because most intelligent people can figure out for themselves that John Lowenstein is a player and would be listed under left fielders, and the Cincinnati Reds are a baseball team of sorts and would be listed in the National League, Western Division, and dumb people don't like the book anyway, so there's no point in trying to explain anything to them. The fourth section consists of general essays not prompted by any one player or team.

The book really has no true beginning, no middle or end, no natural order, any more than a series of conversations that you might have with a friend would have a beginning, a middle or an end. Feel free to start in the middle of the book if you want to. After all, I do.

SECTION

# I

# METHODS

# OLD BUSINESS

The first problem confronting each year's edition of the *Baseball Abstract* is how to explain the things which I have explained before without repeating myself. Back in the days when I was self-publishing the *Abstract*, my solution to this was simply not to explain them at all. I figured that anybody who really wanted to could figure things out. The number of people who really wanted to, unfortunately, was not very large.

I use about a hundred terms and expressions which, unless you have read a previous edition of the *Abstract*, you won't recognize. (A Philadelphia writer sarcastically dubbed the *Abstract* "Baseball's new Bible of Newspeak." I've been trying to persuade Ballantine to include this among the cover quotes.)

In the next few pages, I am going to give very brief definitions of the tools that I use to analyze a baseball team. Some of these tools are formulas, some of them are simply counts of things, some of them are sort of schematic layouts of a baseball team. The methods can be broken down into five general classes:

1) tools that are used to analyze and evaluate hitters;
2) tools that are used to analyze and evaluate pitching;
3) tools that are used to analyze and evaluate defense;
4) tools that are used to analyze and evaluate careers; and
5) tools that are used to compare teams as a whole.

# 1) TOOLS THAT ARE USED TO ANALYZE AND EVALUATE HITTERS

**RUNS CREATED**

Figuring the number of runs created is the beginning of the method that I use to evaluate a hitter. It is my belief that a hitter's job is to create runs, and with that in mind I searched for several years to find a formula which would take the player's totals of singles, doubles, home runs, etc. and translate them into a number of runs. I eventually found a very simple formula which does this with astonishing accuracy. That formula is:

$$\frac{(\text{Hits} + \text{Walks})\,(\text{Total Bases})}{\text{At Bats} + \text{Walks}} = \text{Runs}$$

The way that we know this formula works is by applying it to team and league stats. For example, the best offense in the American League (the offense which scored the most runs) in 1982 was that of the Milwaukee Brewers; the worst, that of the Texas Rangers. The Brewers had 1599 hits, drew 484 walks, totaled 2606 bases, and had 5733 at bats:

$$\frac{(1599 + 484)\,(2606)}{5733 + 484} = 873$$

The Brewers actually scored 891 runs. The Rangers' offensive offense, on the other hand, had a formula projection of 598 runs, and actually scored 590. Because the formula works for teams and for leagues, we assume that it works for individual players as well. If you figure the number of runs created by each member of a team and add them together, you get something very close to the number of runs that the team will actually have scored.

This is a version of the formula that we use when figuring runs created for old-time players or others for whom caught-stealing totals are not available. The stolen-base version of the formula, which is the one in use throughout most of this book, adjusts each element of the formula for stolen-base gains or caught-stealing losses:

$$\frac{(H + W - \text{Caught Stealing})\ (TB + .7\ \text{Stolen Bases})}{AB + W + \text{Caught Stealing}}$$

The major league players creating the most runs in 1982 are listed below

**AMERICAN LEAGUE**

| | Player, Team | Runs Created |
|---|---|---|
| 1. | Robin Yount, Milwaukee | 142 |
| 2. | Dwight Evans, Boston | 130 |
| 3. | Hal McRae, Kansas City | 120 |
| 4. | Eddie Murray, Baltimore | 119 |
| 5. | Cecil Cooper, Milwaukee | 118 |
| 6. | Toby Harrah, Cleveland | 118 |
| 7. | Doug DeCinces, California | 116 |
| 8. | Paul Molitor, Milwaukee | 116 |
| 9. | Brian Downing, California | 110 |
| 10. | Andre Thornton, Cleveland | 108 |

**NATIONAL LEAGUE**

| | Player, Team | Runs Created |
|---|---|---|
| 1. | Al Oliver, Montreal | 124 |
| 2. | Pedro Guerrero, Los Angeles | 118 |
| 3. | Dale Murphy, Atlanta | 114 |
| 4. | Mike Schmidt, Philadelphia | 113 |
| 5. | Jason Thompson, Pittsburgh | 111 |
| 6. | Leon Durham, Chicago | 107 |
| 7. | Gary Carter, Montreal | 105 |
| 8. | Andre Dawson, Montreal | 105 |
| 9. | Bill Madlock, Pittsburgh | 104 |
| 10. | Bill Buckner, Chicago | 100 |

## RUNS CREATED PER GAME

Runs created per game means runs created per 25 outs using the nonstolen-base version of the formula, runs created per 25.5 outs using the stolen-base version. We use 25 or 25.5 outs rather than the 27 that make up a full game because a certain number of these 27 disappear from the traditional stats by runners being removed untimely from the base paths. For example, Rickey Henderson created 93 runs in 1982 while using 435 outs (393 outs while hitting, 42 more by being caught stealing):

$$\frac{93 \times 25.5}{435} = 5.45$$

If an entire team were made up of Rickey Hendersons, they would score 5.45 runs per game. So Rickey's runs per (individual) game are 5.45

## OFFENSIVE WINS AND LOSSES

By putting the runs-created method together with the Pythagorean formula, we can express each player's offensive statistics in terms of the ultimate goal, wins and losses. We assume that the opposition to the hitter is the league and figure his offensive won-lost percentage by this method:

$$\frac{\text{Wins}}{\text{Losses}} = \frac{(\text{Runs Created Per Game})^2}{(\text{League Runs Per Game})^2}$$

Rickey Henderson in 1982 created 5.45 runs per game; the average American League team scored 4.48 runs per game. So his offensive won-lost percentage is

$$\frac{(5.45)^2}{(5.45)^2 + (4.48)^2} = .597$$

Since he made 435 outs and we hold him responsible for one game for each 25.5 outs, we assign Rickey Henderson 17 games. We get his offensive win and loss totals by multiplying the percentage times the number of games:

| Player | Runs Created | Outs | Offensive W/L% | Games | Wins | Losses |
|---|---|---|---|---|---|---|
| R. Henderson | 93 | 435 | .597 | 17 | 10 | 7 |

Rickey's offensive won-lost record is 10-7.

## PARK ADJUSTMENTS

This is not, however, the offensive won and lost record listed for Rickey Henderson in Part IV. As will be discussed in considerable detail as soon as we get through these explanations, ballparks have a large impact on the statistics of the players who play there. A player who creates a 5.15 runs per game in Fenway Park, where runs are plentiful and therefore less valuable, is not equal to a player who creates 5.15 runs per game in the Oakland Mausoleum, where runs are relatively hard to come by.

A chart in *Not of Any General Interest* gives the "Park Adjustment Factors" for all 26 major league parks. It adjusts for what the park does, in a sense, to change the league in which the player competes. For Oakland, it is .95179.

| League Runs per Game | | Park Adjustment Factor | | Runs per Game adjusted for park |
|---|---|---|---|---|
| 4.47709 | X | .95179 | = | 4.26125 |

This is substituted into the offensive won-lost formula. For Rickey, this becomes:

$$\frac{(5.42554)^2}{(5.42554)^2 + (4.26125)^2} = .618$$

Which changes his offensive won-lost record to 11-6.

This completes the evaluative process for the player as a hitter.

## HOME/ROAD AND LEFT-HANDED PITCHING-RIGHT-HANDED PITCHING BREAKDOWNS

Section II of the book breaks the player's performance down in two ways, detailing his home and road batting performance, and his batting record against right-handed pitchers and left-handers pitchers (RHP/LHP). The home/road data I either figure myself or have someone figure for me; for the left/right stuff I am dependent on the generosity of those who have access to the scoresheets, which accounts for some gaps in the data.

**ISOLATED POWER**

Isolated power is defined as that part of slugging percentage which is not batting average. It is extra bases per time at bat.

**POWER/SPEED NUMBER**

Power/Speed number basically is a freak show stat, the sort of thing that has little analytical value. It can be used to draw up lists, and that's about it. What it does is to form a marriage of the player's home-run and stolen-base totals. Thirty home runs and 30 stolen bases is a PSN of 30.0, 20 of each is 20.0, etc. The trick is that you have to do *both* things to rate well, as the power/speed number rates not the power or the speed, but the combination. The formula is:

$$\frac{2(HR \times SB)}{HR + SB}$$

More on PSN in Section IV.

# 2) TOOLS THAT ARE USED TO EVALUATE PITCHERS

**OPPOSITION STOLEN BASES**

I begin by counting things. I go through the box scores for every major league game, and I record several things which should be part of the official record but aren't. I count, for example, how many bases are stolen in the games started by each major-league pitcher. I use these records to evaluate how good a job the pitcher does of holding base runners close.

**DOUBLE PLAY SUPPORT**

You have heard it said that this pitcher gets a lot of ground balls, can get a double play when he needs it. I've got the data, actual counts of the number of double plays turned in the games started by each major league pitcher. The major league pitchers receiving the best double-play support in 1982 were Rick Camp of Atlanta and Rick Honeycutt of Texas; the pitchers receiving the least double play support were Len Barker of Cleveland and Doug Bird of the Cubs.

**PITCHER RUN SUPPORT**

No more need you speculate, reader, about the degree to which a particular pitcher's particular won-lost record is aided by an explosive offense or dragged down by a poor one... No, no more are you at the mercy of sympathetic commentators who try to pin the hard-luck label onto everybody who loses two games 3-2 within a month and passes along every pitcher's assurance that he would have won six more games if they had just scored four runs every time he went to the mound. No sir, now you have the facts to determine for yourself if the man is a victim or a criminal.

Well, some of the facts. Section II also tells you how many runs are scored in support of each major league starting pitcher in 1982, and provides this data back over several years for regular starters. The pitcher receiving the poorest offensive support in the major leagues in 1982 was Bruce Berenyi of the Reds, who was supported by an average of about two and a half runs a game. The most blessed pitcher was Bob McClure of Milwaukee, who had nearly six runs a game to help him to his 12-7 record.

# 3) TOOLS THAT ARE USED TO EVALUATE DEFENSE

**OPPOSITION STOLEN BASES**

As with pitchers, I count (or actually Walt Campbell counts) the number of bases stolen in the games started by each major-league catcher. In the 127 games that Lance Parrish started this year, there were 51 stolen bases by Tiger opponents, 0.40 per start. In the 35 games that he didn't start, there were 32 stolen bases, 0.91 per start. These complete records are given for all 1982 major league catchers, since 1975, in Section III, behind catcher's ratings and comments.

**RANGE FACTOR**

The defensive statistic which I will refer to the most often, probably, is range factor. Range factor is simply the number of plays made per game:

$$\frac{\text{Putouts} + \text{Assists}}{\text{Games}}$$

This simple statistic is, in most cases, an accurate reflection of the amount of ground covered by a player.

## DEFENSIVE EFFICIENCY RECORD

The team equivalent to range factor is defensive efficiency record. For each team, a defensive efficiency record (DER) is given on the appropriate division sheet. This statistic is devised to answer the question: If a ball is put into play against this defense, what percentage of the time does the defense succeed in turning that ball into an out? The San Diego Padres had a defensive efficency in 1982 of .719. This means that when a batted ball was put into play against the Padres, they succeeded in turning that ball into an out 71.9% of the time. The Mets, on the other hand, succeeded in turning hit balls into outs only 69.1% of the time.

Although this difference might seem to be small, it is small in the same way that the difference between having a team batting average of .250 and a team batting average of .280 might seem at a glance, a small difference—one hit every so many at bats. Both differences amount to a little over one hit a game. A defense that can save you one extra hit per game makes all the difference in the world to the pitcher. One hit per game is the difference between Jim Palmer and Ken Forsch; a second hit, the difference between Forsch and Alan Ripley; a third hit, the difference between Ripley and AAA:

**ALLOWED PER NINE INNINGS**

| | Hits | Walks | Home Runs | ERA |
|---|---|---|---|---|
| Jim Palmer | 7.73 | 2.50 | 0.87 | 3.13 |
| Ken Forsch | 8.88 | 2.25 | 0.99 | 3.87 |
| Alan Ripley | 9.54 | 2.79 | 0.88 | 4.26 |

## DEFENSIVE WON-LOST PERCENTAGE

In Section III, part of the player's rating is derived from the defensive won-lost percentage. Defensive won-lost percentages are derived from a series of scales, a 40 point scale, a 30 point scale, a 20 point scale and a 10 point scale. The scales are different for players at each position. An average defensive player will receive 20 points on the 40 point scale, 15 on the 30 point, 10 on the 20 point, 5 on the 10 point. The point awards are added together, and, with the insertion of a decimal point, become the player's defensive won-lost percentage. For example, Buddy Bell receives 34 points (out of a possible 40) for his range afield, 22 points (out of 30) for his fielding percentage, 15 points (out of 20) for the number of double plays he starts and 3 points (out of 10) for the defensive efficiency record of his team. These four add up to 74; his defensive won-lost percentage is .74.

A full listing of factors considered in the defensive ratings at each position is given in *Not of Any General Interest*. Also given there is an outline of the scales used.

## DEFENSIVE SPECTRUM

The defensive spectrum does not apply only to defensive questions, actually, but applies in a more general way to a wide variety of problems confronting a baseball team—to any problem, really, of talent utilization. There exists a spectrum of defensive positions, left to right, which goes something like this:

**DH 1B LF RF 3B CF 2B SS**

Catchers don't count; they are a special case. Along this spectrum, each position makes larger defensive demands than the position preceding it. Those demands, generally speaking, are for speed, agility, reaction time and throwing. This creates a much larger field of available ballplayers at the left end of the spectrum than at the right, a fact which has many important consequences in the business of building a baseball club. These begin with:

1) Players at the left end of the spectrum hit, as a whole, much more than those at the right end. This is because there are so many players available who are physically capable of playing those positions that a team can almost always find somebody who can play the position and also hit.

2) When a team has a shortage of talent—the kind of hole that can keep an otherwise solid team from contending—that hole will almost always be at the right end of the spectrum. This explains why, as is so often observed, pennant winning teams are almost always strong up the middle.

3) There is an inevitable "leftward drift" in any organization, which makes it a requisite of an intelligent trading strategy to fight against that drift.

4) The key to any player's ability to continue to play in the major leagues is his ability to be shifted leftward on the defensive spectrum as he loses range on the field. Suppose that you consider two 30-year-old third basemen of roughly equal ability, one of them a productive hitter who is solid-to-weak defensively, the other a decent hitter who is brilliant on defense. Which will play longer in the major leagues?

The hitter will. His offensive production will enable him to be shifted to first base, where he can play as long as he can hit. By age 33, the better fielder will decline from decent to marginal on offense and from brilliant to solid on defense. By age 35, he will be a former ballplayer.

## DEFENSIVE WON-LOST RECORD

Defensive won-lost records are figured by multiplying the defensive won-lost percentage times a number of games which are assigned to the defense at the position. Per 162 games played at the position, the number of defensive games assigned are:

| 1B | LF | RF | 3B | CF | 2B | C | SS |
|---|---|---|---|---|---|---|---|
| 3 | 4 | 5 | 6 | 6 | 8 | 10 | 11 |

For example, Glenn Hoffmann played 150 games at shortstop last year for Boston. He is assigned ten defensive games:

$$\frac{150 \times 11}{162} = 10.19$$

His defensive won-lost percentage is .43, so his defensive won and lost record, combining these figures, was 4-6.

# 4) TOOLS THAT ARE USED TO ANALYZE AND EVALUATE CAREERS

## CAREER RECORDS IN SEASONAL NOTATION

The bottom line of each player's record box gives the player's record in seasonal notation. The purpose of this gadget is to state the player's career record in a form that is easier to deal with, easier to understand. One hundred sixty two games is considered a "year." The first element of the player's line is the number of "years" that he has played—his career games, divided by 162. The other figures given are the number of at-bat, runs, hits, etc. that the player has had *per 162 games*.

The reason for doing this is that baseball records are understood by most of us with reference to a vast set of single-season standards, not only the major accomplishments like getting 200 hits, 100 RBI, and 37 stolen bases, but also such minor things as 30 doubles and 10 triples. Our familiarity with single-season records is so thorough that we can sense and make sense of such small differences as that between 20 and 25 doubles in a season. We don't have that kind of familiarity with career records; there aren't any standards for doubles hit per 1138 games. The technique of seasonal notation returns that advantage to the career record. For illustration, George Hendrick's career record without seasonal notations is given below:

| G | AB | R | H | 2B | 3B | HR | RBI | SB | Avg |
|---|---|---|---|---|---|---|---|---|---|
| 1463 | 5290 | 712 | 1479 | 242 | 22 | 214 | 823 | 54 | .280 |

In addition to counts of things, there are some formulas and systems which I have developed to analyze specific questions or gain access to general types of questions. We'll start with a few of the former.

## ESTABLISHED PERFORMANCE LEVELS

Established performance levels are a mathematical formulation of a common notion. We might say that Steve Carlton is an established 20-game-winner, or that Rickey Henderson has established the ability to steal over 100 bases a year, or that Steve Garvey is, or was, an established 200-hit-a-year man. There is an implied difference between a player who has done it once and a player who has established that as his normal productive function.

We derive this level, at the moment, by the following method (we'll use hits for purposes of illustration, but the same method is used for all other categories except percentage figures):

$$\frac{1(1980\text{ hits}) + 3(1981\text{ hits}) + 3(1982\text{ hits})}{6}$$

Ordinarily we would multiply the 1981 figure by 2; we use 3 there to adjust for the strike.

Robin Yount's established hit level at the moment is 186.3:

$$\frac{179 + 3(103) + 3(210)}{6} = 186.3$$

A player's established performance level in any area can never be less than 75% of his most recent total. Kent Hrbek's established home run level is 17.25, not 12.00 as would be derived from this formula.

## THE FAVORITE TOY

Established performance levels are used to make estimates of a player's chance of attaining some particular career performance level. What is Rickey Henderson's chance of stealing 1000 bases in his career? What is Robin Yount's chance of getting 3000 career hits? I try to answer those questions by use of a method known as The Favorite Toy.

The player is assigned a number of "years remaining," which is 12.0 if he is 20 years old and 6/10 of a year less for each year that he is older than 20. The player's established performance level is multiplied by his years remaining (YR) to obtain his "projected remaining performance":

| Player | Age | YR | Established Hits Level | Projected Remaining |
|---|---|---|---|---|
| Robin Yount | 26 | 8.4 | 186.3 | 1565 |
| Al Oliver | 35 | 3.0 | 201.8 | 606 |
| Steve Garvey | 33 | 4.2 | 182:3 | 766 |

The projected remaining performance is then compared to the needed performance to estimate the player's chance of reaching the goal. Robin Yount needs 1637 more hits to get 3000. The formula is:

$$\frac{\text{Projected Remaining Hits} - .5\text{ Hits Needed}}{\text{Hits Needed}}$$

Robin Yount's chance of getting 3000 career hits is estimated at 46%.

There are some other rules that are a part of The Favorite Toy which are irrelevant to most cases but absolutely necessary for a few. These are explained in *Not of Any General Interest*.

## VALUE APPROXIMATION METHOD

Finally, the Value Approximation Method. A better classification of the VAM would be not "Methods Used to Evaluate Careers" but "Methods Used to Evaluate Groups of Seasons." There are, however, no other such methods; the Value Approximation Method, as far as I know, is the only tool ever devised to deal with large groups of talent, and in particular with large groups of *unlike* talent.

The VAM evaluates individual seasons by use of a series of crude scales: A player gets 1 point for hitting over .250, 2 for over .275, 3 for over .300 . . . 7 for over .400. Other scales consider games played (1 for 10 games, 2 for 50, 3 for 100, 4 for 130), slugging percentage (1 for .300, 5 for .700), home run percentage (1 for each 2.5 HR/100 at bats), stolen bases (1 for 20, 2 for 50, 3 for 80), walks (1 for each walk per 10 at bats), RBI (1 for having more than you ought to), defensive position (1 or 2 for playing a tough one), fielding average (1 point if above average in each), and position-specific defensive skills (turning the double play, throwing out people). Bonus points are awarded for such things as getting 200 hits or leading the league in RBI. There are different scales, of course, for pitchers.

The system makes no claim to precise or absolute accuracy in specific cases; it is not uncommon for a 14-point season to turn out, on careful examination, to be better than another player's 15-point season. (It would, on the other hand, be decidedly uncommon for a 13-point season to turn out to be better, on careful examination, than a 15-point season.) The system attempts only to sort seasons into groups of obviously similar value. My basic claim is that, if you look at the seasons of a group of players who are valued at 12 or 9 or 5, or whatever, you will find them to be comparable in value.

This method is used in order to assess the total size or weight of a group of seasons. Which farm system has been the most productive in recent years? When is an average player at his peak? How good is a team or a general manager's record in trades? What are the best trading strategies? All of these questions, and many, many more, require the study of large groups of unlike seasons. The Value Approximation Method is the only tool suited to that purpose. It can provide, and it has provided, very convincing answers to questions such as these above.

### CAREER APPROXIMATE VALUE

A new wrinkle this year is Career Approximate Value. Career Value Approximations are found by writing the player's career record into seasonal notation, evaluating the other figures by the ordinary rules of Value Approximation, and multiplying by the number of years—the number of 162-year groups—that the player has played. For example, Henry Aaron's record in seasonal notation is this:

| Years | AB | R | H | 2B | 3B | HR | RBI | SB | Avg | Slugging Pct. | BB |
|---|---|---|---|---|---|---|---|---|---|---|---|
| 20.36 | 607 | 107 | 185 | 31 | 5 | 37 | 113 | 12 | .305 | .555 | 69 |

With the help of a special defensive chart given in *Not of Any General Interest*, the typical Aaron season has an approximate value of 15.75. Since he has 20.36 such seasons, his career approximate value is 15.75 × 20.36 = 321. If figured by individual seasons, his career approximate value is 319.

# 5) TOOLS THAT ARE USED TO EVALUATE TEAMS AS A WHOLE

### THE PYTHAGOREAN FORMULA

The runs-created formula translates bits and pieces of runs into whole runs. The Pythagorean method of won-lost projection translates runs into wins and losses.

The Pythagorean method predicts that the ratio between a team's wins and losses will be the same as the ratio between the square of their runs and the square of their opponent's runs.

$$\frac{\text{Wins}}{\text{Losses}} = \frac{(\text{Runs Scored})^2}{(\text{Opposition Runs})^2}$$

$$\text{Won-Lost Percentage} = \frac{(\text{Runs})^2}{(\text{Runs})^2 + (\text{Opposition Runs})^2}$$

If a team scores 800 runs in a season and allows 700, their won-lost percentage will be about .566, and so they would win about 92 games.

This method has a standard error of about 4.2 wins; we could reduce this slightly by raising runs and opposition runs to a power slightly below 2. But the gain in predictive accuracy is frankly not worth worrying about; the method works very well as it is.

# NEW BUSINESS

This section of the book has no natural order. I guess I'll do it alphabetically.

### 1) ACCOUNT-FORM BOX SCORES

An account-form box score is a method by which, in 30% less space than is used by conventional summary-form box scores, vastly more information about the game can be reported. A full explanation of this method is given in Part IV.

### 2) BALLPARK INFLUENCES

Many of you must believe that I am fascinated with the ways that ballparks shape the statistics of those who play there. Actually, I am rather more inclined to wish that the whole subject would go away, or that there were some Preparation B that we could spray on them ("Shrinks Ballpark Effects *Fast*") so that we could go on to other subjects. But there isn't, and since there isn't the subject is too important to ignore. The ways in which the ballparks alter the game and therefore the statistics of the players who play there are so massive that it is impossible to perceive the abilities of the players accurately without constantly adjusting the lens.

So I have undertaken a kind of consciousness-raising drive on the subject of ballpark effects this year, with the goal of being able to say much less about it in the future. I presented charts of data with each team which summarize the most important effects on different types of offense, on different players, and the various aspects of the park that can cause these effects.

I suppose I should say that my own awareness on this subject is fairly recent. When I began the *Abstract* in 1977, I had been a hard-core baseball fan for many years. But I still thought of ballpark effects, as I suspect many of you do yet, as a marginal effect, the sort of thing that could make a .300 hitter into a .310 hitter and give a power hitter a break on a few longballs. But as I got down more deeply into the evaluation and analysis of player records, it became clear to me that in fact it was much much more than that–that, in fact, the illusions created by park effects were so large that to spend pages and paragraphs making tiny little adjustments for the value of stolen bases or the value of walks or differing numbers of outs used, and yet to ignore these massive illusions, was ludicrous and led inevitably to serious misjudgments. As bothersome as they are, you have to deal with them.

The essential thing that I am trying to show this year is that this is not a theory or a hypothesis or abstract speculation. Fifteen years ago, when a Red Sox pitcher won a 1-0 game in Comiskey Park and said that if he pitched there all the time he'd have a 2.40 ERA just like Joel Horlen and Gary Peters and Tommy John and Wilbur Wood, it was possible to dismiss this as speculation or sour grapes or self-promotion or a gross exaggeration of the effects that a ballpark could have. Solid, comprehensive evidence on the subject was not available. Twenty years ago, when a National League slugger said that he would hit ten more home runs a season if he played in Wrigley Field, if you disagreed with him it was just a matter of you've got your theory and I've got mine. Now it's a matter of you've got your theory and I've got a stack of evidence this high to show that your theory is bunk.

I have tried this year to introduce enough of that evidence, including such things as the complete home and road records of players including Babe Ruth, Joe DiMaggio and Ted Williams, to move the discussion forward a little, and to convince finally the people who still don't believe that Yankee Stadium is tough for a right-handed batter. We've moved beyond the theory stage here;

the facts are known. I'm trying to make a few of them available to you.

I have drawn heavily, in compiling those charts and those comments, on the work of several of my friends and colleagues:

1) Pete Palmer, who figured the career home/road breakdowns that I mentioned before;

2) Craig Wright, who has done a thorough factor-by-factor analysis of the effect of each ballpark on each type of offense;

3) Paul Schwarzenbart, who has done an excellent analysis of the effect of ballparks on National League fielding records; and

4) descriptive comments from many friends of mine about the parks in the cities in which they live, such as Tom Evans in Baltimore and Barry Rubinowitz in Los Angeles, as well as, of course, comments from the players.

### 3) COOPERSTOWN'S TRAIL

Section IV reprints an essay from the 1980 *Abstract* which attempts to set up a point-value system for assessing a player's progress toward the Hall of Fame.

### 4) LATE-INNING RECORDS

A new feature this year of the division sheets are the records of each team in games in which they were ahead, tied or behind after seven innings. I figured some of these a year ago in response to the Goose Gossage number (the Yankees were 51-3 in games in which they led after seven innings), and while my review of the information was not exactly exuberant ("information marginally worth having"), I thought I would follow it for another year or so and see what came of it. What came of it were comments on San Francisco and Seattle, if nothing else.

### 5) THE LAW OF COMPETITIVE BALANCE

The law of competitive balance, in its initial stages, is a way of making sense of some observable facts. Its essential claim is that there exists in the world a negative momentum far more powerful than positive momentum, which acts constantly to reduce the differences between strong teams and weak teams, teams which are ahead and teams which are behind, or good players and poor players. The corollaries are:

1) Every form of strength covers one weakness and creates another, and therefore every form of strength is also a form of weakness and every weakness a strength.

2) The balance of strategies always favors the team which is behind.

3) Psychology tends to pull winners down and push losers upward.

This has tremendous importance for understanding what is likely to unfold during the course of a game or a season.

Long article in Section IV.

### 6) LOG5 METHOD

The log5 method is a way of gauging the odds when two known forces collide. When a .600 ballclub plays a .400 ballclub, how often should the .400 team win? You can figure this by a kind of logarithmic approach, in which you assign a team a log5 or talent weight according to their won-lost percentage. The log5 of a team is *that number which, when added to .5 and divided by the sum, produces the team's won-lost percentage*. The log5 of a .400 team is .333:

$$\frac{.333}{.500 + .333} = .400$$

The log5 of a .600 team is .750. The ratio between the wins of the two teams, matched head to head, will be the same as the ratio of their logs:

$$\frac{.333}{.333 + .750} = .308$$

And the .400 team should win 30.8% of the time.

There is both a theoretical reason why this system has to work, and strong empirical evidence that it *does* work. When I explained these things at some length, some of it unnecessary length, in the 1981 *Baseball Abstract*, the audience reacted as if I was teaching an algebra class rather than talking baseball, so I don't think I'll do that any more. But just to illustrate, how often should the Milwaukee Brewers, a .586 team, beat the Seattle Mariners, a .469 team?

| | |
|---|---|
| Log5 of Milwaukee: | .7077 |
| Log5 of Seattle: | .4416 |
| Success rate for Milwaukee: | .616 |

Actually, you can get the answer quicker, I have recently discovered, without the logarithmic step:

Winning Percentage for Team A =

$$\frac{\text{Wins A} \times \text{Losses B}}{(\text{Wins A} \times \text{Losses B}) + (\text{Wins B} \times \text{Losses A})}$$

For Milwaukee, 95-67, against Seattle, 76-86:

$$\frac{95 \times 86}{95 \times 86 + 67 \times 76} = .616$$

So Milwaukee should win about 61.6 percent of the time. If Pete Vuckovich, 18-6, is facing Rick Honeycutt, 5-17, the probability of Vuckovich winning is 91.1%:

$$\frac{18 \times 17}{18 \times 17 + 6 \times 5} = .911$$

Ignoring, for the moment, that those percentages probably do not represent their true levels of ability.

Dallas Adams, who is a far better mathematician than I am, has taken this method and in essence figured out a way to free it of the assumption that you are in a .500 league, and thus to apply it to other questions. Suppose, for example, that a .320 hitter is facing a pitcher against whom the league's batting average is .208 in a league in which the overall average is .264. What should the hitter's average be against that pitcher, not assuming that there is any particular reason why he would have trouble with him? You can figure that this way:

$$\frac{\frac{.320 \times .208}{.264}}{\frac{.320 \times .208}{.264} + \frac{.680 \times .792}{.736}}$$

The hitter should hit about .256. The formula is:

$$\frac{\frac{\text{Player's Average} \times \text{Pitcher's Average}}{\text{League Average}}}{\frac{\text{Player's Average} \times \text{Pitcher's Average}}{\text{League Average}} + \text{Same thing with everything subtracted from 1}}$$

These methods are very useful as technical controls in certain sorts of studies. For example, suppose that you are studying the question of whether or not power pitchers have an advantage against the Mets, as opposed to control pitchers, or right-handers as opposed to left-handers. Since the pitchers facing the Mets might not be a random selection of pitchers—the other teams might tend to avoid using lefthanders against them, for example—you need to adjust for the ability levels of the two groups. The log5 method makes it pretty simple to do this. How often should Bob Knepper, a 5-15 pitcher, beat the Mets, a 67-95 team?

$$\frac{5 \times 97}{5 \times 97 + 15 \times 65} = .332$$

Knepper should lift his .250 won-lost percentage to .332 against the Mets (now that's bad, when you can only expect to beat the Mets one time in three.) And thus, you can tell whether pitchers like Knepper (in whatever way) beat the Mets more often than they ought to.

**7) PERCENTAGE OF OFFENSIVE VALUE**

A new phrase which you may hear me saying this year is "Hubie Brooks' batting average accounts for 67% of his offensive value" or "Tim Wallach's batting average accounts for only 50% of his offensive value." These figures refer back to the basic design of the player's offensive ability being the product of two things: his ability to get on base and his ability to advance himself or other runners. His batting average represents a part, but only a part, of each of those.

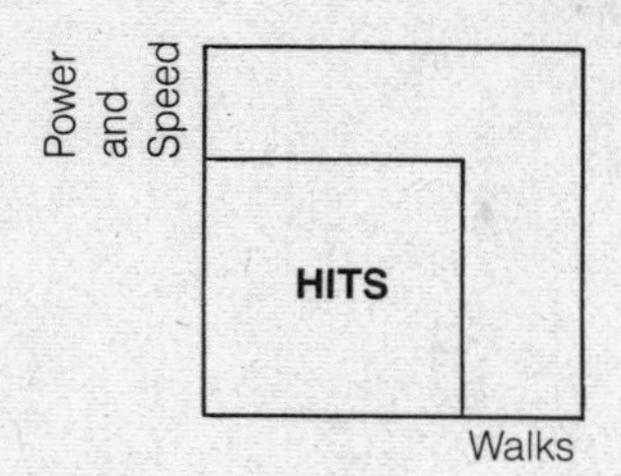


If a player has a lot of power, if he walks a lot, the percentage of this rectangle that is represented by the average alone will be small; if not, it will be large. I figure what the percentage is by figuring out how many runs the player would create if all of his hits were singles and if he had no walks or stolen base attempts. This is simply hits squared divided by at bats. So percentage of offensive value accounted for by batting average is simply hits squared divided by at bats divided by runs created.

It is a method that could easily be misused, actually. One might think that if I said about a .300 hitter that the average was 67% of his value, and about a .250 hitter that it was 50% of his value, that I would be saying that the .250 hitter was as good as the .300 hitter, since .250 is 50% of the same number that .300 is 67% of. But it doesn't work out that way. The method can't be used that literally, but it is a handy way of distinguishing between a player whose batting average represents most of his offensive value, and a player who has a broader base of offensive skills.

**8) RUNS CREATED WITH TECHNICAL ADJUSTMENTS**

An essay in section IV, again, fills you in on the details. As more awkward and time-consuming, but possibly more accurate version of the runs created formula is introduced this year. The formula is:

$$\frac{(H + W + HB - CS)\ (TB + .65\ (SB + SH + SF))}{AB + W\ SH + SF + CS + HB + GDP}$$

The meaning of all of those initials is also explained in section IV.

SECTION

# II

# THE TEAMS

## EXPLANATION OF DIVISION SHEETS

Data on the Division Sheet gives:
*First Chart*—The record of each team in the first half of the season (before the All-Star break) and after, against right-handed pitching and left-handed, in day games and at night and the total record.
*Turnarounds*—The number of times each team has come from one run behind, two runs behind, . . . seven runs behind, and the number of times they have lost after holding a lead of one run, two runs, . . . seven runs. The "total" is the total number of comebacks (or blown leads) plus one for each run of the exchange. To come from four behind and win requires five runs and thus nets five points.
*Defensive Record*—The number of bases stolen against the team, the number of double plays turned by the team, the number of assists by the team's outfielders and the number of sacrifice flies allowed by the team, the team fielding average and the defensive efficiency record and the number of runs allowed by the team. (American League Defensive records also include opposition runners caught stealing and opposition stolen base percentage.)
*Opposition Errors*—The number of errors committed by each team's opponents, and at each position. "Un" is unidentified errors, which result when a player plays two positions in a game and commits an error at one of them.
*Late-Inning Ball Clubs*—The record of each team when the team is ahead after seven innings, tied after seven or behind after seven. The "Net Change" is in half-games.

## EXPLANATION OF PLAYER AND PITCHER DATA

The player and pitcher data boxes given with each team contain the following information.
*Hitters*—Boxes are given for all of the team's regulars and any reserves who could be considered semi-regular. The data given is 1) the number of runs the player has created, 2) the player's record before the All-Star break and after the All-Star break, 3) the player's record in his home park and on the road, 4) the player's batting record against right-handed and left-handed pitching, 5) the player's 1982 record and 6) the player's career record in seasonal notation. The data on who hit what against right-handed and left-handed pitching is obtained from the teams and as such the standards of accuracy and availability, particularly in the National League, are not consistent.

The categories of the record are games, at bats, runs, hits, doubles, triples, home runs, runs batted in, stolen bases and batting average.
*Pitchers*—All available data since 1976 is given for pitchers who made 20 or more starts in 1982. The charts give, for each season, the pitcher's won-lost record, the number of games that he has started, the number of runs scored by his team in games that he started, the average number of runs per start, the number of double plays turned by his team in games that he started and the average per start and the number of bases stolen by his opponents in all of his starts and the average per start. Also given are the pitcher's record in his home park and on the road. Categories are games, innings pitched, wins, losses, won-lost percentage, earned runs allowed and ERA.

# NATIONAL LEAGUE EAST
## DIVISION SHEET

| Team | 1st | 2nd | vs. RHP | vs. LHP | Home | Road | Day | Night | Total | Pct |
|---|---|---|---|---|---|---|---|---|---|---|
| St. Louis | 48-39 | 44-31 | 62-46 | 30-24 | 46-35 | 46-35 | 28-20 | 64-50 | 92-70 | .568 |
| Philadelphia | 47-38 | 42-35 | 71-62 | 18-11 | 51-30 | 38-43 | 27-23 | 62-50 | 89-73 | .549 |
| Montreal | 43-42 | 43-34 | 61-51 | 25-25 | 40-41 | 46-35 | 30-26 | 56-50 | 86-76 | .531 |
| Pittsburgh | 44-40 | 40-38 | 63-53 | 21-25 | 42-39 | 42-39 | 25-22 | 59-56 | 84-78 | .519 |
| Chicago | 36-53 | 37-36 | 52-61 | 21-28 | 38-43 | 35-46 | 52-53 | 21-36 | 73-89 | .451 |
| New York | 40-47 | 25-50 | 51-79 | 14-18 | 33-48 | 32-49 | 25-27 | 40-70 | 65-97 | .401 |

### *TURNAROUNDS*

#### COME FROM BEHIND WINS

| Team | 1 | 2 | 3 | 4 | 5 | 6 | 7 | Total | Points |
|---|---|---|---|---|---|---|---|---|---|
| St. Louis | 24 | 10 | 6 | | | | | 40 | 102 |
| Philadelphia | 19 | 11 | 7 | 2 | | | | 39 | 109 |
| Montreal | 17 | 12 | 4 | 1 | | | | 34 | 91 |
| Pittsburgh | 21 | 11 | 4 | 3 | 3 | | | 42 | 124 |
| Chicago | 11 | 10 | 2 | 3 | 1 | 0 | 1 | 28 | 81 |
| New York | 21 | 8 | 5 | 1 | | | | 35 | 91 |

#### BLOWN LEADS

| 1 | 2 | 3 | 4 | 5 | 6 | 7 | Total | Points |
|---|---|---|---|---|---|---|---|---|
| 17 | 8 | 2 | 1 | 0 | | 1 | 29 | 79 |
| 12 | 9 | 4 | 3 | 2 | | | 30 | 94 |
| 18 | 9 | 4 | 2 | 0 | 1 | 1 | 35 | 104 |
| 24 | 10 | 2 | 2 | 1 | | | 39 | 102 |
| 22 | 7 | 6 | 1 | 1 | | | 37 | 100 |
| 21 | 12 | 6 | 1 | 0 | | | 40 | 107 |

#### DEFENSIVE RECORDS

| Team | OSB | DP | OA/SFA | FAvg | DER | Opposition Runs |
|---|---|---|---|---|---|---|
| St. Louis | 147 | 169 | 33/45 | .981 | .705 | 609 |
| Montreal | 120 | 117 | 28/48 | .980 | .701 | 616 |
| Philadelphia | 150 | 138 | 37/54 | .981 | .688 | 654 |
| Pittsburgh | 102 | 133 | 29/48 | .977 | .690 | 696 |
| Chicago | 153 | 110 | 52/59 | .979 | .689 | 709 |
| New York | 146 | 134 | 46/53 | .972 | .681 | 723 |

#### OPPOSITION ERRORS

| Team | C | 1B | 2B | 3B | SS | LF | CF | RF | P | Un | Total |
|---|---|---|---|---|---|---|---|---|---|---|---|
| New York | 29 | 11 | 20 | 22 | 32 | 8 | 5 | 10 | 17 | 4 | 158 |
| St. Louis | 25 | 15 | 20 | 28 | 20 | 8 | 8 | 11 | 17 | 6 | 158 |
| Pittsburgh | 12 | 13 | 20 | 22 | 21 | 12 | 12 | 5 | 17 | 5 | 139 |
| Philadelphia | 13 | 10 | 20 | 26 | 32 | 4 | 5 | 6 | 17 | 6 | 139 |
| Montreal | 12 | 14 | 23 | 22 | 30 | 10 | 8 | 3 | 9 | 3 | 134 |
| Chicago | 8 | 14 | 18 | 23 | 24 | 6 | 12 | 10 | 12 | 3 | 130 |

#### LATE-INNING BALL CLUBS

| Team | Ahead | Tied | Behind | Net Change |
|---|---|---|---|---|
| Philadelphia | 63-6 | 15- 9 | 11-57 | +11 |
| Pittsburgh | 61-7 | 14- 6 | 9-64 | +10 |
| Montreal | 69-7 | 9-11 | 8-58 | −1 |
| St. Louis | 73-9 | 11-11 | 7-50 | −2 |
| Chicago | 59-6 | 8- 9 | 5-74 | −2 |
| New York | 55-6 | 6-16 | 4-75 | −12 |

# ST. LOUIS CARDINALS

There is only one man in the world, I think, who says "You have to build your ball club to fit your park and your league" more often than I do. That man is Whitey Herzog. Yet the team that he built, a speed-and-defense outfit in a line-drive hitter's park, posted exactly the same 46-35 record in their home park as they did on the road. This presents a little puzzle, and you know how I love puzzles.

I can suggest several answers, which when put together form a credible explanation. One is that the kind of park the Cardinals inhabit, with its very fast artificial turf, puts a premium on outfield defense. Anytime you don't cut the ball off it's two bases, maybe three. Because the Cardinals have so much speed on their roster, one tends to assume that they have a strong defensive outfield—but they don't, at all. Look at them: Lonnie Smith is fast but he falls down with comic regularity, has been known to kick baseballs instead of catching them, and has a poor arm—definitely not a good defensive left fielder. Willie McGee in center field is error-prone, and, though his arm gets good reviews, they are for high, looping throws that do very little damage. Hendrick is an inconsistent right fielder with a mediocre arm. The Cardinals hit 239 doubles, a good total, but they *allowed* 269, a horrible figure. That has to be attributed to their outfield defense.

The Cardinals' defensive strength is in the infield. This is really of more use to them on a slower grass field, which minimizes the damage that a loose cannon shot can do in the outfield, and maximizes the infielder's ability to cut off a ball that might roll through. And the Cards were 27-15 on grass fields, far better than their record on turf.

Second reason: Look at the pitchers. When you take the home run out of the game, that emphasizes the stolen base, the alternative way of getting a runner around. The Cardinals can steal bases, but so can their opponents. Porter doesn't have a gun, by any means. That means that the pitcher has to cut off the running game. The Cardinal starters who do the best job of this, Bob Forsch and John Stuper, were 15-6 with a 3.45 ERA at home (9-10, 3.42 on the road). But the two who do the *worst* job of keeping runners at first, Mura and LaPoint—and both are really bad in that regard—were 6-8 with a 4.32 ERA in Busch, while going 15-6 with a 3.32 mark on the road. (And to show you what kind of a manager we are dealing with here, Herzog gave the two pitchers who are good in Busch 51% more innings in Busch than on the road, and gave the two "road" pitchers 25% more innings on the road. He uses Forsch, vulnerable to the home run, as much as he can in Busch, where home runs just don't fly out much.)

Third point: The Cardinals' power is surprising. They don't hit that many home runs, but that's because they know where they are playing. If they played in a park where the ball would go out, Hendrick and Porter and Hernandez would get some 'taters. They probably have as much real power as Atlanta does, and were only outhomered 46-40 on the road.

Let us back off and run at the general subject of Whitey Herzog's Cardinals from another angle. It is useful, I think, to recall clearly the team that the Cardinals had before Herzog. They were a team of very high batting averages, sustained by occasional 13- and 14-run outbursts, but inconsistent offense and consequently of losing records. Herzog's institution of the running game didn't increase the number of runs that the team scored; indeed, the Cardinals scored quite a few more runs in 1979 and 1980 than they did in 1982. What the aggressive baserunning did was to break up some of the long, long innings that led to 11-3 routs and to replace those runs with one-run innings that cut down on the number of 3-2 losses. It didn't create extra runs, but it rearranged the runs into more productive groups.

Second, the Cardinals B.H. were a team of awesome strengths and gaping weaknesses. They had two #1 catchers on the team, Simmons and Kennedy, but they had no bullpen. They had two right fielders, Durham and Hendrick, but a scar in center. They had three second basemen, Oberkfell, Ramsey and Herr, but a serious shortage of starters. This is, when you think about it, a curious allocation of resources. Herzog was not shy about reacting to that problem, and the 1982 team emerged as one that is most remarkable for its top-to-bottom strength. Did the Cardinals have a player as good as Gary Carter or Andre Dawson, or a pitcher as good as Rogers? If they did, their records hide the fact very well. But when you compare the Cardinals and Expos top-to-bottom, as I did in the Montreal comment, it becomes obvious that that is the secret of the Cards' success. And it is a direct result of Herzog's aggressiveness in reshaping his talent.

At five minutes an evening for four and a half summers, I figure I must have spent about 60 hours listening to Whitey Herzog talk about baseball. I wish I had taken notes. The years 1975 to 1979 were my formative years as a sabermetrician, and I always enjoyed turning on the radio about 7:10 each evening to see if Whitey had been thinking about the same things that I had been thinking about. About 1976, which was the height of the stolen-base mania, I pondered hard on the question of why the stolen base had gone out of the game in the 1920s, and why it came back in the 1960s. I concluded that the biggest factor was the home-run rates; the more reachable the fences were, the more home runs there were, the fewer stolen bases there would be. About a week later Denny Matthews asked Whitey Herzog why he thought there were so many more stolen bases, and Whitey said, "Well, the biggest reason is the ballparks, Denny. They're not building those bandbox ballparks like we played in in the '50s, so you've got to go out and get the runners around some other way." No one will ever be able to convince me that that is not the real explanation, I'm afraid. Many times I heard interviewers toss him questions that were obvious set-ups for preconceived cliché answers. Herzog would refuse to recite the cliché, and instead analyze the matter in terms of what had actually happened or was happening to the ball club. As I am with Earl Weaver, I was amazed not so much at his intelligence, which is impressive in itself, as with the continual freshness and openness of his mind, which would enable him to see things not as retreads of the things which he has always known, but as they really were.

I was appalled, then, to see the account of Herzog's triumph in St. Louis as it filtered through the eyes of the nation's journalists. This is "Whitey Ball," you see; Whitey believes in speed and aggressive base running and line-drive hitting—played that way in Kansas City, plays that way here in St. Louie, too. What absolute malarky. Whitey believes in *winning*. When Whitey was in Kansas City, he fired Charlie Lau, stating as his reason that Charlie wanted to make everybody on the team into a line-drive hitter. (Another reason, I suspect, was the same as the reason for trading Ted Simmons: Lau was creating confusion about who was running the show.) Herzog felt that Lau had made a punch-and-judy hitter out of Brett and was trying to do the same with Clint Hurdle. It is a fact that Brett had his best years after Lau was fired.

But what did one of the nation's best-known sportswriters, who I will be kind enough not to identify, say about all this? That Herzog, after he was fired, "went looking" for a ballpark that would adapt to "his" style of play. He had to have a team that had a lot of young talent, so he could trade them around and come up with what he wanted. He had to have artificial turf, so he would be able to make use of the speedy singles hitters like Willie McGee that he could pick up for free.

Can't you see what is wrong with that? That's Maury Wills you're talking about there, not Whitey Herzog. You remember Maury's book, *How To Steal A Pennant*. Maury was so full of "I'm going to do this" and "I'm going to do that" and "We're going to do this this way" that he was hopelessly unable to deal with the realities of the situation facing him. Intelligent men don't make up stupid conditions like that. Intelligent men adapt to the situation that they are given, take what fate allows them and do what they have to do with it.

A classic case in point and one of the reasons that I decided to study pitchers' records while working on three days rest, four days, etc., was something that Whitey Herzog said one day last year when I happened to pass through St. Louis. He was talking about the difficulties of handling his pitchers, and he said that it was the most awkward staff he'd ever had to deal with because he had a couple of pitchers, chiefly Andujar, who needed a lot of work to stay sharp, and he'd like to work those guys every fourth day, but he had some other pitchers—Forsch and Mura—who needed four or even five days' rest to be effective. I knew from four years of listening to him that he wasn't just blowing smoke, so I thought it might be worthwhile to keep track of how different managers used their staffs. The record for St. Louis, Houston and Atlanta for one 13-day stretch is:

| | ST. LOUIS | | HOUSTON | | ATLANTA | |
|---|---|---|---|---|---|---|
| Day | Starter | Days Rest | Starter | Days Rest | Starter | Days Rest |
| 1 | Andujar | 3 | J. Niekro | 4 | Walk | 4 |
| 2 | Forsch | 5 | Knepper | X | P. Niekro | 4 |
| 3 | | | | | | |
| 4 | LaPoint | 5 | Sutton | 5 | Camp | 4 |
| 5 | Andujar | 3 | Ruhle | 5 | Mahler | 4 |
| 6 | Stuper | 6 | Ryan | 5 | Walk | 4 |
| 7 | Forsch | 4 | J. Niekro | 5 | P. Niekro | 4 |
| 8 | Mura | 7 | Knepper | 5 | Dayley | X |
| 9 | Andujar | 3 | Sutton | 4 | Camp | 4 |
| 10 | Stuper | 3 | Ruhle | 4 | Mahler | 4 |
| 11 | LaPoint | 6 | Ryan | 4 | Walk | 4 |
| 12 | Forsch | 4 | J. Niekro | 4 | P. Niekro | 4 |
| 13 | Andujar | 3 | Knepper | 4 | Dayley | 4 |

Do you see what he was doing? He was spotting Mura, Stuper and LaPoint so that he could keep Andujar working on short rest, Forsch on normal rotation.

What other manager do you know who would be gutty enough to try something like that? Nobody. He saw the situation, he recognized it, he confronted it. He didn't impose any preconceived notions about how to run a pitching staff onto it.

Did it work? Joacquin Andujar pitched 12 times on short rest, had a 2.03 ERA on short rest, and he had a season that is miles above anything he has done before. Bob Forsch never once started on short rest and had his best season in five years. The Cardinals had a staff ERA of 3.37, and I don't know of anybody who cited the Cardinals as having one of the best pitching staffs in the National League before the year started.

There are things that Herzog believes in *a priori*. He believes in building a team that is close-knit. He believes that you can't do anything unless you have players who want to win. He is never afraid to take a chance with an unproven player, if that player has ability and shows desire. He doesn't tell you those things flat out, but they come through plain enough. Those things he would carry with him no matter where he went. But the style of play? The shape of his ball club is the shape of his talent and the shape of his ballpark. Herzog is too smart to believe in building a ball club by trading, or building a ball club from free agency or building a ball club out of the farm system. He believes in building a ball club out of ballplayers. That's all.

Keith HERNANDEZ, First Base

*Runs Created: 96*

| | G | AB | R | H | 2B | 3B | HR | RBI | SB | Avg |
|---|---|---|---|---|---|---|---|---|---|---|
| First Half | 87 | 320 | 45 | 93 | 17 | 2 | 3 | 48 | 12 | .291 |
| Second Half | 73 | 259 | 34 | 80 | 16 | 4 | 4 | 46 | 7 | .309 |
| Home | 81 | 287 | 39 | 77 | 17 | 4 | 4 | 44 | 9 | .268 |
| Road | 79 | 292 | 40 | 96 | 16 | 2 | 3 | 50 | 10 | .329 |
| vs. RHP | | 379 | | 116 | | | 5 | 66 | | .307 |
| vs. LHP | | 200 | | 57 | | | 2 | 28 | | .285 |
| 1982 | 160 | 579 | 79 | 173 | 33 | 6 | 7 | 94 | 19 | .299 |
| 6.85 years | | 563 | 92 | 169 | 37 | 7 | 11 | 83 | 12 | .299 |

Tom HERR, Second Base

*Runs Created: 55*

| | G | AB | R | H | 2B | 3B | HR | RBI | SB | Avg |
|---|---|---|---|---|---|---|---|---|---|---|
| First Half | 61 | 209 | 33 | 50 | 7 | 4 | 0 | 17 | 12 | .239 |
| Second Half | 74 | 284 | 50 | 81 | 12 | 0 | 0 | 19 | 13 | .285 |
| Home | 63 | 236 | 38 | 64 | 10 | 1 | 0 | 19 | 15 | .271 |
| Road | 72 | 257 | 45 | 67 | 9 | 3 | 0 | 17 | 10 | .261 |
| vs. RHP | | 344 | | 101 | | | 0 | 24 | | .294 |
| vs. LHP | | 149 | | 30 | | | 0 | 12 | | .201 |
| 1982 | 135 | 493 | 83 | 131 | 19 | 4 | 0 | 36 | 25 | .266 |
| 2.03 years | | 560 | 82 | 147 | 22 | 9 | 0 | 48 | 29 | .262 |

Ken OBERKFELL, Third Base

*Runs Created: 58*

| | G | AB | R | H | 2B | 3B | HR | RBI | SB | Avg |
|---|---|---|---|---|---|---|---|---|---|---|
| First Half | 66 | 240 | 28 | 68 | 11 | 2 | 1 | 13 | 5 | .283 |
| Second Half | 71 | 230 | 17 | 68 | 11 | 3 | 1 | 21 | 6 | .296 |
| Home | 72 | 235 | 29 | 64 | 13 | 2 | 1 | 16 | 7 | .272 |
| Road | 65 | 235 | 26 | 72 | 9 | 3 | 1 | 18 | 4 | .306 |
| vs. RHP | | 323 | | 107 | | | 2 | 21 | | .331 |
| vs. LHP | | 147 | | 29 | | | 0 | 13 | | .197 |
| 1982 | 137 | 470 | 55 | 136 | 22 | 5 | 2 | 34 | 11 | .289 |
| 3.23 years | | 525 | 67 | 152 | 25 | 7 | 3 | 50 | 10 | .290 |

Ozzie SMITH, Shortstop

*Runs Created: 56*

| | G | AB | R | H | 2B | 3B | HR | RBI | SB | Avg |
|---|---|---|---|---|---|---|---|---|---|---|
| First Half | 84 | 301 | 40 | 78 | 19 | 1 | 2 | 24 | 16 | .259 |
| Second Half | 56 | 187 | 18 | 43 | 5 | 0 | 0 | 19 | 9 | .230 |
| Home | 73 | 246 | 30 | 58 | 12 | 1 | 0 | 19 | 17 | .236 |
| Road | 67 | 242 | 28 | 63 | 12 | 0 | 2 | 24 | 8 | .260 |
| vs. RHP | | 322 | | 78 | | | 0 | 24 | | .242 |
| vs. LHP | | 166 | | 43 | | | 2 | 19 | | .259 |
| 1982 | 140 | 488 | 58 | 121 | 24 | 1 | 2 | 43 | 25 | .248 |
| 4.46 years | | 611 | 73 | 143 | 20 | 5 | 1 | 39 | 39 | .234 |

Lonnie SMITH, Left Field

*Runs Created: 98*

| | G | AB | R | H | 2B | 3B | HR | RBI | SB | Avg |
|---|---|---|---|---|---|---|---|---|---|---|
| First Half | 85 | 324 | 70 | 99 | 20 | 3 | 6 | 43 | 41 | .306 |
| Second Half | 71 | 268 | 50 | 83 | 15 | 5 | 2 | 26 | 27 | .310 |
| Home | .76 | 307 | 62 | 90 | 18 | 8 | 3 | 41 | 37 | .293 |
| Road | 80 | 285 | 58 | 92 | 17 | 0 | 5 | 28 | 31 | .323 |
| vs. RHP | | 402 | | 123 | | | 6 | 50 | | .306 |
| vs. LHP | | 190 | | 59 | | | 2 | 19 | | .311 |
| 1982 | 156 | 592 | 120 | 182 | 35 | 8 | 8 | 69 | 68 | .307 |
| 2.17 years | | 507 | 110 | 159 | 30 | 7 | 6 | 48 | 59 | .314 |

Wllie McGEE, Center Field

*Runs Created: 51*

| | G | AB | R | H | 2B | 3B | HR | RBI | SB | Avg |
|---|---|---|---|---|---|---|---|---|---|---|
| First Half | 53 | 173 | 19 | 55 | 3 | 7 | 0 | 23 | 10 | .318 |
| Second Half | 70 | 249 | 24 | 70 | 9 | 1 | 4 | 33 | 14 | .281 |
| Home | 62 | 220 | 26 | 72 | 7 | 3 | 2 | 30 | 16 | .327 |
| Road | 61 | 202 | 17 | 53 | 5 | 5 | 2 | 26 | 8 | .262 |
| vs. RHP | | 305 | | 93 | | | 2 | 38 | | .305 |
| vs. LHP | | 117 | | 32 | | | 2 | 18 | | .274 |
| 1982 | 123 | 422 | 43 | 125 | 12 | 8 | 4 | 56 | 24 | .296 |
| .076 years | | 555 | 57 | 165 | 16 | 11 | 5 | 74 | 32 | .296 |

George HENDRICK, Right Field

*Runs Created: 76*

| | G | AB | R | H | 2B | 3B | HR | RBI | SB | Avg |
|---|---|---|---|---|---|---|---|---|---|---|
| First Half | 70 | 272 | 34 | 74 | 8 | 2 | 14 | 54 | 1 | .272 |
| Second Half | 66 | 243 | 31 | 71 | 12 | 3 | 5 | 50 | 2 | .292 |
| Home | 70 | 271 | 32 | 79 | 16 | 3 | 10 | 55 | 0 | .292 |
| Road | 66 | 244 | 33 | 66 | 4 | 2 | 9 | 49 | 3 | .270 |
| vs. RHP | | 350 | | 95 | | | 15 | 83 | | .271 |
| vs. LHP | | 165 | | 50 | | | 4 | 21 | | .303 |
| 1982 | 136 | 515 | 65 | 145 | 20 | 5 | 19 | 104 | 3 | .282 |
| 9.03 years | | 586 | 79 | 164 | 27 | 2 | 24 | 91 | 6 | .280 |

Darrell PORTER, Catcher

*Runs Created: 52*

| | G | AB | R | H | 2B | 3B | HR | RBI | SB | Avg |
|---|---|---|---|---|---|---|---|---|---|---|
| First Half | 59 | 195 | 22 | 44 | 10 | 2 | 5 | 24 | 1 | .226 |
| Second Half | 61 | 178 | 24 | 42 | 8 | 3 | 7 | 24 | 0 | .236 |
| Home | 62 | 184 | 17 | 37 | 8 | 3 | 3 | 21 | 0 | .201 |
| Road | 58 | 189 | 29 | 49 | 10 | 2 | 9 | 27 | 1 | .259 |
| vs. RHP | | 297 | | 70 | | | 11 | 35 | | .236 |
| vs. LHP | | 76 | | 16 | | | 1 | 13 | | .211 |
| 1982 | 120 | 373 | 46 | 86 | 18 | 5 | 12 | 48 | 1 | .231 |
| 7.86 years | | 528 | 74 | 131 | 22 | 5 | 17 | 77 | 3 | .248 |

Mike RAMSEY, Outfield

*Runs Created: 21*

| | G | AB | R | H | 2B | 3B | HR | RBI | SB | Avg |
|---|---|---|---|---|---|---|---|---|---|---|
| First Half | 65 | 160 | 13 | 45 | 7 | 2 | 0 | 12 | 6 | .281 |
| Second Half | 47 | 96 | 5 | 14 | 1 | 0 | 1 | 9 | 0 | .146 |
| Home | | | | | | | | | | |
| Road | | | | | | | | | | |
| vs. RHP | | 148 | | 34 | | | 1 | 15 | | .230 |
| vs. LHP | | 108 | | 25 | | | 0 | 6 | | .231 |
| 1982 | 112 | 256 | 18 | 59 | 8 | 2 | 1 | 21 | 6 | .230 |
| 1.42 years | | 360 | 37 | 88 | 13 | 2 | 1 | 27 | 7 | .245 |

Joacquin ANDUJAR

| Year | (W–L) | GS | Run | Avg | DP | Avg | SB | Avg |
|---|---|---|---|---|---|---|---|---|
| 1976 | ( 9-10) | 25 | 75 | 3.00 | 27 | 1.08 | 26 | 1.04 |
| 1977 | (11- 8) | 25 | 110 | 4.40 | 19 | .76 | 23 | .92 |
| 1978 | ( 5- 7) | 13 | 43 | 3.31 | 10 | .77 | 12 | .92 |
| 1979 | (12-12) | 23 | 75 | 3.26 | 20 | .87 | 20 | .87 |
| 1980 | ( 3- 8) | 14 | 49 | 3.50 | 10 | .71 | 19 | 1.36 |
| 1981 | ( 8- 4) | 11 | 48 | 4.36 | 10 | 1.00 | 8 | .73 |
| 1982 | (15-10) | 37 | 147 | 3.94 | 30 | .81 | 27 | .73 |
| 7 years | | 148 | 547 | 3.70 | 125 | ,84 | 135 | .91 |

| | G | IP | W | L | Pct | ER | ERA |
|---|---|---|---|---|---|---|---|
| Home | 19 | 140 | 8 | 5 | .615 | 38 | 2.44 |
| Road | 19 | 125.2 | 7 | 5 | .583 | 35 | 2.51 |

Bob FORSCH

| Year | (W–L) | GS | Run | Avg | DP | Avg | SB | Avg |
|---|---|---|---|---|---|---|---|---|
| 1976 | ( 8-10) | 32 | 151 | 4.72 | 36 | 1.13 | 15 | .47 |
| 1977 | (20- 7) | 35 | 164 | 4.69 | 37 | 1.06 | 21 | .60 |
| 1978 | (11-17) | 34 | 118 | 3.47 | 34 | 1.00 | 36 | 1.06 |
| 1979 | (11-11) | 32 | 136 | 4.25 | 35 | 1.09 | 20 | .62 |
| 1980 | (11-10) | 31 | 168 | 5.42 | 40 | 1.29 | 19 | .61 |
| 1981 | (10- 5) | 20 | 90 | 4.50 | 13 | .65 | 18 | .90 |
| 1982 | (15- 9) | 34 | 148 | 4.35 | 33 | .97 | 26 | .76 |
| 7 years | | 218 | 975 | 4.47 | 228 | 1.05 | 155 | .71 |

| | G | IP | W | L | Pct | ER | ERA |
|---|---|---|---|---|---|---|---|
| Home | 18 | 133.2 | 11 | 2 | .846 | 47 | 3.16 |
| Road | 18 | 99.1 | 4 | 7 | .364 | 43 | 3.90 |

Steve MURA

| Year | (W–L) | GS | Run | Avg | DP | Avg | SB | Avg |
|---|---|---|---|---|---|---|---|---|
| 1978 | ( 0- 2) | 2 | 4 | 2.00 | 2 | 1.00 | 4 | 2.00 |
| 1979 | ( 4- 4) | 5 | 16 | 3.20 | 7 | 1.40 | 6 | 1.20 |
| 1980 | ( 8- 7) | 23 | 93 | 4.04 | 24 | 1.04 | 29 | 1.26 |
| 1981 | ( 5-14) | 22 | 70 | 3.18 | 17 | .77 | 28 | 1.27 |
| 1982 | (12-11) | 30 | 146 | 4.87 | 35 | 1.17 | 38 | 1.27 |
| 5 years | | 82 | 329 | 4.01 | 85 | 1.04 | 105 | 1.28 |

| | G | IP | W | L | Pct | ER | ERA |
|---|---|---|---|---|---|---|---|
| Home | 18 | 83.1 | 3 | 5 | .375 | 43 | 4.64 |
| Road | 17 | 101 | 9 | 6 | .600 | 40 | 3.56 |

John STUPER

| Year | (W–L) | GS | Run | Avg | DP | Avg | SB | Avg |
|---|---|---|---|---|---|---|---|---|
| 1982 | (9-7) | 21 | 73 | 3.48 | 19 | .90 | 8 | .38 |

| | G | IP | W | L | Pct | ER | ERA |
|---|---|---|---|---|---|---|---|
| Home | 13 | 80.1 | 4 | 4 | .500 | 35 | 3.92 |
| Road | 10 | 56.1 | 5 | 3 | .625 | 16 | 2.56 |

Dave LaPOINT

| Year | (W–L) | GS | Run | Avg | DP | Avg | SB | Avg |
|---|---|---|---|---|---|---|---|---|
| 1980 | (1-0) | 3 | 28 | 9.33 | 3 | 1.00 | 4 | 1.34 |
| 1981 | (1-0) | 2 | 14 | 7.00 | 3 | 1.50 | 1 | .50 |
| 1982 | (9-3) | 21 | 100 | 4.76 | 31 | 1.48 | 33 | 1.57 |
| 3 years | | 26 | 142 | 5.43 | 37 | 1.42 | 38 | 1.43 |

| | G | IP | W | L | Pct | ER | ERA |
|---|---|---|---|---|---|---|---|
| Home | 21 | 66.2 | 3 | 3 | .500 | 29 | 3.91 |
| Road | 21 | 86 | 6 | 0 | 1.000 | 29 | 3.03 |

1982 OTHERS

| Pitcher | (W–L) | GS | Run | Avg | DP | Avg | SB | Avg |
|---|---|---|---|---|---|---|---|---|
| Martin | (4-5) | 7 | 30 | 4.29 | 7 | 1.00 | 4 | .57 |
| Rincon | (2-3) | 6 | 23 | 3.83 | 10 | 1.67 | 6 | 1.00 |
| Rasmussen | (1-2) | 3 | 6 | | 4 | | 3 | |
| Kaat | (5-3) | 2 | 8 | | 3 | | 1 | |
| Lahti | (5-4) | 1 | 4 | | 0 | | 1 | |

## ST. LOUIS

*Talent Analysis*

The Cardinals in 1982 possessed 169 points of approximate value, easily the highest total in the National League.

| | AV | % |
|---|---|---|
| Produced by Cardinal system: | 47 | 28% |
| Acquired by trade: | 108 | 64% |
| Purchased or signed from free agency: | 14 | 8% |

They are essentially a trade-built team.

| | | |
|---|---|---|
| Young (Up to age 25): | 17 | 10% |
| Prime (Age 26 to 29): | 105 | 62% |
| Past-prime (Age 30 to 33): | 38 | 22% |
| Old (Age 34 or older): | 9 | 5% |

Most of their players are in their prime; only 28% are past-prime or old.

The Cardinals ranked sixth in the majors in the amount of 1982 talent produced and rank third in talent produced for the period 1979 to 1982.

## BUSCH STADIUM

DIMENSIONS: Normal

SURFACE: Very fast artificial turf

VISIBILITY: The decision in the mid-'70s to close off the center field seats improved the visibility enormously

FOUL TERRITORY: Large; probably the most significant difference between the two Missouri parks

FAVORS:
Hitter/Pitcher—Hitter, but very slightly
Power/Line-drive hitter—Line-drive hitter
Righthander/Lefthander—Neither

TYPES OF OFFENSE AFFECTED: Home runs way down; singles, doubles and triples up

OTHER PARK CHARACTERISTICS: Park completely enclosed and at sea level; air does not move

TYPES OF MARGINAL PLAYERS MOST VALUABLE IN PARK: Speed is essential, offensively and defensively. Herzog has done it exactly right; he is getting tremendous mileage out of speedy line-drive hitters.

PLAYERS ON TEAM HELPED MOST BY PARK: Oberkfell, McGee, Herr

PLAYERS ON TEAM HURT MOST BY PARK: George Hendrick

OTHER COMMENTS: Sometimes, but erroneously, believed to be a pitcher's park. Infield surface is fairly reliable; Cardinals' fielding averages are higher than they would be in most parks. Cardinals' double plays (offensively and defensively) are up 10% at home, the highest of any NL park. Did you know that Busch and Wrigley are the only major large parks which bear the names of commercial products?

## THE GAMES THAT WON IT

On September 13, the Cardinals were in second place. Jack Buck, their fine announcer, had all but declared them dead two weeks earlier. They won 11 of 13 games from that point and moved 6½ games ahead with 7 to play. An account of those 13 games:

| Date | Opponent | Score | Started/Winner | GWRBI (hit) | Inning |
|---|---|---|---|---|---|
| 9-14 | Philadelphia | 2-0 | Stuper | Porter (home run) | 4th |
| 9-15 | Philadelphia | 8-0 | Andujar | Hendrick (single) | 3rd |
| 9-17 | New York | 3-2 | Rasmussen/Sutter | McGee (double) | 10th |
| 9-17 | New York | 7-1 | Mura | Hernandez (sac fly) | 3rd |
| 9-18 | New York | 2-0 | Forsch | Green (home run) | 4th |
| 9-18 | New York | 6-2 | Kaat/Lahti | None (Wilson's error in 2nd) | |
| 9-19 | New York | 3-1 | Stuper | McGee (single) | 4th |
| 9-20 | Philadelphia | 4-1 | Andujar | Hernandez (fielder's choice) | 1st |
| 9-21 | Philadelphia | 2-5 | LOSS Carlton | | |
| 9-22 | Pittsburgh | 2-1 | LaPoint | Herr (single) | 8th |
| 9-23 | Pittsburgh | 3-5 | LOSS Romo | | |
| 9-24 | Chicago | 3-1 | Stuper | Tenace (sac fly) | 8th |
| 9-25 | Chicago | 5-1 | Andujar | Hendrick (single) | 1st |

**HITTERS**

| | G | AB | R | H | 2B | 3B | HR | RBI | SB | Avg |
|---|---|---|---|---|---|---|---|---|---|---|
| Herr | 12 | 42 | 11 | 15 | 2 | 0 | 0 | 3 | 2 | .357 |
| L. Smith | 13 | 49 | 7 | 12 | 2 | 0 | 0 | 5 | 0 | .245 |
| Hernandez | 13 | 37 | 7 | 11 | 1 | 0 | 0 | 5 | 0 | .297 |
| Hendrick | 11 | 40 | 8 | 19 | 3 | 2 | 2 | 12 | 0 | .475 |
| Porter | 10 | 37 | 3 | 8 | 1 | 1 | 1 | 6 | 0 | .216 |
| McGee | 13 | 41 | 2 | 6 | 1 | 0 | 0 | 5 | 2 | .146 |
| Oberkfell | 12 | 33 | 5 | 10 | 2 | 0 | 1 | 3 | 2 | .303 |
| Ramsey | 11 | 37 | 0 | 7 | 1 | 0 | 0 | 2 | 0 | .189 |
| O. Smith | 2 | 8 | 0 | 2 | 0 | 0 | 0 | 0 | 1 | .250 |
| Green | 9 | 15 | 1 | 4 | 1 | 0 | 1 | 2 | 0 | .267 |

**PITCHERS**

| | G | IP | W–L | ERA | Sv |
|---|---|---|---|---|---|
| Andujar | 3 | 25 | 3-0 | 0.73 | 0 |
| Stuper | 3 | 23 | 3-0 | 0.79 | 0 |
| Forsch | 2 | 15 | 1-0 | 1.84 | 0 |
| Rasmussen | 2 | 12 | 0-1 | 2.31 | 0 |
| Sutter | 6 | 11 | 1-0 | 0.00 | 4 |
| Mura | 2 | 9 | 1-0 | 1.04 | 0 |
| Lahti | 2 | 7 | 1-0 | 1.23 | 0 |
| LaPoint | 1 | 8 | 1-0 | 1.13 | 0 |
| Bair | 3 | 7 | 0-0 | 0.00 | 2 |

COMMENTS:

1) MVP—Hendrick? Hendrick or pick-a-pitcher.

2) Ozzie out with injury.

# PHILADELPHIA PHILLIES

The Philadelphia Phillies in 1982 had, to state it delicately, a problem with their lead-off men. The records of the men who batted lead-off for them (while hitting in the #1 spot) are given:

| | G | AB | R | H | 2B | 3B | HR | RBI | SB | Avg |
|---|---|---|---|---|---|---|---|---|---|---|
| Dernier | 81 | 326 | 54 | 81 | 10 | 1 | 4 | 20 | 37 | .248 |
| Rose | 56 | 229 | 22 | 49 | 5 | 2 | 1 | 11 | 1 | .214 |
| Maddox | 15 | 63 | 4 | 19 | 4 | 1 | 0 | 3 | 3 | .302 |
| Gross | 10 | 35 | 2 | 9 | 0 | 0 | 0 | 2 | 2 | .257 |
| DeJesus | 3 | 10 | 0 | 0 | 0 | 0 | 0 | 0 | 0 | .000 |
| Vukovich | 1 | 1 | 0 | 0 | 0 | 0 | 0 | 0 | 0 | .000 |
| Roberts | 1 | 1 | 0 | 0 | 0 | 0 | 0 | 0 | 0 | .000 |
| Unser | 1 | 1 | 0 | 0 | 0 | 0 | 0 | 0 | 0 | .000 |
| Totals | 162 | 666 | 82 | 158 | 19 | 4 | 5 | 36 | 43 | .237 |

The at-bats total indicates that they probably weren't walking very much, either. This put the Phillies' offense in a tremendous hole, from which to have climbed back as high as they did—89 wins—is fairly remarkable. The Phillies' lead-off men missed .300 by the slim margin of 42 hits. If the lead-off man is the foundation of the offense, then everything that follows was built upon an uncomfortably narrow base. The contrast between the Phillies and the Cardinals:

| | St. Louis | Philadelphia |
|---|---|---|
| Runs scored by lead-off men | 125 | 82 |
| Runs scored by players batting second | 110 | 88 |
| Runs scored by spots 3 to 9 | 450 | 494 |

The Phillies had a 47-34 record with Dernier leading off, 30-26 with Rose, 7-7 with Maddox, 5-3 with Gross, 0-3 with Ivan the Terrible.

When I began the *Baseball Abstract* in 1977, my position was that I would not criticize baseball managers. Managers, I reasoned, were professional men. They had seen a lot more baseball games than I had. There was no reason why a team would hire an imbecile to run the show, and therefore it must be assumed that they were not imbeciles. If I were to criticize a baseball manager, why would an interested third party believe that I knew what I was talking about, rather than the manager? Better to remove the discussion to the more impersonal realm of strategies and tactics and definite, quantifiable truths than to join the journalists in discussing individuals. The thing to do with a manager was to try to listen to him and learn from him; better to be a student at his feet than a pygmy at his heels.

And then there was Don Zimmer....

This position has gradually eroded over the years, not entirely of my own choosing. Evaluating managers—evaluating anybody, for that matter—is something that the people who run magazines and talk shows and morning editions always are after you to do. My view of it is that by piling up mountains of facts, making pile after pile of absolutely true, verifiable statements, one builds a little respect in the public's eye, that when you say something people will believe that you know what you're talking about. That respect is the currency by which I live. When I indulge in criticism of managers, I am spending that currency. And editors and talk show hosts... well, the more of it you spend with them the happier they are.

Perhaps, sometimes, I have spent that currency a little foolishly, and will have no one but myself to blame if the public stops believing anything I say. I regret, in particular, an evaluation of Pat Corrales as a manager that appeared in an article in *Sport* magazine last summer. The evaluation said, I think, "D+; has the personality of a doberman pinscher; would be more effective if he were more knowledgeable." That isn't actually what I wrote; what I wrote was funnier than that, but *Sport* was afraid that Corrales would sue them if they printed it. I will respect the advice of their lawyer.

Anyway, Corrales is now under fire for his handling of the Phillies in a pennant race, and I find myself, to my surprise, leaning in the direction of his corner. I simply cannot look at the Philadelphia Phillies of 1982 and see a better team than Corrales got out of them. His managerial performance in Texas looks a lot better when contrasted with the job that Don Zimmer did than it looked when we had only the performance of that team under Billy Hunter to compare it with. I am far from convinced that Corrales is a good manager, but I am not convinced that he isn't, either.

My position with respect to managers now is that I recognize fully that there are many things that they must be able to do that I don't know a thing about. I couldn't begin to help a hitter with his batting stroke. I couldn't teach fundamentals. I couldn't... well, a million things. But between what a manager does for a living and what I do for a living there are certain overlapping areas. It would be silly and false to assume the pretense that the managers, being professional men, know more about all of those things than I do. I work too hard for that. I hope, within those areas of overlapping knowledge, to be able to explain to the public what some of the differences are, what this manager does differently from that one. And I can't resist firing off an opinion now and then; I'm an argumentative SOB by nature.

I can't resolve the issue of how good a manager Corrales is. What I can do, I hope, is put on record a few specific facts that are in some vague way related to the issue. Of the anti-Corrales arguments, I think the most important is that Corrales' failure to rest his regulars in July and August led to their collective and complete collapse in September. But what is the relationship, I wondered, between the number of games a player has played before September, and his performance in that month?

The *Baseball Abstract*, in its first five years, printed each player's record in each month of the season. Going through all of this data, I recorded two things: the number of games that the player had played before September 1 and whether he hit over his average or under his average after September 1. The data:

| Games Played | Players | Up in September | Down in September | % Up |
|---|---|---|---|---|
| 133 or more | 43 | 20 | 23 | 46.5% |
| 127-132 | 126 | 58 | 68 | 46.0% |
| 123-127 | 175 | 81 | 94 | 46.2% |
| 118-122 | 138 | 68 | 70 | 49.3% |
| 113-117 | 95 | 50 | 45 | 52.6% |
| 108-112 | 82 | 43 | 39 | 52.4% |
| 103-107 | 62 | 31 | 31 | 50.0% |

This is not a very important study. It establishes something clearly, but what it establishes is fairly small and fairly obvious: that players who play a lot of games before September do tend to decline in that month. 120 games seems to be about the turning point; above that and a player is likely to have a sub-par September; below that he's in good shape.

Likely, but not *very* likely; 53% to 46% is rather far from a certainty. It seems to me probable that the true effect of overplaying a player is significantly larger than this study shows, for this reason: Most managers presumably are aware of the danger of wearing out a player and allow for it by resting those players who are most likely to tire. Earl Weaver probably realizes that Al Bumbry would tire if you asked him to play 162 games and for that reason he gives Bumbry some time off, so that the effect doesn't show up on him. Those who play over 120 games before September are those who seem to be capable of so doing. The only part of the effect that shows up in the study is that which the managers fail to anticipate, which is probably only a small portion of the whole.

Which doesn't support Corrales at all. No, throwing aside the study, the collapse of the Phillies in mid-September simply looks to me like an ordinary slump. You know, I've noticed that when somebody dies, you always have to connect it to something. You ever notice that? Two years ago this spring, a month after *Sports Illustrated* ran that article about me that gave my career such a boost, a good friend of mine died the most irrational death you can imagine, being killed by a tornado. Whenever we talked about it, we kept coming back to the way that Stan sort of drifted through his life, never married, never launched into a career. It was like he was just waiting to die.

The mind demands to know why the Phillies went through a slump at this particular moment, and whether this or that or the other couldn't have been done to prevent it. But Stan wasn't waiting to die, you know. There is no reasonable or probable connection between the way that he lived and the way that he died, and there is no reasonable or probable connection between the way that Corrales managed and the moment at which the Phillies went into a slump. It is only that the mind must tie a rope between every man and the instrument of his fate.

Pete ROSE, First Base

*Runs Created: 71*

| | G | AB | R | H | 2B | 3B | HR | RBI | SB | Avg |
|---|---|---|---|---|---|---|---|---|---|---|
| First Half | 85 | 335 | 45 | 96 | 16 | 4 | 1 | 31 | 7 | .287 |
| Second Half | 77 | 299 | 35 | 76 | 9 | 0 | 2 | 23 | 1 | .254 |
| Home | 81 | 308 | 31 | 81 | 12 | 1 | 2 | 28 | 3 | .263 |
| Road | 81 | 326 | 49 | 91 | 13 | 3 | 1 | 26 | 5 | .279 |
| vs. RHP | | 501 | | 136 | | | 3 | 37 | | .271 |
| vs. LHP | | 133 | | 36 | | | 0 | 17 | | .271 |
| 1982 | 162 | 634 | 80 | 172 | 25 | 4 | 3 | 54 | 8 | .271 |
| 19.13 years | | 656 | 104 | 202 | 36 | 7 | 8 | 61 | 9 | .308 |

Manny TRILLO, Second Base

*Runs Created: 52*

| | G | AB | R | H | 2B | 3B | HR | RBI | SB | Avg |
|---|---|---|---|---|---|---|---|---|---|---|
| First Half | 76 | 272 | 25 | 72 | 11 | 1 | 0 | 23 | 4 | .265 |
| Second Half | 73 | 277 | 27 | 77 | 13 | 0 | 0 | 16 | 4 | .278 |
| Home | 77 | 266 | 25 | 79 | 14 | 1 | 0 | 21 | 5 | .297 |
| Road | 72 | 283 | 27 | 70 | 10 | 0 | 0 | 18 | 3 | .247 |
| vs. RHP | | 453 | | 124 | | | 0 | 34 | | .274 |
| vs. LHP | | 96 | | 25 | | | 0 | 5 | | .260 |
| 1982 | 149 | 549 | 52 | 149 | 24 | 1 | 0 | 39 | 8 | .271 |
| 7.14 years | | 573 | 56 | 152 | 22 | 4 | 6 | 57 | 7 | .265 |

Mike SCHMIDT, Third Base

*Runs Created: 113*

| | G | AB | R | H | 2B | 3B | HR | RBI | SB | Avg |
|---|---|---|---|---|---|---|---|---|---|---|
| First Half | 71 | 235 | 52 | 68 | 15 | 2 | 10 | 30 | 8 | .289 |
| Second Half | 77 | 279 | 56 | 76 | 11 | 1 | 25 | 57 | 6 | .272 |
| Home | 78 | 264 | 53 | 66 | 13 | 2 | 17 | 43 | 7 | .250 |
| Road | 70 | 250 | 55 | 78 | 13 | 1 | 18 | 44 | 7 | .312 |
| vs. RHP | | 413 | | 114 | | | 25 | 64 | | .276 |
| vs. LHP | | 101 | | 30 | | | 10 | 23 | | .297 |
| 1982 | 148 | 514 | 108 | 144 | 26 | 3 | 35 | 87 | 14 | .280 |
| 9.16 years | | 560 | 105 | 149 | 28 | 4 | 38 | 105 | 17 | .265 |

Ivan DeJESUS, Shortstop

*Runs Created: 53*

| | G | AB | R | H | 2B | 3B | HR | RBI | SB | Avg |
|---|---|---|---|---|---|---|---|---|---|---|
| First Half | 85 | 296 | 27 | 74 | 6 | 4 | 1 | 33 | 13 | .250 |
| Second Half | 76 | 240 | 26 | 54 | 15 | 1 | 2 | 26 | 1 | .225 |
| Home | 81 | 274 | 24 | 60 | 9 | 2 | 1 | 21 | 7 | .219 |
| Road | 80 | 262 | 29 | 68 | 12 | 3 | 2 | 38 | 7 | .260 |
| vs. RHP | | 429 | | 108 | | | 2 | 52 | | .252 |
| vs. LHP | | 107 | | 20 | | | 1 | 7 | | .187 |
| 1982 | 161 | 536 | 53 | 128 | 21 | 5 | 3 | 59 | 14 | .239 |
| 6.09 years | | 586 | 79 | 149 | 23 | 6 | 3 | 39 | 28 | .255 |

Gary MATTHEWS, Left Field

*Runs Created: 95*

| | G | AB | R | H | 2B | 3B | HR | RBI | SB | Avg |
|---|---|---|---|---|---|---|---|---|---|---|
| First Half | 85 | 319 | 47 | 90 | 14 | 0 | 14 | 54 | 13 | .282 |
| Second Half | 77 | 297 | 42 | 83 | 17 | 1 | 5 | 29 | 8 | .279 |
| Home | 81 | 296 | 47 | 89 | 18 | 0 | 10 | 38 | 7 | .301 |
| Road | 81 | 320 | 42 | 84 | 13 | 1 | 9 | 45 | 14 | .263 |
| vs. RHP | | 497 | | 138 | | | 14 | 67 | | .278 |
| vs. LHP | | 119 | | 35 | | | 5 | 16 | | .294 |
| 1982 | 162 | 616 | 89 | 173 | 31 | 1 | 19 | 83 | 21 | .281 |
| 8.92 years | | 603 | 91 | 174 | 28 | 5 | 19 | 83 | 17 | .288 |

### Garry MADDOX, Center Field

*Runs Created: 51*

| | G | AB | R | H | 2B | 3B | HR | RBI | SB | Avg |
|---|---|---|---|---|---|---|---|---|---|---|
| First Half | 60 | 179 | 16 | 50 | 15 | 1 | 3 | 26 | 4 | .279 |
| Second Half | 59 | 233 | 23 | 67 | 12 | 1 | 5 | 35 | 3 | .288 |
| Home | 64 | 212 | 16 | 51 | 11 | 1 | 4 | 27 | 5 | .241 |
| Road | 55 | 200 | 23 | 66 | 16 | 1 | 4 | 34 | 2 | .330 |
| vs. RHP | | 355 | | 99 | | | 7 | 52 | | .279 |
| vs. LHP | | 57 | | 18 | | | 1 | 9 | | .316 |
| 1982 | 119 | 412 | 39 | 117 | 27 | 2 | 8 | 61 | 7 | .284 |
| 9.04 years | | 613 | 77 | 176 | 34 | 7 | 12 | 75 | 26 | .287 |

### Bob DERNIER, Right Field

*Runs Created: 41*

| | G | AB | R | H | 2B | 3B | HR | RBI | SB | Avg |
|---|---|---|---|---|---|---|---|---|---|---|
| First Half | 77 | 279 | 48 | 76 | 9 | 1 | 3 | 18 | 35 | .272 |
| Second Half | 45 | 91 | 8 | 16 | 1 | 1 | 1 | 3 | 7 | .198 |
| Home | 63 | 178 | 32 | 47 | 5 | 0 | 3 | 11 | 23 | .264 |
| Road | 59 | 192 | 24 | 45 | 5 | 2 | 1 | 10 | 19 | .234 |
| vs. RHP | | 271 | | 59 | | | 0 | 9 | | .218 |
| vs. LHP | | 99 | | 33 | | | 4 | 12 | | .333 |
| 1982 | 122 | 370 | 56 | 92 | 10 | 2 | 4 | 21 | 42 | .249 |
| 0.88 years | | 433 | 69 | 113 | 11 | 2 | 5 | 25 | 53 | .260 |

### Bo DIAZ, Catcher

*Runs Created: 76*

| | G | AB | R | H | 2B | 3B | HR | RBI | SB | Avg |
|---|---|---|---|---|---|---|---|---|---|---|
| First Half | 80 | 288 | 49 | 85 | 19 | 0 | 14 | 55 | 3 | .295 |
| Second Half | 64 | 237 | 20 | 66 | 10 | 1 | 4 | 30 | 0 | .278 |
| Home | 74 | 233 | 29 | 74 | 18 | 0 | 11 | 47 | 2 | .318 |
| Road | 70 | 292 | 40 | 77 | 11 | 1 | 7 | 38 | 1 | .264 |
| vs. RHP | | 430 | | 124 | | | 16 | 71 | | .288 |
| vs. LHP | | 95 | | 27 | | | 2 | 14 | | .284 |
| 1982 | 144 | 525 | 69 | 151 | 29 | 1 | 18 | 85 | 3 | .288 |
| 2.12 years | | 507 | 57 | 137 | 31 | 1 | 14 | 79 | 3 | .270 |

### George VUKOVICH, Outfielder

*Runs Created: 40*

| | G | AB | R | H | 2B | 3B | HR | RBI | SB | Avg |
|---|---|---|---|---|---|---|---|---|---|---|
| First Half | 53 | 124 | 18 | 29 | 5 | 2 | 4 | 23 | 1 | .234 |
| Second Half | 70 | 211 | 23 | 62 | 13 | 0 | 2 | 19 | 1 | .294 |
| Home | 60 | 163 | 20 | 46 | 8 | 2 | 3 | 25 | 2 | .282 |
| Road | 63 | 172 | 21 | 45 | 10 | 0 | 3 | 17 | 0 | .262 |
| vs. RHP | | 320 | | 87 | | | 6 | 41 | | .272 |
| vs. LHP | | 15 | | 4 | | | 0 | 1 | | .267 |
| 1982 | 123 | 335 | 41 | 91 | 18 | 2 | 6 | 42 | 2 | .272 |
| 1.36 years | | 308 | 38 | 84 | 14 | 2 | 5 | 40 | 2 | .272 |

### Steve CARLTON

| Year | (W–L) | GS | Run | Avg | DP | Avg | SB | Avg |
|---|---|---|---|---|---|---|---|---|
| 1976 | (20- 7) | 35 | 216 | 6.17 | 31 | .89 | 30 | .86 |
| 1977 | (23-10) | 36 | 175 | 4.86 | 28 | .79 | 34 | .94 |
| 1978 | (16-13) | 34 | 161 | 4.74 | 30 | .88 | 14 | .41 |
| 1979 | (18-11) | 35 | 170 | 4.86 | 30 | .86 | 12 | .34 |
| 1980 | (24- 9) | 38 | 167 | 4.39 | 27 | .71 | 20 | .53 |
| 1981 | (13- 4) | 24 | 106 | 4.42 | 21 | .88 | 13 | .54 |
| 1982 | (23-11) | 38 | 165 | 4.34 | 33 | .87 | 22 | .58 |
| 7 years | | 240 | 1160 | 4.83 | 200 | .83 | 145 | .60 |

| | G | IP | W | L | Pct | ER | ERA |
|---|---|---|---|---|---|---|---|
| Home | 18 | 148 | 13 | 4 | .765 | 41 | 2.55 |
| Road | 20 | 147.2 | 10 | 7 | .588 | 61 | 3.70 |

### Mike KRUKOW

| Year | (W–L) | GS | Run | Avg | DP | Avg | SB | Avg |
|---|---|---|---|---|---|---|---|---|
| 1977 | ( 8-14) | 33 | 139 | 4.21 | 29 | .88 | 42 | 1.27 |
| 1978 | ( 9- 3) | 20 | 89 | 4.45 | 19 | .95 | 19 | .95 |
| 1979 | ( 9- 9) | 28 | 110 | 3.93 | 29 | 1.04 | 24 | .86 |
| 1980 | (10-15) | 34 | 153 | 4.50 | 27 | .79 | 42 | 1.24 |
| 1981 | ( 9- 9) | 25 | 109 | 4.36 | 25 | 1.00 | 30 | 1.20 |
| 1982 | (13-11) | 33 | 136 | 4.12 | 29 | .88 | 38 | 1.15 |
| 6 years | | 173 | 736 | 4.25 | 158 | .91 | 195 | 1.13 |

| | G | IP | W | L | Pct | ER | ERA |
|---|---|---|---|---|---|---|---|
| Home | 15 | 92.1 | 6 | 7 | .462 | 34 | 3.31 |
| Road | 18 | 115.2 | 7 | 4 | .636 | 38 | 2.96 |

### Larry CHRISTENSON

| Year | (W–L) | GS | Run | Avg | DP | Avg | SB | Avg |
|---|---|---|---|---|---|---|---|---|
| 1976 | (13- 8) | 29 | 144 | 4.97 | 27 | .93 | 20 | .69 |
| 1977 | (19- 6) | 34 | 216 | 6.35 | 28 | .82 | 16 | .47 |
| 1978 | (13-14) | 33 | 113 | 3.42 | 25 | .76 | 15 | .46 |
| 1979 | ( 5-10) | 17 | 50 | 2.94 | 16 | .94 | 8 | .47 |
| 1980 | ( 5- 1) | 14 | 70 | 5.00 | 9 | .64 | 10 | .71 |
| 1981 | ( 4- 7) | 15 | 59 | 3.93 | 12 | .80 | 16 | 1.07 |
| 1982 | ( 9-10) | 33 | 135 | 4.09 | 30 | .91 | 23 | .70 |
| 7 years | | 175 | 787 | 4.50 | 147 | .84 | 108 | .62 |

| | G | IP | W | L | Pct | ER | ERA |
|---|---|---|---|---|---|---|---|
| Home | 14 | 96 | 6 | 3 | .667 | 35 | 3.28 |
| Road | 19 | 127 | 3 | 7 | .300 | 51 | 3.54 |

### Dick RUTHVEN

| Year | (W–L) | GS | Run | Avg | DP | Avg | SB | Avg |
|---|---|---|---|---|---|---|---|---|
| 1976 | (14-17) | 36 | 131 | 3.64 | 44 | 1.22 | 41 | 1.14 |
| 1977 | ( 7-13) | 23 | 87 | 3.78 | 13 | .57 | 32 | 1.39 |
| 1978 | (15-11) | 33 | 124 | 3.76 | 33 | 1.00 | 25 | .76 |
| 1979 | ( 7- 5) | 20 | 102 | 5.10 | 11 | .55 | 16 | .80 |
| 1980 | (17-10) | 33 | 154 | 4.67 | 40 | 1.21 | 33 | 1.00 |
| 1981 | (12- 7) | 22 | 109 | 4.95 | 18 | .82 | 36 | 1.64 |
| 1982 | (11-11) | 31 | 122 | 3.94 | 20 | .65 | 36 | 1.16 |
| 7 years | | 198 | 829 | 4.19 | 179 | .91 | 219 | 1.10 |

| | G | IP | W | L | Pct | ER | ERA |
|---|---|---|---|---|---|---|---|
| Home | 18 | 112.2 | 7 | 4 | .636 | 39 | 3.12 |
| Road | 15 | 91.2 | 4 | 7 | .364 | 47 | 4.61 |

### 1982 OTHERS

| Pitcher | (W–L) | GS | Run | Avg | DP | Avg | SB | Avg |
|---|---|---|---|---|---|---|---|---|
| Bystrom | (5-6) | 16 | 66 | 4.13 | 15 | .94 | 21 | 1.31 |
| Denny | (0-2) | 4 | 5 | 1.25 | 2 | .50 | 0 | |
| Farmer | (2-6) | 4 | 18 | 4.50 | 3 | .75 | 6 | 1.50 |
| R. Reed | (5-5) | 2 | 12 | 6.00 | 3 | 1.50 | 2 | 1.00 |
| Baller | (0-0) | 1 | 5 | | 0 | | 2 | |

## PHILADELPHIA

*Talent Analysis*

The Phillies in 1982 possessed 151 points of approximate value:

| | AV | % |
|---|---|---|
| Produced by Phillies' system: | 41 | 27% |
| Acquired by trade: | 98 | 65% |
| Purchased or signed from free agency: | 12 | 8% |

Their percentages are virtually identical to the Cardinals. They are basically a trade-built team.

| | | |
|---|---|---|
| Young (Up to age 25): | 2 | 1% |
| Prime (Age 26 to 29): | 42 | 28% |
| Past-prime (Age 30 to 33): | 70 | 46% |
| Old (Age 34 or older): | 37 | 25% |

71% of their talent is past-prime or old. Only one other National League team, Houston, has even 50% of its talent in those two classes. But I should mention . . . I began writing about the inevitable demise of the Phillies due to aging four years ago, and it hasn't happened yet.

The Phillies ranked fourth in the majors in the amount of 1982 talent produced and rank ninth in the amount produced over for last four seasons.

## VETERAN'S STADIUM

DIMENSIONS: Normal

SURFACE: Artificial; fast carpet

VISIBILITY: —

FOUL TERRITORY: Large

FAVORS:
- Hitter/Pitcher—Hitter
- Power/Line-drive hitter—Power
- Righthander/Lefthander—Neither

TYPES OF OFFENSE AFFECTED: Batting averages not changed, but all types of extra base hits increased

OTHER PARK CHARACTERISTICS: Artificial turf eliminates 14% of infield errors, second-largest effect in league

TYPES OF MARGINAL PLAYERS MOST VALUABLE IN PARK: Line-drive hitters with power

PLAYERS ON TEAM HELPED MOST BY PARK: Gary Matthews

PLAYERS ON TEAM HURT MOST BY PARK: No one seriously

OTHER COMMENTS: Park increases HR by 13%

## THE GAMES THAT LOST IT

On September 10, the Phillies were in first place. As the Cardinals went on a tear, the Phillies lost 8 out of 11 games to drop out of the race. An account of those 11 games:

| Date | Opponent | Score | Starter/Loser | What happened? |
|---|---|---|---|---|
| 9-11 | Pittsburgh | 9-10 | Krukow/Reed | Had 17 hits (Rose had 4) but lost in 9th |
| 9-12 | Pittsburgh | 2-4 | Christenson | 3-run double by Berra |
| 9-13 | St. Louis | 2-0 WIN | Carlton | 3-hit shutout and homer |
| 9-14 | St. Louis | 0-2 | Krukow | Bases loaded DP ball hit by Schmidt in 8th |
| 9-15 | St. Louis | 0-8 | Denny | 3-hit shutout by Andujar |
| 9-17 | Pittsburgh | 2-4 | Carlton | 5th inning HR by Harper |
| 9-18 | Pittsburgh | 5-4 WIN | | Rose homered in 7th to win it |
| 9-19 | Pittsburgh | 1-8 | Krukow | Krukow routed |
| 9-20 | St. Louis | 1-4 | Denny | Andujar sharp; Denny hit hard |
| 9-21 | St. Louis | 5-2 WIN | Carlton | 14 strikeouts |
| 9-22 | Montreal | 4-11 | Ruthven | Speier drove in 8 runs |

**HITTERS**

| | G | AB | R | H | 2B | 3B | HR | RBI | Avg |
|---|---|---|---|---|---|---|---|---|---|
| Maddox | 11 | 43 | 4 | 10 | 3 | 0 | 0 | 3 | .233 |
| Rose | 11 | 39 | 4 | 11 | 0 | 0 | 1 | 7 | .282 |
| Schmidt | 11 | 42 | 4 | 8 | 2 | 0 | 3 | 6 | .190 |
| Matthews | 11 | 39 | 2 | 8 | 1 | 0 | 0 | 2 | .205 |
| Diaz | 6 | 22 | 0 | 1 | 0 | 0 | 0 | 0 | .045 |
| Vukovich | 11 | 30 | 4 | 8 | 1 | 0 | 0 | 1 | .267 |
| Trillo | 11 | 41 | 2 | 10 | 0 | 0 | 0 | 1 | .244 |
| DeJesus | 11 | 33 | 3 | 8 | 2 | 0 | 0 | 6 | .242 |
| Virgil | 7 | 18 | 3 | 7 | 2 | 0 | 1 | 1 | .389 |

**PITCHERS**

| | G | IP | W–L | ERA | Sv |
|---|---|---|---|---|---|
| Carlton | 3 | 23 | 2-1 | 2.35 | 0 |
| Christenson | 2 | 12 | 0-1 | 5.11 | 0 |
| Krukow | 3 | 12 | 0-2 | 10.03 | 0 |
| Farmer | 4 | 9 | 0-0 | 0.96 | 0 |
| Denny | 2 | 7 | 0-2 | 8.59 | 0 |
| Bahnsen | 3 | 7 | 0-0 | 2.70 | 0 |
| Altamirano | 5 | 5 | 0-0 | 3.86 | 0 |
| Ruthven | 2 | 5 | 0-1 | 13.50 | 0 |
| Monge | 3 | 5 | 1-0 | 1.93 | 0 |

COMMENTS:

1) Philly pitchers hit .375 (6-for-16) during the stretch.

2) The Phillies committed only 6 errors during the stretch.

3) Greg Gross was quite effective coming off the bench (4 hits and a sac fly).

4) Schmidt, Matthews, and Diaz combined hit .165 with 8 RBI in 103 at bats.

# MONTREAL EXPOS

In the NL in 1982, the two teams with the best record on grass fields were the Expos (28-14, .667) and the Cardinals (27-15, .643), who play not only on turf but on two of the fastest turfs around. The teams with the two best records while playing on the shaggy linoleum were the Dodgers (25-17, .595) and the Brewers (24-18, .571) both of whom play on grass most of the time.

The Montreal Expos of 1982 were a team that was never out of the pennant race and was never in it. They were never far enough away from the top of the division, from the first of May to the middle of September, that they couldn't have reached the top just by sweeping a couple of quick series. They could never do it. In retrospect, it might have been better for the team had they had a real bad spell, gotten 10 games behind or so and panicked. They never did that, either. They hung around the fringes of the pennant race, without momentum or direction, from beginning to end, waiting for something to happen.

Perhaps I should just skip all of the numbers here, and abandon the floor to those who analyze pennant races in terms of "momentum" and "psychology," "guts" and "desire." It is my belief, as it must be everyone's, that there is a center to a ball club, that that center is formed by the feeling that each player has for the group as a whole. Jim Fanning's obvious failure to take command of the group, by such twerpish habits as changing his second baseman every week and asking his pitchers whether they wanted to pitch to Mike Schmidt or George Vukovich, induced severe doubts in each player about the group as a whole. No center; no momentum; no pennant.

Still, whatever the origin of the Expos' problems, those problems must still take the road of something tangible to make themselves known, as even a ghost must open and close doors and move furniture around or we would never know that there was a ghost there. It is fine to say that the Expos are a better team on paper than the Cardinals, but the Cardinals' approximate value was 169 and the Expos' 157. So what are the differences?

The Expos in 1982 had three players having 15-point seasons (or higher) by the Value Approximation Method. Fourteen points is basically the nominating level for the MVP award. The Cardinals did not have a 15-point player. Do you think that's an accurate comparison? I do. For all the talk you heard about Ozzie and Lonnie and Sutter as MVP candidates, I sure don't think anybody would trade Carter for Ozzie or Dawson for Lonnie, and I wouldn't trade a starter who was 19-8 with a 2.40 ERA for a reliever with Sutter's stats. There were only seven 15-point players in the league, and the Expos had three of them. So then how could the Cardinals be a better team on paper?

| | MONTREAL | | ST. LOUIS | |
|---|---|---|---|---|
| **LINEUP** | | | | |
| **Pos** | **Player** | **AV** | **Player** | **AV** |
| C | Carter | 17 | Porter | 8 |
| 1B | Oliver | 12 | Hernandez | 12 |
| 2B | Flynn | 2 | Herr | 12 |
| 3B | Wallach | 9 | Oberkfell | 9 |
| SS | Speier | 9 | O. Smith | 12 |
| LF | Raines | 11 | L. Smith | 14 |
| CF | Dawson | 15 | McGee | 7 |
| RF | Cromartie | 9 | Hendrick | 11 |
| **PITCHERS** | | | | |
| Ace | Rogers | 16 | Andujar | 12 |
| #2 Starter | Sanderson | 8 | Forsch | 9 |
| #3 Starter | Gullickson | 8 | LaPoint | 7 |
| #4 Starter | Lea | 7 | Mura | 6 |
| Relief Ace | Reardon | 11 | Sutter | 13 |
| Middle Man | Smith | 3 | Bair | 7 |
| Short Man | Fryman | 8 | Kaat | 4 |
| Long Man | Burrios | 3 | Lahti | 4 |
| Spot Starters | Palmer | 3 | Stuper | 5 |
| Others | | | Martin | 1 |
| | | | Rincon | 1 |
| **RESERVES** | | | | |
| C | Blackwell | 0 | Tenace | 4 |
| INF | Gates | 1 | Ramsey | 3 |
| INF | Mills | 1 | Gonzales | 1 |
| OF | White | 1 | Iorg | 3 |
| OF | Youngblood | 1 | Green | 2 |
| OF | Francona | 1 | Landrum | 1 |
| OF | Norman | 1 | Braun | 1 |
| **TOTALS:** | | | | |
| Lineup | | 84 | | 85 |
| Pitchers | | 67 | | 69 |
| Bench | | 6 | | 15 |

My friends who are Expo fans are convinced that too much has been said about the second-base matter already, that the press is using that as a catch-all for problems that really go much deeper. I can't agree with them. The Expos' starting lineup becomes stronger than the Cardinals' if you just pencil in a 7 or an 8—a not-very-good player—at second base. In essence, the Expos had exactly the same problem that the Cardinals had before Herzog: tremendous strength at some positions, which is completely negated by an unnecessary failure to plug a hole, like a girl with flashing eyes and a turned-up nose and three teeth missing. A 7- or 8-point second baseman (Doug Flynn would be about that as a full-time player) isn't difficult to find; nobody should lose a pennant race for the lack of one.

It should also be noted that if there is a moment at which the Expo season went sour, it is, again, related to this problem. The Expos had some defensive maladies stemming from the Al Oliver trade early in the season, but on June 16, they had won 17 out of 26 games (.654 percentage, for about a month) and pulled virtually even with the Cardinals. Terry Francona was injured on that date, and when Tim Raines was sent to left field that ripped the scab off the second base situation. The Expos lost their momentum after that, and they never regained it.

The irony here is that there were national media stories just two years ago about the Expos' glut of young second basemen. Remember those? The theme was:

1) The Expos have a good second baseman already, Rodney Scott.

2) But they've got a kid on their major-league roster, Tony Bernazard, who is good enough to play.

3) And they've got the prospect of the decade at second base for Denver, Tim Raines.

4) And another one at Memphis, Gates, who is too good to be playing at the AA level.

5) And now some kid second baseman named Wallace Johnson is hitting .334 in the rookie league.

What happened? The law of competitive balance. They had so many viable options at second base that they couldn't bring themselves to make a commitment to any one of them. If the Expos had had only one young second baseman, if they had had only Bernazard, or only Raines or even only Gates, they would never have gotten into this mess. They traded Bernazard away because he didn't seem that valuable, they moved Raines to left field because they had other ways of dealing with the second base problem. And then . . . boom. The strength became a weakness.

But that only kept the Expos from having a *stronger* lineup than the Cardinals. Their lineup was still just as strong. The difference is the bench. And that has to reflect on the manager. Are players like Gene Tenace and Dane Iorg and Mike Ramsey really that hard to come by?

What I like about baseball is that it so rarely rises to the level of tragedy, but suspends the shadows of anguish on a tether. It is sad to see such magnificent players as Carter and Dawson and Oliver and Raines and Rogers and Reardon struck down by a needless failure of the organization to provide them with the bit players that they need to make a whole team. Sad, but not tragic. They are too well-paid for tragedy.

Al OLIVER, First Base
*Runs Created: 124*

| | G | AB | R | H | 2B | 3B | HR | RBI | SB | Avg |
|---|---|---|---|---|---|---|---|---|---|---|
| First Half | 84 | 315 | 47 | 101 | 21 | 2 | 14 | 60 | 5 | .321 |
| Second Half | 76 | 302 | 43 | 103 | 22 | 0 | 8 | 49 | 0 | .341 |
| Home | 80 | 296 | 40 | 99 | 20 | 2 | 12 | 64 | 4 | .334 |
| Road | 80 | 321 | 50 | 105 | 23 | 0 | 10 | 45 | 1 | .327 |
| vs. RHP | | 433 | | 144 | | | | | | .333 |
| vs. LHP | | 184 | | 60 | | | | | | .326 |
| 1982 | 160 | 617 | 90 | 204 | 43 | 2 | 22 | 109 | 5 | .331 |
| 12.32 years | | 628 | 86 | 192 | 37 | 6 | 17 | 94 | 7 | .305 |

Doug FLYNN, Second Base
*Runs Created: 29*

| | G | AB | R | H | 2B | 3B | HR | RBI | SB | Avg |
|---|---|---|---|---|---|---|---|---|---|---|
| First Half | 73 | 231 | 10 | 48 | 4 | 1 | 0 | 16 | 5 | .208 |
| Second Half | 73 | 232 | 16 | 56 | 8 | 3 | 0 | 23 | 1 | .241 |
| Home | 75 | 224 | 8 | 42 | 5 | 2 | 0 | 23 | 2 | .188 |
| Road | 71 | 239 | 18 | 62 | 7 | 2 | 0 | 16 | 4 | .259 |
| vs. RHP | | 376 | | 87 | | | | | | .231 |
| vs. LHP | | 87 | | 17 | | | | | | .195 |
| 1982 | 146 | 463 | 26 | 104 | 12 | 4 | 0 | 39 | 6 | .225 |
| 6.17 years | | 483 | 36 | 115 | 14 | 5 | 1 | 39 | 3 | .238 |

Tim WALLACH, Third Base
*Runs Created: 86*

| | G | AB | R | H | 2B | 3B | HR | RBI | SB | Avg |
|---|---|---|---|---|---|---|---|---|---|---|
| First Half | 81 | 297 | 46 | 79 | 16 | 2 | 11 | 48 | 4 | .266 |
| Second Half | 77 | 299 | 43 | 81 | 15 | 1 | 17 | 49 | 2 | .271 |
| Home | 80 | 283 | 44 | 84 | 24 | 1 | 11 | 42 | 3 | .297 |
| Road | 78 | 313 | 45 | 76 | 7 | 2 | 17 | 55 | 3 | .243 |
| vs. RHP | | 451 | | 113 | | | | | | .251 |
| vs. LHP | | 145 | | 47 | | | | | | .324 |
| 1982 | 158 | 596 | 89 | 160 | 31 | 3 | 28 | 97 | 6 | .268 |
| 1.44 years | | 569 | 76 | 147 | 28 | 3 | 23 | 78 | 4 | .259 |

Chris SPEIER, Shortstop
*Runs Created: 58*

| | G | AB | R | H | 2B | 3B | HR | RBI | SB | Avg |
|---|---|---|---|---|---|---|---|---|---|---|
| First Half | 82 | 274 | 19 | 72 | 14 | 2 | 2 | 25 | 0 | .263 |
| Second Half | 74 | 256 | 22 | 64 | 12 | 2 | 5 | 35 | 1 | .250 |
| Home | 79 | 267 | 16 | 63 | 14 | 2 | 2 | 35 | 0 | .236 |
| Road | 77 | 263 | 25 | 73 | 12 | 2 | 5 | 25 | 1 | .278 |
| vs. RHP | | 397 | | 102 | | | | | | .257 |
| vs. LHP | | 133 | | 34 | | | | | | .256 |
| 1982 | 156 | 530 | 41 | 136 | 26 | 4 | 7 | 60 | 1 | .257 |
| 10.34 years | | 562 | 60 | 139 | 23 | 5 | 8 | 56 | 3 | .247 |

Tim RAINES, Left Field
*Runs Created: 95*

| | G | AB | R | H | 2B | 3B | HR | RBI | SB | Avg |
|---|---|---|---|---|---|---|---|---|---|---|
| First Half | 81 | 337 | 43 | 97 | 18 | 3 | 2 | 25 | 39 | .288 |
| Second Half | 75 | 310 | 47 | 82 | 14 | 5 | 2 | 18 | 39 | .265 |
| Home | 76 | 308 | 45 | 84 | 17 | 3 | 1 | 15 | 43 | .273 |
| Road | 80 | 339 | 45 | 95 | 15 | 5 | 3 | 28 | 35 | .280 |
| vs. RHP | | 464 | | 123 | | | | | | .265 |
| vs. LHP | | 183 | | 56 | | | | | | .306 |
| 1982 | 156 | 647 | 90 | 179 | 32 | 8 | 4 | 43 | 78 | .277 |
| 1.64 years | | 599 | 97 | 168 | 28 | 9 | 6 | 49 | 95 | ,281 |

Andre DAWSON, Center Field
*Runs Created: 105*

| | G | AB | R | H | 2B | 3B | HR | RBI | SB | Avg |
|---|---|---|---|---|---|---|---|---|---|---|
| First Half | 75 | 311 | 60 | 95 | 20 | 1 | 11 | 45 | 21 | .305 |
| Second Half | 73 | 297 | 47 | 88 | 17 | 6 | 12 | 38 | 18 | .296 |
| Home | 73 | 297 | 55 | 86 | 17 | 3 | 9 | 36 | 23 | .290 |
| Road | 75 | 311 | 52 | 97 | 20 | 4 | 14 | 47 | 16 | .312 |
| vs. RHP | | 442 | | 142 | | | | | | .321 |
| vs. LHP | | 166 | | 41 | | | | | | .247 |
| 1982 | 148 | 608 | 107 | 183 | 37 | 7 | 23 | 83 | 39 | .301 |
| 5.41 years | | 635 | 96 | 181 | 33 | 9 | 25 | 87 | 34 | .285 |

### Warren CROMARTIE, Right Field

*Runs Created: 69*

| | G | AB | R | H | 2B | 3B | HR | RBI | SB | Avg |
|---|---|---|---|---|---|---|---|---|---|---|
| First Half | 82 | 288 | 36 | 71 | 10 | 2 | 10 | 42 | 3 | .247 |
| Second Half | 62 | 209 | 23 | 55 | 14 | 1 | 4 | 20 | 0 | .263 |
| Home | 72 | 244 | 25 | 60 | 12 | 2 | 4 | 27 | 2 | .246 |
| Road | 72 | 253 | 34 | 66 | 12 | 1 | 10 | 35 | 1 | .261 |
| vs. RHP | | 377 | | 100 | | | | | | .265 |
| vs. LHP | | 120 | | 26 | | | | | | .217 |
| 1982 | 144 | 497 | 59 | 126 | 24 | 3 | 14 | 62 | 3 | .254 |
| 5.67 years | | 606 | 72 | 170 | 35 | 5 | 10 | 58 | 8 | .280 |

### Gary CARTER, Catcher

*Runs Created: 105*

| | G | AB | R | H | 2B | 3B | HR | RBI | SB | Avg |
|---|---|---|---|---|---|---|---|---|---|---|
| First Half | 79 | 284 | 53 | 89 | 19 | 1 | 19 | 55 | 2 | .313 |
| Second Half | 75 | 273 | 38 | 74 | 13 | 0 | 10 | 42 | 0 | .271 |
| Home | 77 | 259 | 50 | 75 | 19 | 1 | 16 | 47 | 1 | .290 |
| Road | 77 | 298 | 41 | 88 | 13 | 0 | 13 | 50 | 1 | .295 |
| vs. RHP | | 402 | | 114 | | | | | | .284 |
| vs. LHP | | 155 | | 49 | | | | | | .316 |
| 1982 | 154 | 557 | 91 | 163 | 32 | 1 | 29 | 97 | 2 | .293 |
| 6.82 years | | 569 | 80 | 153 | 27 | 3 | 25 | 89 | 5 | .269 |

### Joel YOUNGBLOOD, Outfielder

*Runs Created: 25*

| | G | AB | R | H | 2B | 3B | HR | RBI | SB | Avg |
|---|---|---|---|---|---|---|---|---|---|---|
| First Half | 66 | 172 | 18 | 41 | 10 | 0 | 3 | 15 | 0 | .238 |
| Second Half | 54 | 120 | 19 | 29 | 4 | 0 | 0 | 14 | 2 | .242 |
| Home | | | | | | | | | | |
| Road | | | | | | | | | | |
| vs. RHP | | 192 | | 41 | 7 | 0 | 2 | | | .213 |
| vs. LHP | | 100 | | 29 | 7 | 0 | 1 | | | .290 |
| 1982 | 120 | 292 | 37 | 70 | 14 | 0 | 3 | 29 | 2 | .240 |
| 4.51 years | | 459 | 59 | 123 | 25 | 4 | 8 | 50 | 9 | .267 |

### Steve ROGERS

| Year | (W–L) | GS | Run | Avg | DP | Avg | SB | Avg |
|---|---|---|---|---|---|---|---|---|
| 1976 | ( 7-17) | 32 | 92 | 2.88 | 32 | 1.00 | 14 | .44 |
| 1977 | (17-16) | 40 | 155 | 3.88 | 30 | .75 | 26 | .65 |
| 1978 | (13-10) | 29 | 89 | 3.07 | 29 | 1.00 | 11 | .38 |
| 1979 | (13-12) | 37 | 153 | 4.14 | 35 | .95 | 31 | .84 |
| 1980 | (16-11) | 37 | 159 | 4.30 | 24 | .65 | 27 | .73 |
| 1981 | (12- 8) | 22 | 88 | 4.00 | 19 | .86 | 13 | .59 |
| 1982 | (19- 8) | 35 | 149 | 4.26 | 29 | .83 | 25 | .71 |
| 7 years | | 232 | 885 | 3.81 | 198 | .85 | 147 | .63 |

| | G | IP | W | L | Pct | ER | ERA |
|---|---|---|---|---|---|---|---|
| Home | 19 | 146.1 | 6 | 7 | .462 | 49 | 3.01 |
| Road | 16 | 131.1 | 13 | 1 | .929 | 25 | 1.71 |

### Bill GULLICKSON

| Year | (W–L) | GS | Run | Avg | DP | Avg | SB | Avg |
|---|---|---|---|---|---|---|---|---|
| 1980 | (10- 5) | 19 | 86 | 4.53 | 13 | .68 | 16 | .84 |
| 1981 | ( 7- 9) | 22 | 77 | 3.50 | 19 | .86 | 18 | .82 |
| 1982 | (12-14) | 34 | 153 | 4.50 | 21 | .62 | 23 | .68 |
| 3 years | | 75 | 316 | 4.21 | 53 | .71 | 57 | .76 |

| | G | IP | W | L | Pct | ER | ERA |
|---|---|---|---|---|---|---|---|
| Home | 14 | 99.2 | 5 | 5 | .500 | 46 | 4.15 |
| Road | 20 | 137 | 7 | 9 | .438 | 48 | 3.15 |

### Scott SANDERSON

| Year | (W–L) | GS | Run | Avg | DP | Avg | SB | Avg |
|---|---|---|---|---|---|---|---|---|
| 1978 | ( 4- 2) | 9 | 31 | 3.44 | 4 | .44 | 11 | 1.22 |
| 1979 | ( 9- 8) | 24 | 96 | 4.00 | 15 | .62 | 19 | .79 |
| 1980 | (16-11) | 33 | 125 | 3.79 | 24 | .73 | 18 | .55 |
| 1981 | ( 9- 7) | 22 | 107 | 4.86 | 11 | .50 | 9 | .41 |
| 1982 | (12-12) | 32 | 142 | 4.44 | 18 | .56 | 25 | .78 |
| 5 years | | 120 | 501 | 4.18 | 72 | .60 | 82 | .68 |

| | G | IP | W | L | Pct | ER | ERA |
|---|---|---|---|---|---|---|---|
| Home | 20 | 135.2 | 6 | 9 | .400 | 58 | 3.85 |
| Road | 12 | 88.1 | 6 | 3 | .667 | 28 | 2.85 |

### Charlie LEA

| Year | (W–L) | GS | Run | Avg | DP | Avg | SB | Avg |
|---|---|---|---|---|---|---|---|---|
| 1980 | ( 7- 5) | 19 | 87 | 4.58 | 15 | .79 | 13 | .68 |
| 1981 | ( 5- 4) | 11 | 41 | 3.73 | 11 | 1.00 | 7 | .64 |
| 1982 | (12-10) | 27 | 120 | 4.44 | 18 | .67 | 17 | .63 |
| 3 years | | 57 | 248 | 4.35 | 44 | .77 | 37 | .65 |

| | G | IP | W | L | Pct | ER | ERA |
|---|---|---|---|---|---|---|---|
| Home | 11 | 73.2 | 3 | 6 | .333 | 28 | 3.42 |
| Road | 16 | 104 | 9 | 4 | .692 | 36 | 3.12 |

### 1982 OTHERS

| Pitcher | (W–L) | GS | Run | Avg | DP | Avg | SB | Avg |
|---|---|---|---|---|---|---|---|---|
| Burris | (4-14) | 15 | 48 | 3.20 | 11 | .73 | 12 | .80 |
| Palmer | (6- 4) | 13 | 61 | 4.69 | 11 | .85 | 12 | .92 |
| Lerch | (2- 0) | 4 | 22 | 5.50 | 8 | 2.00 | 4 | 1.00 |
| Smith | (2- 4) | 1 | 0 | | 0 | | 0 | |
| Schatzeder | (1- 6) | 1 | 2 | | 0 | | 2 | |

## MONTREAL

*Talent Analysis*

| | AV | % |
|---|---|---|
| Produced by Expos' system: | 107 | 68% |
| Acquired by trade: | 47 | 30% |
| Purchased or signed from free agency: | 3 | 2% |

The Expos are basically a system-built team. Their 107 points of home-grown talent are exceeded by only one NL team, the Dodgers.

| | | |
|---|---|---|
| Young (Up to age 25): | 32 | 20% |
| Prime (Age 26 to 29): | 74 | 47% |
| Past-prime (Age 30 to 33): | 31 | 20% |
| Old (Age 34 or older): | 20 | 13% |

The bulk of the Expos' players are now in their prime.

The Expos ranked eleventh in the major leagues in 1982 talent produced for anybody, and rank fifteenth for the last four years combined.

## OLYMPIC STADIUM

DIMENSIONS: A little short

SURFACE: Turf

VISIBILITY: Very poor—shadows

FOUL TERRITORY: Large

FAVORS:
- Hitter/Pitcher—Pitcher
- Power/Line-drive hitter—Line-drive hitter
- Righthander/Lefthander—Neither

TYPES OF OFFENSE AFFECTED: Does not affect batting averages much, despite fairly short lines (325′) very few home runs are hit here; but triples are up over 20%

OTHER PARK CHARACTERISTICS: Cold weather depresses offense. Not many errors here.

TYPES OF MARGINAL PLAYERS MOST VALUABLE IN PARK: Power pitchers (aided by poor visibility). Quick outfielders with good arms needed to control potential X-base hits. The pattern seems to be that this park helps a player who hits the ball on the ground and hurts a hitter who hits it in the air. This also applies to pitchers; the park helps pitchers like Sanderson, who receive little double-play support and are vulnerable to the home run, but doesn't help a sinker-ball pitcher like Fryman at all.

PLAYERS ON TEAM HELPED MOST BY PARK: Tim Raines, Scott Sanderson

PLAYERS ON TEAM HURT MOST BY PARK: Andre Dawson, Gary Carter

OTHER COMMENTS: Most of the time a park in which there are a lot of home runs will also be a park in which there are a lot of strikeouts; if few home runs, few strikeouts. In Montreal there are many strikeouts but few home runs, and for that reason we can be fairly sure that the players who complain about poor visibility here are justified.

# PITTSBURGH PIRATES

I can't resist doing studies, studies about anything. One time I heard a player say that left-handed pitchers don't find themselves until age 26, and I put about 20 hours into a study designed to figure out whether left-handed pitchers tend to come around at age 26. I felt like a fool, but after all he *did* say it.

Anyway, one thing I've always wondered about was the impact that playing in New York or Los Angeles has on a player's chances of winning a big award. Did Steve Sax beat out Johnnie Ray just because Sax played in Los Angeles and Ray in Pittsburgh and the Dodgers always win the Rookie of the Year Award? Do the Yankees win more than their share of awards? The way I decided to get an angle on this was to set up a point system for, on the one hand, the performance of the ball club, and on the foot, the awards that they have won. In the performance category, a team receives 4 points for winning the league championship, 3 for winning the division and 1 for finishing as the division runner-up. This makes a total of 9 points per league per year, which I figured for all years from 1969 to 1982.

In the awards category, a team receives 4 points for having an MVP, 3 for reeling in a Cy Young Award and 2 for getting a Rookie of the Year citation. Comeback Player of the Year awards are counted the same as moving violations. Again, this creates a pool of 9 points per league per season.

Most teams, it turns out, have won about as many awards as championships. The Baltimore Orioles have won 26½ points worth of performance and 26½ points worth of awards. The Cincinnati Reds rank second in performance points with 25 and second in award points with 25. The Seattle Mariners have totals of 0 and 0. Sixteen teams have totals within four of each other in the two columns. These are:

| Team | Performance | Awards |
|---|---|---|
| Baltimore | 26½ | 26½ |
| Cincinnati | 25 | 25 |
| Los Angeles | 23½ | 20 |
| Philadelphia | 16 | 20 |
| Mets | 8 | 11 |
| St. Louis | 7 | 11 |
| Atlanta | 6½ | 8 |
| San Francisco | 4 | 8 |
| Detroit | 5½ | 5 |
| California | 6½ | 4 |
| Montreal | 5 | 4 |
| Cubs | 3 | 6 |
| Texas | 2½ | 6 |
| White Sox | 1 | 4 |
| Toronto | 0 | 1 |
| Seattle | 0 | 0 |

But there have been some injustices (or what else would you call it when a team ranks 3rd in performance but 16th in recognition?) And that brings us to the Pittsburgh Pirates.

| Performance | |
|---|---|
| Division Champions, 1970 | 3 points |
| League Champions, 1971 | 4 points |
| Division Champions, 1972 | 3 points |
| Division Champions, 1974 | 3 points |
| Division Champions, 1975 | 3 points |
| Division Runners-up, 1976 | 1 point |
| Division Runners-up, 1977 | 1 point |
| Division Runners-up, 1978 | 1 point |
| League Champions, 1979 | 4 points |
| TOTAL PERFORMANCE | 23 points |

| Awards | |
|---|---|
| Most Valuable Player, 1978 | 4 points |
| ½ Most Valuable Player, 1979 | 2 points |
| TOTAL AWARDS | 6 points |

And that's it. No Cy Young Awards, no Rookie of the Year Awards. Among the teams which have done better in award voting than the Pirates are the Minnesota Twins, the Mets, the San Francisco Giants, the Cleveland Indians and, yes, the San Diego Padres. The Twins have 12 award points, twice the Pirates' total, with two wholly-owned MVP awards, a Cy Young Award and a divided Rookie of the Year. The Indians and Padres have never finished as high as second in divisional play, but have still won more awards than the Pirates.

My Kansas City Royals have done almost as badly in award voting as the Pirates, but I'm not allowed to talk about that too much. But the big surprise is that one of baseball's biggest glamour teams, the Yankees, actually make the list of teams which have received *less recognition* than would be justified by their performance.

**ENTITLED TO BITCH**

| | Performance | Awards |
|---|---|---|
| Pirates | 23 | 6 |
| Kansas City | 19 | 6 |
| Oakland | 25 | 14 |
| Yankees | 21 | 14 |
| Astros | 5½ | 0 |

No team has been equally over-blessed, but the teams which are over-drawn at the award bank are:

| | Performance | Awards |
|---|---|---|
| Milwaukee | 6 | 14 |
| Minnesota | 6 | 12 |
| Red Sox | 7½ | 12 |
| Padres | 0 | 7 |
| Indians | 0 | 7 |

I could do a little instant analysis, but most of you could do it equally well. There is no clear pattern of bias against the Midwest and in favor of the East, and indeed for every pattern that you think you can spot, there are two or three "buts" among the ten teams on the two lists.

Should Ray have won the award over Sax? The Dodgers haven't won any more awards than they deserve, but

I would have voted for Ray over Sax to even the scales a bit. You can study their records all night and they don't become distinguishable. I would have voted for Chili Davis over both of them.

Jason THOMPSON, First Base

*Runs Created: 111*

| | G | AB | R | H | 2B | 3B | HR | RBI | SB | Avg |
|---|---|---|---|---|---|---|---|---|---|---|
| First Half | 82 | 299 | 53 | 90 | 19 | 0 | 17 | 55 | 0 | .301 |
| Second Half | 74 | 251 | 34 | 66 | 13 | 0 | 14 | 46 | 1 | .263 |
| Home | 77 | 267 | 48 | 83 | 18 | 0 | 17 | 59 | 0 | .311 |
| Road | 79 | 283 | 39 | 73 | 14 | 0 | 14 | 42 | 0 | .258 |
| vs. RHP | | 399 | | 121 | | | 30 | 88 | | .303 |
| vs. LHP | | 151 | | 35 | | | 1 | 14 | | .232 |
| 1982 | 156 | 550 | 87 | 156 | 32 | 0 | 31 | 101 | 1 | .284 |
| 5.92 years | | 556 | 78 | 148 | 24 | 2 | 27 | 96 | 1 | .266 |

Johnny RAY, Second Base

*Runs Created: 79*

| | G | AB | R | H | 2B | 3B | HR | RBI | SB | Avg |
|---|---|---|---|---|---|---|---|---|---|---|
| First Half | 84 | 339 | 47 | 103 | 16 | 4 | 6 | 37 | 7 | .304 |
| Second Half | 78 | 308 | 32 | 79 | 14 | 3 | 1 | 26 | 9 | .256 |
| Home | 81 | 307 | 51 | 94 | 17 | 5 | 6 | 36 | 9 | .306 |
| Road | 81 | 340 | 28 | 88 | 13 | 2 | 1 | 27 | 7 | .259 |
| vs. RHP | | 476 | | 145 | | | 7 | 51 | | .305 |
| vs. LHP | | 171 | | 37 | | | 0 | 12 | | .216 |
| 1982 | 162 | 647 | 79 | 182 | 30 | 7 | 7 | 63 | 16 | .281 |
| 1.19 years | | 629 | 75 | 174 | 35 | 6 | 6 | 58 | 14 | .276 |

Bill MADLOCK, Third Base

*Runs Created: 104*

| | G | AB | R | H | 2B | 3B | HR | RBI | SB | Avg |
|---|---|---|---|---|---|---|---|---|---|---|
| First Half | 82 | 303 | 50 | 94 | 20 | 0 | 8 | 50 | 10 | .310 |
| Second Half | 72 | 265 | 42 | 87 | 13 | 3 | 11 | 45 | 8 | .328 |
| Home | 77 | 274 | 47 | 93 | 16 | 2 | 13 | 57 | 6 | .339 |
| Road | 77 | 294 | 45 | 88 | 17 | 1 | 6 | 38 | 12 | .299 |
| vs. RHP | | 428 | | 144 | | | 19 | 77 | | .336 |
| vs. LHP | | 140 | | 37 | | | 0 | 18 | | .264 |
| 1982 | 154 | 568 | 92 | 181 | 33 | 3 | 19 | 95 | 18 | .319 |
| 7.47 years | | 594 | 87 | 188 | 33 | 4 | 15 | 77 | 20 | .316 |

Dale BERRA, Shortstop

*Runs Created: 61*

| | G | AB | R | H | 2B | 3B | HR | RBI | SB | Avg |
|---|---|---|---|---|---|---|---|---|---|---|
| First Half | 80 | 266 | 37 | 70 | 16 | 2 | 5 | 30 | 4 | .263 |
| Second Half | 76 | 263 | 27 | 69 | 9 | 3 | 5 | 31 | 2 | .262 |
| Home | 76 | 252 | 27 | 65 | 15 | 5 | 4 | 29 | 2 | .258 |
| Road | 80 | 277 | 37 | 74 | 10 | 0 | 6 | 32 | 4 | .267 |
| vs. RHP | | 373 | | 98 | | | 10 | 47 | | .263 |
| vs. LHP | | 156 | | 41 | | | 0 | 14 | | .263 |
| 1982 | 156 | 529 | 64 | 139 | 25 | 5 | 10 | 61 | 6 | .263 |
| 2.76 years | | 473 | 48 | 112 | 19 | 3 | 10 | 55 | 8 | .238 |

Mike EASLER, Left Field

*Runs Created: 68*

| | G | AB | R | H | 2B | 3B | HR | RBI | SB | Avg |
|---|---|---|---|---|---|---|---|---|---|---|
| First Half | 71 | 232 | 28 | 66 | 11 | 1 | 7 | 30 | 0 | .284 |
| Second Half | 71 | 243 | 24 | 65 | 16 | 1 | 8 | 28 | 1 | .267 |
| Home | 71 | 238 | 32 | 67 | 14 | 2 | 9 | 34 | 0 | .282 |
| Road | 71 | 237 | 20 | 64 | 13 | 0 | 6 | 24 | 1 | .270 |
| vs. RHP | | 411 | | 110 | | | 13 | 50 | | .280 |
| vs. LHP | | 64 | | 21 | | | 2 | 8 | | .328 |
| 1982 | 142 | 475 | 52 | 131 | 27 | 2 | 15 | 58 | 1 | .276 |
| 2.97 years | | 458 | 60 | 134 | 26 | 4 | 16 | 65 | 4 | .293 |

Omar MORENO, Center Field

*Runs Created: 60*

| | G | AB | R | H | 2B | 3B | HR | RBI | SB | Avg |
|---|---|---|---|---|---|---|---|---|---|---|
| First Half | 84 | 356 | 47 | 87 | 9 | 6 | 3 | 29 | 39 | .244 |
| Second Half | 74 | 289 | 35 | 71 | 9 | 3 | 0 | 15 | 21 | .246 |
| Home | 78 | 317 | 49 | 87 | 11 | 8 | 1 | 16 | 29 | .274 |
| Road | 80 | 328 | 33 | 71 | 7 | 1 | 2 | 28 | 31 | .216 |
| vs. RHP | | 469 | | 123 | | | 0 | 37 | | .262 |
| vs. LHP | | 176 | | 35 | | | 0 | 7 | | .199 |
| 1982 | 158 | 645 | 82 | 158 | 18 | 9 | 3 | 44 | 60 | .245 |
| 5.83 years | | 615 | 91 | 157 | 20 | 10 | 4 | 45 | 71 | .255 |

Lee LACY, Right Field

*Runs Created: 56*

| | G | AB | R | H | 2B | 3B | HR | RBI | SB | Avg |
|---|---|---|---|---|---|---|---|---|---|---|
| First Half | 61 | 178 | 36 | 54 | 7 | 1 | 2 | 15 | 26 | .303 |
| Second Half | 60 | 181 | 30 | 58 | 9 | 2 | 3 | 16 | 14 | .320 |
| Home | 60 | 192 | 36 | 64 | 10 | 0 | 4 | 15 | 20 | .333 |
| Road | 61 | 167 | 30 | 48 | 6 | 3 | 1 | 16 | 20 | .287 |
| vs. RHP | | 212 | | 67 | | | 5 | 15 | | .316 |
| vs. LHP | | 147 | | 45 | | | 0 | 16 | | .306 |
| 1982 | 121 | 359 | 66 | 112 | 16 | 3 | 5 | 31 | 40 | .312 |
| 5.80 years | | 439 | 63 | 124 | 20 | 5 | 8 | 44 | 20 | .281 |

Tony PENA, Catcher

*Runs Created: 67*

| | G | AB | R | H | 2B | 3B | HR | RBI | SB | Avg |
|---|---|---|---|---|---|---|---|---|---|---|
| First Half | 73 | 276 | 30 | 88 | 16 | 3 | 6 | 43 | 0 | .319 |
| Second Half | 65 | 221 | 23 | 59 | 12 | 1 | 5 | 20 | 2 | .267 |
| Home | 69 | 241 | 30 | 67 | 11 | 1 | 5 | 28 | 1 | .279 |
| Road | 69 | 256 | 23 | 80 | 17 | 3 | 6 | 35 | 1 | .313 |
| vs. RHP | | 386 | | 109 | | | 4 | 50 | | .282 |
| vs. LHP | | 111 | | 38 | | | 7 | 13 | | .342 |
| 1982 | 138 | 497 | 53 | 147 | 28 | 4 | 11 | 63 | 2 | .296 |
| 1.31 years | | 556 | 53 | 167 | 29 | 5 | 10 | 62 | 2 | .301 |

Rick RHODEN

| Year | (W–L) | GS | Run | Avg | DP | Avg | SB | Avg |
|---|---|---|---|---|---|---|---|---|
| 1976 | (12- 3) | 26 | 121 | 4.65 | 24 | .92 | 11 | .42 |
| 1977 | (16-10) | 31 | 142 | 2.58 | 38 | 1.23 | 23 | .74 |
| 1978 | (10- 8) | 23 | 115 | 5.00 | 15 | .65 | 18 | .78 |
| 1979 | ( 0- 1) | 1 | 1 | | 2 | | 0 | |
| 1980 | ( 7- 5) | 19 | 80 | 4.21 | 21 | 1.11 | 21 | 1.11 |
| 1981 | ( 9- 4) | 21 | 92 | 4.38 | 23 | 1.10 | 8 | .38 |
| 1982 | (11-14) | 35 | 147 | 4.20 | 23 | .66 | 17 | .49 |
| 7 years | | 156 | 698 | 4.97 | 146 | .94 | 98 | .63 |

| | G | IP | W | L | Pct | ER | ERA |
|---|---|---|---|---|---|---|---|
| Home | 17 | 118.2 | 7 | 6 | .538 | 59 | 3.79 |
| Road | 18 | 111.2 | 4 | 8 | .333 | 56 | 4.51 |

## John CANDELARIA

| Year | (W–L) | GS | Run | Avg | DP | Avg | SB | Avg |
|---|---|---|---|---|---|---|---|---|
| 1976 | (16- 7) | 13 | 152 | 4.90 | 28 | .90 | 14 | .45 |
| 1977 | (20- 5) | 33 | 139 | 4.21 | 25 | .76 | 9 | .27 |
| 1978 | (12-11) | 29 | 111 | 3.83 | 31 | 1.07 | 9 | .31 |
| 1979 | (14- 9) | 30 | 138 | 4.60 | 27 | .90 | 9 | .30 |
| 1980 | (11-14) | 34 | 140 | 4.12 | 37 | 1.09 | 12 | .35 |
| 1981 | ( 2- 2) | 6 | 31 | 5.17 | 7 | 1.17 | 1 | .17 |
| 1982 | (12- 7) | 30 | 120 | 4.00 | 32 | 1.07 | 14 | .47 |
| 7 years | | 193 | 831 | 4.31 | 187 | .97 | 68 | .35 |

| | G | IP | W | L | Pct | ER | ERA |
|---|---|---|---|---|---|---|---|
| Home | 17 | 97.1 | 6 | 5 | .545 | 39 | 3.61 |
| Road | 14 | 77.1 | 6 | 2 | .750 | 18 | 2.09 |

## Don ROBINSON

| Year | (W–L) | GS | Run | Avg | DP | Avg | SB | Avg |
|---|---|---|---|---|---|---|---|---|
| 1978 | (14- 6) | 32 | 146 | 4.56 | 22 | .69 | 24 | .75 |
| 1979 | ( 8- 8) | 25 | 126 | 5.04 | 33 | 1.32 | 11 | .44 |
| 1980 | ( 7-10) | 24 | 89 | 3.71 | 16 | .67 | 17 | .71 |
| 1981 | ( 0- 3) | 2 | 10 | 5.00 | 3 | 1.50 | 4 | 2.00 |
| 1982 | (15-13) | 30 | 145 | 4.83 | 19 | .63 | 21 | .70 |
| 5 years | | 113 | 516 | 4.48 | 93 | .82 | 77 | .68 |

| | G | IP | W | L | Pct | ER | ERA |
|---|---|---|---|---|---|---|---|
| Home | 21 | 111.2 | 5 | 8 | .385 | 74 | 5.96 |
| Road | 17 | 115.1 | 10 | 5 | .667 | 34 | 2.65 |

## Larry McWILLIAMS

| Year | (W–L) | GS | Run | Avg | DP | Avg | SB | Avg |
|---|---|---|---|---|---|---|---|---|
| 1978 | (9- 3) | 79 | 79 | 5.27 | 10 | .67 | 8 | .53 |
| 1979 | (3- 2) | 13 | 70 | 5.38 | 9 | .69 | 13 | 1.00 |
| 1980 | (9-14) | 30 | 115 | 3.82 | 22 | .73 | 22 | .73 |
| 1981 | (2- 1) | 5 | 22 | 4.40 | 4 | .80 | 0 | .00 |
| 1982 | (8- 8) | 20 | 76 | 3.80 | 14 | .70 | 10 | .50 |
| 5 years | | 83 | 362 | 4.36 | 59 | .71 | 53 | .64 |

| | G | IP | W | L | Pct | ER | ERA |
|---|---|---|---|---|---|---|---|
| Pittsburgh | 9 | 56.2 | 3 | 2 | .600 | 20 | 3.18 |
| Atlanta | 13 | 27.2 | 1 | 2 | .333 | 12 | 3.90 |
| Road | 24 | 75 | 4 | 3 | .571 | 36 | 4.32 |

## 1982 OTHERS

| Pitcher | (W–L) | GS | Run | Avg | DP | Avg | SB | Avg |
|---|---|---|---|---|---|---|---|---|
| Sarmiento | (9-4) | 17 | 96 | 5.65 | 12 | .71 | 14 | .82 |
| Baumgarten | (0-5) | 10 | 42 | 4.20 | 10 | 1.00 | 10 | 1.00 |
| Solomon | (2-6) | 10 | 47 | 4.70 | 11 | 1.10 | 7 | .70 |
| Moskau | (1-3) | 5 | 25 | 5.00 | 6 | 1.20 | 3 | .60 |
| Griffin | (1-3) | 4 | 18 | 4.50 | 5 | 1.25 | 6 | 1.50 |
| Tunnell | (1-1) | 3 | 16 | 5.33 | 0 | | 1 | |

## PITTSBURGH

*Talent Analysis*

The Pirates in 1982 possessed 151 points of approximate value.

| | AV | % |
|---|---|---|
| Produced by Pirates' system: | 74 | 49% |
| Acquired by trade: | 71 | 47% |
| Purchased or signed from free agency: | 6 | 4% |

The Pirates are a system/trade built team.

| | | |
|---|---|---|
| Young (Up to age 25): | 11 | 8% |
| Prime (Age 26 to 29): | 91 | 60% |
| Past-prime (Age 30 to 33): | 23 | 18% |
| Old (Age 34 or older): | 26 | 17% |

The bulk of the Pirate players are in their prime.

The Pirates' farm system produced 240 points of approximate value, the second-highest total in the majors. Over the years 1979 to 1982, the total approximate value that originates in the Pirates' system is 862 points, easily the highest total in the majors.

## THREE RIVERS STADIUM

DIMENSIONS: Normal

SURFACE: Turf, not exceptionally fast

VISIBILITY: Excellent

FOUL TERRITORY: Fairly large

FAVORS:
Hitter/Pitcher—Hitter
Power/Line-drive hitter—Line-drive hitter
Righthander/Lefthander—Neither

TYPES OF OFFENSE AFFECTED: Increases batting averages 5 to 8 points; increases home runs and doubles a little

OTHER PARK CHARACTERISTICS: —

TYPES OF MARGINAL PLAYERS MOST VALUABLE IN PARK: Line-drive hitters with speed —Lee Lacy

PLAYERS ON TEAM HELPED MOST BY PARK: None affected dramatically

PLAYERS ON TEAM HURT MOST BY PARK: Don Robinson

OTHER COMMENTS: Only artificial surface in the NL which does not help fielders. Poor carpet results in increased errors and sharply decreased double plays.

# CHICAGO CUBS

Bill Buckner remarked last summer that Wrigley Field changed so much from day to day due to winds and other weather factors that "It's like we don't even have a home field." A classic example of a player's alibi being wildly in conflict with the facts. The Cubs' home-field advantage, over the last six years, has been one of the largest in baseball. The home-road records of all National League teams during that time are:

| TEAM | AT HOME | | ON THE ROAD | | IMPROVEMENT | |
|---|---|---|---|---|---|---|
| | W-L | Pct | W-L | Pct | Pct | In Games |
| Houston | 277-179 | .607 | 198-267 | .426 | +43% | +83½ |
| Philadelphia | 293-168 | .636 | 221-235 | .485 | +31% | +69½ |
| CHICAGO | 237-226 | .512 | 178-272 | .396 | +29% | +52½ |
| Pittsburgh | 272-183 | .598 | 223-233 | .489 | +22% | +49½ |
| San Diego | 232-228 | .504 | 184-275 | .401 | +26% | +47½ |
| Los Angeles | 282-180 | .610 | 233-226 | .508 | +20% | +47½ |
| Montreal | 264-195 | .575 | 218-239 | .477 | +21% | +45 |
| Atlanta | 227-224 | .503 | 189-273 | .409 | +23% | +43½ |
| San Francisco | 244-214 | .533 | 209-253 | .452 | +18% | +37 |
| St. Louis | 250-210 | .543 | 213-239 | .470 | +16% | +33 |
| Cincinnati | 254-203 | .556 | 232-227 | .505 | +10% | +23 |
| New York Mets | 191-263 | .421 | 175-284 | .381 | +10% | +18½ |

There are a few other observations to be made about this chart. Although many people tend to ignore the home-field advantage in baseball, almost every team—every team except the Mets—has been a better than .500 team in their home park, while almost every team has been a less-than-.500 team on the road (two exceptions, each by a very thin margin). So if you play .500 ball on the road, you might not win in any given season, but you'll be a contender. I think I wrote something a couple of years ago that if you play .500 ball on the road, you're not likely to win. This is not the first mistake I've ever made, nor the worst. The overall won-lost percentage has been .5500 at home, .4500 on the road, so that one might say accurately that the home field advantage decides one game in ten.

I have written several times that all successful teams tailor their talent to the design of the home park. But there is no strong evidence here that the successful teams do this any more than the unsuccessful teams. If you divide the National League teams into four groups of three teams each, the most successful teams (Los Angeles, Philadelphia and Pittsburgh) have a home-park edge of 24%, the second-most successful group (Cincinnati, Montreal, Houston) an edge of 25%, the third group (St. Louis, San Francisco, Atlanta) of 19%, the fourth group of 25%.

There is some evidence to suggest that the more unique or distinctive a park is, the greater the advantage. The Astrodome is the most forceful park in baseball in its ability to change the way the game is won; the Astros' home-park advantage is huge. Wrigley, obviously, is a unique park and uniquely changes the play of the game. But every park has distinctive features, so how do you measure the uniqueness of a park?

Using the 22% home-park edge, we can construct a chart of how many games you should expect to win at home and on the road in order to post a given overall record:

| If your goal is to win: | You need a home W/L% of: | And a road W/L% of: |
|---|---|---|
| 100 Games | .679 | .556 |
| 90 Games | .611 | .500 |
| 80 Games | .550 | .450 |
| 70 Games | .475 | .389 |
| 60 Games | .407 | .333 |

Over the six seasons, the Cubs scored 2,156 runs in Wrigley Field, 1,566 on the road. Adjusting for a small difference in games played (464 at home, 452 on the road) and for the fact that there is a normal 5½% increase in runs scored at home (5% by game; 10 or 11% by inning), and we conclude that Wrigley has increased the Cubs' offensive output by 27%. They have allowed 2,169 runs in Wrigley, 1,921 on the road. Making the same adjustments, we conclude that Cubs' opponents have increased their offensive output by about 16% in Wrigley, which is still a healthy increase.

Bill BUCKNER, First Base

*Runs Created, 100*

| | G | AB | R | H | 2B | 3B | HR | RBI | SB | Avg |
|---|---|---|---|---|---|---|---|---|---|---|
| First Half | 88 | 355 | 47 | 101 | 20 | 2 | 5 | 50 | 9 | .285 |
| Second Half | 73 | 302 | 46 | 100 | 14 | 3 | 10 | 55 | 6 | .331 |
| Home | 81 | 329 | 52 | 101 | 17 | 1 | 9 | 62 | 6 | .307 |
| Road | 80 | 328 | 41 | 100 | 17 | 4 | 6 | 43 | 9 | .305 |
| vs. RHP | | 476 | | 155 | | | | | | .326 |
| vs. LHP | | 181 | | 46 | | | | | | .254 |
| 1982 | 161 | 657 | 93 | 201 | 34 | 5 | 15 | 105 | 15 | .306 |
| 9.71 years | | 619 | 73 | 184 | 32 | 3 | 11 | 75 | 14 | .298 |

Bump WILLS, Second Base

*Runs Created: 58*

| | G | AB | R | H | 2B | 3B | HR | RBI | SB | Avg |
|---|---|---|---|---|---|---|---|---|---|---|
| First Half | 78 | 280 | 42 | 73 | 10 | 2 | 5 | 25 | 22 | .261 |
| Second Half | 50 | 139 | 22 | 41 | 8 | 2 | 1 | 13 | 13 | .295 |
| Home | 70 | 238 | 42 | 63 | 9 | 3 | 3 | 18 | 18 | .265 |
| Road | 58 | 181 | 22 | 51 | 9 | 1 | 3 | 20 | 17 | .282 |
| vs. RHP | | | | | | | | | | .274 |
| vs. LHP | | | | | | | | | | .263 |
| 1982 | 128 | 419 | 64 | 114 | 18 | 4 | 6 | 38 | 35 | .272 |
| 5.13 years | | 591 | 92 | 157 | 25 | 5 | 7 | 59 | 38 | .266 |

Ryne SANDBERG, Third Base

*Runs Created: 74*

| | G | AB | R | H | 2B | 3B | HR | RBI | SB | Avg |
|---|---|---|---|---|---|---|---|---|---|---|
| First Half | 84 | 332 | 54 | 85 | 16 | 0 | 3 | 23 | 12 | .256 |
| Second Half | 72 | 303 | 49 | 87 | 17 | 5 | 4 | 31 | 20 | .287 |
| Home | 77 | 306 | 57 | 98 | 23 | 3 | 5 | 30 | 20 | .320 |
| Road | 79 | 319 | 46 | 74 | 10 | 4 | 2 | 24 | 12 | .232 |
| vs. RHP | | 470 | | 122 | | | | | | .260 |
| vs. LHP | | 165 | | 50 | | | | | | .303 |
| 1982 | 156 | 635 | 103 | 172 | 33 | 5 | 7 | 54 | 32 | .271 |
| 1.04 years | | 616 | 101 | 166 | 32 | 5 | 7 | 52 | 31 | .270 |

## Larry BOWA, Shortstop

*Runs Created: 46*

| | G | AB | R | H | 2B | 3B | HR | RBI | SB | Avg |
|---|---|---|---|---|---|---|---|---|---|---|
| First Half | 84 | 300 | 29 | 74 | 12 | 4 | 0 | 21 | 5 | .247 |
| Second Half | 58 | 199 | 21 | 49 | 3 | 3 | 0 | 8 | 3 | .246 |
| Home | 71 | 247 | 23 | 65 | 10 | 3 | 0 | 17 | 3 | .263 |
| Road | 71 | 252 | 27 | 58 | 5 | 4 | 0 | 12 | 5 | .230 |
| vs. RHP | | 385 | | 91 | | | | | | .236 |
| vs. LHP | | 114 | | 32 | | | | | | .281 |
| 1982 | 142 | 499 | 50 | 123 | 15 | 7 | 0 | 29 | 8 | .246 |
| 11.61 years | | 630 | 75 | 166 | 19 | 8 | 1 | 39 | 26 | .263 |

## Keith MORELAND, Left Field

*Runs Created: 59*

| | G | AB | R | H | 2B | 3B | HR | RBI | SB | Avg |
|---|---|---|---|---|---|---|---|---|---|---|
| First Half | 84 | 300 | 30 | 81 | 11 | 1 | 11 | 46 | 0 | .270 |
| Second Half | 54 | 176 | 20 | 43 | 6 | 1 | 4 | 22 | 0 | .244 |
| Home | 70 | 239 | 28 | 59 | 10 | 2 | 8 | 37 | 0 | .247 |
| Road | 68 | 237 | 22 | 65 | 7 | 0 | 7 | 31 | 0 | .274 |
| vs. RHP | | 352 | | 86 | | | | | | .244 |
| vs. LHP | | 134 | | 41 | | | | | | .306 |
| 1982 | 138 | 476 | 50 | 124 | 17 | 2 | 15 | 68 | 0 | .261 |
| 1.70 years | | 518 | 48 | 142 | 21 | 2 | 15 | 84 | 2 | .275 |

## Gary WOODS, Center Field

*Runs Created: 30*

| | G | AB | R | H | 2B | 3B | HR | RBI | SB | Avg |
|---|---|---|---|---|---|---|---|---|---|---|
| First Half | 75 | 185 | 20 | 51 | 13 | 0 | 3 | 25 | 3 | .276 |
| Second Half | 42 | 60 | 8 | 15 | 2 | 1 | 1 | 5 | 0 | .250 |
| Home | 57 | 110 | 13 | 27 | 9 | 1 | 2 | 12 | 1 | .245 |
| Road | 50 | 135 | 15 | 39 | 6 | 0 | 2 | 18 | 2 | .289 |
| vs. RHP | | 152 | | 39 | | | | | | .257 |
| vs.LHP | | 93 | | 27 | | | | | | .290 |
| 1982 | 117 | 245 | 28 | 66 | 15 | 1 | 4 | 30 | 3 | .269 |
| 1.63 years | | 406 | 42 | 99 | 21 | 2 | 4 | 45 | 7 | .245 |

## Leon DURHAM, Right Field

*Runs Created: 107*

| | G | AB | R | H | 2B | 3B | HR | RBI | SB | Avg |
|---|---|---|---|---|---|---|---|---|---|---|
| First Half | 82 | 295 | 49 | 89 | 15 | 4 | 12 | 49 | 17 | .302 |
| Second Half | 66 | 244 | 35 | 79 | 18 | 3 | 10 | 41 | 11 | .324 |
| Home | 75 | 281 | 39 | 81 | 18 | 5 | 9 | 41 | 13 | .288 |
| Road | 73 | 258 | 45 | 87 | 15 | 2 | 13 | 49 | 15 | .337 |
| vs. RHP | | 413 | | 131 | | | | | | .317 |
| vs. LHP | | 126 | | 37 | | | | | | .294 |
| 1982 | 148 | 539 | 84 | 168 | 33 | 7 | 22 | 90 | 28 | .312 |
| 2.04 years | | 574 | 82 | 172 | 30 | 8 | 20 | 82 | 30 | .295 |

## Jody DAVIS, Catcher

*Runs Created: 53*

| | G | AB | R | H | 2B | 3B | HR | RBI | SB | Avg |
|---|---|---|---|---|---|---|---|---|---|---|
| First Half | 70 | 226 | 19 | 57 | 10 | 1 | 6 | 24 | 0 | .252 |
| Second Half | 60 | 192 | 22 | 52 | 10 | 1 | 6 | 28 | 0 | .271 |
| Home | 65 | 228 | 21 | 56 | 12 | 0 | 6 | 24 | 0 | .246 |
| Road | 65 | 190 | 20 | 53 | 8 | 2 | 6 | 28 | 0 | .279 |
| vs. RHP | | 313 | | 76 | | | | | | .243 |
| vs. LHP | | 105 | | 33 | | | | | | .314 |
| 1982 | 130 | 418 | 41 | 109 | 20 | 2 | 12 | 52 | 0 | .261 |
| 1.15 years | | 520 | 48 | 135 | 22 | 3 | 14 | 64 | 0 | .259 |

## Jay JOHNSTONE, Outfield

*Runs Created: 38*

| | G | AB | R | H | 2B | 3B | HR | RBI | SB | Avg |
|---|---|---|---|---|---|---|---|---|---|---|
| First Half | 56 | 112 | 15 | 27 | 5 | 1 | 5 | 21 | 0 | .241 |
| Second Half | 63 | 170 | 25 | 41 | 9 | 0 | 5 | 24 | 0 | .241 |
| Chicago | 51 | 144 | 24 | 38 | 4 | 1 | 7 | 23 | 0 | .264 |
| Los Angeles | 9 | 6 | 1 | 1 | 1 | 0 | 0 | 1 | 0 | .167 |
| Road | 59 | 132 | 15 | 29 | 9 | 0 | 3 | 21 | 0 | .220 |
| vs. RHP* | | 243 | | 59 | | | | | | .244 |
| vs. LHP* | | 26 | | 8 | | | | | | .308 |
| 1982 | 119 | 282 | 40 | 68 | 14 | 1 | 10 | 451 | 0 | .241 |
| 9.83 years | | 455 | 56 | 122 | 21 | 4 | 10 | 51 | 5 | .267 |

*with Chicago only

## Ferguson JENKINS

| Year | (W–L) | GS | Run | Avg | DP | Avg | SB | Avg |
|---|---|---|---|---|---|---|---|---|
| 1976 | (12-11) | 29 | 125 | 4.31 | 19 | .66 | 25 | .86 |
| 1977 | (10-10) | 28 | 144 | 5.14 | 31 | 1.11 | 13 | .46 |
| 1978 | (18- 8) | 30 | 149 | 4.97 | 28 | .93 | 19 | .63 |
| 1979 | (16-14) | 37 | 189 | 5.11 | 34 | .92 | 24 | .65 |
| 1980 | (12-12) | 29 | 136 | 4.69 | 31 | 1.07 | 18 | .62 |
| 1981 | ( 5- 8) | 16 | 70 | 4.38 | 20 | 1.25 | 7 | .44 |
| 1982 | (14-15) | 34 | 152 | 4.47 | 22 | .65 | 40 | 1.18 |
| 7 years | | 203 | 965 | 4.75 | 185 | .91 | 146 | .72 |

| | G | IP | W | L | Pct | ER | ERA |
|---|---|---|---|---|---|---|---|
| Home | 19 | 118.1 | 8 | 7 | .533 | 43 | 3.27 |
| Road | 15 | 98.2 | 6 | 8 | .429 | 33 | 3.01 |

## Doug BIRD

| Year | (W–L) | GS | Run | Avg | DP | Avg | SB | Avg |
|---|---|---|---|---|---|---|---|---|
| 1976 | (12-10) | 27 | 112 | 4.15 | 19 | .70 | 17 | .63 |
| 1977 | (11- 4) | 5 | 34 | 6.80 | 3 | .60 | 6 | 1.20 |
| 1978 | ( 6- 6) | 6 | 30 | 5.00 | 1 | .17 | 5 | .83 |
| 1979 | ( 2- 0) | 1 | 6 | | 1 | | 0 | |
| 1980 | ( 3- 0) | 1 | 13 | | 1 | | 0 | |
| 1981 | ( 9- 6) | 16 | 49 | 3.06 | 9 | .56 | 9 | .56 |
| 1982 | ( 9-14) | 33 | 146 | 4.42 | 16 | .48 | 29 | .88 |
| 7 years | | 89 | 390 | 4.38 | 50 | .56 | 66 | .74 |

| | G | IP | W | L | Pct | ER | ERA |
|---|---|---|---|---|---|---|---|
| Home | 20 | 120 | 6 | 10 | .375 | 70 | 5.25 |
| Road | 15 | 71 | 3 | 4 | .429 | 39 | 4.94 |

## Dick NOLES

| Year | (W–L) | GS | Run | Avg | DP | Avg | SB | Avg |
|---|---|---|---|---|---|---|---|---|
| 1979 | ( 3- 4) | 14 | 53 | 3.79 | 11 | .79 | 5 | .36 |
| 1980 | ( 1- 4) | 3 | 19 | 6.33 | 1 | .33 | 7 | 2.33 |
| 1981 | ( 2- 2) | 8 | 37 | 4.63 | 5 | .63 | 11 | 1.38 |
| 1982 | (10-13) | 30 | 123 | 4.10 | 19 | .63 | 34 | 1.13 |
| 4 years | | 55 | 232 | 4.22 | 36 | .65 | 57 | 1.04 |

| | G | IP | W | L | Pct | ER | ERA |
|---|---|---|---|---|---|---|---|
| Home | 15 | 89 | 6 | 4 | .600 | 34 | 3.44 |
| Road | 16 | 82 | 4 | 9 | .308 | 50 | 5.49 |

Randy MARTZ

| Year | (W–L) | GS | Run | Avg | DP | Avg | SB | Avg |
|---|---|---|---|---|---|---|---|---|
| 1980 | ( 1- 2) | 6 | 19 | 3.17 | 4 | .67 | 6 | 1.00 |
| 1981 | ( 5- 7) | 14 | 41 | 2.93 | 13 | .93 | 16 | 1.14 |
| 1982 | (11-10) | 24 | 105 | 4.38 | 26 | 1.08 | 12 | .50 |
| 3 years | | 44 | 165 | 3.75 | 43 | .98 | 34 | .77 |

| | G | IP | W | L | Pct | ER | ERA |
|---|---|---|---|---|---|---|---|
| Home | 16 | 80.1 | 6 | 8 | .429 | 44 | 4.93 |
| Road | 12 | 67.1 | 5 | 2 | .714 | 25 | 3.34 |

1982 OTHERS

| Pitcher | (W–L) | GS | Run | Avg | DP | Avg | SB | Avg |
|---|---|---|---|---|---|---|---|---|
| Ripley | (5-7) | 19 | 63 | 3.32 | 19 | 1.00 | 20 | 1.05 |
| Filer | (1-2) | 8 | 30 | 3.75 | 5 | .63 | 4 | .50 |
| Larson | (0-4) | 6 | 23 | 3.83 | 3 | .50 | 8 | 1.33 |
| Smith | (2-5) | 5 | 19 | 3.80 | 4 | .80 | 5 | 1.00 |
| Kravec | (1-1) | 2 | 11 | 5.50 | 1 | .50 | 1 | .50 |
| Proly | (5-3) | 1 | 4 | | 0 | | 0 | |

## CHICAGO CUBS

*Talent Analysis*

The Cubs in 1982 possessed 146 points of approximate value.

| | AV | % |
|---|---|---|
| Produced by Cubs' system: | 17 | 12% |
| Acquired by trade: | 92 | 63% |
| Purchased or signed from free agency: | 37 | 25% |

The Cubs are beginning to move away from being almost exclusively a trade-built team as is reflected in the money category above. Their most important dollar acquisitions have been Jody Davis, taken from the Mets' organization in a minor league draft, and Ferguson Jenkins.

| | | |
|---|---|---|
| Young (Up to age 25): | 34 | 23% |
| Prime (Age 26 to 29): | 51 | 35% |
| Past-prime (Age 30 to 33): | 32 | 22% |
| Old (Age 34 or older): | 29 | 20% |

42% of the Cubs' 1982 talent was past-prime or old. The norm is 38%.

The Cubs' system ranked twenty-fourth among major league organizations in 1982 talent produced with just 97 points, ahead only of the two 1977 expansion teams. Over the four years 1979 to 1982 they rank twenty-third, ahead of the Yankees. In general I am not a strong advocate of the importance of the farm system, but that clearly has been the dominant failure of the organization.

## WRIGLEY FIELD

DIMENSIONS: Long at lines; normal-to-short in alleys

SURFACE: Grass

VISIBILITY: Excellent

FOUL TERRITORY: Very small

FAVORS:
Hitter/Pitcher—Hitter to extreme degree
Power/Line-drive hitter—Either; helps both greatly
Righthander/Lefthander—Neither

TYPES OF OFFENSE AFFECTED: Lifts batting averages 20-30 points on average; increases doubles by 10-15% and homers by about 40%; infield errors up 7-8%

OTHER PARK CHARACTERISTICS: Lack of night games is a very important factor in the high offensive totals here. You can trace the growth of night baseball directly in the decline of batting averages from the late 1930s to the early 1960s. Besides the better visibility in the daytime, it is also warmer in daytime, and players hit better in warm temperatures, and it is possible that there is some difference in how well the ball travels at night. If Wrigley did get lights, it is probable that the number of runs scored here would decline sharply.

TYPES OF MARGINAL PLAYERS MOST VALUABLE IN PARK: Players, even pinch hitters, with high on-base percentages. In Wrigley, do everything you possibly can to keep an inning alive. Don't bunt, don't try to steal—*hit.* If the Cubs ever had a really good offense they'd score six runs a game. Defensively, the Cubs should concentrate on control pitchers, for the same reason. Stay away from the big innings and you've got a good chance to win.

PLAYERS ON TEAM HELPED MOST BY PARK: All hitters.

PLAYERS ON TEAM HURT MOST BY PARK: All pitchers, but particularly Martz. The Cubs' staff is well designed for the park—control sharp.

# NEW YORK METS

A few random scribblings:

• In the "Does this make any sense to you?" department, an October 18 note from the *Sporting News:*

**Former major leaguer Jack Aker, a manager in the Mets' organization since 1975, was dismissed after leading Tidewater to the International League championship. "Jack Aker has done a fine job," said Mets' Vice President Lou Gorman, "but we felt it was in Jack's best interest to seek challenges in another organization."**

Huh? Is one of us cracking up? What about the best interests of the Mets' organization? Let me get this straight . . . You fired the guy for his own good?

• George Bamberger's handling of his pitching staff can be justified on the grounds, and only on the grounds, of honest experimentation. It's easy to pick a fight with him. His handling of his pitchers was not decisive, bold, imaginative or effective. He worked pitchers on three days' rest early in the season, went to four, then got to using spot starters so that it was often five and six. He failed to make any decisions about who he wanted to sink or swim with, but tried one man and another and another; by the end of the season, almost no one on the staff was pitching as well as he was capable of. He seemed to take forever to recognize Ed Lynch as a pitcher who could help and turned to him basically when he had run out of all other options.

He didn't, in short, do any of the things that I expected him to do. Were this a team that might have been going somewhere, I would be very critical of that.

But if you don't know who your pitchers are, what good does it do to pretend that you do? The Mets weren't any better in '82 than they had been, but they weren't any worse. Bamberger simply made the mistake of getting the team off to a good start, and thus raising expectations.

• What have the Mets done wrong, in adjusting their team to their ballpark? I don't know—maybe it's a Joe Torre characteristic. (The Braves didn't play well in Atlanta last year, either.) I really wasn't aware that the Mets had had such an abnormally small home park advantage until I drew up the chart that accompanies the Cubs' comments.

One thing seems fairly obvious. An essential characteristic of the park is poor visibility. Who is best equipped to take advantage of poor visibility? A pitcher. What type of pitcher? A power pitcher. And who have been the best players in Mets' history? Tom Seaver. Jerry Koosman. Jon Matlack. The Mets as a team have led the NL in pitchers' strikeouts six times. They have finished over .500 all six of those times. They have finished over .500 *without* leading the league in strikeouts only once in their history.

Hmm . . . let's study that a little more systematically. The *Baseball Abstract* for the last three years has presented pitchers' home and road breakdowns. Let's label all of the Mets' pitchers who have averaged less than five strikeouts per nine innings as "control" pitchers and all those with more than five whiffs a game as "power" pitchers and look up their records when they were at home and on the road. The records are given below:

**CONTROL PITCHERS**

| | | IN SHEA | | | | | ON THE ROAD | | | | |
|---|---|---|---|---|---|---|---|---|---|---|---|
| | | IP | ER | W | L | ERA | IP | ER | W | L | ERA |
| 1980 | Bomback | 88 | 34 | 3 | 6 | 3.98 | 75 | 40 | 7 | 2 | 4.80 |
| 1980 | Burris | 63 | 18 | 3 | 8 | 3.94 | 74 | 34 | 3 | 5 | 4.14 |
| 1980 | Hausman | 63 | 18 | 3 | 2 | 2.57 | 59 | 36 | 3 | 3 | 5.49 |
| 1980 | Zachry | 77 | 28 | 3 | 4 | 3.27 | 87 | 27 | 3 | 6 | 2.79 |
| 1981 | Scott | 54 | 27 | 3 | 6 | 4.50 | 82 | 32 | 2 | 4 | 3.51 |
| 1982 | Jones | 47 | 39 | 3 | 8 | 7.47 | 61 | 16 | 4 | 2 | 2.37 |
| 1982 | Scott | 71 | 31 | 4 | 3 | 3.91 | 76 | 53 | 3 | 10 | 6.88 |
| 1982 | Swan | 72 | 31 | 6 | 4 | 3.88 | 94 | 31 | 5 | 3 | 2.96 |
| 1982 | Zachry | 70 | 26 | 3 | 2 | 3.33 | 67 | 36 | 3 | 7 | 4.81 |
| | | 638 | 276 | 32 | 43 | 3.89 | 675 | 305 | 32 | 42 | 4.07 |

**POWER PITCHERS**

| | | IP | ER | W | L | ERA | IP | ER | W | L | ERA |
|---|---|---|---|---|---|---|---|---|---|---|---|
| 1980 | Reardon | 58 | 14 | 5 | 5 | 2.17 | 52 | 18 | 3 | 2 | 3.12 |
| 1980 | Allen | 56 | 17 | 4 | 3 | 2.73 | 41 | 23 | 3 | 7 | 5.05 |
| 1980 | Falcone | 81 | 37 | 6 | 3 | 4.11 | 76 | 42 | 1 | 7 | 4.97 |
| 1980 | Swan | 77 | 27 | 4 | 6 | 3.16 | 51 | 24 | 1 | 3 | 4.24 |
| 1981 | Zachry | 73 | 31 | 5 | 6 | 3.82 | 66 | 33 | 2 | 8 | 4.50 |
| 1982 | Puleo | 94 | 40 | 7 | 4 | 3.83 | 77 | 45 | 2 | 5 | 5.26 |
| 1982 | Falcone | 94 | 40 | 3 | 7 | 3.83 | 77 | 33 | 5 | 3 | 3.86 |
| | | 533 | 206 | 34 | 34 | 3.48 | 443 | 218 | 17 | 35 | 4.46 |

The chart leaves little room for doubt. Every power pitcher on the list has had a better ERA in Shea than on the road, all but one by margins of at least 0.68. The Mets' control type pitchers over the three seasons have improved only infinitesimally in coming home: 32–43, 4.07 ERA on the road; 32–42, 3.89 at home. But the power pitchers, in returning to Shea, have cut a run off their ERA (4.46 to 3.48) and improved their won-lost percentage from .327 to .500. Big difference.

So that would help a little to explain two things:

1) Why have the Mets not had much of a home-park advantage in recent seasons? Answer: They've been trying to build their staff around too many control pitchers.

2) Why wasn't Bamberger successful here? Answer: He likes to work with control pitchers; the park doesn't help them. All of his dramatic successes in Milwaukee and Baltimore were with control pitchers like Mike Caldwell and Ross Grimsley.

Percentages of this size don't add up to substantive explanations of why the Mets are so bad. The Mets are bad because they don't got no ballplayers. But when they start looking for ballplayers . . . well, it's worth knowing.

Dave KINGMAN, First Base

*Runs Created: 66*

| | G | AB | R | H | 2B | 3B | HR | RBI | SB | Avg |
|---|---|---|---|---|---|---|---|---|---|---|
| First Half | 79 | 283 | 47 | 61 | 4 | 1 | 21 | 55 | 3 | .216 |
| Second Half | 70 | 252 | 33 | 48 | 5 | 0 | 16 | 44 | 1 | .190 |
| Home | 73 | 270 | 44 | 58 | 5 | 0 | 19 | 44 | 4 | .215 |
| Road | 76 | 265 | 36 | 51 | 4 | 1 | 18 | 55 | 0 | .192 |
| vs. RHP | | 439 | | 87 | 8 | 1 | 26 | | | .198 |
| vs. LHP | | 96 | | 22 | 1 | 0 | 11 | | | .229 |
| 1982 | 149 | 535 | 80 | 109 | 9 | 1 | 37 | 99 | 4 | .204 |
| 8.59 years | | 550 | 78 | 130 | 20 | 3 | 38 | 102 | 9 | .237 |

Wally BACKMAN, Second Base

*Runs Created: 37*

| | G | AB | R | H | 2B | 3B | HR | RBI | SB | Avg |
|---|---|---|---|---|---|---|---|---|---|---|
| First Half | 73 | 206 | 27 | 58 | 9 | 2 | 1 | 14 | 7 | .282 |
| Second Half | 23 | 55 | 10 | 13 | 4 | 0 | 2 | 8 | 1 | .236 |
| Home | 44 | 114 | 16 | 30 | 3 | 0 | 1 | 7 | 5 | .263 |
| Road | 52 | 147 | 21 | 41 | 10 | 2 | 2 | 15 | 3 | .279 |
| vs. RHP | | 229 | | 68 | 13 | 2 | 3 | | | .297 |
| vs. LHP | | 32 | | 3 | 0 | 0 | 0 | | | .094 |
| 1982 | 96 | 261 | 37 | 71 | 13 | 2 | 3 | 22 | 8 | .272 |
| 0.92 years | | 424 | 59 | 121 | 17 | 3 | 3 | 34 | 12 | .285 |

Hubie BROOKS, Third Base

*Runs Created: 42*

| | G | AB | R | H | 2B | 3B | HR | RBI | SB | Avg |
|---|---|---|---|---|---|---|---|---|---|---|
| First Half | 58 | 210 | 29 | 55 | 10 | 2 | 0 | 24 | 4 | .262 |
| Second Half | 68 | 247 | 21 | 59 | 11 | 0 | 2 | 16 | 2 | .239 |
| Home | 65 | 228 | 17 | 56 | 10 | 2 | 1 | 27 | 4 | .246 |
| Road | 61 | 229 | 23 | 58 | 11 | 0 | 1 | 13 | 2 | .253 |
| vs. RHP | | 372 | | 92 | 17 | 2 | 2 | | | .247 |
| vs. LHP | | 85 | | 22 | 4 | 0 | 0 | | | .259 |
| 1982 | 126 | 457 | 40 | 114 | 21 | 2 | 2 | 40 | 6 | .249 |
| 1.53 years | | 586 | 54 | 163 | 29 | 3 | 5 | 58 | 11 | .278 |

Ron GARDENHIRE, Shortstop

*Runs Created: 33*

| | G | AB | R | H | 2B | 3B | HR | RBI | SB | Avg |
|---|---|---|---|---|---|---|---|---|---|---|
| First Half | 81 | 224 | 18 | 52 | 9 | 1 | 1 | 21 | 3 | .232 |
| Second Half | 60 | 160 | 11 | 40 | 8 | 0 | 2 | 12 | 2 | .250 |
| Home | 70 | 176 | 12 | 37 | 6 | 0 | 1 | 13 | 2 | .210 |
| Road | 71 | 208 | 17 | 55 | 11 | 1 | 2 | 20 | 3 | .264 |
| vs. RHP | | 289 | | 69 | 13 | 1 | 2 | | | .239 |
| vs. LHP | | 95 | | 23 | 4 | 0 | 1 | | | .242 |
| 1982 | 141 | 384 | 29 | 92 | 17 | 1 | 3 | 33 | 5 | .240 |
| 1.04 years | | 415 | 30 | 101 | 17 | 1 | 3 | 35 | 5 | .243 |

George FOSTER, Left Field

*Runs Created: 62*

| | G | AB | R | H | 2B | 3B | HR | RBI | SB | Avg |
|---|---|---|---|---|---|---|---|---|---|---|
| First Half | 84 | 315 | 41 | 89 | 12 | 0 | 10 | 41 | 0 | .283 |
| Second Half | 67 | 235 | 23 | 47 | 11 | 2 | 3 | 29 | 1 | .200 |
| Home | 77 | 280 | 37 | 71 | 11 | 1 | 7 | 36 | 0 | .254 |
| Road | 74 | 270 | 27 | 65 | 12 | 2 | 6 | 34 | 1 | .241 |
| vs. RHP | | 439 | | 104 | 16 | 1 | 9 | | | .237 |
| vs. LHP | | 111 | | 32 | 7 | 1 | 4 | | | .288 |
| 1982 | 151 | 550 | 64 | 136 | 23 | 2 | 13 | 70 | 1 | .247 |
| 9.00 years | | 570 | 84 | 161 | 26 | 4 | 29 | 104 | 5 | .282 |

Mookie WILSON, Center Field

*Runs Created: 78*

| | G | AB | R | H | 2B | 3B | HR | RBI | SB | Avg |
|---|---|---|---|---|---|---|---|---|---|---|
| First Half | 86 | 343 | 46 | 97 | 11 | 4 | 2 | 32 | 28 | .283 |
| Second Half | 73 | 296 | 53 | 81 | 14 | 5 | 3 | 23 | 30 | .274 |
| Home | 80 | 307 | 47 | 85 | 12 | 2 | 2 | 23 | 28 | .277 |
| Road | 79 | 332 | 43 | 93 | 13 | 7 | 3 | 32 | 30 | .280 |
| vs. RHP | | 506 | | 140 | 22 | 7 | 4 | | | .277 |
| vs. LHP | | 133 | | 38 | 3 | 2 | 1 | | | .286 |
| 1982 | 159 | 639 | 90 | 178 | 25 | 9 | 5 | 55 | 58 | .279 |
| 1.72 years | | 623 | 90 | 170 | 22 | 12 | 5 | 42 | 52 | .273 |

Ellis VALENTINE, Right Field

*Runs Created: 40*

| | G | AB | R | H | 2B | 3B | HR | RBI | SB | Avg |
|---|---|---|---|---|---|---|---|---|---|---|
| First Half | 64 | 162 | 16 | 40 | 2 | 0 | 6 | 21 | 0 | .247 |
| Second Half | 47 | 175 | 17 | 57 | 12 | 1 | 2 | 27 | 1 | .326 |
| Home | 52 | 141 | 20 | 45 | 8 | 0 | 4 | 22 | 0 | .319 |
| Road | 59 | 196 | 13 | 52 | 6 | 1 | 4 | 26 | 1 | .265 |
| vs. RHP | | 255 | | 69 | 8 | 0 | 3 | | | .271 |
| vs. LHP | | 82 | | 28 | 6 | 1 | 5 | | | .341 |
| 1982 | 111 | 337 | 33 | 97 | 14 | 1 | 8 | 48 | 1 | .288 |
| 4.92 years | | 581 | 70 | 164 | 32 | 3 | 22 | 87 | 12 | .283 |

John STEARNS, Catcher

*Runs Created: 51*

| | G | AB | R | H | 2B | 3B | HR | RBI | SB | Avg |
|---|---|---|---|---|---|---|---|---|---|---|
| First Half | 74 | 280 | 37 | 84 | 20 | 3 | 3 | 24 | 12 | .300 |
| Second Half | 24 | 72 | 9 | 19 | 5 | 0 | 1 | 4 | 5 | .264 |
| Home | 48 | 160 | 23 | 54 | 13 | 0 | 0 | 12 | 6 | .338 |
| Road | 50 | 192 | 23 | 49 | 12 | 3 | 4 | 16 | 11 | .255 |
| vs. RHP | | 264 | | 81 | 18 | 3 | 4 | | | .307 |
| vs. LHP | | 88 | | 22 | 7 | 0 | 0 | | | .250 |
| 1982 | 98 | 352 | 46 | 103 | 25 | 3 | 4 | 28 | 17 | .293 |
| 4.93 years | | 540 | 66 | 141 | 31 | 2 | 9 | 43 | 18 | .260 |

Bob BAILOR, Futility Player

*Runs Created: 41*

| | G | AB | R | H | 2B | 3B | HR | RBI | SB | Avg |
|---|---|---|---|---|---|---|---|---|---|---|
| First Half | 59 | 192 | 23 | 57 | 8 | 0 | 0 | 19 | 8 | .297 |
| Second Half | 51 | 184 | 21 | 47 | 6 | 1 | 0 | 12 | 12 | .255 |
| Home | 56 | 190 | 19 | 53 | 6 | 0 | 0 | 14 | 7 | .279 |
| Road | 54 | 186 | 25 | 51 | 8 | 1 | 0 | 17 | 13 | .274 |
| vs. RHP | | | | | | | | | | |
| vs. LHP | | | | | | | | | | |
| 1982 | 110 | 376 | 44 | 104 | 14 | 1 | 0 | 31 | 20 | .277 |
| 4.31 years | | 545 | 67 | 122 | 21 | 5 | 2 | 41 | 16 | .224 |

Charles PULEO

| Year | (W–L) | GS | Run | Avg | DP | Avg | SB | Avg |
|---|---|---|---|---|---|---|---|---|
| 1981 | (0-0) | 1 | 2 | | 1 | | 2 | |
| 1982 | (9-9) | 24 | 101 | 4.21 | 22 | .92 | 32 | 1.33 |
| 2 years | | 25 | 103 | 4.12 | 23 | .92 | 34 | 1.36 |

| | G | IP | W | L | Pct | ER | ERA |
|---|---|---|---|---|---|---|---|
| Home | 19 | 94 | 7 | 4 | .636 | 40 | 3.83 |
| Road | 17 | 77 | 2 | 5 | .286 | 45 | 5.26 |

### Pete FALCONE

| Year | (W–L) | GS | Run | Avg | DP | Avg | SB | Avg |
|---|---|---|---|---|---|---|---|---|
| 1976 | (12-16) | 32 | 107 | 3.34 | 26 | .81 | 26 | .81 |
| 1977 | ( 4- 8) | 22 | 117 | 5.32 | 19 | .86 | 16 | .73 |
| 1978 | ( 2- 7) | 14 | 48 | 3.43 | 18 | 1.29 | 7 | .50 |
| 1979 | ( 6-14) | 31 | 106 | 3.42 | 35 | 1.13 | 16 | .52 |
| 1980 | ( 7-10) | 23 | 107 | 4.65 | 24 | 1.04 | 21 | .91 |
| 1981 | ( 5- 3) | 9 | 42 | 4.67 | 6 | .67 | 9 | 1.00 |
| 1982 | ( 8-10) | 23 | 81 | 3.52 | 15 | .65 | 22 | .96 |
| 7 years | | 154 | 607 | 3.94 | 143 | .93 | 117 | .76 |

| | G | IP | W | L | Pct | ER | ERA |
|---|---|---|---|---|---|---|---|
| Home | 19 | 94 | 3 | 7 | .300 | 40 | 3.83 |
| Road | 21 | 77 | 5 | 3 | .625 | 33 | 3.86 |

### Randy JONES

| Year | (W–L) | GS | Run | Avg | DP | Avg | SB | Avg |
|---|---|---|---|---|---|---|---|---|
| 1976 | (22-14) | 40 | 171 | 4.28 | 46 | 1.15 | 21 | .52 |
| 1977 | ( 6-12) | 25 | 73 | 2.92 | 18 | .72 | 20 | .80 |
| 1978 | (13-14) | 36 | 126 | 3.50 | 50 | 1.39 | 14 | .39 |
| 1979 | (11-12) | 39 | 145 | 3.72 | 41 | 1.05 | 28 | .72 |
| 1980 | ( 5-13) | 24 | 72 | 3.00 | 24 | 1.00 | 20 | .83 |
| 1981 | ( 1- 8) | 12 | 35 | 2.92 | 12 | 1.00 | 9 | .75 |
| 1982 | ( 7-10) | 20 | 75 | 3.75 | 23 | 1.15 | 15 | .75 |
| 7 years | | 196 | 697 | 3.56 | 214 | 1.09 | 127 | .65 |

| | G | IP | W | L | Pct | ER | ERA |
|---|---|---|---|---|---|---|---|
| Home | 14 | 47 | 3 | 8 | .273 | 39 | 7.47 |
| Road | 14 | 60.2 | 4 | 2 | .667 | 16 | 2.37 |

### Mickey SCOTT

| Year | (W–L) | GS | Run | Avg | DP | Avg | SB | Avg |
|---|---|---|---|---|---|---|---|---|
| 1979 | (1- 3) | 9 | 45 | 5.00 | 11 | 1.22 | 8 | .89 |
| 1980 | (1- 1) | 6 | 29 | 4.83 | 9 | 1.50 | 4 | .67 |
| 1981 | (5-10) | 23 | 66 | 2.87 | 20 | .87 | 11 | .48 |
| 1982 | (7-13) | 22 | 89 | 4.05 | 12 | .55 | 20 | .91 |
| 4 years | | 60 | 229 | 3.82 | 52 | .87 | 43 | .72 |

| | G | IP | W | L | Pct | ER | ERA |
|---|---|---|---|---|---|---|---|
| Home | 18 | 71.1 | 4 | 3 | .571 | 31 | 3.91 |
| Road | 19 | 75.2 | 3 | 10 | .231 | 53 | 6.88 |

### 1982 OTHERS

| Pitcher | (W–L) | GS | Run | Avg | DP | Avg | SB | Avg |
|---|---|---|---|---|---|---|---|---|
| Zachry | (6- 9) | 16 | 65 | 4.06 | 15 | .94 | 15 | .94 |
| Lynch | (4- 8) | 12 | 43 | 3.58 | 10 | .83 | 0 | .00 |
| Ownbey | (1- 2) | 8 | 36 | 4.50 | 7 | .88 | 13 | 1.63 |
| Gaff | (0- 3) | 5 | 16 | 3.20 | 3 | .60 | 0 | |
| Holman | (2- 1) | 4 | 13 | 3.25 | 3 | .75 | 1 | .25 |
| Terrell | (0- 3) | 3 | 4 | 1.33 | 4 | 1.33 | 6 | 2.00 |
| Orosco | (4-10) | 2 | 9 | 4.50 | 0 | | 0 | |
| Gorman | (1- 1) | 1 | 1 | | 1 | | 0 | |
| Leach | (2- 1) | 1 | 1 | | 0 | | 0 | |

### Craig SWAN

| Year | (W–L) | GS | Run | Avg | DP | Avg | SB | Avg |
|---|---|---|---|---|---|---|---|---|
| 1976 | ( 6- 9) | 22 | 84 | 3.82 | 8 | .36 | 20 | .91 |
| 1977 | ( 9-10) | 24 | 101 | 4.21 | 26 | 1.08 | 27 | 1.13 |
| 1978 | ( 9- 6) | 28 | 105 | 3.75 | 26 | .93 | 21 | .75 |
| 1979 | (14-13) | 35 | 121 | 3.46 | 36 | 1.03 | 31 | .89 |
| 1980 | ( 5- 9) | 21 | 62 | 2.95 | 15 | .71 | 13 | .62 |
| 1981 | ( 0- 2) | 3 | 11 | 3.67 | 2 | .67 | 5 | 1.67 |
| 1982 | (11- 7) | 21 | 73 | 3.57 | 15 | .71 | 22 | 1.05 |
| 7 years | | 154 | 557 | 3.62 | 128 | .83 | 139 | .90 |

| | G | IP | W | L | Pct | ER | ERA |
|---|---|---|---|---|---|---|---|
| Home | 18 | 72 | 6 | 4 | .600 | 31 | 3.88 |
| Road | 19 | 94.1 | 5 | 3 | .625 | 31 | 2.96 |

## NEW YORK METS

*Talent Analysis*

The Mets in 1981 possessed only 125 points of approximate value, easily the lowest total in the National League (the Reds had 133).

| | AV | % |
|---|---|---|
| Produced by Mets' system: | 62 | 50% |
| Acquired by trade: | 60 | 48% |
| Purchased or signed from free agency: | 3 | 2% |

They were built half-and-half, from the system and by trades. Or perhaps "built" is not the right word here.

| | | |
|---|---|---|
| Young (Up to age 25): | 20 | 16% |
| Prime (Age 26 to 29): | 53 | 42% |
| Past-prime (Age 30 to 33): | 49 | 40% |
| Old (Age 34 or older): | 3 | 2% |

They are certainly not a coming team, on the basis of the talent on their 1982 roster.

## SHEA STADIUM

DIMENSIONS: Fairly short

SURFACE: Grass, slow

VISIBILITY: Very poor

FOUL TERRITORY: Extremely large—80° from plate to foul screen

FAVORS:
Hitter/Pitcher—Pitcher
Power/Line-drive hitter—Power
Righthander/Lefthander—Neither

TYPES OF OFFENSE AFFECTED: Reduces all offense except home runs. Reduces batting averages 10-15 points; reduces doubles 8% and triples 25%. Neutral home-run park.

OTHER PARK CHARACTERISTICS: Noise

TYPES OF MARGINAL PLAYERS MOST VALUABLE IN PARK: Sluggers (mobility not crucial)

PLAYERS ON TEAM HELPED MOST BY PARK: Charlie Puleo and Mickey Scott pitched well here

PLAYERS ON TEAM HURT MOST BY PARK: John Stearns

OTHER COMMENTS: Shea increases fielders' errors more than any other NL park except Candlestick

# NATIONAL LEAGUE WEST

## DIVISION SHEET*

| Team | 1st | 2nd | vs. RHP | vs. LHP | Home | Road | Day | Night | Total | Pct |
|---|---|---|---|---|---|---|---|---|---|---|
| Atlanta | 51-33 | 38-40 | 63-58 | 26-15 | 42-39 | 47-34 | 19-22 | 70-51 | 89-73 | .549 |
| Los Angeles | 46-42 | 42-32 | 75-67 | 13- 7 | 43-38 | 45-36 | 23-18 | 65-56 | 88-74 | .543 |
| San Francisco | 42-46 | 45-29 | 61-49 | 26-26 | 45-36 | 42-39 | 35-26 | 52-49 | 87-75 | .537 |
| San Diego | 50-36 | 31-45 | 59-57 | 22-24 | 43-38 | 38-43 | 24-18 | 57-63 | 81-81 | .500 |
| Houston | 37-48 | 40-37 | 58-49 | 19-36 | 43-38 | 34-47 | 14-26 | 63-59 | 77-85 | .475 |
| Cincinnati | 33-53 | 28-48 | 47-71 | 14-30 | 33-48 | 28-53 | 13-34 | 48-67 | 61-101 | .377 |

### *TURNAROUNDS*

| | COME FROM BEHIND WINS | | | | | | | | | BLOWN LEADS | | | | | | | | |
|---|---|---|---|---|---|---|---|---|---|---|---|---|---|---|---|---|---|---|
| Team | 1 | 2 | 3 | 4 | 5 | 6 | 7 | Total | Points | 1 | 2 | 3 | 4 | 5 | 6 | 7 | Total | Points |
| Atlanta | 20 | 12 | 7 | 4 | 3 | | | 46 | 142 | 16 | 12 | 8 | 2 | 1 | | | 39 | 116 |
| Los Angeles | 19 | 9 | 6 | 1 | 1 | | | 36 | 100 | 20 | 15 | 6 | 1 | | | | 42 | 114 |
| San Francisco | 22 | 13 | 6 | 2 | 1 | 1 | 1 | 46 | 138 | 14 | 10 | 5 | 0 | | | | 29 | 78 |
| San Diego | 19 | 8 | 5 | 1 | 0 | 1 | | 34 | 94 | 18 | 19 | 7 | 4 | 1 | | | 39 | 117 |
| Houston | 14 | 10 | 5 | 1 | | | | 30 | 83 | 11 | 11 | 7 | 0 | 2 | 1 | | 32 | 102 |
| Cincinnati | 14 | 6 | 5 | 1 | | | | 26 | 71 | 28 | 8 | 5 | 3 | 1 | | | 45 | 121 |

### DEFENSIVE RECORDS

| Team | OSB | DP | OA/SFA | FAvg | DER | Opposition Runs |
|---|---|---|---|---|---|---|
| Los Angeles | 125 | 131 | 27/35 | .979 | .702 | 612 |
| Houston | 175 | 154 | 28/40 | .978 | .699 | 620 |
| San Diego | 137 | 142 | 38/48 | .976 | .719 | 658 |
| Cincinnati | 147 | 158 | 47/44 | .980 | .685 | 661 |
| San Francisco | 185 | 125 | 40/61 | .973 | .682 | 687 |
| Atlanta | 164 | 186 | 28/45 | .979 | .689 | 702 |

### OPPOSITION ERRORS

| Team | C | 1B | 2B | 3B | SS | LF | CF | RF | P | Un | Total |
|---|---|---|---|---|---|---|---|---|---|---|---|
| Atlanta | 30 | 14 | 17 | 28 | 31 | 8 | 6 | 6 | 16 | 4 | 160 |
| San Diego | 16 | 11 | 27 | 27 | 26 | 13 | 6 | 5 | 23 | 5 | 159 |
| Los Angeles | 13 | 13 | 18 | 20 | 31 | 17 | 6 | 13 | 16 | 2 | 149 |
| Houston | 14 | 15 | 15 | 24 | 28 | 3 | 4 | 2 | 15 | 1 | 121 |
| Cincinnati | 11 | 11 | 13 | 17 | 32 | 14 | 3 | 3 | 17 | 0 | 118 |
| San Francisco | 7 | 11 | 18 | 13 | 24 | 5 | 8 | 4 | 16 | 3 | 109 |

### LATE-INNING BALL CLUBS

| Team | Ahead | Tied | Behind | Net Change |
|---|---|---|---|---|
| San Francisco | 58- 7 | 12- 8 | 17-60 | +14 |
| Atlanta | 68-10 | 12-11 | 9-52 | ± 0 |
| Los Angeles | 72- 8 | 11-10 | 5-56 | − 2 |
| San Diego | 69- 7 | 7-10 | 5-64 | − 5 |
| Cincinnati | 48- 9 | 4- 8 | 8-83 | − 5 |
| Houston | 61-11 | 11-11 | 5-63 | − 6 |

*See explanation of Division Sheet on p. 16

# ATLANTA BRAVES

One of the unique and wonderful things about the 1982 baseball season was that the season of every team worthy of discussion, save Montreal, resolved itself into a very few games in which the team either did it or didn't. Some teams leapt from the starting blocks as if they were on fire ("When you are on fire," Richard Pryor observed, "people will get out of your way"); others sprang from the blocks and fell immediately to their faces. Teams blew very hot and very cold for 145 games, and when they had done so they saw what they had wrought, which was to put about a dozen teams behind them and a short, happy pennant race ahead. Was ever a year so rich in diamond streaks and onyx implosions? Changes that usually evolve over the course of months were compressed into rock-hard crystal moments. My own team, the Royals, had the pennant race in control on September 15, and then lost 10 of 11 games, six to bad teams and the rest to the Angels. In any normal season a collapse of such proportions would have drawn the baleful stares of the nation's press, but in 1982 we were allowed to suffer it alone. In war time, one ceases to wonder at each report of a rifle.

Do not be too quick to suppose that it would be a wonderful world if every season, every pennant race, turned out the way it was in '82, one week to go and all four races still open for business. The NBA has naively supposed that it would be wonderful if every game was decided in the last two minutes. The problem with a 17-game pennant race is that if you know in advance that you're going to wind up with that, it leaves you with 145 games that don't mean a damn thing. Every season isn't like 1982; many pennant races are over by Labor Day, and most are over before the last week of the season. If that wasn't so, if there wasn't the constant danger of being put to sleep by a sudden slump, then the games of May and August would become meaningless, and baseball would atrophy, unable to regain its enthusiasm when the occasion demanded. The 1982 season needed its uniqueness to be so delightful, just as the 1981 season needed its uniqueness to be so painful.

One of the goals that I had in starting a baseball annual, and one that I have never accomplished very well, was to try to put the unique flavor and feel of each season on permanent record. Roger Angell does that rather better than I, I'm afraid. But I can do this much: I can give the public a clearer and accurate record of what actually happened. With several teams—the teams for which there were a few games that wrote the story of the season —this year I am going to use a little space to write the story of those few games into the record.

There was an unmistakeable moment—13 games are not much more than a moment—at which the Atlanta Braves emerged from the cocoon of talent in the shape of a contender. What really happened in those 13 games? That data is given in chart form on page 50.

In a more general way:

1) If there was ever a team effort, this was it. It is extremely difficult to pick a team MVP for the 13 games.

2) The weak part of the Braves' team, the pitching, carried them during this phase. Their team batting average was only .273; their staff ERA was 2.18.

3) The tendency to ascribe the streak to late-game heroics, and thus to the bullpen and to clutch hitting, is clearly a fault of perception. The bullpen did a great job; so did the starters. The games included six come-from-behind victories, about the norm for 13 victories. Only two of those comebacks were in the late innings. The Braves outscored their opponents 22-13 in the first three innings, 20-10 in the middle innings, 24-11 from the seventh inning on.

4) They committed 11 errors and turned 17 double plays in the thirteen games, figures strikingly near their season's averages of .85 errors and 1.16 DP per game.

Did you ever notice how much Joe Torre looks like Rich Little? I keep expecting him to shake his jowls and do a little Trickie Dick for us.

Joe Torre was the National League manager of the year in 1982, or some of the National League managers of the year (I believe there are 27 organizations which give AL and NL manager awards, and in any given season anybody is likely to win one or more of them. I think eventually it's going to wind up like the All-American teams; he's a *consensus* Manager of the Year). I am rather mystified by how these things are decided. There are some managers who are very good at winning these awards. If Bill Virdon gets through a season without being fired, he's an odds-on favorite to be the league manager of the year. Now, I guarantee you that if you poll Bill Virdon's players, *they* will not tell you that he is the best manager there is. If you poll the fans of his hometown team, they will as often as not be after his hide. There is just something about him, or about his teams, or about the relationship between his teams and their records, that habitually impresses some people. Maybe he learned it from Danny Murtaugh. Larry Shephard in 1969 led the Pirates to an 88-74 record, their best in three years, but took a terrible beating from the press and got fired. Danny Murtaugh took over the same team, went 89-73 and was a consensus manager of the year.

Joe Torre, for some reason, is in the same class. He is articulate and polite, but that does not really explain how he was able to take over a team (the 1977 Mets) which was 45 games away from a season in which they had gone 86-76, manage them through consecutive seasons in which they finished 64-98, 66-96, 63-99, 67-95 and 41-62 and still emerge with his reputation untarnished. In New York, no less. Traded Tom Seaver, my butt; they shouldn't have declined by 20 games if they shot Tom Seaver. It wasn't just Seaver; everybody on the team went downhill. George Bamberger took over the team, posted the same kind of record and got catcalls.

Put it on record, anyway, that this is one bandwagon that I'm definitely not jumping on. Torre managed the Atlanta Braves in 1982 very much the way that he managed the New York Mets for four years. He never did establish a starting rotation. He had a red-hot prospect in center field; the kid went into a slump and he gave up on him. He was indecisive, unreliable, continually trying to ride a hot hand. Maybe his style will fit the needs of the Atlanta organization. Casey Stengel never set up a starting rotation in his life; he won the pennant in '57 with no pitcher who started more than 28 times. He never used a set lineup, either; he was always shifting from one guy to the other. He lost big with this style in Brooklyn and Boston, but he posted the greatest record that any manager ever had with the Yankees. Maybe Torre's style just needed the right circumstances to be successful. I'll believe it when I see a little more of it.

Chris CHAMBLISS, First Base

*Runs Created: 79*

| | G | AB | R | H | 2B | 3B | HR | RBI | SB | Avg |
|---|---|---|---|---|---|---|---|---|---|---|
| First Half | 82 | 280 | 28 | 71 | 10 | 2 | 10 | 40 | 2 | .254 |
| Second Half | 75 | 254 | 29 | 73 | 15 | 0 | 10 | 46 | 5 | .287 |
| Home | 78 | 256 | 30 | 73 | 11 | 1 | 11 | 40 | 1 | .285 |
| Road | 79 | 278 | 27 | 71 | 14 | 1 | 9 | 46 | 6 | .255 |
| vs. RHP | | 431 | | 116 | 18 | 2 | 19 | 74 | | .269 |
| vs. LHP | | 103 | | 28 | 7 | 0 | 1 | 12 | | .272 |
| 1982 | 157 | 534 | 57 | 144 | 25 | 2 | 20 | 86 | 7 | .270 |
| 10.56 years | | 610 | 74 | 171 | 32 | 4 | 14 | 77 | 4 | .280 |

Glenn HUBBARD, Second Base

*Runs Created: 60*

| | G | AB | R | H | 2B | 3B | HR | RBI | SB | Avg |
|---|---|---|---|---|---|---|---|---|---|---|
| First Half | 73 | 272 | 39 | 72 | 11 | 0 | 5 | 31 | 3 | .265 |
| Second Half | 72 | 260 | 36 | 60 | 14 | 1 | 4 | 28 | 1 | .231 |
| Home | 71 | 253 | 38 | 64 | 8 | 0 | 6 | 28 | 1 | .253 |
| Road | 74 | 279 | 37 | 68 | 17 | 1 | 2 | 31 | 3 | .244 |
| vs. RHP | | 404 | | 97 | 20 | 1 | 5 | 45 | | .240 |
| vs. LHP | | 128 | | 35 | 5 | 0 | 3 | 14 | | .273 |
| 1982 | 145 | 532 | 75 | 132 | 25 | 1 | 9 | 59 | 4 | .248 |
| 3.10 years | | 585 | 70 | 142 | 24 | 3 | 9 | 57 | 6 | .243 |

Bob HORNER, Third Base

*Runs Created: 82*

| | G | AB | R | H | 2B | 3B | HR | RBI | SB | Avg |
|---|---|---|---|---|---|---|---|---|---|---|
| First Half | 78 | 278 | 53 | 82 | 17 | 0 | 18 | 52 | 1 | .295 |
| Second Half | 62 | 221 | 32 | 48 | 7 | 0 | 14 | 45 | 2 | .235 |
| Home | 75 | 262 | 53 | 62 | 9 | 0 | 25 | 62 | 0 | .237 |
| Road | 65 | 237 | 32 | 68 | 15 | 0 | 7 | 37 | 3 | .287 |
| vs. RHP | | 410 | | 106 | 21 | 0 | 25 | 80 | | .259 |
| vs. LHP | | 89 | | 24 | 3 | 0 | 7 | 17 | | .270 |
| 1982 | 140 | 499 | 85 | 130 | 24 | 0 | 32 | 97 | 3 | .261 |
| 3.41 years | | 608 | 95 | 169 | 24 | 1 | 41 | 114 | 2 | .278 |

Rafael RAMIREZ, Shortstop

*Runs Created: 72*

| | G | AB | R | H | 2B | 3B | HR | RBI | SB | Avg |
|---|---|---|---|---|---|---|---|---|---|---|
| First Half | 84 | 313 | 33 | 81 | 15 | 3 | 3 | 20 | 10 | .259 |
| Second Half | 73 | 296 | 41 | 88 | 9 | 1 | 7 | 32 | 17 | .297 |
| Home | 77 | 295 | 33 | 79 | 18 | 2 | 7 | 31 | 4 | .268 |
| Road | 80 | 314 | 41 | 90 | 6 | 2 | 3 | 21 | 23 | .287 |
| vs. RHP | | 466 | | 121 | 19 | 3 | 6 | 36 | | .260 |
| vs. LHP | | 143 | | 48 | 5 | 1 | 4 | 16 | | .336 |
| 1982 | 157 | 609 | 74 | 169 | 24 | 4 | 10 | 52 | 27 | .278 |
| 1.86 years | | 581 | 65 | 151 | 25 | 4 | 8 | 45 | 19 | .259 |

Jerry ROYSTER, Left Field

*Runs Created: 35*

| | G | AB | R | H | 2B | 3B | HR | RBI | SB | Avg |
|---|---|---|---|---|---|---|---|---|---|---|
| First Half | 44 | 42 | 12 | 7 | 2 | 0 | 0 | 4 | 1 | .167 |
| Second Half | 64 | 219 | 31 | 70 | 11 | 2 | 2 | 21 | 13 | .320 |
| Home | 51 | 129 | 25 | 45 | 10 | 2 | 1 | 17 | 6 | .349 |
| Road | 57 | 132 | 18 | 32 | 3 | 0 | 1 | 8 | 8 | .242 |
| vs. RHP | | 183 | | 50 | 9 | 0 | 1 | 14 | | .273 |
| vs. LHP | | 78 | | 27 | 4 | 2 | 1 | 11 | | .346 |
| 1982 | 108 | 266 | 43 | 77 | 13 | 2 | 2 | 25 | 14 | .295 |
| 5.60 years | | 520 | 72 | 131 | 18 | 5 | 3 | 39 | 28 | .252 |

Dale MURPHY, Center Field

*Runs Created: 114*

| | G | AB | R | H | 2B | 3B | HR | RBI | SB | Avg |
|---|---|---|---|---|---|---|---|---|---|---|
| First Half | 84 | 312 | 61 | 89 | 12 | 1 | 23 | 62 | 7 | .285 |
| Second Half | 178 | 286 | 52 | 79 | 11 | 1 | 13 | 47 | 16 | .276 |
| Home | 81 | 297 | 54 | 92 | 13 | 0 | 24 | 59 | 4 | .310 |
| Road | 81 | 301 | 59 | 76 | 10 | 2 | 12 | 50 | 19 | .252 |
| vs. RHP | | 463 | | 121 | 18 | 1 | 25 | 76 | | .262 |
| vs. LHP | | 135 | | 47 | 5 | 1 | 11 | 35 | | .348 |
| 1982 | 162 | 598 | 113 | 168 | 23 | 2 | 36 | 109 | 23 | .281 |
| 4.41 years | | 588 | 86 | 156 | 22 | 3 | 29 | 92 | 14 | .265 |

Claudell WASHINGTON, Right Field

*Runs Created: 78*

| | G | AB | R | H | 2B | 3B | HR | RBI | SB | Avg |
|---|---|---|---|---|---|---|---|---|---|---|
| First Half | 78 | 304 | 46 | 85 | 15 | 3 | 6 | 36 | 14 | .280 |
| Second Half | 62 | 259 | 48 | 65 | 9 | 3 | 10 | 44 | 19 | .251 |
| Home | 76 | 304 | 49 | 88 | 17 | 2 | 8 | 45 | 15 | .289 |
| Road | 74 | 259 | 45 | 62 | 7 | 4 | 8 | 35 | 18 | .239 |
| vs. RHP | | 451 | | 120 | 22 | 6 | 14 | 62 | | .266 |
| vs. LHP | | 112 | | 30 | 2 | 0 | 2 | 18 | | .268 |
| 1982 | 150 | 563 | 94 | 150 | 24 | 6 | 16 | 80 | 33 | .266 |
| 6.54 years | | 597 | 81 | 166 | 31 | 7 | 12 | 75 | 31 | .279 |

Bruce BENEDICT, Catcher

*Runs Created: 36*

| | G | AB | R | H | 2B | 3B | HR | RBI | SB | Avg |
|---|---|---|---|---|---|---|---|---|---|---|
| First Half | 69 | 233 | 14 | 55 | 10 | 0 | 1 | 27 | 2 | .236 |
| Second Half | 49 | 153 | 20 | 40 | 1 | 1 | 2 | 17 | 2 | .261 |
| Home | 58 | 191 | 20 | 43 | 6 | 1 | 2 | 21 | 1 | .225 |
| Road | 60 | 195 | 14 | 52 | 5 | 0 | 1 | 23 | 3 | .267 |
| vs. RHP | | 282 | | 70 | 7 | 0 | 1 | 32 | | .248 |
| vs. LHP | | 104 | | 25 | 4 | 1 | 2 | 13 | | .240 |
| 1982 | 118 | 386 | 34 | 95 | 11 | 1 | 3 | 44 | 4 | .246 |
| 2.61 years | | 497 | 36 | 124 | 19 | 1 | 4 | 49 | 4 | .249 |

Phil NIEKRO

| Year | (W–L) | GS | Run | Avg | DP | Avg | SB | Avg |
|---|---|---|---|---|---|---|---|---|
| 1976 | (17-11) | 37 | 162 | 4.38 | 24 | .65 | 31 | .84 |
| 1977 | (16-20) | 42 | 170 | 4.05 | 36 | .86 | 49 | 1.17 |
| 1978 | (19-18) | 42 | 152 | 3.62 | 35 | .60 | 43 | 1.02 |
| 1979 | (21-10) | 44 | 199 | 4.52 | 34 | .77 | 46 | 1.05 |
| 1980 | (15-18) | 38 | 131 | 3.45 | 41 | 1.08 | 26 | .68 |
| 1981 | ( 7- 7) | 22 | 87 | 3.95 | 17 | .77 | 23 | 1.05 |
| 1982 | (17- 4) | 35 | 189 | 5.40 | 28 | .80 | 28 | .80 |
| 7 years | | 260 | 1090 | 4.19 | 181 | .70 | 246 | .95 |

| | G | IP | W | L | Pct | ER | ERA |
|---|---|---|---|---|---|---|---|
| Home | 14 | 91 | 3 | 3 | .500 | 51 | 5.04 |
| Road | 21 | 143.1 | 14 | 1 | .933 | 43 | 2.61 |

Rick MAHLER

| Year | (W–L) | GS | Run | Avg | DP | Avg | SB | Avg |
|---|---|---|---|---|---|---|---|---|
| 1981 | (8- 6) | 14 | 32 | 2.29 | 9 | .64 | 15 | 1.07 |
| 1982 | (9-10) | 33 | 152 | 4.61 | 37 | 1.12 | 24 | .73 |
| 2 years | | 47 | 184 | 3.91 | 46 | .98 | 39 | .83 |

| | G | IP | W | L | Pct | ER | ERA |
|---|---|---|---|---|---|---|---|
| Home | 22 | 132 | 7 | 5 | .583 | 48 | 3.27 |
| Road | 17 | 73.1 | 2 | 5 | .286 | 48 | 5.89 |

Bob WALK

| Year | (W–L) | GS | Run | Avg | DP | Avg | SB | Avg |
|---|---|---|---|---|---|---|---|---|
| 1980 | (11- 7) | 27 | 130 | 4.81 | 24 | .89 | 35 | 1.30 |
| 1981 | ( 1- 4) | 8 | 38 | 4.75 | 9 | 1.13 | 7 | .88 |
| 1982 | (11- 9) | 27 | 137 | 5.07 | 29 | 1.07 | 39 | 1.44 |
| 3 years | | 62 | 305 | 4.92 | 62 | 1.00 | 81 | 1.31 |

| | G | IP | W | L | Pct | ER | ERA |
|---|---|---|---|---|---|---|---|
| Home | 15 | 78.1 | 5 | 5 | .500 | 42 | 4.83 |
| Road | 17 | 86 | 6 | 4 | .600 | 47 | 4.92 |

Rick CAMP

| Year | (W–L) | GS | Run | Avg | DP | Avg | SB | Avg |
|---|---|---|---|---|---|---|---|---|
| 1978 | ( 2- 4) | 4 | 13 | 3.25 | 5 | 1.25 | 3 | .75 |
| 1982 | (11-13) | 21 | 64 | 3.05 | 33 | 1.57 | 25 | 1.19 |
| 2 years | | 25 | 77 | 3.08 | 38 | 1.52 | 28 | 1.12 |

| | G | IP | W | L | Pct | ER | ERA |
|---|---|---|---|---|---|---|---|
| Home | 28 | 91.1 | 7 | 5 | .583 | 36 | 3.55 |
| Road | 23 | 86 | 4 | 8 | .333 | 36 | 3.77 |

1982 OTHERS

| Pitcher | (W–L) | GS | Run | Avg | DP | Avg | SB | Avg |
|---|---|---|---|---|---|---|---|---|
| Dayley | (5-6) | 11 | 53 | 4.82 | 14 | 1.27 | 12 | 1.09 |
| Perez | (4-4) | 11 | 44 | 4.00 | 9 | .82 | 8 | .73 |
| Boggs | (2-2) | 10 | 46 | 4.60 | 16 | 1.60 | 16 | 1.60 |
| Cowley | (1-2) | 8 | 32 | 4.00 | 8 | 1.00 | 8 | 1.00 |
| Bedrosian | (8-6) | 3 | 10 | 3.33 | 3 | 1.00 | 3 | 1.00 |
| Hanna | (3-0) | 1 | 4 | | 1 | | 0 | |

## ATLANTA

*Talent Analysis*

The Atlanta Braves in 1982 possessed 157 points of approximate value. This missed being the highest total in the division by one point. That was the only case in which a division-winning team did not have the highest AV total.

| | AV | % |
|---|---|---|
| Produced by Braves' system: | 104 | 66% |
| Acquired by trade: | 41 | 26% |
| Purchased or signed from free agency: | 12 | 8% |

Ted Turner has been one of the prime movers in baseball's rapidly moving inflation rate; it is striking to notice (above) to what little effect. The Braves are one of the most home-grown teams in baseball. Where are all the people he threw the money at?

| | | |
|---|---|---|
| Young (Up to age 25): | 48 | 31% |
| Prime (Age 26 to 29): | 72 | 46% |
| Past-prime (Age 30 to 33): | 13 | 8% |
| Old (Age 34 or older): | 24 | 15% |

The Braves have twice as much young talent as an average team, 48 points AV to 24. 77% of their talent is young or prime; the norm is 62%. And I'm not really sure that Phil Niekro's age is relevant.

## FULTON COUNTY STADIUM

DIMENSIONS: Normal. *Not* short; normal.

SURFACE: Grass; excellent for double plays, ball gets to fielder quickly

VISIBILITY: Good

FOUL TERRITORY: A little small

FAVORS:
Hitter/Pitcher—Hitter, to extreme degree
Power/Line-drive hitter—Both; power more
Righthander/Lefthander—Righthander (see first comment)

TYPES OF OFFENSE AFFECTED: Increases batting averages 25-35 points; increases home runs by *60%*; decreases triples by 40%

TYPES OF MARGINAL PLAYERS MOST VALUABLE IN PARK: One-dimensional sluggers. *Control pitchers*. One- or two-out relief specialists needed to keep game in hand. Sinker ballers.

PLAYERS ON TEAM HELPED MOST BY PARK: Bob Horner, Dale Murphy. All hitters.

PLAYERS ON TEAM HURT MOST BY PARK: Phil Niekro, Tommy Boggs. All pitchers.

OTHER COMMENTS:
1) Craig Wright and I have been having an argument about whether or not there was enough evidence to conclude that the Atlanta park helps a right-handed home run hitter more than a left-hander. The dimensions are the same, but right-handers seem to increase their power output more at home. I felt the evidence was clear before we had 1982 data; Craig didn't. I decided to let the 1982 data rule. Atlanta left-handed regulars in '82 hit 19 home runs on the road, 23 at home, only a 21% increase. Righthanders hit 28 on the road, 63 at home, a 125% increase. Take that, CRW.
2) The fences are reportedly being lifted a few feet to cut down on the home runs hit here in the future.
3) There are more infield errors here than anywhere except San Francisco.
4) The factors causing this park to favor the hitter to such an extent have not yet been fully explained. The warm weather is certainly a factor: Hitters hit far better in warm weather than in cold. The altitude of the park is probably a factor. But whatever it is, it is variable. There are seasons in which those factors, whatever they are, go into almost complete remission.

## JACK RABBIT START

| Date | Opponent | Score | Starter/Winner | GWRBI (hit) | Inning |
|---|---|---|---|---|---|
| 4-6 | at San Diego | 1-0 | Mahler | Hubbard (double) | 5th |
| 4-7 | at San Diego | 6-4 | Walk | Butler (single) | 3rd |
| 4-9 | Houston | 6-2 | Boggs | None (error) | 1st |
| 4-10 | Houston | 8-6 | Bedrosian/McWilliams | Washington (double) | 1st |
| 4-11 | Houston | 5-0 | Mahler | Murphy (homer) | 4th |
| 4-12 | at Cincinnati | 6-1 | Walk | Horner (homer) | 2nd |
| 4-13 | at Cincinnati | 8-5 | Cowley/Garber | Benedict (single) | 7th |
| 4-14 | at Cincinnati | 5-2 | Boggs/Camp | Benedict (walk) | 10th |
| 4-16 | at Houston | 5-3 | Mahler/McWilliams | Horner (double) | 6th |
| 4-17 | at Houston | 2-1 | Walk/Hanna | Horner (double) | 1st |
| 4-18 | at Houston | 6-5 | Cowley/Hrbosky | Pocoroba (double) | 8th |
| 4-20 | Cincinnati | 4-2 | Boggs/Bedrosian | Washington (triple) | 3rd |
| 4-21 | Cincinnati | 4-3 | Mahler/Camp | Washington (single) | 4th |

### HITTERS

| | G | AB | R | H | 2B | 3B | HR | RBI | Avg |
|---|---|---|---|---|---|---|---|---|---|
| Butler | 13 | 53 | 10 | 14 | 0 | 1 | 0 | 7 | .264 |
| Hubbard | 13 | 46 | 7 | 12 | 3 | 0 | 0 | 4 | .261 |
| Washington | 9 | 32 | 3 | 8 | 1 | 1 | 0 | 6 | .250 |
| Horner | 12 | 43 | 8 | 8 | 4 | 0 | 2 | 7 | .186 |
| Murphy | 13 | 43 | 10 | 11 | 2 | 1 | 4 | 12 | .256 |
| Chambliss | 13 | 45 | 7 | 16 | 4 | 0 | 3 | 5 | .356 |
| Benedict | 13 | 41 | 7 | 11 | 4 | 0 | 0 | 5 | .268 |
| Ramirez | 13 | 48 | 7 | 17 | 3 | 3 | 1 | 9 | .354 |

### PITCHERS

| | G | IP | W–L | ERA | Sv |
|---|---|---|---|---|---|
| Mahler | 4 | 27 | 2-0 | 1.98 | 0 |
| Walk | 3 | 19 | 2-0 | 0.96 | 0 |
| Garber | 5 | 11 | 1-0 | 0.00 | 3 |
| Boggs | 3 | 14 | 1-0 | 3.14 | 0 |
| Bedrosian | 3 | 11 | 1-0 | 2.45 | 0 |
| Camp | 7 | 10 | 2-0 | 1.74 | 3 |
| Cowley | 2 | 9 | 0-0 | 4.15 | 0 |

# LOS ANGELES DODGERS

I have it in my head that it was the Los Angeles Dodger organization which began the current movement toward five-man pitching rotations. If this is not correct I will be happy to be instructed on the subject, but as I understand it the Dodgers, following the early retirements of Sandy Koufax and Don Drysdale, decided to go to a five-man pitching rotation while rebuilding the team, shifted briefly back to a four-man staff in 1974, lost Tommy John to an injury in half a season and then didn't win the division in 1975 anyway, so decided to return to the five-man plan. And, to kidnap a metaphor, when Walter O'Malley sneezes, the National League catches a cold.* From the Dodgers using a five-man rotation to the NL using it is not a long step.

Until I decided last spring to do a thorough study of the issue, I really had not taken in the extent to which the four-man pitching rotation had fallen out of favor. My view of the subject, in short, was this:

1) If I have a four-man pitching rotation and you are trying to persuade me to switch to a five-man rotation, what you are saying is that I should take eight starts away from my best starting pitcher, eight away from my second-best starting pitcher, eight away from my third-best starting pitcher, eight away from my fourth-best and give all 32 starts to my fifth-best starting pitcher.

2) Before I am going to do that, I want to see some real good evidence that I am going to get something back in exchange for it.

3) I have not seen any such evidence.

Ergo

4) I wouldn't do it.

I am aware, of course, that the fact that I have not seen any such evidence does not prove that no such evidence exists. The Dodgers usually know what they are doing, and for all I know they may have conducted extensive testing before they decided to do it this way.

Let's make a quick assessment of the direct costs of using a five-man rotation. If we assume that all starters average about seven innings a start (the assumption is wrong but does no significant damage to the conclusion), then if a team has five starters with earned run averages of 2.87, 3.11, 3.36, 3.81 and 4.03, how many runs does it cost them to use a five-man rotation? Answer: 18.48, or about two games a season. It is no great big deal, in other words, so long as you have a respectable fifth starter. Still, 18 runs...well, that's quite a few. The number of runs lost given the ERA combinations of the other NL West teams are given below:

| ERA of: | Atlanta | San Francisco | San Diego | Houston | Cincinnati |
|---|---|---|---|---|---|
| #1 Starter | 3.61 | 3.14 | 3.13 | 2.47 | 2.79 |
| #2 Starter | 3.65 | 4.11 | 4.00 | 3.00 | 3.35 |
| #3 Starter | 4.21 | 4.23 | 4.10 | 3.16 | 3.60 |
| #4 Starter | 4.54 | 4.65 | 4.20 | 3.93 | 3.97 |
| #5 Starter | 4.87 | 5.19 | 4.91 | 4.45 | 5.50 |
| Estimated Loss in Runs on 5-man Rotation | 21.6 | 28.8 | 26.2 | 32.6 | 51.6 |

A clear pattern: the fewer good starters you have, the greater the cost of going to a five-man rotation. Which I guess is obvious.

The next general question is, what are the benefits? Are pitchers more effective on four days rest? How much more effective? How consistent is it among pitchers? Are there some types of pitchers—power pitchers for example—who are more effective on short rest?

To try to answer these questions, I kept track, for the National League, of what each pitcher did while starting on three days rest, four days rest, five days rest or off-rotation. For convenience, I will call three days rest short rest, and five days rest long rest. Everyone's first start is considered to be off-rotation, which increased that total a bit.

My intention was to take the records of pitchers who started a minimum of eight times on short rest and eight times on four days rest and compare their earned run averages to see what the difference was. Unfortunately, to my surprsie, there were only three pitchers in the National League who met that standard: Andujar, Carlton and Phil Niekro. For what it is worth, which problably isn't a hell of a lot, all three of these pitchers had ERAs at least 50 points lower on the three days rest than on four. The one really clear answer that I got was that nobody much pitches on three days and so it is difficult to study what happens to pitchers who do using the current season. The chart below tells that 25 Dodger games in 1982 were started by pitchers working on three days rest, 94 by pitchers on four days rest, 20 by pitchers on five days rest and 23 by pitchers who were off-rotation (the lowest total in the league).

| WEST | | | | | EAST | | | | |
|---|---|---|---|---|---|---|---|---|---|
| | Days Rest | | | | | Days Rest | | | |
| | 3 | 4 | 5 | X | | 3 | 4 | 5 | X |
| Atlanta | 27 | 84 | 17 | 34 | St. Louis | 20 | 85 | 16 | 41 |
| Los Angeles | 25 | 94 | 20 | 23 | Philadelphia | 29 | 81 | 21 | 31 |
| San Francisco | 16 | 72 | 43 | 31 | Montreal | 6 | 85 | 39 | 32 |
| San Diego | 12 | 74 | 40 | 36 | Pittsburgh | 14 | 88 | 24 | 36 |
| Houston | 4 | 99 | 32 | 27 | Chicago | 8 | 90 | 36 | 34 |
| Cincinnati | 6 | 99 | 27 | 30 | New York | 29 | 59 | 32 | 42 |

The good teams had more games started on short rest than the weak teams did, in part (but only in part) because they shifted to four-man rotations once the heavy pennant race started. The Dodgers did, the Phillies did, and Atlanta went to using Niekro on three. Cincinnati and Houston had no reason to bother.

Throughout the league, 10% of starts were made on three days rest, 52% on four, 18% on five and 20% off rotation. Every team in the league had at least twice as

*Since Walter has been dead for two or three years, this perhaps does not bode well for the NL, but you know what I mean.

many pitchers starting on four days rest as on short rest; four days rest was the dominant or preferred pattern for every team. And with the exception of the Mets, who were experimenting with their pitching rotation all summer, every team had around 85 games started by pitchers on four days rest, give or take 14. When a manager could do it that way, he did.

The difference came about, for the most part, in those awkward places in the schedule where a manager had to choose between working somebody on short rest or giving him an extra day off. Some managers would always choose to wait and go on long rest; others would sometimes go ahead and start a pitcher a day early.

If we lower the standard to six starts (instead of eight) to be included in the study, then we have 12 NL pitchers who made a sufficient number of starts on short rest. Of the 12, eight had better earned run averages on short rest than they did on four days. There were three cases where the difference was more than a run, and in all three of those cases the edge was to short rest. The won-lost percentage of the twelve pitchers while starting on short rest was .631 (41-24); on four days rest it was .576 (87-64).

There were 26 pitchers around the league who started a minimum of six times on normal rotation and also on long rest. On balance, these pitchers were slightly more effective on long rest than on rotation. Sixteen of the 26 had lower ERAs on long rest. In toto, the 26 pitchers had a better ERA (3.55-3.66) and won-lost percentage (.514-.484) on five days rest than on four.

So we have somewhat inconsistent evidence; pitchers do better on long rest or short rest than four days, but everybody works on four anyway. It is notable that the pitchers who worked on short rest were by and large very good pitchers, with a .576 won-lost percentage on four days rest, better on three. The pitchers who more often worked on long rest were just average. One of the odd specifics was pitcher Jerry Reuss of the Dodgers. Reuss started 20 times on four days rest, six on short and six on long. His ERA was a run and a half better on either short rest (2.05) or long rest (2.20) than it was on his normal four days rest (3.60). Which probably means absolutely nothing.

If I was looking simply for evidence that pitchers were more effective with an extra day of rest, I would have considered this study a washout. Even if we accepted the most favorable possible conclusion—that there was an 0.11 gain in ERA when working with an extra days rest—that would not come near off-setting the 20-to-50-run loss inherent in shifting to a five-man rotation. Thus the rationale for working with a five-man rotation would appear to depend on one of two arguments: that pitchers who work regularly on short rest grow tired late in the season and thus can cost you a pennant race; or that pitchers who work on short rest are more prone to arm injuries and/or early retirement. Of the first proposition, I would be extremely dubious. Earl Weaver has always used a four-man pitching rotation, and it didn't seem to hurt the Orioles any late in the year. Of the second, I would be much less skeptical. I suspect that there probably is a difference there, that pitchers who work a lot on three days rest probably do run a risk of an early end. But if I was a general manager, I would never make a decision to use a fifth starter on the basis of what I suspect. Unless I saw some real evidence that there was a danger there, I'd stick with a four-man rotation.

This bit of research, as you can probably see, is a companion piece to the comments on Toronto. In all of this discussion, I am struck with one historical coincidence and two anomalies. The coincidence, if it is that, is that although there has been all of this talk about the DH rule ruining pitcher's arms, there are more—no, *far* more—old, veteran, graybeard pitchers around right at this moment than there have ever been at any time in the history of the game. There is no comparison. You look around, you've got Perry, Sutton, Jenkins, John, Carlton, Palmer, Seaver, Ryan, Niekro and Niekro, Fryman, Kaat, Fingers, Rudy May, Koosman, Zahn and a good many others, all 35 or older, many of them still outstanding pitchers. Just 10 years ago, all major league pitchers aged 35 or older won less than 100 games—82, actually—and the only two old pitchers who amounted to anything much were Gibson, who was 36 (and had worked in a five-man rotation for years) and Mike Cuellar, who was 35. While I don't tend to attribute this sudden gathering of old pitchers to the switch to five-man rotations, but to economic factors (*see Gaylord Perry, page 206*) it is quite possible that there is some connection.

The first anomaly, as I mentioned concerning Toronto, is that although the American League has the designated-hitter rule, the National League has almost universally adopted the five-man pitching rotation, while the AL has not. I cannot explain that. It seems backwards.

The second anomaly is that the organizations seem to have adopted a protectionist policy toward their players at a moment when they have just surrendered that which they are attempting to protect. Ten years ago, it was one thing to say that we are using a five-man rotation to protect our pitchers' futures, because that future really belonged to you. You either used it or you traded it; either way it was yours, to do what you would with it. It's not that way any more. What sense would it make for the Toronto Blue Jays to cut Dave Stieb back to 240 innings to protect his future, when it seems to be agreed that his future includes free agency? None at all. What sense does it make for the Dodgers to protect Valenzuela's arm so that four years from now Valenzuela can sell it to the highest bidder? I don't mean to sound callous, but when the economic structure is one that enables the player to say "You've got to give me ever penny that I can get from anybody, and to hell with what happened in the past," that player has got to expect the team to say "You've got to give us every inning that you can pitch, and to hell with your future." The one is the logical complement of the other. I think that baseball management, grounded in economic paternalism for decades, has never been able to make the switch to modern business realism, the foundation of which is greed: that, indeed, is two-thirds of the problem, that management insists on the one hand in fighting hopeless battles to resurrect the old paternalism, and on the other hand in flinging fistfuls of money at the players, half of which is intended to purchase their services, the other half to purchase their affection and loyalty. I think that when baseball management grows up, the four-man rotation is going to make a comeback.

The Dodgers led the league in pinch hitters used,

323; they were, unfortunately, last in the league in pinch hitting success, with a .181 average from the lot. Jorge Orta, the man they brought in to be their top pinch hitter, went 9-for-60 in the role; his lifetime pinch-hitting mark is now .180, on 23-for-128. Orta hit.291 when he wasn't pinch hitting. Rick Monday was 4-for-35 as a pinch hitter (.114), Mike Marshall 3-for-20 (.150), Ken Landreaux 1-for-11 (.091).

Steve GARVEY, First Base

*Runs Created: 79*

| | G | AB | R | H | 2B | 3B | HR | RBI | SB | Avg |
|---|---|---|---|---|---|---|---|---|---|---|
| First Half | 88 | 325 | 35 | 82 | 17 | 1 | 10 | 35 | 2 | .252 |
| Second Half | 74 | 300 | 31 | 94 | 18 | 0 | 6 | 51 | 3 | .313 |
| Home | | 302 | | 86 | | | 5 | 32 | | .285 |
| Road | | 323 | | 90 | | | 11 | 54 | | .279 |
| vs. RHP | | 535 | | 151 | | | 14 | 74 | | .282 |
| vs. LHP | | 90 | | 25 | | | 2 | 12 | | .278 |
| 1982 | 162 | 625 | 66 | 176 | 35 | 1 | 16 | 86 | 5 | .282 |
| 10.66 years | | 614 | 80 | 185 | 31 | 3 | 20 | 93 | 7 | .301 |

Steve SAX, Second Base

*Runs Created: 78*

| | G | AB | R | H | 2B | 3B | HR | RBI | SB | Avg |
|---|---|---|---|---|---|---|---|---|---|---|
| First Half | 85 | 359 | 49 | 100 | 12 | 5 | 0 | 28 | 32 | .279 |
| Second Half | 65 | 279 | 39 | 80 | 11 | 2 | 4 | 19 | 17 | .287 |
| Home | | 311 | | 90 | | | 2 | 19 | | .289 |
| Road | | 327 | | 90 | | | 2 | 28 | | .275 |
| vs. RHP | | 533 | | 151 | | | 4 | 37 | | .283 |
| vs. LHP | | 105 | | 29 | | | 0 | 10 | | .276 |
| 1982 | 150 | 638 | 88 | 180 | 23 | 7 | 4 | 47 | 49 | .282 |
| 1.12 years | | 676 | 92 | 190 | 22 | 6 | 5 | 50 | 48 | .281 |

Ron CEY, Third Base

*Runs Created: 77*

| | G | AB | R | H | 2B | 3B | HR | RBI | SB | Avg |
|---|---|---|---|---|---|---|---|---|---|---|
| First Half | 84 | 312 | 31 | 81 | 15 | 1 | 10 | 34 | 1 | .260 |
| Second Half | 66 | 244 | 31 | 60 | 8 | 0 | 14 | 45 | 2 | .246 |
| Home | | 281 | | 67 | | | 10 | 44 | | .240 |
| Road | | 275 | | 74 | | | 14 | 35 | | .269 |
| vs. RHP | | 470 | | 114 | | | 16 | 60 | | .243 |
| vs. LHP | | 86 | | 27 | | | 8 | 19 | | .314 |
| 1982 | 150 | 556 | 62 | 141 | 23 | 1 | 24 | 79 | 3 | .254 |
| 9.14 years | | 571 | 78 | 151 | 24 | 2 | 25 | 92 | 2 | .264 |

Bill RUSSELL, Shortstop

*Runs Created: 62*

| | G | AB | R | H | 2B | 3B | HR | RBI | SB | Avg |
|---|---|---|---|---|---|---|---|---|---|---|
| First Half | 82 | 244 | 34 | 61 | 9 | 0 | 2 | 22 | 6 | .250 |
| Second Half | 71 | 253 | 30 | 75 | 11 | 2 | 1 | 24 | 4 | .296 |
| Home | | 243 | | 7 | | | 2 | 27 | | .305 |
| Road | | 254 | | 62 | | | 1 | 19 | | .244 |
| vs. RHP | | 416 | | 111 | | | 3 | 41 | | .267 |
| vs. LHP | | 81 | | 25 | | | 0 | 5 | | .309 |
| 1982 | 153 | 497 | 64 | 136 | 20 | 2 | 3 | 46 | 10 | .274 |
| 10.99 years | | 566 | 62 | 150 | 23 | 5 | 4 | 50 | 13 | .265 |

Dusty BAKER, Left Field

*Runs Created: 93*

| | G | AB | R | H | 2B | 3B | HR | RBI | SB | Avg |
|---|---|---|---|---|---|---|---|---|---|---|
| First Half | 77 | 293 | 32 | 86 | 7 | 1 | 16 | 52 | 7 | .294 |
| Second Half | 70 | 277 | 48 | 85 | 12 | 0 | 7 | 36 | 10 | .307 |
| Home | | 290 | | 83 | | | 7 | 43 | | .286 |
| Road | | 280 | | 83 | | | 16 | 45 | | .314 |
| vs. RHP | | 483 | | 140 | | | 17 | 76 | | .290 |
| vs. LHP | | 87 | | 31 | | | 6 | 12 | | .356 |
| 1982 | 147 | 570 | 80 | 171 | 19 | 1 | 23 | 88 | 17 | .300 |
| 9.85 years | | 585 | 80 | 165 | 27 | 2 | 21 | 85 | 13 | .282 |

Ken LANDREAUX, Center Field

*Runs Created: 66*

| | G | AB | R | H | 2B | 3B | HR | RBI | SB | Avg |
|---|---|---|---|---|---|---|---|---|---|---|
| First Half | 71 | 237 | 42 | 74 | 12 | 4 | 2 | 29 | 19 | .312 |
| Second Half | 58 | 224 | 29 | 57 | 11 | 3 | 5 | 21 | 12 | .254 |
| Home | | 209 | | 52 | | | 1 | 14 | | .249 |
| Road | | 252 | | 79 | | | 6 | 36 | | .315 |
| vs. RHP | | 402 | | 118 | | | 6 | 43 | | .294 |
| vs. LHP | | 59 | | 13 | | | 1 | 7 | | .220 |
| 1982 | 129 | 461 | 71 | 131 | 23 | 7 | 7 | 50 | 31 | .284 |
| 3.85 years | | 581 | 78 | 160 | 26 | 9 | 11 | 69 | 20 | .275 |

Pedro GUERRERO, Right Field

*Runs Created: 118*

| | G | AB | R | H | 2B | 3B | HR | RBI | SB | Avg |
|---|---|---|---|---|---|---|---|---|---|---|
| First Half | 80 | 301 | 43 | 87 | 12 | 5 | 16 | 53 | 11 | .289 |
| Second Half | 70 | 274 | 44 | 88 | 15 | 0 | 16 | 47 | 11 | .321 |
| Home | | 286 | | 83 | | | 15 | 50 | | .290 |
| Road | | 289 | | 92 | | | 17 | 50 | | .318 |
| vs. RHP | | 499 | | 153 | | | 26 | 86 | | .307 |
| vs. LHP | | 76 | | 22 | | | 6 | 14 | | .290 |
| 1982 | 150 | 575 | 87 | 175 | 27 | 5 | 32 | 100 | 22 | .304 |
| 2.18 years | | 539 | 78 | 164 | 25 | 4 | 24 | 87 | 14 | .305 |

Mike SCIOSCIA, Catcher

*Runs Created: 33*

| | G | AB | R | H | 2B | 3B | HR | RBI | SB | Avg |
|---|---|---|---|---|---|---|---|---|---|---|
| First Half | 66 | 196 | 20 | 40 | 6 | 1 | 2 | 19 | 1 | .204 |
| Second Half | 63 | 169 | 11 | 40 | 5 | 0 | 3 | 19 | 1 | .237 |
| Home | | 197 | | 47 | | | 2 | 17 | | .239 |
| Road | | 168 | | 33 | | | 3 | 21 | | .196 |
| vs. RHP | | 340 | | 78 | | | 4 | 33 | | .229 |
| vs. LHP | | 25 | | 2 | | | 1 | 5 | | .080 |
| 1982 | 129 | 365 | 31 | 80 | 11 | 1 | 5 | 38 | 2 | .219 |
| 1.70 years | | 464 | 39 | 114 | 15 | 1 | 5 | 44 | 2 | .246 |

Rick MONDAY, Outfield

*Runs Created: 38*

| | G | AB | R | H | 2B | 3B | HR | RBI | SB | Avg |
|---|---|---|---|---|---|---|---|---|---|---|
| First Half | 56 | 119 | 22 | 33 | 4 | 3 | 7 | 28 | 1 | .277 |
| SecondHalf | 48 | 91 | 15 | 21 | 2 | 1 | 4 | 14 | 1 | .231 |
| Home | | 99 | | 24 | | | 7 | 22 | | .242 |
| Road | | 111 | | 30 | | | 4 | 20 | | .277 |
| vs. RHP | | 199 | | 52 | | | 11 | 42 | | .261 |
| vs. LHP | | 11 | | 2 | | | 0 | 0 | | .182 |
| 1982 | 104 | 210 | 37 | 54 | 6 | 4 | 11 | 42 | 2 | .257 |
| 11.46 years | | 516 | 81 | 137 | 21 | 6 | 20 | 65 | 9 | .265 |

### Steve YEAGER, Catcher

*Runs Created: 18*

| | G | AB | R | H | 2B | 3B | HR | RBI | SB | Avg |
|---|---|---|---|---|---|---|---|---|---|---|
| First Half | 44 | 109 | 9 | 30 | 3 | 0 | 2 | 13 | 0 | .275 |
| Second Half | 38 | 87 | 4 | 18 | 2 | 2 | 0 | 5 | 0 | .207 |
| Home | | 76 | | 16 | | | 2 | 8 | | .211 |
| Road | | 120 | | 32 | | | 0 | 10 | | .267 |
| vs. RHP | | 138 | | 31 | | | 0 | 9 | | .225 |
| vs. LHP | | 58 | | 17 | | | 2 | 9 | | .293 |
| 1982 | 82 | 196 | 13 | 48 | 5 | 2 | 2 | 18 | 0 | .245 |
| 6.04 years | | 464 | 49 | 108 | 17 | 2 | 13 | 53 | 2 | .232 |

### Jerry REUSS

| Year | (W–L) | GS | Run | Avg | DP | Avg | SB | Avg |
|---|---|---|---|---|---|---|---|---|
| 1976 | (14- 9) | 29 | 135 | 4.66 | 36 | 1.24 | 15 | .52 |
| 1977 | (10-13) | 33 | 153 | 4.64 | 32 | .97 | 24 | .73 |
| 1978 | ( 3- 2) | 12 | 63 | 5.25 | 10 | .83 | 14 | 1.17 |
| 1979 | ( 7-14) | 21 | 72 | 3.43 | 18 | .86 | 8 | .38 |
| 1980 | (18- 6) | 29 | 126 | 4.34 | 36 | 1.24 | 20 | .69 |
| 1981 | (10- 4) | 22 | 104 | 4.73 | 25 | 1.14 | 6 | .27 |
| 1982 | (18-11) | 37 | 165 | 4.46 | 29 | .78 | 21 | .57 |
| 7 years | | 183 | 808 | 4.42 | 186 | 1.02 | 108 | .59 |

| | G | IP | W | L | Pct | ER | ERA |
|---|---|---|---|---|---|---|---|
| Home | 19 | 126.2 | 9 | 5 | .643 | 37 | 2.63 |
| Road | 20 | 128 | 9 | 6 | .600 | 51 | 3.59 |

### Fernando VALENZUELA

| Year | (W–L) | GS | Run | Avg | DP | Avg | SB | Avg |
|---|---|---|---|---|---|---|---|---|
| 1981 | (13- 7) | 25 | 90 | 3.60 | 13 | .52 | 26 | 1.04 |
| 1982 | (19-13) | 37 | 145 | 3.92 | 33 | .89 | 26 | .70 |
| 2 years | | 62 | 235 | 3.79 | 46 | .74 | 52 | .84 |

| | G | IP | W | L | Pct | ER | ERA |
|---|---|---|---|---|---|---|---|
| Home | 20 | 151 | 10 | 7 | .588 | 50 | 2.98 |
| Road | 17 | 134 | 9 | 6 | .600 | 41 | 2.75 |

### Bob WELCH

| Year | (W–L) | GS | Run | Avg | DP | Avg | SB | Avg |
|---|---|---|---|---|---|---|---|---|
| 1978 | ( 7- 4) | 13 | 52 | 4.00 | 13 | 1.00 | 5 | .38 |
| 1979 | ( 5- 6) | 12 | 44 | 3.67 | 12 | 1.00 | 6 | .50 |
| 1980 | (14- 9) | 32 | 122 | 3.81 | 22 | .69 | 30 | .94 |
| 1981 | ( 9- 5) | 23 | 112 | 4.87 | 15 | .65 | 12 | .52 |
| 1982 | (16-11) | 36 | 163 | 4.53 | 23 | .64 | 22 | .61 |
| 5 years | | 116 | 493 | 4.25 | 85 | .73 | 75 | .65 |

| | G | IP | W | L | Pct | ER | ERA |
|---|---|---|---|---|---|---|---|
| Home | 18 | 124.1 | 7 | 6 | .538 | 36 | 2.61 |
| Road | 18 | 111.1 | 9 | 5 | .643 | 52 | 4.20 |

### Burt HOOTON

| Year | (W–L) | GS | Run | Avg | DP | Avg | SB | Avg |
|---|---|---|---|---|---|---|---|---|
| 1976 | (11-15) | 33 | 128 | 3.88 | 23 | .70 | 29 | .88 |
| 1977 | (12- 7) | 31 | 144 | 4.65 | 27 | .87 | 19 | .61 |
| 1978 | (19-10) | 32 | 118 | 3.69 | 24 | .75 | 25 | .78 |
| 1979 | (11-10) | 29 | 139 | 4.79 | 19 | .66 | 19 | .66 |
| 1980 | (14- 8) | 33 | 139 | 4.21 | 30 | .91 | 42 | 1.27 |
| 1981 | (11- 6) | 23 | 89 | 3.87 | 25 | 1.09 | 23 | 1.00 |
| 1982 | ( 4- 7) | 21 | 81 | 3.86 | 20 | .95 | 26 | 1.24 |
| 7 years | | 202 | 838 | 4.15 | 168 | .83 | 183 | .91 |

| | G | IP | W | L | Pct | ER | ERA |
|---|---|---|---|---|---|---|---|
| Home | 13 | 77 | 4 | 4 | .500 | 32 | 3.74 |
| Road | 8 | 43.2 | 0 | 3 | .00 | 22 | 4.53 |

### 1982 OTHERS

| Pitcher | (W–L) | GS | Run | Avg | DP | Avg | SB | Avg |
|---|---|---|---|---|---|---|---|---|
| Stewart | (9-8) | 14 | 54 | 3.86 | 8 | .57 | 10 | .71 |
| Romo | (1-2) | 6 | 24 | 4.00 | 4 | .67 | 6 | 1.00 |
| Wright | (2-1) | 5 | 27 | 5.40 | 4 | .80 | 7 | 1.40 |
| Power | (1-1) | 4 | 20 | 5.00 | 3 | .75 | 6 | 1.50 |
| Beckwith | (2-1) | 1 | 9 | | 0 | | 1 | |
| Goltz | (0-1) | 1 | 3 | | 1 | | 0 | |

## LOS ANGELES

*Talent Analysis*

The Dodgers possessed 158 points of approximate value in 1982, the highest in the division.

| | AV | % |
|---|---|---|
| Produced by Dodgers' system: | 112 | 71% |
| Acquired by trade: | 39 | 25% |
| Purchased or signed from free agency: | 7 | 4% |

The Dodgers' 71% of their talent which was produced by their own system is the highest figure in baseball.

| | | |
|---|---|---|
| Young (Up to age 25): | 45 | 29% |
| Prime (Age 26 to 29): | 49 | 31% |
| Past-prime (Age 30 to 33): | 49 | 31% |
| Old (Age 34 or older): | 15 | 9% |

The Dodgers' age spectrum reflects a team in transition. They have 45 AV points of young talent, a figure exceeded by only Atlanta and Minnesota, but they also have a slightly above-normal percentage of past-prime and old talent. This leaves them with only 31% of prime talent.

1982 approximate value produced by the Dodgers' system was 247 points, the highest in baseball. For the four years 1979 to 1982, their total has been 751 points, second highest in baseball.

## DODGER STADIUM

DIMENSIONS: Normal.

SURFACE: Grass

VISIBILITY: OK

FOUL TERRITORY: Large

FAVORS:
- Hitter/Pitcher—Pitcher (slightly)
- Power/Line-drive hitter—Power
- Righthander/Lefthander—Neither

TYPES OF OFFENSE AFFECTED: Fewer doubles and triples hit here than anywhere else in the major leagues; eliminates 60% of triples.

OTHER PARK CHARACTERISTICS: Warm weather helps hitters. The range factors of Dodger outfielders are misleading; the small outfield area and sinkerball staff cuts down on outfield opportunities.

TYPES OF MARGINAL PLAYERS MOST VALUABLE IN PARK: Slow, slugging outfielders?

PLAYERS ON TEAM HELPED MOST BY PARK: Bob Welch

PLAYERS ON TEAM HURT MOST BY PARK: Dusty Baker. I really don't know why this park is so poor for Baker when it was a good park for Steve Garvey. They're both slow, right-handed batters—look like similar types of hitters. But Dusty over the last three years has hit .272, .283 and .286 at home, against .315, .356 and .314 marks on the road, and totaled 25 homers in Los Angeles, 36 on the road, while Garvey hit well here.

OTHER COMMENTS: This park does *not* ruin the fielding percentages of Dodger infielders. There are 5% fewer infield errors here than in Dodger road games, possibly due to the official scorers.

## THE GAMES THAT LOST IT

The Dodgers were 3 games ahead on September 20, but then lost eight straight games to hand it to the Braves. An account of those eight games:

| Date | Opponent | Score | Starter/Loser | What Happened? |
|---|---|---|---|---|
| 9-21 | San Diego | 0-2 | Hooton | Montefusco & DeLeon pitched shutout |
| 9-22 | San Diego | 1-2 | Reuss/Niedenfuer | SD scratched run in 10th |
| 9-24 | San Francisco | 2-3 | Welch/Howe | No hits after the fourth |
| 9-25 | San Francisco | 4-5 | Valenzuela | Fernando lost leads in 7th & 8th; errors |
| 9-26 | San Francisco | 2-3 | Hooton | Hooton hit early; no offense |
| 9-27 | Cincinnati | 1-6 | Reuss | Soto in command; Braves in tie |
| 9-28 | Cincinnati | 3-4 | Welch/Stewart | Reds scratched run in 10th; LA loaded bases with none out and didn't score |
| 9-29 | Atlanta | 3-4 | Valenzuela/Forster | Braves scored two in 12th; LA got one but Pedro hit into DP to kill it |

**HITTERS**

| | G | AB | R | H | 2B | 3B | HR | RBI | SB | Avg |
|---|---|---|---|---|---|---|---|---|---|---|
| Sax | 4 | 15 | 1 | 6 | 0 | 0 | 1 | 2 | 3 | .400 |
| Landreaux | 6 | 16 | 1 | 3 | 2 | 0 | 0 | 0 | 0 | .188 |
| Baker | 8 | 34 | 1 | 7 | 1 | 0 | 0 | 1 | 0 | .206 |
| Guerrero | 8 | 32 | 2 | 7 | 0 | 0 | 0 | 3 | 0 | .219 |
| Garvey | 8 | 34 | 1 | 8 | 3 | 0 | 0 | 3 | 0 | .235 |
| Cey | 7 | 23 | 0 | 2 | 0 | 0 | 0 | 0 | 0 | .087 |
| Marshall | 4 | 6 | 1 | 1 | 0 | 0 | 1 | 1 | 0 | .167 |
| Russell | 8 | 30 | 4 | 10 | 1 | 0 | 0 | 3 | 0 | .333 |
| Roenicke | 8 | 12 | 1 | 4 | 0 | 0 | 0 | 0 | 1 | .333 |
| Yeager | 7 | 14 | 0 | 5 | 1 | 1 | 0 | 1 | 0 | .357 |
| Monday | 7 | 12 | 1 | 1 | 0 | 0 | 0 | 0 | 0 | .083 |
| Scioscia | 7 | 12 | 0 | 2 | 0 | 0 | 0 | 1 | 0 | .167 |

**PITCHERS**

| | G | IP | W–L | ERA |
|---|---|---|---|---|
| Valenzuela | 2 | 14 | 0-1 | 3.14 |
| Welch | 2 | 12 | 0-0 | 3.09 |
| Reuss | 2 | 10 | 0-1 | 5.40 |
| Hooton | 2 | 9 | 0-2 | 4.82 |
| Forster | 4 | 7 | 0-1 | 2.45 |
| Stewart | 4 | 6 | 0-1 | 3.00 |
| Niedenfuer | 5 | 7 | 0-1 | 2.45 |
| Howe | 5 | 5 | 0-1 | 1.69 |

COMMENTS:

1) Steve Sax was out of the first five games except for an inning on defense. The men who led off in his absence went 0 for 21, which was probably the one largest key to the slump.

2) Lasorda used 28 pinch hitters in the eight games. They had three hits and no RBI.

3) Note that six of the eight games were 1-run losses. For the rest of the season the Dodgers were one of the best one-run teams in baseball, a 31-27 mark in 1-run decisions overall (31-21 without these six).

# SAN FRANCISCO GIANTS

If you had never heard that the San Francisco manager had once played and coached for Earl Weaver, you wouldn't have to be too smart to figure it out. The signature of Earl Weaver is written large and small all over this team.

First of all, I am, among sabermetricians, not an enthusiastic proponent of walks as an offensive weapon. I think that players who walk a lot tend to be slump-prone. The runs-created method, if used to rate hitters, will rate a player who walks a lot lower than any other reasonably sophisticated offensive rating tool that I know of—lower than Barry Codell's Base-Out Percentage, lower than Boswell's Total Average, lower than Thomas Cover's Offensive Earned Run Average, lower than Pete Palmer's OBA + SP (On Base Average Plus Slugging Percentage). But the public at large doesn't even seem to realize that records are kept of who walks how often, or else thinks that it is just a sort of random result of being at bat when a pitcher is stricken with control trouble. Given that, it must often seem to the public that I am referring to the walks column constantly, overrating all of the people who walk a lot and underrating those who don't.

My view of walks as an offensive weapon is that I don't wish to be an advocate of any position on the subject at all, but. The immense defensive importance of walks is universally assumed. You listen to any game where one team issues four or more walks and loses, and I guarantee you that the announcer will cite the control troubles of the losing pitcher as one of the keys to his defeat (oh, those bases on balls). The fact that bases on balls have both an offensive and a defensive origin—that the batter can do every bit as much to put himself on base by that route as the pitcher can—is equally obvious, and is a fact that any analytical review of the game will constantly thrust upon you. To reach the conclusion that walks have an immense offensive importance is only a tiny logical step. Until the public learns to take that step by itself, it simply is not possible to make any intelligent review of the game without beginning the discussion with that step.

The same, to a much lesser extent, is true of power hitters. The public in general tends to overestimate the value of a high batting average in producing runs, and to underestimate the value of power. As I have tried to explain, to figure the size of the rectangle representing the number of runs that a team will score, you need to know three basic things: The team batting average, how many walks they draw and how much power they have:

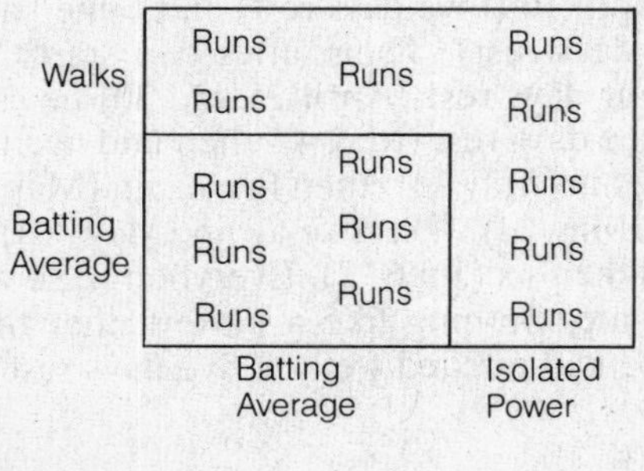

Walks | Runs Runs Runs | Runs Runs
Batting Average | Runs Runs Runs | Runs Runs Runs | Runs Runs Runs
Batting Average | Isolated Power

To put it in a few words, the relationship between a player's batting average and his total offensive value varies immensely from player to player; the two primary factors according to which it varies are the player's isolated power and his walks.

No manager has ever understood this better than Earl Weaver. Craig Wright has described isolated power and walks as the sabermetric virtues, a phrase with which I feel rather uncomfortable; I don't really want to be in the position of advocating one type of offense as opposed to another.

I prefer to think of them as the Earl Weaver virtues. Earl Weaver's teams rarely hit for a high batting average. Only one EW team ever led the league in batting average; usually they were below the league average. Several times, Weaver's teams had fewer hits in the season than did their opponents, and over the course of his career they exceeded their opponents in hits by only 5%. But every team that Earl Weaver managed in the major leagues drew more walks than did their opponents, an average of 24% more. (This has both offensive and defensive components, of course. His hitters drew walks; his pitchers didn't issue them.) All of Weaver's teams but one hit more home runs than their opponents, an average of 22% more.

The San Francisco Giants of 1982 were, down the line, an Earl Weaver team. The team was led by four ballplayers, three of them old, whose batting averages represented an unusually small part of their offensive value —Joe Morgan, Reggie Smith, Darrell Evans and Jack Clark. They all walk a lot, they all have power; they are generally good-percentage base-stealers. And thus:

| | Giants | Giant Opponents | NL Average |
|---|---|---|---|
| Hits | 1393 | 1507 | 1424 |
| Walks | 607 | 466 | 497 |
| Home Runs | 133 | 109 | 108 |
| WINS | 87 | 75 | 81 |

The Giants had 31 fewer hits than an average NL team, 114 fewer than their opponents. But they won.

I should also mention (I should mention it in the interest of fairness, were it not worthy of mention anyway) the one statistic that most amazed me when I received the National League statistic book. Duane Kuiper, with 218 official at bats, drew 32 walks. Duane Kuiper? Yes, he did. He increased his on-base percentage, formerly putrid, to a handsome .377. I have been critical of Kuiper in the past,* but I will be happy to say that that criticism simply does not apply to the new Duane Kuiper. And that remarkable right turn—it is as if Chris Speier had stolen 32 bases—proves beyond any shadow of a doubt that this is not merely the shape of the talent that Robinson happened to have available, but that there is a clear emphasis here in getting on base.

*"A pathetically inept offensive ballplayer at his best" can safely be described as criticism.

As with Weaver, it is offensive and defensive. The pitching staff, with the exception of Rich Gale, is basically a control-pitcher's staff. Bill Laskey walked only 43 men in 189 innings, Atlee Hammaker only 28 in 175, Alan Fowlkes only 24 in 85, Jim Barr 20 in 129. All of these ratios are among the best in the National League.

But what is odd is, is there any Earl Weaver characteristic that this team missed? Look:

1) Earl Weaver's teams always seem to have trouble getting rolling, but come down the stretch like a hurricane. The 1982 Giants were 32-40, a .444 team, on June 25, but went 55-35, .611, thereafter.

2) Earl Weaver's teams, somehow—I haven't figured out how this happens yet—always manage to win more games than they ought to given the number of runs that they score and allow. The '82 Giants out-Earled Earl, managing to exceed their Pythagorean projection by eight full games. They allowed 12 more runs than they scored, but still finished 12 games over .500.

3) Earl Weaver's teams usually play .650 baseball in double headers. The '82 Giants were 8-4, .667, in twin bills.

4) Weaver's teams are usually good-percentage base-stealers, but don't run much. The '82 Giants were fourth in the National League in stolen-base percentage, .707, but were low in the league in the number of stolen-base attempts, 186. They were also last in sacrifice hits.

Earl's teams never play well on artificial turf. The Giants were 20-22 on artificial turf, 67-53 on grass.

5) Weaver's teams almost always do very well in one-run decisions. The Giants were 38-28, third in the league, in one-run games.

And face it, 7) they were in a close pennant race, and they lost it. I have nothing but respect for Earl Weaver, but greater respect for facts, and Earl's record in close pennant races is not, in fact, very good.

We can find a few differences. A key one is the depth of their talent. Weaver's teams in recent years have had about three or four regulars, five at most, with a number of players available and rotating in and out at the other positions in a system that I have described as complex platooning. Robinson, unmistakeably, is trying to get the same system going with the Giants. He had only two players (Clark and Davis) with 500 at-bats, but he had 16 players, more than any other NL team, with 100 or more at-bats. At first base he used Barrios, Bergman, Evans, Leonard, Smith and Summers. It is very clear to me that he is trying to create a cadre of reliable hands that he can call on to play roles as needed within a game, as Lowenstein, Roenicke, Ayala Crowley, Dwyer, *et al* did for Weaver. It is also clear that he hasn't really done it yet, maybe because he hasn't had time to build up a good book on who can hit who. I think if you compared the production of the Giants' left fielders to that of the Orioles, it wouldn't look too good. But if you compared it to the NL average, it probably wouldn't look all that bad, either.

A second key difference seems to be that one essential element of Earl's success is totally missing here. After the 1977 season, when the Orioles lost Ross Grimsley to free agency (they had lost Wayne Garland and Reggie Jackson the year before) many people felt, it is now difficult to recall, that these losses would eventually drag them under. My comment on the subject was:

> *Can the Orioles continue to withstand free agent losses, and win? The Orioles in 1977 turned 189 doubles plays and committed only 106 errors. If they keep that ratio, they're going to keep winning. And the people who are responsible for those remarkable totals are still here.*

The Orioles always turned the double play well, and they never made many errors. Even in recent years, when they have not turned the double play as well, their ratio between these two defensive stats has still been one of the best in baseball. The American League average in '82 was 1.24-1; the Orioles' was 1.39-1, 39% more double plays than errors. And would you like to know what four teams had the best ratios between double plays and errors in 1982? The leaders in the four divisions were St. Louis, (1.36-1), Atlanta (1.36-1), Milwaukee (1.48-1) and California (1.56-1). All four division winners.

The Giants, unfortunately, had the worst ratio between double plays and errors of any major league team, 38% more errors than double plays. This fact, though, is not quite as damaging as it might at first appear. County Stadium in Atlanta is conducive to hitting home runs, Wrigley Field is conducive to high batting averages, the Astrodome is extremely conducive to low ERAs—and Candlestick Park is conducive to errors. A gentleman by the name of Paul Schwarzenbart wrote an excellent article which appeared in the first issue of the *Baseball Analyst*, "Ballpark Effects on Fielding Performance." Not surprisingly, he found that the Giants and their opponents erred 25% more often in Candlestick than in Giant road games, making it easily the most error-filled stadium in the leagues. The park also reduces double plays by about 2%. The reasons for these things are not at all difficult to see, in view of the surface, visibility and wind for which the park is infamous. If the Giants commit a lot of errors over the course of a year, so do their opponents in most seasons. For that reason, the Giants in 1971 were able to win the NL West although they led the league in errors, making them the only team ever to win a division while leading the league in errors.

Still, the fielding is a legitimate problem area. If you park-adjusted error and double-play rates, it would still be a ratio of 0.82-1, and that's still bad. It is definitely an area that needs improvement.

In maintaining the records of how the pitchers were used, it seemed to me early in the season that Robinson's handling of his starting staff was tentative, indecisive, maladroit. A record of Richard Gale's starts and rests through June 12: His first start was on April 10. Then he started on April 16 (Five days rest) and came back on the 20th (three days rest). Then, after two starts "on rotation" (on four days rest; April 25 and 30) he came back again on three days rest (May 4), then had five (May 10), then three again (May 14), then five again (May 20), then three again (May 24), then five again (May 30), then five (June 5) and then six (June 12). Everybody else was pretty much the same, nothing like a pattern that they could rely on. Gale had pitched well on five days rest (5 starts,

2-0 record with 2.56 ERA), but when called to come back on three he was getting hammered (4 starts, 0-4 with 7.71 ERA), which I don't think is too surprising. On balance the staff ERA was near the worst in the league.

This halting, variable use of his starters came to an abrupt end on June 13, when Robinson suddenly fixed his starters on four days rest, running Alan Fowlkes in and out of the rotation to keep the others on the schedule. The chart below breaks the Giants' season down into eighteen 9-game groups and tells how many days of rest the starter of each game had had. If the number of days was not 3, 4, 5 or 6, it is listed as X, meaning the starter was completely off rotation.

| 9 Game Group # | Game # 123 456 789 | Record in These 9 Games | End Date | Record on That Date |
|---|---|---|---|---|
| 1. | xxx x45 455 | 4-5 | April 17 | 4-5 |
| 2. | 443 34x 45x | 3-6 | April 28 | 7-11 |
| 3. | 54x 433 344 | 5-4 | May 7 | 12-15 |
| 4. | 555 443 xx4 | 3-6 | May 16 | 15-21 |
| 5. | 5x5 554 333 | 4-5 | May 25 | 19-26 |
| 6. | 345 555 455 | 5-4 | June 5 | 24-30 |
| 7. | 566 666 454 | 4-5 | June 16 | 28-35 |
| 8. | 445 4x4 444 | 4-5 | June 25 | 32-40 |
| 9. | 444 445 444 | 5-4 | July 4 | 37-44 |
| 10. | 434 444 4x5 | 5-4 | July 16 | 42-48 |
| 11. | xx4 455 443 | 5-4 | July 27 | 47-52 |
| 12. | x44 633 3x4 | 6-3 | August 5 | 53-55 |
| 13. | 554 3x4 444 | 7-2 | August 13 | 60-57 |
| 14. | 445 555 544 | 4-5 | August 23 | 64-62 |
| 15. | 445 55x 45x | 4-5 | Sept. 4 | 68-67 |
| 16. | 44x 4x4 455 | 7-2 | Sept. 14 | 75-69 |
| 17. | 555 x44 655 | 7-2 | Sept. 24 | 82-71 |
| 18. | x44 4x4 444 | 5-4 | October 3 | 87-75 |

You see what happened? Before June 13, the Giants had played 60 games, and had had only 16 pitchers starting on the normal 4-day rest. Through the rest of the year, the majority of their starts were made on four days. And the Giants began to win consistently about a week and a half after the rotation was stabilized.

And who does that remind you of? Sure . . . Earl Weaver uses the most stable starting corps in the majors, has for years. It's rare that you can see a phone call in the records, but you sure can this time. Did this phone conversation actually take place?

FRANK: Hello, Earl?
EARL: Frank, is that you? How's it going, buddy?
FRANK: You need another coach? I'm about to get fired out here.
EARL: Oh? What's the problem?
FRANK: I can't find any pitchers that I can count on. I've tried everything; I've put everybody out there. Nobody can get me into the seventh inning with a chance to win the game.
EARL: Well, have you tried leaving them alone?
FRANK: What's that?
EARL: Frank, it's your team, but I don't believe in doing no experimenting in the middle of the season. I've always believed that you've got to look at the pitchers you've got in camp, make up your mind about who can pitch and who can't, and sink or swim with the best you've got.

If that conversation did not actually occur, it sure *looks* like it did. By June 13th, Frank Robinson had sent to the hill nine starting pitchers—Holland, Fowlkes, Schatzeder, Gale, Barr, Laskey, Hammaker, Martin and Chris. Earl Weaver does not use nine starting pitchers in a year. In the middle of June, Robinson firmly committed himself to Laskey, Gale, Hammaker and Martin, started putting them out there every fifth day regardless of how well they had pitched in their last start. The Giants' staff ERA was 4.06 in late June. It wound up at 3.64.

Finally, I can't tell you how much it pleases me to write this comment. I've been writing basically the same annual comment about the Giants for so long that *I* was getting bored with it. "The Giants are indecisive; they've got the foresight of an earthworm . . . They're continually trying to win pennants that they don't have the talent for. . . . They shuttle people around for no apparent reason." All of this was true for three or four years after it was interesting, and it was hard to write anything else about the team as long as it was true. It was almost embarrassing. My nephew is a Giants fan, he'd say "What'd you write about the Giants this year?" I'd say "Oh, same old stuff." The Giants might have realized they would have trouble getting the same kind of years out of Morgan, Smith, Evans and some others that they got in 1982, and thus they're going to have to try something new to stay in the race in '83. But for the first time in years, they know what they are trying to do,* and they've got a chance at making it work.

I'm not sure how it relates to the other comments here, or for that matter how it relates to the other comments about late-inning production throughout the book, but the Giants were much the best late-inning baseball team in the major leagues last year. The records of all teams in games when they were ahead, behind and tied after seven innings are given on the division sheets. The Giants won 17 games in which they were behind after seven innings, a figure which towers over the division; indeed, over the rest of baseball. Seventeen late-inning rallies is:

1) as many as any other two teams in the division combined;
2) three more than the combined total of Atlanta (9) and LA (5);
3) one less than the combined total of San Diego (5), Houston (5) and Cincinnati (8);
4) Six more than any other team in the league (Philly had 11); and
5) the most in baseball, although Seattle was close with 15.

They also had the best record in the division, 12-8, in games that were tied after seven innings. In the counts of late-inning game-winning RBI, which start with the bottom of the seventh, the Giants had 36. (See chart at top of next page.) The totals of all of the teams around the league are given in the columns at left; the totals of the Giants' players are given in the center column: the individual leaders are given at right.

*Editor's note: Oh yeah? Then how come they let Joe Morgan go?

| Team Totals | | SF Individual Totals | | League Leaders | |
|---|---|---|---|---|---|
| San Francisco | 36 | Clark | 8 | Clark | 8 |
| Philadelphia | 30 | Morgan | 5 | Matthews | 8 |
| Atlanta | 26 | Davis | 4 | | |
| St. Louis | 26 | May | 3 | Chambliss | 5 |
| | | Smith | 3 | Garner | 5 |
| Montreal | 25 | Leonard | 2 | Baker | 5 |
| Pittsburgh | 24 | O'Malley | 2 | Raines | 5 |
| Los Angeles | 22 | Evans | 2 | Cromartie | 5 |
| Chicago | 19 | LeMaster | 1 | Madlock | 5 |
| | | Venable | 1 | Pena | 5 |
| Houston | 19 | Brenly | 1 | Schmidt | 5 |
| San Diego | 18 | Kuiper | 1 | Morgan | 5 |
| New York | 17 | Summers | 1 | Kennedy | 5 |
| Cincinnati | 15 | Bergman | 1 | | |
| | | Pruitt | 1 | | |

## GIANT RECORDS WITH VARIOUS PEOPLE IN AND OUT OF THE LINEUP

| | Record With | Record Without |
|---|---|---|
| Chili Davis | 84-69 | 3- 6 |
| Joe Morgan | 67-53 | 20-22 |
| Jack Clark | 84-70 | 3- 5 |
| Reggie Smith | 55-45 | 32-30 |
| Darrell Evans | 68-58 | 19-17 |
| Jeff Leonard | 42-33 | 45-42 |
| Milt May | 57-41 | 30-34 |
| Johnny LeMaster | 69-58 | 18-17 |
| Dave Bergman | 12-11 | 75-64 |
| Duane Kuiper | 23-22 | 64-53 |
| Jeff Ransom | 5- 8 | 82-67 |
| Champ Summers | 11-19 | 76-56 |
| Guy Slarz | 14-14 | 73-61 |
| Jose Barrios | 2- 2 | 85-73 |
| Jim Wohlford | 27-28 | 60-47 |
| Tom O'Malley | 42-32 | 45-43 |
| Bob Brenly | 26-24 | 61-51 |
| Max Venable | 14- 9 | 73-66 |
| Joe Pettini | 3- 5 | 84-70 |

### Reggie SMITH, First Base

*Runs Created: 62*

| | G | AB | R | H | 2B | 3B | HR | RBI | SB | Avg |
|---|---|---|---|---|---|---|---|---|---|---|
| First Half | 48 | 153 | 19 | 42 | 2 | 0 | 7 | 25 | 2 | .275 |
| Second Half | 58 | 196 | 31 | 57 | 9 | 0 | 11 | 31 | 5 | .291 |
| Home | 54 | 172 | 23 | 48 | 6 | 0 | 10 | 33 | 3 | .279 |
| Road | 52 | 177 | 28 | 51 | 5 | 0 | 8 | 23 | 4 | .288 |
| *vs. RHP | | 253 | | 77* | 8* | 0 | 16 | 47* | | .304 |
| *vs. LHP | | 97 | | 23* | 4* | 0 | 2 | 10* | | .237 |
| 1982 | 106 | 349 | 51 | 99 | 11 | 0 | 18 | 56 | 7 | .284 |
| 12.27 years | | 573 | 92 | 165 | 30 | 5 | 26 | 89 | 11 | .287 |

*I know this doesn't add but it's what they sent me.

### Joe MORGAN, Second Base

*Runs Created: 86*

| | G | AB | R | H | 2B | 3B | HR | RBI | SB | Avg |
|---|---|---|---|---|---|---|---|---|---|---|
| First Half | 66 | 221 | 28 | 62 | 10 | 0 | 7 | 23 | 13 | .281 |
| Second Half | 68 | 242 | 40 | 72 | 9 | 4 | 7 | 38 | 11 | .298 |
| Home | 65 | 223 | 28 | 59 | 7 | 0 | 6 | 29 | 9 | .265 |
| Road | 69 | 240 | 40 | 75 | 12 | 4 | 8 | 32 | 15 | .313 |
| vs. RHP | | 308 | | 87 | 11 | 2 | 8 | 34 | | .282 |
| vs. LHP | | 155 | | 47 | 8 | 2 | 6 | 27 | | .303 |
| 1982 | 134 | 463 | 68 | 134 | 19 | 4 | 14 | 61 | 24 | .289 |
| 14.88 years | | 572 | 103 | 157 | 27 | 6 | 17 | 69 | 45 | .274 |

### Darrell EVANS, Third Base

*Runs Created: 70*

| | G | AB | R | H | 2B | 3B | HR | RBI | SB | Avg |
|---|---|---|---|---|---|---|---|---|---|---|
| First Half | 75 | 250 | 34 | 63 | 12 | 0 | 12 | 27 | 2 | .252 |
| Second Half | 66 | 215 | 30 | 56 | 12 | 4 | 4 | 34 | 3 | .260 |
| Home | 70 | 223 | 27 | 50 | 4 | 1 | 8 | 30 | 2 | .224 |
| Road | 71 | 242 | 37 | 69 | 16 | 3 | 8 | 31 | 3 | .285 |
| vs. RHP | | 303 | | 80 | 14 | 1 | 13 | 35 | | .264 |
| vs. LHP | | 162 | | 39 | 6 | 3 | 3 | 26 | | .241 |
| 1982 | 141 | 465 | 64 | 119 | 20 | 4 | 16 | 61 | 5 | .256 |
| 10.56 years | | 552 | 82 | 139 | 21 | 3 | 22 | 78 | 8 | .251 |

### Johnny LeMASTER, Shortstop

*Runs Created: 32*

| | G | AB | R | H | 2B | 3B | HR | RBI | SB | Avg |
|---|---|---|---|---|---|---|---|---|---|---|
| First Half | 85 | 298 | 27 | 63 | 9 | 1 | 2 | 19 | 10 | .211 |
| Second Half | 45 | 138 | 7 | 31 | 5 | 0 | 0 | 11 | 3 | .225 |
| Home | 67 | 206 | 17 | 48 | 8 | 1 | 1 | 19 | 8 | .233 |
| Road | 63 | 230 | 17 | 46 | 6 | 0 | 1 | 11 | 5 | .200 |
| vs. RHP | | 295 | | 60 | 10 | 1 | 0 | 16 | | .203 |
| vs. LHP | | 141 | | 34 | 4 | 0 | 2 | 14 | | .241 |
| 1982 | 130 | 436 | 34 | 94 | 14 | 1 | 2 | 30 | 13 | .216 |
| 4.33 years | | 482 | 43 | 108 | 19 | 4 | 3 | 37 | 9 | .225 |

### Jeff LEONARD, Left Field

*Runs Created: 37*

| | G | AB | R | H | 2B | 3B | HR | RBI | SB | Avg |
|---|---|---|---|---|---|---|---|---|---|---|
| First Half | 19 | 61 | 8 | 18 | 2 | 0 | 2 | 14 | 6 | .295 |
| Second Half | 61 | 217 | 24 | 54 | 14 | 1 | 7 | 35 | 12 | .249 |
| Home | 43 | 146 | 16 | 37 | 9 | 1 | 4 | 22 | 6 | .253 |
| Road | 37 | 132 | 16 | 35 | 7 | 0 | 5 | 27 | 12 | .265 |
| vs. RHP | | 187 | | 47 | 12 | 1 | 7 | 34 | | .251 |
| vs. LHP | | 91 | | 25 | 4 | 0 | 2 | 15 | | .275 |
| 1982 | 80 | 278 | 32 | 72 | 16 | 1 | 9 | 49 | 18 | .259 |
| 2.25 years | | 483 | 59 | 130 | 23 | 7 | 7 | 66 | 22 | .269 |

### Chili DAVIS, Center Field

*Runs Created: 80*

| | G | AB | R | H | 2B | 3B | HR | RBI | SB | Avg |
|---|---|---|---|---|---|---|---|---|---|---|
| First Half | 86 | 351 | 46 | 98 | 16 | 3 | 10 | 52 | 7 | .279 |
| Second Half | 68 | 290 | 40 | 69 | 11 | 3 | 9 | 24 | 17 | .223 |
| Home | 76 | 306 | 39 | 85 | 10 | 4 | 6 | 27 | 13 | .278 |
| Road | 78 | 335 | 47 | 82 | 17 | 2 | 13 | 49 | 11 | .245 |
| vs. RHP | | 443 | | 109 | 20 | 4 | 16 | 54 | | .246 |
| vs. LHP | | 198 | | 58 | 7 | 2 | 3 | 22 | | .293 |
| 1982 | 154 | 641 | 86 | 167 | 27 | 6 | 19 | 76 | 24 | .261 |
| 1.00 years | | 656 | 87 | 169 | 27 | 6 | 19 | 76 | 24 | .258 |

### Jack CLARK, Right Field

*Runs Created: 98*

| | G | AB | R | H | 2B | 3B | HR | RBI | SB | Avg |
|---|---|---|---|---|---|---|---|---|---|---|
| First Half | 83 | 287 | 45 | 74 | 8 | 1 | 17 | 57 | 4 | .258 |
| Second Half | 74 | 276 | 45 | 80 | 22 | 2 | 10 | 46 | 2 | .290 |
| Home | 79 | 277 | 44 | 74 | 14 | 1 | 9 | 42 | 3 | .267 |
| Road | 78 | 286 | 46 | 80 | 16 | 2 | 18 | 61 | 3 | .280 |
| vs. RHP | | 400 | | 105 | 16 | 2 | 20 | 78 | | .263 |
| vs. LHP | | 163 | | 49 | 14 | 1 | 7 | 25 | | .301 |
| 1982 | 157 | 563 | 90 | 154 | 30 | 3 | 27 | 103 | 6 | .274 |
| 5.26 years | | 577 | 92 | 159 | 31 | 6 | 25 | 92 | 10 | .276 |

### Milt MAY, Catcher

*Runs Created: 46*

| | G | AB | R | H | 2B | 3B | HR | RBI | SB | Avg |
|---|---|---|---|---|---|---|---|---|---|---|
| First Half | 62 | 213 | 16 | 62 | 10 | 0 | 6 | 23 | 0 | .291 |
| Second Half | 52 | 182 | 13 | 42 | 9 | 0 | 3 | 16 | 0 | .231 |
| Home | 50 | 168 | 12 | 37 | 6 | 0 | 4 | 10 | 0 | .220 |
| Road | 64 | 227 | 17 | 67 | 13 | 0 | 5 | 29 | 0 | .295 |
| vs. RHP | | 328 | | 85 | 14 | 0 | 7 | 33 | | .259 |
| vs. LHP | | 67 | | 19 | 5 | 0 | 2 | 6 | | .284 |
| 1982 | 114 | 395 | 29 | 104 | 19 | 0 | 9 | 39 | 0 | .263 |
| 6.60 years | | 515 | 44 | 137 | 21 | 2 | 11 | 63 | 0 | .266 |

### Tom O'MALLEY, Outfield

*Runs Created: 36*

| | G | AB | R | H | 2B | 3B | HR | RBI | SB | Avg |
|---|---|---|---|---|---|---|---|---|---|---|
| First Half | 52 | 170 | 13 | 43 | 9 | 1 | 1 | 14 | 0 | .253 |
| Second Half | 40 | 121 | 13 | 37 | 3 | 3 | 1 | 13 | 0 | .306 |
| Home | 45 | 138 | 14 | 39 | 5 | 3 | 0 | 12 | 0 | .283 |
| Road | 47 | 153 | 12 | 41 | 7 | 1 | 2 | 15 | 0 | .268 |
| vs. RHP | | 196 | | 52 | 5 | 1 | 2 | 14 | | .265 |
| vs. LHP | | 95 | | 28 | 7 | 3 | 0 | 13 | | .295 |
| 1982 | 92 | 291 | 26 | 80 | 12 | 4 | 2 | 27 | 0 | .275 |
| 0.57 years | | 511 | 46 | 140 | 21 | 7 | 4 | 47 | 0 | .275 |

### Bill LASKEY

| Year | (W–L) | GS | Run | Avg | DP | Avg | SB | Avg |
|---|---|---|---|---|---|---|---|---|
| 1982 | (13-12) | 31 | 134 | 4.32 | 23 | .74 | 32 | 1.03 |

| | G | IP | W | L | Pct | ER | ERA |
|---|---|---|---|---|---|---|---|
| Home | 18 | 110.2 | 5 | 8 | .385 | 38 | 3.09 |
| Road | 14 | 78.2 | 8 | 4 | .667 | 28 | 3.20 |

### Rich GALE

| Year | (W–L) | GS | Run | Avg | DP | Avg | SB | Avg |
|---|---|---|---|---|---|---|---|---|
| 1978 | (14- 8) | 30 | 141 | 4.70 | 35 | 1.17 | 18 | .60 |
| 1979 | ( 9-10) | 31 | 184 | 5.94 | 32 | 1.03 | 14 | .45 |
| 1980 | (13- 9) | 28 | 140 | 5.00 | 22 | .79 | 31 | 1.10 |
| 1981 | ( 6- 6) | 15 | 52 | 3.49 | 13 | .87 | 12 | .80 |
| 1982 | ( 7-14) | 29 | 93 | 3.21 | 21 | .72 | 38 | 1.31 |
| 5 years | | 133 | 610 | 4.59 | 123 | .92 | 113 | .85 |

| | G | IP | W | L | Pct | ER | ERA |
|---|---|---|---|---|---|---|---|
| Home | 17 | 83.1 | 5 | 6 | .455 | 36 | 3.89 |
| Road | 16 | 87 | 2 | 8 | .200 | 44 | 4.55 |

### Atlee HAMMAKER

| Year | (W–L) | GS | Run | Avg | DP | Avg | SB | Avg |
|---|---|---|---|---|---|---|---|---|
| 1981 | ( 1-3) | 6 | 23 | 3.83 | 6 | 1.00 | 5 | .83 |
| 1982 | (12-8) | 27 | 105 | 3.89 | 19 | .70 | 33 | 1.22 |
| 2 years | | 33 | 128 | 3.88 | 25 | .76 | 38 | 1.15 |

| | G | IP | W | L | Pct | ER | ERA |
|---|---|---|---|---|---|---|---|
| Home | 15 | 94.1 | 8 | 3 | .727 | 41 | 3.91 |
| Road | 14 | 80.2 | 4 | 5 | .444 | 39 | 4.35 |

### Renie MARTIN

| Year | (W–L) | GS | Run | Avg | DP | Avg | SB | Avg |
|---|---|---|---|---|---|---|---|---|
| 1980 | (10-10) | 20 | 105 | 5.25 | 18 | .90 | 17 | .85 |
| 1982 | ( 7-10) | 25 | 121 | 4.84 | 18 | .72 | 31 | 1.24 |
| 2 years | | 45 | 226 | 5.02 | 36 | .80 | 48 | 1.07 |

| | G | IP | W | L | Pct | ER | ERA |
|---|---|---|---|---|---|---|---|
| Home | 14 | 67.2 | 3 | 6 | .333 | 33 | 4.39 |
| Road | 16 | 73.2 | 4 | 4 | .500 | 40 | 4.89 |

### 1982 OTHERS

| Pitcher | (W–L) | GS | Run | Avg | DP | Avg | SB | Avg |
|---|---|---|---|---|---|---|---|---|
| Fowlkes | ( 4-2) | 15 | 66 | 4.40 | 18 | 1.20 | 24 | 1.60 |
| Barr | ( 4-3) | 9 | 44 | 4.89 | 8 | .89 | 6 | .67 |
| Breining | (11-6) | 9 | 40 | 4.44 | 5 | .56 | 5 | .56 |
| Holland | ( 7-3) | 7 | 31 | 4.43 | 6 | .86 | 6 | .86 |
| Chris | ( 0-2) | 6 | 26 | 4.33 | 3 | .50 | 3 | .50 |
| Schatzeder | ( 1-6) | 3 | 8 | 2.67 | 4 | 1.33 | 2 | .67 |
| Dempsey | ( 0-0) | 1 | 5 | | 0 | | 5 | |

## SAN FRANCISCO

*Talent Analysis*

The Giants possessed 154 points of approximate value in 1982.

| | AV | % |
|---|---|---|
| Produced by Giants' system: | 56 | 36% |
| Acquired by trade: | 69 | 45% |
| Purchased or signed from free agency: | 29 | 19% |
| | | |
| Young (Up to age 25): | 32 | 22% |
| Prime (Age 26 to 29): | 58 | 38% |
| Past-prime (Age 30 to 33): | 33 | 21% |
| Old (Age 34 or older): | 29 | 19% |

In both respects, the Giants are a "non-distinctive" or "typical" ball club.

The Giants' system produced 149 points of approximate value for the 1982 season, the sixteenth highest total in the majors. Over the last four years, they rank 10th with 592. When I began to monitor that, the Giants ranked as the second-most-productive organization, as there was still a lot of talent around from their productive 1960s farm system. Those players have been disappearing rapidly, and the Giants' total has been shrinking. Since most of that value seems to come from players in the generation of Garry Maddox, Gary Matthews, George Foster, Dave Kingman and Gaylord Perry, that figure presumably will continue to shrink.

## CANDLESTICK PARK

DIMENSIONS: Normal

SURFACE: Cobblestones

VISIBILITY: Bad

FOUL TERRITORY: Large

FAVORS:
Hitter/Pitcher—Pitcher
Power/Line-drive hitter—Line-drive hitter; death for power hitters since remodeling in early '70s
Righthander/Lefthander—Neither

TYPES OF OFFENSE AFFECTED: Home runs down by over 20%; triples up by over 20%; errors, if you want to call them offense, are way, way up

OTHER PARK CHARACTERISTICS: A cold park at sea level—a nightmare for hitters

TYPES OF MARGINAL PLAYERS MOST VALUABLE IN PARK: Wind-resistant, as Whitey Herzog said

PLAYERS ON TEAM HELPED MOST BY PARK: Darrell Evans, Joe Morgan (keeps inning going)

PLAYERS ON TEAM HURT MOST BY PARK: Jack Clark, Johnnie LeMaster

# SAN DIEGO PADRES

The San Diego Padres did not lead the league in the number of innings pitched by left-handed pitchers last year—quite. The leaders were Los Angeles (768), San Diego (706) and Pittsburgh (481). I wrote about Dick Williams three years ago that "Even more than he loves sinkerballers, Williams loves left-handed pitching. He accumulates it wherever he goes. The chart below details Williams' history of building left-handed staffs. The columns are:

A) the teams Williams has managed
B) the number of innings that the teams had by left-handed pitchers the year before Williams took over
C) the number of innings that the team had in Williams' first year
D) the number in his second year
E) the number in his third year

| A<br>TEAM | B<br>Before | C<br>1st | D<br>2nd | E<br>3rd |
|---|---|---|---|---|
| Boston | 169 | 183 | 483 | 307 |
| Oakland | 186 | 434 | 618* | 815 |
| California | 600 | 494 | 546 | 512 |
| Montreal | 362 | 181 | 718 | 685 |
| San Diego | 570* | 707 | | |
| Total | 1887 | 1999 | 2320 | 2384 |
| Average | 377 | 400 | 580 | 596 |

*Adjusted for Strike.

The California line is very misleading, because Williams took over the team in midseason and they had disposed of most of the lefthanders who had thrown the 600 innings the year before. It looks as if he was getting rid of lefthanders in Anaheim, when actually he was hauling them in there, too. This causes the average line to understate the trend, which is all right.

Why does he like lefthanders? Probably because 1) they help to cut off the running game, and 2) they help to keep the double play in order. As he stayed in Montreal longer, he began using fewer lefthanders, but then he had Carter and he had a farm system which was cranking out Sandersons and Gullicksons.

One of the favorite aphorisms of the know-it-all and-don't-got-nothing-to-learn baseball fans is that a pitcher is a pitcher; if he can pitch what difference does it make if he is right-handed or left-handed. It is a fact, though, that good teams have a lot more left-handed pitching on them than bad teams; not just *better* left-handed pitching; *more* of it.

How can we show this in convincing and understandable terms? The two charts give the numbers of games started by left-handed pitchers by 80 teams—the four first-place teams from each division for each of the last ten years, and the four last-place teams.

**First Place Teams**

| Year | 1973 | 74 | 75 | 76 | 77 | 78 | 79 | 80 | 81 | 82 | Totals |
|---|---|---|---|---|---|---|---|---|---|---|---|
| AL East | 80 | 116 | 56 | 34 | 58 | 49 | 61 | 110 | 85 | 82 | 731 |
| AL West | 96 | 99 | 80 | 39 | 70 | 73 | 19 | 70 | 5 | 49 | 600 |
| NL East | 102 | 97 | 95 | 95 | 91 | 87 | 50 | 61 | 7 | 30 | 715 |
| NL West | 97 | 83 | 48 | 45 | 64 | 60 | 31 | 1 | 47 | 13 | 489 |
| Totals | 375 | 395 | 279 | 213 | 283 | 269 | 161 | 242 | 144 | 174 | 2535 |

**Last Place Teams**

| | | | | | | | | | | | |
|---|---|---|---|---|---|---|---|---|---|---|---|
| AL East | 25 | 72 | 33 | 58 | 37 | 72 | 50 | 25 | 5 | 7 | 384 |
| AL West | 53 | 60 | 57 | 58 | 56 | 37 | 33 | 66 | 30 | 83 | 533 |
| NL East | 68 | 22 | 57 | 51 | 62 | 43 | 68 | 18 | 14 | 44 | 447 |
| NL West | 61 | 37 | 34 | 16 | 16 | 42 | 31 | 81 | 42 | 34 | 394 |
| Totals | 207 | 191 | 181 | 183 | 171 | 194 | 182 | 190 | 91 | 168 | 1758 |

For the 10 years as a whole, the championship teams have had 2,535 games started by left-handed pitchers; 44% more than the last-place teams (1.75). The averages are 63 per team for first-place teams and 44 per team for last-place teams. The division winners have had more games started by left-handers than the last-place teams in 9 of the 10 years (1979 was the exception) and in all divisions.

I can suggest two reasons for this, both fairly obvious, neither of them a sufficient explanation of the phenomenon:

1) Left-handed pitchers usually are, as a group, slightly better-than-.500 pitchers.

2) Some teams, such as the Astros, are very vulnerable to left-handed pitching, and thus not to have a LHP on your staff prevents you from taking advantage of an opponent's weakness.

Those things don't seem to add up to create a difference as large as the actual difference is. I can not really explain why first-place teams have 40% more left-handed pitching on them than last-place teams. But they do.

Broderick PERKINS, First Base

*Runs Created: 38*

| | G | AB | R | H | 2B | 3B | HR | RBI | SB | Avg |
|---|---|---|---|---|---|---|---|---|---|---|
| First Half | 63 | 187 | 18 | 52 | 5 | 2 | 2 | 23 | 2 | .278 |
| Second Half | 62 | 160 | 14 | 42 | 5 | 2 | 0 | 11 | 0 | .263 |
| Home | 63 | 176 | 17 | 50 | 6 | 2 | 0 | 13 | 0 | .284 |
| Road | 62 | 171 | 15 | 44 | 4 | 2 | 2 | 21 | 2 | .257 |
| vs. RHP | | 273 | | 77 | 9 | 3 | 2 | 26 | | .282 |
| vs. LHP | | 74 | | 17 | 1 | 1 | 0 | 8 | | .230 |
| 1982 | 125 | 347 | 32 | 94 | 10 | 4 | 2 | 34 | 2 | .271 |
| 2.34 years | | 430 | 42 | 118 | 22 | 3 | 3 | 55 | 3 | .276 |

Tim FLANNERY, Second Base

*Runs Created: 40*

| | G | AB | R | H | 2B | 3B | HR | RBI | SB | Avg |
|---|---|---|---|---|---|---|---|---|---|---|
| First Half | 58 | 168 | 25 | 46 | 7 | 1 | 0 | 11 | 0 | .274 |
| Second Half | 64 | 211 | 15 | 54 | 4 | 6 | 0 | 19 | 1 | .256 |
| Home | 63 | 184 | 20 | 51 | 4 | 3 | 0 | 12 | 0 | .277 |
| Road | 59 | 195 | 20 | 49 | 7 | 4 | 0 | 18 | 1 | .251 |
| vs. RHP | | 316 | | 89 | 9 | 6 | 0 | 26 | | .282 |
| vs. LHP | | 63 | | 11 | 2 | 1 | 0 | 4 | | .175 |
| 1982 | 122 | 379 | 40 | 100 | 11 | 7 | 0 | 30 | 1 | .264 |
| 1.70 years | | 472 | 36 | 116 | 16 | 5 | 0 | 38 | 2 | .245 |

Luis SALAZAR, Third Base

*Runs Created: 50*

| | G | AB | R | H | 2B | 3B | HR | RBI | SB | Avg |
|---|---|---|---|---|---|---|---|---|---|---|
| First Half | 80 | 286 | 35 | 65 | 6 | 5 | 5 | 35 | 19 | .227 |
| Second Half | 65 | 238 | 20 | 62 | 9 | 0 | 3 | 27 | 13 | .261 |
| Home | 79 | 287 | 39 | 76 | 9 | 2 | 6 | 40 | 18 | .265 |
| Road | 66 | 237 | 16 | 51 | 6 | 3 | 2 | 22 | 14 | .215 |
| vs. RHP | | 358 | | 78 | 6 | 2 | 5 | 39 | | .218 |
| vs. LHP | | 166 | | 49 | 9 | 3 | 3 | 23 | | .295 |
| 1982 | 145 | 524 | 55 | 127 | 15 | 5 | 8 | 62 | 32 | .242 |
| 1.84 years | | 594 | 65 | 166 | 21 | 10 | 7 | 68 | 29 | .279 |

Garry TEMPLETON, Shortstop

*Runs Created: 53*

| | G | AB | R | H | 2B | 3B | HR | RBI | SB | Avg |
|---|---|---|---|---|---|---|---|---|---|---|
| First Half | 84 | 343 | 51 | 89 | 17 | 7 | 5 | 50 | 16 | .259 |
| Second Half | 57 | 220 | 25 | 50 | 8 | 1 | 1 | 14 | 11 | .227 |
| Home | 71 | 280 | 34 | 59 | 8 | 2 | 2 | 24 | 13 | .211 |
| Road | 70 | 283 | 42 | 80 | 17 | 6 | 4 | 40 | 14 | .283 |
| vs. RHP | | 380 | | 93 | 18 | 5 | 5 | 45 | | .245 |
| vs. LHP | | 183 | | 46 | 7 | 3 | 1 | 19 | | .251 |
| 1982 | 141 | 563 | 76 | 139 | 25 | 8 | 6 | 64 | 27 | .247 |
| 5.27 years | | 674 | 99 | 199 | 29 | 15 | 6 | 66 | 31 | .296 |

Gene RICHARDS, Left Field

*Runs Created: 59*

| | G | AB | R | H | 2B | 3B | HR | RBI | SB | Avg |
|---|---|---|---|---|---|---|---|---|---|---|
| First Half | 59 | 245 | 33 | 76 | 9 | 3 | 1 | 16 | 19 | .310 |
| Second Half | 73 | 276 | 30 | 73 | 4 | 5 | 2 | 12 | 11 | .264 |
| Home | 64 | 242 | 24 | 64 | 7 | 3 | 0 | 13 | 14 | .264 |
| Road | 68 | 279 | 39 | 85 | 6 | 5 | 3 | 15 | 16 | .306 |
| vs. RHP | | 361 | | 99 | 10 | 7 | 2 | 20 | | .274 |
| vs. LHP | | 160 | | 50 | 3 | 1 | 1 | 8 | | .313 |
| 1982 | 132 | 521 | 63 | 149 | 13 | 8 | 3 | 28 | 30 | .286 |
| 5.21 years | | 611 | 86 | 179 | 22 | 12 | 4 | 44 | 44 | .292 |

Ruppert JONES, Center Field

*Runs Created: 64*

| | G | AB | R | H | 2B | 3B | HR | RBI | SB | Avg |
|---|---|---|---|---|---|---|---|---|---|---|
| First Half | 79 | 285 | 54 | 89 | 15 | 1 | 11 | 50 | 14 | .312 |
| Second Half | 37 | 139 | 15 | 31 | 5 | 1 | 1 | 11 | 4 | .223 |
| Home | 57 | 201 | 37 | 66 | 8 | 1 | 6 | 32 | 10 | .328 |
| Road | 59 | 223 | 32 | 54 | 12 | 1 | 6 | 29 | 8 | .242 |
| vs. RHP | | 296 | | 87 | 16 | 0 | 10 | 47 | | .294 |
| vs. LHP | | 128 | | 33 | 4 | 2 | 2 | 14 | | .258 |
| 1982 | 116 | 424 | 69 | 120 | 20 | 2 | 12 | 61 | 18 | .283 |
| 4.83 years | | 599 | 85 | 153 | 30 | 6 | 16 | 72 | 23 | .255 |

Sixto LEZCANO, Right Field

*Runs Created: 87*

| | G | AB | R | H | 2B | 3B | HR | RBI | SB | Avg |
|---|---|---|---|---|---|---|---|---|---|---|
| First Half | 83 | 290 | 46 | 79 | 16 | 4 | 7 | 49 | 2 | .272 |
| Second Half | 55 | 180 | 27 | 57 | 10 | 2 | 9 | 35 | 0 | .317 |
| Home | 61 | 224 | 31 | 60 | 11 | 3 | 5 | 34 | 0 | .268 |
| Road | 67 | 246 | 42 | 76 | 15 | 3 | 11 | 50 | 2 | .309 |
| vs. RHP | | 332 | | 92 | 17 | 4 | 10 | 55 | | .277 |
| vs. LHP | | 138 | | 44 | 9 | 2 | 6 | 29 | | .319 |
| 1982 | 138 | 470 | 73 | 136 | 26 | 6 | 16 | 84 | 2 | .289 |
| 6.14 years | | 555 | 75 | 153 | 27 | 5 | 20 | 79 | 6 | .277 |

Terry KENNEDY, Catcher

*Runs Created: 89*

| | G | AB | R | H | 2B | 3B | HR | RBI | SB | Avg |
|---|---|---|---|---|---|---|---|---|---|---|
| First Half | 81 | 300 | 42 | 84 | 26 | 1 | 10 | 57 | 1 | .280 |
| Second Half | 72 | 262 | 33 | 82 | 16 | 0 | 11 | 40 | 0 | .313 |
| Home | 78 | 287 | 35 | 83 | 19 | 1 | 10 | 51 | 0 | .289 |
| Road | 75 | 275 | 40 | 83 | 23 | 0 | 11 | 46 | 1 | .302 |
| vs. RHP | | 404 | | 116 | 28 | 1 | 17 | 71 | | .287 |
| vs. LHP | | 158 | | 50 | 14 | 0 | 4 | 26 | | .316 |
| 1982 | 153 | 562 | 75 | 166 | 42 | 1 | 21 | 97 | 1 | .295 |
| 2.35 years | | 566 | 62 | 162 | 36 | 2 | 12 | 81 | 0 | .286 |

Tim LOLLAR

| Year | (W–L) | GS | Run | Avg | DP | Avg | SB | Avg |
|---|---|---|---|---|---|---|---|---|
| 1980 | ( 1- 0) | 1 | 2 | | 2 | | 0 | |
| 1981 | ( 2- 8) | 11 | 42 | 3.82 | 10 | .91 | 5 | .45 |
| 1982 | (16- 9) | 34 | 143 | 4.21 | 21 | .62 | 18 | .53 |
| 3 years | | 46 | 187 | 4.07 | 33 | .72 | 23 | .50 |

| | G | IP | W | L | Pct | ER | ERA |
|---|---|---|---|---|---|---|---|
| Home | 18 | 124.1 | 8 | 6 | .571 | 41 | 2.97 |
| Road | 16 | 108.1 | 8 | 3 | .727 | 40 | 3.32 |

John MONTEFUSCO

| Year | (W–L) | GS | Run | Avg | DP | Avg | SB | Avg |
|---|---|---|---|---|---|---|---|---|
| 1976 | (16-14) | 36 | 115 | 3.19 | 27 | .75 | 33 | .92 |
| 1977 | ( 7-12) | 25 | 90 | 3.60 | 12 | .48 | 36 | 1.44 |
| 1978 | (11- 9) | 36 | 153 | 4.25 | 28 | .78 | 45 | 1.25 |
| 1979 | ( 3- 8) | 22 | 72 | 3.27 | 24 | 1.09 | 26 | 1.18 |
| 1980 | ( 4- 8) | 17 | 63 | 3.71 | 15 | .88 | 24 | 1.41 |
| 1981 | ( 2- 3) | 9 | 39 | 4.33 | 11 | 1.22 | 12 | 1.33 |
| 1982 | (10-11) | 32 | 126 | 3.94 | 29 | .91 | 38 | 1.19 |
| 7 years | | 177 | 658 | 3.72 | 146 | .82 | 214 | 1.21 |

| | G | IP | W | L | Pct | ER | ERA |
|---|---|---|---|---|---|---|---|
| Home | 19 | 109.2 | 6 | 6 | .500 | 49 | 4.02 |
| Road | 13 | 74.2 | 4 | 5 | .444 | 33 | 3.98 |

Juan EICHELBERGER

| Year | (W–L) | GS | Run | Avg | DP | Avg | SB | Avg |
|---|---|---|---|---|---|---|---|---|
| 1979 | (0- 0) | 3 | 9 | 3.00 | 5 | 1.67 | 4 | 1.33 |
| 1980 | (1- 1) | 13 | 66 | 5.08 | 15 | 1.15 | 15 | 1.15 |
| 1981 | (8- 8) | 24 | 91 | 3.79 | 21 | .88 | 13 | .54 |
| 1982 | (7-14) | 24 | 96 | 4.00 | 16 | .67 | 24 | 1.00 |
| 4 years | | 64 | 262 | 4.09 | 57 | .89 | 56 | .88 |

| | G | IP | W | L | Pct | ER | ERA |
|---|---|---|---|---|---|---|---|
| Home | 13 | 73.2 | 4 | 4 | .500 | 20 | 2.44 |
| Road | 18 | 104 | 3 | 10 | .231 | 63 | 5.45 |

Chris WELSH

| Year | (W–L) | GS | Run | Avg | DP | Avg | SB | Avg |
|---|---|---|---|---|---|---|---|---|
| 1981 | (6-7) | 19 | 73 | 3.84 | 25 | 1.32 | 13 | .68 |
| 1982 | (8-8) | 20 | 84 | 4.20 | 20 | 1.00 | 8 | .40 |
| 2 years | | 39 | 157 | 4.03 | 45 | 1.15 | 21 | .54 |

| | G | IP | W | L | Pct | ER | ERA |
|---|---|---|---|---|---|---|---|
| Home | 12 | 64.2 | 4 | 4 | .500 | 33 | 4.59 |
| Road | 16 | 74.2 | 4 | 4 | .500 | 43 | 5.18 |

1982 OTHERS

| Pitcher | (W–L) | GS | Run | Avg | DP | Avg | SB | Avg |
|---|---|---|---|---|---|---|---|---|
| Curtis | ( 8-6) | 18 | 86 | 4.78 | 16 | .89 | 16 | .89 |
| Show | (10-6) | 14 | 56 | 4.00 | 13 | .93 | 17 | 1.21 |
| Dravecky | ( 5-3) | 10 | 36 | 3.60 | 12 | 1.20 | 9 | .90 |
| Hawkins | ( 2-5) | 10 | 48 | 4.80 | 9 | .90 | 7 | .50 |

## SAN DIEGO

*Talent Analysis*

The Padres possessed 149 points of approximate value in 1982.

| | AV | % |
|---|---|---|
| Produced by Padres' system: | 51 | 34% |
| Acquired by trade: | 88 | 59% |
| Purchased or signed from free agency: | 10 | 7% |

The Padres are basically a trade-build team.

| | | |
|---|---|---|
| Young (Up to age 25): | 23 | 16% |
| Prime (Age 26 to 29): | 115 | 77% |
| Past-prime (Age 30 to 33): | 6 | 4% |
| Old (Age 34 or older): | 5 | 3% |

The Padres have a greater concentration of talent in the prime ages 25-29 than any other major league team.

San Diego ranked 20th in approximate value produced in 1982, one notch above their placement in talent produced over the four-year period 1979 to 1982.

## JACK MURPHY STADIUM

DIMENSIONS: Normal; long to center

SURFACE: Grass

VISIBILITY: It must be poor. The strikeout-to-walk ratio in Padres' road games last year was 1.50-1; in San Diego it was 1.76-1.

FOUL TERRITORY: Normal

FAVORS:
Hitter/Pitcher—Pitcher
Power/Line-drive hitter—Unsure
Righthander/Lefthander—Neither

TYPES OF OFFENSE AFFECTED: The fences were moved and lowered here a year ago, and it's a little early to make a very good assessment of that issue. On balance, however, the move seems to have had very little effect on run production in the park, which in fact was even lower last year than it has sometimes been in the past. But as best I can tell, the park is now virtually neutral for home runs, but lowers batting averages by about seven points, eliminates 20% of doubles and triples, and (because of the visibility) reduces walks somewhat.

PLAYERS ON TEAM HELPED OR HURT MOST BY PARK: Will not speculate on what types of players might most helped or hurt by the park in its new configuration.

OTHER COMMENTS: This park is at the lowest altitude of any major league park. The ball does not seem to travel well at sea level.

# HOUSTON ASTROS

The Astrodome, suggests Craig Wright, is a baseball time machine, jerking the game back to the days before Babe Ruth, before the home run came and forced all who did not choose to lose to adopt it. It seems an odd phrase for what we think of as an ultramodern structure, with the mythic private apartments of the old judge sealed up behind a concession stand somewhere. One hopes that we will always think of it as ultramodern. If more stadiums like it are built, the state of the art in domed construction will soon move past this; it can retain the ultramodern image only if it represents the furthest point along a road not taken, like the electric car.

But the Astrodome is the one park in baseball in which you simply cannot play long-ball successfully, and this takes the game back to the way it was played long, long ago. The bunt, the hit and run, the squeeze play...in the absence of more powerful weapons, these subtle plays attain a huge significance. In watching the 1980 NL championship games, I understood for the first time what the old-timers who felt that Babe Ruth had ruined the game were talking about. One cannot oppose a home-run hitting offense with a run-at-a-time offense; you'll get beat. Babe Ruth was a cyclone who swept up the precious strategies of the generations before him and scattered them in ruins.

As the mountains make Wyoming folk rugged and the cities make city folk guarded or defensive, this environment, too, shapes the character of its inhabitants. It has always been my feeling that the cliquishness of the Boston Red Sox, their surliness and impatience with the press (granted Ralph Houk has done wonders to control this, but he is the first Sox manager in decades to make any progress on the front), that this was the Curse of Fenway, that it owed its origins to a long-dead architect. An absurd theory? So it sounds, but hear me out. Fenway makes ballplayers look like better hitters than they are. That inflates egos. Inflated egos cause resentment, in particular among those not favored by the park; the team divides into clusters of the favored and the ill-favored.

The Astrodome is a negative image of Fenway, an exactly opposite park in almost every way one can imagine. Beautiful, ugly. Quaint, modern. Vibrant, sterile. Cozy, spacious. Hitter's heaven, hitter's nightmare. And for what were the Astro players of the fine teams of 1978 to 1981 known? Their openness with the press, their closeness and almost family-like atmosphere. Odd, isn't it? As the park knocks 20 points off every player's average, it humbles hitters and it controls egos.

But even more than that, it is my feeling that the mere fact that in Fenway a hitter can create runs *by his own actions* tends to cause Fenway teams to pull apart over time. A key fact about the Astrodome is that it takes three players to make a run. In order to do your job in this park, you have got to see yourself as a part of a plan, a cog in a machine.

My feeling is that, over time, that changes the way that the Astro players think of themselves in relation to their team—but only over time. And thus, I believe, if the Astros are to win it is extremely important for them to keep a team together, to maintain a stable personnel. Tal Smith did that. He took the players who were with the team when he came here in 1975. And then slowly, ever so slowly, he wove new players into the pattern. Art Howe, the first baseman on that team . . . when did he come here? Enos Cabell, Terry Puhl, Cedeno Cruz, Joe Niekro, Ken Forsch, Sambito, J.R. Richard . . . they had all spent years together.

When the new management took over, they felt an immediate need to put their own stamp on the ball club. They weren't bad judges of talent. I don't see any specific trades here that I would regard as being especially bad. But there simply were far too many of them. Sutton . . . in and out; Whoosh. Knight for Cedeno, Thon in at short, Andujar gone, let's try Tony Scott, let's get Phil Garner from Pittsburgh to play second. These men aren't bad ballplayers. But they cannot yet have learned how to add three or four little acts together to make a two-run rally. They don't know what one another can do all that thoroughly. And that is how you have to play ball in the Astrodome.

In Fenway, again, the rule is just the opposite. In Fenway, the longer the players stay together, the more stale and lifeless they become. Fresh talent is constantly needed. After they have a good year or two, they forget all about playing together. Take a look at the teams that have been successful in Fenway Park. The 1975 Red Sox, the last champion, were led by two rookies (Lynn and Rice), and featured prominently a whole list of new and almost-new faces: Rick Burleson, Dwight Evans, Denny Doyle, Cecil Cooper, Rick Wise. The 1975 Red Sox finished 2nd in the league in sacrifice hits, 1st in sac flies.

But the longer this collection of players stayed together, the worse they got. Perhaps it is only a coincidence (I've never been much of an advocate of the bunt), or perhaps it was only Don Zimmer, but they dropped to 10th in the league in sacrifice hits in 1976 and 12th in '77.

Now look at the last Red Sox champion before that, the 1967 team. Again: a lot of new faces on the team (in fact, it was the youngest lineup ever to win the American League flag. Six regulars were 24 or younger.) Again: they finished second in the league in sac hits (they had 85; California had 88) and second in sac flies. Again: the next year they stopped doing these things (fourth in sac hits, sixth in sac flies). Again: the longer the team stayed together, the worse they played.

Now look back to the last previous champion, the 1946 Red Sox. They hold a unique record: Of their eight starters, seven were not with the team the year before. Again: the lineup had some magnificent individual stars. And again, the longer those players stayed together, the worse they played. (Don't have sacrifice totals for them. Sorry.)

As ugly as it seems to many of you, as artificial as it is, the Astrodome should be treasured for the baseball it creates. It is just as unique and just as extreme as Fenway—and in a lot of ways, its baseball is more exciting.

Was there ever a series more magnificent than the 1980 NL playoffs? I feel about the Astrodome much the way I feel about the turf that they invented for it. No, I don't like what it does to the ballparks. Yes, I know about the smell of the grass in Wrigley and Yankee Stadium. Yes, the dryness of Royals Stadium bothers me. But what it does to the *Game*—that, I like. I like it a lot. The speed, the constant danger of the speed, the reflexes, the strategies, the stolen-base attempts—oh, man, I like those a lot. The stadiums that they tore down in the 1960s may be missed forever and I'm sorry I didn't get to see more of them—but I sure don't miss the baseball that they tore down with them. Babe Ruth's game reached its natural culmination in the 1960s, and it had to be the most God-awful boring brand of baseball ever conceived of, a whole decade full of .220-hitting shortstops who negotiated their contracts on whether they'd hit 10 or 13 home runs. If I never see another Dave Nicholson, I think I can live with it. I blame the whole decade on Spike Eckert. Baseball was so boring that people who should have been carrying banners saying, "Hit It Here, Willie" and arguing about who was going to be the NL's Rookie of the Year got all wrapped up in politics instead, and started carrying peace signs and worrying about evil and social injustice and stuff. Attendance suffered. And the nation with it.

Art HOWE, First Base

*Runs Created: 38*

| | G | AB | R | H | 2B | 3B | HR | RBI | SB | Avg |
|---|---|---|---|---|---|---|---|---|---|---|
| First Half | 54 | 181 | 14 | 40 | 4 | 0 | 2 | 19 | 2 | .221 |
| Second Half | 56 | 184 | 15 | 47 | 11 | 1 | 3 | 19 | 0 | .255 |
| Home | | 168 | | 41 | | | 4 | 22 | | .244 |
| Road | | 197 | | 46 | | | 1 | 16 | | .234 |
| vs. RHP | | 266 | | 63 | | | 3 | 26 | | .237 |
| vs. LHP | | 99 | | 24 | | | 2 | 12 | | .242 |
| 1982 | 110 | 365 | 29 | 87 | 15 | 1 | 5 | 38 | 2 | .238 |
| 4.93 years | | 504 | 51 | 132 | 27 | 5 | 8 | 57 | 2 | .263 |

Phil GARNER, Second Base

*Runs Created: 78*

| | G | AB | R | H | 2B | 3B | HR | RBI | SB | Avg |
|---|---|---|---|---|---|---|---|---|---|---|
| First Half | 85 | 328 | 35 | 86 | 20 | 6 | 7 | 44 | 15 | .262 |
| Second Half | 70 | 260 | 30 | 75 | 13 | 2 | 6 | 39 | 9 | .288 |
| Home | | 290 | | 77 | | | 6 | 40 | | .266 |
| Road | | 298 | | 84 | | | 7 | 43 | | .282 |
| vs. RHP | | 409 | | 121 | | | 11 | 64 | | .296 |
| vs. LHP | | 179 | | 40 | | | 2 | 19 | | .223 |
| 1982 | 155 | 588 | 65 | 161 | 33 | 8 | 13 | 83 | 24 | .274 |
| 7.46 years | | 559 | 68 | 147 | 28 | 8 | 10 | 67 | 24 | .263 |

Ray KNIGHT, Third Base

*Runs Created: 83*

| | G | AB | R | H | 2B | 3B | HR | RBI | SB | Avg |
|---|---|---|---|---|---|---|---|---|---|---|
| First Half | 85 | 325 | 47 | 103 | 20 | 3 | 4 | 42 | 1 | .317 |
| Second Half | 73 | 284 | 25 | 76 | 16 | 3 | 2 | 28 | 1 | .268 |
| Home | | 301 | | 81 | | | 0 | 34 | | .269 |
| Road | | 308 | | 98 | | | 6 | 36 | | .318 |
| vs. RHP | | 426 | | 129 | | | 4 | 49 | | .303 |
| vs. LHP | | 183 | | 50 | | | 2 | 21 | | .273 |
| 1982 | 158 | 609 | 72 | 179 | 36 | 6 | 6 | 70 | 2 | .294 |
| 4.65 years | | 502 | 57 | 141 | 31 | 4 | 8 | 60 | 2 | .281 |

Dickie THON, Shortstop

*Runs Created: 68*

| | G | AB | R | H | 2B | 3B | HR | RBI | SB | Avg |
|---|---|---|---|---|---|---|---|---|---|---|
| First Half | 64 | 196 | 25 | 48 | 10 | 3 | 1 | 16 | 13 | .245 |
| Second Half | 72 | 300 | 48 | 89 | 21 | 7 | 2 | 20 | 24 | .297 |
| Home | | 254 | | 80 | | | 1 | 18 | | .315 |
| Road | | 242 | | 57 | | | 2 | 18 | | .236 |
| vs. RHP | | 331 | | 93 | | | 3 | 27 | | .281 |
| vs. LHP | | 165 | | 44 | | | 0 | 9 | | .267 |
| 1982 | 136 | 496 | 73 | 137 | 31 | 10 | 3 | 36 | 37 | .276 |
| 1.85 years | | 494 | 67 | 135 | 28 | 7 | 2 | 34 | 27 | .274 |

Jose CRUZ, Left Field

*Runs Created: 74*

| | G | AB | R | H | 2B | 3B | HR | RBI | SB | Avg |
|---|---|---|---|---|---|---|---|---|---|---|
| First Half | 83 | 310 | 35 | 83 | 16 | 2 | 6 | 47 | 11 | .268 |
| Second Half | 72 | 260 | 27 | 74 | 11 | 0 | 3 | 21 | 10 | .285 |
| Home | | 283 | | 78 | | | 3 | 33 | | .276 |
| Road | | 287 | | 79 | | | 6 | 35 | | .275 |
| vs. RHP | | 384 | | 104 | | | 5 | 47 | | .271 |
| vs. LHP | | 186 | | 53 | | | 4 | 21 | | .285 |
| 1982 | 155 | 570 | 62 | 157 | 27 | 2 | 9 | 68 | 21 | .275 |
| 9.80 years | | 536 | 70 | 151 | 27 | 6 | 11 | 71 | 25 | .281 |

Tony SCOTT, Center Field

*Runs Created: 37*

| | G | AB | R | H | 2B | 3B | HR | RBI | SB | Avg |
|---|---|---|---|---|---|---|---|---|---|---|
| First Half | 78 | 288 | 31 | 71 | 9 | 3 | 0 | 12 | 11 | .247 |
| Second Half | 54 | 172 | 12 | 39 | 7 | 0 | 1 | 17 | 7 | .227 |
| Home | | 209 | | 49 | | | 0 | 14 | | .234 |
| Road | | 251 | | 61 | | | 1 | 15 | | .243 |
| vs. RHP | | 280 | | 60 | | | 0 | 15 | | .214 |
| vs. LHP | | 180 | | 50 | | | 1 | 14 | | .278 |
| 1982 | 132 | 460 | 43 | 110 | 16 | 3 | 1 | 29 | 18 | .239 |
| 5.19 years | | 487 | 58 | 122 | 29 | 5 | 3 | 45 | 23 | .252 |

Terry PUHL, Right Field

*Runs Created: 63*

| | G | AB | R | H | 2B | 3B | HR | RBI | SB | Avg |
|---|---|---|---|---|---|---|---|---|---|---|
| First Half | 80 | 282 | 41 | 69 | 7 | 4 | 7 | 35 | 10 | .245 |
| Second Half | 65 | 225 | 23 | 64 | 10 | 5 | 1 | 15 | 7 | .284 |
| Home | | 271 | | 75 | | | 5 | 28 | | .277 |
| Road | | 236 | | 58 | | | 3 | 22 | | .246 |
| vs. RHP | | 372 | | 103 | | | 6 | 40 | | .277 |
| vs. LHP | | 135 | | 30 | | | 2 | 10 | | .222 |
| 1982 | 145 | 507 | 64 | 133 | 17 | 9 | 8 | 50 | 17 | .262 |
| 4.62 years | | 607 | 86 | 169 | 26 | 7 | 8 | 49 | 30 | .279 |

Alan ASHBY, Catcher

*Runs Created: 44*

| | G | AB | R | H | 2B | 3B | HR | RBI | SB | Avg |
|---|---|---|---|---|---|---|---|---|---|---|
| First Half | 62 | 213 | 24 | 54 | 11 | 2 | 5 | 34 | 2 | .254 |
| Second Half | 38 | 126 | 16 | 33 | 3 | 0 | 7 | 15 | 0 | .262 |
| Home | | 163 | | 37 | | | 5 | 24 | | .227 |
| Road | | 176 | | 50 | | | 7 | 25 | | .284 |
| vs. RHP | | 255 | | 69 | | | 9 | 37 | | .271 |
| vs. LHP | | 84 | | 18 | | | 3 | 12 | | .214 |
| 1982 | 100 | 339 | 40 | 87 | 14 | 2 | 12 | 49 | 2 | .257 |
| 5.01 years | | 495 | 46 | 117 | 22 | 2 | 8 | 58 | 1 | .237 |

Nolan RYAN

| Year | (W–L) | GS | Run | Avg | DP | Avg | SB | Avg |
|---|---|---|---|---|---|---|---|---|
| 1976 | (17-18) | 39 | 107 | 2.74 | 24 | .62 | 51 | 1.31 |
| 1977 | (19-16) | 37 | 147 | 3.97 | 26 | .70 | 42 | 1.14 |
| 1978 | (10-13) | 31 | 125 | 4.03 | 28 | .90 | 63 | 2.03 |
| 1979 | (16-14) | 34 | 167 | 4.91 | 35 | 1.03 | 33 | .97 |
| 1980 | (11-10) | 35 | 140 | 4.00 | 30 | .86 | 30 | .86 |
| 1981 | (11- 5) | 21 | 75 | 3.57 | 15 | .71 | 19 | .90 |
| 1982 | (16-12) | 35 | 134 | 3.83 | 26 | .74 | 41 | 1.17 |
| 7 years | | 232 | 895 | 3.86 | 184 | .79 | 279 | 1.20 |

| | G | IP | W | L | Pct | ER | ERA |
|---|---|---|---|---|---|---|---|
| Home | 15 | 111.1 | 5 | 6 | .455 | 42 | 3.40 |
| Road | 20 | 139 | 11 | 6 | .647 | 46 | 2.98 |

Joe NIEKRO

| Year | (W–L) | GS | Run | Avg | DP | Avg | SB | Avg |
|---|---|---|---|---|---|---|---|---|
| 1977 | (13- 8) | 14 | 63 | 4.50 | 16 | 1.14 | 15 | 1.07 |
| 1978 | (14-14) | 29 | 106 | 3.66 | 18 | .62 | 35 | 1.21 |
| 1979 | (21-11) | 38 | 147 | 3.87 | 42 | 1.11 | 38 | 1.00 |
| 1980 | (20-12) | 36 | 174 | 4.83 | 36 | 1.00 | 36 | 1.00 |
| 1981 | ( 9- 9) | 24 | 93 | 3.88 | 16 | .67 | 26 | 1.08 |
| 1982 | (17-12) | 35 | 119 | 3.40 | 34 | .97 | 37 | 1.06 |
| 6 years | | 176 | 702 | 3.99 | 162 | .92 | 187 | 1.06 |

| | G | IP | W | L | Pct | ER | ERA |
|---|---|---|---|---|---|---|---|
| Home | 18 | 143 | 10 | 5 | .667 | 38 | 2.39 |
| Road | 17 | 127 | 7 | 7 | .500 | 36 | 2.55 |

Bob KNEPPER

| Year | (W–L) | GS | Run | Avg | DP | Avg | SB | Avg |
|---|---|---|---|---|---|---|---|---|
| 1977 | (11- 9) | 27 | 122 | 4.52 | 29 | 1.07 | 27 | 1.00 |
| 1978 | (17-11) | 35 | 125 | 3.57 | 27 | .79 | 26 | .74 |
| 1979 | ( 9-12) | 34 | 162 | 4.76 | 31 | .91 | 26 | .76 |
| 1980 | ( 9-16) | 33 | 123 | 3.73 | 20 | .61 | 41 | 1.24 |
| 1981 | ( 9- 5) | 22 | 63 | 2.86 | 22 | 1.00 | 17 | .77 |
| 1982 | ( 5-15) | 29 | 93 | 3.21 | 30 | 1.03 | 40 | 1.38 |
| 6 years | | 180 | 488 | 3.82 | 159 | .88 | 177 | .98 |

| | G | IP | W | L | Pct | ER | ERA |
|---|---|---|---|---|---|---|---|
| Home | 19 | 94.2 | 3 | 5 | .375 | 46 | 4.37 |
| Road | 14 | 85.1 | 2 | 10 | .167 | 43 | 4.54 |

Vern RUHLE

| Year | (W–L) | GS | Run | Avg | DP | Avg | SB | Avg |
|---|---|---|---|---|---|---|---|---|
| 1976 | ( 9-12) | 32 | 134 | 4.19 | 27 | .84 | 30 | .94 |
| 1977 | ( 3- 5) | 10 | 31 | 3.10 | 11 | 1.10 | 5 | .50 |
| 1978 | ( 3- 3) | 10 | 37 | 3.70 | 7 | .70 | 9 | .90 |
| 1979 | ( 2- 6) | 10 | 34 | 3.40 | 8 | .80 | 5 | .50 |
| 1980 | (12- 4) | 22 | 79 | 3.59 | 24 | 1.09 | 14 | .64 |
| 1981 | ( 4- 6) | 15 | 54 | 3.60 | 15 | 1.00 | 8 | .53 |
| 1982 | ( 9-13) | 21 | 63 | 3.00 | 22 | 1.05 | 14 | .67 |
| 7 years | | 120 | 452 | 3.60 | 114 | .95 | 85 | .71 |

| | G | IP | W | L | Pct | ER | ERA |
|---|---|---|---|---|---|---|---|
| Home | 17 | 75.2 | 5 | 7 | .417 | 30 | 3.57 |
| Road | 14 | 73.1 | 4 | 6 | .400 | 35 | 4.30 |

1982 OTHERS

| Pitcher | (W–L) | GS | Run | Avg | DP | Avg | SB | Avg |
|---|---|---|---|---|---|---|---|---|
| LaCoss | (6-6) | 8 | 32 | 4.00 | 13 | 1.63 | 7 | .88 |
| DiPino | (2-2) | 6 | 23 | 3.83 | 6 | 1.00 | 5 | .83 |
| D. Smith | (5-4) | 1 | 7 | | 1 | | 3 | |

## HOUSTON ASTROS

*Talent Analysis*

The Astros in 1982 possessed 140 points of approximate value.

| | AV | % |
|---|---|---|
| Produced by Astros' system: | 22 | 16% |
| Acquired by trade: | 75 | 53% |
| Purchased or signed from free agency: | 43 | 31% |

The Astros now are a trade-built team. In their championship season, 1980, they were a system-built team (S-44%, T-29%, $-27%).

| | | |
|---|---|---|
| Young (Up to age 25): | 14 | 10% |
| Prime (Age 26 to 29): | 41 | 29% |
| Past-prime (Age 30 to 33): | 36 | 26% |
| Old (Age 34 or older): | 49 | 35% |

The Astros are by far the oldest team in the division.

The Astros' system ranked twenty-second in 1982 talent-produced (116) points and ranks nineteenth over the four-year period 1979 to 1982.

## ASTRODOME

DIMENSIONS: A little long

SURFACE: Turf, fairly fast

VISIBILITY: Not good, some problem with glare

FOUL TERRITORY: —

FAVORS:
Hitter/Pitcher—The best pitcher's park in baseball
Power/Line-drive hitter—Line-drive hitter
Righthander/Lefthander—Neither

TYPES OF OFFENSE AFFECTED: Home runs cut in half. Batting average reduced 15 to 20 points. Doubles down 30% or more. Only triples are increased (20%) due to fast turf and distance of fences.

OTHER PARK CHARACTERISTICS: Ball does not carry.

TYPES OF MARGINAL PLAYERS MOST VALUABLE IN PARK: Good bunters more valuable here than in any other park. Speed and aggressive base running valuable.

PLAYERS ON TEAM HELPED MOST BY PARK: Joe Niekro, LaCoss

PLAYERS ON TEAM HURT MOST BY PARK: Alan Ashby, all hitters

# CINCINNATI REDS

A few notes on the end of the era (and don't kid yourself; it is over).

● Although I'm sure the Reds would prefer to think of themselves as a young team, they had, in fact, the most normal or average age spectrum of any major league team:

| | Reds | Majors as Whole |
|---|---|---|
| Young Talent (Up to age 24) | 16% | 16% |
| Prime Talent (Age 25–29) | 51% | 46% |
| Past-Prime (Age 30–33) | 17% | 24% |
| Old Talent (34 and over) | 16% | 14% |

Speaking of talent breakdowns . . . a year ago I said that 0% of the Reds' talent was purchased or signed from free agency. A Cincinnati sportswriter, in a nice way, pointed to this as an error because of Larry Biittner, but actually that wasn't one of them. Biittner in 1981 batted only 61 times, hit .213 with no homers and 8 RBI, and thus his approximate value was 0.

I don't know how long we want to spend talking about Larry Biittner, but the release of Biittner after he hit .310 strikes me in the same class as the Rangers' mutterings about releasing Jon Matlack, who had a 3.53 ERA on a staff with a 4.28 ERA, or for that matter as Chief Bender's famous radio interview in which he blamed the whole season on three people, none of whom worked in the front office. The disappointment and frustration that the Reds feel is indiscriminate, and attaches itself to everybody on the team. Their judgment is colored, and they begin making talent moves that are objectively irrational. You've got to remind yourself to look at what the player has actually done, and not what you expected him to do.

● The Reds in 1982 had seven players in double figures in stolen bases, tying St. Louis for the league high in that regard (no one else had more than five). But while St. Louis led the league with 200 stolen bases, the Reds were 10th in team stolen bases and had only three more than the league low. The team leader, Eddie Milner, had just 18.

● I was getting on the Astros a little for having too high a turnover rate, but they were reasonable about it. The Reds turned over the team entirely, with just a couple of exceptions, between 1981 and '82. It's tough to blast a team apart and put together an accumulation of players who have no group history without introducing a collective insecurity into the dugout. Herzog's Cardinals, sure, but Herzog did it in two stages, not one, he didn't have a catcher at third base, and he didn't have three unproven players in the lineup. In retrospect, the decline of the Reds seems inevitable. But then, most everything does.

● I think I had a comment somewhere last spring to the effect that the thing to watch for was whether the Reds would still be able to beat lefthanders. I felt that with the departures of Foster, Knight and Collins, the Reds in order to contend would have to establish early that they could still beat a lefthander.

As it turned out, of course, it wasn't a key to the season, as the Reds were too bad to be worrying about stuff like that. They'd have been happy to beat anybody. It was, however, a problem for them. Records against righthanders and lefthanders for the last two seasons:

| | Against RHP | | Against LHP | |
|---|---|---|---|---|
| 1981 | 48–35 | .578 | 18– 7 | .720 |
| 1982 | 47–71 | .398 | 14–30 | .318 |

They declined by .180 against righthanders, by .402 against southpaws, and also were seeing a few more lefthanders.

● The Reds' decline from a .611 won-lost percentage in 1981 to a .377 mark in 1982 is unquestionably a collapse of historic magnitude. A chart of the century's largest one-season declines in won-lost percentage is given below

| Team | From | | | To | | | Down |
|---|---|---|---|---|---|---|---|
| 1. Philadelphia A's | 1914 | 99–53 | .651 | 1915 | 43–109 | .283 | .368 |
| 2. Boston Braves | 1934 | 78–73 | .517 | 1935 | 38–115 | .248 | .269 |
| 3. Cincinnati Reds | 1981 | 66–42 | .611 | 1982 | 61–101 | .377 | .234 |
| 4. Cleveland Indians | 1913 | 86–66 | .566 | 1914 | 51–102 | .333 | .234 |
| 5. Chicago White Sox | 1920 | 96–58 | .623 | 1921 | 52– 92 | .403 | .220 |
| 6. Washington Senators | 1933 | 99–53 | .651 | 1934 | 66– 86 | .434 | .217 |

7. 1905–06 Red Sox, –195; 8. 1917–18 White Sox, –188; 9. 1949–1950 Athletics and 1931–32 Cardinals, –188; 11. 1901–02 Phillies, –184; 12. 1944–45 Reds, –182; 13. 1942–43 Giants, –180; 14. 1919–20 Tigers, –175; 15. 1911–12 Highlanders, –171; 16. 1921–22 Braves, –170; 17. 1908–09 Senators, –169; 18. 1981–82 Oakland, –167; 19. 1942–43 Red Sox, –165; 20. 1912–13 Red Sox, –164; 21. 1901–02 Tigers, 1918–19 Senators, –163; and 1907–08 Athletics, –163; 24. 1909–10 Pirates, –162; 25. 1923–24 Dodgers, –153; 26. 1919–20 Reds, –150; 27. 1903–04 Dodgers, 1976–77 A's, 1951–52 Tigers, –149.

At least six of the collapses, like the Reds' in '82, have primarily economic origins, origins—and, I suspect, outcomes—very similar to the current Reds. The grandest collapse ever (it is all but incomprehensible that this record could ever be challenged) was by the Philadelphia Athletics in 1915. When the Federal League came into existence in 1914, bidding for players drove salaries skyrocketing upward. Connie Mack could not or would not meet the demands of his players and sold them off to other American League teams; he would rather do that, he said, than lose them to the rival league. The A's were a great team, and Mack thought, or said that he thought, that he had retained enough talent to stay in contention. He did keep six or seven key members of the 1914 championship team. Among those he brought in to fill the holes was an aging Nap Lajoie. Still, in view of the team's record of 79 wins and 226 losses over the next two seasons, it seems safe to say that he miscalculated.

So that situation, really, couldn't be much more closely parallel to the Reds' current mess—plug in different names and different numbers and update the details and it's exactly the same story. It was seven years before the A's got out of last place.

The same economic monsoon swamped a couple of other boats. Cy Falkenberg's jump to the new league after a 23–10 season in 1913 was a contributing factor in

Cleveland's somewhat mystifying collapse of 1914. After calm was restored, the Black Sox scandal in 1920 dumped the White Sox, who had purchased some of Mack's stars, into the icy waters of the deep second division. It is a fair tribute to Dick Wagner, I think, to point out that his team went down the tubes faster than the Black Sox.

The 1932 Cardinals fell 29 games when holdouts and contract squabbles forced the trades of Chick Hafey, the 1931 batting champion, and Jim Bottomley—again, a situation very like the current Reds. Wagner can take some solace in this one; the Cardinals were back on top in two years. But the 1902 Philadelphia Phillies, again, faced a very similar situation when their two best outfielders (Ed Delahanty and Elmer Flick) and their two best pitchers (Al Orth and Red Donahue) jumped to the upstart American League. It took the Phillies over ten years to get back in contention. And finally, the Oakland A's just six years ago turned into a pumpkin at the free-agent era's inaugural ball. Whether the A's have recovered yet is highly debatable.

A few brief words about the other 22 Big Bomb teams. Five were wartime teams, either losing their stars or collapsing when the other teams got their's back. Some were just very old teams that wore out together, like the 1934 Senators. Some, such as the 38–115 performance by the Braves in 1935, seem just inexplicable. Several, like the A's in '82, were cases where you had maybe three starting pitchers suddenly gone sour. A contributing factor in several cases was what we'll call the Rick Honeycutt Syndrome, in which a manager refused to get off a dead horse. Some were cases of teams that played .680 or .700 ball for a year coming down to earth. Some were teams which refused to adapt at the opening shot of the lively ball era and were flattened by the teams that did.

Refused to adapt. . . . the words jar me. That's the common thread that runs through all of these, isn't it?

Dan DRIESSEN, First Base

*Runs Created: 80*

| | G | AB | R | H | 2B | 3B | HR | RBI | SB | Avg |
|---|---|---|---|---|---|---|---|---|---|---|
| First Half | 84 | 299 | 40 | 89 | 15 | 1 | 9 | 36 | 6 | .298 |
| Second half | 65 | 217 | 24 | 50 | 10 | 0 | 8 | 21 | 5 | .230 |
| Home | 72 | 253 | 34 | 74 | 12 | 1 | 7 | 29 | 6 | .292 |
| Road | 77 | 263 | 30 | 65 | 13 | 0 | 10 | 28 | 5 | .247 |
| vs. RHP | | 373 | | 109 | | | 15 | 39 | | .292 |
| vs. LHP | | 143 | | 30 | | | 2 | 18 | | .210 |
| 1982 | 149 | 516 | 64 | 139 | 25 | 1 | 17 | 57 | 11 | .269 |
| 7.88 years | | 522 | 73 | 141 | 27 | 3 | 15 | 74 | 18 | .270 |

Ron OESTER, Second Base

*Runs Created: 58*

| | G | AB | R | H | 2B | 3B | HR | RBI | SB | Avg |
|---|---|---|---|---|---|---|---|---|---|---|
| First Half | 85 | 342 | 40 | 88 | 10 | 3 | 3 | 25 | 3 | .257 |
| Second Half | 66 | 207 | 23 | 55 | 9 | 1 | 6 | 22 | 2 | .266 |
| Home | 75 | 274 | 37 | 77 | 14 | 2 | 4 | 25 | 1 | .281 |
| Road | 76 | 275 | 26 | 66 | 5 | 2 | 5 | 22 | 4 | .240 |
| vs. RHP | | 409 | | 109 | | | 9 | 40 | | .268 |
| vs. LHP | | 140 | | 34 | | | 0 | 7 | | .239 |
| 1982 | 151 | 549 | 63 | 143 | 19 | 4 | 9 | 47 | 5 | .260 |
| 2.27 years | | 536 | 66 | 144 | 23 | 6 | 7 | 49 | 6 | .268 |

Johnny BENCH, Third Base

*Runs Created: 50*

| | G | AB | R | H | 2B | 3B | HR | RBI | SB | Avg |
|---|---|---|---|---|---|---|---|---|---|---|
| First Half | 69 | 238 | 25 | 54 | 10 | 0 | 5 | 18 | 1 | .227 |
| Second Half | 50 | 161 | 19 | 49 | 6 | 0 | 8 | 20 | 0 | .304 |
| Home | 58 | 189 | 19 | 49 | 8 | 0 | 5 | 23 | 1 | .259 |
| Road | 61 | 210 | 25 | 54 | 8 | 0 | 8 | 15 | 0 | .257 |
| vs. RHP | | 278 | | 67 | | | 10 | 29 | | .241 |
| vs. LHP | | 121 | | 36 | | | 3 | 9 | | .298 |
| 1982 | 119 | 399 | 44 | 103 | 16 | 0 | 13 | 38 | 1 | .258 |
| 12.64 years | | 581 | 84 | 156 | 29 | 2 | 30 | 105 | 5 | .268 |

Dave CONCEPCION, Shortstop

*Runs Created: 72*

| | G | AB | R | H | 2B | 3B | HR | RBI | SB | Avg |
|---|---|---|---|---|---|---|---|---|---|---|
| First Half | 83 | 328 | 27 | 96 | 12 | 4 | 1 | 34 | 9 | .293 |
| Second Half | 64 | 244 | 21 | 68 | 13 | 0 | 4 | 19 | 4 | .279 |
| Home | 72 | 272 | 28 | 89 | 12 | 3 | 3 | 31 | 8 | .327 |
| Road | 75 | 300 | 20 | 75 | 13 | 1 | 2 | 22 | 5 | .250 |
| vs. RHP | | 407 | | 120 | | | 2 | 37 | | .295 |
| vs. LHP | | 165 | | 44 | | | 3 | 16 | | .267 |
| 1982 | 147 | 572 | 48 | 164 | 25 | 4 | 5 | 53 | 13 | .287 |
| 10.85 years | | 582 | 69 | 159 | 26 | 4 | 8 | 67 | 23 | .273 |

Eddie MILNER, Left Field

*Runs Created: 50*

| | G | AB | R | H | 2B | 3B | HR | RBI | SB | Avg |
|---|---|---|---|---|---|---|---|---|---|---|
| First Half | 80 | 293 | 47 | 80 | 16 | 5 | 4 | 26 | 12 | .273 |
| Second Half | 33 | 114 | 14 | 29 | 7 | 0 | 0 | 5 | 6 | .254 |
| Home | 55 | 194 | 33 | 56 | 14 | 4 | 1 | 16 | 10 | .289 |
| Road | 58 | 213 | 28 | 53 | 9 | 1 | 3 | 15 | 8 | .249 |
| vs. RHP | | 288 | | 75 | | | 4 | 23 | | .260 |
| vs. LHP | | 119 | | 34 | | | 0 | 8 | | .286 |
| 1982 | 113 | 407 | 61 | 109 | 23 | 5 | 4 | 31 | 18 | .268 |
| 0.78 years | | 532 | 80 | 141 | 31 | 6 | 5 | 41 | 23 | .265 |

Cesar CEDENO, Center Field

*Runs Created: 68*

| | G | AB | R | H | 2B | 3B | HR | RBI | SB | Avg |
|---|---|---|---|---|---|---|---|---|---|---|
| First Half | 75 | 268 | 32 | 81 | 19 | 1 | 7 | 36 | 8 | .302 |
| Second Half | 63 | 224 | 20 | 61 | 16 | 0 | 1 | 21 | 8 | .272 |
| Home | 75 | 276 | 33 | 84 | 23 | 1 | 6 | 37 | 12 | .304 |
| Road | 63 | 216 | 19 | 58 | 12 | 0 | 2 | 20 | 4 | .269 |
| vs. RHP | | 360 | | 102 | | | 4 | 41 | | .260 |
| vs. LHP | | 132 | | 40 | | | 4 | 16 | | .303 |
| 1982 | 138 | 492 | 52 | 142 | 35 | 1 | 8 | 57 | 16 | .289 |
| 10.19 years | | 611 | 92 | 177 | 37 | 6 | 17 | 82 | 49 | .289 |

Paul HOUSEHOLDER, Right Field

*Runs Created: 35*

| | G | AB | R | H | 2B | 3B | HR | RBI | SB | Avg |
|---|---|---|---|---|---|---|---|---|---|---|
| First Half | 69 | 160 | 17 | 30 | 1 | 2 | 4 | 14 | 6 | .188 |
| Second Half | 69 | 257 | 23 | 58 | 10 | 3 | 5 | 20 | 11 | .226 |
| Home | 71 | 165 | 22 | 43 | 6 | 4 | 6 | 23 | 8 | .261 |
| Road | 67 | 252 | 18 | 45 | 5 | 1 | 3 | 11 | 9 | .179 |
| vs. RHP | | 276 | | 50 | | | 4 | 20 | | .181 |
| vs. LHP | | 141 | | 38 | | | 5 | 14 | | .270 |
| 1982 | 138 | 417 | 40 | 88 | 11 | 5 | 9 | 34 | 17 | .211 |
| 1.12 years | | 474 | 49 | 105 | 14 | 5 | 10 | 45 | 19 | .222 |

Alex TREVINO, Catcher

*Runs Created: 34*

| | G | AB | R | H | 2B | 3B | HR | RBI | SB | Avg |
|---|---|---|---|---|---|---|---|---|---|---|
| First Half | 67 | 214 | 12 | 55 | 4 | 0 | 0 | 19 | 2 | .257 |
| Second Half | 53 | 141 | 12 | 34 | 6 | 3 | 1 | 14 | 1 | .241 |
| Home | 64 | 194 | 12 | 51 | 7 | 2 | 0 | 21 | 2 | .263 |
| Road | 56 | 161 | 12 | 38 | 3 | 1 | 1 | 12 | 1 | .236 |
| vs. RHP | | 267 | | 69 | | | 0 | 24 | | .258 |
| vs. LHP | | 88 | | 20 | | | 1 | 9 | | .227 |
| 1982 | 120 | 355 | 24 | 89 | 10 | 3 | 1 | 33 | 3 | .251 |
| 2.27 years | | 475 | 41 | 123 | 15 | 3 | 0 | 44 | 4 | .258 |

Mario SOTO

| Year | (W–L) | GS | Run | Avg | DP | Avg | SB | Avg |
|---|---|---|---|---|---|---|---|---|
| 1977 | ( 2- 6) | 10 | 40 | 4.00 | 11 | 1.10 | 9 | .90 |
| 1978 | ( 1- 0) | 1 | 5 | | 0 | | 1 | |
| 1980 | (10- 8) | 12 | 54 | 4.50 | 4 | .33 | 13 | 1.08 |
| 1981 | (12- 9) | 25 | 105 | 4.20 | 19 | .76 | 29 | 1.16 |
| 1982 | (14-13) | 34 | 130 | 3.82 | 20 | .59 | 27 | .79 |
| 5 years | | 82 | 334 | 4.07 | 54 | .66 | 79 | .96 |

| | G | IP | W | L | Pct | ER | ERA |
|---|---|---|---|---|---|---|---|
| Home | 17 | 137 | 9 | 5 | .643 | 41 | 2.69 |
| Road | 17 | 120.2 | 5 | 8 | .385 | 39 | 2.91 |

Bruce BERENYI

| Year | (W–L) | GS | Run | Avg | DP | Avg | SB | Avg |
|---|---|---|---|---|---|---|---|---|
| 1980 | (2- 2) | 6 | 32 | 5.33 | 8 | 1.33 | 14 | 2.33 |
| 1981 | (9- 6) | 20 | 88 | 4.40 | 17 | .85 | 25 | 1.25 |
| 1982 | (9-18) | 34 | 88 | 2.59 | 39 | 1.15 | 45 | 1.32 |
| 3 years | | 60 | 208 | 3.47 | 64 | 1.07 | 84 | 1.40 |

| | G | IP | W | L | Pct | ER | ERA |
|---|---|---|---|---|---|---|---|
| Home | 17 | 119.2 | 4 | 10 | .286 | 45 | 3.38 |
| Road | 17 | 102.2 | 5 | 8 | .385 | 38 | 3.33 |

Frank PASTORE

| Year | (W–L) | GS | Run | Avg | DP | Avg | SB | Avg |
|---|---|---|---|---|---|---|---|---|
| 1979 | ( 7- 2) | 9 | 40 | 4.44 | 5 | .56 | 8 | .89 |
| 1980 | (13- 7) | 27 | 119 | 4.41 | 19 | .70 | 21 | .78 |
| 1981 | ( 4- 9) | 22 | 92 | 4.18 | 22 | 1.00 | 19 | .86 |
| 1982 | ( 8-13) | 29 | 114 | 3.93 | 31 | 1.07 | 25 | .86 |
| 4 years | | 87 | 365 | 4.20 | 77 | .89 | 73 | .84 |

| | G | IP | W | L | Pct | ER | ERA |
|---|---|---|---|---|---|---|---|
| Home | 16 | 115.1 | 5 | 7 | .417 | 44 | 3.43 |
| Road | 13 | 73 | 3 | 6 | .333 | 39 | 4.81 |

Tom SEAVER

| Year | (W–L) | GS | Run | Avg | DP | Avg | SB | Avg |
|---|---|---|---|---|---|---|---|---|
| 1976 | (14-11) | 34 | 119 | 3.50 | 28 | .82 | 27 | .79 |
| 1977 | (21- 6) | 33 | 153 | 4.64 | 14 | .42 | 22 | .67 |
| 1978 | (16-14) | 36 | 143 | 3.97 | 21 | .58 | 29 | .81 |
| 1979 | (16- 6) | 32 | 156 | 4.88 | 33 | 1.03 | 28 | .88 |
| 1980 | (10- 8) | 26 | 116 | 4.46 | 18 | .69 | 32 | 1.23 |
| 1981 | (14- 2) | 23 | 115 | 5.00 | 21 | .91 | 25 | 1.09 |
| 1982 | ( 5-13) | 21 | 69 | 3.29 | 17 | .81 | 18 | .86 |
| 7 years | | 205 | 871 | 4.25 | 152 | .74 | 181 | .88 |

| | G | IP | W | L | Pct | ER | ERA |
|---|---|---|---|---|---|---|---|
| Home | 9 | 44 | 3 | 6 | .333 | 29 | 5.93 |
| Road | 12 | 67.1 | 2 | 7 | .222 | 39 | 5.21 |

Bob SHIRLEY

| Year | (W–L) | GS | Run | Avg | DP | Avg | SB | Avg |
|---|---|---|---|---|---|---|---|---|
| 1977 | (12-18) | 35 | 130 | 3.71 | 36 | 1.03 | 23 | .66 |
| 1978 | ( 8-11) | 20 | 80 | 4.00 | 19 | .95 | 11 | .55 |
| 1979 | ( 8-16) | 25 | 106 | 4.24 | 19 | .76 | 9 | .36 |
| 1980 | (11-12) | 12 | 43 | 3.58 | 7 | .58 | 16 | 1.33 |
| 1981 | ( 6- 4) | 11 | 50 | 4.55 | 11 | 1.00 | 9 | .82 |
| 1982 | ( 8-13) | 20 | 53 | 2.65 | 16 | .80 | 9 | .45 |
| 6 years | | 123 | 462 | 3.76 | 108 | .88 | 77 | .62 |

| | G | IP | W | L | Pct | ER | ERA |
|---|---|---|---|---|---|---|---|
| Home | 17 | 74.2 | 4 | 3 | .571 | 31 | 3.74 |
| Road | 24 | 78 | 4 | 10 | .286 | 30 | 3.46 |

1982 OTHERS

| Pitcher | (W–L) | GS | Run | Avg | DP | Avg | SB | Avg |
|---|---|---|---|---|---|---|---|---|
| Leibrandt | (5-7) | 11 | 45 | 4.09 | 14 | 1.27 | 13 | 1.18 |
| Harris | (2-6) | 10 | 35 | 3.50 | 11 | 1.10 | 7 | .70 |
| Sherrer | (0-1) | 2 | 7 | 3.50 | 3 | 1.50 | 3 | 1.50 |
| Price | (3-4) | 1 | 4 | | 0 | | 0 | |

## CINCINNATI REDS

*Talent Analysis*

The Cincinnati Reds in 1982 possessed only 133 points of approximate value.

| | AV | % |
|---|---|---|
| Produced by Reds' system: | 98 | 74% |
| Acquired by trade: | 32 | 24% |
| Purchased or signed from free agency: | 3 | 2% |

The 74% system figure is the highest in the National League.

The Reds' organization ranked third in the major leagues in 1982 in talent produced with 207 approximate value. Over the four years 1979 to 1982, they rank 6th with 751.

## RIVERFRONT STADIUM

DIMENSIONS: Normal

SURFACE: Hard turf

VISIBILITY: Acceptable

FOUL TERRITORY: Small

FAVORS:
Hitter/Pitcher—Neither
Power/Line-drive hitter—Neither
Righthander/Lefthander—Neither

OTHER PARK CHARACTERISTICS: Fewer infield errors, but also fewer double plays than any other NL park. Ball bounces so high off the turf that it doesn't get to infielder as fast as it might. The park may lower batting averages a point or five for the same reason.

TYPES OF MARGINAL PLAYERS MOST VALUABLE IN PARK: I don't know

PLAYERS ON TEAM HELPED MOST BY PARK: Oester

PLAYERS ON TEAM HURT MOST BY PARK: Bench

OTHER COMMENTS: The peculiarity of this essentially featureless ballpark is that players who don't have much power seem to homer more often in this park than on the road, but the true power hitters who have played here, like Foster and Bench, have not done well in the park at all.

# AMERICAN LEAGUE EAST

## DIVISION SHEET*

| Team | 1st | 2nd | vs. RHP | vs. LHP | Home | Road | Day | Night | Total | Pct |
|---|---|---|---|---|---|---|---|---|---|---|
| Milwaukee | 48-35 | 47-32 | 61-49 | 34-18 | 48-34 | 47-33 | 27-22 | 68-45 | 95-67 | .586 |
| Baltimore | 44-38 | 50-30 | 63-48 | 31-20 | 53-28 | 41-40 | 24-14 | 70-54 | 94-68 | .580 |
| Boston | 49-36 | 40-37 | 61-51 | 28-22 | 49-32 | 40-41 | 34-19 | 55-54 | 89-73 | .549 |
| Detroit | 42-41 | 41-38 | 61-59 | 22-20 | 47-34 | 36-45 | 24-27 | 59-52 | 83-79 | .512 |
| New York | 39-42 | 40-41 | 51-51 | 28-32 | 42-39 | 37-44 | 15-20 | 64-63 | 79-83 | .488 |
| Cleveland | 41-41 | 37-43 | 56-54 | 22-30 | 41-40 | 37-44 | 22-24 | 56-60 | 78-84 | .481 |
| Toronto | 37-47 | 41-37 | 43-40 | 35-44 | 44-37 | 34-47 | 30-28 | 48-56 | 78-84 | .481 |

### *TURNAROUNDS*

#### COME FROM BEHIND WINS

| Team | 1 | 2 | 3 | 4 | 5 | 6 | 7 | Total | Points |
|---|---|---|---|---|---|---|---|---|---|
| Milwaukee | 23 | 16 | 3 | 3 | | | | 45 | 111 |
| Baltimore | 21 | 18 | 4 | 3 | | | | 46 | 127 |
| Boston | 19 | 14 | 7 | 2 | 2 | 1 | | 45 | 137 |
| Detroit | 22 | 13 | 4 | 0 | 1 | | | 40 | 105 |
| New York | 16 | 10 | 2 | 2 | 0 | 1 | 1 | 32 | 95 |
| Cleveland | 14 | 11 | 5 | 1 | 1 | | | 32 | 92 |
| Toronto | 19 | 15 | 3 | 0 | 1 | | | 38 | 101 |

#### BLOWN LEADS

| Team | 1 | 2 | 3 | 4 | 5 | 6 | 7 | Total | Points |
|---|---|---|---|---|---|---|---|---|---|
| Milwaukee | 16 | 14 | 5 | 0 | 0 | 1 | | 36 | 101 |
| Baltimore | 18 | 8 | 4 | 3 | 3 | | | 36 | 109 |
| Boston | 12 | 10 | 1 | 1 | 2 | | | 26 | 75 |
| Detroit | 14 | 8 | 6 | 3 | 1 | 0 | 1 | 33 | 105 |
| New York | 16 | 8 | 5 | 2 | | | | 31 | 86 |
| Cleveland | 18 | 14 | 5 | 2 | 1 | | | 40 | 110 |
| Toronto | 20 | 10 | 4 | 1 | 1 | 1 | | 37 | 104 |

#### DEFENSIVE RECORDS

| Team | OSB | OCS | OSB% | DP | OA/SFA | FAvg | DER | Opposition Runs |
|---|---|---|---|---|---|---|---|---|
| Detroit | 84 | 63 | .571 | 165 | 41/34 | .981 | .719 | 685 |
| Baltimore | 98 | 51 | .657 | 140 | 25/46 | .984 | .714 | 687 |
| Toronto | 78 | 46 | .629 | 146 | 29/31 | .987 | .704 | 701 |
| Boston | 101 | 55 | .647 | 172 | 34/43 | .981 | .685 | 713 |
| New York | 98 | 44 | .690 | 158 | 44/59 | .979 | .685 | 716 |
| Milwaukee | 121 | 62 | .661 | 185 | 42/51 | .980 | .697 | 717 |
| Cleveland | 125 | 60 | .676 | 127 | 24/66 | .980 | .700 | 748 |

#### OPPOSITION ERRORS

| Team | C | 1B | 2B | 3B | SS | LF | CF | RF | P | Un | Total |
|---|---|---|---|---|---|---|---|---|---|---|---|
| Milwaukee | 17 | 20 | 16 | 28 | 32 | 10 | 9 | 6 | 13 | 2 | 153 |
| Cleveland | 12 | 21 | 25 | 25 | 19 | 8 | 8 | 5 | 12 | 3 | 138 |
| Toronto | 11 | 8 | 17 | 23 | 34 | 5 | 8 | 4 | 19 | 3 | 132 |
| New York | 7 | 14 | 8 | 27 | 30 | 3 | 5 | 13 | 20 | 1 | 128 |
| Detroit | 7 | 11 | 17 | 18 | 24 | 11 | 10 | 9 | 11 | 2 | 120 |
| Boston | 5 | 12 | 13 | 23 | 34 | 7 | 4 | 7 | 10 | 4 | 119 |
| Baltimore | 8 | 8 | 9 | 21 | 36 | 12 | 6 | 3 | 6 | 5 | 114 |

#### LATE-INNING BALL CLUBS

| Team | Ahead | Tied | Behind | Net Change |
|---|---|---|---|---|
| Boston | 68- 7 | 13- 6 | 7-59 | +7 |
| Toronto | 55- 8 | 16-10 | 7-66 | +5 |
| Baltimore | 74- 9 | 13- 7 | 7-52 | +4 |
| Cleveland | 56-10 | 11- 9 | 10-64 | +2 |
| Milwaukee | 76- 8 | 14-13 | 5-46 | −2 |
| Detroit | 68- 8 | 7-10 | 8-61 | −3 |
| New York | 60- 5 | 11-17 | 7-59 | −4 |

*See explanation of Division Sheet on p. 16

# MILWAUKEE BREWERS

Most ball games, as we all know, are decided in the late innings, unless of course they aren't. That's why you can't win a pennant anymore without a good bullpen. Dallas Green's statement upon taking over the Cubbies: It is known around the league that if you keep the game close the Cubs will beat themselves in the late innings. Doug Rader, in taking over Texas: I was a good player at the end of the game, when it meant something. An article in Ozark Airlines in-flight magazine asserts blandly that 75% of all games are decided in the last two innings. Oh yes, there is no doubt about it: in barrooms and press boxes, in the carpool and in the bleachers and wherever baseball teams are analyzed, the late innings are in ascendancy, the bullpen is the crucial factor; don't tell me about Ben Ogilvie's batting average, I want to know what he hits in the late innings with men on base.

But is it? Which of the following statements, do you suppose, are true?

1) Most ballgames are decided in the late innings.
2) Most ballgames are decided in the early innings.
3) There is comparatively little difference between a good team and a bad team as to what they do in the early innings; most of the spread occurs from the seventh inning on. That is why the bullpen has become so important.
4) Modern bullpens are so good that it is difficult to rally in the late innings against most teams, and for that reason the crucial innings in the largest share of ballgames are the first five.

I hope, eventually, to find convincing evidence to support one or more of those statements. One way in which this can be done is to study the divergence of a team's won-lost record from .500 throughout the progression of a ball game. If it is true, for example, that most ball games are decided late, then the divergence should come late.

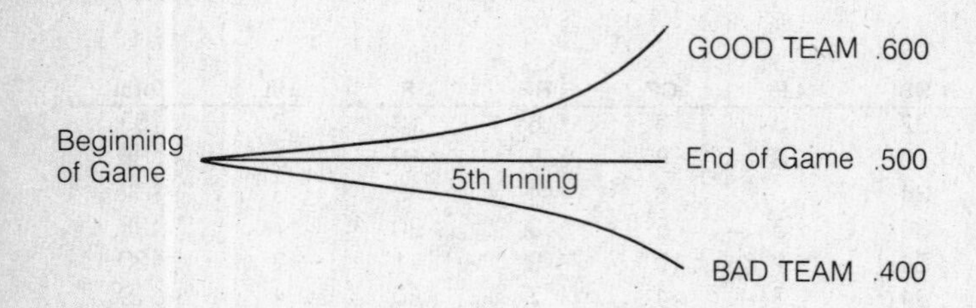


If, on the other hand, most ball games are decided early, then most of the divergence should come early.

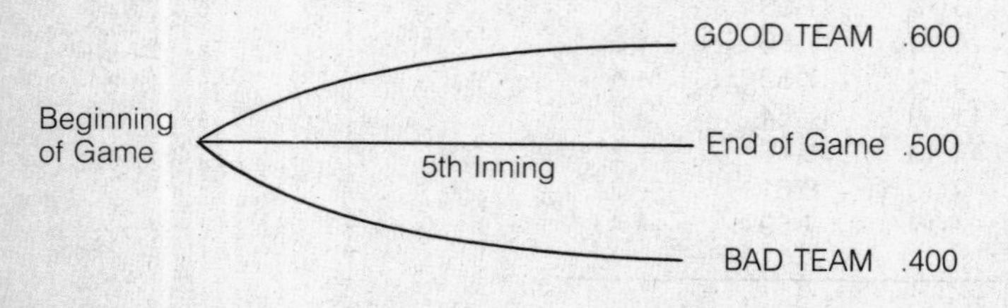


If one inning is as important as another, then the graph should be a straight line.

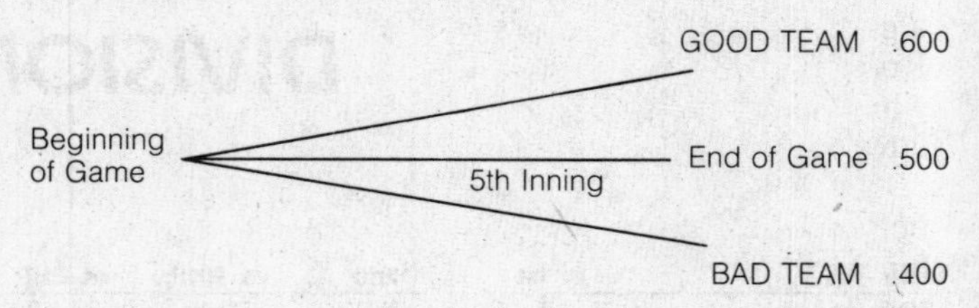


In order to draw these graphs, we need to figure out what each team's record would be if the game ended after one inning, two innings, three innings . . . eight innings, nine innings.

Which brings us to the Milwaukee Brewers. *With or without Rollie Fingers, the Milwaukee Brewers are not a good late-inning ball club*. In their 163 games in 1982, the Brewers were ahead after six innings 90 times and behind only 50; they were tied the other 23. Had they only split the ties from that point on, the Brewers would have won over 100 ballgames. They actually won 95. Throughout the first six innings of the game, the Brewers moved further and further away from .500:

| Record after: | Ahead | Behind | Tied | Divergence |
|---|---|---|---|---|
| 1 inning | 48 | 38 | 77 | +10 |
| 2 innings | 65 | 43 | 55 | +22 |
| 3 innings | 80 | 51 | 32 | +29 |
| 4 innings | 85 | 51 | 27 | +34 |
| 5 innings | 88 | 52 | 23 | +36 |
| 6 innings | 90 | 50 | 23 | +40 |

But after the sixth, they lost ground, drifting back toward .500:

| Record after: | Ahead | Behind | Tied | Divergence |
|---|---|---|---|---|
| 7 innings | 84 | 50 | 29 | +34 |
| 8 innings | 91 | 49 | 23 | +42 |
| 9 innings | 90 | 53 | 20 | +37 |
| Final Record | 95 | 67 | 1 | +28 |

So the Brewers' pattern, actually, is *more* extreme than the one which would support the early-innings thesis:

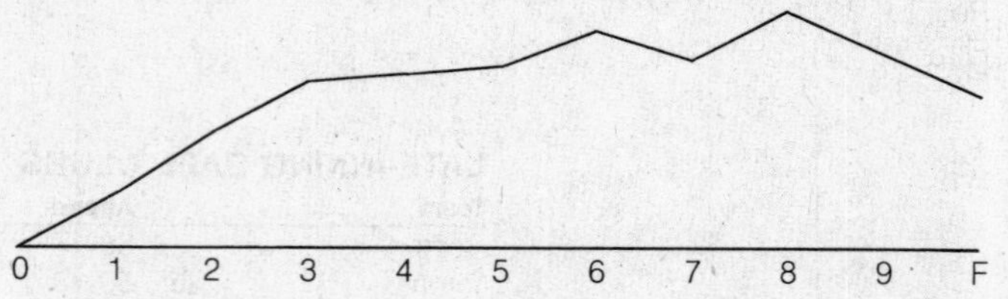


Almost incredibly, the Brewers were able to beat the opposition more consistently in just three innings than they could in all nine. After three innings they were 29 games over .500; they wound up 28 over.

Rollie Fingers last pitched on September 2. On September 2, the Brewers were +36 through six innings and

+25 in final. After September 2, they were +4 through six and +3 in final scores. The pattern didn't change in September.

OK, it is a long step between what is true for one team, and what is true in general. I did, however, figure a couple of other teams. The Baltimore Orioles are a team very unlike the Brewers in what would seem to be the most revelant ways. Unlike the Brewers, the Orioles lack a grade-A reliever (You're welcome, Tippy). Unlike the Brewers, the Orioles have an awesome bench, a bench which seems to be about nine-deep in people who can hit late-inning three-run homers.

But. Like the Brewers, the Orioles actually had a better record through six innings than they did through nine. I know it doesn't sound right; I read the box scores, too. I know it seems like the Orioles pull an unbelievable number of games out of the fire in the 8th inning, but the facts are and if you don't believe it count 'em yourself, the Baltimore Orioles actually lost ground to the opposition after the sixth inning. The complete chart is given below; they were +28 after six innings, +26 after the game.

| | Ahead | Behind | Tied | Divergence |
|---|---|---|---|---|
| Record after 1 inning | 42 | 37 | 84 | +5 |
| Record after 2 innings | 68 | 50 | 45 | +18 |
| Record after 3 innings | 70 | 60 | 33 | +10 |
| Record after 4 innings | 78 | 60 | 25 | +18 |
| Record after 5 innings | 83 | 60 | 20 | +23 |
| Record after 6 innings | 84 | 56 | 23 | +28 |
| Record after 7 innings | 84 | 59 | 20 | +25 |
| Record after 8 innings | 84 | 59 | 20 | +25 |
| Record after 9 innings | 86 | 64 | 13 | +22 |
| Final record | 94 | 68 | 1 | +26 |

Well, what about a *bad* team. Do they lose most of their games late, or what? Chief Bender blamed three people for the disastrous 1982 season of the Cincinnati Reds, one of them, inevitably, a relief pitcher (Jim Kern). Here is the chart of the Reds' regress through the game:

| | Ahead | Behind | Tied | Divergence |
|---|---|---|---|---|
| Record after 1 inning | 37 | 40 | 85 | -3 |
| Record after 2 innings | 48 | 64 | 50 | -16 |
| Record after 3 innings | 53 | 73 | 36 | -20 |
| Record after 4 innings | 61 | 79 | 22 | -18 |
| Record after 5 innings | 64 | 81 | 17 | -17 |
| Record after 6 innings | 60 | 89 | 13 | -29 |
| Record after 7 innings | 57 | 91 | 12 | -34 |
| Record after 8 innings | 55 | 96 | 11 | -41 |
| Record after 9 innings | 53 | 90 | 19 | -37 |
| Final record | 61 | 101 | | -40 |

The Reds were a legitimately bad late-inning ball club, with a further deterioration of 11 games (or half games) after the sixth inning. Yet even so, the lion's share of their divergence from .500 comes very early in the game. They are 20 games away from .500 by the third inning, and move 20 more in the last six. How can you blame the bullpen for the failures of a team which is ahead after the seventh inning only 57 times?

Among these three teams, then, there is a very clear pattern. All three teams revealed their identity in the very first inning; the good teams pull ahead in the first, the bad one drops behind in the first. All have moved decisively in the direction of their fate by the second inning; all, in fact, are 16 or more games away from .500 that early.

I want to move slowly here. Three teams do not make for an exhaustive study of the issue. There probably are teams which win the pennant by dominating the late innings:

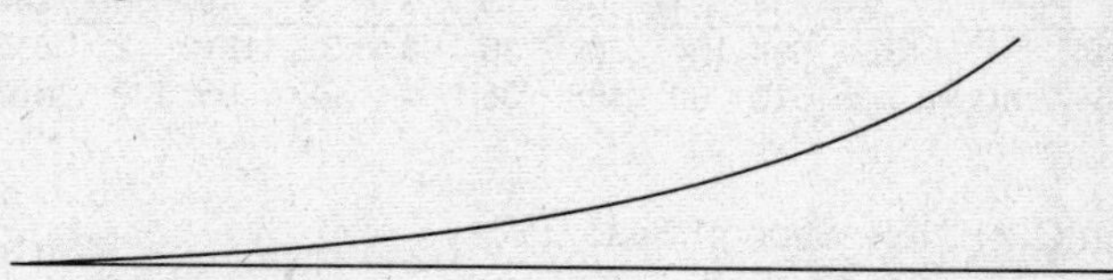

There probably are teams which lose the pennant due to their inability to get out of the late innings with a lead:

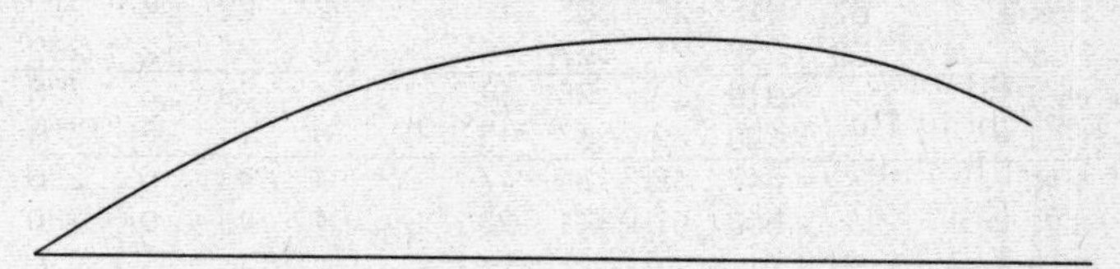

I want to do some more studies and find out how many of every type of pattern there are.

But these findings are, at the least, curiously discordant with the supposition that the late innings are crucial. It seems that every analysis of a pennant race begins or ends with a concession that of course what it all comes down to is a battle of the bullpens. But if you actually look, it is surprisingly easy to find championship teams which lack an outstanding reliever. The Royals won the AL West in 1976, 77, and 78 with spotty relief work from Mark Littell, Doug Bird and Al Hrabosky. Quick now, who were the top relievers for the NL Champion Dodgers in '77 and '78? (Charlie Hough and Mike Garman in '77, Terry Forster in '78). When the Dodgers won the World's Championship in '81 their top reliever had 8 saves. The Angels last year won 93 games with a terrible bullpen; the A's had the best record in the American League in '81 with no bullpen at all. The Red Sox' top reliever in '75 was Dick Drago (2-2, 15 saves and a 3.82 ERA). In 1971 the Giants' ace was Jerry Johnson. In the last 12 real seasons (1970-1982, except 1981), 12 teams have won their divisions with no pitcher getting more than 15 saves, and 40% of division champions have had no pitcher with 20 saves.

I'm not saying the bullpen isn't important. It is; the question is whether it is especially important, more so than any other position. I hear people say all the time that somebody isn't going to win the pennant because they lack an outstanding reliever; I can't remember hearing anybody say that somebody isn't going to win because they lack an outstanding second baseman. I don't see any evidence to justify that distinction.

The Milwaukee/California play-off series was the first post-season series matching two expansion teams.

Cecil COOPER, First Base

*Runs Created: 118*

| | G | AB | R | H | 2B | 3B | HR | RBI | SB | Avg |
|---|---|---|---|---|---|---|---|---|---|---|
| First Half | 77 | 321 | 55 | 103 | 23 | 1 | 19 | 68 | 2 | .321 |
| Second Half | 78 | 333 | 49 | 102 | 15 | 2 | 13 | 53 | 0 | .306 |
| Home | 78 | 317 | 48 | 96 | 16 | 2 | 12 | 53 | 2 | .303 |
| Road | 77 | 337 | 56 | 109 | 22 | 1 | 20 | 68 | 0 | .323 |
| vs. RHP | | 420 | 70 | 139 | 25 | 2 | 24 | 72 | 2 | .331 |
| vs. LHP | | 234 | 34 | 66 | 13 | 1 | 9 | 49 | 0 | .282 |
| 1982 | 155 | 654 | 104 | 205 | 38 | 3 | 32 | 121 | 2 | .313 |
| 7.64 years | | 610 | 90 | 188 | 36 | 4 | 22 | 95 | 9 | .308 |

Jim GANTNER, Second Base

*Runs Created: 55*

| | G | AB | R | H | 2B | 3B | HR | RBI | SB | Avg |
|---|---|---|---|---|---|---|---|---|---|---|
| First Half | 60 | 195 | 18 | 60 | 8 | 1 | 3 | 17 | 1 | .308 |
| Second Half | 72 | 252 | 30 | 72 | 9 | 1 | 1 | 26 | 5 | .286 |
| Home | 67 | 215 | 27 | 65 | 11 | 1 | 2 | 22 | 4 | .302 |
| Road | 65 | 232 | 21 | 67 | 6 | 1 | 2 | 21 | 2 | .289 |
| vs. RHP | | 319 | 39 | 95 | 14 | 2 | 4 | 29 | 3 | .298 |
| vs. LHP | | 128 | 9 | 37 | 3 | 0 | 0 | 14 | 3 | .289 |
| 1982 | 132 | 447 | 48 | 132 | 17 | 2 | 4 | 43 | 6 | .295 |
| 3.23 years | | 506 | 57 | 141 | 20 | 3 | 4 | 48 | 9 | .280 |

Paul MOLITOR, Third Base

*Runs Created: 115*

| | G | AB | R | H | 2B | 3B | HR | RBI | SB | Avg |
|---|---|---|---|---|---|---|---|---|---|---|
| First Half | 81 | 327 | 68 | 97 | 12 | 4 | 10 | 34 | 17 | .297 |
| Second Half | 79 | 339 | 68 | 104 | 14 | 4 | 9 | 37 | 24 | .307 |
| Home | 80 | 318 | 75 | 101 | 19 | 6 | 9 | 36 | 19 | .318 |
| Road | 80 | 348 | 61 | 100 | 7 | 2 | 10 | 35 | 22 | .287 |
| vs. RHP | | 441 | 92 | 133 | 16 | 7 | 15 | 57 | 28 | .302 |
| vs. LHP | | 225 | 44 | 68 | 10 | 1 | 4 | 14 | 13 | .302 |
| 1982 | 160 | 666 | 136 | 201 | 26 | 8 | 19 | 71 | 41 | .302 |
| 3.70 years | | 668 | 114 | 199 | 32 | 8 | 12 | 63 | 40 | .297 |

Robin YOUNT, Shortstop

*Runs Created: 142*

| | G | AB | R | H | 2B | 3B | HR | RBI | SB | Avg |
|---|---|---|---|---|---|---|---|---|---|---|
| First Half | 78 | 318 | 56 | 104 | 21 | 8 | 15 | 57 | 5 | .327 |
| Second Half | 78 | 317 | 73 | 106 | 25 | 4 | 14 | 57 | 9 | .334 |
| Home | 78 | 394 | 55 | 95 | 25 | 5 | 9 | 55 | 8 | .313 |
| Road | 78 | 331 | 74 | 115 | 21 | 7 | 20 | 59 | 6 | .347 |
| vs. RHP | | 435 | 76 | 139 | 29 | 5 | 22 | 85 | 8 | .320 |
| vs. LHP | | 200 | 53 | 71 | 17 | 7 | 7 | 29 | 6 | .355 |
| 1982 | 156 | 635 | 129 | 210 | 46 | 12 | 29 | 114 | 14 | .331 |
| 7.65 years | | 634 | 89 | 178 | 33 | 7 | 13 | 72 | 15 | .281 |

Ben OGLIVIE, Left Field

*Runs Created: 86*

| | G | AB | R | H | 2B | 3B | HR | RBI | SB | Avg |
|---|---|---|---|---|---|---|---|---|---|---|
| First Half | 83 | 321 | 45 | 84 | 13 | 0 | 19 | 56 | 2 | .262 |
| Second Half | 76 | 281 | 47 | 63 | 9 | 1 | 15 | 46 | 1 | .224 |
| Home | 79 | 284 | 47 | 75 | 18 | 1 | 16 | 50 | 2 | .264 |
| Road | 80 | 318 | 45 | 72 | 4 | 0 | 18 | 52 | 1 | .226 |
| vs. RHP | | 383 | 65 | 99 | 12 | 1 | 25 | 72 | 3 | .258 |
| vs. LHP | | 219 | 27 | 48 | 10 | 0 | 9 | 30 | 0 | .219 |
| 1982 | 159 | 602 | 92 | 147 | 22 | 1 | 34 | 102 | 3 | .244 |
| 7.99 years | | 545 | 77 | 148 | 26 | 3 | 24 | 83 | 10 | .272 |

Gorman THOMAS, Center Field

*Runs Created: 95*

| | G | AB | R | H | 2B | 3B | HR | RBI | SB | Avg |
|---|---|---|---|---|---|---|---|---|---|---|
| First Half | 79 | 290 | 46 | 71 | 14 | 0 | 22 | 56 | 0 | .245 |
| Second Half | 79 | 277 | 50 | 68 | 15 | 1 | 17 | 56 | 3 | .245 |
| Home | 82 | 287 | 48 | 67 | 14 | 1 | 19 | 61 | 1 | .233 |
| Road | 76 | 280 | 48 | 72 | 15 | 0 | 20 | 51 | 2 | .257 |
| vs. RHP | | 369 | 57 | 88 | 18 | 1 | 24 | 74 | 3 | .238 |
| vs. LHP | | 198 | 39 | 51 | 11 | 0 | 15 | 38 | 0 | .258 |
| 1982 | 158 | 567 | 96 | 139 | 29 | 1 | 39 | 112 | 3 | .245 |
| 6.25 years | | 518 | 77 | 121 | 26 | 2 | 32 | 92 | 5 | .235 |

Charlie MOORE, Right Field

*Runs Created: 45*

| | G | AB | R | H | 2B | 3B | HR | RBI | SB | Avg |
|---|---|---|---|---|---|---|---|---|---|---|
| First Half | 65 | 231 | 35 | 58 | 9 | 3 | 4 | 27 | 1 | .251 |
| Second Half | 68 | 225 | 18 | 58 | 13 | 1 | 2 | 18 | 1 | .258 |
| Home | 66 | 223 | 25 | 56 | 12 | 2 | 3 | 22 | 0 | .251 |
| Road | 67 | 233 | 28 | 60 | 10 | 2 | 3 | 23 | 2 | .258 |
| vs. RHP | | 283 | 34 | 70 | 15 | 3 | 2 | 28 | 2 | .247 |
| vs. LHP | | 173 | 19 | 46 | 7 | 1 | 4 | 17 | 0 | .266 |
| 1982 | 133 | 456 | 53 | 116 | 22 | 4 | 6 | 45 | 2 | .254 |
| 5.41 years | | 485 | 56 | 128 | 22 | 5 | 5 | 49 | 6 | .264 |

Ted SIMMONS, Catcher

*Runs Created: 75*

| | G | AB | R | H | 2B | 3B | HR | RBI | SB | Avg |
|---|---|---|---|---|---|---|---|---|---|---|
| First Half | 72 | 277 | 36 | 72 | 15 | 0 | 14 | 45 | 0 | .260 |
| Second Half | 65 | 262 | 37 | 73 | 13 | 0 | 9 | 52 | 0 | .279 |
| Home | 69 | 265 | 29 | 67 | 14 | 0 | 7 | 39 | 0 | .253 |
| Road | 68 | 274 | 44 | 78 | 14 | 0 | 16 | 58 | 0 | .285 |
| vs. RHP | | 357 | 47 | 95 | 21 | 0 | 13 | 56 | 0 | .266 |
| vs. LHP | | 182 | 26 | 50 | 7 | 0 | 10 | 41 | 0 | .275 |
| 1982 | 137 | 539 | 73 | 145 | 28 | 0 | 23 | 97 | 0 | .269 |
| 11.12 years | | 598 | 77 | 174 | 34 | 4 | 19 | 98 | 1 | .291 |

Roy HOWELL, Designated Hitter

*Runs Created: 32*

| | G | AB | R | H | 2B | 3B | HR | RBI | SB | Avg |
|---|---|---|---|---|---|---|---|---|---|---|
| First Half | 45 | 125 | 17 | 32 | 5 | 1 | 3 | 14 | 0 | .256 |
| Second Half | 53 | 175 | 14 | 46 | 6 | 1 | 1 | 24 | 0 | .263 |
| Home | 50 | 152 | 13 | 34 | 4 | 0 | 0 | 16 | 0 | .224 |
| Road | 48 | 148 | 18 | 44 | 7 | 2 | 4 | 22 | 0 | .297 |
| vs. RHP | | 277 | 28 | 68 | 10 | 2 | 3 | 34 | 0 | .245 |
| vs. LHP | | 23 | 3 | 10 | 1 | 0 | 1 | 4 | 0 | .435 |
| 1982 | 98 | 300 | 31 | 78 | 11 | 2 | 4 | 38 | 0 | .260 |
| 6.02 years | | 570 | 64 | 149 | 28 | 4 | 12 | 68 | 1 | .262 |

Mike CALDWELL

| Year | (W–L) | GS | Run | Avg | DP | Avg | SB | Avg |
|---|---|---|---|---|---|---|---|---|
| 1977 | ( 5- 8) | 12 | 48 | 4.00 | 16 | 1.33 | 6 | .50 |
| 1978 | (22- 9) | 34 | 145 | 4.25 | 30 | .88 | 10 | .29 |
| 1979 | (16- 6) | 30 | 159 | 5.30 | 34 | 1.13 | 13 | .43 |
| 1980 | (13-11) | 33 | 192 | 5.82 | 48 | 1.45 | 12 | .36 |
| 1981 | (11- 9) | 23 | 107 | 4.54 | 25 | 1.09 | 8 | .35 |
| 1982 | (17-13) | 34 | 164 | 4.82 | 43 | 1.26 | 9 | .26 |
| 6 years | | 166 | 815 | 4.91 | 196 | 1.18 | 58 | .35 |

| | G | IP | W | L | Pct | ER | ERA |
|---|---|---|---|---|---|---|---|
| Home | 21 | 162.2 | 11 | 8 | .579 | 62 | 3.43 |
| Road | 14 | 95.1 | 6 | 5 | .545 | 50 | 4.72 |

Doc MEDICH

| Year | (W–L) | GS | Run | Avg | DP | Avg | SB | Avg |
|---|---|---|---|---|---|---|---|---|
| 1976 | ( 8-11) | 26 | 85 | 3.27 | 19 | .73 | 19 | .73 |
| 1977 | (12- 7) | 29 | 154 | 5.31 | 26 | .90 | 29 | 1.00 |
| 1978 | ( 9- 8) | 22 | 94 | 4.27 | 23 | 1.05 | 11 | .50 |
| 1979 | (10- 7) | 19 | 97 | 5.11 | 17 | .89 | 6 | .32 |
| 1980 | (14-11) | 32 | 167 | 5.22 | 36 | 1.11 | 20 | .62 |
| 1981 | (10- 6) | 20 | 92 | 4.60 | 13 | .65 | 8 | .40 |
| 1982 | (12-15) | 31 | 119 | 3.84 | 37 | 1.19 | 32 | 1.03 |
| 7 years | | 179 | 808 | 4.51 | 171 | .96 | 125 | .70 |

| | G | IP | W | L | Pct | ER | ERA |
|---|---|---|---|---|---|---|---|
| Milwaukee | 5 | 40.1 | 2 | 2 | .500 | 18 | 4.02 |
| Texas | 10 | 67.1 | 5 | 3 | .625 | 20 | 2.67 |
| Road | 16 | 78 | 5 | 10 | .333 | 66 | 7.62 |

Pete VUCKOVICH

| Year | (W–L) | GS | Run | Avg | DP | Avg | SB | Avg |
|---|---|---|---|---|---|---|---|---|
| 1977 | ( 7- 7) | 8 | 33 | 4.13 | 11 | 1.38 | 1 | .12 |
| 1978 | (12-12) | 23 | 71 | 3.07 | 20 | .87 | 18 | .78 |
| 1979 | (15-10) | 32 | 159 | 4.97 | 22 | .69 | 18 | .56 |
| 1980 | (12- 9) | 30 | 133 | 4.43 | 26 | .87 | 25 | .83 |
| 1981 | (14- 4) | 23 | 115 | 5.00 | 30 | 1.30 | 13 | .57 |
| 1982 | (18- 6) | 30 | 157 | 5.23 | 34 | 1.13 | 35 | 1.17 |
| 6 years | | 146 | 668 | 4.58 | 143 | .98 | 110 | .75 |

| | G | IP | W | L | Pct | ER | ERA |
|---|---|---|---|---|---|---|---|
| Home | 13 | 105.1 | 7 | 3 | .700 | 31 | 2.65 |
| Road | 17 | 118.1 | 11 | 3 | .786 | 52 | 3.96 |

Moose HAAS

| Year | (W–L) | GS | Run | Avg | DP | Avg | SB | Avg |
|---|---|---|---|---|---|---|---|---|
| 1977 | (10-12) | 32 | 130 | 4.06 | 29 | .91 | 26 | .81 |
| 1978 | ( 2- 3) | 6 | 46 | 7.67 | 6 | 1.00 | 4 | .67 |
| 1979 | (11-11) | 28 | 146 | 5.21 | 24 | .86 | 25 | .89 |
| 1980 | (16-15) | 33 | 117 | 3.55 | 41 | 1.24 | 19 | .58 |
| 1981 | (11- 7) | 22 | 101 | 4.59 | 21 | .95 | 17 | .77 |
| 1982 | (11- 8) | 27 | 148 | 5.48 | 27 | 1.00 | 18 | .67 |
| 6 years | | 148 | 688 | 4.65 | 148 | 1.00 | 109 | .74 |

| | G | IP | W | L | Pct | ER | ERA |
|---|---|---|---|---|---|---|---|
| Home | 12 | 81.2 | 5 | 4 | .556 | 37 | 4.19 |
| Road | 20 | 111.2 | 6 | 4 | .600 | 59 | 4.76 |

Bob McCLURE

| Year | (W–L) | GS | Run | Avg | DP | Avg | SB | Avg |
|---|---|---|---|---|---|---|---|---|
| 1980 | ( 5-8) | 5 | 18 | 3.60 | 4 | .80 | 6 | 1.20 |
| 1982 | (12-7) | 26 | 155 | 5.96 | 25 | .96 | 12 | .46 |
| 2 years | | 31 | 173 | 5.58 | 29 | .94 | 18 | .58 |

| | G | IP | W | L | Pct | ER | ERA |
|---|---|---|---|---|---|---|---|
| Home | 17 | 86.2 | 6 | 4 | .600 | 41 | 4.26 |
| Road | 17 | 86 | 6 | 3 | .667 | 40 | 4.19 |

Randy LERCH

| Year | (W–L) | GS | Run | Avg | DP | Avg | SB | Avg |
|---|---|---|---|---|---|---|---|---|
| 1977 | (10- 6) | 28 | 139 | 4.96 | 35 | 1.25 | 32 | 1.14 |
| 1978 | (11- 8) | 28 | 150 | 5.36 | 22 | .79 | 22 | .79 |
| 1979 | (10-13) | 35 | 150 | 4.29 | 35 | 1.00 | 29 | .79 |
| 1980 | ( 4-14) | 22 | 83 | 3.77 | 16 | .73 | 31 | 1.41 |
| 1981 | ( 7- 9) | 18 | 65 | 3.61 | 23 | 1.28 | 14 | .78 |
| 1982 | ( 8- 7) | 24 | 138 | 5.75 | 33 | 1.38 | 26 | 1.08 |
| 6 years | | 155 | 725 | 4.68 | 164 | 1.06 | 154 | .99 |

| | G | IP | W | L | Pct | ER | ERA |
|---|---|---|---|---|---|---|---|
| Home | DATA UNAVAILABLE (and who cares anyway?) | | | | | | |
| Road | | | | | | | |

Don SUTTON

| Year | (W–L) | GS | Run | Avg | DP | Avg | SB | Avg |
|---|---|---|---|---|---|---|---|---|
| 1976 | (21-10) | 34 | 132 | 3.88 | 28 | .82 | 25 | .74 |
| 1977 | (14- 8) | 33 | 159 | 4.82 | 20 | .61 | 34 | 1.03 |
| 1978 | (15-11) | 34 | 150 | 4.41 | 22 | .65 | 28 | .82 |
| 1979 | (12-15) | 32 | 139 | 4.34 | 21 | .66 | 28 | .88 |
| 1980 | (13- 5) | 31 | 105 | 3.39 | 18 | .58 | 34 | 1.10 |
| 1981 | (11- 9) | 23 | 89 | 3.87 | 11 | .48 | 6 | .26 |
| 1982 | (17- 9) | 34 | 159 | 4.68 | 34 | 1.00 | 34 | 1.00 |
| 7 years | | 221 | 933 | 4.22 | 154 | .70 | 187 | .85 |

| | G | IP | W | L | Pct | ER | ERA |
|---|---|---|---|---|---|---|---|
| Milwaukee | 4 | 33 | 3 | 1 | .750 | 10 | 2.73 |
| Houston | 16 | 124.2 | 7 | 3 | .700 | 31 | 2.24 |
| Road | 14 | 92 | 7 | 5 | .583 | 44 | 4.30 |

1982 OTHERS

| Pitcher | (W–L) | GS | Run | Avg | DP | Avg | SB | Avg |
|---|---|---|---|---|---|---|---|---|
| Slaton | (10-6) | 7 | 40 | 5.71 | 12 | 1.71 | 2 | .29 |
| Augustine | ( 1-3) | 2 | 7 | 3.50 | 3 | 1.50 | 0 | |

## MILWAUKEE

*Talent Analysis*

The Brewers possessed 183 points of approximate value in 1982. This is the highest total in the major leagues not only in 1982, but in the four years that I have been keeping track of that.

| | AV | % |
|---|---|---|
| Produced by Brewers' system: | 84 | 46% |
| Acquired by trade: | 93 | 51% |
| Purchased or signed from free agency: | 6 | 3% |

They are a system-and-trade-built team.

| | | |
|---|---|---|
| Young (Up to age 25): | 2 | 1% |
| Prime (Age 26 to 29): | 89 | 49% |
| Past-prime (Age 30 to 33): | 80 | 44% |
| Old (Age 34 or older): | 12 | 6% |

The Brewers are definitely not a young team, not quite an old team. 50% of their talent is past prime or old; the norm is 38%.

The Brewers' system contributed 134 points of approximate value to the majors in 1982. This ranks them 18th among the 26 teams—and, again, emphasizes that producing talent is not the dominant feature of successful organizations.

## MILWAUKEE COUNTY STADIUM

DIMENSIONS: Short down the lines

SURFACE: Grass

VISIBILITY: —

FOUL TERRITORY: —

FAVORS:
Hitter/Pitcher—Pitcher
Power/Line-drive hitter—Neither
Righthander/Lefthander—Neither

TYPES OF OFFENSE AFFECTED: Reduces runs scored by about 7% and home runs by about 12%

PLAYERS ON TEAM HELPED MOST BY PARK: Vuckovich

PLAYERS ON TEAM HURT MOST BY PARK: Cecil Cooper, Ted Simmons, Robin Yount

OTHER COMMENTS: Well, I've said it before, so I won't hammer on it, but despite all of the hitters who have had great years here, it is *not* a bandbox park by any stretch of the imagination. Aaron, Matthews, Oglivie, Thomas—they all hit most of their home runs on the road. Take a gander at Robin Yount's road statistics.

# BALTIMORE ORIOLES

I wanted to begin the discussion of the Baltimore Orioles and their remarkable little exmanager by putting on record a breakdown of the number of times who scored how many runs in one inning. Earl Weaver and Gene Mauch, as I suppose you know, represent the extreme opposite positions of an old, old argument. Many of the strategic tools in baseball, most prominently the sacrifice bunt and the stolen base, are plays to increase one's chances of scoring one run in the inning. An unfortunate side-effect is that they decrease the chance of scoring 3 or 4 or 5 runs in an inning, since the runner risks or forfeits one of the outs in the inning without doing anything to increase anybody else's chance of scoring. That's why "the book" says that you don't try to steal when you're three or four runs behind.

Anyway, as the public now understands, thanks to Thomas Boswell, Weaver believes that the probable loss on the third or fourth run in the inning is more important than the probable gain on the first, and thus he makes very limited use of the first-run strategies. Mauch makes very extensive use of them, and in particular of the sac bunt. While I don't want to speak for the entire field, I think that it is safe to say that every sabermetrician who has studied the issue agrees with Weaver.

But sabermetrics is a new science, and it is possible, I suppose, that what we believe now will not be what we believe ten years from now. Certainly nobody wants to close off the issue without examining it thoroughly. And that is what this data is doing here. Because one of the things that one needs to know, in order to take a full look at the issue, is how many times a big-inning team does score 3 or 4 or 5 runs in an inning, and how many times a Gene Mauch team scores one in an inning.

This, then, is the data for the American League in 1982:

**NUMBER OF TIMES SCORED**

*X RUNS IN AN INNING*

| Team | 1 | 2 | 3 | 4 | 5 | 6 | 7 | 8 | 9 | 10 | 11 |
|---|---|---|---|---|---|---|---|---|---|---|---|
| Milwaukee | 237 | 131 | 53 | 27 | 13 | 5 | 3 | 0 | 1 | | |
| Baltimore | 218 | 102 | 62 | 22 | 9 | 3 | 1 | 1 | | | |
| Boston | 211 | 100 | 48 | 23 | 12 | 4 | 2 | 1 | | | |
| Detroit | 227 | 128 | 39 | 17 | 6 | 2 | 0 | 1 | 0 | 0 | 1 |
| New York | 221 | 84 | 50 | 21 | 11 | 4 | 1 | | | | |
| Cleveland | 217 | 115 | 34 | 17 | 3 | 6 | 1 | 1 | | | |
| Toronto | 229 | 97 | 48 | 15 | 2 | 0 | 2 | | | | |
| California | 283 | 114 | 39 | 20 | 10 | 4 | 2 | 1 | 0 | 1 | |
| Kansas City | 236 | 100 | 52 | 26 | 11 | 3 | 1 | 1 | | | |
| Chicago | 226 | 108 | 52 | 21 | 14 | 2 | 2 | 1 | | | |
| Seattle | 228 | 85 | 38 | 15 | 6 | 1 | 5 | 1 | | | |
| Oakland | 232 | 105 | 40 | 17 | 11 | 1 | | | | | |
| Minnesota | 199 | 91 | 38 | 19 | 10 | 6 | | | | | |
| Texas | 208 | 83 | 28 | 19 | 6 | 2 | 2 | | | | |

The most basic reaction is that this does verify the images that we had of Weaver and Mauch. Mauch's team had over seven times as many one-run innings as three-run innings, 283-39; Weaver's team had a ratio of 3½ to 1, 218-62. The numbers of runs involved are similar. The Angels had 65 more runs one at a time, the Orioles 69 more in 3-run volleys.

As a one-run-at-a-time team, the Angels stand out like a Puerto Rican at a Republican convention. While 10 of the other 13 teams had 217 to 237 one-run innings and the Brewers were second-high in the league at 237, the Angels had 283 one-run innings. The Orioles, on the other hand, don't stand out in any particular respect as a big-innings team. The data from the chart above is organized in the one below. The Big-Inning Percentage is the percentage of all runs scored in innings of three or more.

| Team | Total Runs | Total Innings In Which Scored | Runs Scored Per Inning | Big Inning % |
|---|---|---|---|---|
| Milwaukee | 891 | 470 | 1.90 | 44.0 |
| Baltimore | 774 | 418 | 1.85 | 45.5 |
| Boston | 753 | 401 | 1.88 | 45.4 |
| Detroit | 729 | 421 | 1.73 | 33.7 |
| New York | 709 | 392 | 1.81 | 45.1 |
| Cleveland | 683 | 394 | 1.73 | 34.6 |
| Toronto | 651 | 393 | 1.66 | 35.0 |
| California | 814 | 474 | 1.72 | 37.2 |
| Kansas City | 784 | 430 | 1.82 | 44.4 |
| Chicago | 786 | 426 | 1.85 | 43.8 |
| Seattle | 651 | 379 | 1.72 | 38.9 |
| Oakland | 691 | 406 | 1.70 | 36.0 |
| Minnesota | 657 | 363 | 1.81 | 42.0 |
| Texas | 590 | 348 | 1.70 | 36.6 |

The Orioles did have the highest big inning percentage in the league, but only by the thinnest possible margin, and their number of runs scored per inning is in the middle of the big-inning group. There is an unusually clear natural grouping of the two types. Milwaukee, Baltimore, Boston, New York, Kansas City, Chicago and Minnesota are big-inning teams, the others are not. All of the big-inning teams score 42 to 46% of their runs in innings of three or more; all of the others are below 39%. All of the big-inning teams score at least 1.81 runs per inning when they score; all of the others are at 1.73 or below. The surprise in the lot is to see Kansas City in the big-inning group, but that is clearly where they belong.

The big-inning teams average 85 wins and 765 runs scored; the others average 77 wins and 687 runs scored. This must be assumed to mean nothing at all, because being a big-inning team is not strictly a choice. If you don't have the horses, you can't just decide that you're going to have big innings. However, there *is* a choice involved. We will call the combined number of sacrifice hits and caught stealing "First-Run Outs," which is shorthand for "outs invested by the manager in first-run strategies."

| BIG—INNING TEAMS | | OTHER TEAMS | |
|---|---|---|---|
| Team | First-Run Outs | Team | First-Run Outs |
| Milwaukee | 108 | California | 167 |
| Baltimore | 95 | Detroit | 107 |
| Boston | 92 | Cleveland | 142 |
| New York | 100 | Toronto | 129 |
| Kansas City | 80 | Oakland | 137 |
| Chicago | 112 | Seattle | 124 |
| Minnesota | 55 | Texas | 109 |

The big-inning teams invested an average of only 92 outs in first-run strategies; the other teams invested an average of 131, or nearly half again as many. The big-inning teams did ground into more double plays than the one-run teams, by an average of 139 to 117 (though a large share of that, again, was created by the fact that the big-inning teams were better teams with more people on base).

I don't have any striking conclusion to draw here. I just have a feeling that somebody who is analyzing offensive decisions someday will find this information awfully valuable, so I wanted to make it available.

A year ago I commented concerning the Orioles that while most managers will rest their regulars in the second game of a double-header, Earl Weaver would often rest his regulars in the *first* game of the twin-bill. By using his complex platooning Weaver would be able to select a first-game lineup which was as strong, in the circumstances, as any lineup would be, and then he would have a clear advantage in the second game. I noted that his record in double-headers was always outstanding—about 50 points better than his record in all games, which ain't bad itself—and I speculated that if you checked, you would find that the Orioles were around their usual won-lost percentage in the first games of double-headers, and picked up the edge in the nightcap.

Well, somebody did, and they are. A man by the name of Clem Comly, of Wallingford, Pennsylvania, figured the Orioles' record in double-headers from 1974 to 1980, broken down by first game, second game, home, road, early season, and late season. The Orioles in that period were 49-33 in the first games of double-headers, a .598 won-lost percentage, but 54-28 in the second games, a .659 percentage. Their overall won-lost percentage for those seven years was .584. All differences, as Mr. Comly notes, are well within the range of chance. He also observes that the Orioles' second-game superiority all comes late in the season, and wonders therefore if the reason for it might not be the depth of their starters.

He did the work; he deserves to have his opinion heard. But I don't buy it. First of all, I don't think that the Orioles' starting pitching is unusually deep, at all; in fact, I think it is unusually shallow. The Orioles, year in and year out, concentrate more of their starts into four or five pitchers than any other team in the American League, and have exceptionally few games which are started by any other pitcher. But more than that, this is not a randomly observed occurrence for which we are now seeking an explanation, but rather a phenomenon which I speculated *should* occur, and which Mr. Comly has confirmed *does* occur. You're going to have a hell of a time convincing me that it occurs for some other reason than the one I suggested. I suggested that the Orioles should dominate the second games of double-headers because Weaver handles his people in such a way that it minimizes the cost of fatigue. Mr. Comly's finding that the Orioles' second-game edge occurs late in the season—the O's were 39-11 in the second games of double headers after the first of July—gibes perfectly with that explanation, if we assume that fatigue is more of a factor late in the season than it is early.

Why did the Orioles under Weaver always play so well late in the year, and so badly early in the year? I promised a thorough study of the effects of fatigue in a pennant race sometime, and I haven't done it this year. What I have done is a brief study of the in-season records of half the teams, the NL West and the AL East. I used the years 1971 to 1980.

Almost every team seemed to hold to a pronounced in-season pattern throughout the decade. The Cincinnati Reds started slowly year in and year out, and hit their stride about mid-July. (See below)

Consider the number of games involved here: that .539 percentage in April represents over a season's worth of April games; the .636 percentage in August covers nearly two seasons. Are these differences statistically significant? Well, if you compare a 103-59 team (.636) to an 87-75 team (.537), do you wonder whether the difference between them is significant? The Reds had a .600 or better won-lost percentage in August in nine of the ten seasons; they had a .600 won-lost percentage in April only three times.

The team that the Reds were locked in combat with, the Dodgers, maintained an opposite pattern. (See below)

The Dodgers had a better record on May 31 than they would finish the year with in nine of the ten seasons.

Why? I couldn't say that I know. One suggestion for why the Orioles start so badly is that the inclement Aprils of the East Coast disrupt their schedule to such a point that it makes it difficult to get rolling. It is a fact that the Orioles played an average of 18 games a year in April and 26 in May, while the Dodgers played 21 and 27.

It is also true that the San Francisco Giants, averaging 21 in April and 28 in May, played well early in the season. The Padres, who had the same averages, didn't; the Dodgers had to have somebody to beat. The Astros,

| | April | May | June | July | August | September | October | Total |
|---|---|---|---|---|---|---|---|---|
| Reds | 104-89 | 153-121 | 160-124 | 174-119 | 182-104 | 157-109 | 10-5 | 940-670 |
| | .539 | .558 | .563 | .594 | .636 | .593 | .667 | .584 |

| | April | May | June | July | August | September | October | Total |
|---|---|---|---|---|---|---|---|---|
| Los Angeles | 103-80 | 160-111 | 196-133 | 140-137 | 167-117 | 162-113 | 10-7 | 915-698 |
| | .619 | .590 | .523 | .505 | .588 | .589 | .588 | .567 |

|  | April | May | June | July | August | September | October | Total |
|---|---|---|---|---|---|---|---|---|
| Cincinnati | 193 .539 | 274 .558 | 284 .563 | 293 .594 | 286 .636 | 265 .593 | 15 .663 | 1610 .584 |
| Houston | 211 .545 | 268 .466 | 275 .505 | 294 .486 | 283 .516 | 264 .500 | 16 .357 | 1611 .501 |
| Los Angeles | 210 .619 | 271 .590 | 279 .523 | 277 .505 | 284 .588 | 275 .589 | 17 .588 | 1613 .567 |
| Atlanta | 197 .416 | 270 .407 | 288 .493 | 287 .481 | 285 .477 | 264 .443 | 16 .313 | 1607 .454 |
| San Francisco | 206 .500 | 279 .516 | 285 .463 | 286 .536 | 278 .464 | 272 .441 | 15 .467 | 1611 .486 |
| San Diego | 206 .379 | 283 .452 | 280 .421 | 280 .429 | 282 .411 | 262 .412 | 16 .563 | 1609 .421 |
| Baltimore | 179 .508 | 263 .529 | 281 .594 | 288 .601 | 287 .596 | 288 .646 | 14 .643 | 1600 .585 |
| Boston | 173 .503 | 266 .568 | 272 .592 | 301 .532 | 291 .574 | 287 .551 | 17 .412 | 1607 .554 |
| Milwaukee | 166 .524 | 268 .459 | 283 .530 | 300 .460 | 306 .444 | 273 .432 | 15 .467 | 1611 .471 |
| New York | 182 .511 | 271 .546 | 278 .565 | 293 .549 | 286 .573 | 279 .609 | 18 .500 | 1607 .561 |
| Cleveland | 173 .405 | 265 .498 | 281 .473 | 292 .449 | 299 .502 | 276 .424 | 15 .467 | 1601 .462 |
| Detroit | 171 .515 | 263 .483 | 284 .500 | 296 .533 | 300 .487 | 278 .446 | 17 .529 | 1609 .493 |
| Toronto | 80 .425 | 107 .327 | 110 .373 | 113 .345 | 117 .410 | 111 .288 | 8 .500 | 646 .361 |

who never lose a game to the weather, have the same pattern as the Dodgers, at a lower level. The Yankees, who also lose a lot of games early in the year, had pretty much the same pattern as the Orioles. All the details and more are shown in the chart above; categories are games played and won-lost percentages in the month:

These charts qualify for inclusion in the *Abstract* because they contain clearly nonrandom patterns of significant import in calculating the dynamics of a pennant race. Or you will have to convince me that, over the course of more than 200 games, the fact that Houston played better than Cincinnati in April is merely a random coincidence.

Anyway, there are several theories about why the Orioles have the in-season pattern that they do. Various people attribute it to:

1) the schedule;
2) the depth of the Orioles' pitchers;
3) reduction of fatigue due to platooning;
4) Weaver's patience with his starting corps;
5) the increased importance of fundamentals late in the season;
6) other changes in what types of offense work best at various times of the season; and
7) that the Orioles had a few big players who were consistent slow starters.

What do I attribute it to? I don't know. All of these theories, you see, can be checked out. All of them have logical consequences which you can check out if you really want to know. And that is what is frustrating about being a sabermetrician—having so many more records and so many more theories than you can possibly ever study. There are so many tracks in the snow that you can't begin to follow them all, and you never know for sure which track will lead you to the quarry.

Back to the serious business.

The only question in my mind concerning the Baltimore Orioles in the post-Weaver era is whether they will fall apart this year or next. The problems that this team presents to the incoming manager are immense. If Singleton doesn't bounce back, an ordinary season from the platooning leftfielders could leave Murray and Ripken as the Orioles' offense. At this writing (mid-December) there is either no third baseman or no shortstop; there is no surplus of talent anywhere that can be used to plug the gap without opening another one. The starting rotation is mediocre to bad. The best starter is a 37-year-old man who probably shouldn't pitch more than 225 innings. The center fielder is washed up; the man ticketed to replace him isn't going to hit.

Weaver disguised these weaknesses with a shell game of incomprehensible complexity. Nobody else knows that trick. It is a team built of, by, and for Earl Weaver. Even if it were a good team—which it isn't, without Earl Weaver—the new manager would still find himself at the controls of a machine custom-built for somebody else.

The demise of this team is not inevitable in 1983. Maybe Gary Roenicke, given more playing time, will break loose and drive in 110 runs, draw 120 walks. Disco Dan could make a comeback. That would give the Orioles three big bats in the middle of their lineup, which if the pitching rotation were to hold up for a year might keep them in contention.

I've got doubts about that. I'd say it's 60-40 this year, the 60% being for a target of 88 wins or above, the 40% heading for 75. For 1984, it's 50-50. But there is no doubt in my mind that the public is shortly going to find out just how good a manager Earl Weaver is.

Eddie MURRAY, First Base

*Runs Created: 119*

|  | G | AB | R | H | 2B | 3B | HR | RBI | SB | Avg |
|---|---|---|---|---|---|---|---|---|---|---|
| First Half | 71 | 242 | 35 | 74 | 17 | 1 | 13 | 50 | 3 | .306 |
| Second Half | 80 | 308 | 52 | 100 | 13 | 0 | 19 | 60 | 4 | .325 |
| Home | 79 | 287 | 55 | 97 | 14 | 0 | 18 | 58 | 4 | .338 |
| Road | 72 | 263 | 32 | 77 | 16 | 1 | 14 | 52 | 3 | .293 |
| vs. RHP |  | 366 | 60 | 106 | 20 | 0 | 21 | 78 | 6 | .290 |
| vs. LHP |  | 184 | 27 | 68 | 10 | 1 | 11 | 32 | 1 | .370 |
| 1982 | 151 | 550 | 87 | 174 | 30 | 1 | 32 | 110 | 7 | .316 |
| 5.48 years |  | 616 | 91 | 182 | 33 | 2 | 30 | 107 | 6 | .295 |

Rich DAUER, Second Base

*Runs Created: 70*

|  | G | AB | R | H | 2B | 3B | HR | RBI | SB | Avg |
|---|---|---|---|---|---|---|---|---|---|---|
| First Half | 80 | 306 | 46 | 89 | 16 | 0 | 5 | 26 | 0 | .291 |
| Second Half | 78 | 252 | 29 | 67 | 8 | 2 | 3 | 31 | 0 | .266 |
| Home | 80 | 274 | 38 | 70 | 12 | 1 | 4 | 32 | 0 | .255 |
| Road | 78 | 284 | 37 | 86 | 12 | 1 | 4 | 25 | 0 | .303 |
| vs. RHP |  | 384 | 48 | 103 | 13 | 1 | 4 | 28 | 0 | .268 |
| vs. LHP |  | 174 | 27 | 53 | 11 | 1 | 4 | 19 | 0 | .305 |
| 1982 | 158 | 558 | 75 | 156 | 24 | 2 | 8 | 57 | 0 | .280 |
| 4.86 years |  | 569 | 71 | 151 | 29 | 1 | 7 | 60 | 1 | .265 |

Cal RIPKEN, Third Base/Shortstop

*Runs Created: 89*

| | G | AB | R | H | 2B | 3B | HR | RBI | SB | Avg |
|---|---|---|---|---|---|---|---|---|---|---|
| First Half | 80 | 297 | 39 | 80 | 19 | 4 | 11 | 46 | 2 | .269 |
| Second Half | 80 | 301 | 51 | 78 | 13 | 1 | 17 | 47 | 1 | .259 |
| Home | 80 | 289 | 38 | 71 | 14 | 1 | 11 | 48 | 2 | .246 |
| Road | 80 | 309 | 52 | 87 | 18 | 4 | 17 | 45 | 1 | .282 |
| vs. RHP | | 429 | 60 | 110 | 24 | 4 | 16 | 64 | 2 | .256 |
| vs. LHP | | 169 | 30 | 48 | 8 | 1 | 12 | 29 | 1 | .284 |
| 1982 | 160 | 598 | 90 | 158 | 32 | 5 | 28 | 93 | 3 | .264 |
| 1.13 years | | 564 | 81 | 144 | 28 | 4 | 25 | 82 | 3 | .256 |

Len SAKATA, Shortstop

*Runs Created: 40*

| | G | AB | R | H | 2B | 3B | HR | RBI | SB | Avg |
|---|---|---|---|---|---|---|---|---|---|---|
| First Half | 68 | 197 | 24 | 49 | 9 | 1 | 2 | 13 | 5 | .249 |
| Second Half | 68 | 146 | 16 | 40 | 9 | 0 | 4 | 18 | 2 | .274 |
| Home | 71 | 152 | 22 | 42 | 5 | 1 | 3 | 12 | 6 | .276 |
| Road | 65 | 191 | 18 | 47 | 13 | 0 | 3 | 19 | 1 | .246 |
| vs. RHP | | 198 | 21 | 51 | 14 | 1 | 3 | 18 | 6 | .258 |
| vs. LHP | | 145 | 19 | 38 | 4 | 0 | 3 | 13 | 1 | .262 |
| 1982 | 136 | 343 | 40 | 89 | 18 | 1 | 6 | 31 | 7 | .259 |
| 2.01 years | | 409 | 46 | 93 | 16 | 2 | 7 | 35 | 8 | .226 |

John LOWENSTEIN, Left Field

*Runs Created: 79*

| | G | AB | R | H | 2B | 3B | HR | RBI | SB | Avg |
|---|---|---|---|---|---|---|---|---|---|---|
| First Half | 58 | 151 | 33 | 46 | 5 | 1 | 13 | 33 | 0 | .305 |
| Second Half | 64 | 171 | 36 | 57 | 10 | 1 | 11 | 33 | 7 | .333 |
| Home | 60 | 153 | 33 | 48 | 6 | 0 | 10 | 34 | 4 | .314 |
| Road | 62 | 169 | 36 | 55 | 9 | 2 | 14 | 32 | 3 | .325 |
| vs. RHP | | 315 | 69 | 102 | 15 | 2 | 24 | 65 | 7 | .324 |
| vs. LHP | | 7 | 0 | 1 | 0 | 0 | 0 | 1 | 0 | .143 |
| 1982 | 122 | 322 | 69 | 103 | 15 | 2 | 24 | 66 | 7 | .320 |
| 6.96 years | | 412 | 61 | 105 | 16 | 2 | 13 | 50 | 18 | .254 |

Dan FORD, Right Field

*Runs Created: 42*

| | G | AB | R | H | 2B | 3B | HR | RBI | SB | Avg |
|---|---|---|---|---|---|---|---|---|---|---|
| First Half | 70 | 268 | 28 | 67 | 19 | 2 | 6 | 33 | 2 | .250 |
| Second Half | 53 | 153 | 18 | 32 | 2 | 1 | 4 | 10 | 3 | .209 |
| Home | 61 | 192 | 21 | 39 | 6 | 1 | 5 | 16 | 2 | .203 |
| Road | 62 | 229 | 25 | 60 | 15 | 2 | 5 | 27 | 3 | .262 |
| vs. RHP | | 241 | 21 | 52 | 11 | 2 | 3 | 24 | 2 | .216 |
| vs. LHP | | 180 | 25 | 47 | 10 | 1 | 7 | 19 | 3 | .261 |
| 1982 | 123 | 421 | 46 | 99 | 21 | 3 | 10 | 43 | 5 | .235 |
| 6.15 years | | 584 | 85 | 158 | 29 | 6 | 18 | 82 | 8 | .271 |

Gary ROENICKE, Center Field

*Runs Created: 70*

| | G | AB | R | H | 2B | 3B | HR | RBI | SB | Avg |
|---|---|---|---|---|---|---|---|---|---|---|
| First Half | 67 | 208 | 30 | 52 | 11 | 0 | 15 | 44 | 2 | .250 |
| Second Half | 70 | 185 | 28 | 54 | 14 | 1 | 6 | 30 | 4 | .292 |
| Home | 67 | 183 | 27 | 44 | 12 | 0 | 6 | 33 | 2 | .240 |
| Road | 70 | 210 | 31 | 62 | 13 | 1 | 15 | 41 | 4 | .295 |
| vs. RHP | | 240 | 30 | 63 | 14 | 0 | 13 | 50 | 5 | .263 |
| vs. LHP | | 153 | 28 | 43 | 11 | 1 | 8 | 24 | 1 | .281 |
| 1982 | 137 | 393 | 58 | 106 | 25 | 1 | 21 | 74 | 6 | .270 |
| 3.27 years | | 438 | 62 | 113 | 23 | 1 | 20 | 63 | 3 | .258 |

Rick DEMPSEY, Catcher

*Runs Created: 40*

| | G | AB | R | H | 2B | 3B | HR | RBI | SB | Avg |
|---|---|---|---|---|---|---|---|---|---|---|
| First Half | 63 | 186 | 22 | 40 | 5 | 0 | 5 | 18 | 0 | .215 |
| Second Half | 62 | 158 | 13 | 48 | 10 | 1 | 0 | 18 | 0 | .304 |
| Home | 65 | 168 | 13 | 46 | 8 | 0 | 2 | 20 | 0 | .274 |
| Road | 60 | 176 | 22 | 42 | 7 | 1 | 3 | 16 | 0 | .239 |
| vs. RHP | | 214 | 25 | 56 | 7 | 1 | 3 | 21 | 0 | .262 |
| vs. LHP | | 130 | 10 | 32 | 8 | 0 | 2 | 15 | 0 | .246 |
| 1982 | 125 | 344 | 35 | 88 | 15 | 1 | 5 | 36 | 0 | .256 |
| 5.73 years | | 451 | 48 | 109 | 21 | 2 | 7 | 41 | 3 | .241 |

Ken SINGLETON, Designated Hitter

*Runs Created: 75*

| | G | AB | R | H | 2B | 3B | HR | RBI | SB | Avg |
|---|---|---|---|---|---|---|---|---|---|---|
| First Half | 81 | 299 | 40 | 82 | 14 | 0 | 6 | 42 | 0 | .274 |
| Second Half | 75 | 262 | 31 | 59 | 13 | 2 | 8 | 35 | 0 | .225 |
| Home | 79 | 272 | 43 | 64 | 12 | 1 | 9 | 43 | 0 | .235 |
| Road | 77 | 289 | 28 | 77 | 15 | 1 | 5 | 34 | 0 | .266 |
| vs. RHP | | 414 | 62 | 115 | 22 | 1 | 14 | 64 | 0 | .278 |
| vs. LHP | | 147 | 9 | 26 | 5 | 1 | 0 | 13 | 0 | .177 |
| 1982 | 156 | 561 | 71 | 141 | 27 | 2 | 14 | 77 | 0 | .251 |
| 11.24 years | | 562 | 81 | 161 | 26 | 2 | 20 | 84 | 2 | .287 |

Dennis MARTINEZ

| Year | (W–L) | GS | Run | Avg | DP | Avg | SB | Avg |
|---|---|---|---|---|---|---|---|---|
| 1977 | (14- 7) | 13 | 77 | 5.92 | 17 | 1.31 | 5 | .39 |
| 1978 | (16-11) | 38 | 173 | 4.55 | 43 | 1.13 | 28 | .74 |
| 1979 | (15-16) | 39 | 156 | 4.00 | 35 | .90 | 36 | .92 |
| 1980 | ( 6- 4) | 12 | 53 | 4.42 | 13 | 1.09 | 14 | 1.17 |
| 1981 | (14- 5) | 24 | 105 | 4.38 | 18 | .75 | 18 | .75 |
| 1982 | (16-12) | 39 | 184 | 4.72 | 34 | .87 | 35 | .90 |
| 6 years | | 165 | 748 | 4.50 | 160 | .97 | 136 | .82 |

| | G | IP | W | L | Pct | ER | ERA |
|---|---|---|---|---|---|---|---|
| Home | 23 | 135.1 | 10 | 4 | .714 | 74 | 4.92 |
| Road | 17 | 116.2 | 6 | 8 | .429 | 44 | 3.39 |

Scott McGREGOR

| Year | (W–L) | GS | Run | Avg | DP | Avg | SB | Avg |
|---|---|---|---|---|---|---|---|---|
| 1977 | ( 3- 5) | 5 | 22 | 4.40 | 3 | .60 | 1 | .20 |
| 1978 | (15-13) | 32 | 115 | 3.59 | 31 | .97 | 10 | .31 |
| 1979 | (13- 6) | 23 | 112 | 4.87 | 21 | .91 | 8 | .35 |
| 1980 | (20- 8) | 36 | 194 | 5.39 | 38 | 1.06 | 15 | .42 |
| 1981 | (13- 5) | 22 | 97 | 4.41 | 26 | 1.18 | 10 | .45 |
| 1982 | (14-12) | 37 | 175 | 4.73 | 28 | .76 | 17 | .46 |
| 6 years | | 155 | 715 | 4.61 | 147 | .95 | 61 | .39 |

| | G | IP | W | L | Pct | ER | ERA |
|---|---|---|---|---|---|---|---|
| Home | 20 | 120 | 7 | 6 | .538 | 60 | 4.50 |
| Road | 17 | 106.1 | 7 | 6 | .538 | 56 | 4.74 |

Mike FLANAGAN

| Year | (W–L) | GS | Run | Avg | DP | Avg | SB | Avg |
|---|---|---|---|---|---|---|---|---|
| 1977 | (15-10) | 33 | 149 | 4.52 | 45 | 1.36 | 18 | .55 |
| 1978 | (19-15) | 40 | 170 | 4.25 | 45 | 1.12 | 14 | .35 |
| 1979 | (23- 9) | 38 | 186 | 4.89 | 42 | 1.11 | 11 | .29 |
| 1980 | (16-13) | 37 | 166 | 4.49 | 42 | 1.14 | 18 | .49 |
| 1981 | ( 9- 6) | 20 | 83 | 4.15 | 23 | 1.15 | 4 | .20 |
| 1982 | (15-11) | 35 | 164 | 4.69 | 33 | .94 | 17 | .49 |
| 6 years | | 203 | 918 | 4.52 | 230 | 1.13 | 82 | .40 |

| | G | IP | W | L | Pct | ER | ERA |
|---|---|---|---|---|---|---|---|
| Home | 18 | 120 | 9 | 4 | .692 | 50 | 3.75 |
| Road | 18 | 116 | 6 | 7 | .462 | 54 | 4.19 |

Jim PALMER

| Year | (W–L) | GS | Run | Avg | DP | Avg | SB | Avg |
|---|---|---|---|---|---|---|---|---|
| 1976 | (22-13) | 40 | 133 | 3.33 | 34 | .85 | 36 | .90 |
| 1977 | (20-11) | 39 | 164 | 4.21 | 33 | .85 | 18 | .46 |
| 1978 | (21-12) | 38 | 141 | 3.71 | 38 | 1.00 | 21 | .55 |
| 1979 | (10- 6) | 22 | 124 | 5.64 | 24 | 1.09 | 8 | .36 |
| 1980 | (16-10) | 33 | 167 | 5.06 | 33 | 1.00 | 24 | .73 |
| 1981 | ( 7- 8) | 22 | 91 | 4.14 | 28 | 1.27 | 13 | .59 |
| 1982 | (15- 5) | 32 | 150 | 4.69 | 24 | .75 | 12 | .38 |
| 7 years | | 226 | 970 | 4.29 | 214 | .95 | 132 | .58 |

| | G | IP | W | L | Pct | ER | ERA |
|---|---|---|---|---|---|---|---|
| Home | 15 | 106.1 | 7 | 4 | .636 | 33 | 2.79 |
| Road | 21 | 120.2 | 8 | 1 | .889 | 46 | 3.43 |

1982 OTHERS

| Pitcher | (W–L) | GS | Run | Avg | DP | Avg | SB | Avg |
|---|---|---|---|---|---|---|---|---|
| Stewart | (10-9) | 12 | 58 | 4.83 | 12 | 1.00 | 11 | .92 |
| Davis | ( 8-4) | 8 | 43 | 5.38 | 7 | .88 | 6 | .75 |

## BALTIMORE

*Talent Analysis*

The Orioles in 1982 possessed 175 points of approximate value.

| | AV | % |
|---|---|---|
| Produced by Orioles' system: | 105 | 64% |
| Acquired by trade: | 46 | 28% |
| Purchased or signed from free agency: | 14 | 8% |

They are a system-built team.

| | | |
|---|---|---|
| Young (Up to age 25): | 19 | 12% |
| Prime (Age 26 to 29): | 68 | 41% |
| Past-prime (Age 30 to 33): | 38 | 23% |
| Old (Age 34 or older): | 40 | 24% |

They are a little older than average.

The Orioles' system produced 169 points worth of talent for the 1982 season. This ranked eighth in the major leagues. Over the last four years, they rank twelfth.

## MEMORIAL STADIUM

DIMENSIONS: Short at the lines

SURFACE: Grass

VISIBILITY: Poor, particularly in daytime

FOUL TERRITORY: Normal to large

FAVORS:
Hitter/Pitcher—Pitcher
Power/Line-drive hitter—Power
Righthander/Lefthander—Neither

TYPES OF OFFENSE AFFECTED: Reduces batting averages 10 to 15 points; reduces home runs 5 to 7%, but the park still favors a short-sequence offense

OTHER PARK CHARACTERISTICS: The high concrete walls slanting across the outfield ricochet everything toward center and allow the Orioles to bunch their outfielders, effectively eliminating the power alleys. Triples are down 40% in this park. This also enables the Orioles to survive without a fast defensive outfield.

TYPES OF MARGINAL PLAYERS MOST VALUABLE IN PARK: Sluggers with limited mobility

PLAYERS ON TEAM HELPED MOST BY PARK: Dennis Martinez

PLAYERS ON TEAM HURT MOST BY PARK: Rich Dauer

# BOSTON RED SOX

There is only one man in baseball today, I think, who has a position all to himself. That man, of course, is Bob Stanley, and his unique role is that of Long Reliever Who Can Actually Pitch. He represents a new strategy, and thus a new series of questions, a new series of evaluative problems for sabermetricians. How valuable is Stanley to the Red Sox? Should he have been considered for the Cy Young Award? Would he be more valuable to the team as a starter? Is this a coming strategy?

I wouldn't exactly say that the designated-hitter rule brought Bob Stanley's role into existence, but the DH rule is compatible with the use of a quality pitcher as a long reliever, in several ways. The most important is that the rule makes it possible to keep a long reliever in the game when you are behind. In the NL, if you get 3 or 4 runs behind you are compelled to pinch hit for the pitcher almost every time he comes up. That simple fact has always put the possibility of using a quality pitcher in that role out of the question.

There are a couple of other things . . . The DH rule reduces the number of pinch hitters and defensive substitutes needed, and thus clears space on the roster for another specialty to evolve. The DH rule increases the number of runs scored, and thus presumably increases the chance that you can come back and win even if you get behind early, hence making it more profitable to invest a good pitcher in the effort to keep the game in hand. On certain teams, at least, on Boston and Milwaukee and Kansas City. On the Texas Rangers, a good long relief man would be about as much use to you as a Brockabrella in a hailstorm.

Whether or not this new strategy will take hold, it seems safe to say, will not be determined by mathematical inference. I believe in the Natural Selection of Strategies. If a team tries something and wins, other teams will follow; if a team tries something and loses, nobody else imitates it. If the imitating team tries it and goes into a slump, they'll stop; if they try it and get hot, they'll keep it up. Successful managers stay around while unsuccessful managers learn to sell insurance, and therefore the strategies of the successful managers stay around, too. By small degrees and over a painfully long period of time, the best strategies come into use and the worst die out, and all a sabermetrician can do is speed up the process a little.

This one, anyway, seems to be catching on. Slaton was doing the same job for Milwaukee much of the year, Armstrong for Kansas City part of the year. Ralph Houk received a lot of praise for his handling of the bullpen last year.

Well, I don't mean to duck the argument. I've got one real serious reservation about Houk's use of his bullpen. I think there is a strong tendency, in any hitter's park, to go to the bullpen too often and too early. I think that that destroys the starting corps over the course of a season. It is an unavoidable fact that the teams which play in the best hitter's parks in baseball—Fenway, Wrigley, County Stadium in Atlanta, Tiger Stadium—win obviously fewer championships than their share, and that the group of teams which play in the pitcher's parks—Yankee, Memorial in Baltimore, Dodger Stadium are in the group—win more than their share. I think that there is a connection. I think that it is easier to build and maintain a starting rotation in a pitcher's park than it is in one that favors the hitter. There is no getting around it: When you take a pitcher out of the game in the fourth or fifth inning, you are telling that pitcher that he has failed. As far as I'm concerned, the less often you have to tell him that, the better. What I would want my manager to tell his pitchers is this: "Look, this park isn't going to give you any breaks. The hitter sees the ball great here. Sometimes you're going to get a little pop foul that would get you out of the inning anywhere else, and it's going to get into the stands. Fly balls are going to bounce off the wall for doubles, and sometimes they're going to glide on out of here. You're going to give up some runs. I am *not* going to come and get you whenever you get into trouble. Sometimes you're going to give up five or six or even seven runs, and I'm going to tell you to tough it out." What Houk is telling his pitchers, by going to the bullpen so early, is just the opposite. I think I'd use Bob Stanley to improve the starting rotation, rather than using him to weaken it.

I am presenting with the Red Sox this year the career records at home and on the road of several Red Sox stars, past and present (see pages 87-88). I did the same with the Yankees. I purchased this data from the man who compiled it, Pete Palmer. I am presenting it here as a part of my campaign to put to rest the last doubts that some people still have about the fundamental fact that ballparks dramatically alter the records of those who play there. But mostly I'm presenting them because I think they're fascinating. I mean, people like to argue about whether this guy was helped by Fenway or that guy was or how much, or how do Ted Williams and Joe DiMaggio compare when you get them out of their home parks, or how many home runs would Babe Ruth have hit if it hadn't been for Yankee Stadium, or is Yankee really that tough for a right-handed batter, or does Fenway help a singles hitter like Pesky or lefthander like Yaz or Lynn? I was excited when I found out that somebody really had the goods on these matters. I wish I had room to print a lot more of it. Hope you share a little of that excitement.

The Red Sox set a major league for grounding into double plays, 171 as a team.

## **TED WILLIAMS** CAREER HOME AND ROAD BREAKDOWNS

| | *In Fenway Park* | | | | | | | | | *On The Road* | | | | | | | | |
|---|---|---|---|---|---|---|---|---|---|---|---|---|---|---|---|---|---|---|
| **Year** | **G** | **AB** | **R** | **H** | **2B** | **3B** | **HR** | **RBI** | **Avg** | **G** | **AB** | **R** | **H** | **2B** | **3B** | **HR** | **RBI** | **Avg** |
| 1938 | 75 | 277 | 74 | 95 | 22 | 5 | 14 | 68 | .343 | 74 | 288 | 57 | 90 | 22 | 6 | 17 | 77 | .313 |
| 1940 | 76 | 297 | 69 | 101 | 28 | 5 | 9 | 60 | .340 | 68 | 264 | 65 | 92 | 15 | 9 | 14 | 53 | .348 |
| 1941 | 75 | 243 | 72 | 104 | 21 | 2 | 19 | 62 | .428 | 68 | 213 | 63 | 81 | 12 | 1 | 18 | 58 | .380 |
| 1942 | 75 | 261 | 73 | 93 | 21 | 3 | 16 | 68 | .356 | 75 | 261 | 68 | 93 | 13 | 2 | 20 | 69 | .356 |
| 1946 | 76 | 266 | 74 | 98 | 21 | 4 | 18 | 69 | .368 | 74 | 248 | 68 | 78 | 16 | 4 | 20 | 54 | .315 |
| 1947 | 81 | 277 | 67 | 92 | 24 | 6 | 16 | 63 | .332 | 75 | 251 | 58 | 89 | 16 | 3 | 16 | 51 | .355 |
| 1948 | 66 | 239 | 57 | 88 | 23 | 1 | 9 | 66 | .368 | 71 | 270 | 67 | 100 | 21 | 2 | 16 | 61 | .370 |
| 1949 | 77 | 272 | 87 | 95 | 27 | 1 | 23 | 86 | .349 | 78 | 294 | 63 | 99 | 12 | 2 | 20 | 73 | .337 |
| 1950 | 43 | 160 | 50 | 57 | 13 | 0 | 16 | 56 | .356 | 46 | 174 | 32 | 49 | 11 | 1 | 12 | 41 | .282 |
| 1951 | 73 | 268 | 69 | 108 | 22 | 3 | 18 | 81 | .403 | 75 | 263 | 40 | 61 | 6 | 1 | 12 | 45 | .232 |
| 1952 | 4 | 6 | 1 | 3 | 0 | 0 | 1 | 3 | .500 | 2 | 4 | 1 | 1 | 0 | 1 | 0 | 0 | .250 |
| 1953 | 19 | 47 | 10 | 17 | 4 | 0 | 8 | 18 | .362 | 18 | 44 | 7 | 20 | 2 | 0 | 5 | 16 | .455 |
| 1954 | 58 | 186 | 48 | 69 | 12 | 0 | 16 | 39 | .371 | 59 | 200 | 45 | 64 | 11 | 1 | 13 | 50 | .320 |
| 1955 | 54 | 172 | 48 | 67 | 11 | 1 | 15 | 47 | .390 | 44 | 148 | 29 | 47 | 10 | 2 | 13 | 36 | .318 |
| 1956 | 72 | 205 | 39 | 74 | 19 | 2 | 10 | 43 | .361 | 64 | 195 | 32 | 64 | 9 | 0 | 14 | 39 | .328 |
| 1957 | 63 | 206 | 42 | 83 | 19 | 0 | 12 | 36 | .403 | 69 | 214 | 54 | 80 | 9 | 1 | 26 | 51 | .374 |
| 1958 | 66 | 207 | 47 | 68 | 14 | 2 | 10 | 41 | .329 | 63 | 204 | 34 | 67 | 9 | 0 | 16 | 44 | .328 |
| 1959 | 52 | 134 | 14 | 37 | 10 | 0 | 3 | 21 | .276 | 51 | 138 | 18 | 32 | 5 | 0 | 7 | 22 | .232 |
| 1960 | 60 | 164 | 32 | 54 | 8 | 0 | 15 | 38 | .329 | 53 | 146 | 24 | 44 | 7 | 0 | 14 | 34 | .301 |
| Career | 1165 | 3887 | 973 | 1403 | 319 | 35 | 248 | 965 | .361 | 1127 | 3819 | 825 | 1251 | 206 | 36 | 273 | 874 | .328 |

## **BOBBY DOERR** CAREER HOME AND ROAD BREAKDOWNS

| | *In Fenway Park* | | | | | | | | | *On The Road* | | | | | | | | |
|---|---|---|---|---|---|---|---|---|---|---|---|---|---|---|---|---|---|---|
| **Year** | **G** | **AB** | **R** | **H** | **2B** | **3B** | **HR** | **RBI** | **Avg** | **G** | **AB** | **R** | **H** | **2B** | **3B** | **HR** | **RBI** | **Avg** |
| 1937 | 22 | 52 | 11 | 12 | 1 | 1 | 2 | 8 | .231 | 33 | 95 | 11 | 21 | 4 | 0 | 0 | 6 | .221 |
| 1938 | 74 | 259 | 39 | 84 | 20 | 4 | 5 | 43 | .324 | 71 | 250 | 31 | 63 | 6 | 3 | 0 | 37 | .252 |
| 1939 | 59 | 239 | 37 | 78 | 11 | 0 | 7 | 44 | .326 | 68 | 286 | 38 | 89 | 17 | 2 | 5 | 29 | .311 |
| 1940 | 76 | 291 | 47 | 87 | 20 | 3 | 16 | 61 | .299 | 75 | 304 | 40 | 86 | 17 | 7 | 6 | 44 | .283 |
| 1941 | 66 | 238 | 39 | 77 | 21 | 2 | 11 | 54 | .324 | 66 | 262 | 35 | 64 | 7 | 2 | 5 | 39 | .244 |
| 1942 | 72 | 257 | 40 | 88 | 26 | 3 | 8 | 55 | .342 | 72 | 288 | 31 | 70 | 9 | 2 | 7 | 47 | .243 |
| 1943 | 77 | 295 | 36 | 85 | 20 | 2 | 9 | 38 | .288 | 78 | 309 | 42 | 78 | 12 | 1 | 7 | 37 | .252 |
| 1944 | 74 | 276 | 60 | 97 | 19 | 8 | 11 | 57 | .351 | 51 | 192 | 35 | 55 | 11 | 2 | 4 | 24 | .286 |
| 1946 | 78 | 303 | 65 | 95 | 25 | 2 | 13 | 72 | .314 | 73 | 280 | 30 | 63 | 9 | 7 | 5 | 44 | .225 |
| 1947 | 81 | 316 | 53 | 87 | 14 | 7 | 12 | 60 | .275 | 65 | 245 | 26 | 58 | 9 | 3 | 5 | 35 | .237 |
| 1948 | 72 | 257 | 57 | 82 | 17 | 2 | 19 | 71 | .319 | 68 | 270 | 37 | 68 | 6 | 4 | 8 | 40 | .252 |
| 1949 | 72 | 276 | 53 | 83 | 21 | 3 | 9 | 52 | .301 | 67 | 265 | 38 | 84 | 9 | 6 | 9 | 57 | .317 |
| 1950 | 77 | 305 | 68 | 105 | 19 | 7 | 18 | 86 | .344 | 72 | 281 | 35 | 67 | 10 | 4 | 9 | 34 | .238 |
| 1951 | 54 | 190 | 29 | 59 | 12 | 2 | 5 | 42 | .311 | 52 | 212 | 31 | 57 | 9 | 0 | 8 | 31 | .269 |
| Career | 954 | 3554 | 634 | 1119 | 246 | 46 | 145 | 743 | .315 | 911 | 3539 | 460 | 923 | 135 | 43 | 78 | 504 | .261 |

## **FRED LYNN** CAREER HOME AND ROAD BREAKDOWNS

| | *At Home* | | | | | | | | | *On The Road* | | | | | | | | |
|---|---|---|---|---|---|---|---|---|---|---|---|---|---|---|---|---|---|---|
| **Year** | **G** | **AB** | **R** | **H** | **2B** | **3B** | **HR** | **RBI** | **Avg** | **G** | **AB** | **R** | **H** | **2B** | **3B** | **HR** | **RBI** | **Avg** |
| 1974 | 8 | 23 | 3 | 10 | 1 | 1 | 1 | 6 | .435 | 7 | 20 | 2 | 8 | 1 | 1 | 1 | 4 | .400 |
| 1975 | 76 | 266 | 54 | 98 | 29 | 4 | 9 | 53 | .368 | 69 | 262 | 49 | 77 | 18 | 3 | 12 | 52 | .294 |
| 1976 | 63 | 239 | 45 | 86 | 21 | 6 | 4 | 39 | .360 | 69 | 268 | 31 | 73 | 11 | 2 | 6 | 26 | .272 |
| 1977 | 61 | 227 | 45 | 71 | 20 | 3 | 10 | 45 | .313 | 68 | 270 | 36 | 58 | 9 | 2 | 8 | 31 | .215 |
| 1978 | 76 | 276 | 47 | 86 | 19 | 2 | 11 | 47 | .312 | 74 | 265 | 28 | 75 | 14 | 1 | 11 | 35 | .283 |
| 1979 | 77 | 277 | 76 | 107 | 30 | 0 | 28 | 83 | .386 | 70 | 254 | 40 | 70 | 12 | 1 | 11 | 39 | .276 |
| 1980 | 51 | 174 | 33 | 60 | 18 | 3 | 6 | 32 | .345 | 59 | 241 | 34 | 65 | 14 | 0 | 6 | 29 | .270 |
| 1981* | 39 | 125 | 14 | 34 | 5 | 0 | 3 | 17 | .272 | 37 | 131 | 14 | 22 | 3 | 1 | 2 | 17 | .168 |
| 1982* | 71 | 251 | 51 | 73 | 18 | 1 | 13 | 48 | .291 | 67 | 221 | 38 | 68 | 20 | 0 | 8 | 38 | .308 |
| Career | 522 | 1858 | 368 | 625 | 161 | 20 | 85 | 370 | .336 | 520 | 1932 | 272 | 516 | 102 | 11 | 65 | 268 | .267 |

*The Big A

**JOHN PESKY** CAREER HOME AND ROAD BREAKDOWNS

| | *At Home* | | | | | | | | | *On The Road* | | | | | | | | |
|---|---|---|---|---|---|---|---|---|---|---|---|---|---|---|---|---|---|---|
| **Year** | **G** | **AB** | **R** | **H** | **2B** | **3B** | **HR** | **RBI** | **Avg** | **G** | **AB** | **R** | **H** | **2B** | **3B** | **HR** | **RBI** | **Avg** |
| 1942 | 74 | 303 | 49 | 94 | 13 | 5 | 1 | 18 | .310 | 73 | 317 | 56 | 111 | 16 | 4 | 1 | 33 | .350 |
| 1946 | 77 | 315 | 70 | 107 | 18 | 2 | 2 | 36 | .340 | 76 | 306 | 45 | 101 | 25 | 2 | 0 | 19 | .330 |
| 1947 | 81 | 330 | 62 | 109 | 12 | 4 | 0 | 24 | .330 | 74 | 308 | 44 | 98 | 15 | 4 | 0 | 15 | .318 |
| 1948 | 74 | 283 | 62 | 84 | 15 | 5 | 0 | 32 | .297 | 69 | 282 | 62 | 75 | 11 | 1 | 3 | 23 | .266 |
| 1949 | 76 | 315 | 62 | 110 | 19 | 4 | 0 | 41 | .349 | 72 | 289 | 49 | 75 | 8 | 3 | 2 | 28 | .260 |
| 1950 | 65 | 246 | 74 | 82 | 12 | 3 | 1 | 29 | .333 | 62 | 244 | 38 | 71 | 10 | 3 | 0 | 20 | .291 |
| 1951 | 65 | 260 | 48 | 83 | 10 | 4 | 2 | 27 | .319 | 66 | 220 | 45 | 67 | 10 | 2 | 1 | 14 | .305 |
| 1952* | 48 | 122 | 23 | 31 | 4 | 0 | 1 | 9 | .254 | 46 | 122 | 13 | 24 | 2 | 0 | 0 | 2 | .197 |
| 1953* | 50 | 141 | 26 | 45 | 12 | 0 | 2 | 14 | .319 | 53 | 167 | 17 | 45 | 10 | 1 | 0 | 10 | .269 |
| 1954* | 28 | 57 | 7 | 11 | 0 | 2 | 1 | 5 | .193 | 41 | 118 | 15 | 32 | 4 | 1 | 0 | 5 | .271 |
| Career | 638 | 2372 | 483 | 756 | 115 | 29 | 10 | 235 | .319 | 632 | 2373 | 384 | 699 | 111 | 21 | 7 | 169 | .295 |

*Left Fenway during 1952 season.

**CARL YASTRZEMSKI** CAREER HOME AND ROAD BREAKDOWNS

| | *In Fenway Park* | | | | | | | | | *On The Road* | | | | | | | | |
|---|---|---|---|---|---|---|---|---|---|---|---|---|---|---|---|---|---|---|
| **Year** | **G** | **AB** | **R** | **H** | **2B** | **3B** | **HR** | **RBI** | **Avg** | **G** | **AB** | **R** | **H** | **2B** | **3B** | **HR** | **RBI** | **Avg** |
| 1961 | 73 | 287 | 30 | 91 | 18 | 5 | 6 | 41 | .317 | 75 | 296 | 41 | 64 | 13 | 1 | 5 | 39 | .216 |
| 1962 | 79 | 316 | 64 | 108 | 27 | 5 | 11 | 52 | .342 | 81 | 330 | 35 | 83 | 16 | 1 | 8 | 42 | .252 |
| 1963 | 74 | 282 | 50 | 89 | 24 | 2 | 6 | 36 | .316 | 77 | 288 | 41 | 94 | 16 | 1 | 8 | 32 | .326 |
| 1964 | 75 | 286 | 40 | 83 | 20 | 7 | 6 | 39 | .290 | 76 | 281 | 37 | 81 | 9 | 2 | 9 | 28 | .288 |
| 1965 | 74 | 266 | 51 | 88 | 30 | 2 | 16 | 53 | .331 | 59 | 228 | 27 | 66 | 15 | 1 | 4 | 19 | .289 |
| 1966 | 80 | 305 | 48 | 99 | 25 | 1 | 11 | 53 | .325 | 80 | 289 | 33 | 66 | 14 | 1 | 5 | 27 | .228 |
| 1967 | 81 | 286 | 66 | 95 | 16 | 1 | 27 | 74 | .332 | 80 | 293 | 46 | 34 | 15 | 3 | 17 | 47 | .321 |
| 1968 | 80 | 264 | 48 | 75 | 15 | 1 | 11 | 42 | .284 | 77 | 275 | 42 | 87 | 17 | 1 | 12 | 32 | .316 |
| 1969 | 81 | 297 | 48 | 83 | 16 | 1 | 21 | 55 | .279 | 81 | 306 | 48 | 71 | 12 | 1 | 19 | 56 | .232 |
| 1970 | 81 | 272 | 62 | 96 | 15 | 0 | 22 | 61 | .353 | 80 | 294 | 63 | 90 | 14 | 0 | 18 | 41 | .306 |
| 1971 | 75 | 257 | 47 | 72 | 15 | 0 | 7 | 42 | .280 | 73 | 251 | 28 | 57 | 6 | 2 | 8 | 28 | .227 |
| 1972 | 69 | 247 | 46 | 71 | 15 | 2 | 5 | 41 | .287 | 56 | 208 | 24 | 49 | 3 | 0 | 7 | 27 | .236 |
| 1973 | 74 | 247 | 40 | 70 | 12 | 3 | 8 | 46 | .283 | 78 | 293 | 42 | 90 | 13 | 1 | 11 | 49 | .307 |
| 1974 | 77 | 256 | 48 | 83 | 13 | 1 | 5 | 43 | .324 | 71 | 259 | 45 | 72 | 12 | 1 | 10 | 36 | .278 |
| 1975 | 77 | 274 | 56 | 75 | 16 | 1 | 8 | 43 | .274 | 72 | 269 | 35 | 71 | 14 | 0 | 6 | 17 | .264 |
| 1976 | 74 | 255 | 37 | 81 | 17 | 1 | 10 | 56 | .318 | 81 | 291 | 34 | 65 | 6 | 1 | 11 | 46 | .223 |
| 1977 | 78 | 282 | 58 | 99 | 16 | 0 | 14 | 67 | .351 | 72 | 276 | 41 | 66 | 11 | 3 | 14 | 35 | .239 |
| 1978 | 72 | 265 | 37 | 77 | 14 | 1 | 7 | 39 | .291 | 72 | 258 | 33 | 68 | 7 | 1 | 10 | 42 | .264 |
| 1979 | 75 | 262 | 34 | 79 | 15 | 1 | 15 | 55 | .302 | 72 | 256 | 35 | 61 | 13 | 0 | 6 | 32 | .238 |
| 1980 | 54 | 176 | 19 | 47 | 8 | 1 | 5 | 21 | .267 | 51 | 188 | 30 | 53 | 13 | 0 | 10 | 29 | .282 |
| 1981 | 46 | 158 | 20 | 46 | 11 | 1 | 3 | 33 | .291 | 45 | 180 | 16 | 37 | 3 | 0 | 4 | 20 | .206 |
| 1982 | 66 | 224 | 27 | 69 | 10 | 1 | 7 | 36 | .308 | 65 | 235 | 26 | 57 | 12 | 0 | 9 | 36 | .243 |
| Career | 1615 | 5774 | 976 | 1776 | 368 | 38 | 231 | 1028 | .308 | 1574 | 5844 | 802 | 1542 | 254 | 21 | 211 | 760 | .264 |

Dave STAPLETON, First Base

*Runs Created: 64*

| | G | AB | R | H | 2B | 3B | HR | RBI | SB | Avg |
|---|---|---|---|---|---|---|---|---|---|---|
| First Half | 85 | 328 | 37 | 81 | 14 | 0 | 8 | 37 | 1 | .247 |
| Second Half | 65 | 210 | 29 | 61 | 14 | 1 | 6 | 28 | 1 | .290 |
| Home | 76 | 271 | 40 | 78 | 15 | 0 | 7 | 35 | 1 | .288 |
| Road | 74 | 267 | 26 | 64 | 13 | 1 | 7 | 30 | 1 | .240 |
| vs. RHP | | 371 | 54 | 101 | 16 | 1 | 10 | 48 | 0 | .272 |
| vs. LHP | | 167 | 12 | 41 | 12 | 0 | 4 | 17 | 2 | .246 |
| 1982 | 150 | 538 | 66 | 142 | 28 | 1 | 14 | 65 | 2 | .264 |
| 2.15 years | | 624 | 80 | 180 | 36 | 3 | 14 | 71 | 2 | .288 |

Jerry REMY, Second Base

*Runs Created: 70*

| | G | AB | R | H | 2B | 3B | HR | RBI | SB | Avg |
|---|---|---|---|---|---|---|---|---|---|---|
| First Half | 80 | 322 | 47 | 90 | 9 | 1 | 0 | 29 | 9 | .280 |
| Second Half | 75 | 314 | 42 | 88 | 13 | 2 | 0 | 18 | 7 | .280 |
| Home | 81 | 334 | 49 | 93 | 10 | 1 | 0 | 28 | 6 | .278 |
| Road | 74 | 302 | 40 | 85 | 12 | 2 | 0 | 19 | 10 | .281 |
| vs. RHP | | 446 | 66 | 125 | 16 | 3 | 0 | 32 | 15 | .280 |
| vs. LHP | | 190 | 23 | 53 | 6 | 0 | 0 | 15 | 1 | .279 |
| 1982 | 155 | 636 | 89 | 178 | 22 | 3 | 0 | 47 | 16 | .280 |
| 6.04 years | | 622 | 87 | 172 | 20 | 5 | 1 | 46 | 32 | .276 |

Carney LANSFORD, Third Base

*Runs Created: 77*

| | G | AB | R | H | 2B | 3B | HR | RBI | SB | Avg |
|---|---|---|---|---|---|---|---|---|---|---|
| First Half | 64 | 243 | 26 | 70 | 11 | 2 | 3 | 28 | 7 | .288 |
| Second Half | 64 | 239 | 39 | 75 | 17 | 2 | 8 | 35 | 2 | .314 |
| Home | 62 | 231 | 38 | 76 | 17 | 2 | 4 | 30 | 4 | .329 |
| Road | 66 | 251 | 27 | 69 | 11 | 2 | 7 | 33 | 5 | .275 |
| vs. RHP | | 365 | 56 | 113 | 26 | 4 | 8 | 47 | 8 | .310 |
| vs. LHP | | 117 | 9 | 32 | 2 | 0 | 3 | 16 | 1 | .274 |
| 1982 | 128 | 482 | 65 | 145 | 28 | 4 | 11 | 63 | 9 | .301 |
| 4.07 years | | 636 | 96 | 186 | 32 | 4 | 14 | 80 | 19 | .292 |

Glenn HOFFMAN, Shortstop

*Runs Created: 36*

| | G | AB | R | H | 2B | 3B | HR | RBI | SB | Avg |
|---|---|---|---|---|---|---|---|---|---|---|
| First Half | 84 | 295 | 40 | 69 | 18 | 2 | 5 | 37 | 0 | .234 |
| Second Half | 66 | 174 | 13 | 29 | 5 | 0 | 2 | 12 | 0 | .167 |
| Home | 74 | 230 | 30 | 52 | 12 | 2 | 6 | 37 | 0 | .226 |
| Road | 76 | 239 | 23 | 46 | 11 | 0 | 1 | 12 | 0 | .192 |
| vs. RHP | | 315 | 39 | 68 | 10 | 2 | 6 | 38 | 0 | .216 |
| vs. LHP | | 154 | 14 | 30 | 13 | 0 | 1 | 11 | 0 | .195 |
| 1982 | 150 | 469 | 53 | 98 | 23 | 2 | 7 | 49 | 0 | .209 |
| 2.11 years | | 485 | 56 | 115 | 23 | 3 | 6 | 53 | 1 | .238 |

Jim RICE, Left Field

*Runs Created: 104*

| | G | AB | R | H | 2B | 3B | HR | RBI | SB | Avg |
|---|---|---|---|---|---|---|---|---|---|---|
| First Half | 77 | 297 | 43 | 87 | 12 | 2 | 12 | 48 | 0 | .293 |
| Second Half | 68 | 276 | 43 | 90 | 12 | 3 | 12 | 49 | 0 | .326 |
| Home | 77 | 306 | 51 | 101 | 11 | 4 | 9 | 49 | 0 | .330 |
| Road | 68 | 267 | 35 | 76 | 13 | 1 | 15 | 48 | 0 | .285 |
| vs. RHP | | 418 | 75 | 131 | 14 | 3 | 22 | 71 | 0 | .313 |
| vs. LHP | | 155 | 11 | 46 | 10 | 2 | 2 | 26 | 0 | .297 |
| 1982 | 145 | 573 | 86 | 177 | 24 | 5 | 24 | 97 | 0 | .309 |
| 7.28 years | | 633 | 101 | 196 | 29 | 8 | 33 | 114 | 7 | .305 |

Rick MILLER, Center Field

*Runs Created: 41*

| | G | AB | R | H | 2B | 3B | HR | RBI | SB | Avg |
|---|---|---|---|---|---|---|---|---|---|---|
| First Half | 72 | 227 | 33 | 62 | 6 | 0 | 3 | 21 | 1 | .273 |
| Second Half | 63 | 182 | 17 | 42 | 7 | 2 | 1 | 17 | 4 | .231 |
| Home | 64 | 168 | 23 | 42 | 6 | 2 | 1 | 16 | 3 | .250 |
| Road | 71 | 241 | 27 | 62 | 7 | 0 | 3 | 22 | 1 | .257 |
| vs. RHP | | 328 | 45 | 86 | 11 | 2 | 4 | 30 | 4 | .262 |
| vs. LHP | | 81 | 5 | 18 | 2 | 0 | 0 | 8 | 1 | .222 |
| 1982 | 135 | 409 | 50 | 104 | 13 | 2 | 4 | 38 | 5 | .254 |
| 7.67 years | | 451 | 64 | 121 | 19 | 4 | 4 | 43 | 10 | .267 |

Dwight EVANS, Right Field

*Runs Created: 130*

| | G | AB | R | H | 2B | 3B | HR | RBI | SB | Avg |
|---|---|---|---|---|---|---|---|---|---|---|
| First Half | 85 | 316 | 59 | 93 | 20 | 4 | 14 | 46 | 2 | .294 |
| Second Half | 77 | 292 | 63 | 91 | 15 | 4 | 21 | 58 | 1 | .312 |
| Home | 81 | 304 | 72 | 95 | 23 | 4 | 21 | 61 | 0 | .313 |
| Road | 81 | 304 | 50 | 89 | 12 | 4 | 14 | 43 | 3 | .293 |
| vs. RHP | | 436 | 94 | 131 | 21 | 4 | 28 | 73 | 2 | .300 |
| vs. LHP | | 172 | 28 | 53 | 14 | 4 | 7 | 31 | 1 | .308 |
| 1982 | 162 | 608 | 122 | 184 | 35 | 8 | 35 | 104 | 3 | .303 |
| 8.23 years | | 537 | 84 | 144 | 30 | 5 | 22 | 74 | 6 | .269 |

Rich GEDMAN, Catcher

*Runs Created: 28*

| | G | AB | R | H | 2B | 3B | HR | RBI | SB | Avg |
|---|---|---|---|---|---|---|---|---|---|---|
| First Half | 61 | 213 | 23 | 59 | 12 | 2 | 4 | 23 | 0 | .277 |
| Second Half | 31 | 76 | 7 | 13 | 5 | 0 | 0 | 3 | 0 | .171 |
| Home | 48 | 147 | 21 | 44 | 14 | 2 | 1 | 18 | 0 | .299 |
| Road | 44 | 142 | 9 | 28 | 3 | 0 | 3 | 8 | 0 | .197 |
| vs. RHP | | 250 | 30 | 64 | 17 | 2 | 4 | 25 | 0 | .256 |
| vs. LHP | | 39 | 0 | 8 | 0 | 0 | 0 | 1 | 0 | .205 |
| 1982 | 92 | 289 | 30 | 72 | 17 | 2 | 4 | 26 | 0 | .249 |
| 1.01 years | | 513 | 54 | 135 | 32 | 2 | 9 | 53 | 0 | .263 |

Carl YASTRZEMSKI, Designated Hitter

*Runs Created: 70*

| | G | AB | R | H | 2B | 3B | HR | RBI | SB | Avg |
|---|---|---|---|---|---|---|---|---|---|---|
| First Half | 69 | 239 | 29 | 71 | 10 | 1 | 11 | 45 | 0 | .297 |
| Second Half | 62 | 220 | 24 | 55 | 12 | 0 | 5 | 27 | 0 | .250 |
| Home | 66 | 224 | 27 | 69 | 10 | 1 | 7 | 36 | 0 | .308 |
| Road | 65 | 235 | 26 | 57 | 12 | 0 | 9 | 36 | 0 | .243 |
| vs. RHP | | 394 | 50 | 110 | 19 | 1 | 14 | 55 | 0 | .279 |
| vs. LHP | | 65 | 3 | 16 | 3 | 0 | 2 | 17 | 0 | .246 |
| 1982 | 131 | 459 | 53 | 126 | 22 | 1 | 16 | 72 | 0 | .275 |
| 19.69 years | | 590 | 90 | 165 | 32 | 3 | 23 | 91 | 9 | .280 |

Wade BOGGS, Infield

*Runs Created: 61*

| | G | AB | R | H | 2B | 3B | HR | RBI | SB | Avg |
|---|---|---|---|---|---|---|---|---|---|---|
| First Half | 34 | 97 | 15 | 34 | 4 | 0 | 1 | 9 | 0 | .351 |
| Second Half | 70 | 241 | 36 | 84 | 10 | 1 | 4 | 35 | 1 | .349 |
| Home | 55 | 180 | 34 | 64 | 12 | 1 | 4 | 30 | 1 | .356 |
| Road | 49 | 158 | 17 | 54 | 2 | 0 | 1 | 14 | 0 | .342 |
| vs. RHP | | 233 | 38 | 83 | 10 | 1 | 5 | 32 | 1 | .356 |
| vs. LHP | | 105 | 13 | 35 | 4 | 0 | 0 | 12 | 0 | .333 |
| 1982 | 104 | 338 | 51 | 118 | 14 | 1 | 5 | 44 | 1 | .349 |
| 0.64 years | | 528 | 80 | 184 | 22 | 2 | 8 | 69 | 2 | .349 |

Dennis ECKERSLEY

| Year | (W–L) | GS | Run | Avg | DP | Avg | SB | Avg |
|---|---|---|---|---|---|---|---|---|
| 1976 | (13-12) | 30 | 112 | 3.73 | 19 | .63 | 41 | 1.37 |
| 1977 | (14-13) | 33 | 133 | 4.03 | 22 | .67 | 37 | 1.12 |
| 1978 | (20- 8) | 35 | 173 | 4.94 | 28 | .80 | 28 | .80 |
| 1979 | (17-10) | 33 | 171 | 5.18 | 26 | .79 | 34 | 1.03 |
| 1980 | (12-14) | 30 | 124 | 4.13 | 23 | .77 | 34 | 1.13 |
| 1981 | ( 9- 8) | 23 | 111 | 4.83 | 17 | .74 | 38 | 1.65 |
| 1982 | (13-13) | 33 | 124 | 3.76 | 26 | .79 | 25 | .76 |
| 7 years | | 217 | 948 | 4.37 | 161 | .74 | 237 | 1.09 |

| | G | IP | W | L | Pct | ER | ERA |
|---|---|---|---|---|---|---|---|
| Home | 19 | 128.2 | 8 | 7 | .533 | 58 | 4.06 |
| Road | 14 | 95.2 | 5 | 6 | .455 | 35 | 3.29 |

### Mike TORREZ

| Year | (W–L) | GS | Run | Avg | DP | Avg | SB | Avg |
|---|---|---|---|---|---|---|---|---|
| 1976 | (16-12) | 39 | 158 | 4.05 | 43 | 1.10 | 25 | .64 |
| 1977 | (17-13) | 35 | 170 | 4.86 | 31 | .89 | 19 | .54 |
| 1978 | (16-13) | 36 | 192 | 5.33 | 39 | 1.08 | 38 | 1.06 |
| 1979 | (16-13) | 36 | 218 | 6.06 | 36 | 1.00 | 31 | .86 |
| 1980 | ( 9-16) | 32 | 157 | 4.91 | 45 | 1.41 | 14 | .44 |
| 1981 | (10- 3) | 22 | 116 | 5.27 | 23 | 1.05 | 12 | .55 |
| 1982 | ( 9- 9) | 31 | 178 | 5.74 | 33 | 1.06 | 21 | .68 |
| 7 years | | 231 | 1189 | 5.15 | 250 | 1.08 | 160 | .69 |

| | G | IP | W | L | Pct | ER | ERA |
|---|---|---|---|---|---|---|---|
| Home | 15 | 80 | 3 | 4 | .429 | 43 | 4.84 |
| Road | 16 | 95.2 | 6 | 5 | .545 | 59 | 5.55 |

### John TUDOR

| Year | (W–L) | GS | Run | Avg | DP | Avg | SB | Avg |
|---|---|---|---|---|---|---|---|---|
| 1979 | ( 1- 2) | 6 | 25 | 4.17 | 6 | 1.00 | 4 | .67 |
| 1980 | ( 8- 5) | 13 | 61 | 4.69 | 15 | 1.15 | 5 | .38 |
| 1981 | ( 4- 3) | 11 | 56 | 5.09 | 10 | .91 | 3 | .27 |
| 1982 | (13-10) | 30 | 135 | 4.50 | 29 | .97 | 16 | .53 |
| 4 years | | 60 | 277 | 4.62 | 60 | 1.00 | 28 | .47 |

| | G | IP | W | L | Pct | ER | ERA |
|---|---|---|---|---|---|---|---|
| Home | 17 | 104 | 7 | 6 | .538 | 53 | 4.59 |
| Road | 15 | 91.2 | 6 | 4 | .600 | 26 | 2.55 |

### Chuck RAINEY

| Year | (W–L) | GS | Run | Avg | DP | Avg | SB | Avg |
|---|---|---|---|---|---|---|---|---|
| 1979 | (8-5) | 16 | 76 | 4.75 | 25 | 1.56 | 5 | .31 |
| 1980 | (8-3) | 13 | 70 | 5.38 | 26 | 2.00 | 7 | .54 |
| 1981 | (0-1) | 2 | 9 | 4.50 | 1 | .50 | 0 | .00 |
| 1982 | (7-5) | 25 | 123 | 4.92 | 28 | 1.12 | 22 | .88 |
| 4 years | | 56 | 278 | 4.96 | 80 | 1.45 | 34 | .61 |

| | G | IP | W | L | Pct | ER | ERA |
|---|---|---|---|---|---|---|---|
| Home | 14 | 65.2 | 2 | 1 | .667 | 41 | 5.62 |
| Road | 13 | 63.1 | 5 | 4 | .556 | 31 | 4.41 |

### 1982 OTHERS

| Pitcher | (W–L) | GS | Run | Avg | DP | Avg | SB | Avg |
|---|---|---|---|---|---|---|---|---|
| Hurst | (3-7) | 19 | 86 | 4.53 | 25 | 1.32 | 9 | .47 |
| Ojeda | (4-6) | 14 | 65 | 4.64 | 17 | 1.21 | 6 | .43 |
| Denman | (3-4) | 9 | 41 | 4.56 | 6 | .67 | 2 | .22 |
| Boyd | (0-1) | 1 | 1 | | 2 | | 0 | |

## BOSTON

*Talent Analysis*

The Red Sox in 1982 possessed 163 points of approximate value.

| | AV | % |
|---|---|---|
| Produced by Red Sox' system: | 109 | 67% |
| Acquired by trade: | 41 | 25% |
| Purchased or signed from free agency: | 13 | 8% |

They are built from within.

| | | |
|---|---|---|
| Young (Up to age 25): | 27 | 17% |
| Prime (Age 26 to 29): | 83 | 51% |
| Past-prime (Age 30 to 33): | 24 | 15% |
| Old (Age 34 or older): | 29 | 18% |

They are a little bit younger than average; it's a pretty standard age spectrum.

The Red Sox system produced 200 approximate value for 1982, fifth highest in the majors. The four-year total is 719, the fourth highest in baseball.

## FENWAY PARK

DIMENSIONS: Fabled

SURFACE: Grass

VISIBILITY: Perfect

FOUL TERRITORY: Tiny

FAVORS:
Hitter/Pitcher—Hitter
Power/Line-drive hitter—Both
Righthander/Lefthander—Righthander for power; lefthander for average

TYPES OF OFFENSE AFFECTED: Increases batting averages by, conservatively, 20 points. The Red Sox hit .294 in Fenway last year, .255 on the road; their opponents hit .285 in Fenway, .266 on the road. Increases doubles by over 30%. Increases home runs by 20% (maybe 25 to 30% for righthanders, less for lefties).

OTHER PARK CHARACTERISTICS: Too numerous to mention

TYPES OF MARGINAL PLAYERS MOST VALUABLE IN PARK: Control pitchers, left-handed pinch hitters

PLAYERS ON TEAM HELPED MOST BY PARK: Yaz, Rice

PLAYERS ON TEAM HURT MOST BY PARK: Pitchers, but Red Sox pitchers generally are not hurt by the park as much as their hitters are helped by it

OTHER COMMENTS: Craig Wright points out that it is a common misconception that you have to play longball in this park. Actually, it is a park in which a long-sequence offense can do very well.

# DETROIT TIGERS

The American League Red Book in 1982 had a picture of Lee MacPhail receiving something called the "John E. Fetzer Award." If an award is ever given for baseball's silliest and least-desirable award, I nominate the John E. Fetzer. Who the hell wants to win an award named after John E. Fetzer? What is it given for, anyway? "Long and Meritorious Service"? Are the people who clean the men's room eligible? What's the difference between the John E. Fetzer Award and the Joe Cronin Award? Is there any one of you who can tell me A) who won the John E. Fetzer Award in 1981, or B) who is likely to win it next year?

Sorry, Mr. MacPhail. Didn't mean to denigrate your award, there.

Note the strong similarity between the basic offensive line of the Tigers and the Orioles, in all categories except runs scored and stolen bases:

| | G | AB | R | H | 2B | 3B | HR | RBI | SB | Avg |
|---|---|---|---|---|---|---|---|---|---|---|
| Detroit | 162 | 5590 | 729 | 1489 | 237 | 40 | 177 | 684 | 93 | .266 |
| Baltimore | 163 | 5557 | 774 | 1478 | 259 | 27 | 179 | 735 | 49 | .266 |

The Tigers had 2337 total bases to the Orioles' 2328; the slugging percentages were .418 and .419.

Every bit of new knowledge that comes into popular circulation kills off a dozen myths or so, and that is why people are so reluctant to learn sometimes, that they love those myths and they treasure them. Things that people cannot quite see or touch or measure—these are the common man's link with profundity. So you ask a dozen Tiger fans why that happened, how the Orioles could score 45 more runs with the same batting average, virtually the same home-run count, equivalent totals of doubles and triples, and the Tigers with nearly twice as many stolen bases, and five fans will tell you that the Tigers didn't hit with runners on base and left too many people out there, and four will tell you about hitting behind the runner and giving yourself up to move base runners around (those things, you know, that the Orioles do so well), and two will cite base-running blunders, and one will ramble on in a general way about executing fundamentals and making better use of the hit and run. And people love these myths, and all of those things may be true but you could boil the truth in all of them down to tallow and you wouldn't be able to make a candle out of it, when the reason for that difference is in fact quite obvious. The Orioles drew 634 walks last year, the Tigers only 470. Divide the difference by four and you've got the difference between the two offenses.

I have made some critical remarks in the past about the Tigers' defensive positioning. Whitey Herzog and Dick Williams and Earl Weaver and Ralph Houk—all my heroes, so to speak—are hard-working students of where the ball is hit by whom and against whom; they keep charts and they use them. If you watch the Tigers on defense, they simply don't adjust. Enos Cabell at third will pull in to guard against the bunt and will guard the lines in the late innings; Trammell adjusts a step or two depending on where Cabell is, and Herndon will back up a couple of steps for Jim Rice or Eddie Murray. But basically, they use the same defense for everybody, George Brett or Rich Dauer. And if you listen to Sparky Anderson talk on the subject, it is obvious that he knows as much about where a hitter is likely to hit the ball as he knows about the ovulation cycle of an orangutan.

It is very important to note, with respect to those remarks (which I do not intend to retract, because they are true), that the Tigers had the best defensive efficiency record, .719, of any American League team. That is to say, when a hit ball is put into play against them, Sparky's Tigers are more likely to turn that ball into an out than is any other American League defense.

What does that mean? That defensive positioning is not as important as I've always believed it to be? Very possibly, yes. But I have mentioned in the past that the surprise in figuring defensive efficiency records has always been the extent to which the best teams were the teams whose outfielders covered a lot of ground. I wouldn't have expected that. I would have expected the dominant pattern to be that the teams with the great shortstops and second basemen would be the most effective at preventing hits.

Anyway, if you look at the Tigers, what do you see? Three center fielders. Actually, with Wilson and Gibson in center, the Tigers had *four* bona fide center fielders on their roster. Chet Lemon played center for the White Sox for five years, Herndon for two years for the Giants. And neither one of them was that bad a center fielder, although they both had weaknesses. All three had very good range factors in '82. In the NL, it's the same thing. The team with the highest DER isn't St. Louis, with the great defensive infield, but San Diego—and again, all three of their outfielders make a lot of plays. Don't let the terminology throw you: "a high DER" just means that the opposition gets very few hits; a "good range factor" just means that the outfielders make a lot of plays. It can't be a coincidence.

Like Toronto, the Tigers worked more pitchers on three days' rest than any National League team. Jack Morris started ten times on three days' rest, Petry nine times.

I really hate to rip Sparky all the time. I'm not kidding; I detest it. I've reached the point at which everything the man does irritates me, but he still seems like a nice guy. I'm not a negative person. But you've got a ball club here that's playing 15 games a year below their ability. I can't just pretend I don't see it. Eventually Sparky is going to get fired (wouldn't you think?) and then the truth of what I am saying will become generally known.

Tiger lead-off men hit 19 home runs last year.

**HANK GREENBERG:** CAREER HOME AND ROAD BREAKDOWNS

| | *In Tiger Stadium* | | | | | | | | | *On The Road* | | | | | | | | |
|---|---|---|---|---|---|---|---|---|---|---|---|---|---|---|---|---|---|---|
| **Year** | **G** | **AB** | **R** | **H** | **2B** | **3B** | **HR** | **RBI** | **Avg** | **G** | **AB** | **R** | **H** | **2B** | **3B** | **HR** | **RBI** | **Avg** |
| 1930 | 1 | 1 | 0 | 0 | 0 | 0 | 0 | 0 | .000 | 0 | 0 | 0 | 0 | 0 | 0 | 0 | 0 | .000 |
| 1933 | 59 | 225 | 38 | 66 | 16 | 3 | 9 | 47 | .293 | 58 | 224 | 21 | 69 | 17 | 0 | 3 | 40 | .308 |
| 1934 | 79 | 302 | 73 | 110 | 41 | 4 | 15 | 78 | .364 | 74 | 291 | 45 | 91 | 22 | 3 | 11 | 61 | .313 |
| 1935 | 79 | 307 | 62 | 100 | 23 | 8 | 18 | 86 | .326 | 73 | 312 | 59 | 103 | 23 | 8 | 18 | 84 | .330 |
| 1936 | 3 | 8 | 3 | 4 | 0 | 2 | 1 | 5 | .500 | 9 | 38 | 7 | 12 | 6 | 0 | 1 | 15 | .316 |
| 1937 | 77 | 295 | 81 | 113 | 27 | 8 | 25 | 101 | .383 | 77 | 299 | 56 | 87 | 22 | 6 | 15 | 82 | .291 |
| 1938 | 79 | 277 | 77 | 97 | 9 | 1 | 39 | 92 | .350 | 76 | 279 | 67 | 78 | 14 | 3 | 19 | 54 | .280 |
| 1939 | 65 | 229 | 51 | 77 | 21 | 3 | 16 | 57 | .336 | 73 | 271 | 61 | 79 | 21 | 4 | 17 | 55 | .292 |
| 1940 | 74 | 279 | 84 | 110 | 28 | 4 | 27 | 98 | .394 | 74 | 294 | 45 | 85 | 22 | 4 | 14 | 52 | .289 |
| 1941 | 15 | 52 | 11 | 15 | 4 | 1 | 2 | 12 | .288 | 4 | 15 | 1 | 3 | 1 | 0 | 0 | 0 | .200 |
| 1945 | 43 | 150 | 29 | 555 | 15 | 2 | 7 | 37 | .367 | 35 | 120 | 18 | 29 | 5 | 0 | 6 | 23 | .242 |
| 1946 | 72 | 257 | 46 | 71 | 8 | 2 | 29 | 76 | .276 | 70 | 266 | 45 | 74 | 21 | 3 | 15 | 51 | .278 |
| 1947* | 66 | 212 | 43 | 58 | 6 | 0 | 18 | 48 | .274 | 59 | 190 | 28 | 42 | 7 | 2 | 7 | 26 | .221 |
| Career | 712 | 2594 | 598 | 876 | 198 | 38 | 205 | 733 | .338 | 682 | 2599 | 453 | 752 | 181 | 33 | 126 | 543 | .289 |

*In Pittsburgh, actually

Enos CABBEL, First Base

*Runs Created: 43*

| | G | AB | R | H | 2B | 3B | HR | RBI | SB | Avg |
|---|---|---|---|---|---|---|---|---|---|---|
| First Half | 74 | 301 | 30 | 84 | 11 | 3 | 2 | 26 | 7 | .279 |
| Second Half | 51 | 163 | 15 | 37 | 6 | 0 | 0 | 11 | 8 | .227 |
| Home | 62 | 229 | 19 | 57 | 8 | 0 | 2 | 21 | 4 | .249 |
| Road | 63 | 235 | 26 | 64 | 9 | 3 | 0 | 16 | 11 | .272 |
| vs. RHP | | 281 | 25 | 72 | 10 | 2 | 0 | 20 | 12 | .256 |
| vs. LHP | | 183 | 20 | 49 | 7 | 1 | 2 | 17 | 3 | .268 |
| 1982 | 125 | 464 | 45 | 121 | 17 | 3 | 2 | 37 | 15 | .261 |
| 7.51 years | | 601 | 76 | 164 | 26 | 6 | 6 | 59 | 28 | .272 |

Alan TRAMMELL, Shortstop

*Runs Created: 64*

| | G | AB | R | H | 2B | 3B | HR | RBI | SB | Avg |
|---|---|---|---|---|---|---|---|---|---|---|
| First Half | 81 | 244 | 27 | 50 | 15 | 0 | 3 | 30 | 5 | .205 |
| Second Half | 76 | 245 | 39 | 76 | 19 | 3 | 6 | 27 | 14 | .310 |
| Home | 80 | 239 | 39 | 72 | 21 | 2 | 5 | 32 | 10 | .301 |
| Road | 77 | 250 | 27 | 54 | 13 | 1 | 4 | 25 | 9 | .216 |
| vs. RHP | | 346 | 44 | 89 | 21 | 2 | 6 | 38 | 18 | .257 |
| vs. LHP | | 143 | 22 | 37 | 13 | 1 | 3 | 19 | 1 | .259 |
| 1982 | 157 | 489 | 66 | 126 | 34 | 3 | 9 | 57 | 19 | .258 |
| 4.37 years | | 547 | 80 | 149 | 22 | 5 | 6 | 54 | 14 | .272 |

Lou WHITAKER, Second Base

*Runs Created: 84*

| | G | AB | R | H | 2B | 3B | HR | RBI | SB | Avg |
|---|---|---|---|---|---|---|---|---|---|---|
| First Half | 81 | 268 | 25 | 68 | 8 | 2 | 5 | 27 | 3 | .254 |
| Second Half | 71 | 292 | 51 | 92 | 14 | 6 | 10 | 38 | 8 | .315 |
| Home | 75 | 276 | 37 | 80 | 10 | 6 | 9 | 32 | 3 | .290 |
| Road | 77 | 284 | 39 | 80 | 12 | 2 | 6 | 33 | 8 | .282 |
| vs. RHP | | 412 | 56 | 116 | 16 | 7 | 12 | 45 | 10 | .282 |
| vs. LHP | | 148 | 20 | 44 | 6 | 1 | 3 | 20 | 1 | .297 |
| 1982 | 152 | 560 | 76 | 160 | 22 | 8 | 15 | 65 | 11 | .286 |
| 4.22 years | | 548 | 81 | 148 | 19 | 7 | 6 | 59 | 13 | .271 |

Larry HERNDON, Left Field

*Runs Created: 95*

| | G | AB | R | H | 2B | 3B | HR | RBI | SB | Avg |
|---|---|---|---|---|---|---|---|---|---|---|
| First Half | 84 | 320 | 49 | 94 | 9 | 8 | 15 | 44 | 9 | .294 |
| Second Half | 73 | 294 | 43 | 85 | 12 | 5 | 8 | 44 | 3 | .289 |
| Home | 78 | 287 | 43 | 86 | 6 | 5 | 9 | 34 | 5 | .300 |
| Road | 79 | 327 | 49 | 93 | 15 | 8 | 14 | 54 | 7 | .284 |
| vs. RHP | | 429 | 62 | 117 | 13 | 6 | 17 | 61 | 9 | .273 |
| vs. LHP | | 185 | 30 | 62 | 8 | 7 | 6 | 27 | 3 | .335 |
| 1982 | 157 | 614 | 92 | 179 | 21 | 13 | 23 | 88 | 12 | .292 |
| 5.25 years | | 523 | 65 | 143 | 19 | 10 | 9 | 52 | 14 | .273 |

Tom BROOKENS, Third Base

*Runs Created: 36*

| | G | AB | R | H | 2B | 3B | HR | RBI | SB | Avg |
|---|---|---|---|---|---|---|---|---|---|---|
| First Half | 74 | 171 | 20 | 45 | 6 | 0 | 4 | 19 | 4 | .263 |
| Second Half | 66 | 227 | 20 | 47 | 9 | 3 | 5 | 39 | 1 | .207 |
| Home | 70 | 203 | 21 | 45 | 7 | 2 | 4 | 27 | 5 | .222 |
| Road | 70 | 195 | 19 | 47 | 8 | 1 | 5 | 31 | 0 | .241 |
| vs. RHP | | 248 | 22 | 53 | 8 | 2 | 7 | 36 | 2 | .214 |
| vs. LHP | | 150 | 18 | 39 | 7 | 1 | 2 | 22 | 3 | .260 |
| 1982 | 140 | 398 | 40 | 92 | 15 | 3 | 9 | 58 | 5 | .231 |
| 2.61 years | | 512 | 56 | 130 | 21 | 6 | 10 | 65 | 13 | .255 |

Kirk GIBSON, Center Field

*Runs Created: 38*

| | G | AB | R | H | 2B | 3B | HR | RBI | SB | Avg |
|---|---|---|---|---|---|---|---|---|---|---|
| First Half | 69 | 266 | 34 | 74 | 16 | 2 | 8 | 35 | 9 | .278 |
| Second Half | – | – | – | – | – | – | – | – | – | – |
| Home | 32 | 129 | 18 | 35 | 4 | 1 | 4 | 19 | 2 | .271 |
| Road | 37 | 137 | 16 | 39 | 12 | 1 | 4 | 16 | 7 | .285 |
| vs. RHP | | 172 | 21 | 54 | 13 | 2 | 6 | 23 | 6 | .314 |
| vs. LHP | | 94 | 13 | 20 | 3 | 0 | 2 | 12 | 3 | .213 |
| 1982 | 69 | 266 | 34 | 74 | 16 | 2 | 8 | 35 | 9 | .278 |
| 1.33 years | | 579 | 76 | 169 | 24 | 5 | 20 | 72 | 25 | .291 |

## Chet LEMON, Right Field

*Runs Created: 66*

| | G | AB | R | H | 2B | 3B | HR | RBI | SB | Avg |
|---|---|---|---|---|---|---|---|---|---|---|
| First Half | 69 | 241 | 36 | 56 | 10 | 0 | 5 | 18 | 0 | .232 |
| Second Half | 56 | 195 | 39 | 60 | 10 | 1 | 14 | 34 | 1 | .308 |
| Home | 66 | 219 | 38 | 65 | 9 | 0 | 12 | 25 | 1 | .297 |
| Road | 59 | 217 | 37 | 51 | 11 | 1 | 7 | 27 | 0 | .235 |
| vs. RHP | | 300 | 47 | 78 | 14 | 0 | 13 | 34 | 0 | .260 |
| vs. LHP | | 136 | 28 | 38 | 6 | 1 | 6 | 18 | 1 | .279 |
| 1982 | 125 | 436 | 75 | 116 | 20 | 1 | 19 | 52 | 1 | .266 |
| 5.61 years | | 576 | 85 | 164 | 35 | 5 | 16 | 71 | 8 | .285 |

## Lance PARRISH, Catcher

*Runs Created: 85*

| | G | AB | R | H | 2B | 3B | HR | RBI | SB | Avg |
|---|---|---|---|---|---|---|---|---|---|---|
| First Half | 63 | 217 | 40 | 70 | 10 | 1 | 13 | 36 | 2 | .323 |
| Second Half | 70 | 269 | 35 | 68 | 9 | 1 | 19 | 51 | 1 | .253 |
| Home | 67 | 238 | 41 | 64 | 11 | 1 | 22 | 54 | 2 | .269 |
| Road | 66 | 248 | 34 | 74 | 8 | 1 | 10 | 33 | 1 | .298 |
| vs. RHP | | 340 | 48 | 89 | 12 | 1 | 20 | 55 | 3 | .262 |
| vs. LHP | | 146 | 27 | 49 | 7 | 1 | 12 | 32 | 0 | .336 |
| 1982 | 133 | 486 | 75 | 138 | 19 | 2 | 32 | 87 | 3 | .284 |
| 3.78 years | | 586 | 81 | 156 | 29 | 4 | 27 | 87 | 5 | .266 |

## Mike IVIE, Designated Hitter

*Runs Created: 34*

| | G | AB | R | H | 2B | 3B | HR | RBI | SB | Avg |
|---|---|---|---|---|---|---|---|---|---|---|
| First Half | 48 | 174 | 26 | 42 | 7 | 1 | 12 | 33 | 0 | .241 |
| Second Half | 32 | 85 | 9 | 18 | 5 | 0 | 2 | 5 | 0 | .212 |
| Home | 42 | 132 | 22 | 26 | 4 | 0 | 10 | 22 | 0 | .197 |
| Road | 38 | 127 | 13 | 34 | 8 | 1 | 4 | 16 | 0 | .268 |
| vs. RHP | | 145 | 16 | 32 | 6 | 1 | 5 | 20 | 0 | .221 |
| vs. LHP | | 114 | 19 | 28 | 6 | 0 | 9 | 18 | 0 | .246 |
| 1982 | 80 | 259 | 35 | 60 | 12 | 1 | 14 | 38 | 0 | .232 |
| 5.17 years | | 512 | 59 | 138 | 25 | 3 | 16 | 78 | 4 | .270 |

## Jack MORRIS

| Year | (W–L) | GS | Run | Avg | DP | Avg | SB | Avg |
|---|---|---|---|---|---|---|---|---|
| 1977 | ( 1- 1) | 6 | 21 | 3.50 | 3 | .50 | 5 | .83 |
| 1978 | ( 3- 5) | 7 | 35 | 5.00 | 7 | 1.00 | 3 | .43 |
| 1979 | (17- 7) | 27 | 138 | 5.11 | 33 | 1.22 | 14 | .52 |
| 1980 | (16-15) | 36 | 164 | 4.56 | 35 | .97 | 31 | .86 |
| 1981 | (14- 7) | 25 | 133 | 5.32 | 33 | 1.32 | 16 | .64 |
| 1982 | (17-16) | 37 | 151 | 4.08 | 32 | .86 | 15 | .41 |
| 6 years | | 138 | 642 | 4.65 | 143 | 1.04 | 84 | .61 |

| | G | IP | W | L | Pct | ER | ERA |
|---|---|---|---|---|---|---|---|
| Home | 19 | 138.1 | 9 | 6 | .600 | 53 | 3.51 |
| Road | 18 | 128 | 8 | 10 | .444 | 67 | 4.71 |

## Dan PETRY

| Year | (W–L) | GS | Run | Avg | DP | Avg | SB | Avg |
|---|---|---|---|---|---|---|---|---|
| 1979 | ( 6-5) | 15 | 62 | 4.13 | 16 | 1.07 | 8 | .53 |
| 1980 | (10-9) | 25 | 122 | 4.88 | 32 | 1.28 | 16 | .64 |
| 1981 | (10-9) | 22 | 72 | 3.27 | 25 | 1.14 | 8 | .36 |
| 1982 | (15-9) | 35 | 176 | 5.03 | 38 | 1.09 | 16 | .46 |
| 4 years | | 97 | 432 | 4.45 | 111 | 1.14 | 48 | .49 |

| | G | IP | W | L | Pct | ER | ERA |
|---|---|---|---|---|---|---|---|
| Home | 16 | 122.2 | 8 | 2 | .800 | 33 | 2.42 |
| Road | 19 | 123.1 | 7 | 7 | .500 | 55 | 4.01 |

## Milt WILCOX

| Year | (W–L) | GS | Run | Avg | DP | Avg | SB | Avg |
|---|---|---|---|---|---|---|---|---|
| 1977 | ( 6-12) | 13 | 64 | 4.92 | 8 | .62 | 9 | .69 |
| 1978 | (13-12) | 27 | 118 | 4.37 | 21 | .78 | 9 | .33 |
| 1979 | (12-10) | 29 | 126 | 4.34 | 30 | 1.03 | 19 | .66 |
| 1980 | (13-11) | 31 | 182 | 5.87 | 27 | .87 | 20 | .65 |
| 1981 | (12- 9) | 24 | 82 | 3.42 | 25 | 1.04 | 12 | .50 |
| 1982 | (12-10) | 29 | 144 | 4.97 | 34 | 1.17 | 13 | .45 |
| 6 years | | 91 | 400 | 4.40 | 107 | 1.18 | 45 | .50 |

| | G | IP | W | L | Pct | ER | ERA |
|---|---|---|---|---|---|---|---|
| Home | 13 | 93 | 6 | 5 | .545 | 31 | 3.00 |
| Road | 16 | 100.2 | 6 | 5 | .545 | 47 | 4.20 |

## Jerry UJDUR

| Year | (W–L) | GS | Run | Avg | DP | Avg | SB | Avg |
|---|---|---|---|---|---|---|---|---|
| 1980 | ( 1- 0) | 2 | 13 | 6.50 | 2 | 1.00 | 0 | – |
| 1981 | ( 0- 0) | 4 | 19 | 4.75 | 2 | .50 | 2 | .50 |
| 1982 | (10-10) | 25 | 104 | 4.16 | 29 | 1.16 | 19 | .76 |
| 3 years | | 31 | 136 | 4.39 | 33 | 1.06 | 21 | .68 |

| | G | IP | W | L | Pct | ER | ERA |
|---|---|---|---|---|---|---|---|
| Home | 13 | 92.1 | 3 | 6 | .333 | 42 | 4.09 |
| Road | 12 | 85.2 | 7 | 4 | .636 | 31 | 3.26 |

## 1982 OTHERS

| Pitcher | (W–L) | GS | Run | Avg | DP | Avg | SB | Avg |
|---|---|---|---|---|---|---|---|---|
| Pashnick | (4-4) | 13 | 53 | 4.08 | 10 | .77 | 5 | .38 |
| Underwood | (4-8) | 12 | 52 | 4.33 | 12 | 1.00 | 10 | 1.00 |
| Rucker | (5-6) | 4 | 14 | 3.50 | 3 | .75 | 1 | .25 |
| Rozema | (3-0) | 2 | 6 | 3.00 | 0 | | 1 | |
| Tobik | (4-9) | 1 | 7 | | 1 | | 0 | |
| Saucier | (3-1) | 1 | 5 | | 1 | | 1 | |
| Gumpert | (0-0) | 1 | 4 | | 0 | | 0 | |
| Berenguer | (0-0) | 1 | 6 | | 0 | | 0 | |
| James | (0-2) | 1 | 7 | | 0 | | 2 | |

## DETROIT TIGERS

*Talent Analysis*

The Tigers possessed 164 points of approximate value.

| | AV | % |
|---|---|---|
| Produced by Tigers' system: | 110 | 67% |
| Acquired by trade: | 38 | 23% |
| Purchased or signed from free agency: | 16 | 10% |

The Tigers are a system-built team.

| | | |
|---|---|---|
| Young (Up to age 25): | 31 | 19% |
| Prime (Age 26 to 29): | 103 | 63% |
| Past-prime (Age 30 to 33): | 26 | 16% |
| Old (Age 34 or older): | 4 | 2% |

The Tigers remain a young team.

The Tiger system could claim 155 approximate value output in 1982, the twelfth highest total in the majors. Over the last four years their total is 620, which ranks eighth.

## TIGER STADIUM

DIMENSIONS: Short in the alleys and in right field

SURFACE: Grass

VISIBILITY: Superb

FOUL TERRITORY: Small

FAVORS:
Hitter/Pitcher—Pitcher
Power/Line-drive hitter—Power
Righthander/Lefthander—Lefthander

TYPES OF OFFENSE AFFECTED: Home runs, up 20-25%; mostly by lefties; a fairly neutral park for a right-handed batter

TYPES OF MARGINAL PLAYERS MOST VALUABLE IN PARK: Left-handed power

PLAYERS ON TEAM HELPED MOST BY PARK: Well, there was Jason Thompson, and there was Richie Hebner . . . Trammell seems to hit well here

PLAYERS ON TEAM HURT MOST BY PARK: None much

OTHER COMMENTS: Sometimes you just can't figure stats. The Tiger pitchers walked 284 men at home, 270 on the road. They were hammered for 100 home runs at home, just 72 on the road. Yet somehow, they cut their ERA from 4.20 on the road to 3.45 at home.

# NEW YORK YANKEES

Like a great work of literature, it can only be fully appreciated with the benefit of hindsight. As Bob Lemon is let out to pasture, let it be noted that in 1977, Bob Lemon won 90 games with this lineup:

| | |
|---|---|
| 1B | Jim Spencer |
| 2B | Jorge Orta |
| 3B | Eric Soderholm |
| SS | Alan Bannister |
| LF | Ralph Garr |
| CF | Chet Lemon |
| RF | Richie Zisk |
| C | Jim Essian |
| DH | Oscar Gamble |

His starting rotation was Francisco Barrios, Steve Stone, Ken Kravec and Chris Knapp. His relief ace was Lerrin LaGrow.

How? He had a bad infield, a bad outfield, an awful starting rotation and Jim Essian at catcher. Kravec had the best ERA of any starter, 4.10. The team finished last in the league in double plays, first in errors, and last in stolen bases. The pitching staff threw three shutouts. It had to be one of the best managerial accomplishments of the decade.

Lemon also brought the Royals in in 1971 at 85–76 with a team prominently featuring Gail Hopkins, Paul Schaal, Joe Keough, Jerry May, Bob Oliver and Ed Kirkpatrick. His top home-run hitter that year hit 15, and only one other player was in double figures. The only starters to win more than eight games were Dick Drago and Mike Hedlund. The more you look at these accomplishments, the more remarkable they seem.

My friend Randy Spence, who is an excellent chess player, once told me that each game of chess is like an intense, ferocious argument without words—an argument about how chess should be played. In the ledger of bad ideas of historical magnitude, enter now the name of George Steinbrenner, cited for his 1981 argument that the era of the home run was over, and that the Yankees were to become a slashing, speed-based team in tune with the 1980s. The chance that this would work was roughly equal to the chance that Ronald Reagan might elope with Joan Baez. All successful ball teams adjust to the design of their home park, and this park is not designed for speed. It is designed for left-handed power. And no Yankee team has ever won a pennant—not even once—without having that left-handed power, and a bunch of it. Throughout their history, the periods when they have not had left-handed power and the periods when they have not won coincide perfectly.

Besides that, however, there is another problem. You cannot win a pennant by stealing bases. Nobody ever has, nobody ever will. It cannot be done. It is an argument that cannot be won, a position that cannot be defended.

There are people in the world who want to say that stolen bases are really the key to a modern offense because I saw Rickey Henderson play 18 times this year and this happened and that happened and . . . Let them go. But if you begin at the beginning of the subject, asking "How important are stolen bases, relative to other types of offense?" you can get answers to that question in any number of ways, correlation studies, building simulated offenses, dissecting offensive sequences, dozens of others. Anything you do—anything at all, anything you can devise, if it has even a reasonable degree of intellectual integrity—will lead you to the same conclusion. Stolen bases, compared to any other type of offense, are trivial. They create virtually no runs on balance; they have very little to do with who wins and loses.

I've introduced several of these studies in past *Abstracts*, and probably I should reintroduce them because there weren't an awful lot of people who read the book at that time. But anyway, as I said, there's no shortage. Another way to study the impact of each type of offensive weapon is to study what happened to the teams which used them. What happens to teams which lead the league in stolen bases, for example? Since the 1969 expansion, nine teams which have led their leagues in stolen bases have also won their divisions. Eleven stolen base leaders have finished second, none third, none fourth, two fifth and six sixth. That is an "average finish" of 2.75.

How does this compare to the teams leading in the other offensive categories? Take a look:

| Average Finish of Team Leading In: | |
|---|---|
| Runs Scored | 2.11 |
| Triples | 2.32 |
| Slugging Percentage | 2.43 |
| Home Runs | 2.43 |
| Doubles | 2.46 |
| Batting Average | 2.50 |
| Walks | 2.69 |
| Stolen Bases | 2.75 |

In all cases of ties, I used the higher figure; for example, St. Louis and San Diego tied for the NL lead in triples in 1982, so I used St. Louis, first, instead of San Diego, fourth.

Anyway, teams leading the league in stolen bases, even in this "speed era," have done worse than teams leading the league in any other major offensive category.

That is only half the study. The other half is a look at how teams finishing *last* in the league in stolen bases have done in the same 1969 to 1982 period. That chart is given below:

| | |
|---|---|
| Triples | 3.50 |
| Stolen Bases | 3.54 |
| Home Runs | 4.39 |
| Walks | 4.50 |
| Doubles | 5.11 |
| Runs Scored | 5.36 |
| Slugging Average | 5.39 |
| Batting Average | 5.43 |

This time stolen bases are edged out by their partner, triples, as the least important offensive category. But teams finishing last in the league in stolen bases and triples are able to win far more consistently than teams finishing last in any other category.

We can combine these two studies into one by figuring the average distance between the teams finishing first in the league and those finishing last. It makes sense, don't you think, that the more important an offensive category is, the greater would be the average distance between the teams doing well in that category and the teams doing poorly? Those distances are:

| | |
|---|---|
| Runs Scored (5.36 – 2.11) | 3.25 |
| Slugging Percentage (5.39 – 2.43) | 2.96 |
| Batting Average (5.43 – 2.50) | 2.93 |
| Doubles (5.11 – 2.50) | 2.68 |
| Home Runs (4.39 – 2.43) | 1.96 |
| Walks (4.50 – 2.69) | 1.81 |
| Triples (3.50 – 2.32) | 1.18 |
| Stolen Bases (3.54 – 2.75) | 0.79 |

One of the things that I like about this study is that it also refutes many of the side-issues which are so often used to confuse the issue. People say, for example, that stolen bases are important because they intimidate the opposition. Intimidating the opposition is nice, but winning is more the point of the game. If, in fact, stolen bases had intimidation value that paid off in the win column, then that would cause those teams to finish higher in the standings, would cause the gaps between the teams which have speed and those that do not to grow larger. People say that speed is valuable because it pays off in opposition errors. Well, that's great, but *why don't they win*? People say that speed is important because it enables people to go from first to third on a single, that it is important because it can be used in defense as well as offense. But this method of measuring its importance wouldn't care *why* it was important, and as such it throws a road block in front of any and all of those arguments.

OK, that's only one study; it might be wrong. Let's do another one. Remember my friend's comment about each chess match being an argument? Well, let us say the same thing about every baseball game. Let us say that Kansas City is playing Milwaukee. Kansas City steals more bases than Milwaukee; Milwaukee hits more home runs than Kansas City. Kansas City is "arguing" that stolen bases are more important, so every time Kansas City beats Milwaukee, we consider that a victory for stolen bases; when Milwaukee wins it's a victory for power. Kansas City won 7 of the 12 matchups, and speed leads 7-5.

But suppose that we do this for every possible contrasting match-up—that is, for every American League game in which one team has more power and the other team has more speed. There were 596 such games in 1982. The teams with higher seasonal stolen base totals won 263—a miserable .441 won-lost percentage.

OK, perhaps that is not a revelation, as who actually believes that stolen bases are more important than home runs? So we extend the method to compare teams having an edge in stolen bases to teams having an edge in each of the other offensive categories. We find:

| | Wins | Losses | W/L% |
|---|---|---|---|
| Stolen Bases Against Triples | 214 | 244 | .467 |
| Stolen Bases Against Slugging Percentage | 310 | 388 | .451 |
| Stolen Bases Against Home Runs | 263 | 333 | .441 |
| Stolen Bases Against Doubles | 250 | 337 | .426 |
| Stolen Bases Against Batting Average | 252 | 360 | .412 |
| Stolen Bases Against Runs Scored | 231 | 337 | .407 |

Some of you who are especially sharp are wondering if this effect was caused simply because the Oakland A's, who led the league in stolen bases, were a bad team. That's an intelligent objection. But if you throw out all games involving the A's and recompute the won-lost percentages, you get: against triples, .479; against slugging percentage, .450; against home runs, .450; against doubles, .427; against batting average, .409; against runs scored, .416. Teams stealing a lot of bases lose, consistently, to teams holding an advantage in any other offensive category.

Sure, the stolen base is more important in the National League than it is in the American League. Sure, it plays a role in the offense. But don't say that St. Louis "ran to the World's Championship." The Cardinals had an awful lot of plusses besides stolen bases. Their approximate value, which in essence is simply a careful count of the plusses, was easily the highest in the National League, and would have been if they had been last in the league in stolen bases.

Steinbrenner, at this writing, gives evidence of having returned to the real world. At the beginning of the free agent season, I felt that there were three people out there who could save the Yankees: Thompson, Bannister and Kemp. I felt that if the Yankees could get two out of the three, they would be back in contention. If they were shut out, they might as well put their head between their knees and kiss their dynasty goodbye. If they got one of the three, then it should be interesting.

The one they got was Kemp. Kemp is an outstanding hitter, a far better hitter than the public realizes. He hits for a good average, he walks a lot, he's an RBI man. He has always hit well in Yankee Stadium. (His career batting average there is .324, 36/111, whereas it is .234 against the Yankees in other parks.) He is a hard-nosed type who does not figure to be affected by the pressure of being a free agent in New York. He deals well with left-handed pitching. With Winfield coming up ahead of him and Baylor behind, he will drive in over 100 runs unless he is injured, and he is not injury-prone. If the pitching can be patched up at all, it figures to be an interesting summer in the Bronx.

**JOE DiMAGGIO** CAREER HOME AND ROAD BREAKDOWNS

| | *In Yankee Stadium* | | | | | | | | | *On The Road* | | | | | | | | |
|---|---|---|---|---|---|---|---|---|---|---|---|---|---|---|---|---|---|---|
| **Year** | **G** | **AB** | **R** | **H** | **2B** | **3B** | **HR** | **RBI** | **Avg** | **G** | **AB** | **R** | **H** | **2B** | **3B** | **HR** | **RBI** | **Avg** |
| 1936 | 67 | 288 | 51 | 90 | 18 | 8 | 8 | 53 | .313 | 71 | 349 | 81 | 116 | 26 | 7 | 21 | 72 | .332 |
| 1937 | 77 | 306 | 83 | 105 | 16 | 8 | 19 | 80 | .343 | 74 | 315 | 68 | 110 | 19 | 7 | 27 | 87 | .349 |
| 1938 | 74 | 296 | 67 | 104 | 23 | 8 | 15 | 75 | .351 | 71 | 303 | 62 | 90 | 9 | 5 | 17 | 65 | .297 |
| 1939 | 64 | 237 | 46 | 83 | 16 | 1 | 12 | 50 | .350 | 56 | 225 | 62 | 93 | 16 | 5 | 18 | 76 | .413 |
| 1940 | 63 | 234 | 40 | 84 | 12 | 6 | 16 | 67 | .359 | 69 | 274 | 53 | 95 | 16 | 3 | 15 | 66 | .347 |
| 1941 | 76 | 292 | 60 | 101 | 21 | 6 | 16 | 69 | .346 | 63 | 249 | 62 | 92 | 22 | 5 | 14 | 56 | .369 |
| 1942 | 77 | 305 | 51 | 89 | 15 | 6 | 8 | 55 | .292 | 77 | 305 | 72 | 97 | 14 | 7 | 13 | 59 | .318 |
| 1946 | 66 | 254 | 37 | 666 | 8 | 6 | 8 | 35 | .260 | 66 | 249 | 44 | 80 | 12 | 2 | 17 | 60 | .321 |
| 1947 | 70 | 252 | 49 | 77 | 18 | 5 | 9 | 51 | .306 | 71 | 282 | 48 | 91 | 13 | 5 | 11 | 46 | .323 |
| 1948 | 77 | 294 | 54 | 92 | 10 | 8 | 15 | 70 | .313 | 76 | 300 | 56 | 98 | 16 | 3 | 24 | 85 | .327 |
| 1949 | 37 | 127 | 25 | 41 | 7 | 3 | 5 | 23 | .323 | 39 | 145 | 33 | 53 | 7 | 3 | 9 | 44 | .366 |
| 1950 | 65 | 242 | 48 | 67 | 11 | 6 | 9 | 47 | .277 | 74 | 283 | 66 | 91 | 22 | 4 | 23 | 75 | .322 |
| 1951 | 67 | 233 | 37 | 61 | 11 | 2 | 8 | 45 | .262 | 49 | 182 | 35 | 48 | 11 | 2 | 4 | 26 | .264 |
| Career | 880 | 3360 | 648 | 1060 | 186 | 73 | 148 | 720 | .315 | 856 | 3461 | 742 | 1154 | 203 | 58 | 213 | 817 | .333 |

**LOU GEHRIG** CAREER HOME AND ROAD BREAKDOWNS

| | *In Yankee Stadium* | | | | | | | | | *On The Road* | | | | | | | | |
|---|---|---|---|---|---|---|---|---|---|---|---|---|---|---|---|---|---|---|
| **Year** | **G** | **AB** | **R** | **H** | **2B** | **3B** | **HR** | **RBI** | **Avg** | **G** | **AB** | **R** | **H** | **2B** | **3B** | **HR** | **RBI** | **Avg** |
| 1923 | 6 | 4 | 0 | 1 | 1 | 0 | 0 | 2 | .250 | 7 | 22 | 6 | 10 | 3 | 1 | 1 | 7 | .455 |
| 1924 | 4 | 6 | 2 | 4 | 0 | 0 | 0 | 2 | .067 | 6 | 6 | 0 | 2 | 1 | 0 | 0 | 3 | .333 |
| 1925 | 68 | 237 | 41 | 66 | 14 | 5 | 11 | 42 | .278 | 58 | 200 | 32 | 63 | 9 | 5 | 9 | 26 | .315 |
| 1926 | 75 | 270 | 62 | 81 | 19 | 12 | 4 | 44 | .300 | 80 | 302 | 73 | 98 | 28 | 8 | 12 | 63 | .325 |
| 1927 | 77 | 277 | 71 | 96 | 16 | 8 | 24 | 77 | .347 | 78 | 307 | 78 | 122 | 36 | 10 | 23 | 98 | .397 |
| 1928 | 77 | 262 | 62 | 97 | 26 | 5 | 12 | 66 | .370 | 77 | 300 | 77 | 113 | 21 | 8 | 15 | 76 | .377 |
| 1929 | 77 | 271 | 60 | 85 | 13 | 7 | 21 | 76 | .314 | 77 | 282 | 67 | 81 | 20 | 2 | 14 | 50 | .287 |
| 1930 | 76 | 270 | 59 | 94 | 16 | 10 | 14 | 57 | .348 | 78 | 311 | 84 | 126 | 26 | 7 | 27 | 117 | .405 |
| 1931 | 77 | 304 | 83 | 92 | 12 | 10 | 24 | 86 | .303 | 78 | 315 | 80 | 119 | 19 | 5 | 22 | 98 | .378 |
| 1932 | 77 | 289 | 59 | 88 | 13 | 6 | 12 | 60 | .304 | 79 | 307 | 79 | 120 | 29 | 3 | 22 | 91 | .391 |
| 1933 | 75 | 281 | 59 | 85 | 112 | 4 | 17 | 69 | .302 | 77 | 312 | 79 | 113 | 29 | 8 | 15 | 70 | .362 |
| 1934 | 77 | 290 | 68 | 120 | 20 | 4 | 30 | 98 | .414 | 77 | 289 | 60 | 90 | 20 | 2 | 19 | 67 | .311 |
| 1935 | 74 | 253 | 45 | 71 | 8 | 5 | 15 | 45 | .281 | 75 | 282 | 80 | 105 | 18 | 5 | 15 | 74 | .372 |
| 1936 | 77 | 267 | 81 | 94 | 11 | 1 | 27 | 71 | .352 | 78 | 312 | 86 | 111 | 26 | 6 | 22 | 81 | .386 |
| 1937 | 79 | 275 | 68 | 104 | 13 | 3 | 24 | 93 | .378 | 78 | 294 | 70 | 96 | 24 | 6 | 13 | 66 | .327 |
| 1938 | 79 | 287 | 61 | 88 | 12 | 3 | 16 | 58 | .307 | 78 | 289 | 54 | 82 | 20 | 3 | 13 | 56 | .284 |
| 1939 | 5 | 18 | 1 | 3 | 0 | 0 | 0 | 1 | .167 | 3 | 10 | 1 | 1 | 0 | 0 | 0 | 0 | .100 |
| Career | 1080 | 3861 | 882 | 1269 | 206 | 83 | 251 | 947 | .329 | 1084 | 4140 | 1006 | 1452 | 329 | 79 | 242 | 1043 | .351 |

**BILL DICKEY** CAREER HOME AND ROAD BREAKDOWNS

| | *In Yankee Stadium* | | | | | | | | | *On The Road* | | | | | | | | |
|---|---|---|---|---|---|---|---|---|---|---|---|---|---|---|---|---|---|---|
| **Year** | **G** | **AB** | **R** | **H** | **2B** | **3B** | **HR** | **RBI** | **Avg** | **G** | **AB** | **R** | **H** | **2B** | **3B** | **HR** | **RBI** | **Avg** |
| 1928 | 7 | 11 | 1 | 3 | 1 | 1 | 0 | 2 | .273 | 3 | 4 | 0 | 0 | 0 | 0 | 0 | 0 | .000 |
| 1929 | 66 | 227 | 30 | 71 | 9 | 4 | 5 | 31 | .313 | 64 | 220 | 30 | 74 | 21 | 2 | 5 | 34 | .331 |
| 1930 | 51 | 158 | 26 | 54 | 11 | 5 | 3 | 40 | .342 | 58 | 208 | 29 | 70 | 14 | 2 | 2 | 25 | .337 |
| 1931 | 67 | 252 | 37 | 79 | 9 | 6 | 4 | 38 | .313 | 63 | 225 | 28 | 77 | 8 | 4 | 2 | 40 | .342 |
| 1932 | 51 | 183 | 35 | 59 | 9 | 1 | 7 | 32 | .322 | 57 | 240 | 31 | 32 | 11 | 3 | 8 | 52 | .306 |
| 1933 | 63 | 213 | 25 | 66 | 9 | 3 | 9 | 45 | .310 | 67 | 265 | 33 | 86 | 15 | 5 | 5 | 52 | .325 |
| 1934 | 55 | 211 | 23 | 56 | 10 | 1 | 6 | 30 | .265 | 49 | 184 | 33 | 71 | 14 | 3 | 6 | 42 | .386 |
| 1935 | 58 | 211 | 31 | 64 | 12 | 2 | 11 | 35 | .303 | 62 | 237 | 23 | 61 | 14 | 4 | 3 | 46 | .257 |
| 1936 | 51 | 191 | 43 | 67 | 10 | 2 | 14 | 52 | .351 | 61 | 232 | 56 | 86 | 16 | 6 | 8 | 55 | .371 |
| 1937 | 72 | 270 | 47 | 94 | 13 | 1 | 21 | 85 | .348 | 68 | 260 | 40 | 82 | 22 | 11 | 8 | 48 | .315 |
| 1938 | 64 | 213 | 50 | 76 | 9 | 1 | 23 | 83 | .357 | 68 | 241 | 34 | 66 | 18 | 3 | 4 | 32 | .274 |
| 1939 | 65 | 217 | 48 | 58 | 5 | 1 | 19 | 49 | .267 | 63 | 263 | 50 | 87 | 18 | 2 | 5 | 56 | .331 |
| 1940 | 57 | 194 | 23 | 45 | 5 | 0 | 5 | 31 | .232 | 49 | 178 | 22 | 47 | 6 | 1 | 4 | 23 | .264 |
| 1941 | 59 | 187 | 15 | 55 | 10 | 3 | 5 | 40 | .294 | 50 | 161 | 20 | 44 | 5 | 3 | 2 | 31 | .273 |
| 1942 | 43 | 140 | 14 | 43 | 4 | 1 | 1 | 16 | .307 | 39 | 128 | 14 | 36 | 9 | 0 | 1 | 21 | .281 |
| 1943 | 46 | 129 | 13 | 44 | 6 | 1 | 2 | 14 | .341 | 39 | 113 | 16 | 41 | 12 | 1 | 2 | 19 | .363 |
| 1946 | 32 | 78 | 6 | 20 | 4 | 0 | 0 | 7 | .256 | 22 | 56 | 4 | 15 | 4 | 0 | 2 | 3 | .268 |
| Career | 907 | 3085 | 467 | 954 | 136 | 32 | 135 | 630 | .309 | 882 | 3215 | 463 | 1015 | 207 | 40 | 67 | 579 | .316 |

**BABE RUTH** CAREER HOME AND ROAD BREAKDOWNS

1914-19, old Fenway; 1920-22, Polo Grounds; 1923-34, Yankee Stadium; 1935, Braves Field

| | *At Home* | | | | | | | | | *On The Road* | | | | | | | | |
|---|---|---|---|---|---|---|---|---|---|---|---|---|---|---|---|---|---|---|
| **Year** | **G** | **AB** | **R** | **H** | **2B** | **3B** | **HR** | **RBI** | **Avg** | **G** | **AB** | **R** | **H** | **2B** | **3B** | **HR** | **RBI** | **Avg** |
| 1914 | 5 | 10 | 1 | 2 | 1 | 0 | 0 | 0 | .200 | 0 | 0 | 1 | 0 | 0 | 0 | 0 | 0 | .000 |
| 1915 | 18 | 41 | 8 | 15 | 4 | 1 | 1 | | .366 | 24 | 51 | 8 | 14 | 6 | 0 | 3 | | .275 |
| 1916 | 34 | 66 | 10 | 14 | 5 | 1 | 0 | | .212 | 33 | 70 | 8 | 23 | 0 | 2 | 3 | | .329 |
| 1917 | 26 | 57 | 8 | 21 | 4 | 1 | 1 | | .368 | 26 | 66 | 6 | 19 | 2 | 2 | 1 | | .288 |
| 1918 | 48 | 145 | 28 | 45 | 14 | 8 | 0 | | .310 | 47 | 172 | 22 | 50 | 12 | 3 | 11 | | .291 |
| 1919 | 63 | 200 | 47 | 65 | 19 | 6 | 9 | | .325 | 67 | 232 | 56 | 74 | 15 | 6 | 20 | | .319 |
| 1920 | 60 | 204 | 77 | 81 | 21 | 6 | 29 | 71 | .397 | 76 | 254 | 81 | 91 | 15 | 3 | 25 | 66 | .358 |
| 1921 | 78 | 255 | 94 | 103 | 24 | 7 | 32 | 81 | .404 | 74 | 285 | 83 | 101 | 20 | 9 | 27 | 90 | .354 |
| 1922 | 53 | 195 | 40 | 58 | 7 | 5 | 14 | 45 | .297 | 57 | 211 | 54 | 70 | 17 | 3 | 21 | 54 | .332 |
| 1923 | 76 | 246 | 74 | 101 | 26 | 7 | 19 | 63 | .411 | 76 | 276 | 78 | 104 | 19 | 6 | 22 | 68 | .377 |
| 1924 | 78 | 260 | 70 | 99 | 18 | 4 | 24 | 71 | .381 | 75 | 269 | 73 | 101 | 21 | 3 | 22 | 50 | .375 |
| 1925 | 56 | 203 | 35 | 59 | 8 | 1 | 11 | 34 | .291 | 42 | 156 | 26 | 45 | 4 | 1 | 14 | 32 | .288 |
| 1926 | 75 | 241 | 68 | 88 | 13 | 2 | 23 | 76 | .365 | 77 | 254 | 71 | 96 | 17 | 3 | 24 | 70 | .378 |
| 1927 | 73 | 253 | 82 | 94 | 10 | 4 | 28 | 70 | .372 | 78 | 287 | 76 | 98 | 19 | 4 | 32 | 94 | .341 |
| 1928 | 77 | 260 | 76 | 86 | 8 | 4 | 29 | 70 | .331 | 77 | 276 | 87 | 87 | 21 | 4 | 25 | 72 | .315 |
| 1929 | 60 | 218 | 50 | 72 | 7 | 3 | 21 | 66 | .330 | 75 | 281 | 71 | 100 | 19 | 3 | 25 | 88 | .356 |
| 1930 | 72 | 244 | 72 | 91 | 13 | 5 | 26 | 75 | .373 | 73 | 274 | 78 | 95 | 15 | 4 | 23 | 78 | .347 |
| 1931 | 75 | 267 | 72 | 96 | 11 | 0 | 24 | 78 | .360 | 70 | 267 | 77 | 103 | 20 | 3 | 22 | 85 | .386 |
| 1932 | 72 | 239 | 62 | 78 | 6 | 2 | 19 | 69 | .326 | 61 | 218 | 58 | 78 | 7 | 3 | 22 | 68 | .358 |
| 1933 | 68 | 214 | 51 | 68 | 9 | 1 | 22 | 56 | .318 | 69 | 245 | 46 | 70 | 12 | 2 | 12 | 47 | .286 |
| 1934 | 69 | 190 | 47 | 56 | 11 | 2 | 13 | 50 | .295 | 56 | 175 | 31 | 49 | 6 | 2 | 9 | 34 | .280 |
| 1935 | 11 | 25 | 6 | 6 | 0 | 0 | 2 | 4 | .240 | 17 | 47 | 7 | 7 | 0 | 0 | 4 | 8 | .149 |
| Career | 1253 | 4033 | 1078 | 1398 | 239 | 70 | 347 | 1037 + | .347 | 1250 | 4366 | 1097 | 1475 | 267 | 66 | 367 | 1004 + | .338 |
| In Yankee | 851 | 2835 | 759 | 988 | 140 | 35 | 259 | 778 | .349 | 829 | 2978 | 772 | 1026 | 180 | 38 | 252 | 786 | .345 |

Willie RANDOLPH, Second Base

*Runs Created: 71*

| | G | AB | R | H | 2B | 3B | HR | RBI | SB | Avg |
|---|---|---|---|---|---|---|---|---|---|---|
| First Half | 74 | 280 | 44 | 75 | 10 | 3 | 2 | 26 | 6 | .268 |
| Second Half | 70 | 273 | 41 | 80 | 11 | 1 | 1 | 10 | 10 | .293 |
| Home | 74 | 270 | 43 | 81 | 10 | 4 | 1 | 14 | 10 | .300 |
| Road | 70 | 283 | 42 | 74 | 11 | 0 | 2 | 22 | 6 | .261 |
| vs. RHP | | 333 | 55 | 96 | 11 | 1 | 1 | 23 | 14 | .288 |
| vs. LHP | | 220 | 30 | 59 | 10 | 3 | 2 | 13 | 2 | .268 |
| 1982 | 144 | 553 | 85 | 155 | 21 | 4 | 3 | 36 | 16 | .280 |
| 5.95 years | | 595 | 99 | 161 | 23 | 8 | 4 | 49 | 30 | .271 |

Ken GRIFFEY, Right Field

*Runs Created: 65*

| | G | AB | R | H | 2B | 3B | HR | RBI | SB | Avg |
|---|---|---|---|---|---|---|---|---|---|---|
| First Half | 63 | 245 | 39 | 71 | 13 | 2 | 4 | 20 | 7 | .290 |
| Second Half | 64 | 239 | 31 | 63 | 10 | 0 | 8 | 34 | 3 | .264 |
| Home | 64 | 243 | 37 | 65 | 12 | 2 | 8 | 32 | 5 | .267 |
| Road | 63 | 241 | 33 | 69 | 11 | 0 | 4 | 22 | 5 | .286 |
| vs. RHP | | 306 | 47 | 87 | 16 | 1 | 9 | 43 | 9 | .284 |
| vs. LHP | | 178 | 23 | 47 | 7 | 1 | 3 | 11 | 1 | .264 |
| 1982 | 127 | 484 | 70 | 134 | 23 | 2 | 12 | 54 | 10 | .277 |
| 7.25 years | | 599 | 102 | 182 | 31 | 9 | 10 | 66 | 22 | .304 |

Graig NETTLES, Third Base

*Runs Created: 50*

| | G | AB | R | H | 2B | 3B | HR | RBI | SB | Avg |
|---|---|---|---|---|---|---|---|---|---|---|
| First Half | 59 | 208 | 21 | 47 | 6 | 1 | 6 | 26 | 1 | .226 |
| Second Half | 63 | 197 | 26 | 47 | 5 | 1 | 12 | 29 | 0 | .239 |
| Home | 67 | 222 | 24 | 47 | 8 | 1 | 10 | 27 | 0 | .212 |
| Road | 55 | 183 | 23 | 47 | 3 | 1 | 8 | 28 | 1 | .257 |
| vs. RHP | | 249 | 33 | 59 | 5 | 2 | 15 | 41 | 0 | .237 |
| vs. LHP | | 156 | 14 | 35 | 6 | 0 | 3 | 14 | 1 | .224 |
| 1982 | 122 | 405 | 47 | 94 | 11 | 2 | 18 | 55 | 1 | .232 |
| 12.30 years | | 574 | 78 | 144 | 21 | 2 | 26 | 82 | 3 | .250 |

Rick CERONE, Catcher

*Runs Created: 25*

| | G | AB | R | H | 2B | 3B | HR | RBI | SB | Avg |
|---|---|---|---|---|---|---|---|---|---|---|
| First Half | 25 | 86 | 7 | 20 | 0 | 0 | 1 | 8 | 0 | .233 |
| Second Half | 64 | 214 | 22 | 48 | 10 | 0 | 4 | 20 | 0 | .224 |
| Home | 46 | 158 | 13 | 35 | 5 | 0 | 1 | 12 | 0 | .222 |
| Road | 43 | 142 | 16 | 33 | 5 | 0 | 4 | 16 | 0 | .232 |
| vs. RHP | | 182 | 17 | 35 | 4 | 0 | 3 | 15 | 0 | .192 |
| vs. LHP | | 118 | 12 | 33 | 6 | 0 | 2 | 13 | 0 | .280 |
| 1982 | 89 | 300 | 29 | 68 | 10 | 0 | 5 | 28 | 0 | .227 |
| 3.56 years | | 543 | 57 | 132 | 26 | 3 | 9 | 64 | 1 | .243 |

Oscar GAMBLE, Designated Hitter

*Runs Created: 63*

| | G | AB | R | H | 2B | 3B | HR | RBI | SB | Avg |
|---|---|---|---|---|---|---|---|---|---|---|
| First Half | 53 | 158 | 23 | 38 | 12 | 1 | 7 | 26 | 5 | .241 |
| Second Half | 55 | 158 | 26 | 48 | 9 | 1 | 11 | 31 | 1 | .304 |
| Home | 54 | 142 | 25 | 40 | 13 | 1 | 11 | 33 | 1 | .282 |
| Road | 54 | 174 | 24 | 46 | 8 | 1 | 7 | 24 | 5 | .264 |
| vs. RHP | | 282 | 42 | 74 | 19 | 2 | 15 | 47 | 6 | .262 |
| vs. LHP | | 34 | 7 | 12 | 2 | 0 | 3 | 10 | 0 | .353 |
| 1982 | 108 | 316 | 49 | 86 | 21 | 2 | 18 | 57 | 6 | .272 |
| 8.56 years | | 473 | 69 | 128 | 20 | 3 | 21 | 69 | 5 | .270 |

Roy SMALLEY, Shortstop

*Runs Created: 71*

| | G | AB | R | H | 2B | 3B | HR | RBI | SB | Avg |
|---|---|---|---|---|---|---|---|---|---|---|
| First Half | 71 | 236 | 25 | 56 | 6 | 1 | 8 | 28 | 0 | .237 |
| Second Half | 71 | 250 | 30 | 69 | 8 | 1 | 12 | 39 | 0 | .276 |
| Home | 70 | 236 | 23 | 66 | 7 | 2 | 8 | 33 | 0 | .280 |
| Road | 72 | 250 | 32 | 59 | 7 | 0 | 12 | 34 | 0 | .236 |
| vs. RHP | | 298 | 38 | 81 | 10 | 0 | 16 | 48 | 0 | .272 |
| vs. LHP | | 188 | 17 | 44 | 4 | 2 | 4 | 19 | 0 | .234 |
| 1982 | 142 | 486 | 55 | 125 | 14 | 2 | 20 | 67 | 0 | .257 |
| 6.34 years | | 585 | 78 | 151 | 24 | 3 | 15 | 72 | 3 | .259 |

Dave WINFIELD, Left Field

*Runs Created: 100*

| | G | AB | R | H | 2B | 3B | HR | RBI | SB | Avg |
|---|---|---|---|---|---|---|---|---|---|---|
| First Half | 65 | 254 | 40 | 75 | 13 | 2 | 15 | 47 | 4 | .295 |
| Second Half | 75 | 285 | 44 | 76 | 11 | 6 | 22 | 59 | 1 | .267 |
| Home | 71 | 272 | 38 | 78 | 9 | 4 | 14 | 53 | 2 | .287 |
| Road | 69 | 267 | 46 | 73 | 15 | 4 | 23 | 53 | 3 | .273 |
| vs. RHP | | 331 | 51 | 94 | 20 | 7 | 18 | 66 | 5 | .284 |
| vs. LHP | | 208 | 33 | 57 | 4 | 1 | 19 | 40 | 0 | .274 |
| 1982 | 140 | 539 | 84 | 151 | 24 | 8 | 37 | 106 | 5 | .280 |
| 8.41 years | | 586 | 87 | 166 | 27 | 6 | 24 | 95 | 18 | .284 |

Jerry MUMPHREY, Center Field

*Runs Created: 83*

| | G | AB | R | H | 2B | 3B | HR | RBI | SB | Avg |
|---|---|---|---|---|---|---|---|---|---|---|
| First Half | 46 | 180 | 19 | 51 | 4 | 4 | 0 | 17 | 7 | .283 |
| Second Half | 77 | 297 | 57 | 92 | 20 | 6 | 9 | 51 | 4 | .310 |
| Home | 65 | 243 | 47 | 78 | 13 | 6 | 6 | 36 | 6 | .321 |
| Road | 58 | 234 | 29 | 65 | 11 | 4 | 3 | 32 | 5 | .278 |
| vs. RHP | | 312 | 56 | 105 | 19 | 7 | 8 | 56 | 10 | .337 |
| vs. LHP | | 165 | 20 | 38 | 5 | 3 | 1 | 12 | 1 | .230 |
| 1982 | 123 | 477 | 76 | 143 | 24 | 10 | 9 | 68 | 11 | .300 |
| 5.46 years | | 537 | 74 | 154 | 22 | 7 | 5 | 54 | 26 | .288 |

Lou PINIELLA, Designated Hitter

*Runs Created: 41*

| | G | AB | R | H | 2B | 3B | HR | RBI | SB | Avg |
|---|---|---|---|---|---|---|---|---|---|---|
| First Half | 55 | 144 | 19 | 43 | 9 | 1 | 3 | 25 | 0 | .299 |
| Second Half | 47 | 117 | 14 | 37 | 8 | 0 | 3 | 12 | 0 | .316 |
| Home | 53 | 127 | 11 | 35 | 7 | 1 | 1 | 17 | 0 | .276 |
| Road | 49 | 134 | 22 | 45 | 10 | 0 | 5 | 20 | 0 | .336 |
| vs. RHP | | 52 | 6 | 15 | 1 | 0 | 1 | 8 | 0 | .288 |
| vs. LHP | | 209 | 27 | 65 | 16 | 1 | 5 | 29 | 0 | .311 |
| 1982 | 102 | 261 | 33 | 80 | 17 | 1 | 6 | 37 | 0 | .307 |
| 10.28 years | | 548 | 61 | 159 | 28 | 4 | 10 | 72 | 3 | .290 |

Dave COLLINS, Scapegoat

*Runs Created: 35*

| | G | AB | R | H | 2B | 3B | HR | RBI | SB | Avg |
|---|---|---|---|---|---|---|---|---|---|---|
| First Half | 62 | 199 | 24 | 49 | 6 | 2 | 1 | 12 | 8 | .246 |
| Second Half | 49 | 149 | 17 | 39 | 6 | 1 | 2 | 13 | 5 | .262 |
| Home | 60 | 185 | 28 | 52 | 8 | 3 | 2 | 13 | 9 | .281 |
| Road | 51 | 163 | 13 | 36 | 4 | 0 | 1 | 12 | 4 | .221 |
| vs. RHP | | 196 | 29 | 53 | 7 | 2 | 3 | 18 | 9 | .270 |
| vs. LHP | | 152 | 12 | 35 | 5 | 1 | 0 | 7 | 4 | .230 |
| 1982 | 111 | 348 | 41 | 88 | 12 | 3 | 3 | 25 | 13 | .253 |
| 5.47 years | | 520 | 74 | 142 | 19 | 5 | 4 | 38 | 41 | .274 |

Ron GUIDRY

| Year | (W–L) | GS | Run | Avg | DP | Avg | SB | Avg |
|---|---|---|---|---|---|---|---|---|
| 1977 | (16- 7) | 25 | 118 | 4.72 | 19 | .76 | 10 | .40 |
| 1978 | (25- 3) | 35 | 165 | 4.71 | 26 | .74 | 9 | .26 |
| 1979 | (18- 8) | 30 | 137 | 4.57 | 32 | 1.07 | 6 | .20 |
| 1980 | (17-10) | 29 | 152 | 5.24 | 31 | 1.07 | 7 | .24 |
| 1981 | (11- 5) | 21 | 83 | 3.95 | 20 | .95 | 7 | .33 |
| 1982 | (14- 8) | 33 | 181 | 5.48 | 29 | .88 | 19 | .58 |
| 6 years | | 173 | 836 | 4.83 | 157 | .91 | 58 | .34 |

| | G | IP | W | L | Pct | ER | ERA |
|---|---|---|---|---|---|---|---|
| Home | 17 | 113.1 | 6 | 5 | .545 | 45 | 3.57 |
| Road | 17 | 108.2 | 8 | 3 | .727 | 49 | 4.06 |

Dave RIGHETTI

| Year | (W–L) | GS | Run | Avg | DP | Avg | SB | Avg |
|---|---|---|---|---|---|---|---|---|
| 1979 | ( 0- 1) | 3 | 10 | 3.33 | 3 | 1.00 | 7 | 2.33 |
| 1981 | ( 8- 4) | 15 | 58 | 3.87 | 7 | .47 | 9 | .60 |
| 1982 | (11-10) | 27 | 112 | 4.15 | 20 | .74 | 23 | .85 |
| Career | | 45 | 180 | 4.00 | 30 | .67 | 39 | .87 |

| | G | IP | W | L | Pct | ER | ERA |
|---|---|---|---|---|---|---|---|
| Home | 19 | 103 | 7 | 4 | .636 | 37 | 3.23 |
| Road | 14 | 80 | 4 | 6 | .400 | 40 | 4.50 |

Mike MORGAN

| Year | (W–L) | GS | Run | Avg | DP | Avg | SB | Avg |
|---|---|---|---|---|---|---|---|---|
| 1978 | (0- 3) | 3 | 6 | 2.00 | 2 | .67 | 5 | 1.67 |
| 1979 | (2-10) | 13 | 35 | 2.69 | 23 | 1.77 | 8 | .62 |
| 1980 | (7-11) | 23 | 91 | 3.96 | 27 | 1.17 | 15 | .65 |
| Career | | 39 | 132 | 3.38 | 52 | 1.33 | 28 | .72 |

| | G | IP | W | L | Pct | ER | ERA |
|---|---|---|---|---|---|---|---|
| Home | 12 | 67.1 | 2 | 6 | .250 | 34 | 4.54 |
| Road | 18 | 83 | 5 | 5 | .500 | 39 | 4.23 |

1982 OTHERS

| Pitcher | (W–L) | GS | Run | Avg | DP | Avg | SB | Avg |
|---|---|---|---|---|---|---|---|---|
| Rawley | (11-10) | 17 | 78 | 4.29 | 18 | 1.06 | 9 | .53 |
| Erickson | ( 4- 5) | 11 | 38 | 3.45 | 8 | .73 | 5 | .45 |
| Alexander | ( 1- 7) | 11 | 34 | 3.09 | 11 | 1.00 | 9 | .82 |
| May | ( 6- 6) | 6 | 23 | 3.83 | 5 | .83 | 5 | .83 |
| Howell | ( 2- 3) | 6 | 39 | 6.50 | 4 | .67 | 6 | 1.00 |
| Pacella | ( 0- 1) | 1 | 1 | 1.00 | 1 | 1.00 | 2 | 2.00 |

## NEW YORK YANKEES

*Talent Analysis*

The New York Yankees possessed 161 points of approximate value in 1982.

| | AV | % |
|---|---|---|
| Produced by Yankees' system: | 11 | 7% |
| Acquired by trade: | 96 | 60% |
| Purchased or signed from free agency: | 54 | 33% |

The Yankees have less home-grown talent on their roster than any other major league team, now having dropped far behind even Toronto and Seattle. In the money category, they rank behind California.

| | | |
|---|---|---|
| Young (Up to age 25): | 14 | 9% |
| Prime (Age 26 to 29): | 63 | 39% |
| Past-prime (Age 30 to 33): | 54 | 34% |
| Old (Age 34 or older): | 30 | 19% |

They are a fairly old team, but not unusually so. They rank twelfth in the league in the amount of young and prime talent.

Despite the rave notices to Willie McGee and others, the Yankee system could claim only 118 approximate value of its own in the majors in '82. This ranks twenty-first among the 26 teams, although it is on the way up. They are twenty-fourth over the last four years.

## YANKEE STADIUM

DIMENSIONS: Short to lines; cavernous in center

SURFACE: Grass

VISIBILITY: OK

FOUL TERRITORY: Large

FAVORS:
Hitter/Pitcher—Pitcher
Power/Line-drive hitter—Power
Righthander/Lefthander—Of course

TYPES OF OFFENSE AFFECTED: Net effects are small; individual effects are very pronounced. It cuts the home run frequency of a right-handed batter virtually in half, but gives it back to left-handers.

OTHER PARK CHARACTERISTICS: Dangerous people

TYPES OF MARGINAL PLAYERS MOST VALUABLE IN PARK: Lefthanded power hitters

PLAYERS ON TEAM HELPED MOST BY PARK: Guidry

PLAYERS ON TEAM HURT MOST BY PARK: Winfield

OTHER COMMENTS: Yankee, as you can see on the home/road breakdowns given for Ruth and Gehrig, was never a great park for left-handed batters, by any means. It is an excellent park for a left-handed batter who pulls the ball severely, as Nettles does and Dickey could for a few years. But for a true left-handed power hitter, it's really still a below-average park; it "favors" the lefthander only in that it doesn't choke him, as it does a righthander. Any right-handed batter who ever played here was a lot better than his statistics said —including DiMaggio. And be sure you take a look at Lou Gehrig's 1927 and 1930 records on the road.

# CLEVELAND INDIANS

Manny Trillo, it should be noted, was strictly a throw-in in what was described in the papers as the Manny Trillo trade. Manny's been a good ballplayer, but he's a 32-year-old glove man who wants a big contract to stay with the team more than a year. Nobody much wants him. The essence of the swap was Hayes-for-Franco, a rare exchange of two true blue-chip prospects. The Phillies must have decided that Franco couldn't play short, or they wouldn't have thrown in the change to make the deal.

The Cleveland Indians are baseball's first bionic baseball team, if the image does not imply too much force or energy, a team assembled from the living scraps and donated parts of other baseball teams, without a heart or a soul or a reason for living, that you can tell. Mike Ferraro's assignment is to impart these things to them. I interpreted Ferraro's signing as a good omen for the organization, as I regard Ferraro as one of the best managerial prospects around. Then came the winter meetings, and the illusion that something might be different now was shattered. Ferraro will almost have to play Trillo at second, for a year, which will hurt Perconte's chances of making it a year from now.

The Indians are the most difficult team in baseball to describe because their essential feature is that they are featureless, that they have no dominant character or type. They are not an old team nor a young team. They are not a power team nor a line-drive team, not an offensive team nor a pitching-and-defense team. You tell me: Do they have a particularly strong or a particularly weak infield or outfield? Do they have a past or a future? Is there anything to distinguish their starting rotation or their bullpen? They are not strong up the middle nor especially strong at the corner positions. They should change their name to the Cleveland Blahs. They'd probably get sued by a Blah Association and have to have a Blah Appreciation Day to settle the case, bring in a Blah singer (Jerry Vale) and a Blah actor and actress (Robert Wagner and Lois Nettleton), a Blah politician (Thomas Eagleton) and maybe some Blah ballplayers out of the past (Larry Brown, Duke Sims, Chuck Hinton).

What I want to know is, exactly what does Gabe Paul have to do before he gets fired? Trade Len Barker to the Yankees for Bye-Bye Balboni? Get arrested? Die? Trade Bo Diaz for Lary Sorensen? Deal off Von Hayes? At what point do you cry "Uncle"?

This is the man who, with the Indians heading into a crunching part of the schedule with seven pitchers on their roster, refused to call up a pitcher because he said the work would be good for them. This is the man who made his manager play the 1982 season with 11 minor leaguers on the roster.

There is still some good young talent on this team. I think Ferraro will do a good job with them. But "a good job" means 86 or 88 wins and third place if Andre Thornton and Toby Harrah don't go in the tank, 80 wins if they do. If I was an Indians' fan, I know exactly what I would do. I would set to work and build the largest, loudest and most abrasive fan organization in the world. It might not accomplish anything tangible, but it would serve a useful purpose anyway. It would prevent me from resorting to mayhem to put an end to the Chinese water torture of Gabe Paul's trades.

The Cleveland Indians turned *61* fewer double plays than their opponents in 1982, 127 to 188. No other team in the league was worse than −31.

**A TYPICAL CLEVELAND INDIANS LINEUP**

*(Date of this exact lineup: August 11)*

| | G | AB | R | H | 2B | 3B | HR | RBI | SB | Avg |
|---|---|---|---|---|---|---|---|---|---|---|
| Lead-off Man | 104 | 379 | 50 | 89 | 12 | 3 | 3 | 25 | 33 | .235 |
| Second Hitter | 162 | 602 | 100 | 183 | 29 | 4 | 25 | 78 | 17 | .304 |
| Third Hitter | 160 | 591 | 67 | 160 | 26 | 1 | 4 | 65 | 2 | .271 |
| Clean-up | 161 | 589 | 90 | 161 | 26 | 1 | 32 | 116 | 6 | .273 |
| Batting Fifth | 47 | 120 | 11 | 25 | 4 | 0 | 2 | 11 | 0 | .208 |
| Batting Sixth | 125 | 416 | 40 | 107 | 13 | 5 | 2 | 26 | 3 | .257 |
| Batting Seventh | 152 | 562 | 71 | 152 | 18 | 2 | 8 | 44 | 12 | .270 |
| Batting Eighth | 113 | 323 | 33 | 81 | 18 | 0 | 5 | 34 | 3 | .251 |
| Batting Ninth | 112 | 276 | 34 | 74 | 12 | 1 | 0 | 21 | 9 | .268 |

If you understand this lineup, please do not explain it to anyone.

Mike HARGROVE, First Base

*Runs Created: 75*

| | G | AB | R | H | 2B | 3B | HR | RBI | SB | Avg |
|---|---|---|---|---|---|---|---|---|---|---|
| First Half | 83 | 317 | 39 | 86 | 9 | 1 | 2 | 35 | 1 | .271 |
| Second Half | 77 | 274 | 28 | 74 | 17 | 0 | 2 | 30 | 1 | .270 |
| Home | 79 | 276 | 32 | 72 | 14 | 0 | 0 | 38 | 0 | .271 |
| Road | 81 | 315 | 35 | 88 | 12 | 1 | 4 | 27 | 2 | .279 |
| vs. RHP | | 379 | | 109 | 20 | 0 | 3 | | | .288 |
| vs. LHP | | 212 | | 51 | 6 | 1 | 1 | | | .241 |
| 1982 | 160 | 591 | 67 | 160 | 26 | 1 | 4 | 65 | 2 | .271 |
| 7.98 years | | 559 | 82 | 164 | 27 | 3 | 9 | 70 | 3 | .293 |

Toby HARRAH, Third Base

*Runs Created: 118*

| | G | AB | R | H | 2B | 3B | HR | RBI | SB | Avg |
|---|---|---|---|---|---|---|---|---|---|---|
| First Half | 83 | 325 | 67 | 108 | 13 | 3 | 17 | 48 | 6 | .332 |
| Second Half | 79 | 277 | 33 | 75 | 16 | 1 | 8 | 30 | 11 | .271 |
| Home | 81 | 298 | 57 | 100 | 15 | 2 | 17 | 45 | 9 | .336 |
| Road | 81 | 304 | 43 | 83 | 14 | 2 | 8 | 33 | 8 | .273 |
| vs. RHP | | 406 | | 117 | 18 | 2 | 17 | | | .288 |
| vs. LHP | | 196 | | 66 | 11 | 2 | 8 | | | .337 |
| 1982 | 162 | 602 | 100 | 183 | 29 | 4 | 25 | 78 | 17 | .309 |
| 10.54 years | | 563 | 85 | 151 | 23 | 3 | 16 | 72 | 20 | .268 |

Mike FISCHLIN, Shortstop

*Runs Created: 31*

| | G | AB | R | H | 2B | 3B | HR | RBI | SB | Avg |
|---|---|---|---|---|---|---|---|---|---|---|
| First Half | 50 | 110 | 14 | 32 | 3 | 1 | 0 | 10 | 5 | .291 |
| Second Half | 62 | 166 | 20 | 42 | 9 | 0 | 0 | 11 | 4 | .253 |
| Home | 54 | 122 | 15 | 36 | 6 | 1 | 0 | 10 | 4 | .295 |
| Road | 58 | 154 | 19 | 38 | 6 | 0 | 0 | 11 | 5 | .247 |
| vs. RHP | | 159 | | 38 | 9 | 0 | 0 | | | .239 |
| vs. LHP | | 117 | | 36 | 3 | 1 | 0 | | | .308 |
| 1982 | 112 | 276 | 34 | 74 | 12 | 1 | 0 | 21 | 9 | .268 |
| 1.19 years | | 354 | 34 | 82 | 12 | 1 | 0 | 22 | 11 | .230 |

Miguel DILONE, Left Field

*Runs Created: 37*

| | G | AB | R | H | 2B | 3B | HR | RBI | SB | Avg |
|---|---|---|---|---|---|---|---|---|---|---|
| First Half | 56 | 222 | 31 | 48 | 9 | 2 | 3 | 15 | 14 | .216 |
| Second Half | 48 | 157 | 19 | 41 | 3 | 1 | 0 | 10 | 19 | .261 |
| Home | 50 | 176 | 26 | 44 | 3 | 1 | 2 | 10 | 16 | .250 |
| Road | 54 | 203 | 24 | 45 | 9 | 2 | 1 | 15 | 17 | .222 |
| vs. RHP | | 278 | | 71 | 8 | 3 | 0 | | | .255 |
| vs. LHP | | 101 | | 18 | 4 | 0 | 0 | | | .178 |
| 1982 | 104 | 379 | 50 | 89 | 12 | 3 | 3 | 25 | 33 | .235 |
| 3.65 years | | 447 | 69 | 122 | 15 | 5 | 1 | 29 | 59 | .272 |

Rick MANNING, Center Field

*Runs Created: 65*

| | G | AB | R | H | 2B | 3B | HR | RBI | SB | Avg |
|---|---|---|---|---|---|---|---|---|---|---|
| First Half | 75 | 291 | 37 | 79 | 11 | 2 | 4 | 20 | 11 | .271 |
| Second Half | 77 | 271 | 34 | 73 | 7 | 0 | 4 | 24 | 1 | .269 |
| Home | 76 | 275 | 32 | 71 | 8 | 0 | 1 | 18 | 5 | .258 |
| Road | 76 | 287 | 39 | 81 | 10 | 2 | 7 | 26 | 7 | .282 |
| vs. RHP | | 347 | | 94 | 14 | 1 | 6 | | | .271 |
| vs. LHP | | 215 | | 58 | 4 | 1 | 2 | | | .270 |
| 1982 | 152 | 562 | 71 | 152 | 18 | 2 | 8 | 44 | 12 | .270 |
| 6.25 years | | 609 | 77 | 160 | 22 | 5 | 6 | 52 | 22 | .263 |

Von HAYES, Right Field

*Runs Created: 63*

| | G | AB | R | H | 2B | 3B | HR | RBI | SB | Avg |
|---|---|---|---|---|---|---|---|---|---|---|
| First Half | 78 | 282 | 36 | 71 | 14 | 3 | 8 | 51 | 20 | .252 |
| Second Half | 72 | 245 | 29 | 61 | 11 | 0 | 6 | 31 | 12 | .249 |
| Home | 76 | 257 | 30 | 68 | 17 | 3 | 3 | 38 | 15 | .265 |
| Road | 74 | 270 | 35 | 64 | 8 | 0 | 11 | 44 | 17 | .237 |
| vs. RHP | | 359 | | 91 | 18 | 1 | 11 | | | .253 |
| vs. LHP | | 168 | | 41 | 7 | 2 | 3 | | | .244 |
| 1982 | 150 | 527 | 65 | 132 | 25 | 3 | 14 | 82 | 32 | .250 |
| 1.19 years | | 535 | 72 | 135 | 28 | 4 | 13 | 83 | 34 | .252 |

Ron HASSEY, Catcher

*Runs Created: 41*

| | G | AB | R | H | 2B | 3B | HR | RBI | SB | Avg |
|---|---|---|---|---|---|---|---|---|---|---|
| First Half | 58 | 175 | 17 | 34 | 6 | 0 | 2 | 17 | 1 | .194 |
| Second Half | 55 | 148 | 16 | 47 | 12 | 0 | 3 | 17 | 2 | .318 |
| Home | 54 | 146 | 13 | 30 | 7 | 0 | 2 | 13 | 2 | .205 |
| Road | 59 | 177 | 20 | 51 | 11 | 0 | 3 | 21 | 1 | .288 |
| vs. RHP | | 272 | | 65 | 14 | 0 | 4 | | | .239 |
| vs. LHP | | 51 | | 16 | 4 | 0 | 1 | | | .314 |
| 1982 | 113 | 323 | 33 | 81 | 18 | 0 | 5 | 34 | 3 | .251 |
| 2.49 years | | 482 | 28 | 132 | 22 | 2 | 8 | 66 | 2 | .273 |

Alan BANNISTER, Second Base/Outfield

*Runs Created: 45*

| | G | AB | R | H | 2B | 3B | HR | RBI | SB | Avg |
|---|---|---|---|---|---|---|---|---|---|---|
| First Half | 64 | 214 | 33 | 59 | 11 | 1 | 3 | 27 | 16 | .276 |
| Second Half | 37 | 134 | 7 | 34 | 5 | 0 | 1 | 14 | 2 | .254 |
| Home | 47 | 153 | 18 | 38 | 6 | 0 | 2 | 24 | 9 | .248 |
| Road | 54 | 195 | 22 | 55 | 10 | 1 | 2 | 17 | 9 | .282 |
| vs. RHP | | | | | | | | | | |
| vs. LHP | | | | | | | | | | |
| 1982 | 101 | 348 | 40 | 93 | 16 | 1 | 4 | 41 | 18 | .267 |
| 4.58 years | | 519 | 74 | 140 | 24 | 5 | 2 | 50 | 20 | .270 |

Andre THORNTON, Designated Hitter

*Runs Created: 108*

| | G | AB | R | H | 2B | 3B | HR | RBI | SB | Avg |
|---|---|---|---|---|---|---|---|---|---|---|
| First Half | 83 | 304 | 55 | 91 | 15 | 0 | 20 | 68 | 3 | .299 |
| Second Half | 78 | 285 | 35 | 70 | 11 | 1 | 12 | 48 | 3 | .246 |
| Home | 80 | 289 | 41 | 74 | 11 | 1 | 16 | 62 | 5 | .256 |
| Road | 81 | 300 | 49 | 87 | 15 | 0 | 16 | 54 | 1 | .290 |
| vs. RHP | | 397 | | 97 | 14 | 0 | 21 | | | .244 |
| vs. LHP | | 192 | | 64 | 12 | 1 | 11 | | | .333 |
| 1982 | 161 | 589 | 90 | 161 | 26 | 1 | 32 | 116 | 6 | .273 |
| 6.11 years | | 532 | 85 | 136 | 27 | 3 | 27 | 92 | 5 | .255 |

Len BARKER

| Year | (W–L) | GS | Run | Avg | DP | Avg | SB | Avg |
|---|---|---|---|---|---|---|---|---|
| 1977 | ( 4- 1) | 3 | 23 | 7.67 | 4 | 1.33 | 0 | .00 |
| 1979 | ( 6- 6) | 19 | 86 | 4.53 | 22 | 1.16 | 17 | .89 |
| 1980 | (19-12) | 36 | 165 | 4.58 | 20 | .56 | 56 | 1.56 |
| 1981 | ( 8- 7) | 22 | 117 | 5.32 | 6 | .27 | 13 | .59 |
| 1982 | (15-11) | 33 | 153 | 4.64 | 19 | .58 | 26 | .79 |
| 5 years | | 123 | 544 | 4.42 | 71 | .58 | 102 | .83 |

| | G | IP | W | L | Pct | ER | ERA |
|---|---|---|---|---|---|---|---|
| Home | 17 | 132 | 7 | 6 | .538 | 52 | 3.55 |
| Road | 16 | 112.2 | 8 | 5 | .615 | 54 | 4.31 |

Lary SORENSEN

| Year | (W–L) | GS | Run | Avg | DP | Avg | SB | Avg |
|---|---|---|---|---|---|---|---|---|
| 1977 | ( 7-10) | 20 | 78 | 3.90 | 20 | 1.00 | 4 | .20 |
| 1978 | (18-12) | 36 | 163 | 4.53 | 22 | .63 | 15 | .42 |
| 1979 | (15-14) | 34 | 155 | 4.56 | 38 | 1.12 | 14 | .41 |
| 1980 | (12-10) | 29 | 149 | 5.14 | 39 | 1.34 | 6 | .21 |
| 1981 | ( 7- 7) | 23 | 94 | 4.09 | 25 | 1.09 | 16 | .70 |
| 1982 | (10-15) | 30 | 139 | 4.63 | 39 | 1.30 | 15 | .50 |
| Career | | 172 | 778 | 4.52 | 183 | 1.06 | 70 | .41 |

| | G | IP | W | L | Pct | ER | ERA |
|---|---|---|---|---|---|---|---|
| Home | 17 | 95.1 | 5 | 6 | .455 | 61 | 5.76 |
| Road | 15 | 94 | 5 | 9 | .357 | 57 | 5.46 |

Rick SUTCLIFFE

| Year | (W–L) | GS | Run | Avg | DP | Avg | SB | Avg |
|---|---|---|---|---|---|---|---|---|
| 1976 | ( 0- 0) | 1 | 1 | | 2 | | 1 | |
| 1979 | (17-10) | 30 | 162 | 5.40 | 21 | .70 | 25 | .83 |
| 1980 | ( 3- 9) | 10 | 50 | 5.00 | 9 | .90 | 19 | 1.90 |
| 1981 | ( 2- 2) | 6 | 16 | 2.67 | 5 | .83 | 6 | 1.00 |
| 1982 | (14- 8) | 27 | 122 | 4.52 | 21 | .78 | 27 | 1.00 |
| Career | | 74 | 351 | 4.74 | 58 | .78 | 78 | 1.05 |

| | G | IP | W | L | Pct | ER | ERA |
|---|---|---|---|---|---|---|---|
| Home | 18 | 116 | 7 | 3 | .706 | 39 | 3.03 |
| Road | 16 | 100 | 7 | 5 | .583 | 32 | 2.88 |

Rick WAITS

| Year | (W–L) | GS | Run | Avg | DP | Avg | SB | Avg |
|---|---|---|---|---|---|---|---|---|
| 1976 | ( 7- 9) | 22 | 70 | 3.18 | 29 | 1.32 | 13 | .59 |
| 1977 | ( 9- 7) | 16 | 69 | 4.31 | 20 | 1.25 | 11 | .69 |
| 1978 | (13-15) | 33 | 134 | 4.06 | 37 | 1.12 | 23 | .70 |
| 1979 | (16-13) | 34 | 158 | 4.67 | 38 | 1.12 | 26 | .76 |
| 1980 | (13-14) | 33 | 145 | 4.39 | 35 | 1.06 | 15 | .45 |
| 1981 | ( 8-10) | 21 | 80 | 3.81 | 17 | .81 | 14 | .67 |
| 1982 | ( 2-13) | 21 | 81 | 3.86 | 17 | .81 | 18 | .86 |
| 7 years | | 180 | 737 | 4.09 | 193 | 1.07 | 120 | .67 |

| | G | IP | W | L | Pct | ER | ERA |
|---|---|---|---|---|---|---|---|
| Home | 14 | 66 | 1 | 8 | .111 | 43 | 5.86 |
| Road | 11 | 49 | 1 | 5 | .167 | 26 | 4.78 |

John DENNY

| Year | (W–L) | GS | Run | Avg | DP | Avg | SB | Avg |
|---|---|---|---|---|---|---|---|---|
| 1976 | (11- 9) | 30 | 126 | 4.20 | 36 | 1.20 | 11 | .37 |
| 1977 | ( 8- 8) | 26 | 157 | 6.04 | 25 | .96 | 18 | .69 |
| 1978 | (14-11) | 33 | 134 | 4.06 | 36 | 1.09 | 29 | .88 |
| 1979 | ( 8-11) | 31 | 139 | 4.48 | 38 | 1.23 | 17 | .55 |
| 1980 | ( 8- 6) | 16 | 66 | 4.12 | 24 | 1.50 | 14 | .88 |
| 1981 | (10- 6) | 19 | 80 | 4.21 | 27 | 1.42 | 7 | .37 |
| 1982 | ( 6-13) | 25 | 109 | 4.36 | 16 | .64 | 13 | .52 |
| 7 years | | 180 | 811 | 4.50 | 202 | 1.12 | 109 | .61 |

1982 OTHERS

| Pitcher | (W–L) | GS | Run | Avg | DP | Avg | SB | Avg |
|---|---|---|---|---|---|---|---|---|
| Whitson | (4-2) | 9 | 29 | 3.22 | 5 | .56 | 8 | .89 |
| Anderson | (3-4) | 5 | 13 | 2.60 | 6 | 1.20 | 2 | .40 |
| Blyleven | (2-2) | 4 | 22 | 5.50 | 1 | .25 | 7 | 1.75 |
| Brennen | (4-2) | 4 | 12 | 3.00 | 2 | .50 | 2 | .50 |
| Heaton | (0-2) | 4 | 8 | 2.00 | 1 | .25 | 2 | .50 |
| Bohnet | (0-0) | 3 | 12 | 4.00 | 0 | | 0 | |
| Reed | (1-1) | 1 | 1 | | 2 | | 2 | |

## CLEVELAND

*Talent Analysis*

The Indians possessed 135 points of approximate value in 1982.

| | AV | % |
|---|---|---|
| Produced by Indians' system: | 35 | 26% |
| Acquired by trade: | 99 | 73% |
| Purchased or signed from free agency: | 1 | 1% |

The Indians are the one major league team with the largest share of their talent acquired by trade.

| | | |
|---|---|---|
| Young (Up to age 25): | 11 | 8% |
| Prime (Age 26 to 29): | 72 | 53% |
| Past-prime (Age 30 to 33): | 52 | 39% |
| Old (Age 34 or older): | 0 | 0% |

The Indians' farm system ranked nineteenth in 1982 talent produced, 130 approximate value. Over the four years, 1979 to 1983, they rank eighteenth.

## MUNICIPAL STADIUM

DIMENSIONS: Normal—short at lines

SURFACE: Grass

VISIBILITY: Poor

FOUL TERRITORY: —

FAVORS:
Hitter/Pitcher—Neither
Power/Line-drive hitter—Neither
Righthander/Lefthander—Righthander

TYPES OF OFFENSE AFFECTED: Averages up just a bit; doubles and triples way down

OTHER PARK CHARACTERISTICS: The wind off the lake cuts into the home run output of a lefthander pretty sharply (Von Hayes hit only 3 homers here, 11 on the road). It's a good home run park for a righthander, or a lefthander if the wind isn't blowing.

TYPES OF MARGINAL PLAYERS MOST VALUABLE IN PARK: Righthanded power hitters

PLAYERS ON TEAM HELPED MOST BY PARK: Toby Harrah

PLAYERS ON TEAM HURT MOST BY PARK: Ron Hassey

# TORONTO BLUE JAYS

Before one can attempt to say anything intelligent about the effects of the designated hitter rule, it is necessary to stop and recall the climate of speculation near hysteria into which the rule was born. Volumes were written in the winter of 1972-73 about how this rule was going to change the game. People wrote that the DH rule would take the bunt out of the game. They wrote that it would keep old hitters around until they were 50. They wrote that it would destroy competitive balance (because the good organizations would have an extra hitter to get in the lineup but the poor wouldn't). Some people argued that the DH rule would actually drive offensive totals downward (by keeping the good pitchers in the game longer). Some argued that it was a ruse to keep salaries down (I can't remember why). One of the loudest complaints was that beanball wars would get out of hand; an extension therefrom was that teams would divide into factions of hitters and pitchers. There was a general agreement that this was only a foot in the door, and that other gadgets were sure to follow.

In the climate of the times, it was inevitable that anything that happened in the American League was going to be laid at the door of the DH. If, in 1973, an American League hitter had hit .400, if a pitcher had won 30 games, if a team had won 112 games, if the American League had won the All-Star Game, if a batter had been killed by a pitch; if Mark Belanger had won the batting title or the Cleveland Indians the pennant, it is absolutely certain that these effects would have been traced, somehow, to That Rule. If there had been three separate incidents of chimpanzees getting loose on the field, if there had been an outbreak of diarrhea among second basemen, if a terrorist group had occupied Fenway Park, it is extremely likely that these things would have been attributed to the rule. That is not a joke; it is an absurd reality. Can you not see the editorial of, say, Dick U. Oldsportswriter, on the Monday morning after the Fenway terrorists surrendered:

> *But what can the fuzzy-thinking old men who run baseball expect when they kidnap the game itself, subvert its rules to serve their own ends, but that desperate and fuzzy-thinking young men will do the same thing? Baseball does not belong to the men who have seized its rules and destroyed its traditions any more than Fenway belongs to the Petrocellites. I see the tragedy in Fenway and the DH rule as being two horrible symptoms of the same disease.*

OK, OK, I'm pushing my luck. Anyway, what happened in 1973 was that the American League had 13 20-game winners, and the National League had but one. Inevitably, a logical bridge was established between the two: the DH rule was making it vastly easier to win 20 games.

I am unsure whether this connection is 100% a fiction, or only 95. I know it is at least 95. Consider the following facts, or deny them:

1) The number of 20-game winners in the American League immediately before the DH rule was adopted was already at historic highs. The 1971 total was 11, the highest in 50 years; the 1972 total would have been in double figures had not a strike wiped out the first 10 days of the schedule.

2) The National League level of 20-game winners happened, by a coincidence clearly irrelevant to the DH rule, to be at a historic low in the period just after the rule was adopted.

3) In 1973, no National League pitcher started more than 40 times, while 15 AL pitchers *averaged* over 40 starts apiece. This, again, is clearly irrelevant to the DH rule.

The myth that the DH rule was making it vastly easier to win 20 games took root because no one bothered to examine the facts.

All of this is merely a preface to the current controversy. The DH rule is now supposed to be doing something else to pitchers. Tony Kubek is convinced that the DH rule is ruining pitchers' arms. "You see pitchers, like Christenson and Candelaria, coming back from arm injuries in the National League. You don't see that happen in the American League." Or "I remember talking to Catfish Hunter just after the rule was adopted, and he said 'I'm going to get more starts, more wins, and make more money.' Well, he did, but he sure paid a price for it, didn't he?" Run that by me again real slow, Tony; how does the DH rule get more starts for a pitcher? By keeping them in the game longer, the DH should reduce the number of starts that a pitcher can make. Sure, Catfish blew out early, but so did Andy Messersmith in the NL, and Don Gullett and Randy Jones.

But if there is a danger there, then the Toronto Blue Jays are tempting fate. The sudden improvement of 1982 was attributable in very large measure to three very hard-working, very young arms attached to Clancy, Stieb and Leal. Among them they started 55 times on three days rest, surely the highest total in baseball. What is the danger? *Is* the DH rule causing pitchers like these three to burn out faster than they normally would?

One way that we can study this issue is by looking at the turnover in starting pitchers in the two leagues. If Kubek is right, if the DH rule is ruining pitchers' arms, then if we draw up lists of the pitchers who pitch 200 innings in each league, the names of the AL pitchers should have less of a tendency to repeat on the list than do the NL pitchers. We can provide an insight into the general question by breaking it down into a lot of smaller but more specific questions, such as: Of all American League pitchers who pitch 200 innings in a season, what percentage will pitch 200 innings again three years later? Four years later? One year later? How about the National League pitchers?

Well, I have done these studies, and Kubek apparently has a point. The rate of season-to-season turnover of 200-innings pitchers is consistently higher in the American League than it is in the National, by a margin that certainly appears to be significant. The rate of one-year turnover is higher, the rate of two-year turnover is higher, the rates of three-year, four-year, five-year, six-year, seven-year, eight-year or nine-year turnover are higher, as best I can measure them, in the American League.

To pick one item from the chart: if a National League pitcher pitches 200 innings in a season, the chance that he will also pitch 200 innings in a season five years later is 38%. But if an American League pitcher pitches 200 innings in a season, the chance that he will pitch 200 innings in a season five years later is only 23%.

To compile the chart below, what I did was to draw up a list of all the pitchers who pitched 200 innings in the American League in 1973 and then to check to see how many of these pitchers pitched 200 innings (in either league) in 1974, 1975, 1976, . . . 1982. 133 innings was used as the 200-inning standard for 1981. Then I did the same thing for 1974, checking to see how many of the pitchers worked 200 innings again in 1975, 1976, . . . 1982. I repeated the process for both leagues and for every season since the DH rule was adopted. To make nine-year comparisons, there was only one group of pitchers to work with (1982 as compared to 1973), but to make the eight-year comparison, there was twice as much data (1981 as compared to 1973 and 1982 as compared to 1974), and so on . . . to make the one-year-later comparisons, there were nine years worth of data.

The data is summarized in the chart below. The columns are:

1) the number of American League 200-inning pitchers who could be studied for the time-frame given;
2) the number of those pitchers repeating as 200-inning pitchers in the relevant year;
3) the number of National League 200-inning pitchers who could be studied for the time frame given;
4) the number of NL hurlers repeating as 200-inning men;
5) the AL percentage; and
6) the NL percentage.

**200-INNING PITCHERS**

| | AL | | NL | | | |
|---|---|---|---|---|---|---|
| | Pitchers | Repeats | Pitchers | Repeats | AL % | NL % |
| 1 year later | 271 | 156 | 258 | 157 | 57.6 | 60.9 |
| 2 years later | 242 | 106 | 231 | 121 | 43.8 | 52.4 |
| 3 years later | 210 | 79 | 205 | 93 | 37.6 | 45.4 |
| 4 years later | 184 | 55 | 178 | 71 | 29.9 | 39.9 |
| 5 years later | 155 | 36 | 149 | 56 | 23.2 | 37.6 |
| 6 years later | 122 | 24 | 123 | 38 | 19.7 | 30.9 |
| 7 years later | 90 | 15 | 94 | 27 | 16.7 | 28.7 |
| 8 years later | 61 | 7 | 67 | 15 | 11.5 | 22.4 |
| 9 years later | 29 | 3 | 34 | 6 | 10.3 | 17.6 |

As you can see on the chart, the National League percentages are higher all up and down the list. It is worth noting that the short-term and medium-term differences here persist if you break the ten year period of the DH rule down into shorter groups. For example, when you ask how many of the AL pitchers were still pitching regularly four years later, the answer is 31% (28 of 90) when 1973-75 is compared to 1977-79, and 29% when 1976-78 is compared to 1980-82. The National League answers are 40% for the period 1973-75, and 39% from 1976-78. This is true throughout; the NL averages are higher all across the board.

I am still unconvinced that this difference is caused by the DH rule. I might suggest that it is possible that the difference in pitcher durability was caused by the fact that the American League is more of a curve-ball pitcher's league than the NL. The strange thing is that one would think that, with the DH rule, American League teams would have been the first to abandon the four-man starting rotation; but it doesn't seem to have happened that way. Only 10% of NL starts in 1982 were made on three days rest. I don't know what the percentage is in the AL, but it is certainly higher than 10%. It is possible that the difference is caused by a random imbalance in which league has had the ten most durable pitchers in baseball (remember, since we are talking about 258 NL pitcher/seasons and not 258 different pitchers, each pitcher is considered in the data for each season that he pitches 200 innings, which magnifies the effect that a Steve Carlton or a Don Sutton has on the chart). It is possible that the only difference is that Billy Martin has been in the American League all these years.

And it is possible that a frog could fly an airplane if you could only get the instructions translated into froggie. What I actually *know* is that American League starting pitchers *have* been less durable than their National League counterparts since the DH rule was adopted. Kubek is *not* imagining it. Since the DH rule is the most obvious and most visible reason why this might be so, I think this study shifts the burden of proof onto those who would deny Kubek's position. And I don't have any proof to give them.

The Toronto Blue Jays are likely to decline in 1983, it seems. A Toronto sportswriter by the name of Bryan Johnson wrote a column at the close of last season (October 14, *Globe and Mail*) in which he used the Pythagorean formula to make an observation about the Blue Jays. His notion was that since the Blue Jays runs scored and allowed totals ordinarily would project to about 75 wins, and the Blue Jays actually won 78 games, the law of averages was against their winning as many games again next year.

There is an inference there which goes, intentionally or by accident, beyond anything that I have actually written. That a team which scores 651 runs and allows 701 could ordinarily expect to win 75 games, not 78, I know, but that teams which win more games than their projection in one season tend to decline in the next, I don't know or did not. Johnson assumed (I think) that because the Blue Jays exceeded their expectation, they must have been somewhat lucky, and that they could not expect to be similarly lucky next season. That makes sense, but does it hold up? Is it not possible that getting more wins than your share out of a given number of runs is in some way a talent and thus something which is steady from year to year?

Pete Palmer, in examining a variety of runs-to-wins projection methods, has produced a computer printout which lists the projected and actual won-lost percentages from every team in this century, and this makes it fairly easy to check out Johnson's thesis. I performed two tests. In the first, I recorded the won-lost records of all National League teams from 1900 to 1980 which had actual won-lost percentages at least .040 (about six games) better than their Pythagorean projections. There were 42 such teams. In the following seasons, 29 of those teams declined, 13 improved. The 42 teams declined by a total of 203 games. Conclusion: Johnson certainly seems to have a point. Teams which win more games than their Pythagorean expectation *are* lucky, by and large, and luck does *not* hold up from year to year.

There are few enough things to baseball which have predictive significance in any degree that the discovery of a new one, however small, is a fairly exciting moment in the life of a sabermetrician. Think about it: if you find a team that wins three or four more games than they ought to by the formula $R^2/(R^2+OR^2) = W/L\%$, you can bet that that team will decline in the following season, and make money. This brings about the second study, which is moved in three ways closer to the Blue Jays. In the first study, I used only teams which were .040 better than their projection; the Blue Jays were not that far over their heads. So in the second study, I cut the limit to +.020. The second study was done with the American League teams, and using only teams since 1960.

There were 50 teams in the second study. Fifteen of them improved in the following seasons, 33 declined and two posted the same record. There was a net loss, again, of 203 games. So the Blue Jays are 2-1 favorites, essentially, to win fewer than 78 games in 1983. We'll call it the Johnson Effect.

I see something that can off-set that, if the Blue Jays will seize on it. The Blue Jays' good news of 1982 is being interpreted as bad news in 1983, and it should be. But I look at the Toronto designated-hitter stats, which are so bad they're funny, and I can just as easily see bad news becoming good news. Blue Jay designated hitters created only 54 runs while using up 470 outs, which is the bad news. An average DH created 86 runs. But if the Blue Jays are finally serious about improving themselves, and it appears that they are, then how hard can it be to find a designated hitter who can improve the team by three or four games? The Karl Pagels, the Jim Tracys, the Ken Phelpses and Tucker Asfords and Randy Basses, these guys are always around, if you need one. Mike Easler was in that class for years, as was Gary Gray. The problem they have is that ordinarily nobody needs them. I can't believe that the Blue Jays couldn't find one if they looked around hard enough. I can't believe that you couldn't go to the winter meetings and pick up one of those guys in exchange for a ride to the airport. All right, I'm overstating it, but the point is that if you're losing games because you haven't got a center fielder or a catcher or a shortstop or a relief ace, then you've got real problems, because those people are hard to come up with. But if you're losing games because you need a DH—well, by comparison, that's good news.

**TORONTO BLUE JAYS**

| | Record With | Record Without |
|---|---|---|
| Alfredo Griffin | 78-84 | – – |
| Damaso Garcia | 70-71 | 8-13 |
| Lloyd Moseby | 61-67 | 17-17 |
| Wayne Nordhagen | 19-23 | 59-61 |
| Jesse Barfield | 53-52 | 25-32 |
| Barry Bonnell | 52-56 | 26-28 |
| Willie Upshaw | 78-81 | 0- 3 |
| Buck Martinez | 35-43 | 43-41 |
| Garth Iorg | 45-52 | 33-32 |
| Al Woods | 27-28 | 51-56 |
| John Mayberry | 4- 7 | – – |
| Ernie Whitt | 38-38 | 40-46 |
| Rance Mulliniks | 39-39 | 39-45 |
| Hosken Powell | 38-38 | 40-46 |
| Otto Velez | 6-10 | 72-74 |
| Dave Revering | 18-19 | 60-65 |
| Anthony Johnson | 14-17 | 64-67 |
| Leon Roberts | 17-12* | 61-72 |
| Glenn Adams | 8-10 | 70-74 |
| Gene Petralli | 6- 5 | 72-79 |
| Dave Baker | 3- 3 | 75-81 |

*Leon Roberts argument for the MVP award.

Willie UPSHAW, First Base

*Runs Created: 82*

| | G | AB | R | H | 2B | 3B | HR | RBI | SB | Avg |
|---|---|---|---|---|---|---|---|---|---|---|
| First Half | 82 | 291 | 39 | 84 | 12 | 6 | 12 | 45 | 1 | .289 |
| Second Half | 78 | 289 | 38 | 71 | 13 | 1 | 9 | 30 | 7 | .246 |
| Home | 79 | 290 | 40 | 89 | 13 | 7 | 11 | 46 | 3 | .307 |
| Road | 81 | 290 | 37 | 66 | 12 | 0 | 10 | 29 | 5 | .228 |
| vs. RHP | | 320 | 50 | 83 | 9 | 7 | 15 | 48 | 6 | .259 |
| vs. LHP | | 260 | 27 | 72 | 16 | 0 | 6 | 27 | 2 | .277 |
| 1982 | 160 | 580 | 77 | 155 | 25 | 7 | 21 | 75 | 8 | .267 |
| 2.16 years | | 452 | 59 | 111 | 18 | 5 | 13 | 50 | 7 | .246 |

Damaso GARCIA, Second Base

*Runs Created: 80*

| | G | AB | R | H | 2B | 3B | HR | RBI | SB | Avg |
|---|---|---|---|---|---|---|---|---|---|---|
| First Half | 81 | 347 | 47 | 106 | 18 | 2 | 4 | 27 | 21 | .305 |
| Second Half | 66 | 250 | 42 | 79 | 14 | 1 | 1 | 15 | 33 | .316 |
| Home | 72 | 289 | 48 | 96 | 19 | 1 | 3 | 23 | 23 | .332 |
| Road | 75 | 308 | 41 | 89 | 13 | 2 | 2 | 19 | 31 | .289 |
| vs. RHP | | 331 | 55 | 99 | 21 | 1 | 5 | 26 | 34 | .299 |
| vs. LHP | | 266 | 34 | 86 | 11 | 2 | 0 | 16 | 20 | .323 |
| 1982 | 147 | 597 | 89 | 185 | 32 | 3 | 5 | 42 | 54 | .310 |
| 2.35 years | | 625 | 73 | 178 | 30 | 5 | 4 | 45 | 35 | .284 |

Rance MULLINIKS, Third Base

*Runs Created: 37*

| | G | AB | R | H | 2B | 3B | HR | RBI | SB | Avg |
|---|---|---|---|---|---|---|---|---|---|---|
| First Half | 64 | 164 | 20 | 38 | 13 | 0 | 1 | 19 | 1 | .232 |
| Second Half | 48 | 147 | 12 | 38 | 12 | 0 | 3 | 16 | 2 | .259 |
| Home | 62 | 174 | 19 | 42 | 14 | 0 | 2 | 24 | 2 | .241 |
| Road | 50 | 137 | 13 | 34 | 11 | 0 | 2 | 11 | 1 | .248 |
| vs. RHP | | 278 | 29 | 68 | 24 | 0 | 4 | 34 | 3 | .245 |
| vs. LHP | | 33 | 3 | 8 | 1 | 0 | 0 | 1 | 0 | .242 |
| 1982 | 112 | 311 | 32 | 76 | 25 | 0 | 4 | 35 | 3 | .244 |
| 1.99 years | | 436 | 48 | 103 | 24 | 2 | 5 | 41 | 3 | .236 |

Alfredo GRIFFIN, Shortstop

*Runs Created: 45*

| | G | AB | R | H | 2B | 3B | HR | RBI | SB | Avg |
|---|---|---|---|---|---|---|---|---|---|---|
| First Half | 84 | 282 | 27 | 67 | 11 | 4 | 0 | 23 | 4 | .238 |
| Second Half | 78 | 257 | 30 | 63 | 9 | 4 | 1 | 25 | 6 | .245 |
| Home | 81 | 266 | 37 | 69 | 15 | 6 | 0 | 26 | 4 | .259 |
| Road | 81 | 273 | 20 | 61 | 5 | 2 | 1 | 22 | 6 | .223 |
| vs. RHP | | 303 | 32 | 78 | 10 | 4 | 1 | 30 | 5 | .257 |
| vs. LHP | | 236 | 25 | 52 | 10 | 4 | 0 | 18 | 5 | .220 |
| 1982 | 162 | 539 | 57 | 130 | 20 | 8 | 1 | 48 | 10 | .241 |
| 3.72 years | | 606 | 64 | 152 | 24 | 11 | 1 | 39 | 16 | .251 |

Hosken POWELL, Left Field

*Runs Created: 30*

| | G | AB | R | H | 2B | 3B | HR | RBI | SB | Avg |
|---|---|---|---|---|---|---|---|---|---|---|
| First Half | 60 | 128 | 21 | 36 | 6 | 2 | 0 | 8 | 3 | .281 |
| Second Half | 52 | 137 | 22 | 37 | 7 | 2 | 3 | 18 | 1 | .270 |
| Home | 60 | 143 | 25 | 39 | 7 | 1 | 2 | 17 | 0 | .273 |
| Road | 52 | 122 | 18 | 34 | 6 | 3 | 1 | 9 | 4 | .279 |
| vs. RHP | | 256 | 40 | 71 | 12 | 4 | 3 | 24 | 4 | .277 |
| vs. LHP | | 9 | 3 | 2 | 1 | 0 | 0 | 2 | 0 | .222 |
| 1982 | 112 | 265 | 43 | 73 | 13 | 4 | 3 | 26 | 4 | .275 |
| 3.42 years | | 507 | 69 | 133 | 23 | 5 | 5 | 45 | 12 | .263 |

Lloyd MOSEBY, Center Field

*Runs Created: 50*

| | G | AB | R | H | 2B | 3B | HR | RBI | SB | Avg |
|---|---|---|---|---|---|---|---|---|---|---|
| First Half | 78 | 251 | 24 | 55 | 11 | 4 | 6 | 24 | 2 | .219 |
| Second Half | 69 | 236 | 27 | 60 | 9 | 5 | 3 | 28 | 9 | .254 |
| Home | 71 | 221 | 27 | 56 | 8 | 5 | 4 | 24 | 7 | .253 |
| Road | 76 | 266 | 24 | 59 | 12 | 4 | 5 | 28 | 4 | .222 |
| vs. RHP | | 318 | 35 | 78 | 13 | 4 | 3 | 29 | 10 | .245 |
| vs. LHP | | 169 | 16 | 37 | 7 | 5 | 6 | 23 | 1 | .219 |
| 1982 | 147 | 487 | 51 | 115 | 20 | 9 | 9 | 52 | 11 | .236 |
| 2.23 years | | 562 | 59 | 131 | 27 | 5 | 12 | 63 | 12 | .233 |

Jesse BARFIELD, Right Field

*Runs Created: 63*

| | G | AB | R | H | 2B | 3B | HR | RBI | SB | Avg |
|---|---|---|---|---|---|---|---|---|---|---|
| First Half | 71 | 205 | 29 | 54 | 8 | 2 | 8 | 33 | 1 | .263 |
| Second Half | 68 | 189 | 25 | 43 | 5 | 0 | 10 | 25 | 0 | .228 |
| Home | 64 | 173 | 27 | 43 | 2 | 0 | 11 | 32 | 0 | .249 |
| Road | 75 | 221 | 27 | 54 | 11 | 2 | 7 | 26 | 1 | .244 |
| vs. RHP | | 148 | 17 | 33 | 3 | 1 | 3 | 16 | 1 | .223 |
| vs. LHP | | 246 | 37 | 64 | 10 | 1 | 15 | 42 | 0 | .260 |
| 1982 | 139 | 394 | 54 | 97 | 13 | 2 | 18 | 58 | 1 | .246 |
| 1.04 years | | 486 | 59 | 116 | 15 | 4 | 19 | 64 | 5 | .240 |

Barry BONNELL, Left Field

*Runs Created: 52*

| | G | AB | R | H | 2B | 3B | HR | RBI | SB | Avg |
|---|---|---|---|---|---|---|---|---|---|---|
| First Half | 77 | 246 | 39 | 80 | 17 | 1 | 4 | 33 | 5 | .325 |
| Second Half | 63 | 191 | 20 | 48 | 9 | 2 | 2 | 16 | 9 | .251 |
| Home | 72 | 222 | 24 | 56 | 15 | 1 | 4 | 23 | 4 | .252 |
| Road | 68 | 215 | 35 | 72 | 11 | 2 | 2 | 26 | 10 | .335 |
| vs. RHP | | 186 | 24 | 48 | 7 | 0 | 1 | 18 | 8 | .258 |
| vs. LHP | | 251 | 35 | 80 | 19 | 3 | 5 | 31 | 6 | .319 |
| 1982 | 140 | 437 | 59 | 128 | 26 | 3 | 6 | 49 | 14 | .293 |
| 4.20 years | | 516 | 62 | 138 | 23 | 4 | 9 | 57 | 11 | .268 |

Ernie WHITT, Catcher

*Runs Created: 40*

| | G | AB | R | H | 2B | 3B | HR | RBI | SB | Avg |
|---|---|---|---|---|---|---|---|---|---|---|
| First Half | 67 | 178 | 20 | 46 | 7 | 1 | 7 | 21 | 2 | .258 |
| Second Half | 38 | 106 | 8 | 28 | 7 | 1 | 4 | 21 | 1 | .264 |
| Home | 55 | 150 | 17 | 41 | 10 | 2 | 8 | 23 | 1 | .273 |
| Road | 50 | 134 | 11 | 33 | 4 | 0 | 3 | 19 | 2 | .246 |
| vs. RHP | | 249 | 25 | 69 | 12 | 2 | 10 | 36 | 2 | .277 |
| vs. LHP | | 35 | 3 | 5 | 2 | 0 | 1 | 6 | 1 | .143 |
| 1982 | 105 | 284 | 28 | 74 | 14 | 2 | 11 | 42 | 3 | .261 |
| 1.96 years | | 427 | 38 | 103 | 20 | 2 | 10 | 52 | 5 | .240 |

Jim CLANCY

| Year | (W–L) | GS | Run | Avg | DP | Avg | SB | Avg |
|---|---|---|---|---|---|---|---|---|
| 1977 | ( 4- 9) | 13 | 50 | 3.85 | 6 | .46 | 8 | .62 |
| 1978 | (10-12) | 30 | 101 | 3.37 | 34 | 1.14 | 20 | .67 |
| 1979 | ( 2- 7) | 11 | 39 | 3.55 | 12 | 1.09 | 6 | .55 |
| 1980 | (13-16) | 34 | 111 | 3.26 | 30 | .88 | 11 | .32 |
| 1981 | ( 6-12) | 22 | 80 | 3.64 | 24 | 1.09 | 12 | .55 |
| 1982 | (16-14) | 40 | 172 | 4.30 | 42 | 1.05 | 13 | .33 |
| 6 years | | 150 | 553 | 3.69 | 148 | .99 | 70 | .47 |

| | G | IP | W | L | Pct | ER | ERA |
|---|---|---|---|---|---|---|---|
| Home | 21 | 118.1 | 7 | 8 | .467 | 63 | 4.79 |
| Road | 19 | 148.1 | 9 | 6 | .600 | 47 | 2.85 |

Dave STIEB

| Year | (W–L) | GS | Run | Avg | DP | Avg | SB | Avg |
|---|---|---|---|---|---|---|---|---|
| 1979 | ( 8- 8) | 18 | 82 | 4.56 | 24 | 1.33 | 9 | .50 |
| 1980 | (12-15) | 32 | 124 | 3.88 | 46 | 1.44 | 20 | .62 |
| 1981 | (11-10) | 25 | 70 | 2.80 | 28 | 1.12 | 11 | .44 |
| 1982 | (17-14) | 38 | 149 | 3.92 | 32 | .84 | 11 | .29 |
| 4 years | | 103 | 425 | 4.13 | 130 | 1.26 | 51 | .50 |

| | G | IP | W | L | Pct | ER | ERA |
|---|---|---|---|---|---|---|---|
| Home | 17 | 129.1 | 8 | 6 | .571 | 46 | 3.20 |
| Road | 21 | 159 | 9 | 8 | .529 | 58 | 3.32 |

Luis LEAL

| Year | (W–L) | GS | Run | Avg | DP | Avg | SB | Avg |
|---|---|---|---|---|---|---|---|---|
| 1980 | ( 3- 4) | 10 | 55 | 5.50 | 14 | 1.40 | 8 | .80 |
| 1981 | ( 7-13) | 19 | 58 | 3.05 | 15 | .79 | 10 | .53 |
| 1982 | (12-15) | 38 | 161 | 4.24 | 28 | .74 | 28 | .74 |
| 3 years | | 67 | 274 | 4.09 | 57 | .85 | 46 | .69 |

| | G | IP | W | L | Pct | ER | ERA |
|---|---|---|---|---|---|---|---|
| Home | 19 | 130.2 | 8 | 3 | .727 | 47 | 3.24 |
| Road | 21 | 119 | 4 | 12 | .250 | 62 | 4.69 |

Jim GOTT

| Year | (W–L) | GS | Run | Avg | DP | Avg | SB | Avg |
|---|---|---|---|---|---|---|---|---|
| 1982 | ( 5-10) | 23 | 73 | 3.17 | 20 | .87 | 15 | .65 |

| | G | IP | W | L | Pct | ER | ERA |
|---|---|---|---|---|---|---|---|
| Home | 15 | 72.2 | 3 | 5 | .375 | 33 | 4.09 |
| Road | 15 | 63.1 | 2 | 5 | .286 | 34 | 4.83 |

1982 OTHERS

| Pitcher | (W–L) | GS | Run | Avg | DP | Avg | SB | Avg |
|---|---|---|---|---|---|---|---|---|
| Bomback | (1-5) | 8 | 29 | 3.63 | 11 | 1.38 | 2 | .25 |
| Eichhorn | (0-3) | 7 | 27 | 3.86 | 6 | .86 | 5 | .71 |
| Garvin | (1-1) | 4 | 21 | 5.25 | 2 | .50 | 5 | 1.25 |
| Jackson | (8-8) | 2 | 11 | 5.50 | 2 | 1.00 | 0 | 2.00 |
| Geisel | (1-1) | 2 | 8 | 4.00 | 1 | .50 | 0 | .50 |

## TORONTO BLUE JAYS

*Talent Analysis*

The Blue Jays possessed 148 points of approximate value in 1982.

| | AV | % |
|---|---|---|
| Produced by Blue Jays' system: | 41 | 28% |
| Acquired by trade: | 63 | 42% |
| Purchased or signed from free agency: | 18 | 12% |
| Retained from expansion draft: | 26 | 18% |
| Young (Up to age 25): | 31 | 21% |
| Prime (Age 26 to 29): | 93 | 63% |
| Past-prime (Age 30 to 33): | 24 | 16% |
| Old (Age 34 or older): | 0 | 0% |

The Blue Jays are one of the youngest teams in baseball.

The Blue Jays' system produced 47 points of approximate value for the 1982 season, 10 points more than Seattle. The figures for both teams are growing rapidly.

## EXHIBITION STADIUM

DIMENSIONS: Normal

SURFACE: Turf

VISIBILITY: Excellent

FOUL TERRITORY: —

FAVORS:
- Hitter/Pitcher—Pitcher
- Power/Line-drive hitter—Line-drive
- Righthander/Lefthander—Neither

TYPES OF OFFENSE AFFECTED: Batting averages up a few points, doubles and triples up around 15%; most similar to Three Rivers Stadium

TYPES OF MARGINAL PLAYERS MOST VALUABLE IN PARK: Recommend speed for the outfield. Hosken Powell may be a good example of a player who can help you here.

PLAYERS ON TEAM HELPED MOST BY PARK: Upshaw

PLAYERS ON TEAM HURT MOST BY PARK: Jim Clancy; Bonnell has not hit well here

OTHER COMMENTS: The Blue Jays haven't yet collected any of the kind of hitters who should do well here, the line-drive hitters with some pop in their bat (Brett, Kemp, McRae, Fisk, D. Parker, K. Hernandez, Cooper). If they ever get one of these guys he'll win some batting championships, because the park will give him a few points.

# AMERICAN LEAGUE WEST
## DIVISION SHEET*

| Team | 1st | 2nd | vs. RHP | vs. LHP | Home | Road | Day | Night | Total | Pct |
|---|---|---|---|---|---|---|---|---|---|---|
| California | 49-37 | 44-32 | 63-40 | 30-29 | 52-29 | 41-40 | 23-18 | 70-51 | 93-69 | .574 |
| Kansas City | 47-37 | 43-35 | 59-46 | 31-26 | 56-25 | 34-47 | 17-23 | 73-49 | 90-72 | .556 |
| Chicago | 45-37 | 42-38 | 57-51 | 30-24 | 49-31 | 38-44 | 23-19 | 64-56 | 87-75 | .537 |
| Seattle | 45-41 | 31-45 | 54-57 | 22-29 | 42-39 | 34-47 | 14-15 | 62-71 | 76-86 | .469 |
| Oakland | 38-50 | 30-44 | 45-62 | 23-32 | 36-45 | 32-49 | 27-32 | 41-62 | 68-94 | .420 |
| Texas | 35-46 | 29-52 | 50-77 | 14-21 | 38-43 | 26-55 | 14-20 | 50-78 | 64-98 | .395 |
| Minnesota | 28-59 | 32-43 | 39-67 | 21-35 | 37-44 | 23-58 | 18-31 | 42-71 | 60-102 | .370 |

### *TURNAROUNDS*

| | COME FROM BEHIND WINS | | | | | | | | | BLOWN LEADS | | | | | | | | |
|---|---|---|---|---|---|---|---|---|---|---|---|---|---|---|---|---|---|---|
| Team | 1 | 2 | 3 | 4 | 5 | 6 | 7 | Total | Points | 1 | 2 | 3 | 4 | 5 | 6 | 7 | Total | Points |
| California | 26 | 4 | 9 | 2 | 2 | | | 43 | 122 | 20 | 9 | 8 | 1 | 1 | 1 | | 40 | 117 |
| Kansas City | 14 | 9 | 5 | 1 | 2 | 1 | | 32 | 99 | 11 | 9 | 5 | 2 | | | | 27 | 79 |
| Chicago | 23 | 4 | 5 | 2 | 4 | | | 38 | 96 | 24 | 13 | 7 | | | | | 44 | 115 |
| Oakland | 15 | 14 | 1 | 2 | 3 | | | 35 | 104 | 22 | 14 | 3 | 1 | 4 | | | 44 | 127 |
| Seattle | 14 | 15 | 8 | 2 | | | | 39 | 115 | 21 | 6 | 1 | 3 | 2 | | | 33 | 91 |
| Texas | 15 | 5 | 1 | 0 | 1 | | | 22 | 55 | 21 | 12 | 4 | 1 | 1 | | | 39 | 105 |
| Minnesota | 15 | 7 | 5 | 0 | 0 | 1 | | 28 | 78 | 23 | 20 | 4 | 0 | 1 | 1 | | 49 | 135 |

### DEFENSIVE RECORDS

| Team | OSB | OCS | OSB% | DP | OA/SFA | FAvg | DER | Opposition Runs |
|---|---|---|---|---|---|---|---|---|
| California | 66 | 77 | .462 | 168 | 29/32 | .983 | .706 | 670 |
| Chicago | 102 | 59 | .637 | 173 | 27/41 | .976 | .682 | 710 |
| Seattle | 118 | 51 | .698 | 158 | 48/33 | .978 | .695 | 712 |
| Kansas City | 85 | 53 | .616 | 140 | 21/54 | .979 | .712 | 717 |
| Texas | 93 | 59 | .612 | 168 | 41/51 | .981 | .685 | 749 |
| Oakland | 97 | 58 | .626 | 137 | 29/54 | .974 | .700 | 819 |
| Minnesota | 128 | 57 | .692 | 162 | 39/45 | .982 | .702 | 819 |

### OPPOSITION ERRORS

| Team | C | 1B | 2B | 3B | SS | LF | CF | RF | P | Un | Total |
|---|---|---|---|---|---|---|---|---|---|---|---|
| Chicago | 23 | 14 | 22 | 25 | 18 | 10 | 5 | 5 | 23 | 1 | 146 |
| Kansas City | 13 | 19 | 19 | 23 | 25 | 2 | 10 | 5 | 7 | 8 | 131 |
| Seattle | 11 | 13 | 22 | 16 | 29 | 4 | 5 | 14 | 11 | 4 | 129 |
| California | 13 | 12 | 13 | 19 | 30 | 3 | 13 | 9 | 11 | 4 | 127 |
| Oakland | 12 | 10 | 13 | 18 | 28 | 9 | 5 | 7 | 10 | 5 | 117 |
| Texas | 11 | 6 | 15 | 15 | 26 | 6 | 3 | 9 | 15 | 3 | 109 |
| Minnesota | 5 | 7 | 13 | 30 | 26 | 3 | 3 | 2 | 6 | 0 | 95 |

### LATE-INNING BALL CLUBS

| Team | Ahead | Tied | Behind | Net Change |
|---|---|---|---|---|
| Kansas City | 73- 4 | 12- 8 | 5-60 | + 5 |
| Seattle | 54- 6 | 7-11 | 15-69 | + 5 |
| Chicago | 69- 5 | 11-10 | 6-60 | + 2 |
| Texas | 48- 7 | 11- 8 | 5-83 | + 1 |
| California | 76- 8 | 8-11 | 8-50 | − 3 |
| Oakland | 53-11 | 8- 8 | 7-74 | − 4 |
| Minnesota | 52- 7 | 2-16 | 6-79 | −15 |

*See explanation of Division Sheet on p. 16

# CALIFORNIA ANGELS

A linguistic point . . . After the split into divisions in 1969, nobody was quite sure whether the term *pennant* could or could not be applied to a divisional championship. There is no logical reason why it couldn't; a pennant is a flag given to the team which wins, and the title itself by extension. But as the usage has developed, it isn't employed that way. I think this is unfortunate. I was listening to the broadcast of the Angels' game on October 2 when they finally wrapped it up, and you could tell that the announcer desperately wanted to say "The Angels win the pennant!" but couldn't. "Divisional title," the substitute, sounds awkward and unduly diminished for what is, after all, the main work of the season, the goal of the 162-game chase.

In May, Reggie Jackson will become the first ballplayer to strike out 2000 times in his career.

Somebody asked me to keep track of how often the Angels won when Reggie hit a home run. This isn't very hard to count, but it only becomes meaningful when compared to the other members of the team, hence the chart below. 24 of Reggie's 39 HR were hit in wins, 15 in losses;

| | W | L | Pct. |
|---|---|---|---|
| Grich | 13 | 5 | .722 |
| Downing | 19 | 9 | .679 |
| Baylor | 16 | 8 | .667 |
| DeCinces | 19 | 11 | .633 |
| Lynn | 13 | 8 | .619 |
| Reggie | 24 | 15 | .615 |
| Others | 17 | 9 | .654 |

Despite the continuing disparity in performance, American League West teams drew more fans to the park in 1982 than those in the AL East, 11,573,922 to 11,494,313. This is the first time the West teams have outdrawn the East; the West's share of the attendance in 1980 was only 43.1%, and their best ever to that point was 46.9% in 1973. The West's share jumped to 49.2% in '81 and 50.2% last year.

Gene Mauch had a beautiful line last fall when somebody asked him if he wouldn't almost have been happier losing than having to face all those questions about what does it feel like after all these years. Gene didn't like that question either, so he snapped, "Nobody in this room is smart enough to analyze me." Nobody in the world is smart enough to figure out why Gene Mauch does some of the things he does, including Gene Mauch.

Mauch has been managing in the major leagues long enough to have become a legend in his own time. He hasn't *become* one, of course, but he's been managing that long. You want to know how long Gene Mauch has been managing in the major leagues, consider this: Alvin Dark played for him. Mauch might have become a legend—he certainly had the personality for it—if only he had won a little more often.

But, as I am so fond of saying, records are only meaningful in the context in which they are compiled, and that is no less true for Gene Mauch's wins and losses than it is for Bob Horner's home-run rates or Pete Vuckovich's wins and losses. And in the context in which it has come, Gene Mauch's record ain't half bad. The chart below gives his record in detail.

| | BEFORE Mauch | Mauch | AFTER Mauch |
|---|---|---|---|
| Philadelphia | 134-176 .432 | 645-684 .485 | 113-148 .433 |
| Montreal | 398-563 .398 | 499-627 .443 | 130-194 .401 |
| Minnesota | 158-163 .492 | 378-394 .490 | 124-183 .404 |
| California | 175-194 .474 | 122-103 .542 | |

Column 1: The teams that Gene Mauch has managed.

Column 2: The record (wins, losses, won-lost percentage) of the team in the two years before Mauch took over. In Philadelphia, where Mauch became manager two games into the season, this record is for two years and two games. In California, it is for two years and 47 games. And in Montreal, where Mauch managed an expansion franchise from its beginning, I substituted the average record of an expansion team over its first six years in the "Before Mauch" category.

Column 3: The teams' records (wins, losses, won-lost percentage) under Gene Mauch.

Column 4: The teams' records (same) in the two years after Mauch left. In Philadelphia, "two years" meant one year, 109 games. In Minnesota, it meant two years, 37 games.

Mauch took over a terrible team in Philadelphia, and had them in contention in three years; he left and the team was as bad as ever. That is a fact. His record in Montreal is far better than the normal performance of an expansion team. That is a fact. He took over a sub-.500 team in Minnesota, and, despite a steady bleeding of talent, had them in two pennant races before the hemorrhaging became uncontrollable. That is a fact, or at least a characterization of it that no one could argue with. He took over a highly talented team of chronic under-achievers in California, and he won 93 games and a divisional title with them. That is a fact. That he is under .500 lifetime as a manager, that he went 20 years without winning anything . . . these are also facts. But that he should have done this in 1964 or that he should have won so many games in 1977; these are only opinions.

And I have my opinion, too. Gene Mauch's problem, in short, is that he has taken over too many challenges and not enough ball clubs. Mauch's reputation as a manager, and even as a managerial prospect before he was a manager, was good enough to have given him some choice in which jobs he took. Mauch was either too impatient to wait for a good job to be offered, or he was too arrogant to realize that even he could not lift a bad team single-handedly all the way over the pack. But there never was anybody in the room who was smart enough to tell him that.

A bad manager? Not at all; a good judge of talent, an excellent psychologist and motivator, a fine handler of pitchers who built generally superb bullpens, an intense and capable in-game strategist who worked too hard on that phase of the job, and did not always respect its limitations. A master of details, a master of small things. He may have analyzed ball games somewhat better than he analyzed pennant races. I am a little sad to see him depart the scene without one of those rings on his finger. For his arrogance, he paid with his reputation.

Rod CAREW, First Base

*Runs Created: 78*

| | G | AB | R | H | 2B | 3B | HR | RBI | SB | Avg |
|---|---|---|---|---|---|---|---|---|---|---|
| First Half | 75 | 277 | 43 | 82 | 13 | 1 | 1 | 21 | 7 | .296 |
| Second Half | 63 | 246 | 45 | 85 | 12 | 4 | 2 | 23 | 3 | .346 |
| Home | 64 | 226 | 42 | 78 | 14 | 1 | 1 | 20 | 2 | .345 |
| Road | 74 | 297 | 46 | 89 | 11 | 4 | 2 | 24 | 8 | .300 |
| vs. RHP | | 361 | 64 | 128 | 20 | 3 | 2 | 28 | 10 | .355 |
| vs. LHP | | 162 | 24 | 39 | 5 | 2 | 1 | 16 | 0 | .241 |
| 1982 | 138 | 523 | 88 | 167 | 25 | 5 | 3 | 44 | 10 | .310 |
| 13.09 years | | 617 | 95 | 204 | 30 | 8 | 7 | 69 | 26 | .331 |

Bobby GRICH, Second Base

*Runs Created: 82*

| | G | AB | R | H | 2B | 3B | HR | RBI | SB | Avg |
|---|---|---|---|---|---|---|---|---|---|---|
| First Half | 78 | 281 | 35 | 75 | 16 | 4 | 8 | 38 | 2 | .267 |
| Second Half | 67 | 225 | 39 | 57 | 12 | 1 | 11 | 27 | 1 | .253 |
| Home | 73 | 252 | 37 | 65 | 13 | 4 | 8 | 32 | 3 | .258 |
| Road | 72 | 254 | 37 | 67 | 15 | 1 | 11 | 33 | 0 | .264 |
| vs. RHP | | 308 | 45 | 77 | 15 | 3 | 12 | 43 | 2 | .250 |
| vs. LHP | | 198 | 29 | 55 | 13 | 2 | 7 | 22 | 1 | .278 |
| 1982 | 145 | 506 | 74 | 132 | 28 | 5 | 19 | 65 | 3 | .261 |
| 9.44 years | | 570 | 84 | 151 | 27 | 5 | 18 | 70 | 10 | .267 |

Doug DeCINCES, Third Base

*Runs Created: 116*

| | G | AB | R | H | 2B | 3B | HR | RBI | SB | Avg |
|---|---|---|---|---|---|---|---|---|---|---|
| First Half | 85 | 310 | 43 | 83 | 21 | 4 | 10 | 47 | 3 | .268 |
| Second Half | 68 | 265 | 51 | 90 | 21 | 1 | 20 | 50 | 4 | .340 |
| Home | 74 | 266 | 43 | 82 | 18 | 1 | 17 | 53 | 4 | .308 |
| Road | 79 | 309 | 51 | 91 | 24 | 4 | 13 | 44 | 3 | .294 |
| vs. RHP | | 362 | 54 | 101 | 23 | 4 | 17 | 66 | 5 | .279 |
| vs. LHP | | 213 | 40 | 72 | 19 | 1 | 13 | 31 | 2 | .338 |
| 1982 | 153 | 575 | 94 | 173 | 42 | 5 | 30 | 97 | 7 | .301 |
| 6.24 years | | 560 | 75 | 146 | 33 | 3 | 22 | 79 | 7 | .261 |

Tim FOLI, Shortstop

*Runs Created: 38*

| | G | AB | R | H | 2B | 3B | HR | RBI | SB | Avg |
|---|---|---|---|---|---|---|---|---|---|---|
| First Half | 84 | 270 | 33 | 77 | 8 | 2 | 2 | 34 | 1 | .285 |
| Second Half | 66 | 210 | 13 | 44 | 6 | 0 | 1 | 22 | 2 | .210 |
| Home | 75 | 232 | 24 | 62 | 8 | 1 | 1 | 29 | 2 | .267 |
| Road | 75 | 248 | 22 | 59 | 6 | 1 | 2 | 27 | 0 | .238 |
| vs. RHP | | 303 | 30 | 78 | 11 | 2 | 2 | 43 | 1 | .257 |
| vs. LHP | | 177 | 16 | 43 | 3 | 0 | 1 | 13 | 1 | .243 |
| 1982 | 150 | 480 | 46 | 121 | 14 | 2 | 3 | 56 | 2 | .252 |
| 9.43 years | | 585 | 57 | 147 | 23 | 2 | 2 | 48 | 8 | .251 |

Brian DOWNING, Left Field

*Runs Created: 110*

| | G | AB | R | H | 2B | 3B | HR | RBI | SB | Avg |
|---|---|---|---|---|---|---|---|---|---|---|
| First Half | 82 | 329 | 55 | 94 | 19 | 2 | 13 | 33 | 1 | .286 |
| Second Half | 76 | 294 | 54 | 81 | 18 | 0 | 15 | 51 | 1 | .276 |
| Home | 79 | 315 | 59 | 93 | 19 | 1 | 15 | 40 | 1 | .295 |
| Road | 79 | 308 | 50 | 82 | 18 | 1 | 13 | 44 | 1 | .266 |
| vs. RHP | | 402 | 67 | 105 | 24 | 1 | 19 | 58 | 1 | .261 |
| vs. LHP | | 221 | 42 | 70 | 13 | 1 | 9 | 26 | 1 | .317 |
| 1982 | 158 | 623 | 109 | 175 | 37 | 2 | 28 | 84 | 2 | .281 |
| 6.27 years | | 515 | 73 | 137 | 23 | 1 | 13 | 65 | 5 | .267 |

Fred LYNN, Center Field

*Runs Created: 88*

| | G | AB | R | H | 2B | 3B | HR | RBI | SB | Avg |
|---|---|---|---|---|---|---|---|---|---|---|
| First Half | 78 | 277 | 49 | 80 | 24 | 1 | 9 | 31 | 7 | .289 |
| Second Half | 60 | 195 | 40 | 61 | 14 | 0 | 12 | 55 | 0 | .313 |
| Home | 71 | 251 | 51 | 73 | 18 | 1 | 13 | 48 | 3 | .291 |
| Road | 67 | 221 | 38 | 68 | 20 | 0 | 8 | 38 | 4 | .308 |
| vs. RHP | | 316 | 65 | 102 | 29 | 1 | 14 | 54 | 7 | .323 |
| vs. LHP | | 156 | 24 | 39 | 9 | 0 | 7 | 32 | 0 | .250 |
| 1982 | 138 | 472 | 89 | 141 | 38 | 1 | 21 | 86 | 7 | .299 |
| 6.43 years | | 589 | 100 | 178 | 41 | 5 | 23 | 99 | 8 | .301 |

Reggie JACKSON, Right Field

*Runs Created: 104*

| | G | AB | R | H | 2B | 3B | HR | RBI | SB | Avg |
|---|---|---|---|---|---|---|---|---|---|---|
| First Half | 77 | 269 | 40 | 69 | 2 | 0 | 20 | 47 | 2 | .257 |
| Second Half | 76 | 261 | 52 | 77 | 15 | 1 | 19 | 54 | 2 | .295 |
| Home | 76 | 267 | 46 | 76 | 7 | 1 | 21 | 53 | 1 | .285 |
| Road | 77 | 263 | 46 | 70 | 10 | 0 | 18 | 48 | 3 | .266 |
| vs. RHP | | 326 | 65 | 93 | 12 | 0 | 25 | 73 | 4 | .285 |
| vs. LHP | | 204 | 27 | 53 | 5 | 1 | 14 | 28 | 0 | .260 |
| 1982 | 153 | 530 | 92 | 146 | 17 | 1 | 39 | 101 | 4 | .275 |
| 13.40 years | | 577 | 95 | 157 | 28 | 3 | 35 | 103 | 16 | .272 |

Bob BOONE, Catcher

*Runs Created: 49*

| | G | AB | R | H | 2B | 3B | HR | RBI | SB | Avg |
|---|---|---|---|---|---|---|---|---|---|---|
| First Half | 75 | 241 | 15 | 66 | 11 | 0 | 1 | 29 | 0 | .274 |
| Second Half | 68 | 231 | 27 | 55 | 6 | 0 | 6 | 29 | 0 | .238 |
| Home | 71 | 224 | 22 | 59 | 7 | 0 | 5 | 27 | 0 | .263 |
| Road | 72 | 248 | 20 | 62 | 10 | 0 | 2 | 31 | 0 | .250 |
| vs. RHP | | 321 | 25 | 79 | 13 | 0 | 4 | 36 | 0 | .246 |
| vs. LHP | | 151 | 17 | 42 | 4 | 0 | 3 | 22 | 0 | .278 |
| 1982 | 143 | 472 | 42 | 121 | 17 | 0 | 7 | 58 | 0 | .256 |
| 7.83 years | | 532 | 50 | 138 | 24 | 3 | 9 | 66 | 3 | .259 |

Don BAYLOR, Designated Hitter

*Runs Created: 84*

| | G | AB | R | H | 2B | 3B | HR | RBI | SB | Avg |
|---|---|---|---|---|---|---|---|---|---|---|
| First Half | 84 | 339 | 38 | 92 | 14 | 0 | 13 | 53 | 5 | .271 |
| Second Half | 73 | 269 | 42 | 68 | 10 | 1 | 11 | 40 | 5 | .253 |
| Home | 80 | 305 | 42 | 80 | 10 | 1 | 13 | 47 | 8 | .262 |
| Road | 77 | 303 | 38 | 80 | 14 | 0 | 11 | 46 | 2 | .264 |
| vs. RHP | | 369 | 56 | 98 | 13 | 1 | 16 | 61 | 9 | .266 |
| vs. LHP | | 239 | 24 | 62 | 11 | 0 | 8 | 32 | 1 | .259 |
| 1982 | 157 | 608 | 80 | 160 | 24 | 1 | 24 | 93 | 10 | .263 |
| 9.21 years | | 593 | 88 | 157 | 26 | 2 | 23 | 89 | 28 | .264 |

## Ken FORSCH

| Year | (W–L) | GS | Run | Avg | DP | Avg | SB | Avg |
|---|---|---|---|---|---|---|---|---|
| 1977 | ( 5- 8) | 5 | 8 | 1.60 | 6 | 1.20 | 2 | .40 |
| 1978 | (10- 6) | 6 | 18 | 3.00 | 4 | .67 | 4 | .67 |
| 1979 | (11- 6) | 24 | 108 | 4.50 | 23 | .96 | 14 | .58 |
| 1980 | (12-13) | 32 | 114 | 3.56 | 25 | .78 | 27 | .84 |
| 1981 | (11- 7) | 20 | 96 | 4.80 | 25 | 1.25 | 13 | .65 |
| 1982 | (13-11) | 35 | 167 | 4.77 | 27 | .77 | 18 | .51 |
| 6 years | | 122 | 511 | 4.19 | 110 | .90 | 78 | .64 |

| | G | IP | W | L | Pct | ER | ERA |
|---|---|---|---|---|---|---|---|
| Home | 22 | 128.1 | 9 | 6 | .600 | 57 | 4.00 |
| Road | 15 | 99.2 | 4 | 5 | .444 | 41 | 3.70 |

## Geoff ZAHN

| Year | (W–L) | GS | Run | Avg | DP | Avg | SB | Avg |
|---|---|---|---|---|---|---|---|---|
| 1977 | (12-14) | 32 | 155 | 4.84 | 40 | 1.25 | 17 | .53 |
| 1978 | (14-14) | 35 | 144 | 4.14 | 48 | 1.37 | 13 | .37 |
| 1979 | (13- 7) | 24 | 115 | 4.79 | 36 | 1.50 | 4 | .17 |
| 1980 | (14-18) | 35 | 157 | 4.49 | 51 | 1.46 | 20 | .57 |
| 1981 | (10-11) | 25 | 139 | 5.56 | 30 | 1.20 | 9 | .36 |
| 1982 | (18- 8) | 34 | 190 | 5.59 | 41 | 1.21 | 10 | .29 |
| 6 years | | 185 | 900 | 4.86 | 246 | 1.33 | 73 | .39 |

| | G | IP | W | L | Pct | ER | ERA |
|---|---|---|---|---|---|---|---|
| Home | 16 | 116 | 10 | 1 | .909 | 37 | 2.87 |
| Road | 18 | 113.1 | 8 | 7 | .533 | 58 | 4.61 |

## Mike WITT

| Year | (W–L) | GS | Run | Avg | DP | Avg | SB | Avg |
|---|---|---|---|---|---|---|---|---|
| 1981 | (8-9) | 21 | 95 | 4.52 | 23 | 1.10 | 20 | .95 |
| 1982 | (8-6) | 26 | 123 | 4.73 | 27 | 1.04 | 11 | .42 |
| Career | | 47 | 218 | 4.64 | 50 | 1.06 | 31 | .66 |

| | G | IP | W | L | Pct | ER | ERA |
|---|---|---|---|---|---|---|---|
| Home | 15 | 93.2 | 5 | 3 | .625 | 27 | 2.59 |
| Road | 18 | 86 | 3 | 3 | .500 | 43 | 4.50 |

## Steve RENKO

| Year | (W–L) | GS | Run | Avg | DP | Avg | SB | Avg |
|---|---|---|---|---|---|---|---|---|
| 1976 | ( 8-12) | 28 | 89 | 3.18 | 13 | .46 | 17 | .61 |
| 1977 | ( 7- 2) | 16 | 75 | 4.69 | 13 | .81 | 9 | .56 |
| 1978 | ( 6-12) | 25 | 77 | 3.08 | 20 | .80 | 23 | .92 |
| 1979 | (11- 9) | 27 | 145 | 5.37 | 16 | .59 | 22 | .81 |
| 1980 | ( 9- 9) | 23 | 101 | 4.39 | 29 | 1.26 | 8 | .35 |
| 1981 | ( 8- 4) | 15 | 66 | 4.40 | 13 | .87 | 8 | .53 |
| 1982 | (11- 6) | 23 | 111 | 4.82 | 20 | .87 | 9 | .39 |
| 7 years | | 157 | 664 | 4.23 | 124 | .79 | 96 | .61 |

| | G | IP | W | L | Pct | ER | ERA |
|---|---|---|---|---|---|---|---|
| Home | 16 | 92 | 6 | 2 | .750 | 37 | 3.62 |
| Road | 15 | 64 | 5 | 4 | .556 | 40 | 5.63 |

## Tommy JOHN

| Year | (W–L) | GS | Run | Avg | DP | Avg | SB | Avg |
|---|---|---|---|---|---|---|---|---|
| 1976 | (10-10) | 31 | 108 | 3.48 | 33 | 1.06 | 26 | .84 |
| 1977 | (20- 7) | 31 | 159 | 5.13 | 41 | 1.32 | 12 | .39 |
| 1978 | (17-10) | 30 | 150 | 5.00 | 38 | 1.27 | 22 | .73 |
| 1979 | (21- 9) | 36 | 172 | 4.78 | 56 | 1.56 | 11 | .31 |
| 1980 | (22- 9) | 36 | 189 | 5.25 | 47 | 1.31 | 4 | .11 |
| 1981 | ( 9- 8) | 20 | 74 | 3.70 | 27 | 1.35 | 9 | .45 |
| 1982 | (14-12) | 33 | 149 | 4.51 | 39 | 1.18 | 11 | .33 |
| 7 years | | 217 | 1001 | 4.61 | 281 | 1.29 | 95 | .43 |

| | G | IP | W | L | Pct | ER | ERA |
|---|---|---|---|---|---|---|---|
| New York | 15 | 110.1 | 6 | 6 | .500 | 42 | 3.86 |
| California | 4 | 15.2 | 2 | 1 | .667 | 10 | 5.74 |
| Road | 18 | 95.2 | 6 | 5 | .545 | 39 | 3.72 |

## 1982 OTHERS

| Pitcher | (W–L) | GS | Run | Avg | DP | Avg | SB | Avg |
|---|---|---|---|---|---|---|---|---|
| Kison | (10-5) | 16 | 93 | 5.81 | 17 | 1.06 | 8 | .50 |
| Moreno | ( 3-7) | 8 | 24 | 3.00 | 6 | .75 | 4 | .50 |
| Goltz | ( 8-5) | 7 | 40 | 5.71 | 10 | 1.43 | 0 | .00 |
| Tiant | ( 2-2) | 5 | 27 | 5.40 | 4 | .80 | 3 | .60 |
| Steirer | (11-0) | 1 | 7 | | 0 | | 0 | |

## CALIFORNIA

*Talent Analysis*

The California Angels possessed 179 points of approximate value in 1982.

| | AV | % |
|---|---|---|
| Produced by system: | 16 | 9% |
| Acquired by trade: | 80 | 45% |
| Purchased or signed from free agency: | 83 | 46% |

The Angels had more purchased talent than any other team.

| | | |
|---|---|---|
| Young (Up to age 25): | 7 | 4% |
| Prime (Age 26 to 29): | 20 | 11% |
| Past-prime (Age 30 to 33): | 89 | 50% |
| Old (Age 34 or older): | 63 | 35% |

With 85% of their talent old or past-prime, the Angels are easily the oldest team in the major leagues.

The Angels' system ranked fourteenth in the amount of 1982 talent produced, 152; over the last four years they rank thirteenth with 566.

## ANAHEIM STADIUM

DIMENSIONS: Normal

SURFACE: Grass

VISIBILITY: Poor

FOUL TERRITORY: —

FAVORS:
Hitter/Pitcher—Neither
Power/Line-drive hitter—Power
Righthander/Lefthander—Neither

TYPES OF OFFENSE AFFECTED: Cuts doubles and triples a little; a pretty decent home-run park

PLAYERS ON TEAM HELPED MOST BY PARK: Geoff Zahn

PLAYERS ON TEAM HURT MOST BY PARK: No one

OTHER COMMENTS: This used to be very much a pitcher's park, but it was remodeled to put extra seats in the house a few years ago and apparently is a neutral park now

## THE GAMES THAT WON IT

On September 17, the Angels were two games behind the Royals. In the next 10 games they won eight times, including four straight victories over Kansas City, to virtually clinch the division. An account of those 10 games:

| Date | Opponent | Score | Started/Winner | GWRBI (hit) | Inning |
|---|---|---|---|---|---|
| 9-18 | Toronto | 8-6 | Witt/Sanchez | Lynn (2-run single) | 9th |
| 9-19 | Toronto | 5-1 | Kison | DeCinces (ground ball) | 1st |
| 9-20 | Kansas City | 3-2 | Zahn | Foli (home run) | 5th |
| 9-21 | Kansas City | 2-1 | Forsch | Sconiers (single) | 9th |
| 9-22 | Kansas City | 8-5 | John | DeCinces (home run) | 1st |
| 9-23 | Texas | 4-5 | Loss | Renko blasted in start; Witt pitched super but lost | |
| 9-24 | Texas | 10-1 | Kison | Carew (fly ball) | 3rd |
| 9-25 | Texas | 6-5 | Zahn/Goltz | Downing (hit by pitcher) | 7th |
| 9-26 | Texas | 5-7 | Loss | Forsch (0-6 after three) | |
| 9-27 | Kansas City | 3-2 | John | Baylor (single) | 7th |

### HITTERS

| | G | AB | R | H | 2B | 3B | HR | RBI | Avg |
|---|---|---|---|---|---|---|---|---|---|
| Carew | 9 | 36 | 5 | 12 | 1 | 2 | 1 | 5 | .333 |
| DeCinces | 10 | 40 | 8 | 12 | 3 | 0 | 4 | 9 | .300 |
| Reggie | 10 | 34 | 5 | 4 | 1 | 0 | 2 | 4 | .118 |
| Downing | 10 | 38 | 4 | 13 | 4 | 0 | 1 | 7 | .342 |
| Lynn | 9 | 32 | 5 | 11 | 0 | 0 | 1 | 4 | .344 |
| Grich | 9 | 31 | 3 | 5 | 1 | 0 | 0 | 1 | .161 |
| Foli | 8 | 23 | 3 | 7 | 0 | 0 | 1 | 4 | .304 |
| Boone | 10 | 28 | 2 | 9 | 1 | 0 | 0 | 1 | .321 |
| Baylor | 8 | 30 | 7 | 8 | 0 | 0 | 1 | 4 | .267 |

### PITCHERS

| | G | IP | W | L | ERA | Sv |
|---|---|---|---|---|---|---|
| Kison | 2 | 17 | 2 | 0 | 0.53 | 0 |
| John | 2 | 13 | 2 | 0 | 4.05 | 0 |
| Zahn | 2 | 14 | 1 | 0 | 4.61 | 0 |
| Forsch | 2 | 12 | 1 | 1 | 4.63 | 0 |
| Sanchez | 4 | 7 | 1 | 0 | 0.00 | 2 |
| Goltz | 2 | 7 | 1 | 0 | 0.00 | 1 |
| Witt | 2 | 7 | 0 | 1 | 3.86 | 0 |

COMMENTS:

1) Tim Foli's home run was probably the biggest hit of the year.

2) The Angels were the only team whose offense carried them during their games-that-won-it stretch.

3) Daryl Sconiers beat the Royals on September 21 with his first hit of the season.

# KANSAS CITY ROYALS

Kansas City catchers and outfielders combined threw out only 71 baserunners in 1982, easily the lowest total in the league. I use that as an estimate of the number of opposing runners removed on the basepaths...

Among the pleasures of being a Royals' fan, few rank any higher than turning on the radio each evening to receive the 7 o'clock greeting of Mr. Denny Matthews. My goal about each team is to try to bring to light something about the team which is not generally known. After years of post-season play with basically the same team, not much about the Royals has slipped through the network of the country's information services. But behind their microphone, all but unknown to the nation, sits one of the most skilled and gifted men that the craft has ever produced.

His gifts, I suppose, are moderate, if well adapted to the task. His voice has a pleasant timbre that suggests a cheerful occasion. Its natural inflection rises and falls constantly, so that over the course of countless hours it acquires neither the grating quality of forced enthusiasm nor the drone of forced interest. He has a dry, understated humor that drifts through much of his audience undetected. One cannot learn these things at a microphone; they are given. But heck, I talk to people with pleasant voices every day, and Denny isn't Bob Uecker, by any means. These are not the things that lift him out of the class of the competent announcers, and into the class of the great ones.

Fred White, the Royals' other announcer, is good too. But what are the acquired skills, I got to wondering, that make an announcer? If Denny and Fred are not quite paragons of the things a baseball announcer should be, they are an acceptable substitute. So what do they have, exactly?

1) (And by far the most important) An intense focus on the game that is being played in front of them. I score games sometimes, even over the radio, and when I do I try to record a variety of information other than the stuff you can get out of the records. Sometimes I try to do this with other announcers, and I am amazed at the information they leave out. "Base hit!" says the announcer. Base hit? Where? Scooting by the shortstop into center? Drilled to left? I'll be listening to another game, and there will be runners on first and third in the fifth, and I will wonder if the manager is going to bring the infield in—and be astounded that the announcer doesn't tell me. There will be a single to center and I will be sitting there trying to visualize the play, and when I look for the throw... no throw. The voice has not told me where the throw went. I find out two pitches into the next batter that the other runner is now on third, and I wonder if the announcer didn't see him go over there, or what? The color man breaks in and tells you that the runner was able to get to third base because he was off with the pitch. Well, if he was off with the pitch, why didn't you tell me? This leaves me wondering if he was off with the pitch the previous two times, when the ball was fouled off.

And you know why so many announcers don't tell you these things? *Because they don't see them.* Because they haven't ever learned, really, to become the eyes of the listeners. I was just amazed, in the World Series, when an announcer told us that Darrell Porter's batting stance "looks a lot like Rod Carew's." Darrell Porter's tense, pigeon-toed, cocked-arm, locked-wrist stance like Rod Carew's pointed lead foot, loose wrist, relaxed batting style? They have open stances and they crouch a little and they point the bat in the air. That's the end of the similarities. I saw an American League rookie do an absolutely perfect impression of Rickey Henderson at the plate last summer and the announcer's comment was "Hm. Funny-looking batting stance."

Denny Matthews tells you, batter after batter:

1) What the pitch was.
2) Where the pitch was.
3) What kind of a swing the batter had at it (fought it off, flicked at it, tried to hold up, had a good rip but swung over it).
4) Where the defense is.
5) What the runner does.
6) Where the hit goes.
7) Where the throw goes.

If the wind is blowing in, he tells you; if it shifts, you hear about it. He describes the batting stance of each player, in very specific terms as well as the impression it gives, once each year. He describes the delivery of the pitcher in specific terms. If the throw to first was a low throw or a high throw or a wide throw or a good throw, he tells you. If the fielder fields the ball on the second hop or the third hop, on a high hop or a short hop, to his left or to his right, he tells you. If the batter breaks his bat, if he squirts the ball off the end of the bat, he tells you. In the batter's first at-bat, he tells you what the batter has done in the last few games; after that, he tells you what the hiter has done earlier in the game. After awhile, you get used to knowing stuff like that.

There is one thing that happens about every week that tips you off on how intense Mr. Matthew's concentration on the game is. What does your announcer say when the scoreboard count gets mixed up? Does he never notice it, and just read the count off the board? Does he say, "Now wait a minute... I thought the third pitch was called a strike." Does he debate the color man about what the count was? Denny dismisses it with a six-word phrase: The scoreboard has the count wrong.

2) The other main thing that I like about Denny is the things he *doesn't* say because he is too busy describing what he sees. Let's go back to the first-and-third situation where the announcer doesn't tell us what happened. What is he saying, while he is not telling us where the hit went and where the runner went and where the throw went? The worst announcers, and you know they do it, will launch into a sermonette about a) the character of the man who got the hit, or b) the bad run of luck we've been having lately, how we're in one of these stretches

that balls like that that aren't really hit that well just fall in between the fielders. The competent announcers tell you what they see, and then break into generalities about the people involved in the play, and talk about "concentration" and "fundamentals" and stuff.

Some people actually criticize Matthews because he's not judgmental about what he sees. They want the announcer to tell them that Ron LeFlore has a bad arm; and Denny will tell them that the throw was off-line, and then move on. But what is an announcer doing, when he makes those sort of judgments? My view is, if the announcer sees the man make a poor throw, he should say so at the time; if he doesn't see it, he shouldn't be talking about it. I don't want an announcer passing on to me the stuff he heard in a bar last week. I don't want to know what some scout said about the guy's arm. I can make those judgments for myself; indeed, I prefer to. That's all right if the announcer knows what he's talking about, but two times in three he doesn't.

3) Denny works consciously against the pace of the game. If the game is dull, he starts giving you more and more information about the game, the players. When the game is on the line, he lets the situation speak for itself. If it's a blowout, he starts telling stories.

Nobody's perfect. He moans a lot about the length of the games and how slow the pitcher is working, and I wish he'd shut up about it. A lot of the fans complain about his giving meaningless stats, and I think sometimes that the stats he gives are not always meaningful (but then again, he doesn't state them in a way that makes that judgment for you). But he works hard at his craft; he truly loves the game. He gets his ego and his theories and his preconceptions out of the way, and becomes a tube through which the game splashes out into your room, pure and clean and complete. That's too easy for most announcers, and too hard.

I score baseball games all kinds of different ways. Sometimes I score by where the ball lands on the field. Sometimes I score pitch by pitch. Sometimes I focus on the pitcher, try to "code" his delivery. Sometimes I keep a record of the position of the defense. Sometimes I try to focus on the communication of the players one to another, put down the pen and put the glasses on the third base coach for an inning. Boring; back to scoring.

Anyway, I do all of this mostly because it helps me to see things that I wasn't seeing before. I always have dreams, though, of sorting through all of the scoresheets, organizing them according to types of scoring in use and diagramming them in such a way as to learn all kinds of keen stuff. As a practical matter, I've only got so many hours, and the scoresheets from 80 or 90 Royals games a year, all scored in different ways and some of them over the radio, are not the greatest source of potential understanding of the game that you could find.

I did, however, locate 47 games from last year in which I used a "hit-location" scoring system. This might be used to answer certain questions:

*Q. Where do most hits on the field land?*

These 47 games had 888 hits, 461 for the Royals, 427 against. The 12 largest "holes" in the defense:

1) Straight up the middle, between the second baseman and the shortstop at ground level (108 hits; 107 singles and one triple. Robin Yount smoked one up the middle when Amos was playing him to pull).

2) All infield hits, if lumped together, accounted for 91 hits. All were singles.

3) 90 hits fell in front of the left fielder (87 singles, 3 doubles).

4) 76 hits fell in front of the center fielder (75 singles and a triple).

5) 66 hits went in the hole between shortstop and third base (65 singles and a double).

6) 63 hits fell in front of the right fielder (58 singles, two doubles, two triples and an inside-the-park home run. Steve Hammond apparently never saw it.)

7) 55 hits went into the gap in right (30 singles, 17 doubles, 8 triples).

8) 50 hits fell between the left fielder and the left-field line (16 singles, 34 doubles).

9) 47 hits went on the ground between the first baseman and the second baseman (45 singles and 2 doubles).

10) 41 hits fell between the right fielder and the right-field line (11 singles, 26 doubles, 2 triples, 2 home runs).

11) 40 hits went into the gap in left (17 singles, 18 doubles, 5 triples).

12) 30 hits went between the third baseman and the third-base line (7 singles, 23 doubles).

This doesn't include home runs over the fences (48 to left, 30 to right, 26 from left-center to right-center).

There are some mild surprises here. I am surprised that more hits go up the middle than through the hole. If organized into groups:

| | Singles | Doubles | Triples | Home Runs |
|---|---|---|---|---|
| Infield hits | 91 | 0 | 0 | 0 |
| Through the infield | 219 | 3 | 1 | 0 |
| Down the lines | 36 | 84 | 3 | 2 |
| In front of the outfield | 220 | 5 | 3 | 1 |
| In the gaps | 47 | 36 | 13 | 0 |
| Over the outfield | 0 | 18 | 2 | 0 |
| Over the fences | 0 | 0 | 0 | 104 |
| | 613 | 146 | 22 | 107 |

*Q. Where are the differences between the Royals and their opponents?*

1) The largest difference by far is in the number of hits going up the middle. The Royals had a 67-41 edge in those hits. In part this is a reflection of the Royals' offense, which has several players who hit the ball right up the middle. In some part it is probably a credit to Frank White, but in large part it seems to be a reflection of U.L. Washington's positioning. While KC had well over twice as many hits going up the middle as in the hole (67-29), their opponents were nearly even (41-37). If you count hits going on either side of the shortstop, the Royals had a 95-79 advantage over their opponents; on either side of the second baseman, a 94-63 edge. (Maybe Frank did earn that Gold Glove.)

2) The Royals had a 54-37 advantage in infield hits (speed, of course), including a 10-2 edge in infield hits fielded by the pitcher.

3) In these 47 games, the opponents had no hits—none—going between the Royals first baseman and the

first-base line. The Royals had 5 such hits (3 for extra bases).

4) The Royals had a 19-11 edge in balls going between the third baseman and the third-base line.

5) KC trailed their opponents in hits dropping in front of the outfielders, 43-47 in left, 37-39 in center and 27-36 in right field, a total of 107-122.

6) The Royals also had fewer hits in the gaps than their opponents (which I find very surprising, since KC is known as a team of "gap" hitters with speed in the outfield). They trailed 16-24 in the left-field gap, and 25-30 in the right-field gap.

7) The Royals trailed 51-56 in home runs. They trailed 21-27 in home runs to left, but led 19-12 in home runs to right.

All of these facts are capable of innumerable interpretations. I will emulate Denny Matthews, and let you figure them out.

In the Royals' years as a powerhouse, 1976-1980, they had a large home-field advantage, but never as large as last year, when they were 56-25 in Royals Stadium, the best home record in baseball, but a dismal 34-47 on the road, the 18th-best road record in baseball. Well, tied for 18th with Seattle, Toronto and Houston. The Royals' *offense* was always well adapted to their stadium, which minimizes power, but their pitching staff was not. In a park like Royals Stadium, the edge is to a control pitcher who is vulnerable to the home run (like Forsch in St. Louis), because the park minimizes this weakness. That wasn't really the character of their pitching staff in their glory years, but as they have gotten older they have moved in that direction. So now the staff, too, is well-adapted to the stadium—but they give up so many home runs on the road (99 last year, highest in the league) that they just get blown out a lot.

**GEORGE BRETT** CAREER HOME AND ROAD BREAKDOWNS

| | *In Royals Stadium* | | | | | | | | | *On The Road* | | | | | | | | |
|---|---|---|---|---|---|---|---|---|---|---|---|---|---|---|---|---|---|---|
| **Year** | **G** | **AB** | **R** | **H** | **2B** | **3B** | **HR** | **RBI** | **Avg** | **G** | **AB** | **R** | **H** | **2B** | **3B** | **HR** | **RBI** | **Avg** |
| 1973 | 6 | 15 | 1 | 0 | 0 | 0 | 0 | 0 | .000 | 7 | 25 | 1 | 5 | 2 | 0 | 0 | 0 | .200 |
| 1974 | 64 | 216 | 22 | 67 | 16 | 4 | 0 | 22 | .310 | 69 | 241 | 27 | 62 | 5 | 1 | 2 | 25 | .257 |
| 1975 | 81 | 309 | 46 | 112 | 22 | 10 | 2 | 48 | .362 | 78 | 325 | 38 | 83 | 13 | 3 | 9 | 41 | .255 |
| 1976 | 80 | 313 | 57 | 115 | 23 | 5 | 6 | 43 | .367 | 79 | 332 | 37 | 100 | 11 | 9 | 1 | 24 | .301 |
| 1977 | 70 | 285 | 53 | 96 | 17 | 11 | 9 | 43 | .337 | 69 | 279 | 52 | 80 | 15 | 2 | 13 | 45 | .287 |
| 1978 | 67 | 261 | 50 | 92 | 31 | 6 | 4 | 41 | .352 | 61 | 249 | 29 | 58 | 14 | 2 | 5 | 21 | .233 |
| 1979 | 78 | 324 | 67 | 121 | 23 | 14 | 11 | 62 | .373 | 76 | 321 | 52 | 91 | 19 | 6 | 12 | 45 | .283 |
| 1980 | 61 | 235 | 44 | 92 | 18 | 6 | 13 | 63 | .391 | 56 | 214 | 43 | 83 | 15 | 3 | 11 | 55 | .388 |
| 1981 | 43 | 159 | 17 | 53 | 13 | 5 | 2 | 21 | .333 | 46 | 188 | 25 | 56 | 14 | 2 | 4 | 22 | .298 |
| 1982 | 73 | 275 | 47 | 75 | 12 | 5 | 9 | 45 | .273 | 71 | 277 | 54 | 91 | 20 | 4 | 12 | 37 | .329 |
| Career | 623 | 2392 | 404 | 823 | 175 | 66 | 56 | 347 | .344 | 612 | 2451 | 358 | 709 | 128 | 34 | 69 | 315 | .289 |

Willie AIKENS, First Base

*Runs Created: 73*

| | G | AB | R | H | 2B | 3B | HR | RBI | SB | Avg |
|---|---|---|---|---|---|---|---|---|---|---|
| First Half | 68 | 240 | 22 | 60 | 16 | 0 | 4 | 30 | 0 | .250 |
| Second Half | 66 | 226 | 28 | 71 | 13 | 1 | 13 | 44 | 0 | .314 |
| Home | 70 | 250 | 34 | 77 | 13 | 1 | 11 | 46 | 0 | .308 |
| Road | 64 | 216 | 16 | 54 | 16 | 0 | 6 | 28 | 0 | .250 |
| vs. RHP | 96 | 312 | 35 | 95 | 23 | 1 | 12 | 54 | 0 | .304 |
| vs. LHP | 38 | 154 | 15 | 36 | 6 | 0 | 5 | 20 | 0 | .234 |
| 1982 | 134 | 466 | 50 | 131 | 29 | 1 | 17 | 74 | 0 | 281 |
| 3.36 years | | 544 | 68 | 149 | 27 | 0 | 22 | 93 | 1 | .273 |

George BRETT, Third Base

*Runs Created: 107*

| | G | AB | R | H | 2B | 3B | HR | RBI | SB | Avg |
|---|---|---|---|---|---|---|---|---|---|---|
| First Half | 79 | 306 | 57 | 92 | 17 | 6 | 10 | 42 | 3 | .301 |
| Second Half | 65 | 246 | 44 | 74 | 15 | 3 | 11 | 40 | 3 | .301 |
| Home | 73 | 275 | 47 | 75 | 12 | 5 | 9 | 45 | 4 | .273 |
| Road | 71 | 277 | 54 | 91 | 20 | 4 | 12 | 37 | 2 | .329 |
| vs. RHP | 93 | 349 | 70 | 111 | 23 | 7 | 16 | 60 | 4 | .318 |
| vs. LHP | 51 | 203 | 31 | 55 | 9 | 2 | 5 | 22 | 2 | .271 |
| 1982 | 144 | 552 | 101 | 166 | 32 | 9 | 21 | 82 | 6 | .301 |
| 7.62 years | | 635 | 100 | 201 | 40 | 13 | 16 | 87 | 17 | .316 |

Frank WHITE, Second Base

*Runs Created: 76*

| | G | AB | R | H | 2B | 3B | HR | RBI | SB | Avg |
|---|---|---|---|---|---|---|---|---|---|---|
| First Half | 74 | 270 | 41 | 83 | 25 | 4 | 3 | 25 | 5 | .307 |
| Second Half | 71 | 254 | 30 | 73 | 20 | 2 | 8 | 31 | 5 | .287 |
| Home | 76 | 269 | 46 | 86 | 29 | 5 | 7 | 39 | 4 | .320 |
| Road | 69 | 255 | 24 | 70 | 16 | 1 | 4 | 17 | 6 | .275 |
| vs. RHP | 91 | 345 | 48 | 98 | 24 | 4 | 6 | 32 | 7 | .284 |
| vs. LHP | 54 | 179 | 23 | 58 | 21 | 2 | 5 | 24 | 3 | .324 |
| 1982 | 145 | 524 | 71 | 156 | 45 | 6 | 11 | 56 | 10 | .298 |
| 7.58 years | | 520 | 65 | 134 | 26 | 5 | 8 | 54 | 18 | .258 |

U.L. WASHINGTON, Shortstop

*Runs Created: 63*

| | G | AB | R | H | 2B | 3B | HR | RBI | SB | Avg |
|---|---|---|---|---|---|---|---|---|---|---|
| First Half | 45 | 145 | 12 | 42 | 5 | 2 | 0 | 16 | 5 | .290 |
| Second Half | 74 | 292 | 52 | 83 | 14 | 1 | 10 | 44 | 18 | .284 |
| Home | 55 | 192 | 28 | 54 | 9 | 1 | 2 | 26 | 13 | .281 |
| Road | 64 | 245 | 36 | 71 | 10 | 2 | 8 | 34 | 10 | .290 |
| vs. RHP | 78 | 282 | 35 | 75 | 11 | 2 | 1 | 36 | 15 | .266 |
| vs. LHP | 41 | 155 | 29 | 50 | 8 | 1 | 9 | 24 | 8 | .323 |
| 1982 | 119 | 437 | 64 | 125 | 19 | 3 | 10 | 60 | 23 | .286 |
| 3.40 years | | 512 | 66 | 135 | 20 | 7 | 6 | 52 | 22 | .263 |

Willie WILSON, Left Field

*Runs Created: 93*

| | G | AB | R | H | 2B | 3B | HR | RBI | SB | Avg |
|---|---|---|---|---|---|---|---|---|---|---|
| First Half | 60 | 259 | 33 | 89 | 8 | 8 | 1 | 23 | 14 | .344 |
| Second Half | 76 | 326 | 54 | 105 | 11 | 7 | 2 | 23 | 23 | .322 |
| Home | 68 | 288 | 50 | 100 | 9 | 6 | 2 | 26 | 26 | .347 |
| Road | 68 | 297 | 37 | 94 | 10 | 9 | 1 | 20 | 11 | .316 |
| vs. RHP | 82 | 364 | 60 | 131 | 12 | 12 | 3 | 29 | 34 | .360 |
| vs. LHP | 54 | 221 | 27 | 63 | 7 | 3 | 0 | 17 | 3 | .285 |
| 1982 | 136 | 585 | 87 | 194 | 19 | 15 | 3 | 46 | 37 | .332 |
| 4.35 years | | 587 | 101 | 183 | 20 | 12 | 3 | 44 | 66 | .312 |

Amos OTIS, Center Field

*Runs Created: 67*

| | G | AB | R | H | 2B | 3B | HR | RBI | SB | Avg |
|---|---|---|---|---|---|---|---|---|---|---|
| First Half | 76 | 290 | 50 | 87 | 18 | 2 | 9 | 56 | 7 | .300 |
| Second Half | 49 | 185 | 23 | 49 | 7 | 1 | 2 | 32 | 2 | .265 |
| Home | 60 | 220 | 41 | 71 | 14 | 2 | 5 | 44 | 6 | .323 |
| Road | 65 | 255 | 32 | 65 | 11 | 1 | 6 | 44 | 3 | .255 |
| vs. RHP | 74 | 307 | 46 | 85 | 16 | 2 | 8 | 66 | 7 | .277 |
| vs. LHP | 51 | 168 | 27 | 51 | 9 | 1 | 3 | 22 | 2 | .304 |
| 1982 | 125 | 475 | 73 | 136 | 25 | 3 | 11 | 88 | 9 | .286 |
| 11.48 years | | 596 | 92 | 167 | 31 | 6 | 17 | 83 | 29 | .279 |

Jerry MARTIN, Right Field

*Runs Created: 65*

| | G | AB | R | H | 2B | 3B | HR | RBI | SB | Avg |
|---|---|---|---|---|---|---|---|---|---|---|
| First Half | 82 | 300 | 26 | 81 | 13 | 1 | 6 | 35 | 1 | .270 |
| Second Half | 65 | 219 | 26 | 57 | 9 | 0 | 9 | 30 | 0 | .260 |
| Home | 75 | 264 | 27 | 65 | 9 | 0 | 6 | 32 | 1 | .246 |
| Road | 72 | 255 | 25 | 73 | 13 | 1 | 9 | 33 | 0 | .286 |
| vs. RHP | 83 | 314 | 32 | 81 | 12 | 0 | 8 | 37 | 1 | .258 |
| vs. LHP | 64 | 205 | 20 | 57 | 10 | 1 | 7 | 28 | 0 | .278 |
| 1982 | 147 | 519 | 52 | 138 | 22 | 1 | 15 | 65 | 1 | .266 |
| 5.89 years | | 427 | 56 | 108 | 22 | 3 | 14 | 56 | 6 | .254 |

John WATHAN, Catcher

*Runs Created: 55*

| | G | AB | R | H | 2B | 3B | HR | RBI | SB | Avg |
|---|---|---|---|---|---|---|---|---|---|---|
| First Half | 71 | 278 | 53 | 74 | 5 | 2 | 1 | 29 | 26 | .266 |
| Second Half | 50 | 170 | 26 | 47 | 6 | 1 | 2 | 22 | 10 | .276 |
| Home | 65 | 233 | 46 | 73 | 7 | 1 | 2 | 31 | 18 | .313 |
| Road | 56 | 215 | 33 | 48 | 4 | 2 | 1 | 20 | 18 | .223 |
| vs. RHP | 74 | 287 | 50 | 75 | 5 | 2 | 2 | 31 | 20 | .261 |
| vs. LHP | 47 | 161 | 29 | 46 | 6 | 1 | 1 | 20 | 16 | .286 |
| 1982 | 121 | 448 | 79 | 121 | 11 | 3 | 3 | 51 | 36 | .270 |
| 3.55 years | | 494 | 64 | 136 | 16 | 6 | 5 | 59 | 20 | .276 |

Hal McRAE, Designated Hitter

*Runs Created: 120*

| | G | AB | R | H | 2B | 3B | HR | RBI | SB | Avg |
|---|---|---|---|---|---|---|---|---|---|---|
| First Half | 84 | 321 | 45 | 101 | 21 | 5 | 14 | 79 | 2 | .315 |
| Second Half | 75 | 292 | 46 | 88 | 25 | 3 | 13 | 54 | 2 | .301 |
| Home | 80 | 304 | 45 | 91 | 25 | 4 | 12 | 68 | 2 | .299 |
| Road | 79 | 309 | 46 | 98 | 21 | 4 | 15 | 65 | 2 | .317 |
| vs. RHP | 100 | 404 | 61 | 123 | 29 | 8 | 13 | 85 | 3 | .304 |
| vs. LHP | 59 | 209 | 30 | 66 | 17 | 0 | 14 | 48 | 1 | .316 |
| 1982 | 159 | 613 | 91 | 189 | 46 | 8 | 27 | 133 | 4 | .308 |
| 9.75 years | | 583 | 78 | 169 | 40 | 6 | 16 | 88 | 11 | .290 |

Larry GURA

| Year | (W–L) | GS | Run | Avg | DP | Avg | SB | Avg |
|---|---|---|---|---|---|---|---|---|
| 1977 | ( 8- 5) | 6 | 29 | 4.83 | 5 | .83 | 0 | .00 |
| 1978 | (16- 4) | 26 | 115 | 4.42 | 22 | .85 | 12 | .46 |
| 1979 | (13-12) | 33 | 180 | 5.45 | 32 | .97 | 20 | .61 |
| 1980 | (18-10) | 36 | 188 | 5.22 | 33 | .92 | 19 | .53 |
| 1981 | (11- 8) | 23 | 84 | 3.65 | 20 | .87 | 7 | .30 |
| 1982 | (18-12) | 37 | 185 | 5.00 | 29 | .78 | 10 | .27 |
| 6 years | | 161 | 781 | 4.85 | 141 | .88 | 68 | .42 |

| | G | IP | W | L | Pct | ER | ERA |
|---|---|---|---|---|---|---|---|
| Home | 22 | 152 | 11 | 6 | .647 | 64 | 3.79 |
| Road | 15 | 96 | 7 | 6 | .538 | 47 | 4.41 |

Vida BLUE

| Year | (W–L) | GS | Run | Avg | DP | Avg | SB | Avg |
|---|---|---|---|---|---|---|---|---|
| 1976 | (18-13) | 37 | 141 | 3.81 | 26 | .70 | 26 | .70 |
| 1977 | (14-19) | 38 | 120 | 3.16 | 24 | .63 | 25 | .66 |
| 1978 | (18-10) | 35 | 136 | 3.89 | 30 | .86 | 22 | .63 |
| 1979 | (14-14) | 34 | 167 | 4.91 | 31 | .91 | 20 | .59 |
| 1980 | (14-10) | 31 | 101 | 3.26 | 22 | .71 | 16 | .52 |
| 1981 | ( 8- 6) | 18 | 55 | 3.06 | 18 | 1.00 | 13 | .72 |
| 1982 | (13-12) | 31 | 135 | 4.35 | 23 | .74 | 12 | .39 |
| 7 years | | 224 | 855 | 3.81 | 151 | .67 | 134 | .60 |

| | G | IP | W | L | Pct | ER | ERA |
|---|---|---|---|---|---|---|---|
| Home | 14 | 92.2 | 7 | 4 | .636 | 25 | 2.43 |
| Road | 17 | 88.1 | 6 | 8 | .429 | 51 | 5.20 |

Paul SPLITTORFF

| Year | (W–L) | GS | Run | Avg | DP | Avg | SB | Avg |
|---|---|---|---|---|---|---|---|---|
| 1976 | (11- 8) | 23 | 97 | 4.22 | 24 | 1.04 | 25 | 1.09 |
| 1977 | (16- 6) | 37 | 202 | 5.46 | 28 | .76 | 19 | .51 |
| 1978 | (19-13) | 38 | 181 | 4.76 | 42 | 1.11 | 14 | .37 |
| 1979 | (15-17) | 35 | 173 | 4.94 | 39 | 1.11 | 20 | .57 |
| 1980 | (14-11) | 33 | 154 | 4.67 | 36 | 1.09 | 16 | .48 |
| 1981 | ( 5- 5) | 15 | 70 | 4.67 | 16 | 1.07 | 15 | 1.00 |
| 1982 | (10-10) | 28 | 139 | 4.96 | 27 | .96 | 16 | .57 |
| 7 years | | 209 | 1016 | 4.86 | 212 | 1.01 | 125 | .60 |

| | G | IP | W | L | Pct | ER | ERA |
|---|---|---|---|---|---|---|---|
| Home | 12 | 68 | 4 | 5 | .444 | 32 | 4.20 |
| Road | 17 | 94 | 6 | 5 | .545 | 41 | 3.93 |

Dennis LEONARD

| Year | (W–L) | GS | Run | Avg | DP | Avg | SB | Avg |
|---|---|---|---|---|---|---|---|---|
| 1976 | (17- 9) | 34 | 184 | 5.41 | 23 | .68 | 33 | .97 |
| 1977 | (20-12) | 37 | 165 | 4.46 | 37 | 1.00 | 13 | .35 |
| 1978 | (21-17) | 40 | 183 | 4.58 | 30 | .75 | 20 | .50 |
| 1979 | (14-12) | 32 | 165 | 5.16 | 22 | .69 | 7 | .22 |
| 1980 | (20-11) | 38 | 201 | 5.29 | 31 | .82 | 23 | .61 |
| 1981 | (13-11) | 26 | 88 | 3.38 | 22 | .85 | 15 | .58 |
| 1982 | (10- 6) | 21 | 124 | 5.90 | 20 | .95 | 15 | .71 |
| 7 years | | 228 | 1110 | 4.87 | 185 | .81 | 126 | .55 |

| | G | IP | W | L | Pct | ER | ERA |
|---|---|---|---|---|---|---|---|
| Home | 13 | 82.1 | 7 | 3 | .700 | 41 | 4.48 |
| Road | 8 | 48.1 | 3 | 3 | .500 | 33 | 6.15 |

1982 OTHERS

| Pitcher | (W–L) | GS | Run | Avg | DP | Avg | SB | Avg |
|---|---|---|---|---|---|---|---|---|
| Frost | (6-6) | 14 | 66 | 4.71 | 13 | .93 | 11 | .79 |
| Black | (4-6) | 14 | 49 | 3,50 | 11 | .79 | 10 | .71 |
| Creel | (1-4) | 6 | 20 | 3.33 | 5 | .83 | 4 | .67 |
| Castro | (3-2) | 4 | 25 | 6.25 | 3 | .75 | 4 | 1.00 |
| Botelho | (2-1) | 4 | 26 | 6.50 | 4 | 1.00 | 2 | .50 |
| Hood | (4-0) | 3 | 15 | 5.00 | 5 | 1.67 | 1 | .33 |

## KANSAS CITY

*Talent Analysis*

The Royals possessed 168 points of approximate value in 1982.

| | AV | % |
|---|---|---|
| Produced by the system: | 87 | 52% |
| Acquired by trade: | 69 | 41% |
| Purchased or signed from free agency: | 12 | 7% |

A farm-built team.

| | | |
|---|---|---|
| Young (Up to age 25): | 5 | 3% |
| Prime (Age 26 to 29): | 75 | 45% |
| Past-prime (Age 30 to 33): | 45 | 27% |
| Old (Age 34 or older): | 43 | 26% |

The Royals have become an old team.

The system produced 164 points of value in '82; this ranks tenth. Over the period 1979 to 1982 their 561 total ranks fourteenth.

## ROYALS STADIUM

DIMENSIONS: Normal; deep in alleys

SURFACE: Turf, very fast but not extremely hard

VISIBILITY: Excellent

FOUL TERRITORY: Small

FAVORS:
Hitter/Pitcher—Hitter
Power/Line-drive hitter—Line-drive
Righthander/Lefthander—Neither

TYPES OF OFFENSE AFFECTED: Worst home run park in AL, but wonderful park for doubles and triples; raises overall batting averages 8 to 12 points

OTHER PARK CHARACTERISTICS: Like Busch Stadium, turf is extremely hot in day games— so hot as to create serious fatigue problems if you're not careful

TYPES OF MARGINAL PLAYERS MOST VALUABLE IN PARK: Outfield defense is paramount; Geronimo and Martin valuable additions. If you don't have defense in the outfield you will not win in this park, period.

PLAYERS ON TEAM HELPED MOST BY PARK: Brett before 1980; Wathan, Blue, Leonard

PLAYERS ON TEAM HURT MOST BY PARK: Aikens, Otis, Washington

OTHER COMMENTS: The Royals' home-park edge is much larger than it would be if they were in the NL. There are several similar parks in the NL, but none in the AL, and many AL teams simply lack the personnel to adjust to the park. Defensive positioning in this park means playing the infield deep and the outfield shallow and near the lines, but you can't do that unless you have infielders who can close the gap in a hurry. Teams like Baltimore, Cleveland and Detroit simply have no options that work in this park.

## THE GAMES THAT LOST IT

The Royals led the division by two games on September 15, but lost 10 of 11 games, leaving them suddenly with no real chance. An account of those 11 games:

| Date | Opponent | Score | Starter/Loser | What Happened |
|---|---|---|---|---|
| 9-16 | Seattle | 2-4 | Leonard | Joe Simpson, 2-run triple in 9th |
| 9-17 | Minnesota | 4-5 | Splittorff | Four-run third |
| 9-18 | Minnesota | 5-11 | Blue | 6-0 after 3 |
| 9-19 | Minnesota | 4-9 | Castro | 7-0 after 5; Gaeti Grand Slam |
| 9-20 | California | 2-3 | Gura | Tim Foli |
| 9-21 | California | 1-2 | Leonard/Quiz | Sconiers' single in 9th |
| 9-22 | California | 5-8 | Blue | 5-1 after 2 |
| 9-24 | Oakland | 7-4 | Win | Gura, early lead |
| 9-25 | Oakland | 3-10 | Leonard | Two 5-run innings |
| 9-26 | Oakland | 4-5 | Castro/Quiz | Blew a 4-0 lead |
| 9-27 | California | 2-3 | Blue | Led 2-0, didn't hold it; two errors by Brett |

**HITTERS**

| | G | AB | R | H | 2B | 3B | HR | RBI | SB | Avg |
|---|---|---|---|---|---|---|---|---|---|---|
| Wilson | 11 | 44 | 4 | 11 | 0 | 0 | 0 | 1 | 2 | .250 |
| Washington | 11 | 43 | 7 | 13 | 1 | 0 | 4 | 8 | 0 | .302 |
| Brett | 11 | 44 | 5 | 10 | 1 | 0 | 0 | 3 | 0 | .227 |
| McRae | 9 | 44 | 5 | 14 | 5 | 0 | 1 | 4 | 0 | .318 |
| White | 8 | 26 | 2 | 6 | 0 | 0 | 2 | 2 | 0 | .231 |
| Aikens | 4 | 10 | 1 | 4 | 0 | 0 | 1 | 1 | 0 | .400 |
| Martin | 10 | 32 | 3 | 10 | 1 | 0 | 3 | 4 | 0 | .313 |
| Otis | 7 | 25 | 3 | 8 | 0 | 0 | 2 | 6 | 0 | .320 |
| Wathan | 10 | 35 | 2 | 4 | 0 | 0 | 0 | 2 | 1 | .114 |

**PITCHERS**

| | G | IP | W | L | ERA |
|---|---|---|---|---|---|
| Leonard | 3 | 19 | 0 | 2 | 5.68 |
| Blue | 3 | 11 | 0 | 3 | 9.82 |
| Gura | 2 | 14 | 1 | 1 | 3.86 |
| Quiz | 5 | 8 | 0 | 2 | 3.24 |
| Castro | 2 | 9 | 0 | 1 | 6.00 |
| Armstrong | 2 | 8 | 0 | 0 | 5.62 |
| Hood | 3 | 7 | 0 | 0 | 7.71 |
| Splittorff | 1 | 3 | 0 | 1 | 12.00 |

COMMENTS:

1) Royals outscored 46-25 in the first five innings, 14-18 after that.

2) Injury to Aikens, who was on a tear at the time, very key to the stretch, but the Royals scored enough runs (39 in 11 games) to win some games in this period. Injuries also benched Otis, White and McRae during part of the period.

3) An obvious pattern during this time was that the Royals, perhaps aware of their pitching problems, were trying to make very difficult defensive plays rather than taking an out at first base. A classic was a first-inning play on September 18, when with a runner out and men on first and third, Kent Hrbek chopped the ball toward third. Vida Blue cut it off and had a play at first, but he tried to make the play at third and threw it away. That's a suicidal play. If you take the play at first you've got two out and two on; if you throw late to third you've got the bases loaded and one out. I know that a player doesn't have time to pull out his pocket calculator and figure the percentages, but they'd been taking the play that they could make all year, and in this period . . . September 17, Leonard tried to make a play at second on a bad bunt, threw late and put himself in a none-out, two-on situation; September 19, U.L. Washington set-up a three-run third inning when he *twice* tried to make the play at second and missed; September 21, Leonard faked to second on a bunt play and threw it in the dirt. And on and on.

# CHICAGO WHITE SOX

I wrote one of the early Charlie-Lau-is-a-genius stories for the *Baseball Bulletin* in 1976, before the Royals had won the first of the division championships that would provide a showcase for his hitting pupils. He was popular in Kansas City; the players thought he was brilliant; he was a pleasant man who seemed to have nothing better to do than stop and talk to me. As I do now—as all people who think for themselves do, I suppose—he tended to speak in his own language, throwing around now-familiar Lauish phrases like . . . oh, I can never remember. I don't understand them anyway, just as I imagine Charlie doesn't have the foggiest notion about the meaning of AV or the $\log^5$ method.

What I do understand, though, is records, and I thought it would be fun to construct a record for Charlie, follow around the first $100,000-a-year batting coach from team to team and see how much hitting has gone on. His first experience was a highly successful one.

TEAM: Baltimore, 1969

| | Runs Scored | Batting Avg | W-L | Runs Position | Offensive W/L% |
|---|---|---|---|---|---|
| Pre-LAU 2 years | 654 | .240 | 76-85 | 4th | .547 |
| Pre-LAU 1 year | 579 | .225 | 91-71 | 3rd | .524 |
| Lau | 779 | .265 | 109-53 | 2nd | .586 |
| Post-LAU 1 year | 792 | .257 | 108-59 | 1st | .585 |
| Post-LAU 2 years | 742 | .261 | 101-57 | 1st | .602 |

There are a lot of qualifiers that go with this. The AL redefined the strike zone in '69 and run production was way up all around the league. 1969 was Earl Weaver's first full year in Baltimore. Frank Robinson battled an injury in 1968 and had the worst year of his career, came back strong in '69. Charlie didn't teach Frank to hit. The Orioles finished fourth in the league in runs scored in 1967, third in '68, second in '69, first in '70, so how much importance can you attribute to Charlie's coming in '69?

These are quibbles about whether or not the improvement can be credited to him—but they did improve. His second try was not as successful.

TEAM: Oakland, 1970

| | Runs Scored | Batting Avg | W-L | Runs Position | Offensive W/L% |
|---|---|---|---|---|---|
| Pre-LAU 2 years | 569 | .240 | 82-80 | 4th | .512 |
| Pre-LAU 1 year | 740 | .249 | 88-74 | 4th | .561 |
| Lau | 678 | .249 | 89-73 | 5th | .518 |
| Post-LAU 1 year | 691 | .252 | 101-60 | 3rd | .558 |
| Post-LAU 2 years | 604 | .240 | 93-62 | 2nd | .558 |

Not a disastrous year, but a young team failed to improve, and they failed to improve because the offense had a bad year.

It was his work in his third assignment that earned his reputation.

TEAM: Kansas City, 1971 to 1978

| | Runs Scored | Batting Avg | W-L | Runs Position | Offensive W/L% |
|---|---|---|---|---|---|
| Pre-LAU 2 years | 586 | .240 | 69-93 | 9th | .441 |
| Pre-LAU 1 year | 611 | .244 | 65-97 | 12th | .456 |
| Lau 1 | 603 | .250 | 85-76 | 8th | .490 |
| Lau 2 | 580 | .255 | 76-78 | 3rd | .541 |
| Lau 3* | 755 | .261 | 88-74 | 2nd | .549 |
| Lau 4 | 667 | .259 | 77-85 | 7th | .509 |
| Lau 5** | 710 | .261 | 91-71 | 5th | .516 |
| Lau 6 | 713 | .269 | 90-72 | 4th | .547 |
| Lau 7 | 822 | .277 | 102-60 | 5th | .556 |
| Lau 8 | 743 | .268 | 92-70 | 3rd | .543 |
| Post-LAU 1 year | 851 | .282 | 85-77 | 2nd | .559 |
| Post-LAU 2 years | 809 | .286 | 97-65 | 4th | .551 |

*KC moved to Royals Stadium; DH rule adopted
**Minor league hitting instructor most of season; recalled late in July.

Again, one can argue about Lau's role in the improvement of Kansas City. One thing that got me started doing this was that the team as a whole and Brett in particular had their best years after Charlie left. Still, they did improve under him, and that was enough to get him rehired.

TEAM: New York Yankees, 1979 to 1981

| | Runs Scored | Batting Avg | W-L | Runs Position | Offensive W/L% |
|---|---|---|---|---|---|
| Pre-LAU 2 years | 831 | .281 | 100-62 | 4th | .562 |
| Pre-LAU 1 year | 735 | .267 | 100-63 | 4th | .535 |
| Lau 1 | 734 | .266 | 89-71 | 9th | .491 |
| Lau 2 | 820 | .267 | 103-59 | 2nd | .558 |
| Lau 3 | 421 | .252 | 59-48 | 11th | .482 |
| Post-LAU 1 year | 709 | .256 | 79-83 | 8th | .488 |

The low point of the record. The Yankees deteriorated offensively in his hands. But his reputation continued to grow, and thus the big contract.

TEAM: Chicago White Sox, 1982

| | Runs Scored | Batting Avg | W-L | Runs Position | Offensive W/L% |
|---|---|---|---|---|---|
| Pre-LAU 2 years | 587 | .257 | 70-90 | 14th | .399 |
| Pre-LAU 1 year | 476 | .272 | 54-52 | 3rd | .548 |
| Lau 1 | 786 | .286 | 87-75 | 3rd | .540 |

The White Sox did not improve offensively, despite the additions of Paciorek and Kemp to the lineup. Their batting average went up, but in relation to the league their run production did not advance.

A great coach? The record does not prove that. But I began this research with a quiet suspicion that Lau was a charlatan, a front-runner with a clever knack for getting a job with coming organizations, making friends with the good young hitters, and taking credit for their success. The record certainly does not prove that. The mere fact that good organizations have hired him speaks well for him.

He has been associated with 12 winning teams in the last 14 years, with a combined record of 1,237 wins and 965 losses—an average of 90-72. How many hitting coaches have even been *employed* for the last 14 years? It cannot safely be said that he is a genius, but it can safely be said that he works at analyzing hitters, and that he has had some fresh ideas on the subject, that those ideas work for some people. That much safely, and more if you like him. His low-key, wait-for-them-to-come-to-you approach probably helps keep the lid on the clubhouse. It's a good record.

I suppose I should put on record that I think the White Sox are now clearly the team of the future in the AL West. California will spend most of the decade paying for the 1982 title; Kansas City is fighting to hold on without enough obvious young talent to make it a good bet. The Mariners . . . if you can't afford to keep a Floyd Bannister you've got no business owning a baseball team. The other teams are all four years away, and the White Sox will march into the breach.

Tom PACIORER, First Base
*Runs Created: 65*

| | G | AB | R | H | 2B | 3B | HR | RBI | SB | Avg |
|---|---|---|---|---|---|---|---|---|---|---|
| First Half | 72 | 262 | 31 | 81 | 16 | 3 | 6 | 37 | 3 | .309 |
| Second Half | 32 | 120 | 18 | 38 | 11 | 1 | 5 | 18 | 0 | .317 |
| Home | 50 | 178 | 24 | 50 | 12 | 3 | 0 | 17 | 3 | .281 |
| Road | 54 | 204 | 25 | 69 | 15 | 1 | 11 | 38 | 0 | .338 |
| vs. RHP | | 260 | 30 | 78 | 16 | 2 | 8 | 41 | 0 | .300 |
| vs. LHP | | 122 | 19 | 41 | 11 | 2 | 3 | 14 | 3 | .336 |
| 1982 | 104 | 382 | 49 | 119 | 27 | 4 | 11 | 55 | 3 | .312 |
| 5.92 years | | 478 | 58 | 135 | 28 | 4 | 11 | 60 | 7 | .283 |

Tony BERNAZARD, Second Base
*Runs Created: 75*

| | G | AB | R | H | 2B | 3B | HR | RBI | SB | Avg |
|---|---|---|---|---|---|---|---|---|---|---|
| First Half | 81 | 325 | 56 | 86 | 17 | 4 | 5 | 34 | 9 | .265 |
| Second Half | 56 | 215 | 34 | 52 | 8 | 5 | 6 | 22 | 2 | .242 |
| Home | 64 | 241 | 41 | 56 | 8 | 7 | 1 | 18 | 2 | .232 |
| Road | 73 | 299 | 49 | 82 | 17 | 2 | 10 | 38 | 9 | .274 |
| vs. RHP | | 367 | 60 | 93 | 19 | 7 | 9 | 40 | 6 | .253 |
| vs. LHP | | 173 | 30 | 45 | 6 | 2 | 2 | 16 | 5 | .260 |
| 1982 | 137 | 540 | 90 | 138 | 25 | 9 | 11 | 56 | 11 | .256 |
| 2.14 years | | 536 | 84 | 139 | 22 | 7 | 11 | 54 | 12 | .259 |

Aurelio RODRIGUEZ, Third Base
*Runs Created: 24*

| | G | AB | R | H | 2B | 3B | HR | RBI | SB | Avg |
|---|---|---|---|---|---|---|---|---|---|---|
| First Half | 46 | 69 | 7 | 8 | 2 | 0 | 0 | 2 | 0 | .133 |
| Second Half | 72 | 197 | 17 | 54 | 13 | 1 | 3 | 29 | 0 | .274 |
| Home | 61 | 135 | 10 | 35 | 6 | 1 | 0 | 14 | 0 | .259 |
| Road | 57 | 122 | 14 | 27 | 9 | 0 | 3 | 17 | 0 | .221 |
| vs. RHP | | 154 | 13 | 36 | 11 | 1 | 1 | 21 | 0 | .234 |
| vs. LHP | | 103 | 11 | 26 | 4 | 0 | 2 | 10 | 0 | .252 |
| 1982 | 118 | 257 | 24 | 62 | 15 | 1 | 3 | 31 | 0 | .241 |
| 12.04 years | | 500 | 47 | 120 | 22 | 4 | 9 | 50 | 3 | .239 |

Vance LAW, Shortstop
*Runs Created: 45*

| | G | AB | R | H | 2B | 3B | HR | RBI | SB | Avg |
|---|---|---|---|---|---|---|---|---|---|---|
| First Half | 35 | 88 | 11 | 27 | 5 | 0 | 1 | 9 | 2 | .307 |
| Second Half | 79 | 271 | 29 | 74 | 15 | 1 | 4 | 45 | 2 | .273 |
| Home | 57 | 172 | 22 | 54 | 11 | 1 | 2 | 22 | 2 | .314 |
| Road | 57 | 187 | 18 | 47 | 9 | 0 | 3 | 32 | 2 | .251 |
| vs. RHP | | 239 | 25 | 70 | 12 | 0 | 1 | 27 | 2 | .293 |
| vs. LHP | | 120 | 15 | 31 | 8 | 1 | 4 | 27 | 2 | .258 |
| 1982 | 114 | 359 | 40 | 101 | 20 | 1 | 5 | 54 | 4 | .281 |
| 1.04 years | | 479 | 50 | 122 | 21 | 4 | 5 | 58 | 7 | .254 |

Bill ALMON, Shortstop
*Runs Created: 33*

| | G | AB | R | H | 2B | 3B | HR | RBI | SB | Avg |
|---|---|---|---|---|---|---|---|---|---|---|
| First Half | 75 | 238 | 35 | 65 | 9 | 3 | 4 | 21 | 9 | .273 |
| Second Half | 36 | 70 | 5 | 14 | 1 | 1 | 0 | 5 | 1 | .200 |
| Home | 50 | 136 | 19 | 41 | 5 | 2 | 2 | 13 | 6 | .301 |
| Road | 61 | 172 | 21 | 38 | 5 | 2 | 2 | 13 | 4 | .221 |
| vs. RHP | | 208 | 27 | 53 | 6 | 2 | 4 | 18 | 5 | .255 |
| vs. LHP | | 100 | 13 | 26 | 4 | 2 | 0 | 8 | 5 | .260 |
| 1982 | 111 | 308 | 40 | 79 | 10 | 4 | 4 | 26 | 10 | .256 |
| 4.38 years | | 486 | 56 | 126 | 16 | 5 | 3 | 35 | 17 | .259 |

Steve KEMP, Left Field
*Runs Created: 92*

| | G | AB | R | H | 2B | 3B | HR | RBI | SB | Avg |
|---|---|---|---|---|---|---|---|---|---|---|
| First Half | 81 | 292 | 43 | 86 | 12 | 0 | 8 | 51 | 4 | .295 |
| Second Half | 79 | 288 | 48 | 80 | 11 | 1 | 11 | 47 | 3 | .278 |
| Home | 79 | 274 | 42 | 71 | 7 | 1 | 4 | 42 | 4 | .259 |
| Road | 81 | 306 | 49 | 95 | 16 | 0 | 15 | 56 | 3 | .310 |
| vs. RHP | | 376 | 59 | 10 | 17 | 0 | 15 | 63 | 5 | .293 |
| vs. LHP | | 204 | 32 | 56 | 6 | 1 | 4 | 35 | 2 | .275 |
| 1982 | 160 | 580 | 91 | 166 | 23 | 1 | 19 | 98 | 7 | .286 |
| 5.21 years | | 592 | 90 | 168 | 26 | 4 | 21 | 100 | 6 | .284 |

Rudy LAW, Center Field
*Runs Created: 56*

| | G | AB | R | H | 2B | 3B | HR | RBI | SB | Avg |
|---|---|---|---|---|---|---|---|---|---|---|
| First Half | 56 | 92 | 15 | 27 | 4 | 1 | 1 | 11 | 13 | .293 |
| Second Half | 65 | 244 | 40 | 80 | 11 | 7 | 2 | 21 | 23 | .328 |
| Home | 59 | 162 | 26 | 51 | 7 | 4 | 0 | 11 | 19 | .315 |
| Road | 62 | 174 | 29 | 56 | 8 | 4 | 3 | 21 | 17 | .322 |
| vs. RHP | | 267 | 48 | 86 | 14 | 6 | 2 | 25 | 32 | .322 |
| vs. LHP | | 69 | 7 | 21 | 1 | 2 | 1 | 7 | 4 | .304 |
| 1982 | 121 | 336 | 55 | 107 | 15 | 8 | 3 | 32 | 36 | .318 |
| 1.61 years | | 457 | 70 | 131 | 12 | 8 | 3 | 35 | 49 | .287 |

Ron LeFLORE, Center Field
*Runs Created: 42*

| | G | AB | R | H | 2B | 3B | HR | RBI | SB | Avg |
|---|---|---|---|---|---|---|---|---|---|---|
| First Half | 68 | 279 | 47 | 81 | 12 | 4 | 4 | 22 | 23 | .290 |
| Second Half | 23 | 55 | 9 | 15 | 3 | 0 | 0 | 3 | 5 | .273 |
| Home | 43 | 162 | 27 | 50 | 7 | 2 | 3 | 14 | 10 | .309 |
| Road | 48 | 172 | 31 | 46 | 8 | 2 | 1 | 11 | 18 | .267 |
| vs. RHP | | 210 | 39 | 61 | 8 | 3 | 3 | 20 | 20 | .290 |
| vs. LHP | | 124 | 19 | 35 | 7 | 1 | 1 | 5 | 8 | .282 |
| 1982 | 91 | 334 | 58 | 96 | 15 | 4 | 4 | 25 | 28 | .287 |
| 6.78 years | | 658 | 108 | 189 | 25 | 8 | 9 | 52 | 67 | .288 |

Carlton FISK, Catcher

*Runs Created: 67*

| | G | AB | R | H | 2B | 3B | HR | RBI | SB | Avg |
|---|---|---|---|---|---|---|---|---|---|---|
| First Half | 68 | 234 | 29 | 61 | 7 | 0 | 7 | 30 | 8 | .261 |
| Second Half | 67 | 242 | 37 | 66 | 10 | 3 | 7 | 35 | 9 | .273 |
| Home | 68 | 237 | 33 | 65 | 9 | 2 | 7 | 38 | 8 | .274 |
| Road | 67 | 239 | 33 | 62 | 8 | 1 | 7 | 27 | 9 | .259 |
| vs. RHP | | 324 | 38 | 84 | 9 | 1 | 9 | 40 | 11 | .259 |
| vs. LHP | | 152 | 28 | 43 | 8 | 2 | 5 | 25 | 6 | .283 |
| 1982 | 135 | 476 | 66 | 127 | 17 | 3 | 14 | 65 | 17 | .267 |
| 8.08 years | | 570 | 91 | 163 | 29 | 5 | 23 | 84 | 10 | .281 |

Harold BAINES, Right Field

*Runs Created: 93*

| | G | AB | R | H | 2B | 3B | HR | RBI | SB | Avg |
|---|---|---|---|---|---|---|---|---|---|---|
| First Half | 81 | 300 | 40 | 81 | 17 | 4 | 11 | 56 | 6 | .270 |
| Second Half | 80 | 308 | 49 | 84 | 12 | 4 | 14 | 49 | 4 | .273 |
| Home | 80 | 288 | 42 | 83 | 15 | 4 | 11 | 54 | 5 | .288 |
| Road | 81 | 320 | 47 | 82 | 14 | 4 | 14 | 51 | 5 | .256 |
| vs. RHP | | 407 | 54 | 108 | 21 | 5 | 16 | 69 | 6 | .265 |
| vs. LHP | | 201 | 35 | 57 | 8 | 3 | 9 | 36 | 4 | .284 |
| 1982 | 161 | 608 | 89 | 165 | 29 | 8 | 25 | 105 | 10 | .271 |
| 2.37 years | | 582 | 79 | 156 | 27 | 9 | 20 | 82 | 8 | .268 |

Greg LUZINSKI, Designated Hitter

*Runs Created: 101*

| | G | AB | R | H | 2B | 3B | HR | RBI | SB | Avg |
|---|---|---|---|---|---|---|---|---|---|---|
| First Half | 82 | 320 | 50 | 95 | 20 | 1 | 11 | 65 | 0 | .297 |
| Second Half | 77 | 263 | 37 | 75 | 17 | 0 | 7 | 37 | 1 | .285 |
| Home | 78 | 274 | 53 | 89 | 22 | 0 | 13 | 62 | 1 | .325 |
| Road | 81 | 309 | 34 | 81 | 15 | 1 | 5 | 40 | 0 | .262 |
| vs. RHP | | 396 | 56 | 110 | 20 | 1 | 12 | 68 | 1 | .278 |
| vs. LHP | | 187 | 31 | 60 | 17 | 0 | 6 | 34 | 0 | .321 |
| 1982 | 159 | 583 | 87 | 170 | 37 | 1 | 18 | 102 | 1 | .292 |
| 9.58 years | | 584 | 79 | 164 | 32 | 2 | 27 | 102 | 3 | .281 |

Dewey HOYT

| Year | (W–L) | GS | Run | Avg | DP | Avg | SB | Avg |
|---|---|---|---|---|---|---|---|---|
| 1980 | ( 9- 3) | 12 | 51 | 4.33 | 12 | 1.00 | 10 | .83 |
| 1981 | ( 9- 3) | 1 | 0 | | 0 | | 0 | |
| 1982 | (19-15) | 32 | 170 | 5.31 | 30 | .94 | 26 | .81 |
| Career | | 45 | 221 | 4.91 | 42 | .93 | 36 | .80 |

| | G | IP | W | L | Pct | ER | ERA |
|---|---|---|---|---|---|---|---|
| Home | 19 | 122.2 | 13 | 3 | .813 | 48 | 3.52 |
| Road | 20 | 117 | 6 | 12 | .333 | 46 | 3.54 |

Richard DOTSON

| Year | (W–L) | GS | Run | Avg | DP | Avg | SB | Avg |
|---|---|---|---|---|---|---|---|---|
| 1979 | ( 2- 0) | 5 | 30 | 6.00 | 7 | 1.40 | 5 | 1.00 |
| 1980 | (12-10) | 32 | 145 | 4.53 | 28 | .88 | 36 | 1.12 |
| 1981 | ( 9- 8) | 24 | 134 | 5.58 | 28 | 1.17 | 19 | .79 |
| 1982 | (11-15) | 31 | 128 | 4.13 | 28 | .90 | 25 | .81 |
| Career | | 92 | 437 | 4.75 | 91 | .99 | 85 | .92 |

| | G | IP | W | L | Pct | ER | ERA |
|---|---|---|---|---|---|---|---|
| Home | 16 | 97.2 | 3 | 9 | .250 | 38 | 3.50 |
| Road | 18 | 99 | 8 | 6 | .571 | 46 | 4.18 |

Britt BURNS

| Year | (W–L) | GS | Run | Avg | DP | Avg | SB | Avg |
|---|---|---|---|---|---|---|---|---|
| 1978 | ( 0- 2) | 2 | 3 | 1.50 | 0 | .00 | 1 | .50 |
| 1980 | (15-13) | 33 | 99 | 3.00 | 29 | .88 | 21 | .64 |
| 1981 | (10- 6) | 23 | 95 | 4.13 | 21 | .91 | 20 | .87 |
| 1982 | (13- 5) | 28 | 144 | 5.14 | 22 | .79 | 14 | .50 |
| Career | | 86 | 341 | 3.97 | 72 | .84 | 56 | .65 |

| | G | IP | W | L | Pct | ER | ERA |
|---|---|---|---|---|---|---|---|
| Home | 13 | 82.2 | 7 | 2 | .778 | 43 | 4.68 |
| Road | 15 | 86.2 | 6 | 3 | .667 | 33 | 3.43 |

Dennis LAMP

| Year | (W–L) | GS | Run | Avg | DP | Avg | SB | Avg |
|---|---|---|---|---|---|---|---|---|
| 1977 | ( 0- 2) | 3 | 10 | 3.33 | 4 | 1.33 | 1 | .33 |
| 1978 | ( 7-15) | 36 | 133 | 3.69 | 35 | .97 | 40 | 1.11 |
| 1979 | (11-10) | 32 | 142 | 4.44 | 40 | 1.25 | 21 | .66 |
| 1980 | (10-14) | 37 | 155 | 4.19 | 29 | .78 | 41 | 1.11 |
| 1981 | ( 7- 6) | 10 | 30 | 3.00 | 10 | 1.00 | 12 | 1.20 |
| 1982 | (11- 8) | 27 | 140 | 5.19 | 32 | 1.19 | 17 | .63 |
| Career | | 145 | 610 | 4.21 | 150 | 1.03 | 132 | .91 |

| | G | IP | W | L | Pct | ER | ERA |
|---|---|---|---|---|---|---|---|
| Home | 24 | 108 | 5 | 4 | .556 | 48 | 4.00 |
| Road | 21 | 81.2 | 6 | 4 | .600 | 36 | 3.97 |

1982 OTHERS

| Pitcher | (W–L) | GS | Run | Avg | DP | Avg | SB | Avg |
|---|---|---|---|---|---|---|---|---|
| Trout | ( 6- 9) | 19 | 80 | 4.21 | 22 | 1.16 | 11 | .58 |
| Koosman | (11- 7) | 19 | 107 | 5.63 | 24 | 1.26 | 2 | .11 |
| Barnes | ( 0- 2) | 2 | 4 | 2.00 | 1 | .50 | 0 | .00 |
| Escarrega | ( 1- 3) | 2 | 5 | 2.50 | 2 | 1.00 | 3 | 1.50 |
| Siwy | ( 0- 0) | 1 | 4 | | 1 | | 2 | |
| Kern | ( 2- 1) | 1 | 4 | | 1 | | 1 | |

## CHICAGO WHITE SOX

*Talent Analysis*

The Chicago White Sox possessed 157 points of approximate value in 1982.

| | AV | % |
|---|---|---|
| Produced by system: | 48 | 31% |
| Acquired by trade: | 87 | 55% |
| Purchased or signed from free agency: | 22 | 14% |

They are a trade-built team.

| | | |
|---|---|---|
| Young (Up to age 25): | 41 | 26% |
| Prime (Age 26 to 29): | 66 | 42% |
| Past-prime (Age 30 to 33): | 21 | 13% |
| Old (Age 34 or older): | 29 | 19% |

Their young percentage is high. Only 32% of their talent is past-prime or old; the norm is 38%.

## COMISKEY PARK

DIMENSIONS: They were very long; reportedly shorter this year.

SURFACE: Grass

VISIBILITY: —

FOUL TERRITORY: Large

FAVORS:
Hitter/Pitcher—Neither; well, the pitcher, but only to a slight degree
Power/Line-drive hitter—Line-drive in the past
Righthander/Lefthander—Neither

TYPES OF OFFENSE AFFECTED: Cut home runs about 20% before 1983, but doubles and triples were up, triples way up

PLAYERS HELPED MOST BY PARK: Baines, Hoyt

PLAYERS HURT MOST BY PARK: Kemp and Paciork, the newcomers, didn't hit well here, which I suppose is to be expected

MARGINAL PLAYERS MOST VALUABLE: Who knows with the new dimensions

# SEATTLE MARINERS

Just a few notes....

• The Seattle turf seems to be the fastest turf for a runner in the American League, possibly in baseball. As I mentioned concerning Texas, teams which play on artificial turf generally improve their stolen-base percentage when at home. But few improve it as much as the Mariners:

| | SB% On the Road | SB% At Home |
|---|---|---|
| Seattle | 50.9 | 72.8 |
| Kansas City | 73.6 | 73.4 |
| Minnesota | 51.4 | 55.6 |
| Toronto | 58.1 | 61.0 |

The Mariners also reduced their grounded-into-double-plays total from 64 to 49 in coming home, despite having far more runners on at home. The other three teams grounded into 1% more double plays at home than on the road.

• I had some harsh comments about Lachemann's lineup selection. I didn't mean to imply that he's not a good manager. He got an awful lot of mileage out of some marginal players like Todd Cruz, Jim Beattie, Gaylord and Rick Sweet by accepting their weaknesses and making use of their strengths. They won 76 games last year without a really good player on the team. But if he can keep the team near .500 without Bannister and Bochte, he's a wizard.

• The Mariners were the best late-inning ballclub in the American League. They won 15 games in which they were behind after seven innings (league high), and had 23 late-inning game-winning RBIs. (California was the only team in the division with more, 26.) They led the league in one-run victories, 31. In fact, to have finished with the record that they had, given the shape they were in after two innings, is remarkable.

| Record After | Ahead | Behind | Tied | W/L% (if ties are split) |
|---|---|---|---|---|
| 1st Inning | 30 | 42 | 90 | .463 |
| 2nd Inning | 38 | 71 | 53 | .398 |
| 3rd Inning | 44 | 78 | 40 | .395 |
| 4th Inning | 48 | 76 | 40 | .420 |
| 5th Inning | 61 | 78 | 23 | .448 |
| 6th Inning | 58 | 84 | 20 | .420 |
| 7th Inning | 60 | 84 | 18 | .426 |
| 8th Inning | 60 | 80 | 23 | .441 |
| 9th Inning | 67 | 74 | 21 | .478 |
| Final Record | 76 | 86 | | .469 |

What sort of record would you expect a team to have that was ahead 38 times and behind 71 after two innings? About 55-107, I'd say. The Mariners got steadily better from then on.

One tends to attribute the bad starts to poor lineup selection leading to too few first-inning runs, and the great late-inning record to the great bullpen. The Mariners did score only 67 first-inning runs, while the Toronto Blue Jays, who scored exactly the same number of runs overall, scored 84 in the first. They scored in the first about the same number of times, but the Blue Jays scored more when they did. But if you notice, the real problem wasn't the first inning, it was the second, and a lot of the business of getting back into the game was accomplished by the fifth inning. So it would seem that something else—luck, perhaps—emphasized a pattern that should have occurred anyway.

Some of the things you see, looking over the accounts of the games the Mariners took late....Todd Cruz's name comes up a lot, Gary Gray's, and there seem to be about ten games that they won on late-inning errors.

• The Mariners first-inning run production improved dramatically late in the season, when Edler came up and began platooning at third base and hitting second.

• The Mariners have Julio Cruz, who is one of the best base stealers ever to play the game, and Bobby Brown, who stole 28 bases in 34 attempts. They managed to negate this advantage completely with 10 stolen base attempts by Castillo (he was 2 for 10), 12 by Todd Cruz (2 for 12), 7 by Dave Henderson (2 for 7) and 22 by Joe Simpson (8 for 22).

• The Mariners' raising of the fences last year seems to have done little, if anything, to reduce the number of home runs hit here. From 1977 through 1981, there were 789 home runs in the Kingdome, as opposed to 515 in Mariner road games. Adjusting for a small difference in the number of games, the park increased home-run production by 51%. Last year they raised the fences, but there were 182 home runs hit here, as opposed to 121 on the road, a 50% increase. Further, batting averages in the park went up and the K/W ratio improved, suggesting that something may have been done that improved visibility.*

So now you've got a power/speed park. Ah, but where is Bobby Bonds when you need him?

*I am informed now that a curtain which was put up to reduce glare was removed in August of 1981, with the result being greatly improved visibility for the hitters and fielders. Apparently this has also reduced the "Bermuda triangle" effect.

Gary GRAY, First Base

*Runs Created: 34*

| | G | AB | R | H | 2B | 3B | HR | RBI | SB | Avg |
|---|---|---|---|---|---|---|---|---|---|---|
| First Half | 41 | 149 | 13 | 39 | 10 | 0 | 2 | 18 | 0 | .262 |
| Second Half | 38 | 120 | 13 | 30 | 4 | 2 | 5 | 11 | 1 | .250 |
| Home | 46 | 153 | 17 | 41 | 8 | 1 | 5 | 18 | 1 | .268 |
| Road | 33 | 116 | 9 | 28 | 6 | 1 | 2 | 11 | 0 | .241 |
| vs. RHP | | 159 | 15 | 45 | 10 | 1 | 3 | 19 | 0 | .283 |
| vs. LHP | | 110 | 11 | 24 | 4 | 1 | 4 | 10 | 1 | .218 |
| 1982 | 79 | 269 | 26 | 69 | 14 | 2 | 7 | 29 | 1 | .257 |
| 1.30 years | | 481 | 50 | 115 | 18 | 2 | 19 | 55 | 4 | .240 |

Julio CRUZ, Second Base

*Runs Created: 63*

| | G | AB | R | H | 2B | 3B | HR | RBI | SB | Avg |
|---|---|---|---|---|---|---|---|---|---|---|
| First Half | 82 | 303 | 46 | 74 | 7 | 1 | 5 | 27 | 24 | .244 |
| Second Half | 71 | 246 | 37 | 59 | 15 | 4 | 3 | 22 | 22 | .240 |
| Home | 74 | 263 | 51 | 67 | 13 | 2 | 8 | 32 | 28 | .255 |
| Road | 79 | 286 | 32 | 66 | 9 | 3 | 0 | 17 | 18 | .231 |
| vs. RHP | | 350 | 48 | 73 | 9 | 2 | 1 | 19 | 33 | .209 |
| vs. LHP | | 199 | 35 | 60 | 13 | 3 | 7 | 30 | 13 | .302 |
| 1982 | 153 | 549 | 83 | 133 | 22 | 5 | 8 | 49 | 46 | .242 |
| 4.20 years | | 592 | 90 | 144 | 18 | 4 | 4 | 36 | 61 | .243 |

Manny CASTILLO, Third Base

*Runs Created: 46*

| | G | AB | R | H | 2B | 3B | HR | RBI | SB | Avg |
|---|---|---|---|---|---|---|---|---|---|---|
| First Half | 67 | 265 | 27 | 71 | 15 | 1 | 0 | 30 | 0 | .268 |
| Second Half | 70 | 241 | 22 | 59 | 14 | 0 | 3 | 19 | 2 | .245 |
| Home | 67 | 242 | 25 | 62 | 13 | 1 | 3 | 26 | 2 | .256 |
| Road | 70 | 264 | 24 | 68 | 16 | 0 | 0 | 23 | 0 | .258 |
| vs. RHP | | 388 | 39 | 103 | 22 | 0 | 2 | 41 | 2 | .265 |
| vs. LHP | | 118 | 10 | 27 | 7 | 1 | 0 | 8 | 0 | .229 |
| 1982 | 137 | 506 | 49 | 130 | 29 | 1 | 3 | 49 | 2 | .257 |
| 0.90 years | | 573 | 56 | 147 | 32 | 1 | 3 | 54 | 2 | .256 |

Todd CRUZ, Shortstop

*Runs Created: 42*

| | G | AB | R | H | 2B | 3B | HR | RBI | SB | Avg |
|---|---|---|---|---|---|---|---|---|---|---|
| First Half | 68 | 252 | 24 | 60 | 9 | 1 | 7 | 20 | 0 | .238 |
| Second Half | 68 | 240 | 20 | 53 | 11 | 1 | 9 | 37 | 2 | .221 |
| Home | 62 | 229 | 20 | 49 | 10 | 0 | 8 | 22 | 1 | .214 |
| Road | 74 | 263 | 24 | 64 | 10 | 2 | 8 | 35 | 1 | .243 |
| vs. RHP | 83 | 327 | 27 | 79 | 11 | 2 | 11 | 36 | 1 | .242 |
| vs. LHP | 53 | 165 | 17 | 34 | 9 | 0 | 5 | 21 | 1 | .206 |
| 1982 | 136 | 492 | 44 | 113 | 20 | 2 | 16 | 57 | 2 | .230 |
| 1.86 years | | 509 | 44 | 117 | 22 | 2 | 11 | 52 | 2 | .230 |

Bruce BOCHTE, Left Field

*Runs Created: 78*

| | G | AB | R | H | 2B | 3B | HR | RBI | SB | Avg |
|---|---|---|---|---|---|---|---|---|---|---|
| First Half | 79 | 289 | 27 | 88 | 13 | 0 | 5 | 40 | 6 | .304 |
| Second Half | 65 | 220 | 31 | 63 | 8 | 0 | 7 | 30 | 2 | .286 |
| Home | 71 | 242 | 35 | 84 | 14 | 0 | 7 | 40 | 3 | .347 |
| Road | 73 | 267 | 23 | 67 | 7 | 0 | 5 | 30 | 5 | .251 |
| vs. RHP | 93 | 330 | 37 | 96 | 14 | 0 | 9 | 45 | 6 | .291 |
| vs. LHP | 51 | 179 | 21 | 55 | 7 | 0 | 3 | 25 | 2 | .307 |
| 1982 | 144 | 509 | 58 | 151 | 21 | 0 | 12 | 70 | 8 | .297 |
| 6.96 years | | 565 | 69 | 162 | 28 | 3 | 11 | 72 | 5 | .286 |

Dave HENDERSON, Center Field

*Runs Created: 45*

| | G | AB | R | H | 2B | 3B | HR | RBI | SB | Avg |
|---|---|---|---|---|---|---|---|---|---|---|
| First Half | 51 | 157 | 29 | 44 | 9 | 1 | 9 | 27 | 0 | .280 |
| Second Half | 52 | 167 | 18 | 38 | 8 | 0 | 5 | 21 | 2 | .228 |
| Home | 49 | 158 | 26 | 36 | 10 | 0 | 8 | 27 | 2 | .228 |
| Road | 54 | 166 | 21 | 46 | 7 | 1 | 6 | 21 | 0 | .277 |
| vs. RHP | 45 | 161 | 26 | 40 | 6 | 0 | 6 | 26 | 1 | .248 |
| vs. LHP | 58 | 163 | 21 | 42 | 11 | 1 | 8 | 22 | 1 | .258 |
| 1982 | 103 | 324 | 47 | 82 | 17 | 1 | 14 | 48 | 2 | .253 |
| 1.01 years | | 446 | 63 | 102 | 20 | 1 | 20 | 60 | 4 | .229 |

Al COWENS, Right Field

*Runs Created: 85*

| | G | AB | R | H | 2B | 3B | HR | RBI | SB | Avg |
|---|---|---|---|---|---|---|---|---|---|---|
| First Half | 84 | 324 | 39 | 89 | 21 | 5 | 12 | 44 | 2 | .275 |
| Second Half | 61 | 236 | 33 | 62 | 18 | 3 | 8 | 34 | 9 | .263 |
| Home | 75 | 291 | 36 | 86 | 22 | 3 | 13 | 50 | 4 | .296 |
| Road | 70 | 269 | 36 | 65 | 17 | 5 | 7 | 28 | 7 | .242 |
| vs. RHP | 86 | 313 | 45 | 93 | 23 | 5 | 16 | 55 | 6 | .256 |
| vs. LHP | 59 | 197 | 27 | 58 | 16 | 3 | 4 | 12 | 5 | .294 |
| 1982 | 145 | 560 | 72 | 151 | 39 | 8 | 20 | 78 | 11 | .270 |
| 7.32 years | | 563 | 74 | 156 | 26 | 8 | 10 | 72 | 14 | .277 |

Rick SWEET, Catcher

*Runs Created: 27*

| | G | AB | R | H | 2B | 3B | HR | RBI | SB | Avg |
|---|---|---|---|---|---|---|---|---|---|---|
| First Half | 30 | 91 | 15 | 28 | 5 | 0 | 3 | 11 | 0 | .308 |
| Second Half | 57 | 167 | 14 | 38 | 1 | 1 | 1 | 13 | 3 | .228 |
| Home | 40 | 117 | 18 | 35 | 4 | 0 | 3 | 13 | 2 | .299 |
| Road | 47 | 141 | 11 | 31 | 2 | 1 | 1 | 11 | 1 | .220 |
| vs. RHP | 85 | 234 | 28 | 64 | 6 | 1 | 4 | 21 | 3 | .274 |
| vs. LHP | 2 | 24 | 1 | 2 | 0 | 0 | 0 | 3 | 0 | .083 |
| 1982 | 87 | 258 | 29 | 66 | 6 | 1 | 4 | 24 | 3 | .256 |
| 1.07 years | | 452 | 41 | 108 | 13 | 1 | 5 | 33 | 4 | .240 |

Richie ZISK, Designated Hitter

*Runs Created: 85*

| | G | AB | R | H | 2B | 3B | HR | RBI | SB | Avg |
|---|---|---|---|---|---|---|---|---|---|---|
| First Half | 66 | 252 | 24 | 67 | 10 | 0 | 7 | 24 | 0 | .266 |
| Second Half | 64 | 251 | 37 | 80 | 18 | 1 | 14 | 38 | 2 | .319 |
| Home | 62 | 242 | 25 | 65 | 19 | 0 | 8 | 28 | 1 | .269 |
| Road | 68 | 261 | 36 | 82 | 9 | 1 | 13 | 34 | 1 | .314 |
| vs. RHP | 78 | 324 | 38 | 93 | 17 | 1 | 14 | 44 | 2 | .287 |
| vs. LHP | 52 | 179 | 23 | 54 | 11 | 0 | 7 | 18 | 0 | .302 |
| 1982 | 130 | 503 | 61 | 147 | 28 | 1 | 21 | 62 | 2 | .292 |
| 8.41 years | | 578 | 77 | 167 | 28 | 3 | 23 | 90 | 1 | .290 |

Floyd BANNISTER

| Year | (W–L) | GS | Run | Avg | DP | Avg | SB | Avg |
|---|---|---|---|---|---|---|---|---|
| 1977 | ( 8- 9) | 23 | 134 | 5.83 | 17 | .74 | 21 | .91 |
| 1978 | ( 3- 9) | 16 | 46 | 2.88 | 13 | .81 | 19 | 1.19 |
| 1979 | (10-15) | 30 | 117 | 3.90 | 22 | .73 | 30 | 1.00 |
| 1980 | ( 9-13) | 32 | 107 | 3.34 | 27 | .84 | 28 | .88 |
| 1981 | ( 9- 9) | 20 | 69 | 3.45 | 14 | .70 | 12 | .60 |
| 1982 | (12-13) | 35 | 161 | 4.60 | 24 | .69 | 26 | .74 |
| Career | | 156 | 634 | 4.06 | 117 | .75 | 136 | .87 |

| | G | IP | W | L | Pct | ER | ERA |
|---|---|---|---|---|---|---|---|
| Home | 17 | 120 | 5 | 8 | .385 | 50 | 3.75 |
| Road | 18 | 127 | 7 | 5 | .583 | 44 | 3.12 |

Gaylord PERRY

| Year | (W–L) | GS | Run | Avg | DP | Avg | SB | Avg |
|---|---|---|---|---|---|---|---|---|
| 1976 | (15-14) | 32 | 120 | 3.75 | 19 | .59 | 19 | .59 |
| 1977 | (15-12) | 34 | 133 | 3.91 | 37 | 1.09 | 4 | .11 |
| 1978 | (21- 6) | 37 | 162 | 4.38 | 36 | .97 | 29 | .78 |
| 1979 | (12-11) | 32 | 104 | 3.25 | 29 | .91 | 24 | .75 |
| 1980 | (10-13) | 32 | 136 | 4.25 | 35 | 1.09 | 12 | .38 |
| 1981 | ( 8- 9) | 23 | 99 | 4.30 | 18 | .78 | 7 | .30 |
| 1982 | (10-12) | 32 | 128 | 4.00 | 32 | 1.00 | 18 | .56 |
| 7 years | | 222 | 882 | 3.97 | 206 | .93 | 113 | .51 |

| | G | IP | W | L | Pct | ER | ERA |
|---|---|---|---|---|---|---|---|
| Home | 16 | 108.2 | 5 | 4 | .554 | 59 | 4.89 |
| Road | 16 | 108 | 5 | 8 | .385 | 47 | 3.92 |

Mike MOORE

| Year | (W–L) | GS | Run | Avg | DP | Avg | SB | Avg |
|---|---|---|---|---|---|---|---|---|
| 1982 | ( 7-14) | 27 | 95 | 3.52 | 21 | .78 | 25 | .93 |

| | G | IP | W | L | Pct | ER | ERA |
|---|---|---|---|---|---|---|---|
| Home | 15 | 73.1 | 5 | 6 | .455 | 42 | 5.15 |
| Road | 13 | 71 | 2 | 8 | .200 | 44 | 5.58 |

Jim BEATTIE

| Year | (W–L) | GS | Run | Avg | DP | Avg | SB | Avg |
|---|---|---|---|---|---|---|---|---|
| 1978 | ( 6- 9) | 22 | 91 | 4.14 | 15 | .68 | 15 | .68 |
| 1979 | ( 3- 6) | 13 | 53 | 4.08 | 16 | 1.23 | 14 | 1.08 |
| 1980 | ( 5-15) | 29 | 124 | 4.28 | 37 | 1.28 | 24 | .83 |
| 1981 | ( 3- 2) | 9 | 31 | 3.44 | 6 | .67 | 6 | .67 |
| 1982 | ( 8-12) | 26 | 99 | 3.81 | 23 | .88 | 24 | .92 |
| Career | | 99 | 398 | 4.02 | 97 | .98 | 83 | .84 |

| | G | IP | W | L | Pct | ER | ERA |
|---|---|---|---|---|---|---|---|
| Home | 14 | 86.2 | 4 | 6 | .400 | 33 | 3.45 |
| Road | 14 | 85.2 | 4 | 6 | .400 | 31 | 3.26 |

1982 OTHERS

| Pitcher | (W–L) | GS | Run | Avg | DP | Avg | SB | Avg |
|---|---|---|---|---|---|---|---|---|
| Nelson | (6-9) | 19 | 75 | 3.95 | 22 | 1.16 | 14 | .74 |
| Stoddard | (3-3) | 9 | 30 | 3.33 | 12 | 1.33 | 3 | .33 |
| Nunez | (1-2) | 5 | 25 | 5.00 | 5 | 1.00 | 3 | .60 |
| Clark | (5-2) | 5 | 23 | 4.60 | 8 | 1.60 | 1 | .20 |
| Bordi | (0-2) | 2 | 7 | 3.50 | 2 | 1.00 | 2 | 1.00 |
| Stanton | (2-4) | 1 | 3 | | 1 | | 0 | |
| Anderson | (0-0) | 1 | 5 | | 1 | | 0 | |

## SEATTLE

*Talent Analysis*

The Mariners possessed 150 of approximate value in 1982.

| | AV | % |
|---|---|---|
| Produced by Mariners' system: | 28 | 19% |
| Acquired by trade: | 68 | 45% |
| Purchased or signed from free agency: | 43 | 29% |
| Retained from expansion draft: | 11 | 7% |

They are a trade-built team. Their system, trade, money and expansion percentages over the last four years:

| | 1979 | 1980 | 1981 | 1982 |
|---|---|---|---|---|
| System | 6% | 4% | 5% | 19% |
| Trade | 48% | 49% | 49% | 45% |
| Money | 21% | 26% | 31% | 29% |
| Expansion | 26% | 20% | 15% | 7% |

They are moving toward a system-built team, but it's years away yet.

| | | |
|---|---|---|
| Young (Up to age 25): | 26 | 17% |
| Prime (Age 26 to 29): | 89 | 59% |
| Past-prime (Age 30 to 33): | 28 | 19% |
| Old (Age 34 or older): | 7 | 5% |

They're a young team.

## KINGDOME

DIMENSIONS: Short

SURFACE: Turf

VISIBILITY: Has been poor

FOUL TERRITORY: Small

FAVORS:
Hitter/Pitcher—Hitter
Power/Line-drive hitter—Power
Righthander/Lefthander—Neither

TYPES OF OFFENSE AFFECTED: Home runs way up, triples down; there are a lot of walks here, for some reason . . . the mound may be funny

PLAYERS ON TEAM HELPED MOST BY PARK: Bochte, Cowens

PLAYERS ON TEAM HURT MOST BY PARK: Zisk hasn't hit at all well here—60 points better on road the last two years

# OAKLAND A'S

Will someone please explain this to me? In 1981 the Oakland A's stole 98 bases, fourth highest total in the American League, but hit a league-leading 104 home runs and posted the best won-lost record in the league. In 1982, they soared to a major-league leading total of 232 stolen bases, but dropped to sixth in the league in home runs and fell off to a dismal 68-94 record.

After the season, team prez Roy Eisenhardt announced that the A's were going to rebuild their team concentrating on, in the order he said them, speed, pitching and defense.

Jimmy Sexton, an A's scrub, set a major league record in '82 when he stole 16 bases without being caught stealing.

A year ago and two, in writing about the Oakland A's, I put forward the thesis that Billy Martin's handling of his pitching staff was that of a man who did not quite believe in the existence of the future. Martin once had Mickey Lolich pitch over 700 innings for him in two seasons, worked Joe Coleman over 280 for three years in a row, gave Ferguson Jenkins 328 innings, Catfish Hunter 328, and in 1980 set some bizarre records by dragging 94 complete games out of young starters. All of the pitchers who had done this for him the past, I pointed out, had paid a price for it two or three years down the line.

In view of what happened to the Oakland A's pitching staff in 1982, this thesis seems to have been not only tenable, but prescient. I wish I was as smart every day as I was the day I wrote that. And yet, oddly, it is for these comments, and not for any genuinely silly and stupid things that I write during the course of a year, that I have been drawing fire. With the A's pitching staff wobbling and poised to fall, Bruce Jenkins of the *San Francisco Chronicle* devoted several hundred words in the May 25 green pages to argue that "A closer examination of the records . . . reveals that James' theory makes no sense at all." Presumably following Jenkins' lead, Peter Gammons ruled in *The Sporting News* that "most of James' examples are invalid."

They were not invalid, Peter, because they were not examples. Jenkins wrote that "to illustrate, James inspected the careers of 12 pitchers who had great years for Martin, worked a high number of innings, and then declined over the next two or three years. The conclusion: Martin burns them out." That's absolutely false; it is *not* what I wrote, at all. It involves a critical misunderstanding.

That misunderstanding came about for three reasons, two of them trivial: I didn't write it as carefully as I should have, and he didn't read it as carefully as he should have. The important misunderstanding is this: there is a very basic difference between being a sabermetrician and being a sportswriter. Jenkins failed to recognize that difference, and grafted the expectations of a sportswriter on the work of a sabermetrician, thus making it in his mind something that it was not. The difference, as I explained it in the letter to the reader in the 1981 *Abstract:*

> *Sportswriters characteristically begin their analysis with a* position on an issue; *sabermetrics begins with the issue itself. The most over-used form in journalism is the diatribe, the endless impassioned and quasi-logical pitches for the cause of the day—Mike Norris for the Cy Young Award, Rickey Henderson for MVP, Gil Hodges for the Hall of Fame, everybody for lower salaries and let's all line up against the DH. Sportswriting "analysis" is largely an adversarial process, with the most successful sportswriter being the one who is the most effective advocate of his position. I personally, of course, have positions which I advocate from time to time, but sabermetrics by its nature is unemotional, noncommittal. The sportswriter attempts to be a good lawyer, the sabermetrician, a fair judge.*

Simply put, I would never make a prior assumption that Billy Martin burns out his pitchers and then draw up a list of "examples" (as Gammons thought) "to illustrate" (as Jenkins thought) the position. A sportswriter would do it that way; I would not. I didn't set out to demonstrate that Martin burns out his pitchers, but to *examine the evidence* on the issue. I used these 12 pitchers on the list because *these are the only pitchers there are who are relevant to the subject* (or, rather, the only ones there were at the time. There are 16 now.) There were 12 pitchers who had pitched 220 or more innings in a season for Billy Martin through 1979; there were 12 pitchers on the list. All 12 of those pitchers, with the arguable exception of Jim Kaat, went through a sharp down phase in their careers two or three years after the season in which they pitched the most innings for Martin. All of them, now 16 for 16; there is no evidence to put on the other side. These quibbles about "But this guy didn't have a sore arm" and "But this guy had a sore arm even before Martin managed him" and "This guy wasn't that good anyway" don't have anything to do with the subject. They might explain *any* of the declines, but there remains the damning consistency.

Granted, I should have made the fact that this was a comprehensive list, not a selected list, clear at the time. But there are other things that I did not say, either. I didn't say the A's were going to have sore arms; I didn't say they were going to have tired arms. It could be that the damage to a pitcher's arm could show up not as an injury, but as a loss of three to five miles off the fastball. It is possible that the damage that is done to arms is done not by throwing too many innings, but by throwing too many of the curve balls that Martin so dearly loves. It is very possible that the relevant indicator is not the total number of innings pitched, but the number of innings pitched when the pitcher is tired. (Remember the burst of 12- and 14-inning complete games here in 1980?) It is very possible that *I DON'T KNOW* what causes Martin's pitchers to fall apart after a couple of good years, and indeed that I never pretended to know.

Look, I'm well aware that I'm not always right. I

make a lot of mistakes; when somebody points them out to me, I own up cheerfully. Inconsistency is a euphemism for growth. But not this time, buddy, not this time. This time I recognized a pattern in Martin's history. I foresaw the consequences of it, and I wrote it up and had it out a year before it manifested itself. That pattern I did not imagine, as I often do; that pattern is *real*. Through the almost impenetrable clouds of enthusiasm and hype that were surrounding Billy Martin, I stared hard and I foresaw the end in great detail. I saw the method and the instrument of his demise, the role that his temper would play; I saw the thinnesss of his talent that he had so brilliantly disguised. And I deserve to hear some credit for it, and not this silly misguided carping.

Dan MEYER, First Base
*Runs Created: 38*

| | G | AB | R | H | 2B | 3B | HR | RBI | SB | Avg |
|---|---|---|---|---|---|---|---|---|---|---|
| First Half | 68 | 217 | 18 | 57 | 14 | 2 | 5 | 40 | 1 | .263 |
| Second Half | 52 | 166 | 10 | 35 | 3 | 1 | 3 | 19 | 0 | .211 |
| Home | 64 | 200 | 12 | 51 | 5 | 3 | 3 | 31 | 1 | .255 |
| Road | 56 | 183 | 16 | 41 | 12 | 0 | 5 | 28 | 0 | .224 |
| vs. RHP | | 340 | 25 | 81 | 15 | 2 | 8 | 50 | 1 | .238 |
| vs. LHP | | 43 | 3 | 11 | 2 | 1 | 0 | 9 | 0 | .256 |
| 1982 | 120 | 383 | 28 | 92 | 17 | 3 | 8 | 59 | 1 | .240 |
| 6.27 years | | 563 | 63 | 144 | 23 | 5 | 14 | 71 | 10 | .256 |

Davey LOPES, Second Base
*Runs Created: 51*

| | G | AB | R | H | 2B | 3B | HR | RBI | SB | Avg |
|---|---|---|---|---|---|---|---|---|---|---|
| First Half | 69 | 239 | 32 | 61 | 10 | 1 | 6 | 22 | 16 | .255 |
| Second | 59 | 211 | 26 | 48 | 9 | 2 | 5 | 20 | 12 | .227 |
| Home | 65 | 220 | 25 | 50 | 4 | 2 | 5 | 23 | 12 | .227 |
| Road | 63 | 230 | 33 | 59 | 15 | 1 | 6 | 19 | 16 | .257 |
| vs. RHP | | 274 | 31 | 62 | 11 | 1 | 9 | 31 | 17 | .226 |
| vs. LHP | | 176 | 27 | 47 | 8 | 2 | 2 | 11 | 11 | .267 |
| 1982 | 128 | 450 | 58 | 109 | 19 | 3 | 11 | 42 | 28 | .242 |
| 8.24 years | | 612 | 99 | 159 | 22 | 5 | 13 | 52 | 54 | .261 |

Wayne GROSS, Third Base
*Runs Created: 47*

| | G | AB | R | H | 2B | 3B | HR | RBI | SB | Avg |
|---|---|---|---|---|---|---|---|---|---|---|
| First Half | 68 | 206 | 17 | 52 | 7 | 0 | 3 | 15 | 0 | .252 |
| Second Half | 61 | 180 | 26 | 45 | 7 | 0 | 6 | 26 | 3 | .250 |
| Home | 67 | 206 | 25 | 52 | 10 | 0 | 3 | 13 | 2 | .252 |
| Road | 62 | 180 | 18 | 45 | 4 | 0 | 6 | 28 | 1 | .250 |
| vs. RHP | | 341 | 38 | 91 | 13 | 0 | 9 | 38 | 3 | .267 |
| vs. LHP | | 45 | 5 | 6 | 1 | 0 | 0 | 3 | 0 | .133 |
| 1982 | 129 | 386 | 43 | 97 | 14 | 0 | 9 | 41 | 3 | .251 |
| 4.54 years | | 490 | 56 | 115 | 20 | 2 | 17 | 60 | 4 | .235 |

Fred STANLEY, Shortstop
*Runs Created: 16*

| | G | AB | R | H | 2B | 3B | HR | RBI | SB | Avg |
|---|---|---|---|---|---|---|---|---|---|---|
| First Half | 52 | 126 | 16 | 24 | 4 | 0 | 0 | 7 | 0 | .190 |
| Second Half | 49 | 102 | 17 | 20 | 3 | 0 | 2 | 10 | 0 | .196 |
| Home | 52 | 113 | 13 | 21 | 4 | 0 | 1 | 11 | 0 | .186 |
| Road | 49 | 115 | 20 | 23 | 3 | 0 | 1 | 6 | 0 | .200 |
| vs. RHP | | 139 | 17 | 21 | 3 | 0 | 1 | 7 | 0 | .151 |
| vs. LHP | | 89 | 16 | 23 | 4 | 0 | 1 | 10 | 0 | .258 |
| 1982 | 101 | 228 | 33 | 44 | 7 | 0 | 2 | 17 | 0 | .193 |
| 5.04 years | | 327 | 39 | 71 | 8 | 1 | 2 | 24 | 2 | .216 |

Rickey HENDERSON, Left Field
*Runs Created: 93*

| | G | AB | R | H | 2B | 3B | HR | RBI | SB | Avg |
|---|---|---|---|---|---|---|---|---|---|---|
| First Half | 88 | 323 | 78 | 89 | 15 | 4 | 7 | 35 | 84 | .276 |
| Second Half | 61 | 213 | 41 | 54 | 9 | 0 | 3 | 16 | 46 | .254 |
| Home | 79 | 281 | 62 | 78 | 12 | 2 | 5 | 25 | 63 | .278 |
| Road | 70 | 255 | 57 | 65 | 12 | 2 | 5 | 26 | 67 | .255 |
| vs. RHP | | 331 | 84 | 89 | 14 | 2 | 7 | 30 | 89 | .269 |
| vs. LHP | | 205 | 35 | 54 | 10 | 2 | 3 | 21 | 41 | .263 |
| 1982 | 149 | 536 | 119 | 143 | 24 | 4 | 10 | 51 | 130 | .267 |
| 3.11 years | | 611 | 118 | 178 | 25 | 6 | 8 | 53 | 103 | .291 |

Dwayne MURPHY, Center Field
*Runs Created: 83*

| | G | AB | R | H | 2B | 3B | HR | RBI | SB | Avg |
|---|---|---|---|---|---|---|---|---|---|---|
| First Half | 81 | 293 | 49 | 68 | 5 | 1 | 16 | 60 | 16 | .232 |
| Second Half | 70 | 250 | 35 | 62 | 11 | 0 | 11 | 34 | 10 | .248 |
| Home | 77 | 276 | 46 | 65 | 7 | 0 | 15 | 46 | 15 | .236 |
| Road | 74 | 267 | 38 | 65 | 9 | 1 | 12 | 48 | 11 | .243 |
| vs. RHP | | 341 | 56 | 83 | 12 | 0 | 18 | 57 | 20 | .243 |
| vs. LHP | | 202 | 28 | 47 | 4 | 1 | 9 | 37 | 6 | .233 |
| 1982 | 151 | 543 | 84 | 130 | 16 | 1 | 27 | 94 | 26 | .239 |
| 3.69 years | | 527 | 81 | 134 | 15 | 3 | 18 | 72 | 21 | .254 |

Tony ARMAS, Right Field
*Runs Created: 63*

| | G | AB | R | H | 2B | 3B | HR | RBI | SB | Avg |
|---|---|---|---|---|---|---|---|---|---|---|
| First Half | 72 | 290 | 30 | 66 | 12 | 2 | 11 | 41 | 2 | .288 |
| Second Half | 66 | 246 | 28 | 59 | 7 | 0 | 17 | 48 | 0 | .240 |
| Home | 77 | 297 | 25 | 59 | 12 | 1 | 14 | 45 | 0 | .199 |
| Road | 61 | 239 | 33 | 66 | 7 | 1 | 14 | 44 | 2 | .276 |
| vs. RHP | | 344 | 37 | 78 | 12 | 2 | 19 | 65 | 2 | .227 |
| vs. LHP | | 192 | 21 | 47 | 7 | 0 | 9 | 24 | 0 | .245 |
| 1982 | 138 | 536 | 58 | 125 | 19 | 2 | 28 | 89 | 2 | .233 |
| 4.31 years | | 578 | 62 | 145 | 20 | 4 | 26 | 87 | 4 | .251 |

Mike HEATH, Catcher
*Runs Created: 34*

| | G | AB | R | H | 2B | 3B | HR | RBI | SB | Avg |
|---|---|---|---|---|---|---|---|---|---|---|
| First Half | 44 | 140 | 18 | 34 | 10 | 2 | 0 | 17 | 4 | .243 |
| Second Half | 57 | 178 | 25 | 43 | 8 | 2 | 3 | 22 | 4 | .242 |
| Home | 49 | 149 | 24 | 38 | 6 | 1 | 3 | 20 | 6 | .255 |
| Road | 52 | 169 | 19 | 39 | 12 | 3 | 0 | 19 | 2 | .231 |
| vs. RHP | | 210 | 27 | 48 | 9 | 3 | 1 | 26 | 8 | .229 |
| vs. LHP | | 108 | 16 | 29 | 9 | 1 | 2 | 13 | 0 | .269 |
| 1982 | 101 | 318 | 43 | 77 | 18 | 4 | 3 | 39 | 8 | .242 |
| 2.37 years | | 538 | 51 | 130 | 19 | 3 | 6 | 58 | 6 | .243 |

Jeff BURROUGHS, Designated Hitter
*Runs Created: 58*

| | G | AB | R | H | 2B | 3B | HR | RBI | SB | Avg |
|---|---|---|---|---|---|---|---|---|---|---|
| First Half | 47 | 79 | 10 | 18 | 3 | 1 | 4 | 16 | 0 | .228 |
| Second Half | 66 | 206 | 32 | 61 | 10 | 1 | 12 | 32 | 1 | .296 |
| Home | 51 | 108 | 16 | 26 | 3 | 0 | 6 | 15 | 1 | .241 |
| Road | 62 | 177 | 26 | 53 | 10 | 2 | 10 | 33 | 0 | .299 |
| vs. RHP | | 154 | 26 | 43 | 4 | 1 | 11 | 31 | 1 | .279 |
| vs. LHP | | 131 | 16 | 36 | 9 | 1 | 5 | 17 | 0 | .275 |
| 1982 | 113 | 285 | 42 | 79 | 13 | 2 | 16 | 48 | 1 | .277 |
| 8.79 years | | 554 | 74 | 145 | 23 | 2 | 25 | 90 | 2 | .261 |

Matt KEOUGH

| Year | (W–L) | GS | Run | Avg | DP | Avg | SB | Avg |
|---|---|---|---|---|---|---|---|---|
| 1977 | ( 1- 2) | 6 | 20 | 3.33 | 5 | .83 | 9 | 1.50 |
| 1978 | ( 8-15) | 32 | 97 | 3.03 | 34 | 1.06 | 22 | .69 |
| 1979 | ( 2-17) | 28 | 83 | 2.96 | 30 | 1.07 | 23 | .82 |
| 1980 | (16-13) | 32 | 128 | 4.00 | 24 | .75 | 18 | .56 |
| 1981 | (10- 6) | 19 | 90 | 4.74 | 17 | .89 | 5 | .26 |
| 1982 | (11-18) | 34 | 149 | 4.38 | 30 | .88 | 18 | .53 |
| 6 years | | 151 | 567 | 3.75 | 140 | .93 | 95 | .63 |

| | G | IP | W | L | Pct | ER | ERA |
|---|---|---|---|---|---|---|---|
| Home | 15 | 82 | 3 | 10 | .231 | 61 | 6.59 |
| Road | 19 | 127.1 | 8 | 8 | .500 | 72 | 5.09 |

Rick LANGFORD

| Year | (W–L) | GS | Run | Avg | DP | Avg | SB | Avg |
|---|---|---|---|---|---|---|---|---|
| 1977 | ( 8-19) | 31 | 106 | 3.42 | 26 | .84 | 17 | .55 |
| 1978 | ( 7-13) | 24 | 60 | 2.50 | 14 | .58 | 9 | .38 |
| 1979 | (12-16) | 29 | 105 | 3.62 | 20 | .69 | 11 | .38 |
| 1980 | (19-12) | 33 | 148 | 4.48 | 28 | .85 | 6 | .18 |
| 1981 | (12-10) | 24 | 96 | 4.00 | 17 | .71 | 6 | .25 |
| 1982 | (11-16) | 31 | 132 | 4.26 | 24 | .77 | 11 | .35 |
| 6 years | | 172 | 647 | 3.76 | 129 | .75 | 59 | .34 |

| | G | IP | W | L | Pct | ER | ERA |
|---|---|---|---|---|---|---|---|
| Home | 18 | 137 | 7 | 8 | .467 | 58 | 3.81 |
| Road | 14 | 100.1 | 4 | 8 | .333 | 53 | 4.75 |

Mike NORRIS

| Year | (W–L) | GS | Run | Avg | DP | Avg | SB | Avg |
|---|---|---|---|---|---|---|---|---|
| 1977 | ( 2- 7) | 12 | 42 | 3.50 | 11 | .92 | 11 | .92 |
| 1978 | ( 0- 5) | 5 | 13 | 2.60 | 5 | 1.00 | 6 | 1.20 |
| 1979 | ( 5- 8) | 18 | 67 | 3.72 | 11 | .61 | 11 | .61 |
| 1980 | (22- 9) | 33 | 155 | 4.70 | 24 | .73 | 16 | .48 |
| 1981 | (12- 9) | 23 | 95 | 4.13 | 14 | .61 | 16 | .70 |
| 1982 | ( 7-11) | 28 | 109 | 3.89 | 28 | 1.00 | 20 | .71 |
| 6 years | | 119 | 481 | 4.04 | 93 | .78 | 80 | .67 |

| | G | IP | W | L | Pct | ER | ERA |
|---|---|---|---|---|---|---|---|
| Home | 14 | 73.2 | 2 | 7 | .222 | 38 | 4.64 |
| Road | 14 | 92.2 | 5 | 4 | .556 | 50 | 4.86 |

Steve McCATTY

| Year | (W–L) | GS | Run | Avg | DP | Avg | SB | Avg |
|---|---|---|---|---|---|---|---|---|
| 1977 | ( 0- 0) | 2 | 9 | 4.50 | 2 | 1.00 | 3 | 1.50 |
| 1979 | (11-12) | 23 | 94 | 4.09 | 16 | .70 | 25 | 1.09 |
| 1980 | (14-14) | 31 | 159 | 5.13 | 19 | .61 | 29 | .94 |
| 1981 | (14- 7) | 22 | 95 | 4.32 | 10 | .45 | 9 | .41 |
| 1982 | ( 6- 3) | 20 | 113 | 5.65 | 17 | .85 | 15 | .75 |
| 5 years | | 98 | 470 | 4.80 | 64 | .65 | 81 | .83 |

| | G | IP | W | L | Pct | ER | ERA |
|---|---|---|---|---|---|---|---|
| Home | 10 | 68 | 5 | 1 | .833 | 26 | 3.44 |
| Road | 11 | 60.2 | 1 | 2 | .333 | 31 | 4.60 |

Brian KINGMAN

| Year | (W–L) | GS | Run | Avg | DP | Avg | SB | Avg |
|---|---|---|---|---|---|---|---|---|
| 1979 | ( 8- 7) | 17 | 72 | 4.24 | 9 | .53 | 9 | .53 |
| 1980 | ( 8-20) | 30 | 86 | 2.87 | 18 | .60 | 15 | .50 |
| 1981 | ( 3- 6) | 15 | 54 | 3.60 | 14 | .93 | 8 | .53 |
| 1982 | ( 4-12) | 20 | 73 | 3.65 | 17 | .85 | 12 | .60 |
| 4 years | | 82 | 285 | 3.48 | 58 | .71 | 44 | .54 |

| | G | IP | W | L | Pct | ER | ERA |
|---|---|---|---|---|---|---|---|
| Home | 12 | 77.1 | 2 | 6 | .250 | 32 | 3.72 |
| Road | 11 | 45.1 | 2 | 6 | .250 | 29 | 5.76 |

1982 OTHERS

| Pitcher | (W–L) | GS | Run | Avg | DP | Avg | SB | Avg |
|---|---|---|---|---|---|---|---|---|
| Underwood | (10-6) | 10 | 45 | 4.50 | 7 | .70 | 4 | .40 |
| Conroy | ( 2-2) | 5 | 24 | 4.80 | 3 | .60 | 3 | .60 |
| Baker | ( 1-1) | 3 | 10 | 3.33 | 2 | .67 | 4 | 1.33 |
| Codiroli | ( 1-2) | 3 | 6 | 2.00 | 2 | .67 | 2 | .67 |
| Hanna | ( 0-4) | 2 | 3 | 1.50 | 2 | 1.00 | 2 | 1.00 |
| McLaughlin | ( 0-4) | 2 | 6 | 3.00 | 1 | .50 | 1 | .50 |
| Jones | ( 3-1) | 2 | 13 | 6.50 | 2 | 1.00 | 1 | .50 |
| Beard | (10-9) | 2 | 5 | 2.50 | 2 | 1.00 | 4 | 2.00 |

## OAKLAND

*Talent Analysis*

The A's possessed only 122 points of approximate value in 1982.

| | AV | % |
|---|---|---|
| Produced by system: | 60 | 49% |
| Acquired by trade: | 49 | 40% |
| Purchased or signed from free agency: | 13 | 11% |

They are primarily a system-built team.

| | | |
|---|---|---|
| Young (Up to age 25): | 23 | 61% |
| Prime (Age 26 to 29): | 61 | 50% |
| Past-prime (Age 30 to 33): | 26 | 21% |
| Old (Age 34 or older): | 12 | 10% |

They are a young team.

The A's system accounted for 166 points of approximate value in 1982, the ninth highest total in baseball. That figure is shrinking as players from the Reggie-era are passing away. Over the four year period they rank fifth with 711.

## OAKLAND COLISEUM

DIMENSIONS: Normal

SURFACE: Grass

VISIBILITY: Poor

FOUL TERRITORY: Immense. The foul territory may be the largest factor depressing batting averages here.

FAVORS:
Hitter/Pitcher—Pitcher (very much)
Power/Line-drive hitter—Power
Righthander/Lefthander—Neither

TYPES OF OFFENSE AFFECTED: Batting averages down about 20 points, doubles down 15%, triples 25%, home runs 10%. Even if it cut all equally, that would "favor" power because if you cut home runs 10%, that only decreases runs resulting from home runs by about 10%, while if you cut singles by 10%, that reduces runs resulting from singles by 20 or 30%. But actually, it reduces home runs less than other types of offense, so it is strictly a power-hitter's park. The A's positively cannot build a championship team without adapting to that reality.

PLAYERS ON TEAM HELPED MOST BY PARK: Langford, McCatty

PLAYERS ON TEAM HURT MOST BY PARK: Dwayne Murphy

OTHER COMMENTS: 3-1 against Carney Lansford hitting .300 in this park. He has hit well here in the past (.303 on 24/79 over the last three years); he's a legitimate hitter going into his option year, and I don't figure him for a crash—maybe .275, .285 with better power than in Fenway. But he's not going to win the batting championship here.

# TEXAS RANGERS

The most interesting work that is being done in sabermetrics these days is not being done by me. I still work as hard as ever—indeed, harder (that is the problem)—but I have entered a more mature phase of my career, in which I am making a living by pushing forward the ideas that I developed in the lazy years from 1975–1978.

Which is not meant to imply that the work of Craig Wright is not mature. Craig is a sabermetrician in the employ of the Texas Rangers, a good friend of mine, and a brilliant analyst of the game. You know how that goes—"intelligent" means that he agrees with me; "brilliant" means that I agree with him but I never would have thought of it myself. We don't agree on everything, actually; Craig thinks stolen bases are more important than I do, for one thing. His employment inside O.B. forces him to take baseball science into areas of practical considerations that I either have never taken a fancy to, never wanted to bother with or never realized were important. It is an understatement to say that he has a much clearer idea of the needs of a baseball organization than I have.

A lot of his work, unfortunately, must be shielded from public view for the benefit of the Rangers. I wrote something a couple of years ago (or if I didn't, I intended to) about the potential of sabermetrics for diagnosing what has gone wrong when a player's performance goes sour. If a player hits .280 one year and .230 the next, you have got to be able to figure what he is doing different. It can't just happen without leaving any clues. We've got films, we've got radar guns, we've got more records than you can shake a dog at. We've got a million witnesses. Is his batting average off at home and on the road? Is it off at day and at night? Is it off against righthanders and lefthanders? How often is the batter pulling the ball this year, and how often did he pull it last year? How often is he hitting it on the ground this year, and how often last year? Is he seeing more breaking balls? Is he getting behind in the count more? Is he swinging at more high strikes? Has there been any change in his personal habits? Is he hitting as well with men on base?

No matter what is going wrong, you have got to be able to find it, if you want to badly enough. There have been cases where Craig has been able to do exactly that, get out there in the snow and track the problem to its very source.

And that, of course, is all I can say about that. At the heart of each problem is a player's weakness, and I can't be pointing the finger at the weaknesses of the Texas Rangers. But I can give a few other specific examples of things that I have learned.

You remember the argument about range factors in last year's *Abstract*? Is Buddy Bell's very high range factor an illusion created by there being a lot of balls hit in his direction because of the Ranger staff? Craig keeps track of where balls are hit (so do I, but he uses his own system, not mine). He does it for all Ranger games. There were 634 balls hit between the shortstop and the third base line against the Rangers last year, 639 by the Rangers. But whereas Ranger opponents made plays on 63.7% of these balls (407 of 639), Ranger third basemen made plays on 68.5% of them (434 of 634). That figure was 69.8% when Bell was in the lineup, 59.0% when he wasn't. There were only 103 hits in the hole against the Rangers in 1982, 139 by them—but Buddy Bell made far more plays than the opposing third basemen. Bell's high range factor is a reflection of one thing and one thing only: his range afield.

We knew that range factors were valid anyway; we just have better proof of it now. What is more important than that is that we have a verifiable way of translating Bell's defensive stats into a number of runs prevented. Bell prevented 34 opposition hits as opposed to an average third baseman. By playing an extra step off the line, he allowed 3 extra doubles, meaning that he is 37 singles better than average third basemen (13 runs) minus 3 doubles (−1.6 runs), leaving him 11½ runs better, defensively, than the opposing third baseman. (Just decided to check something out . . . Bell's defensive won-lost record in 1982 was 4-1. That's a game and a half over .500; at 8 runs per game, that means 12 runs! Man, I never dreamed the defensive won-lost percentage would work *that* well.)

Obviously, every Ranger is not spectacular with the glove, and again I cannot use Craig's data to point the finger at their weaknesses. But the potential value of that data, both to the Rangers and to sabermetricians, is immense.

I have attributed the reappearance of the running game in recent years almost solely to declining home-run rates. Craig has convinced me that a much larger share of it is due to the simple physical fact that you can run faster on artificial turf than you can on grass. Well, I can't find the data, but take my word for it—stolen-base percentages are way up on artificial turf.

Craig has demonstrated, to my surprise, that almost all managers who are successful in the major leagues a) managed in the minors first, and b) were successful there too.

He has taken the lists that I provide of the value produced by each system, and analyzed the characteristics of those systems which produce talent and those which don't. He has contributed heavily to my understanding of the effects of ballparks. He has pointed out to me something that seems now obvious—that those outfielders who have poor-arm reps but throw out a lot of baserunners, like LeFlore, Gene Richards and Lonnie Smith, are invariably fast runners and get assists because they can cut off the ball quicker than a runner thinks they will. In large ways and small, I've learned a lot from talking to him.

But one thing I learned from Craig was not from anything he told me. My own conclusion: The Texas Rangers Era of Disintegration ended with the elevation of Joe Klein to General Manager. There is no doubt in my mind. I talk to Craig about every week; I know what he is working on, I have an idea what's going on in the organization. The day that Klein took over, the things that Craig was working on spun around 180 degrees; all of a sudden, instead of fighting little skirmishes over misutilization of talent or trying to stave off silly trades, the organization looked square in the face of the problems confronting them, and began an orderly process of addressing these problems. They conducted a thorough, intelligent search for a manager and hired a good man for all the right reasons. Instead of looking for a scapegoat, they reviewed the needs of the team on the field, identified their weaknesses—correctly—and carefully researched their options for correcting them. When they weren't able to make the trades they wanted, they didn't drive the Rangermobile off a cliff, make a stupid trade just to be making one. I don't know when or if they will ever win the division; one must reckon with time, chance, and economics. But they're going to be back in the frenzy in a couple of years.

Dave HOSTETLER, First Base

*Runs Created: 54*

| | G | AB | R | H | 2B | 3B | HR | RBI | SB | Avg |
|---|---|---|---|---|---|---|---|---|---|---|
| First Half | 41 | 144 | 28 | 40 | 5 | 2 | 12 | 26 | 1 | .278 |
| Second Half | 72 | 274 | 25 | 57 | 7 | 1 | 10 | 41 | 1 | .208 |
| Home | 55 | 194 | 21 | 46 | 4 | 0 | 10 | 31 | 2 | .237 |
| Road | 58 | 224 | 32 | 51 | 8 | 3 | 12 | 36 | 0 | .228 |
| vs. RHP | | 304 | 41 | 77 | 8 | 3 | 18 | 56 | 2 | .253 |
| vs. LHP | | 114 | 12 | 20 | 4 | 0 | 4 | 11 | 0 | .175 |
| 1982 | 113 | 418 | 53 | 97 | 12 | 3 | 22 | 67 | 2 | .232 |
| 0.73 years | | 581 | 74 | 137 | 16 | 4 | 32 | 93 | 3 | .238 |

Mike RICHARDT, Second Base

*Runs Created: 34*

| | G | AB | R | H | 2B | 3B | HR | RBI | SB | Avg |
|---|---|---|---|---|---|---|---|---|---|---|
| First Half | 44 | 152 | 9 | 34 | 4 | 0 | 1 | 19 | 1 | .224 |
| Second Half | 75 | 250 | 25 | 63 | 6 | 0 | 2 | 24 | 8 | .252 |
| Home | 57 | 188 | 14 | 44 | 2 | 0 | 0 | 17 | 4 | .234 |
| Road | 62 | 214 | 20 | 53 | 8 | 0 | 3 | 26 | 5 | .248 |
| vs. RHP | | 290 | 23 | 76 | 9 | 0 | 3 | 39 | 6 | .262 |
| vs. LHP | | 112 | 11 | 21 | 1 | 0 | 0 | 4 | 3 | .188 |
| 1982 | 119 | 402 | 34 | 97 | 10 | 0 | 3 | 43 | 9 | .241 |
| 0.87 years | | 544 | 41 | 130 | 14 | 0 | 4 | 59 | 10 | .239 |

Buddy BELL, Third Base

*Runs Created: 86*

| | G | AB | R | H | 2B | 3B | HR | RBI | SB | Avg |
|---|---|---|---|---|---|---|---|---|---|---|
| First Half | 81 | 315 | 35 | 94 | 16 | 0 | 10 | 39 | 4 | .298 |
| Second Half | 67 | 222 | 27 | 65 | 11 | 2 | 3 | 28 | 1 | .293 |
| Home | 74 | 264 | 26 | 80 | 14 | 1 | 3 | 31 | 2 | .303 |
| Road | 74 | 273 | 36 | 79 | 13 | 1 | 10 | 36 | 3 | .289 |
| vs. RHP | | 418 | 45 | 123 | 21 | 1 | 9 | 50 | 5 | .294 |
| vs. LHP | | 119 | 17 | 36 | 6 | 1 | 4 | 17 | 0 | .303 |
| 1982 | 148 | 537 | 62 | 159 | 27 | 2 | 13 | 67 | 5 | .296 |
| 9.40 years | | 614 | 78 | 175 | 28 | 4 | 13 | 75 | 4 | .285 |

Billy SAMPLE, Left Field

*Runs Created: 46*

| | G | AB | R | H | 2B | 3B | HR | RBI | SB | Avg |
|---|---|---|---|---|---|---|---|---|---|---|
| First Half | 47 | 167 | 31 | 52 | 10 | 1 | 7 | 17 | 6 | .311 |
| Second Half | 50 | 193 | 25 | 42 | 4 | 1 | 3 | 12 | 4 | .218 |
| Home | 57 | 203 | 37 | 55 | 9 | 1 | 7 | 22 | 5 | .271 |
| Road | 40 | 157 | 19 | 39 | 5 | 1 | 3 | 7 | 5 | .248 |
| vs. RHP | | 274 | 47 | 75 | 10 | 1 | 9 | 22 | 10 | .274 |
| vs. LHP | | 86 | 9 | 19 | 4 | 1 | 1 | 7 | 0 | .221 |
| 1982 | 97 | 360 | 56 | 94 | 14 | 2 | 10 | 29 | 10 | .261 |
| 2.46 years | | 461 | 74 | 128 | 26 | 2 | 9 | 45 | 12 | .277 |

George WRIGHT, Center Field

*Runs Created: 61*

| | G | AB | R | H | 2B | 3B | HR | RBI | SB | Avg |
|---|---|---|---|---|---|---|---|---|---|---|
| First Half | 72 | 254 | 31 | 59 | 10 | 5 | 4 | 27 | 2 | .232 |
| Second Half | 78 | 303 | 38 | 88 | 10 | 0 | 7 | 23 | 1 | .290 |
| Home | 76 | 284 | 35 | 66 | 9 | 2 | 3 | 18 | 3 | .232 |
| Road | 74 | 273 | 34 | 81 | 11 | 3 | 8 | 32 | 0 | .297 |
| vs. RHP | | 391 | 44 | 96 | 9 | 5 | 4 | 32 | 2 | .246 |
| vs. LHP | | 166 | 25 | 51 | 11 | 0 | 7 | 18 | 1 | .307 |
| 1982 | 150 | 557 | 69 | 147 | 20 | 5 | 11 | 50 | 3 | .264 |
| 0.93 years | | 599 | 74 | 158 | 22 | 5 | 12 | 54 | 3 | .264 |

Larry PARRISH, Right Field

*Runs Created: 57*

| | G | AB | R | H | 2B | 3B | HR | RBI | SB | Avg |
|---|---|---|---|---|---|---|---|---|---|---|
| First Half | 55 | 171 | 21 | 36 | 3 | 0 | 6 | 25 | 1 | .211 |
| Second Half | 73 | 269 | 38 | 80 | 12 | 0 | 11 | 37 | 4 | .297 |
| Home | 60 | 204 | 28 | 55 | 8 | 0 | 6 | 26 | 1 | .270 |
| Road | 68 | 236 | 31 | 61 | 7 | 0 | 11 | 36 | 4 | .258 |
| vs. RHP | | 321 | 38 | 89 | 10 | 0 | 12 | 50 | 5 | .277 |
| vs. LHP | | 119 | 21 | 27 | 5 | 0 | 5 | 12 | 0 | .227 |
| 1982 | 128 | 440 | 59 | 116 | 15 | 0 | 17 | 62 | 5 | .264 |
| 6.76 years | | 570 | 71 | 150 | 33 | 4 | 17 | 75 | 3 | .263 |

Jim SUNDBERG, Catcher

*Runs Created: 55*

| | G | AB | R | H | 2B | 3B | HR | RBI | SB | Avg |
|---|---|---|---|---|---|---|---|---|---|---|
| First Half | 71 | 251 | 16 | 64 | 9 | 1 | 5 | 20 | 1 | .255 |
| Second Half | 68 | 219 | 21 | 54 | 13 | 4 | 5 | 27 | 1 | .247 |
| Home | 66 | 217 | 21 | 50 | 11 | 3 | 3 | 20 | 0 | .230 |
| Road | 73 | 253 | 16 | 68 | 11 | 2 | 7 | 27 | 2 | .269 |
| vs. RHP | | 363 | 27 | 87 | 12 | 5 | 8 | 38 | 2 | .240 |
| vs. LHP | | 107 | 10 | 31 | 10 | 0 | 2 | 9 | 0 | .290 |
| 1982 | 139 | 470 | 37 | 118 | 22 | 5 | 10 | 47 | 2 | .251 |
| 7.82 years | | 520 | 55 | 134 | 22 | 3 | 7 | 55 | 2 | .258 |

Lamar JOHNSON, Designated Hitter

*Runs Created: 36*

| | G | AB | R | H | 2B | 3B | HR | RBI | SB | Avg |
|---|---|---|---|---|---|---|---|---|---|---|
| First Half | 62 | 193 | 24 | 49 | 5 | 0 | 5 | 23 | 2 | .254 |
| Second Half | 43 | 131 | 13 | 35 | 6 | 0 | 2 | 15 | 1 | .267 |
| Home | 55 | 172 | 16 | 44 | 6 | 0 | 2 | 19 | 2 | .256 |
| Road | 50 | 152 | 21 | 40 | 5 | 0 | 5 | 19 | 1 | .263 |
| vs. RHP | | 201 | 22 | 53 | 6 | 0 | 3 | 21 | 2 | .264 |
| vs. LHP | | 123 | 15 | 31 | 5 | 0 | 4 | 17 | 1 | .252 |
| 1982 | 105 | 324 | 37 | 84 | 11 | 0 | 7 | 38 | 3 | .259 |
| 4.89 years | | 538 | 60 | 154 | 25 | 3 | 13 | 78 | 5 | .287 |

John GRUBB, Designated Hitter

*Runs Created: 48*

| | G | AB | R | H | 2B | 3B | HR | RBI | SB | Avg |
|---|---|---|---|---|---|---|---|---|---|---|
| First Half | 59 | 172 | 20 | 54 | 7 | 1 | 2 | 17 | 0 | .314 |
| Second Half | 44 | 136 | 15 | 32 | 6 | 2 | 1 | 9 | 0 | .235 |
| Home | 50 | 149 | 18 | 42 | 7 | 1 | 2 | 13 | 0 | .282 |
| Road | 53 | 159 | 17 | 44 | 6 | 2 | 1 | 13 | 0 | .277 |
| vs. RHP | | 281 | 33 | 79 | 10 | 2 | 2 | 23 | 0 | .281 |
| vs. LHP | | 27 | 2 | 7 | 3 | 1 | 1 | 3 | 0 | .259 |
| 1982 | 103 | 308 | 35 | 86 | 13 | 3 | 3 | 26 | 0 | .279 |
| 6.56 years | | 513 | 68 | 144 | 26 | 4 | 10 | 53 | 4 | .280 |

Charlie HOUGH

| Year | (W–L) | GS | Run | Avg | DP | Avg | SB | Avg |
|---|---|---|---|---|---|---|---|---|
| 1979 | ( 7- 5) | 14 | 83 | 5.93 | 12 | .86 | 15 | 1.07 |
| 1980 | ( 3- 5) | 3 | 15 | 5.00 | 2 | .67 | 4 | 1.33 |
| 1981 | ( 4- 1) | 5 | 24 | 4.80 | 5 | 1.00 | 3 | .60 |
| 1982 | (16-13) | 34 | 146 | 4.29 | 30 | .88 | 26 | .76 |
| 4 years | | 56 | 268 | 4.78 | 49 | .87 | 48 | .85 |

| | G | IP | W | L | Pct | ER | ERA |
|---|---|---|---|---|---|---|---|
| Home | 19 | 130.1 | 9 | 6 | .600 | 55 | 3.80 |
| Road | 15 | 97.2 | 7 | 7 | .500 | 45 | 4.15 |

Frank TANANA

| Year | (W–L) | GS | Run | Avg | DP | Avg | SB | Avg |
|---|---|---|---|---|---|---|---|---|
| 1976 | (19-10) | 34 | 129 | 3.79 | 16 | .47 | 40 | 1.18 |
| 1977 | (15- 9) | 31 | 149 | 4.81 | 24 | .77 | 12 | .39 |
| 1978 | (18-12) | 33 | 158 | 4.79 | 19 | .58 | 22 | .67 |
| 1979 | ( 7- 5) | 17 | 83 | 4.88 | 15 | .88 | 13 | .76 |
| 1980 | (11-12) | 31 | 150 | 4.84 | 28 | .90 | 24 | .77 |
| 1981 | ( 4-10) | 23 | 97 | 4.22 | 24 | 1.04 | 20 | .87 |
| 1982 | ( 7-18) | 30 | 99 | 3.30 | 27 | .90 | 14 | .47 |
| 7 years | | 199 | 865 | 4.35 | 153 | .77 | 145 | .73 |

| | G | IP | W | L | Pct | ER | ERA |
|---|---|---|---|---|---|---|---|
| Home | 15 | 99.2 | 2 | 10 | .167 | 43 | 3.88 |
| Road | 15 | 94.2 | 5 | 8 | .385 | 48 | 4.56 |

Rick HONEYCUTT

| Year | (W–L) | GS | Run | Avg | DP | Avg | SB | Avg |
|---|---|---|---|---|---|---|---|---|
| 1977 | ( 0- 1) | 3 | 10 | 3.33 | 2 | .67 | 2 | .67 |
| 1978 | ( 5-11) | 24 | 97 | 4.04 | 25 | 1.04 | 14 | .58 |
| 1979 | (11-12) | 29 | 122 | 4.21 | 32 | 1.10 | 17 | .59 |
| 1980 | (10-17) | 30 | 97 | 3.23 | 40 | 1.33 | 16 | .53 |
| 1981 | (11- 6) | 20 | 85 | 4.25 | 21 | 1.05 | 4 | .20 |
| 1982 | ( 5-17) | 26 | 88 | 3.38 | 35 | 1.35 | 11 | .42 |
| Career | | 132 | 499 | 3.78 | 155 | 1.17 | 64 | .48 |

| | G | IP | W | L | Pct | ER | ERA |
|---|---|---|---|---|---|---|---|
| Home | 16 | 89.2 | 3 | 10 | .231 | 53 | 5.32 |
| Road | 14 | 74.1 | 2 | 7 | .222 | 43 | 5.21 |

1982 OTHERS

| Pitcher | (W–L) | GS | Run | Avg | DP | Avg | SB | Avg |
|---|---|---|---|---|---|---|---|---|
| Matlack | ( 7-7) | 14 | 48 | 3.43 | 12 | .86 | 7 | .50 |
| Butcher | ( 1-5) | 13 | 52 | 4.00 | 13 | 1.00 | 4 | .31 |
| Schmidt | ( 4-6) | 8 | 27 | 3.38 | 4 | .50 | 6 | .75 |
| Smithson | ( 3-4) | 8 | 25 | 3.13 | 8 | 1.00 | 4 | .50 |
| Mason | ( 1-2) | 4 | 19 | 4.75 | 6 | 1.50 | 2 | .50 |
| Comer | ( 1-6) | 3 | 10 | 3.33 | 4 | 1.33 | 1 | .33 |
| Darwin | (10-8) | 1 | 2 | | 0 | | 0 | |

## TEXAS RANGERS

*Talent Analysis*

The Texas Rangers in 1982 possessed 123 points of approximate value.

| | AV | % |
|---|---|---|
| Produced by system: | 53 | 43% |
| Acquired by trade: | 48 | 39% |
| Purchased or signed from free agency: | 22 | 18% |

They are essentially a trade-built team.

| | | |
|---|---|---|
| Young (Up to age 25): | 16 | 13% |
| Prime (Age 26 to 29): | 55 | 45% |
| Past-prime (Age 30 to 33): | 42 | 34% |
| Old (Age 34 or older): | 10 | 8% |

42% of their talent is past-prime or old; the norm is 38%.

The Rangers' system ranked thirteenth in 1982 approximate value produced, 153 points, and ranks eleventh over the four-year period.

## ARLINGTON STADIUM

DIMENSIONS: Normal

SURFACE: Grass

VISIBILITY: Poor

FOUL TERRITORY: —

FAVORS:
Hitter/Pitcher—Pitcher
Power/Line-drive hitter—Line-drive
Righthander/Lefthander—Neither

TYPES OF OFFENSE AFFECTED: Home runs, triples both reduced sharply

OTHER PARK CHARACTERISTICS: The wind blows in from right field here; however, the notion that because of this the park discriminates against a lefthander is without foundation.

TYPES OF MARGINAL PLAYERS MOST VALUABLE IN PARK: Unknown

PLAYERS ON TEAM HELPED MOST BY PARK: Darwin, Hough

PLAYERS ON TEAM HURT MOST BY PARK: George Wright, Sundberg

OTHER COMMENTS: This park has always had a reputation for being a pitcher's park, a reputation that was *not* supported by the statistical evidence. However, two years ago the fences were moved out in the power alleys (10 feet), and the number of runs scored has dived sharply, more than should be caused by a 10-foot adjustment of the fences, leaving no doubt that it is now a pitcher's park.

# MINNESOTA TWINS

The 1982 season was, I believe, the best year for rookies since 1964. The 1964 rookie explosion is something that constantly draws at me, fascinates me so that on any busy day every other month I am compelled to go back and spend half-an-hour or an hour reaffirming the details of it in my mind, being reassured that there really was a season once in which:

a) Two rookies (Tony Oliva and Dick Allen) had seasons which were among rookiedom's ten greatest ever.

b) There were at a minimum six and possibly as many as eleven rookies who in any normal season would have been absolutely automatic rookie-of-the-year selections.

c) Every single team, with the arguable exception of Detroit, had at least one rookie who was one of their ten most valuable players.

d) Several teams had three of four rookies who were among their ten most valuable players.

e) There were probably 40 or 50 players who had rookie seasons at least comparable to the weakest rookie-of-the-year selections.

f) A dozen or more other players came up who didn't have outstanding rookie seasons, but were destined for outstanding or even great careers.

I don't know why this all fascinates me so. I do know that I should write it up and get it out of my system, but it has such marginal relevance to the present . . . well, I'll do a historical *Abstract* sometime and get to it then.

Anyway, the 1982 rookie crop, while it does not begin to compare to that outburst, compares very favorably to any since. The Minnesota Twins were the center of this new group, and if you doubt that it is an impressive rookie crew, tell me if you can deny either of the following two statements:

1) Gary Gaetti was the Twins' third- or fourth-most exciting rookie, definitely behind Hrbek and Brunansky and possibly, according to taste, behind Washington, Eisenreich or Laudner.

2) Gary Gaetti could very possibly hit 300 or 400 home runs in the major leagues.

This brings up the question of what are the most impressive one-team, one-season rookie crops ever. One could measure this by use of the value approximation method—one season AV judging them as rookies, career AV for evaluating how it all turns out. The Twins in 1982 had 66 points of approximate value from their rookies, over half of their team AV. (This can be figured by the lists of AV in *Not of Any General Interest*.) What is the all-time record? I don't know. But some of the greatest rookie crews that I do know about include:

| Year | Team | | Top Rookies |
|---|---|---|---|
| 1982 | Minnesota | 66 | Hrbek (12), Brunansky (10), Gaetti (9) |
| 1960 | Baltimore | 57 | Hansen (14), Estrada (12), Gentile (11) |
| 1937 | Boston | 47 | Turner (17), Fette (15), V. DiMaggio (11) |
| 1958 | San Francisco | 43 | Cepeda (12), Davenport (9), 2 with (8) |
| 1942 | St. Louis | 43 | Beasley (15), Musial (12), 2 with (5) |
| 1929 | Cleveland | 38 | Averill (15), Ferrell (15), Gardner (4) |
| 1978 | Detroit | 35 | Whitaker (11), Trammell (11), Parrish (5) |
| 1975 | Boston | 32 | Lynn (17), Rice (13), Burton (2) |

The fact that I cannot find a team which has had more production from a group of rookies, in a couple of hours poking around looking for one, does not powerfully suggest that no such team exists. If you were to do an exhaustive study, make up an all-time top ten, it is possible that none of these teams would make it. But all the same, 66 approximate value points of rookie output ain't hay.

There are a couple of other points suggested by this list. I note that almost all of these teams came from extremely productive four- or five-year eras for the organization, so much so that in several cases I was unsure which season I should figure. Detroit had the three mentioned plus Jack Morris and Kip Young in '78, but they also had Steve Kemp and Dave Rozema in '77, Jason Thompson and Mark Fidrych in '76, and several others just before or after. Boston surrounded Rice and Lynn with Burleson, Cooper, Evans, Oglivie and several others popping out of that system in about three years. And both of these lists would be dwarfed by the talent produced by the Giants in the late fifties.

And yet, despite all that talent, these teams were not, as a group, on the road to greatness. The records of these teams over the four following years were:

| | | That Year | | Next | | Next | | Next | | Next | |
|---|---|---|---|---|---|---|---|---|---|---|---|
| Year | Team | W-L | Position | W-L | Position | W-L | Position | W-L | Position | W-L | Position |
| 1928 | Cleveland | 81-71 | 3rd | 81-73 | 4th | 78-76 | 4th | 87-65 | 4th | 75-76 | 4th |
| 1937 | Boston | 79-73 | 5th | 77-75 | 5th | 63-88 | 7th | 65-87 | 7th | 62-92 | 7th |
| 1942 | St. Louis | 106-48 | 1st | 105-49 | 1st | 105-49 | 1st | 95-59 | 2nd | 95-59 | 1st |
| 1958 | San Francisco | 80-74 | 3rd | 83-71 | 3rd | 79-75 | 5th | 85-69 | 3rd | 103-62 | 1st |
| 1960 | Baltimore | 89-65 | 2nd | 95-67 | 3rd | 77-85 | 7th | 86-76 | 4th | 97-65 | 3rd |
| 1975 | Boston | 95-65 | 1st | 83-79 | 3rd | 97-64 | 2nd | 99-64 | 2nd | 91-69 | 3rd |
| 1978 | Detroit | 86-76 | 5th | 85-76 | 5th | 84-78 | 5th | 60-49 | 4th | 83-79 | 4th |

Which, in its turn, suggests a couple of other conclusions. At the time that the Tiger farm system was going through this phase where they were kicking out a LeFlore or a Petry or a Whitaker every year, I believed that this accumulation of talent must inevitably, in time, return the Tigers to the top of the division. In view of what I see in this chart, the fact that that did not happen does not seem very surprising. It didn't happen to the Red Sox either, or the Giants or even the Orioles. I believe that I was making exactly the same mistake that the teams themselves were making, which is one of the mistakes that the Twins are making. We all overestimated the importance of talent in building a championship team, and underestimated the importance of other factors, chiefly good management. Indeed, reviewing the things that I have written over the last five or six years, I think that I repeated that mistake many times, most recently just a year ago, when I picked the Montreal Expos to win the NL West, knowing full well that the Expos were being managed by an amateur. (There is probably an Expo team, say '77 or so, which could have gone on this list.) I think that I was making basically the same mistake when I foresaw the demise of the Philadelphia Phillies, about 1979, when their talent pool seemed to be evaporating.

I am also reminded of a study I did three years ago which correlated the total approximate value produced by each major league team with the number of wins posted by the teams. The correlation, surprisingly, was very slight. In simple English, those teams which had produced the most talent out of their own farm systems were, on the whole, only very slightly better than those teams which had produced the *least* talent. Producing talent seemed to have little to do with winning ball games. I found that conclusion, at the time, too surprising to accept. But I'm a lot closer to accepting it now.

My wife helps me a little bit with the stat work, compiling charts and stuff. She says that if she doesn't know what a category means, doesn't know whether it's good to be high or low, she just looks for Minnesota.

I was in the press box at a game last September at which it was announced that one of the teams had a record of 38-10 in games of which they scored in the first inning. This is one of those statistics at which everyone scratches their head and agrees that it sounds impressive, but what does it mean? I haven't discovered an answer to that question, but I have discovered some facts which are along the road to an answer, and collected some data by which to erect standards in the area, so come along...

The team, as you could probably guess, was the Royals, and the Royals are indeed a very good first-inning team.

The chart at right presents, in order:

1) The number of times that each American League team scored in the first inning in 1982.
2) Their won-lost record when they did.
3) Their won-lost percentage when they did.
4) Their won-lost record when they didn't.
5) Their won-lost percentage when they didn't.
6) The difference between their won-lost percentage when they did and when they didn't, which I will call, in the text following, their "first-inning importance."

| Team | 1 | 2 | 3 | 4 | 5 | 6 |
|---|---|---|---|---|---|---|
| Milwaukee | 60 | 46-14 | .767 | 49-53 | .480 | .287 |
| Kansas City | 59 | 45-14 | .763 | 45-58 | .436 | .327 |
| California | 58 | 41-17 | .707 | 52-52 | .500 | .207 |
| | | | | | | |
| Chicago | 56 | 36-20 | .643 | 51-55 | .481 | .162 |
| Baltimore | 54 | 37-17 | .685 | 57-51 | .528 | .157 |
| Oakland | 53 | 28-25 | .528 | 40-69 | .367 | .161 |
| Cleveland | 51 | 30-21 | .588 | 48-63 | .432 | .156 |
| | | | | | | |
| New York | 47 | 33-14 | .702 | 46-69 | .400 | .202 |
| Boston | 43 | 29-14 | .674 | 60-59 | .504 | .170 |
| Seattle | 43 | 27-16 | .628 | 49-70 | .412 | .216 |
| Toronto | 42 | 27-15 | .643 | 51-69 | .425 | .218 |
| | | | | | | |
| Texas | 41 | 26-15 | .634 | 38-83 | .314 | .320 |
| Detroit | 37 | 25-12 | .676 | 58-67 | .464 | .212 |
| MINNESOTA | 31 | 12-19 | .387 | 48-83 | .366 | .021 |
| | | | | | | |
| Total | 675 | 442-233 | .655 | 692-901 | .434 | .221 |

There are several patterns here, some of which make sense and some of which don't. The three teams which scored most often in the first inning were, in order, Milwaukee, Kansas City, and California. The three teams which were most successful when they did score in the first inning were, in order, Milwaukee, Kansas City, and California. The team which scored the least often in the first was Minnesota; the team which was least successful when they did score in the first inning was Minnesota. I couldn't give you a decent explanation of why this happens.

There are two things that one can *almost* say here—that any team is a winning team when they score in the first inning, and that no team is a winning team when they don't. (One exception, two exceptions.) I think that is an important addition to the discussion earlier (*see Milwaukee, page 76*) about the importance of the early and late innings.

The Minnesota Twins stand apart on these lists, to an almost absurd degree. They scored in the first inning only 31 times, easily the lowest total in the league. Were it not for Sparky Anderson's rather novel ideas on lineup selection, no other team would have been in the thirties. And while only one other team was below .588 in those games when they did score in the first, the Twins were at .387. But the really amazing one is this list of the smallest first-inning importance:

| | |
|---|---|
| Chicago | .162 |
| Oakland | .161 |
| Baltimore | .157 |
| Cleveland | .156 |
| Minnesota | .021 |

Now *that's* dominating the category.

Why? To every other team, even to the other teams which were nearly as bad as the Twins, the first inning was important. But to the Twins, a first-inning run seemed to mean nothing. There's no apparent reason for that. One can say that the Twin's pitching staff was so bad that there was no hope of winning even with a head start. But there is no evidence to support this among the other teams with poor pitching staffs. The two teams with the highest first-inning importance in the league were Kansas

City, which was 10th in the league in ERA, and Texas, which was 12th. One of those teams had a very good offense, the other a very bad one. Why is the first inning so important to Texas, and why isn't it important to Baltimore? What's the key?

Well, maybe it doesn't mean anything. (But if it's meaningless, why the big spread in column six?) This notion of first-inning importance starts another chain of thought, which is that this would be another way of contrasting the importance of the early innings with that of the late. Let's pick a late inning—the eighth suggests itself—and see what teams' records were when they did and did not score then. Categories are the same as the earlier charts.

**8th Inning Scores**

| Team | 1 | 2 | 3 | 4 | 5 | 6 |
|---|---|---|---|---|---|---|
| Milwaukee | 57 | 42-15 | .737 | 53-52 | .505 | .232 |
| California | 52 | 36-15 | .692 | 57-53 | .518 | .174 |
| Oakland | 49 | 27-22 | .551 | 41-72 | .363 | .188 |
| | | | | | | |
| Detroit | 48 | 32-16 | .667 | 51-63 | .447 | .220 |
| Boston | 47 | 33-14 | .702 | 56-59 | .487 | .215 |
| Kansas City | 44 | 30-14 | .682 | 60-58 | .508 | .174 |
| New York | 42 | 31-11 | .738 | 48-72 | .400 | .338 |
| | | | | | | |
| Chicago | 41 | 28-13 | .683 | 59-62 | .488 | .195 |
| Baltimore | 40 | 28-12 | .700 | 66-56 | .541 | .159 |
| Minnesota | 40 | 19-21 | .475 | 41-81 | .336 | .139 |
| | | | | | | |
| Toronto | 40 | 25-15 | .625 | 53-69 | .434 | .191 |
| Seattle | 37 | 23-14 | .622 | 53-72 | .424 | .198 |
| Cleveland | 36 | 26-10 | .722 | 52-72 | .413 | .309 |
| | | | | | | |
| Total | 610 | 401-209 | .657 | 733-925 | .442 | .215 |

The Twins, again, were the only team in the league which could not post a winning record even given a run in the inning. Again, the inning was less important to them than to any other team.

It appears, on the basis of the two charts, that a run in the eighth will do almost exactly as much to win a game for you as a run in the first. Teams which scored in the first won 65.5% of the time. Teams which scored in the eight won 65.7% of the time. To the extent that there is a difference in the importance of the two innings, it is that there are more runs scored in the first and therefore it attains that significance a little more often.

This is not to deny that there are late-inning situations in which games are absolutely decided. Of course there are. Having the same importance *in retrospect* is not having the same importance at the time. It might be accurate to say that 15% of the runs that are scored in the first inning turn out to have won the ballgame, while 15% of those which are scored in the eight actually win them. Of 100 first-inning runs, all are equal at the time, but 15 are distinguished later; of 100 in the 8th, 15 are immediately meaningful. But immediacy is not the same as value.

The overrating of the late innings in contrast with the early, I think, is very much like the overrating of RBI and RBI men in comparison to the men who get rallies started. Early in the rally, late in the rally; early in the game, late in the game. People are always fascinated by "payoff" statistics, by wins and losses as opposed to ERA, by who caught the touchdown pass. Mazerkoski was the hero; who remembers Hal Smith? If the food is good you tip the waitress. Sabermetricians are an odd lot. We always want to know what the recipe was.

Kent HRBEK, First Base

*Runs Created: 94*

| | G | AB | R | H | 2B | 3B | HR | RBI | SB | Avg |
|---|---|---|---|---|---|---|---|---|---|---|
| First Half | 74 | 292 | 48 | 97 | 12 | 4 | 17 | 60 | 2 | .332 |
| Second Half | 66 | 240 | 34 | 63 | 9 | 0 | 6 | 32 | 1 | .263 |
| Home | 73 | 272 | 50 | 86 | 11 | 4 | 11 | 46 | 0 | .316 |
| Road | 67 | 260 | 32 | 74 | 10 | 0 | 12 | 46 | 3 | .285 |
| vs. RHP | | 347 | 55 | 102 | 11 | 3 | 19 | 62 | 3 | .294 |
| vs. LHP | | 185 | 27 | 58 | 10 | 1 | 4 | 30 | 0 | .314 |
| 1982 | 140 | 532 | 82 | 160 | 21 | 4 | 23 | 92 | 3 | .301 |
| 1.01 years | | 593 | 86 | 174 | 26 | 4 | 24 | 98 | 3 | .294 |

John CASTINO, Second Base

*Runs Created: 41*

| | G | AB | R | H | 2B | 3B | HR | RBI | SB | Avg |
|---|---|---|---|---|---|---|---|---|---|---|
| First Half | 57 | 203 | 21 | 45 | 6 | 0 | 3 | 20 | 0 | .222 |
| Second Half | 60 | 207 | 27 | 54 | 6 | 6 | 3 | 17 | 2 | .261 |
| Home | 58 | 194 | 25 | 47 | 9 | 3 | 2 | 18 | 2 | .242 |
| Road | 59 | 216 | 23 | 52 | 3 | 3 | 4 | 19 | 0 | .241 |
| vs. RHP | | 273 | 33 | 66 | 8 | 4 | 5 | 30 | 0 | .242 |
| vs. LHP | | 137 | 15 | 33 | 4 | 2 | 1 | 7 | 2 | .241 |
| 1982 | 117 | 410 | 48 | 99 | 12 | 6 | 6 | 37 | 2 | .241 |
| 3.19 years | | 542 | 64 | 150 | 17 | 9 | 9 | 59 | 6 | .276 |

Gary GAETTI, Third Base

*Runs Created: 61*

| | G | AB | R | H | 2B | 3B | HR | RBI | SB | Avg |
|---|---|---|---|---|---|---|---|---|---|---|
| First Half | 74 | 244 | 32 | 53 | 15 | 1 | 13 | 38 | 0 | .217 |
| Second Half | 71 | 264 | 27 | 64 | 10 | 3 | 12 | 46 | 0 | .242 |
| Home | 76 | 268 | 35 | 63 | 13 | 3 | 15 | 46 | 0 | .235 |
| Road | 69 | 240 | 24 | 54 | 12 | 1 | 10 | 38 | 0 | .225 |
| vs. RHP | | 341 | 40 | 74 | 16 | 1 | 11 | 46 | 0 | .217 |
| vs. LHP | | 167 | 19 | 43 | 9 | 3 | 14 | 38 | 0 | .257 |
| 1982 | 145 | 508 | 59 | 117 | 25 | 4 | 25 | 84 | 0 | .230 |
| 0.95 years | | 562 | 66 | 128 | 26 | 4 | 28 | 92 | 0 | .229 |

Ron WASHINGTON, Shortstop

*Runs Created: 48*

| | G | AB | R | H | 2B | 3B | HR | RBI | SB | Avg |
|---|---|---|---|---|---|---|---|---|---|---|
| First Half | 75 | 289 | 32 | 84 | 14 | 5 | 3 | 25 | 2 | .291 |
| Second Half | 44 | 162 | 16 | 38 | 3 | 1 | 2 | 14 | 1 | .235 |
| Home | 53 | 197 | 19 | 48 | 6 | 2 | 4 | 18 | 2 | .244 |
| Road | 66 | 254 | 29 | 74 | 11 | 4 | 1 | 21 | 1 | .291 |
| vs. RHP | | 315 | 31 | 82 | 13 | 4 | 4 | 33 | 3 | .260 |
| vs. LHP | | 136 | 17 | 40 | 4 | 2 | 1 | 6 | 0 | .294 |
| 1982 | 119 | 451 | 48 | 122 | 17 | 6 | 5 | 39 | 3 | .271 |
| 0.97 years | | 571 | 62 | 153 | 21 | 7 | 5 | 46 | 8 | .267 |

### Gary WARD, Left Field

*Runs Created: 101*

| | G | AB | R | H | 2B | 3B | HR | RBI | SB | Avg |
|---|---|---|---|---|---|---|---|---|---|---|
| First Half | 78 | 291 | 41 | 77 | 13 | 1 | 12 | 36 | 9 | .265 |
| Second Half | 74 | 279 | 44 | 88 | 20 | 6 | 16 | 55 | 4 | .315 |
| Home | 80 | 290 | 45 | 90 | 22 | 5 | 16 | 56 | 7 | .310 |
| Road | 72 | 280 | 40 | 75 | 11 | 2 | 12 | 35 | 6 | .268 |
| vs. RHP | | 372 | 54 | 107 | 19 | 4 | 18 | 55 | 11 | .288 |
| vs. LHP | | 198 | 31 | 58 | 14 | 3 | 10 | 36 | 2 | .293 |
| 1982 | 152 | 570 | 85 | 165 | 33 | 7 | 28 | 91 | 13 | .289 |
| 1.61 years | | 571 | 87 | 165 | 29 | 9 | 20 | 81 | 11 | .289 |

### Bobby MITCHELL, Center Field

*Runs Created: 45*

| | G | AB | R | H | 2B | 3B | HR | RBI | SB | Avg |
|---|---|---|---|---|---|---|---|---|---|---|
| First Half | 55 | 191 | 19 | 43 | 3 | 3 | 1 | 11 | 4 | .225 |
| Second Half | 69 | 263 | 29 | 70 | 8 | 3 | 1 | 17 | 4 | .266 |
| Home | 58 | 203 | 24 | 63 | 7 | 3 | 1 | 14 | 3 | .310 |
| Road | 66 | 251 | 24 | 50 | 4 | 3 | 1 | 14 | 5 | .199 |
| vs. RHP | | 346 | 32 | 81 | 10 | 4 | 2 | 20 | 7 | .234 |
| vs. LHP | | 108 | 16 | 32 | 1 | 2 | 0 | 8 | 1 | .296 |
| 1982 | 124 | 454 | 48 | 113 | 11 | 6 | 2 | 28 | 8 | .249 |
| 0.88 years | | 528 | 56 | 131 | 13 | 7 | 2 | 32 | 9 | .247 |

### Tom BRUNANSKY, Right Field

*Runs Created: 80*

| | G | AB | R | H | 2B | 3B | HR | RBI | SB | Avg |
|---|---|---|---|---|---|---|---|---|---|---|
| First Half | 53 | 186 | 31 | 50 | 9 | 1 | 10 | 21 | 0 | .269 |
| Second Half | 74 | 277 | 46 | 76 | 21 | 0 | 10 | 25 | 1 | .274 |
| Home | 63 | 233 | 36 | 63 | 19 | 1 | 10 | 23 | 0 | .270 |
| Road | 64 | 230 | 41 | 63 | 11 | 0 | 10 | 23 | 1 | .274 |
| vs. RHP | | 314 | 44 | 81 | 20 | 0 | 11 | 25 | 0 | .258 |
| vs. LHP | | 149 | 33 | 45 | 10 | 1 | 9 | 21 | 1 | .302 |
| 1982 | 127 | 463 | 77 | 126 | 30 | 1 | 20 | 46 | 1 | .272 |
| 0.85 years | | 584 | 99 | 154 | 35 | 1 | 27 | 61 | 2 | .264 |

### Tim LAUDNER, Catcher

*Runs Created: 39*

| | G | AB | R | H | 2B | 3B | HR | RBI | SB | Avg |
|---|---|---|---|---|---|---|---|---|---|---|
| First Half | 41 | 129 | 17 | 34 | 9 | 0 | 4 | 17 | 0 | .264 |
| Second Half | 52 | 177 | 20 | 44 | 10 | 1 | 3 | 16 | 0 | .249 |
| Home | 48 | 148 | 16 | 40 | 11 | 1 | 2 | 13 | 0 | .270 |
| Road | 45 | 158 | 21 | 38 | 8 | 0 | 5 | 20 | 0 | .241 |
| vs. RHP | | 221 | 26 | 57 | 11 | 1 | 5 | 23 | 0 | .258 |
| vs. LHP | | 85 | 11 | 21 | 8 | 0 | 2 | 10 | 0 | .247 |
| 1982 | 93 | 306 | 37 | 78 | 19 | 1 | 7 | 33 | 0 | .255 |
| 0.66 years | | 529 | 62 | 129 | 32 | 2 | 14 | 58 | 0 | .244 |

### Randy JOHNSON, Designated Hitter

*Runs Created: 33*

| | G | AB | R | H | 2B | 3B | HR | RBI | SB | Avg |
|---|---|---|---|---|---|---|---|---|---|---|
| First Half | 62 | 184 | 23 | 50 | 9 | 0 | 8 | 28 | 0 | .272 |
| Second Half | 27 | 51 | 3 | 8 | 1 | 0 | 2 | 4 | 0 | .157 |
| Home | 45 | 116 | 20 | 34 | 7 | 0 | 7 | 17 | 0 | .293 |
| Road | 44 | 119 | 6 | 24 | 3 | 0 | 3 | 15 | 0 | .202 |
| vs. RHP | | 224 | 26 | 58 | 10 | 0 | 10 | 32 | 0 | .259 |
| vs. LHP | | 11 | 0 | 0 | 0 | 0 | 0 | 0 | 0 | .000 |
| 1982 | 89 | 235 | 26 | 58 | 10 | 0 | 10 | 32 | 0 | .247 |
| 0.62 years | | 411 | 42 | 100 | 16 | 0 | 16 | 57 | 0 | .243 |

### Brad HAVENS

| Year | (W–L) | GS | Run | Avg | DP | Avg | SB | Avg |
|---|---|---|---|---|---|---|---|---|
| 1981 | ( 3- 6) | 12 | 32 | 2.67 | 8 | .67 | 10 | .83 |
| 1982 | (10-14) | 32 | 128 | 4.00 | 24 | .75 | 30 | .94 |
| Career | | 44 | 160 | 3.64 | 32 | .73 | 40 | .91 |

| | G | IP | W | L | Pct | ER | ERA |
|---|---|---|---|---|---|---|---|
| Home | 17 | 110 | 6 | 8 | .429 | 42 | 3.44 |
| Road | 16 | 98.2 | 4 | 6 | .400 | 58 | 5.29 |

### Al WILLIAMS

| Year | (W–L) | GS | Run | Avg | DP | Avg | SB | Avg |
|---|---|---|---|---|---|---|---|---|
| 1980 | ( 6- 2) | 9 | 55 | 6.11 | 10 | 1.11 | 4 | .44 |
| 1981 | ( 6-10) | 22 | 94 | 4.27 | 29 | 1.32 | 20 | .91 |
| 1982 | ( 9- 7) | 26 | 120 | 4.26 | 26 | 1.00 | 26 | 1.00 |
| Career | | 57 | 269 | 4.72 | 65 | 1.14 | 50 | .88 |

| | G | IP | W | L | Pct | ER | ERA |
|---|---|---|---|---|---|---|---|
| Home | 15 | 91.2 | 7 | 5 | .583 | 44 | 4.32 |
| Road | 11 | 62 | 2 | 2 | .500 | 28 | 4.06 |

### Bobby CASTILLO

| Year | (W–L) | GS | Run | Avg | DP | Avg | SB | Avg |
|---|---|---|---|---|---|---|---|---|
| 1977 | ( 1- 0) | 1 | 3 | | 0 | | 0 | |
| 1981 | ( 2- 4) | 1 | 3 | | 3 | | 0 | |
| 1982 | (13-11) | 25 | 104 | 4.16 | 23 | .92 | 13 | .52 |
| Career | | 27 | 110 | 4.07 | 26 | .96 | 13 | .48 |

| | G | IP | W | L | Pct | ER | ERA |
|---|---|---|---|---|---|---|---|
| Home | 18 | 112.2 | 9 | 3 | .750 | 48 | 3.83 |
| Road | 22 | 106 | 4 | 8 | .333 | 41 | 3.58 |

### Frank VIOLA

| Year | (W–L) | GS | Run | Avg | DP | Avg | SB | Avg |
|---|---|---|---|---|---|---|---|---|
| 1982 | ( 4-10) | 22 | 93 | 4.33 | 24 | 1.09 | 18 | .82 |

| | G | IP | W | L | Pct | ER | ERA |
|---|---|---|---|---|---|---|---|
| Home | 13 | 72 | 1 | 8 | .111 | 50 | 6.25 |
| Road | 9 | 54 | 3 | 2 | .600 | 23 | 3.83 |

### 1982 OTHERS

| Pitcher | (W–L) | GS | Run | Avg | DP | Avg | SB | Avg |
|---|---|---|---|---|---|---|---|---|
| O'Connor | (8- 9) | 19 | 79 | 4.16 | 24 | 1.26 | 11 | .58 |
| Redfern | (5-11) | 13 | 49 | 3.77 | 16 | 1.23 | 7 | .54 |
| Erickson | (4- 3) | 7 | 39 | 5.57 | 6 | .86 | 2 | .29 |
| Jackson | (0- 5) | 7 | 12 | 1.71 | 11 | 1.57 | 6 | .86 |
| Felton | (0-13) | 6 | 14 | 2.33 | 6 | 1.00 | 8 | 1.33 |
| Filson | (0- 2) | 3 | 10 | 3.33 | 2 | .67 | 2 | .67 |
| Pacella | (1- 2) | 1 | 2 | | 1 | | 2 | |
| Cooper | (0- 1) | 1 | 7 | | 0 | | 0 | |

## MINNESOTA TWINS

*Talent Analysis*

The Twins' possessed 126 points of approximate value in 1982.

| | AV | % |
|---|---|---|
| Produced by the Twins' system: | 66 | 52% |
| Acquired by trade: | 48 | 38% |
| Purchased or signed from free agency: | 12 | 10% |

Most of their spots were filled from the system.

| | | |
|---|---|---|
| Young (Up to age 25): | 59 | 47% |
| Prime (Age 26 to 29): | 60 | 48% |
| Past-prime (Age 30 to 33): | 7 | 5% |
| Old (Age 34 or older): | 0 | 0% |

The Twins are the youngest team in baseball.

| | AV | Rank |
|---|---|---|
| 1982 talent produced by Twins' system | 140 | 17th |
| 1979-82 talent produced by system | 517 | 17th |

## HUBIE DOME

DIMENSIONS: Short, and weird

SURFACE: Turf

VISIBILITY: Probably not as good as has been reported. The strikeout-to-walk ratio in games here was markedly worse than the strikeout-to-walk ratio in Twins road games.

FOUL TERRITORY: Small

FAVORS:
Hitter/Pitcher—Hitter
Power/Line-drive hitter—Power
Lefthander/Righthander—Neither that one can tell yet

TYPES OF OFFENSE AFFECTED: On initial information, batting averages up about 5 points, power up 16%; surprisingly, doubles and triples look like they are way up

TYPES OF MARGINAL PLAYERS MOST VALUABLE: I would presume, sluggers. That is a tentative opinion.

PLAYERS ON TEAM HELPED MOST BY PARK: Castillo, Mitchell, Havens

PLAYERS ON TEAM HURT MOST BY PARK: Viola, Davis

OTHER COMMENTS: The degree to which this park favors power hitters does not appear to be nearly as large as was at first supposed. To hit home runs and to give up a lot of home runs is the true character of the Minnesota ball club, and not an illusion created by the park. The Twins gave up 98 home runs on the road, more than anyone except Kansas City.

Section

# III

# PLAYER RATINGS

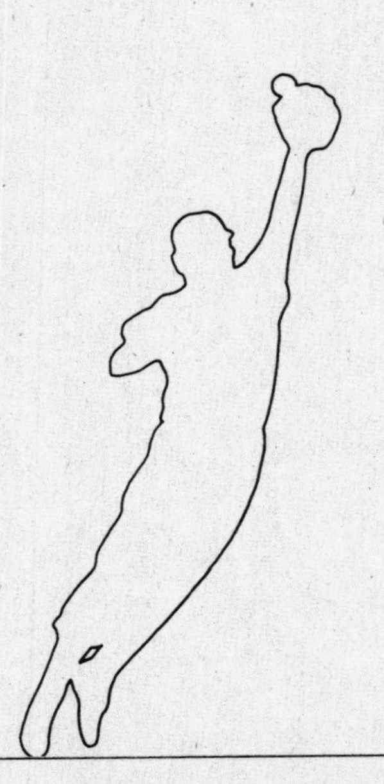

# HOW THE PLAYERS ARE RATED THIS TIME

I have been doing a player-ratings-and-comments section now for four years, and have yet to use a rating system twice. I will never use exactly the same rating method year after year, because I will (I hope) always be learning more about the game, about the relative importance of various factors in the game and the ways that things can be measured. Thus I will (I hope) always be including new information into the ratings. But I believe that I have hit upon a form now that is capable of growth, a form viable enough to evolve over a period of years into a comprehensive and accurate assessment of the abilities of each player.

After each player's name, a won-lost record is given in parenthesis. These figures represent the number of wins and the number of losses that the player has contributed to his team over the last two years, offensively and defensively. Since each game is seen both offensively and defensively, the total for each team in each year is 324, not 162. This system is a development of the one that was used last year, but rather than rehash here what was said last year, let me trace briefly all of the stages that lead to these ratings. More details on each step are given elsewhere in the book; if they're not given this year then they were given last year, and if they weren't given last year they will be given next year.

### TO EVALUATE THE PLAYER OFFENSIVELY

1) Figure the number of runs the player created in 1981.
   · *Eddie Murray created 72 runs in 1981.*
2) Translate this into a number of runs per (25.5-out) game.
   · *Eddie Murray created 6.77 runs per (individual) game.*
3) Figure the league average of runs per game.
   · *The AL average in 1981 was 4.075 runs per game.*
4) Adjust this for the park the player played in.
   · *Memorial Stadium reduced offense by 10%. The adjusted average is 3.89 runs per game.*
5) Express the player's runs per game as a won-lost percentage, by use of the Pythagorean method.
   · *Murray's offensive won-lost percentage was .753.*
6) Assign the player an area of responsibility of one game per 25.5 outs used.
   · *Murray used 270 outs.*
   · *We assign him the responsibility for 11 games.*
7) Make a won-lost record out of that.
   · *Murray's 1981 won-lost record was 8-3.*
8) Repeat the process for 1982.
   · *Murray's 1982 won-lost record was 12-3.*
   · *Take my word for it.*

### HOW THE DEFENSIVE RATINGS ARE DERIVED

1) Each player is rated on four defensive categories, which are different at each position. The categories for a shortstop are A) Range factor minus double plays per game; B) Double plays per game, divided by the team average of hits and walks allowed per game; C) Fielding Percentage; and D) the defensive efficiency record of the team. The considerations for each position, and also the charts by which these factors are changed into a won-lost percentage, are given in *Not of Any General Interest*.
2) Subtract the player's errors and double plays from his total chances, and divide by the number of games that he has played.
   · *Ozzie Smith in 1982 made 5.129 non-double-play chances per game.*
3) If the player played on artificial turf, add 2%. If he played on grass, subtract 2%.
   · *Ozzie's figure is increased to 5.232.*
4) Award the point value given in the defensive-ratings

chart in *Not of Any General Interest.*
· *Ozzie is awarded 36 points out of a possible 40 for his range afield.*

5) Figure how many double plays per game the player has made.
   · *Ozzie was involved in 0.72 DP per game.*
6) Divide by the average number of hits plus walks allowed by the team.
   · *The Cardinals allowed 11.86 baserunners per game.*
   · *Ozzie removed 6.12% of those players from the bases.*
7) Adjust this for the park the man plays in.
   · *Busch Stadium increases double plays by 10%.*
   · *Ozzie's DP rate is adjusted to .0582.*
8) Award the number of points given in the chart.
   · *Ozzie is awarded 20 points out of a possible 30 for his DP%.*
9) Look up the player's fielding percentage.
   · *Ozzie fielded .984.*
10) Adjust this for the park in which he plays.
   · *Busch Stadium reduces infield errors by about 8%.*
   · *Ozzie's fielding average is adjusted to .983.*
11) Award the appropriate number of points.
   · *Ozzie gets 15 points out of a possible 20 for his fielding percentage.*
12) Locate the team's Defensive Efficiency Record.
   · *The Cardinal's DER was .705.*
13) Award the appropriate points.
   · *Six.*
14) Add up all points awarded.
   · *36 + 20 + 15 + 6 = 77*
15) Throw in a decimal point.
   · *Ozzie Smith's 1982 defensive won-lost percentage was .77.*
16) Assign a shortstop a defensive area of responsibility of 11 games per 162 played at the position. (Reason for 11 games explained shortly.)
   · *Ozzie played 139 games; he is held responsible for nine defensive games.*
17) Make a won-lost record out of those two.
   · *Ozzie's 1982 defensive won-lost record is 7-2.*
18) Repeat the process for 1981.
   · *Ozzie's 1981 defensive won-lost record was 5-2.*
   · Please *take my word for it.*

A team in a season has 324 "games" in this process, 162 offensive and 162 defensive. The even balance of offense and defense, again, is not an assumption but a conclusion that you can verify in any number of ways. Of the 162 "defensive games," the pitcher is assumed to be responsible for about two-thirds, or 109 of 162. That is an assumption or an estimate, and it can't be verified. Of the 53 remaining defensive games, the shortstop is assigned the most, 11, and the first baseman the fewest, 3.

## HOW THE RATINGS ARE COMBINED INTO RANKINGS

In the simplest case, you simply add the four won-lost marks together and that's the player's total wins and losses. However, there is a continual rounding error to be dealt with—8 wins and 3 losses do not produce a .753 won-lost percentage, but .727—and to minimize the effect of this, we carry decimals through on the four rankings and round off at the end. For example, Sixto Lezcano:

| | Games | Percentage | Raw W-L | Precise Wins |
|---|---|---|---|---|
| 1981 Offensive | 6 | .625 | 4-2 | 3.750 |
| 1981 Defensive | 2 | .46 | 1-1 | 0.92 |
| 1982 Offensive | 13 | .752 | 10-3 | 9.776 |
| 1982 Defensive | 4 | .69 | 3-1 | 2.76 |
| Total Record | 25 | .688 | 18-7 | 17.206 |

So we list his record as 17-8, rather than 18-7, because the rounding error is smaller.

The players are listed, then, according to the random chance that a .400 team would post their record in the same number of decisions. You have to have some way to adjust for the size of a player's contribution; a player who hits .300 with 15 home runs in 300 at-bats is not as valuable as a player who hits .300 with 30 home runs in 600 at-bats. A rookie has not proven as much as a player who performs at the same level for two seasons. A traditional mathematical test of the worth of data is the chance that it could occur at random. I reason

1) That a replacement-level player is about a .400 player.
2) That the value of a player is measured by the extent to which he has proven that he is not a replacement-level player.
3) The smaller the chance that a replacement-level player would post this record, the better the player.

The chance that a .400 team would win 17 or more out of any 25 games is .0042. Lezcano therefore is ranked below Jack Clark, 23-12 (.00323) and ahead of George Hendrick, 19-11 (.00830).

At the conclusion of each player's comment, two more won-lost records are given in parenthesis, and these are usually not identified. There are the player's two-year offensive won-lost totals, which come first, and the two-year defensive won-lost totals, which come second. Jack Clark's offensive won-lost records were 8-3 in 1981 and 11-5 in 1982, a total of 19-8. His defensive totals were 2-1 in '81 and 3-2 in '82, a total of 5-3. So at the end of Clark's comment there is a parenthesis reading, "(19-8; 5-3)."

# FOREWORD TO CATCHERS COMMENTS

The defensive won-lost charts used this year are the same as they were last year at all positions except one, catcher. A year ago the considerations were:

| | |
|---|---|
| 40 point | Opposition Stolen Bases Per Game |
| 30 point | Assists Per Game |
| 20 point | Fielding Percentage |
| 10 point | Team Earned Run Average |

A year ago, on his own, Walt Campbell figured the earned run averages of each team with each starting catcher. The differences were surprisingly large and consistent; almost every team had a better ERA with their #1 catcher in the lineup than without him; often the differences were quite large, even when the #2 catcher was used 50 or 60 games. I was intrigued enough to have this data figured again this year (this time by Randy Lakeman), and the same was true again. Cleveland's ERA with their #1 catcher, Ron Hassey, was 3.68; in 49 games with the rookie Chris Bando, it was 4.48; in 22 games with Bill Nahorodny, 5.09. Milwaukee's ERA was best with Simmons in the lineup, Kansas City's with Wathan, Atlanta's with Benedict, etc...with a few exceptions. Two of the most prominent exceptions, Detroit without Parrish and Pittsburgh without Pena, joined the minority in both seasons.

Convinced that something real was being measured there, I promoted "Team ERA with Catcher in Lineup" to the #2 consideration in the rankings:

| | |
|---|---|
| 40 point | Opposition Stolen Bases Per Game |
| 30 point | Team ERA with this Catcher |
| 20 point | Fielding Percentage |
| 10 point | Assists Per Game |

I also felt that the old ranking, by weighting both opposition stolen bases and assists heavily, put too much weight on the catcher's throwing ability. To help you evaluate this information yourself, and because I think the data is interesting, I also included the chart "Records with Different Starting Catchers" at the end of the Catchers section, and before the OSB records.

There would be a real danger in making too many of these kinds of changes, which is that you could wind up rating all of the people who play for the teams with the best ERAs as good players, and all of the players who play for poor teams as poor players. Most of the really surprising ratings in this book are ones in which a highly visible player, somebody who plays for a championship team or perennial contender, is rated below a virtually unknown player from a poorer team. People will be surprised that I rate Dickie Thon higher than Ozzie Smith, surprised that I rate just about everybody higher than Charlie Moore, in large part because they have seen Ozzie Smith, and they have seen Charlie Moore, and they are aware of what those players can do, when they are not equally aware of what other players can do. Lord, do you think Charlie Moore was the only right fielder in the American League who ever cut loose a good throw? To watch the World Series, you'd have thought he was. I think if Dickie Thon was on a championship team and Ozzie Smith was on a didn't-run-too-hard team, people would laugh at you for suggesting that Smith was a better all-around player.

Anyway, by overlooking those objections in the case of catchers, I am suggesting that the impact that the catcher has on the defensive play of his team is so large that it is fair, uniquely, to evaluate him by how well his team does. The logical implication is that the defensive impact of the catcher is larger than that of anyone else, even the shortstop. I'm not at all sure about that. But I am sure that the defensive won-lost method for catchers needed some adjustments, and these are the ones that I chose.

On a larger issue, I think that this method of analysis—studying the records of teams with and without somebody in the lineup—probably has far more potential than I have realized in the past. My attitude has always been that the impact of any one player on a team's won-lost record is fairly small, that the games he misses might be a non-random selection due to platooning or injuries at a time when the team was or was not playing well or "pattern resting" of one kind or another, or that by simple chance the impact of a player's absence from the lineup might not show up in the space of the 15 or 20 games a year that he missed. I think in retrospect that in saying these things I was doing something that I often lecture other people about doing, which is to focus on the problems that the method presents, rather than focusing on the potential that it has. That just blocks you from learning.

What is the probability that the Montreal Expos would play better in ten games with Gary Carter than in ten games without him? To figure that, I made the most conservative possible assumptions. I assume that the Expos would be able to replace him with a player with a .400 offensive won-lost percentage. I assumed that there would be no defensive decline. I assumed, naturally, that there would be no psychological effect of his absence.

Using these assumptions, I estimated that the Expos' offense would decline by 0.362 runs per game when he was out of the lineup. This would lower the Expos' won-lost percentage by about .043. In a ten-game stretch:

| | |
|---|---|
| Probability of Better Record with Carter: | .487 |
| Probability of Same Record with and without: | .174 |
| Probability of Better Record without Carter: | .339 |

Given more realistic assumptions—that the replacement player can't hit a lick, that there is a defensive drop-off as well as an offensive, that looking at the issue over the course of several years you should have a hundred or more "out games" to deal with—it would seem to me that the impact of the loss of such a player could not fail to show up in the records.

As to the problem of platooning...Again, it doesn't seem to be as prohibitive as all that. The abilities of the players seem to have a surprising tendency to show through. I presented with the teams the won-lost records of Toronto and San Francisco with everybody in and out of the lineup. In both cases, there were "advantage records" going both ways. Toronto, for example, had a better record with the left-handed Rance Mullinicks than with the right-handed Garth Iorg, but a better record with the right-handed Jesse Barfield than with the left-handed Hosken Powell. (Wonder what the odds are on a team platooning four people named Rance, Garth, Jesse and Hosken?)

Carrying it one step further, what if you kept track of the offensive decline and the defensive decline? If the offensive decline is larger than that which can reasonably be ascribed to the player's own hitting, then isn't that a way of measuring the psychological impact of his loss on the rest of the team? And if it isn't larger, then doesn't that make you wonder why?

That's intriguing, but it's small stuff, because we can evaluate offensive production awfully well anyway, having very well-designed statistics on the subject. The really exciting thing is the potential of such a method for analyzing defensive play. There is an awful lot that we don't know about defense. Suppose that we used the known and knowable facts of offensive ability to ascertain that the offensive decline when a given type of hitter—like say Mike Schmidt—is out of the lineup is 0.79 runs per game. We know so much about offense that, applying whatever controls turn out to be necessary, we have to be able to do that. Suppose, then, that we apply exactly the same methods to find the defensive decline when a *defensive* star is out of the lineup? How many runs does that cost you? Make a list of all the Gold Glove winners from 1970 to the present, and at each position you will have hundreds of games when a Gold Glove defensive player was out of the lineup. Find those games, and figure out how much of an increase there is in runs allowed when the player is out of the lineup. At each position, I assure you, you will find an increase in runs allowed when the Gold Glover is out of the lineup. This would answer a whole lot of questions. How many runs does a Gold Glove shortstop save for his team, on average? A Gold Glove catcher? What is the defensive value of a good second baseman as opposed to a good third baseman? How large is the defensive difference as opposed to the offensive difference?

I get letters every week telling me that, in compiling the ratings, I underestimate defense and overrate the good hitters as opposed to the glove men. People love to say that it doesn't matter that much what a second baseman hits, because his glove work is so much more important than his hitting. My reply is always (when I get around to replying, which is certainly not always) that 1) I used to think the same thing, before I studied the issue; 2) how do you know this, and 3) prove it. Nobody has ever been able to. Sabermetrics is a science; it's not a bull session. I only write like it was bull-session because I don't like the way scientists write.

But now I will go one step further, and tell you *how* you can prove it. I will reverse my position, admit that I was wrong, acknowledge that defense is more important than offense at second base, if you do one simple thing: Prove to me that the defensive loss when a slick-fielding second baseman is out of the lineup is larger than the offensive loss when a good-hitting second baseman is out, and you win the argument.

# CATCHERS

### 1. *Gary CARTER, Montreal (28-14)*

Had the best defensive won-lost percentage of any catcher in baseball, as he did a year ago. I wonder who saves more runs for his team, Carter or Ozzie Smith? It would be close . . . in the last two years, the Expos are 6-14 (.300) with Carter out of the lineup . . . I think he was obviously the best player in the National League in 1982, and that he is one of the six greatest catchers ever to play the game (Bench, Berra, Dickey, Cochrane, Campanella) . . . you've got to wonder how long he can catch 150 games a year without damaging his career. (Offensive 18-9; Defensive 10-5)

### 2. *Terry KENNEDY, San Diego (25-17)*

The offensive portion of his won-lost mark (18-9) matches Carter's for the two seasons combined; his defense is getting there . . . he no longer reminds one of Milt May, at all. May got to the stage that Kennedy was at a year ago, but then never got beyond it . . . His arm is not great, but Williams uses control-type pitchers who negate the running game . . . The Padres are 9-1 in the games that Doug Gwosdz has started over the last two years. (18-9, 7-8)

### 3. *Lance PARRISH, Detroit (22-16)*

I mentioned a year ago that the Tigers were 18-3 (in '81) in games that Parrish did not start. Both I and a researcher for *Sports Illustrated* went over a list of those 21 games, and couldn't find any pattern that would explain this, no tendency to have Fahey catch Jack Morris's games or anything like that.

Well, it happened again last year. With Parrish as the starting catcher, the Tigers were 61-66, a .480 team; without him they were 22-13, .629. That's 40-16 without Parrish over two years; sub-.500 by nine games with him. How do you explain something like that?

I don't know if this is fair or not, but I remember a couple of years ago when the Tigers started the season with Roger Craig calling pitches from the bench. Doesn't that strike you as an expression of a lack of confidence in Parrish's ability to call a game? The Tigers had a 3.92 ERA with Parrish as a starting catcher, 2.98 with Wockenfuss, 3.84 with Fahey.

In some measure this is a quibble. We can prove that Parrish is an outstanding hitter, we can prove that he cuts off the running game, we can see how well he blocks the plate. We cannot prove that he is or is not an inept handler of pitchers, and so we have to rate him high. But if it's causing you to lose games, it's no quibble. (14-10; 8-6)

### 4. *Bo DIAZ, Philadelphia (19-13)*

Pat Corrales last spring described Bo Diaz as the best young catcher in baseball. Also, one might add, the *oldest* young catcher in baseball. Diaz is now 30, a year younger than Darrell Porter, a year older than Gary Carter. But Corrales deserves a lot of credit for this remarkable season. Corrales got in Diaz' corner years ago, has been telling anybody who would listen that Diaz was going to be an outstanding catcher. You can't reasonably dissociate Corrales' enthusiastic support for Diaz from the season that he had, but many people never make the connection at all, and instead blame Corrales for burning out Diaz, by not giving him more days off in August. O.K., Diaz did collapse late in the year, so that's fair, but on balance he had a season that was far above any reasonable expectation. (13-7; 6-6)

### 5. *Jim SUNDBERG, Texas (20-18)*

Holds the Texas franchise records for games played, at-bats, hits, doubles, triples and total bases. Will add the RBI record this summer with his thirty-first, giving him 462 in his career (Toby Harrah had 461 as a Ranger).

Cut to 131 games caught last year; could be reasonably described as the hardest-working catcher ever, with six seasons catching 90% of his team's games . . . there are more catchers around now catching 140 or 145 games or 150 or 155 than there have ever been. You could attribute this to better protective gear, or possibly draw a link to free agency (see comment on Dodgers). . . . Sundberg has gone through a mid-summer swoon in his hitting every year since 1979. Last year was classic: he hit .345 in April, .265 in May, but .215 in June, only .160 in July, then recovered to .255, .295 in August and September. That has been his pattern; in '80 he hit .313 in April, .300 in May, but .152 in June; he hit .210 in June of '79, .208 in June of '77. (13-11; 8-6)

### 6. *Carlton FISK, Chicago White Sox (20-18)*

Arm came back somewhat last year; defensive rating also helped by the change in the defensive won-lost percentage system . . . stole 17 bases in 19 attempts . . . even I approve of that kind of base stealing. (13-11; 8-6)

### 7. *Tony PENA, Pittsburgh (17-15)*

Seems to take stolen base attempts as a personal insult . . . the Pirates' best hitter against lefthanders. The last two years has hit .338, .342 against lefthanders, with .281 and .282 averages against righthanders, and last year hit seven home runs against lefties, which is more than any other three Pirates combined. His home run rates were 1 per 16 at-bats against lefties, 1 per 92 against righthanders. There is no question but what a lefty should walk Pena and pitch to Jason Thompson. Against righthanders Thompson hit 21 points higher and had seven times as much power. But against lefties, Antonio hit 110 points higher with nine times as much power as Thompson. . . The two great young catchers in the N.L., Pena and Terry Kennedy, both have the same birthday. . . . Pena still has a lot of rough edges in his defense . . . wonder why the Pirates signed Tenace? They've already got three young catchers, four if you count Harper. Maybe they're going to play him in right field. . . (11-9; 6-6)

### 8. *Alan ASHBY, Houston (16-14)*

Has made a remarkable metamorphosis since he began just four or five years ago as a .210-hitting glove man. He started hitting for a decent average, became a good judge of the strike zone, and last year he hit 12 homers in 399 at-bats. But now his glove work has gone to pot; opponents stole 1.16 bases a game against him (Milt May was 1.17, the worst in the leagues), and the team played way better with Pujols or Knicely in the lineup than they did with Ashby. (11-7; 5-7)

### 9. *Darrell PORTER, St. Louis (14-12)*

Well Jeez, Darrell, if you were going to win the World Series for somebody, why couldn't it have been for us? We're the ones who took you in when you were down and out, watched you grow into a star, stayed behind you and poured out our warmth and friendship when you had your troubles. You go put yourself in an institution and not one joke did I ever hear about it in Kansas City. You had a miserable year for us, we didn't boo you.

The national media chose Willie Wilson to be the goat in the 1980 World Series, but anybody who has studied the scoresheets knows who really lost that series for the Royals. Twice you come tiptoeing into home plate like an old lady trying to sneak into bed with the gardener; you bat eight times with men on base and don't drive in one damn run, and you don't throw worth a hoot. We didn't need you to be the series MVP—Amos was taking care of that—we just needed you to do your part. And then the St. Louis fans give you absolute hell for two years, and you give them a World's Championship—their (ouch) ninth. There's no justice. (9-7; 5-5)

### 10. *Milt MAY, San Francisco (17-16)*

He is very far from the Earl Weaver-type catcher that I would suspect Robinson may be looking for, a good handler of pitchers who can keep the double play in order. But Robinson doesn't have one of those; May is the best he has. (12-8; 6-7)

### 11. *John STEARNS, New York (15-14)*

Does this say "Mets" all over it? John Stearns had 103 hits last year, and vaulted from tenth to seventh on the list of the Mets' leaders. The men he passed were Rusty Staub, Tommy Agee and Wayne Garrett... (10-8, 4-5)

### 12. *Rick DEMPSEY, Baltimore (16-16)*

Still has the best career OSB rate in the majors, allowing .45 stolen bases per game (.46 in '82)...probably had his best offensive season in '82... hit .344 in day games. (8-10; 8-6)

### *13. Mike SCIOSCIA, Los Angeles (16-17)*

His year wasn't all *that* bad. He walked enough to have an on-base percentage over .300 (Yeager's was .295) and also drove in more runs per at-bat than Yeager. . . . Yeager does have an edge defensively, but I still think Scioscia's going to be a good player. (8-11; 7-7)

### *14. Ted SIMMONS, Milwaukee (19-21)*

The year, when you look at it closely, isn't all that good. . . . He had 97 RBI, but batting behind three players who had 616 hits and 155 walks, how impressive is that? His .312 on-base percentage is about the same as Scioscia's, his power wasn't tremendous, and he grounded into 20 double plays. He's a good hitter, but way behind Parrish and Carter and Stearns and Diaz and Kennedy, and not any better than Pena, Porter, Ashby and Fisk. When you combine that with the dismal '81 season, you get this rating. . .

One of the many wonderful moments in the movie *Ragtime* occurs just after the terrorist group has seized the library, and Jimmy Cagney, the police chief, has arrived on the scene. A stranger breaks through the crowd and informs Cagney with great urgency that he is curator of the library, and that it is a priceless collection that must be handled with the utmost of care. Well, says Cagney, why don't you go tell those fellows that? To which the poor man replies, are you trying to be funny? And Cagney replies, my good man, so long as those guys are in there, you are not the cur-a-tor of anything.

I was just amazed last summer by the intensity of the anti-Herzog, pro-Simmons sentiment in St. Louis. The Cardinals had the best record in the division in '81 and were in contention all the way last year, but every time they lost two games in a row all the Simba-ites would come out of the woodwork.

But look at the situation, as it must have looked to Herzog. You've got a highly talented team that isn't winning. The team doesn't hustle; it doesn't execute fundamentals; it doesn't play very good defense. You've got a player who is universally recognized as the leader of that team. He is a public idol. He is on the board of directors of the art museum. He is, reportedly, good buddies with the owner. He is a .300 hitter with power. But, unfortunately, he is a catcher, and he is not a good one. So you sign another catcher, and you tell him that, for the good of the team, he is going to have to move. And he says, "No, I won't do it. The hell with what's good for the team." What are you going to do?

I don't know what you'd do, but I know what I would do. If I had to trade that man for five cents on the dollar, I'd trade him. You don't have to be in baseball to relate to that circumstance. Suppose that you are the new manager of an office, or a loading dock, or the new plant manager in a factory, and things aren't running worth a hoot, and people are bitching and moaning a lot instead of working together, and you approach your highest-paid employee, who is also the most popular, visible man in the organization, and who is also a friend of your boss, and you tell him that you're going to assign him some different duties. And he tells you to stick it. What are you going to do?

*De facto* authority, that is the message. You either get rid of that son of a bitch, or you accept the fact that he is running the show and you are not. If Whitey Herzog didn't have the guts to run Ted Simmons out of St. Louis, he might as well have quit on the spot. Because if he didn't, from that moment on he was not the man-a-ger of anything. (13-14; 6-7)

### *15. Jody DAVIS, Chicago (14-15)*

The Cubs may be shaping up as a decent up-the-middle team. Well, it's premature to talk about it that way, I guess, but they've got three real good "maybes" up the center of the diamond—Davis, Mel Hall in center, Sandberg as a shortstop or second baseman. Davis figures to be in the top 10 at his position in a year or two, and that's championship quality. (8-9; 6-6)

### *16. Bruce BENEDICT, Atlanta (16-18)*

Hit .407 in September (24 for 59) . . . the Braves had a 67-43 record with Benedict in the lineup, which is the best record that any team in the majors had with their #1 catcher. They were 22-30 without him . . . would move up a lot if he could just keep his average around .275. (9-12;7-6)

### *17. Ernie WHITT, Toronto (11-12)*

The platoon combination of Whitt and Martinez totaled 21 homers, 79 RBI in 1982, after just 5 homers and 37 RBI in '81 . . . it's hard to see how they're going to repeat . . . Buck Martinez' stolen base rates are exceptionally good and have been getting better throughout the years. He didn't really throw that well when he was in Kansas City . . . the Blue Jays were a little better with Whitt in the lineup than Martinez. But they were both pretty amazing for a couple of true castoffs. (6-7; 5-5)

### *18. Bob BOONE, California (16-19)*

The man responsible for the Angels' fine record against base stealers was not Bob Boone, but Gene Mauch. Mauch insists that his pitchers eliminate the leg kick with runners on first, which makes it all but impossible to run against his teams. When he was in Minnesota, the Twins were the best team in the league against base stealers, although there was no publicity given to that category then. They had the second-best record in the league against base stealers in '78 (behind Texas), the best record in '79, the second-best record in '80 (behind New York). When Mauch moved to California, the best record in the league against base stealers moved to California. Butch Wynegar's opposition-stolen-base rate shot up 60% after Mauch left Minnesota, and Boone was being robbed blind in Philly, so it obviously is not the catcher, but Mauch's pitchers, who are doing this. (7-14; 8-6)

### *19. Alejandro TREVINO, Cincinnati (11-13)*

I think I referred to him somewhere as a terrible ballplayer, which is laying it on a bit thick. He's a pretty good defensive player and not the worst in the league or on the team with the bat. But he's about even with Steve Nicosia, and Nicosia doesn't seem to be going anywhere . . . the real trouble is, Trevino's too small to catch every day, and there's a big drop-off when he's out. Among them Trevino, Van Gorder and O'Berry had 537 at bats, hit .231 with 1 homer and 43 RBI, scored 33 runs and grounded into 21 double-plays. (6-8; 5-5)

***20. John WATHAN, Kansas City (15-19)***

The same injury that kept him from stealing 50 bases also kept him from setting a record for grounding into double plays. He had 26 double plays in 448 at bats, an amazing 1-for-17 ratio. He completes his swing with his ankles twisted, has to recover before he can get out of the box. If you watch his feet in batting practice it's real obvious . . . the rookie who filled in for him while he was out, Don Slaught, out-hit him .278–.271, hit as many home runs in 115 at-bats as Wathan did in 448, grounded into double plays less than half as often, made only one error in 43 games (Wathan had 10 in 120 games) and had a super 0.39 OSB game rate. Wathan handles the pitching staff better and the team played better with him in the lineup, so I'm not calling for the change to be made, but I'm not exactly dreading it when it has to be made, either . . . (9-13; 5-7)

***21. Ron HASSEY, Cleveland (11-14)***

I should have known that Bo Diaz was a good catcher when the Indians decided to keep Hassey and trade Diaz . . . Hassey's not bad, decent defense and can get on base. But he's been inconsistent with the bat, last year .194 before the All-Star break, .318 after. Is 30 years old and hasn't really established himself. (7-9; 5-4)

***22. Mike HEATH, Oakland (13-17)***

Is listed at 5'11", 176 pounds. Can that be right? I thought he was about 6'5", 220. . . 27 now, looks like he might settle in and have a Jim Hegan-type career. Excellent arm, blocks the plate well, but fielded .973 last year, which is awful. . . (7-12; 6-5)

***23. Rick SWEET, Seattle (6-7)***

Listed as a switch hitter, but was basically the left-handed part of a platoon arrangement. Went 2-for-24 against lefties . . . the team had a far better ERA (3.43) with Sweet as the starting catcher than they did with Bulling (3.98) or Essian (4.33). There is no obvious explanatory pattern, such as Sweet catching Bannister's games or something. (3-5; 3-2)

***24. Rick CERONE, New York Yankees (10-15)***

Cerone and Wynegar are a natural platoon combination, although they weren't used that way in '82 because one or the other was generally injured. Cerone hit .192 against righthanders, .280 against lefties; Wynegar hit .315 against righthanders, .250 against lefties. Wynegar has hit better against righthanders and Cerone against lefthanders every year, at least since 1979, when I began collecting data.

A lot of the public probably thinks that Cerone is the better player because he had the one good year in New York in '80, but as that season gets further behind us it begins to look more and more like a fluke. His other batting averages in the major leagues are .200, .223, .239, .244, .227; his highest average in the minors was .254. There just isn't anything else in his career to suggest that he is the kind of player who could hit .277 with 85 RBI. Wynegar is an inch behind him defensively, but a yard ahead of him offensively. He hits for a better average (.256 lifetime), walks three times as much, doesn't ground into as many double plays. By far the biggest difference between them is that Wynegar would get on base 50 or 60 more times over the course of a season . . . The Yankees were 41-46 (.471) with Cerone in the lineup, 31-28 (.525) with Wynegar. (5-11; 5-4)

***25. Rich GEDMAN, Boston (9-14)***

Again, the unrated player, Garry Allenson, rates the edge, this time because of defense. The Red Sox were a .588 team (50-35) and had a staff ERA of 3.73 with Allenson in the lineup, but were 37-39 and jumped to 4.48 with Gedman. Allenson also had a far better OSB rate. . . I'm not crazy about either one of them, but if Gedman doesn't hit, it's an easy choice. Although Allenson hit only .205, his on-base percentage and his RBI rate were still better than Gedman's. (6-8; 3-6)

***26. Tim LAUDNER, Minnesota (6-11)***

Name rhymes with "Podner." (4-6; 2-5)

## RECORDS WITH DIFFERENT STARTING CATCHERS

### AMERICAN LEAGUE

| *Baltimore* | W–L | Pct | ERA |
|---|---|---|---|
| Rick Dempsey | 61-40 | .604 | 3.83 |
| Joe Nolan | 33-28 | .541 | 4.25 |

| *Boston* | W–L | Pct | ERA |
|---|---|---|---|
| Gary Allenson | 50-35 | .588 | 3.73 |
| Rich Gedman | 37-39 | .487 | 4.48 |
| Marc Sullivan | 1-0 | 1.000 | 0.00 |
| Roger La Francois | 1-0 | 1.000 | 1.67 |

| *California* | W–L | Pct | ERA |
|---|---|---|---|
| Bob Boone | 84-55 | .604 | 3.80 |
| Joe Ferguson | 9-14 | .391 | 3.97 |

| *Chicago* | W–L | Pct | ERA |
|---|---|---|---|
| Carlton Fisk | 70-59 | .543 | 3.92 |
| Marc Hill | 14-12 | .538 | 3.51 |
| Marv Foley | 3-4 | .429 | 4.41 |

| *Cleveland* | W–L | Pct | ERA |
|---|---|---|---|
| Ron Hassey | 49-42 | .538 | 3.68 |
| Chris Bando | 21-28 | .429 | 4.48 |
| Bill Nahorodny | 8-14 | .364 | 5.09 |

| *Detroit* | W–L | Pct | ERA |
|---|---|---|---|
| Lance Parrish | 61-66 | .480 | 3.92 |
| Bill Fahey | 10- 7 | .588 | 2.98 |
| John Wockenfuss | 12- 6 | .667 | 3.84 |

| *Kansas City* | W–L | Pct | ERA |
|---|---|---|---|
| John Wathan | 69-47 | .595 | 3.94 |
| Don Slaught | 15-17 | .469 | 4.44 |
| Jamie Quirk | 6- 8 | .429 | 4.46 |

| *Milwaukee* | W–L | Pct | ERA |
|---|---|---|---|
| Ted Simmons | 72-47 | .605 | 3.81 |
| Ned Yost | 14-14 | .500 | 4.77 |
| Charlie Moore | 9- 6 | .600 | 3.95 |

| *Minnesota* | W–L | Pct | ERA |
|---|---|---|---|
| Tim Laudner | 34-55 | .382 | 4.79 |
| Sal Butera | 12-30 | .286 | 4.90 |
| Butch Wynegar | 9-14 | .391 | 4.91 |
| Ray Smith | 5- 3 | .625 | 2.44 |

| *New York* | W–L | Pct | ERA |
|---|---|---|---|
| Rick Cerone | 41-46 | .471 | 3.77 |
| Butch Wynegar | 31-28 | .525 | 4.22 |
| Barry Foote | 5- 8 | .385 | 4.34 |
| Domingo Ramos | 2- 1 | .667 | 4.47 |

| *Oakland* | W–L | Pct | ERA |
|---|---|---|---|
| Mike Heath | 34-43 | .442 | 4.22 |
| Jeff Newman | 26-39 | .400 | 4.96 |
| Bob Kearney | 8-12 | .400 | 4.43 |

| *Seattle* | W–L | Pct | ERA |
|---|---|---|---|
| Rick Sweet | 32-32 | .500 | 3.43 |
| Terry Bulling | 24-26 | .480 | 3.98 |
| Jim Essian | 17-25 | .405 | 4.33 |
| Orlando Mercado | 3- 2 | .600 | 3.56 |
| Dan Firova | 0- 1 | .000 | 9.00 |

| *Texas* | W–L | Pct | ERA |
|---|---|---|---|
| Jim Sundberg | 49-80 | .380 | 4.38 |
| Don Werner | 9-10 | .474 | 4.37 |
| Bobby Johnson | 6- 8 | .429 | 3.26 |

| *Toronto* | W–L | Pct | ERA |
|---|---|---|---|
| Ernie Whitt | 37-39 | .487 | 4.02 |
| Buck Martinez | 35-42 | .455 | 3.92 |
| Gene Petralli | 6- 3 | .667 | 3.69 |

## NATIONAL LEAGUE

| *Atlanta* | W–L | Pct | ERA |
|---|---|---|---|
| Bruce Benedict | 67-43 | .609 | 3.62 |
| Biff Pocoroba | 12-17 | .414 | 4.09 |
| Matt Sinatro | 10-13 | .435 | 4.46 |

| *Chicago* | W–L | Pct | ERA |
|---|---|---|---|
| Jody Davis | 56-64 | .467 | 4.10 |
| Keith Moreland | 16-23 | .410 | 3.38 |
| Butch Benton | 0- 1 | .000 | 4.00 |
| Larry Cox | 1- 1 | .500 | 3.71 |

| *Cincinnati* | W–L | Pct | ERA |
|---|---|---|---|
| Alex Trevino | 44-59 | .427 | 3.33 |
| Dave Van Gorder | 14-31 | .311 | 4.10 |
| Mike O'Berry | 3-11 | .214 | 4.68 |

| *Houston* | W–L | Pct | ERA |
|---|---|---|---|
| Alan Ashby | 40-50 | .444 | 3.75 |
| Luis Pujols | 29-27 | .518 | 3.00 |
| Alan Knicely | 8- 8 | .500 | 3.04 |

| *Los Angeles* | W–L | Pct | ERA |
|---|---|---|---|
| Mike Scioscia | 57-50 | .533 | 3.39 |
| Steve Yeager | 31-23 | .574 | 3.05 |
| Don Crow | 0- 1 | .000 | 1.00 |

| *Montreal* | W–L | Pct | ERA |
|---|---|---|---|
| Gary Carter | 82-69 | .543 | 3.13 |
| Tim Blackwell | 4- 6 | .400 | 5.42 |
| Brad Gulden | 0- 1 | .000 | 10.13 |

| *New York* | W–L | Pct | ERA |
|---|---|---|---|
| John Stearns | 32-47 | .405 | 4.06 |
| Ron Hodges | 28-37 | .431 | 3.87 |
| Bruce Bochy | 5-11 | .313 | 3.08 |
| Ronn Reynolds | 0- 2 | .000 | 3.71 |

| *Philadelphia* | W–L | Pct | ERA |
|---|---|---|---|
| Bo Diaz | 77-58 | .570 | 3.37 |
| Ozzie Virgil | 11-15 | .423 | 5.00 |
| Dave Roberts | 1- 0 | 1.000 | 0.00 |

| *Pittsburgh* | W–L | Pct | ERA |
|---|---|---|---|
| Tony Pena | 67-59 | .532 | 3.94 |
| Steve Nicosia | 15-17 | .469 | 3.35 |
| Adalberto Ortiz | 2- 2 | .500 | 3.55 |

| *St. Louis* | W–L | Pct | ERA |
|---|---|---|---|
| Darrell Porter | 62-46 | .574 | 3.36 |
| Gene Tenace | 19-13 | .592 | 3.45 |
| Orlando Sanchez | 2- 3 | .400 | 2.93 |
| Glenn Brummer | 9- 8 | .529 | 3.42 |

| *San Diego* | W–L | Pct | ERA |
|---|---|---|---|
| Terry Kennedy | 70-64 | .522 | 3.42 |
| Steve Swisher | 6-12 | .333 | 4.20 |
| Doug Gwosdz | 4- 0 | 1.000 | 1.25 |
| Ron Tingley | 1- 5 | .167 | 5.26 |

| *San Francisco* | W–L | Pct | ERA |
|---|---|---|---|
| Milt May | 58-43 | .574 | 3.52 |
| Bob Brenly | 24-24 | .500 | 3.76 |
| Jeff Ransom | 5- 8 | .385 | 4.19 |

## OPPOSITION STOLEN BASES

Categories in the Opposition Stolen Base records give the number of games each man started as a catcher, the number of bases stolen by the opposition in those games, and the per game average. Asterisks indicate league leadership.

**Gary ALLENSON**

| Year | Team | League | GS | SB | Avg |
|---|---|---|---|---|---|
| 1979 | Boston | A | 83 | 59 | .71 |
| 1980 | Boston | A | 19 | 11 | .58 |
| 1981 | Boston | A | 40 | 36 | .90 |
| 1982 | Boston | A | 86 | 41 | .48 |
| 4 years | | | 228 | 147 | .64 |

**Alan ASHBY**

| Year | Team | League | GS | SB | Avg |
|---|---|---|---|---|---|
| 1975 | Cleveland | A | 82 | 64 | .78 |
| 1976 | Cleveland | A | 73 | 75 | 1.03 |
| 1977 | Toronto | A | 121 | 67 | .56 |
| 1978 | Toronto | A | 79 | 51 | .65 |
| 1979 | Houston | N | 103 | 70 | .68 |
| 1980 | Houston | N | 105 | 100 | .95 |
| 1981 | Houston | N | 74 | 59 | .80 |
| 1982 | Houston | N | 90 | 104 | 1.16 |
| 8 years | | | 727 | 590 | .81 |

**Chris BANDO**

| Year | Team | League | GS | SB | Avg |
|---|---|---|---|---|---|
| 1981 | Cleveland | A | 8 | 4 | .50 |
| 1982 | Cleveland | A | 49 | 24 | .49 |
| 2 years | | | 57 | 28 | .49 |

**Bruce BENEDICT**

| Year | Team | League | GS | SB | Avg |
|---|---|---|---|---|---|
| 1978 | Atlanta | N | 16 | 15 | .94 |
| 1979 | Atlanta | N | 69 | 64 | .93 |
| 1980 | Atlanta | N | 111 | 81 | .73 |
| 1981 | Atlanta | N | 86 | 83 | .97 |
| 1982 | Atlanta | N | 111 | 96 | .86 |
| 5 years | | | 393 | 339 | .86 |

**Butch BENTON**

| Year | Team | League | GS | SB | Avg |
|---|---|---|---|---|---|
| 1980 | New York | N | 5 | 5 | 1.00 |
| 1982 | Chicago | N | 1 | 2 | 2.00 |
| 2 years | | | 6 | 7 | 1.17 |

**Tim BLACKWELL**

| Year | Team | League | GS | SB | Avg |
|---|---|---|---|---|---|
| 1975 | Boston | A | 37 | 35 | .95 |
| 1976 | Philadelphia | N | 2 | 3 | 1.50 |
| 1977 | Phil/Montreal | N | 5 | 13 | 2.60 |
| 1978 | Chicago | N | 34 | 28 | .82 |
| 1979 | Chicago | N | 39 | 36 | .92 |
| 1980 | Chicago | N | 93 | 92 | .99 |
| 1981 | Chicago | N | 47 | 63 | 1.34 |
| 1982 | Montreal | N | 8 | 14 | 1.75 |
| 8 years | | | 265 | 284 | 1.07 |

**Bruce BOCHY**

| Year | Team | League | GS | SB | Avg |
|---|---|---|---|---|---|
| 1978 | Houston | N | 45 | 46 | 1.02 |
| 1979 | Houston | N | 37 | 40 | 1.08 |
| 1980 | Houston | N | 2 | 1 | .50 |
| 1982 | New York | N | 16 | 16 | 1.00 |
| 4 years | | | 100 | 103 | 1.03 |

**Bob BOONE**

| Year | Team | League | GS | SB | Avg |
|---|---|---|---|---|---|
| 1975 | Philadelphia | N | 81 | 31 | .38 |
| 1976 | Philadelphia | N | 97 | 79 | .57 |
| 1977 | Philadelphia | N | 119 | 79 | .56 |
| 1978 | Philadelphia | N | 117 | 68 | .58 |
| 1979 | Philadelphia | N | 110 | 54 | .49* |
| 1980 | Philadelphia | N | 130 | 123 | .95 |
| 1981 | Philadelphia | N | 64 | 77 | 1.20 |
| 1982 | California | A | 138 | 48 | .35* |
| 8 years | | | 857 | 535 | .62 |

**Bob BRENLY**

| Year | Team | League | GS | SB | Avg |
|---|---|---|---|---|---|
| 1981 | San Francisco | N | 10 | 7 | .70 |
| 1982 | San Francisco | N | 48 | 53 | 1.10 |
| 2 years | | | 58 | 60 | 1.03 |

**Glenn BRUMMER**

| Year | Team | League | GS | SB | Avg |
|---|---|---|---|---|---|
| 1981 | St. Louis | N | 7 | 9 | 1.29 |
| 1982 | St. Louis | N | 15 | 11 | .73 |
| 2 years | | | 22 | 20 | .91 |

**Sal BUTERA**

| Year | Team | League | GS | SB | Avg |
|---|---|---|---|---|---|
| 1980 | Minnesota | A | 28 | 16 | .57 |
| 1981 | Minnesota | A | 51 | 23 | .45 |
| 1982 | Minnesota | A | 42 | 29 | .69 |
| 3 years | | | 121 | 68 | .56 |

**Gary CARTER**

| Year | Team | League | GS | SB | Avg |
|---|---|---|---|---|---|
| 1975 | Montreal | N | 55 | 21 | .38 |
| 1976 | Montreal | N | 54 | 27 | .50 |
| 1977 | Montreal | N | 142 | 110 | .77 |
| 1978 | Montreal | N | 147 | 80 | .54* |
| 1979 | Montreal | N | 135 | 75 | .56 |
| 1980 | Montreal | N | 146 | 94 | .64* |
| 1981 | Montreal | N | 99 | 53 | .54* |
| 1982 | Montreal | N | 154 | 106 | .69 |
| 8 years | | | 932 | 566 | .61 |

**Rick CERONE**

| Year | Team | League | GS | SB | Avg |
|---|---|---|---|---|---|
| 1975 | Cleveland | A | 3 | 2 | .67 |
| 1976 | Cleveland | A | 4 | 4 | 1.00 |
| 1977 | Toronto | A | 28 | 10 | .36 |
| 1978 | Toronto | A | 79 | 48 | .61 |
| 1979 | Toronto | A | 133 | 69 | .52 |
| 1980 | New York | A | 146 | 56 | .38* |
| 1981 | New York | A | 65 | 34 | .52 |
| 1982 | New York | A | 86 | 55 | .64 |
| 8 years | | | 544 | 278 | .51 |

**Larry COX**

| Year | Team | League | GS | SB | Avg |
|---|---|---|---|---|---|
| 1975 | Philadelphia | N | 1 | 0 | .00 |
| 1977 | Seattle | A | 30 | 27 | .90 |
| 1978 | Chicago | N | 40 | 31 | .78 |
| 1979 | Seattle | A | 87 | 79 | .91 |
| 1980 | Seattle | A | 86 | 60 | .70 |
| 1981 | Texas | A | 5 | 7 | 1.40 |
| 1982 | Chicago | N | 2 | 4 | 2.00 |
| 8 years | | | 251 | 208 | .83 |

**Donald CROW**

| Year | Team | League | GS | SB | Avg |
|---|---|---|---|---|---|
| 1982 | Los Angeles | N | 1 | 4 | 4.00 |

**Jody DAVIS**

| Year | Team | League | GS | SB | Avg |
|---|---|---|---|---|---|
| 1981 | Chicago | N | 53 | 38 | .72 |
| 1982 | Chicago | N | 120 | 93 | .78 |
| 2 years | | | 173 | 131 | .76 |

**Rick DEMPSEY**

| Year | Team | League | GS | SB | Avg |
|---|---|---|---|---|---|
| 1975 | New York | A | 11 | 8 | .73 |
| 1976 | NY/Baltimore | A | 59 | 27 | .46 |
| 1977 | Baltimore | A | 84 | 30 | .36 |
| 1978 | Baltimore | A | 130 | 62 | .48* |
| 1979 | Baltimore | A | 113 | 47 | .42* |
| 1980 | Baltimore | A | 95 | 50 | .53 |
| 1981 | Baltimore | A | 72 | 32 | .44 |
| 1982 | Baltimore | A | 101 | 46 | .46 |
| 8 years | | | 665 | 302 | .45 |

**Bo DIAZ**

| Year | Team | League | GS | SB | Avg |
|---|---|---|---|---|---|
| 1978 | Cleveland | A | 39 | 23 | .59 |
| 1979 | Cleveland | A | 11 | 11 | 1.00 |
| 1980 | Cleveland | A | 52 | 40 | .77 |
| 1981 | Cleveland | A | 42 | 20 | .48 |
| 1982 | Philadelphia | N | 135 | 115 | .85 |
| 5 years | | | 279 | 209 | .75 |

**Jim ESSIAN**

| Year | Team | League | GS | SB | Avg |
|---|---|---|---|---|---|
| 1976 | Chicago | A | 64 | 45 | .70 |
| 1977 | Chicago | A | 105 | 75 | .71 |
| 1978 | Oakland | A | 88 | 57 | .65 |
| 1979 | Oakland | A | 66 | 60 | .91 |
| 1980 | Oakland | A | 66 | 30 | .45 |
| 1981 | Chicago | A | 17 | 11 | .65 |
| 1982 | Seattle | A | 43 | 53 | 1.23 |
| 7 years | | | 449 | 331 | .74 |

**Bill FAHEY**

| Year | Team | League | GS | SB | Avg |
|---|---|---|---|---|---|
| 1975 | Texas | A | 10 | 12 | 1.20 |
| 1976 | Texas | A | 23 | 21 | .91 |
| 1977 | Texas | A | 21 | 17 | .81 |
| 1979 | San Diego | N | 54 | 41 | .76 |
| 1980 | San Diego | N | 67 | 66 | .99 |
| 1981 | Detroit | A | 19 | 13 | .68 |
| 1982 | Detroit | A | 17 | 12 | .71 |
| 7 years | | | 211 | 182 | .86 |

**Joe FERGUSON**

| Year | Team | League | GS | SB | Avg |
|---|---|---|---|---|---|
| 1975 | Los Angeles | N | 31 | 13 | .42 |
| 1976 | LA/St. Louis | N | 56 | 35 | .62 |
| 1977 | Houston | N | 117 | 92 | .79 |
| 1978 | Houston/LA | N | 102 | 69 | .68 |
| 1979 | Los Angeles | N | 62 | 52 | .84 |
| 1980 | Los Angeles | N | 50 | 56 | 1.12 |
| 1981 | California | A | 8 | 5 | .62 |
| 1982 | California | A | 24 | 18 | .75 |
| 8 years | | | 450 | 340 | .76 |

**Carlton FISK**

| Year | Team | League | GS | SB | Avg |
|---|---|---|---|---|---|
| 1975 | Boston | A | 68 | 34 | .50 |
| 1976 | Boston | A | 130 | 89 | .68* |
| 1977 | Boston | A | 149 | 61 | .41 |
| 1978 | Boston | A | 150 | 102 | .68 |
| 1979 | Boston | A | 34 | 24 | .71 |
| 1980 | Boston | A | 112 | 73 | .65 |
| 1981 | Chicago | A | 89 | 64 | .72 |
| 1982 | Chicago | A | 129 | 79 | .61 |
| 8 years | | | 861 | 526 | .61 |

**Marvis FOLEY**

| Year | Team | League | GS | SB | Avg |
|---|---|---|---|---|---|
| 1978 | Chicago | A | 9 | 13 | 1.44 |
| 1979 | Chicago | A | 29 | 26 | .90 |
| 1980 | Chicago | A | 40 | 30 | .75 |
| 1982 | Chicago | A | 7 | 5 | .71 |
| 4 years | | | 85 | 74 | .87 |

**Barry FOOTE**

| Year | Team | League | GS | SB | Avg |
|---|---|---|---|---|---|
| 1975 | Montreal | N | 103 | 51 | .50 |
| 1976 | Montreal | N | 91 | 62 | .68 |
| 1977 | Montreal/Phil | N | 17 | 7 | .41 |
| 1978 | Philadelphia | N | 11 | 8 | .73 |
| 1979 | Chicago | N | 121 | 75 | .62 |
| 1980 | Chicago | N | 52 | 44 | .85 |
| 1981 | Chicago | N | 6 | 2 | .33 |
| 1981 | New York | A | 31 | 23 | .74 |
| 1982 | New York | A | 14 | 7 | .50 |
| 8 years | | | 446 | 279 | .63 |

**Rich GEDMAN**

| Year | Team | League | GS | SB | Avg |
|---|---|---|---|---|---|
| 1980 | Boston | A | 2 | 2 | 1.00 |
| 1981 | Boston | A | 57 | 51 | .89 |
| 1982 | Boston | A | 74 | 60 | .81 |
| 3 years | | | 133 | 113 | .85 |

**Doug GWOSDZ**

| Year | Team | League | GS | SB | Avg |
|---|---|---|---|---|---|
| 1981 | San Diego | N | 6 | 3 | .50 |
| 1982 | San Diego | N | 4 | 1 | .25 |
| 2 years | | | 10 | 4 | .40 |

**Ron HASSEY**

| Year | Team | League | GS | SB | Avg |
|---|---|---|---|---|---|
| 1978 | Cleveland | A | 23 | 18 | .78 |
| 1979 | Cleveland | A | 61 | 50 | .82 |
| 1980 | Cleveland | A | 103 | 77 | .75 |
| 1981 | Cleveland | A | 53 | 23 | .43 |
| 1982 | Cleveland | A | 91 | 85 | .93 |
| 5 years | | | 331 | 253 | .76 |

**Mike HEATH**

| Year | Team | League | GS | SB | Avg |
|---|---|---|---|---|---|
| 1978 | New York | A | 23 | 12 | .52 |
| 1979 | Oakland | A | 18 | 13 | .72 |
| 1980 | Oakland | A | 43 | 23 | .53 |
| 1981 | Oakland | A | 76 | 34 | .45 |
| 1982 | Oakland | A | 77 | 37 | .48 |
| 5 years | | | 237 | 119 | .50 |

**Marc HILL**

| Year | Team | League | GS | SB | Avg |
|---|---|---|---|---|---|
| 1975 | San Francisco | N | 47 | 31 | .66 |
| 1976 | San Francisco | N | 41 | 27 | .66 |
| 1977 | San Francisco | N | 95 | 84 | .88 |
| 1978 | San Francisco | N | 105 | 90 | .86 |
| 1979 | San Francisco | N | 53 | 42 | .79 |
| 1980 | SF/Seattle | N/A | 33 | 25 | .76 |
| 1982 | Chicago | A | 26 | 17 | .65 |
| 7 years | | | 400 | 316 | .79 |

**Ron HODGES**

| Year | Team | League | GS | SB | Avg |
|---|---|---|---|---|---|
| 1975 | New York | N | 8 | 8 | 1.00 |
| 1976 | New York | N | 44 | 28 | .64 |
| 1977 | New York | N | 22 | 20 | .91 |
| 1978 | New York | N | 25 | 25 | 1.00 |
| 1979 | New York | N | 17 | 14 | .82 |
| 1980 | New York | N | 9 | 9 | 1.00 |
| 1981 | New York | N | 5 | 7 | 1.40 |
| 1982 | New York | N | 65 | 63 | .97 |
| 8 years | | | 195 | 174 | .89 |

**Bob JOHNSON**

| Year | Team | League | GS | SB | Avg |
|---|---|---|---|---|---|
| 1981 | Texas | A | 3 | 2 | .67 |
| 1982 | Texas | A | 14 | 6 | .43 |
| 2 years | | | 17 | 8 | .47 |

**Bob KEARNEY**

| Year | Team | League | GS | SB | Avg |
|---|---|---|---|---|---|
| 1982 | Oakland | A | 20 | 12 | .60 |

**Terry KENNEDY**

| Year | Team | League | GS | SB | Avg |
|---|---|---|---|---|---|
| 1978 | St. Louis | N | 9 | 5 | .56 |
| 1979 | St. Louis | N | 27 | 21 | .78 |
| 1980 | St. Louis | N | 38 | 50 | 1.32 |
| 1981 | San Diego | N | 97 | 84 | .87 |
| 1982 | San Diego | N | 133 | 102 | .77 |
| 5 years | | | 304 | 262 | .86 |

**Alan KNICELY**

| Year | Team | League | GS | SB | Avg |
|---|---|---|---|---|---|
| 1981 | Houston | N | 1 | 0 | .00 |
| 1982 | Houston | N | 16 | 12 | .75 |
| 2 years | | | 17 | 12 | .71 |

**Roger LaFRANCOIS**

| Year | Team | League | GS | SB | Avg |
|---|---|---|---|---|---|
| 1982 | Boston | A | 1 | 0 | .00 |

**Tim LAUDNER**

| Year | Team | League | GS | SB | Avg |
|---|---|---|---|---|---|
| 1981 | Minnesota | A | 10 | 6 | .60 |
| 1982 | Minnesota | A | 89 | 74 | .83 |
| 2 years | | | 99 | 80 | .81 |

**Buck MARTINEZ**

| Year | Team | League | GS | SB | Avg |
|---|---|---|---|---|---|
| 1975 | Kansas City | A | 70 | 66 | .94 |
| 1976 | Kansas City | A | 86 | 77 | .90 |
| 1977 | Kansas City | A | 22 | 14 | .64 |
| 1978 | Milwaukee | A | 85 | 44 | .52 |
| 1979 | Milwaukee | A | 67 | 35 | .52 |
| 1980 | Milwaukee | A | 74 | 37 | .50 |
| 1981 | Toronto | A | 44 | 25 | .57 |
| 1982 | Toronto | A | 80 | 30 | .38 |
| 8 years | | | 528 | 328 | .62 |

**Milt MAY**

| Year | Team | League | GS | SB | Avg |
|---|---|---|---|---|---|
| 1975 | Houston | N | 99 | 66 | .67 |
| 1976 | Detroit | A | 6 | 4 | .67 |
| 1977 | Detroit | A | 108 | 62 | .57 |
| 1978 | Detroit | A | 88 | 54 | .61 |
| 1979 | Detroit/Chicago | A | 61 | 42 | .69 |
| 1980 | San Francisco | N | 94 | 89 | .95 |
| 1981 | San Francisco | N | 86 | 87 | 1.01 |
| 1982 | San Francisco | N | 101 | 118 | 1.17 |
| 8 years | | | 643 | 522 | .81 |

**Orlando MERCADO**

| Year | Team | League | GS | SB | Avg |
|---|---|---|---|---|---|
| 1982 | Seattle | A | 5 | 3 | .60 |

**Charlie MOORE**

| Year | Team | League | GS | SB | Avg |
|---|---|---|---|---|---|
| 1975 | Milwaukee | A | 40 | 29 | .72 |
| 1976 | Milwaukee | A | 46 | 44 | .96 |
| 1977 | Milwaukee | A | 118 | 81 | .69 |
| 1978 | Milwaukee | A | 74 | 36 | .49 |
| 1979 | Milwaukee | A | 89 | 61 | .69 |
| 1980 | Milwaukee | A | 78 | 39 | .50 |
| 1981 | Milwaukee | A | 29 | 18 | .62 |
| 1982 | Milwaukee | A | 17 | 5 | .29 |
| 8 years | | | 491 | 313 | .64 |

**Keith MORELAND**

| Year | Team | League | GS | SB | Avg |
|---|---|---|---|---|---|
| 1979 | Philadelphia | N | 12 | 14 | 1.17 |
| 1980 | Philadelphia | N | 31 | 38 | 1.23 |
| 1981 | Philadelphia | N | 42 | 44 | 1.05 |
| 1982 | Chicago | N | 39 | 54 | 1.38 |
| 4 years | | | 124 | 150 | 1.21 |

**Bill NAHARODNY**

| Year | Team | League | GS | SB | Avg |
|---|---|---|---|---|---|
| 1977 | Chicago | A | 7 | 6 | .86 |
| 1978 | Chicago | A | 98 | 80 | .82 |
| 1979 | Chicago | A | 44 | 48 | 1.09 |
| 1980 | Atlanta | N | 38 | 42 | 1.08 |
| 1982 | Cleveland | N | 22 | 13 | .59 |
| 5 years | | | 209 | 188 | .90 |

**Jeff NEWMAN**

| Year | Team | League | GS | SB | Avg |
|---|---|---|---|---|---|
| 1976 | Oakland | A | 24 | 13 | .54 |
| 1977 | Oakland | A | 41 | 27 | .66 |
| 1978 | Oakland | A | 44 | 29 | .66 |
| 1979 | Oakland | A | 78 | 43 | .55 |
| 1980 | Oakland | A | 53 | 33 | .62 |
| 1981 | Oakland | A | 33 | 15 | .45 |
| 1982 | Oakland | A | 65 | 48 | .74 |
| 7 years | | | 338 | 208 | .62 |

**Steve NICOSIA**

| Year | Team | League | GS | SB | Avg |
|---|---|---|---|---|---|
| 1978 | Pittsburgh | N | 1 | 2 | 2.00 |
| 1979 | Pittsburgh | N | 54 | 28 | .52 |
| 1980 | Pittsburgh | N | 52 | 36 | .69 |
| 1981 | Pittsburgh | N | 49 | 38 | .78 |
| 1982 | Pittsburgh | N | 31 | 22 | .71 |
| 5 years | | | 187 | 126 | .67 |

**Joe NOLAN**

| Year | Team | League | GS | SB | Avg |
|---|---|---|---|---|---|
| 1977 | Atlanta | N | 13 | 19 | 1.46 |
| 1978 | Atlanta | N | 52 | 55 | 1.06 |
| 1979 | Atlanta | N | 58 | 78 | 1.34 |
| 1980 | Atl/Cincin | N | 45 | 71 | 1.58 |
| 1981 | Cincinnati | N | 63 | 67 | 1.06 |
| 1982 | Baltimore | A | 62 | 52 | .84 |
| 6 years | | | 293 | 342 | 1.17 |

**Mike O'BERRY**

| Year | Team | League | GS | SB | Avg |
|---|---|---|---|---|---|
| 1979 | Boston | A | 19 | 11 | .58 |
| 1980 | Chicago | N | 15 | 15 | 1.00 |
| 1981 | Cincinnati | N | 38 | 31 | .82 |
| 1982 | Cincinnati | N | 14 | 8 | .57 |
| 4 years | | | 86 | 65 | .76 |

**Adalberto ORTIZ**

| Year | Team | League | GS | SB | Avg |
|---|---|---|---|---|---|
| 1982 | Pittsburgh | N | 4 | 2 | .50 |

**Lance PARRISH**

| Year | Team | League | GS | SB | Avg |
|---|---|---|---|---|---|
| 1978 | Detroit | A | 74 | 31 | .42 |
| 1979 | Detroit | A | 135 | 71 | .53 |
| 1980 | Detroit | A | 114 | 56 | .49 |
| 1981 | Detroit | A | 88 | 44 | .50 |
| 1982 | Detroit | A | 127 | 51 | .40 |
| 5 years | | | 538 | 253 | .47 |

**Tony PENA**

| Year | Team | League | GS | SB | Avg |
|---|---|---|---|---|---|
| 1980 | Pittsburgh | N | 5 | 6 | 1.20 |
| 1981 | Pittsburgh | N | 54 | 28 | .50 |
| 1982 | Pittsburgh | N | 127 | 78 | .61* |
| 3 years | | | 186 | 112 | .60 |

**Gene PETRALLI**

| Year | Team | League | GS | SB | Avg |
|---|---|---|---|---|---|
| 1982 | Toronto | A | 8 | 6 | .75 |

**Biff POCOROBA**

| Year | Team | League | GS | SB | Avg |
|---|---|---|---|---|---|
| 1975 | Atlanta | N | 50 | 59 | 1.18 |
| 1976 | Atlanta | N | 52 | 34 | .64 |
| 1977 | Atlanta | N | 86 | 101 | 1.17 |
| 1978 | Atlanta | N | 78 | 82 | 1.05 |
| 1979 | Atlanta | N | 6 | 7 | 1.17 |
| 1980 | Atlanta | N | 9 | 13 | 1.44 |
| 1981 | Atlanta | N | 6 | 3 | .50 |
| 1982 | Atlanta | N | 29 | 42 | 1.45 |
| 8 years | | | 316 | 341 | 1.08 |

**Darrell PORTER**

| Year | Team | League | GS | SB | Avg |
|---|---|---|---|---|---|
| 1975 | Milwaukee | A | 120 | 86 | .72 |
| 1976 | Milwaukee | A | 105 | 87 | .83 |
| 1977 | Kansas City | A | 121 | 60 | .50 |
| 1978 | Kansas City | A | 141 | 76 | .53 |
| 1979 | Kansas City | A | 141 | 64 | .45 |
| 1980 | Kansas City | A | 80 | 39 | .49 |
| 1981 | St. Louis | N | 51 | 41 | .80 |
| 1982 | St. Louis | N | 108 | 94 | .87 |
| 8 years | | | 867 | 547 | .63 |

**Luis PUJOLS**

| Year | Team | League | GS | SB | Avg |
|---|---|---|---|---|---|
| 1978 | Houston | N | 47 | 56 | 1.19 |
| 1979 | Houston | N | 22 | 18 | .82 |
| 1980 | Houston | N | 56 | 56 | 1.00 |
| 1981 | Houston | N | 35 | 23 | .66 |
| 1982 | Houston | N | 56 | 59 | 1.05 |
| 5 years | | | 216 | 212 | .98 |

**Jamie QUIRK**

| Year | Team | League | GS | SB | Avg |
|---|---|---|---|---|---|
| 1979 | Kansas City | A | 2 | 1 | .50 |
| 1980 | Kansas City | A | 11 | 13 | 1.18 |
| 1981 | Kansas City | A | 15 | 13 | .87 |
| 1982 | Kansas City | A | 14 | 11 | .79 |
| 4 years | | | 42 | 38 | .90 |

**Robert RAMOS**

| Year | Team | League | GS | SB | Avg |
|---|---|---|---|---|---|
| 1978 | Montreal | N | 1 | 1 | 1.00 |
| 1980 | Montreal | N | 9 | 9 | 1.00 |
| 1981 | Montreal | N | 9 | 10 | 1.11 |
| 1982 | New York | A | 3 | 1 | .33 |
| 4 years | | | 22 | 21 | .95 |

**Jeff RANSOM**

| Year | Team | League | GS | SB | Avg |
|---|---|---|---|---|---|
| 1981 | San Francisco | N | 3 | 5 | 1.67 |
| 1982 | San Francisco | N | 13 | 14 | 1.08 |
| 2 years | | | 16 | 19 | 1.19 |

**Ronn REYNOLDS**

| Year | Team | League | GS | SB | Avg |
|---|---|---|---|---|---|
| 1982 | New York | N | 2 | 1 | .50 |

**Dave ROBERTS**

| Year | Team | League | GS | SB | Avg |
|---|---|---|---|---|---|
| 1977 | San Diego | N | 43 | 36 | .84 |
| 1978 | San Diego | N | 30 | 15 | .50 |
| 1979 | Texas | A | 9 | 4 | .44 |
| 1980 | Texas | A | 16 | 11 | .69 |
| 1982 | Philadelphia | N | 1 | 3 | 3.00 |
| 5 years | | | 99 | 69 | .70 |

**Orlando SANCHEZ**

| Year | Team | League | GS | SB | Avg |
|---|---|---|---|---|---|
| 1981 | St. Louis | N | 9 | 8 | .89 |
| 1982 | St. Louis | N | 6 | 11 | 1.83 |
| 2 years | | | 15 | 19 | 1.27 |

**Mike SCIOSCIA**

| Year | Team | League | GS | SB | Avg |
|---|---|---|---|---|---|
| 1980 | Los Angeles | N | 44 | 49 | 1.11 |
| 1981 | Los Angeles | N | 87 | 64 | .74 |
| 1982 | Los Angeles | N | 107 | 84 | .79 |
| 3 years | | | 238 | 197 | .83 |

**Ted SIMMONS**

| Year | Team | League | GS | SB | Avg |
|---|---|---|---|---|---|
| 1975 | St. Louis | N | 148 | 99 | .67 |
| 1976 | St. Louis | N | 107 | 62 | .58 |
| 1977 | St. Louis | N | 139 | 96 | .69 |
| 1978 | St. Louis | N | 119 | 120 | 1.01 |
| 1979 | St. Louis | N | 118 | 100 | .85 |
| 1980 | St. Louis | N | 121 | 116 | .96 |
| 1981 | Milwaukee | A | 73 | 47 | .64 |
| 1982 | Milwaukee | A | 119 | 94 | .79 |
| 8 years | | | 944 | 734 | .78 |

**Matt SINATRO**

| Year | Team | League | GS | SB | Avg |
|---|---|---|---|---|---|
| 1981 | Atlanta | N | 10 | 4 | .40 |
| 1982 | Atlanta | N | 22 | 26 | 1.18 |
| 2 years | | | 32 | 30 | .94 |

**Don SLAUGHT**

| Year | Team | League | GS | SB | Avg |
|---|---|---|---|---|---|
| 1982 | Kansas City | A | 31 | 12 | .39 |

**Ray SMITH**

| Year | Team | League | GS | SB | Avg |
|---|---|---|---|---|---|
| 1981 | Minnesota | A | 13 | 7 | .54 |
| 1982 | Minnesota | A | 8 | 3 | .38 |
| 2 years | | | 21 | 10 | .48 |

**John STEARNS**

| Year | Team | League | GS | SB | Avg |
|---|---|---|---|---|---|
| 1975 | New York | N | 46 | 40 | .87 |
| 1976 | New York | N | 29 | 17 | .59 |
| 1977 | New York | N | 116 | 85 | .73 |
| 1978 | New York | N | 134 | 87 | .65 |
| 1979 | New York | N | 113 | 99 | .88 |
| 1980 | New York | N | 70 | 60 | .86 |
| 1981 | New York | N | 63 | 44 | .70 |
| 1982 | New York | N | 79 | 66 | .84 |
| 8 years | | | 650 | 498 | .77 |

**Marc SULLIVAN**

| Year | Team | League | GS | SB | Avg |
|---|---|---|---|---|---|
| 1982 | Boston | A | 1 | 0 | .00 |

**Jim SUNDBERG**

| Year | Team | League | GS | SB | Avg |
|---|---|---|---|---|---|
| 1975 | Texas | A | 149 | 78 | .52 |
| 1976 | Texas | A | 134 | 98 | .73 |
| 1977 | Texas | A | 136 | 47 | .35* |
| 1978 | Texas | A | 146 | 74 | .51 |
| 1979 | Texas | A | 144 | 74 | .51 |
| 1980 | Texas | A | 147 | 101 | .69 |
| 1981 | Texas | A | 97 | 40 | .41* |
| 1982 | Texas | A | 129 | 74 | .57 |
| 8 years | | | 1082 | 586 | .54 |

**Richard SWEET**

| Year | Team | League | GS | SB | Avg |
|---|---|---|---|---|---|
| 1982 | Seattle | A | 64 | 33 | .52 |

**Gene TENACE**

| Year | Team | League | GS | SB | Avg |
|---|---|---|---|---|---|
| 1975 | Oakland | A | 110 | 68 | .62 |
| 1976 | Oakland | A | 62 | 43 | .69 |
| 1977 | San Diego | N | 87 | 70 | .80 |
| 1978 | San Diego | N | 56 | 47 | .84 |
| 1979 | San Diego | N | 78 | 41 | .53 |
| 1980 | San Diego | N | 81 | 75 | .93 |
| 1981 | St. Louis | N | 36 | 30 | .83 |
| 1982 | St. Louis | N | 33 | 31 | .94 |
| 8 years | | | 543 | 405 | .75 |

**Ron TINGLEY**

| Year | Team | League | GS | SB | Avg |
|---|---|---|---|---|---|
| 1982 | San Diego | N | 7 | 13 | 1.86 |

**Alejandro TREVINO**

| Year | Team | League | GS | SB | Avg |
|---|---|---|---|---|---|
| 1978 | New York | N | 3 | 0 | .00 |
| 1979 | New York | N | 33 | 22 | .67 |
| 1980 | New York | N | 78 | 58 | .74 |
| 1981 | New York | N | 37 | 17 | .46 |
| 1982 | Cincinnati | N | 104 | 89 | .86 |
| 5 years | | | 255 | 186 | .73 |

**David VAN GORDER**

| Year | Team | League | GS | SB | Avg |
|---|---|---|---|---|---|
| 1982 | Cincinnati | N | 44 | 50 | 1.14 |

**Osvaldo VIRGIL**

| Year | Team | League | GS | SB | Avg |
|---|---|---|---|---|---|
| 1982 | Philadelphia | N | 26 | 32 | 1.23 |

**John WATHAN**

| Year | Team | League | GS | SB | Avg |
|---|---|---|---|---|---|
| 1976 | Kansas City | A | 8 | 4 | .50 |
| 1977 | Kansas City | A | 19 | 10 | .53 |
| 1978 | Kansas City | A | 16 | 12 | .75 |
| 1979 | Kansas City | A | 18 | 7 | .39 |
| 1980 | Kansas City | A | 71 | 57 | .80 |
| 1981 | Kansas City | A | 68 | 44 | .65 |
| 1982 | Kansas City | A | 117 | 62 | .53 |
| 7 years | | | 317 | 196 | .62 |

**Don WERNER**

| Year | Team | League | GS | SB | Avg |
|---|---|---|---|---|---|
| 1978 | Cincinnati | N | 37 | 36 | .97 |
| 1980 | Cincinnati | N | 19 | 28 | 1.47 |
| 1982 | Texas | A | 19 | 11 | .58 |
| 3 years | | | 75 | 75 | 1.00 |

**Ernie WHITT**

| Year | Team | League | GS | SB | Avg |
|---|---|---|---|---|---|
| 1978 | Toronto | A | 1 | 0 | .00 |
| 1979 | Toronto | A | 92 | 73 | .79 |
| 1981 | Toronto | A | 60 | 28 | .47 |
| 1982 | Toronto | A | 74 | 43 | .58 |
| 4 years | | | 227 | 144 | .63 |

**John WOCKENFUSS**

| Year | Team | League | GS | SB | Avg |
|---|---|---|---|---|---|
| 1975 | Detroit | A | 33 | 27 | .82 |
| 1976 | Detroit | A | 44 | 40 | .91 |
| 1977 | Detroit | A | 33 | 19 | .58 |
| 1979 | Detroit | A | 18 | 16 | .89 |
| 1980 | Detroit | A | 23 | 18 | .78 |
| 1981 | Detroit | A | 2 | 1 | .50 |
| 1982 | Detroit | A | 18 | 20 | 1.11 |
| 7 years | | | 171 | 141 | .82 |

**Butch WYNEGAR**

| Year | Team | League | GS | SB | Avg |
|---|---|---|---|---|---|
| 1976 | Minnesota | A | 133 | 124 | .93 |
| 1977 | Minnesota | A | 138 | 80 | .58 |
| 1978 | Minnesota | A | 121 | 72 | .60 |
| 1979 | Minnesota | A | 141 | 60 | .43 |
| 1980 | Minnesota | A | 133 | 60 | .45 |
| 1981 | Minnesota | A | 36 | 29 | .81 |
| 1982 | Minnesota/NY | A | 82 | 57 | .70 |
| 7 years | | | 784 | 482 | .61 |

**Steve YEAGER**

| Year | Team | League | GS | SB | Avg |
|---|---|---|---|---|---|
| 1975 | Los Angeles | N | 131 | 50 | .38 |
| 1976 | Los Angeles | N | 108 | 51 | .47* |
| 1977 | Los Angeles | N | 118 | 70 | .59 |
| 1978 | Los Angeles | N | 72 | 39 | .54 |
| 1979 | Los Angeles | N | 89 | 54 | .61 |
| 1980 | Los Angeles | N | 66 | 57 | .86 |
| 1981 | Los Angeles | N | 23 | 14 | .61 |
| 1982 | Los Angeles | N | 54 | 37 | .69 |
| 8 years | | | 661 | 372 | .56 |

**Ned YOST**

| Year | Team | League | GS | SB | Avg |
|---|---|---|---|---|---|
| 1980 | Milwaukee | A | 10 | 5 | .50 |
| 1981 | Milwaukee | A | 7 | 4 | .57 |
| 1982 | Milwaukee | A | 27 | 19 | .70 |
| 3 years | | | 44 | 28 | .64 |

# FIRST BASEMEN

### 1. *Eddie MURRAY, Baltimore (23-8)*

A year ago I made a flip comment that in 1986 Eddie Murray would become the first player to get 100 career game-winning RBI. Actually, after three years of official GWs, it is shaping up as a three-horse race:

| | '80 | '81 | '82 | Total |
|---|---|---|---|---|
| 1. Jack Clark | 18 | 11 | 21 | 50 |
| 2. Eddie Murray | 16 | 10 | 20 | 46 |
| 3. Keith Hernandez | 13 | 10 | 21 | 44 |
| 4. Dusty Baker | 17 | 8 | 16 | 41 |
| 5. Mike Schmidt | 17 | 10 | 13 | 40 |
| Andre Dawson | 17 | 9 | 14 | 40 |
| 7. Gary Matthews | 13 | 9 | 17 | 39 |
| 8. Cecil Cooper | 11 | 11 | 15 | 37 |
| 9. Singleton, Baylor, Luzinski, Simmons | | | | 36 |

The National Leaguers have an edge in that the DH rule creates a wider dispersion of GWRBI. In plain English, the DH rule creates more runs, but no more GW runs, hence a smaller percentage of one's RBI will be game-winning. And somebody *might* make it in 1985. (Offensive 20-6; Defensive 3-2)

### 2. *Keith HERNANDEZ, St. Louis (23-10)*

The seventh game of the World Series was played on Keith Hernandez' birthday in '82, and Keith had a pretty good day, with two hits, two walks and two RBI. This, along with a couple of other times that I noticed somebody having a good B'Day, got me to wondering if there was a significant birthday effect. It seems credible that there might be; after all, birthdays are important to a lot of people, and researchers have found that old people are much more likely to die just after a birthday than just before. That seems on the surface of it less plausible than that somebody might get an extra single on the day.

Anyway, it's a "hit." I made up a list of all of the regulars who were included in the 1982 *Who's Who In Baseball*, and who had birthdays for April to October 3, arranged them in order, and began compiling the statistics of people who were celebrating their birthdays. Here's what they did:

| G | AB | R | H | 2B | 3B | HR | RBI | SB | Avg |
|---|---|---|---|---|---|---|---|---|---|
| 89 | 285 | 59 | 96 | 17 | 6 | 12 | 48 | 13 | .337 |

Birthday boys hit .350 in April, .375 in May, .419 in June,

.286 in July, .299 in August, .302 in September and .333 in October.

I had intended to form a control on this study by weighting each player's season performance by the number of at-bats on his birthday and thus finding the "expected daily performance" for the group of players studied. This, however, was quite unnecessary in view of the results. Since *nobody* in the study was a .337 hitter with a .565 slugging percentage, it was obvious that the *average* player in the study couldn't be a .337 hitter with a .565 slugging percentage.

So what I did instead was to rerun the study from the 1980 season. This produced:

| G | AB | R | H | 2B | 3B | HR | RBI | SB | Avg |
|---|---|---|---|---|---|---|---|---|---|
| 70 | 248 | 22 | 72 | 10 | 1 | 8 | 31 | 4 | .290 |

This is a lot less dramatic, but again, the average player in the study obviously is not a .290 hitter.

Two players in the 1982 study—Gene Richards and Al Bumbry—had four hits on their birthdays, and how many times do you do that in a season, anyway? Willie Upshaw hit a game-winning three-run triple on his birthday, Phil Garner a three-run homer (on his birthday in 1980 Garner hit *two* home runs), Keith Moreland a home run, Doug Flynn a game-winning single. On their birthdays Ken Oberkfell went 3-for-3, Ron Oester, Paul Molitor and Willie Wilson 3-for-5; George Brett tripled and homered to drive in three runs and Terry Kennedy doubled and homered to drive in three. Ken Singleton broke out of a terrible slump with a two-run homer; Jim Sundberg, Lamar Johnson and Jerry Mumphrey homered. George Vukovich pinch-hit and homered; Mike Ramsey came off the bench and went 2-for-2. Dusty Baker drove in two runs, Johnnie LeMaster had a game-winning single. Dickie Thon singled, doubled and tripled for three RBI. Andre Dawson and Andre Thornton both went 3-for-5 with four RBI and a homer plus some doubles on their days.

I'll try to check it again next year, but for now I'd say that there was definite "birthday effect there." And if you're a gambler it might not be a bad idea to keep a list of pitcher's birthdays around, either. (20-8; 3-2)

### 3. *Al OLIVER, Montreal (21-9)*

He made 19 errors, the most by any first baseman in four years. Most were early in the summer, and at least three of those errors led directly to Expo losses (April 15, wild throw on sac bunt; May 12, two runs scored when failed to handle good ball; August 20, error cost a run that put game into extra innings). It's not his fault, of course; that's what you get when you assign a player to do OJT in regular season play.

I think I wrote a year ago that all players are in decline by the age of 35. Oliver is 36, and he sure seems to be hiding it well. Three years ago, pooh-poohing the notion that Oliver was an unrecognized superstar, I observed that "Al Oliver has never led either league in anything. He has never driven in 100 runs in a season; he has never scored 100. He has never had 200 hits in a season." That was an accurate summation of Al Oliver's career up to age 33, but it just doesn't apply any more, nor does the argument that went with it. Now he has driven in 100 runs twice, won a batting championship and some other league titles, run his chances of getting 3000 career hits up from 17% to 43%. He has become a great ballplayer at an age when everybody, almost, is in decline. You've got to admire him for it. (19-8; 1-2)

### 4. *Cecil COOPER, Milwaukee (23-11)*

There is one big difference between Murray (32 HR, 110 RBI, .316) and Cooper (32, 121, .313), and that is on-base percentage: Murray, .395; Cooper, .345. Murray is also a better percentage base stealer, has better defensive stats and gets a few more game-winners. It doesn't take Cooper out of the class of great ballplayers, but it does move Murray to the head of the class. (21-8; 3-2)

### 5. *Jason THOMPSON, Pittsburgh (18-8)*

Still has a lot of trouble with lefthanders, homered only once against them last year, twice in '81. After the awesome first month (.710 slugging and more than an RBI per game), his final stats last year wound up almost exactly where they were in '77. (16-6; 2-2)

### 6. *Bill BUCKNER, Chicago (22-13)*

Set a major league record with 159 assists at first. Green insists that his pitchers always cover first on a GB3, so much so that even Pete Rose, who covers as much ground as any other flower, led the league in assists when he was there... Coming off his first 200-hit season, he has definitely emerged as a 3000-hit candidate. The chart that keeps track of that for him shows this since 1977:

| Year | Age | Hits | Career Hits | Projected Remaining | 3000 Chance |
|---|---|---|---|---|---|
| 1977 | 27 | 121 | 958 | 1065 | .02 |
| 1978 | 28 | 144 | 1102 | 1040 | .05 |
| 1979 | 29 | 168 | 1270 | 1004 | .08 |
| 1980 | 30 | 187 | 1457 | 1041 | .17 |
| 1981 | 31 | 131 | 1588 | 1010 | .22 |
| 1982 | 32 | 201 | 1789 | 946 | .28 |

He would have been in much better shape before '77 but for injuries. But at the age he's reached now, he'll have to stay healthy to have a shot. (19-11; 3-2)

### 7. *Tom PACIOREK, Chicago (15-8)*

Batting average for the last two seasons is .319, and with power (.180 isolated power, .499 slugging). Grounded into only six double plays and was hit by a pitch nine times... did not hit a home run and averaged only .281 in Chicago, with 11 home runs and a .338 average on the road. Might be helped by the new dimensions this year. The random chance that a player who hits 11 home runs would just happen to hit all of them on the road is less than 1 in 2000. (15-6; 1-1)

### 8. *Rod CAREW, California (17-10)*

A year ago in an article for *Sports Illustrated*, I commented that Rod Carew's batting average (in 1981) was about 110 points higher in games that were decided by four or more runs than it was in close games. There was something of an ethical question involved in writing this, because I wasn't sure in my own mind exactly how meaningful this fact was. Since pitchers' duels are always close games, most players' batting averages would be a little lower in close games, so the comparison is a somewhat loaded one. Besides, and particularly with a rally-starter as opposed to a rally-finisher, there is a real danger of confusing cause and effect here. What the statistic could show is that when Carew gets four hits in a game, the game doesn't tend to be close. And I knew that if I wrote that, people would leap directly from "Rod Carew's batting average in 1981 was around .250 in close games" to "Rod Carew doesn't hit in the clutch."

I eventually decided it was legitimate enough to use, for three reasons:

1) The Angels as a team were legitimately awful in close games; they won most of the time when the game wasn't close, lost most of the time when it was. The overall won-lost percentage is .500 in close games or in blowouts, so that's not any kind of illusion. I decided that it was legitimate to point the finger at the players who hit in routs and didn't hit in close games.

2) Carew had hit about .250 in close games, but about .290 in games that the Angels *lost* by four runs or more. I couldn't explain that away.

3) The imbalanced-offense effect would explain a 15-point difference in batting, not a 110-point difference.

So I used it, but I decided that I would check to see what the same data was in 1982, and report on it whether the split was there or whether it wasn't. It wasn't. Rod Carew in 1982 hit .323 in close games, .312 in games that were decided by four runs or more. In one-run games, he hit .357 (55 for 154). The Angels as a team were still bad in one-run games (22-24; they were 71-45 in other games), but this time it wasn't Rodney's fault. (15-10; 2-2)

### *9. Chris CHAMBLISS, Atlanta (19-13)*

Atlanta had an estimated *52* 3-6-3 (first to short to first) or 3-6-1 double plays last year, nine more than any other NL team, three more than Boston . . . 20 home runs in '82 set a career high for him. (16-11; 3-2)

### *10. Kent HRBEK, Minnesota (13-7)*

I'm sure all of the publicity given to the balls flying out of the Humpdome has caused some people to dismiss Hrbek's impressive stats, but he actually hit more home runs on the road than in Minnesota (12-11). His batting average increase at home wasn't extraordinary, either, 31 points. I think both Hrbek and Ripken will be great ballplayers. It's a pity the American League couldn't have given no Cy Young Award and two Rookie-of-the-Year awards. (11-6; 2-1)

### *11. Steve GARVEY, Los Angeles (20-15)*

The worst strikeout-to-walk ratio (8.6-1) in the National League if you adjust for intentional walks (Willie McGee is a little worse without the adjustment) . . . A lot of people have interpreted Garvey's late-season rush as evidence that he has found himself, that, after struggling for nigh-on two years, he has remembered some missing element of the program and can be expected to be back to the 200-hit, 100-RBI level in '83. That may be the way it is, but Garvey has always closed with a rush. In 1976 he hit .377 after September 1 to bring a .304 average to .317; in 1977 he hit .378 in September to lift a .280 average to .297; in 1978 he hit .430 in September to haul his average from .293 to .316. Last year was just the same thing at a lower level; he hit .328 in the last month to bring him from .271 to .282. His complete record in September from 1978 to the present is worth a look:

| Year | G | AB | R | H | 2B | 3B | HR | RBI | SB | Avg |
|---|---|---|---|---|---|---|---|---|---|---|
| 1975 | 24 | 97 | 16 | 34 | 8 | 1 | 4 | 20 | 0 | .351 |
| 1976 | 32 | 114 | 18 | 43 | 7 | 1 | 3 | 14 | 6 | .377 |
| 1977 | 29 | 111 | 14 | 42 | 3 | 0 | 5 | 18 | 3 | .378 |
| 1978 | 29 | 107 | 15 | 46 | 9 | 1 | 3 | 22 | 2 | .430 |
| 1979 | 28 | 100 | 13 | 31 | 5 | 0 | 5 | 24 | 0 | .310 |
| 1980 | 33 | 128 | 15 | 41 | 9 | 0 | 4 | 14 | 1 | .320 |
| 1981 | 32 | 116 | 17 | 33 | 3 | 0 | 3 | 12 | 1 | .284 |
| 1982 | 29 | 119 | 16 | 39 | 7 | 0 | 3 | 22 | 0 | .328 |

To Garvey's credit, he has gone through this annual drive in the heat of an annual pennant race; and the hotter the race has been, the hotter Garvey has been. In 1981 the Dodgers were playing for nothing, and that is the one year that Garvey didn't do much in September.

Oh—I should note, I did *not* say, ever, that Steve Garvey was overrated. Indeed, I went out of my way to say that he wasn't overrated; NBC just mixed up the quote.

What is it about Senator Garvey that rings so false when you know in your heart that it is probably as genuine as the contented look on the face of a cow and as deeply held as Halloween candy in the hand of a child? I have a cousin who strikes me exactly the same way, and I'll bet you do too; we'll call mine Wally. Wally graduated from high school with highest Hosannahs and went straight to Harvard, where he met and married a reasonably pretty girl with an awfully sensible head on her, and then he got his master's degree and went to work in corporate America, shinnying rapidly up the ladder of success and making oodles of money and saving it so that his children will never have to worry about who will pay for their next orthodontist's appointment. Wally is an awfully nice man and he has never said an unkind word to me in his life, and he is brilliant, and I avoid him at all costs. There is something about the very sensibleness of his life that seems to any normal person to be almost accusatory, for sometimes I am chubby while he retains an accusing trimness, and sometimes I am underemployed while he rests in accusingly attainable affluence, and sometimes I might neglect to have my teeth looked at for a decade or two because of an irrational fear of dentists while I know without a thought that if Wally had such a fear he would deal with it directly, and if he didn't his wife would spin him around and kick him in the butt and send him on the way to his appointment anyway, so that you would never know the difference.

It does not ring false, perhaps, but hollow, that since the very essence of life is a mystery, life seems unreal without self-doubt, and we must see that self-doubt in others before we can accept that they share our humanity. Garvey never allows the question marks to rise into his eyes or to afflict his performance, and thus he seems . . . what is it that people say about him? Plastic? A robot? A programmed performer? How can he be a human without doubting himself, without yielding to periods of frustration and futile anger? It is not only Garvey's chin which seems chiseled in granite, but his values, which were given to him while he was in grade school along with the rest of us. But while the rest of us have eroded ours by turning them over and over and examining them in different ways, Garvey seems, impossibly, to have let his stay untested and unworn.

One might think that when this period is in the past Garvey shall be humanized somewhat by what the networks refer to as his "mental torment," by his accompanying sub-Garvey seasons. Self-doubt comes directly from pain, as ashes are left by a fire. What is so unnerving about Wally and Steve is to think that they have never lost a year or two out of their lives because they were wondering about something, got their values confused, never sifted through the ashes before. 1981 and 1982 were the years Garvey lost in the fire, and one might hope that he will have the sense not to hide that from us. Welcome, Steve; welcome to the human race. (17-13; 3-2)

### *12. Mike HARGROVE, Cleveland (18-13)*

The answer to a trivia question: Who was the American League's Rookie of the Year in George Brett's rookie season? There are a lot of parallels in their careers since then. After hitting for no power as rookies, each hit 11 home runs with a .300+ average in 1975, each dropped off to seven home runs in 1976 (Brett led the league for the first time in batting, Hargrove for the first time in walks). Both had their worst seasons ever in 1978, and both had their best seasons in 1980. (14-12; 3-2)

### *13. Willie AIKENS, Kansas City (16-11)*

Saved his season with a very good August and a .373, eight-homer September. Stats on July 31 were .253 with five homers and 37 RBI.

Just for posterity's sake . . . I noted a year ago that Willie had never hit a triple in the major leagues, and wondered in print if this was a record. It was. I made a journey through the encyclopedia to check, and with the help of an old box score concluded that the previous record of the sort was held by Ed (faster than a speeding bureaucracy) Herrmann, who tripled in his third at-bat on May 4, 1973, 1,282 at bats into his career. Herrmann, who may have been the slowest player I ever saw, was eventually to amass four triples lifetime.

Anyway, Willie had topped this nonperformance by the beginning of 1982, and I pointed this out in a note for *Sports Illustrated*. This apparently didn't set too well with Aikens, and there was a stretch early in the season (June 6 to 12, to be specific) in which Willie was thrown out three times in a week trying to stretch a triple into a triple. Toward the end of a 14-1 rout in Yankee Stadium he hit a massive, high drive to right center, a thing of beauty it was, which bounced off the wall and away from Dave Collins. Collins ran it down and three-hopped it to the vicinity of the shortstop, who chased it down and relayed it to third. It was a close play, but I thought he was safe.

It was August the 20th, and the wife and I were for some odd reason up in the cheap seats, when the historic moment finally arrived. It was Willie's 1717th career at-bat. Gus Triandos was not in attendance. Willie speared a fastball and launched it straight toward the tacky water fountains in center field. Susie and I both realized before Willie was out of the batter's box that if it didn't clear the wall this might be *it*, and so we jumped to our feet and began screaming wildly for Willie to get it in gear. This drew considerable consternation from the surrounding fans, most of whom I think were there on a bus tour or something, because it was 11 to 3 in the bottom of the seventh and nobody had seen anything worth cheering about since the departure of Chico Escarrega in the fifth. Rudy Law was in center field, which will not come as a surprise to those of you who have seen Rudy Law throw. There was a play, but it wasn't close.

Willie in 1982 was taking a lot of crap for his fielding, for which I feel personally responsible, but the strange thing was that he was fielding a lot better than he ever has before. If he was an F three years ago and a D- in '81, he was . . . what, a D+ last year? It wasn't that bad. But he wasn't hitting a lick for four months, and when you don't hit that magnifies the other weaknesses in your game. I really like the guy; he seems hard-working and dedicated. It's fun to watch him struggle so hard to overcome his inherent limitations; almost inspiring, in a comical way. I'd a lot rather have him out there than Mike Squires. (15-8; 2-2)

### *14. Dan DRIESSEN, Cincinnati (16-11)*

I really can't understand the decision to keep this guy in the lineup at the cost of Bench. The Reds screwed up Bench's career at a point when it should have had five good years left because they didn't want to fool with this sub-.270-hitting non-RBI man . . . led the league in fielding percentage. (13-9; 3-2)

### *15. Pete ROSE, Philadelphia (20-16)*

Phillies again were low in the league in 3-6-3 double plays . . . Wonder who will retire his uniform number? Cincinnati? Philadelphia? Both? Neither? . . . number of doubles hit has dropped sharply the last two seasons . . .

There has been some controversy about Corrales' decision to sit down Rose a few games in '83 (or, conversely, *not* to sit him down a few games in '82). But if there was ever a case of mere numbers leaving no doubt about what should be done, this is it. Rose has been a great September hitter all his life. In 1977 he hit .365 after September 1, in 1978 .315, in 1979 .421 (51-for-121). But in 1980 he turned 39, and his September average dropped to .234; in 1982, it dropped to .222. Nobody likes getting older. But when you've got a 40+ year old player playing 162 games and not hitting a lick at the end of the year, you've got to make a connection.

• Rose had 1,702 hits by the age of 29, an impressive total but not one of the 10 highest ever (the #10 man is Richie Ashburn, who had 1,766). Rose's one-time teammate, Vada Pinson, had 1,881 by age 29. But Pete now has 2,167 hits *since* turning 30, which is the fourth highest total ever, behind Sammie Rice (2,561), Cap Anson (2,546) and Honus Wagner (2,214).

• A man by the name of David Frank of Olney, Maryland, has done an unbelievably thorough breakdown of Rose's career, and can tell you how many times Rose has had one hit in a game, two hits in a game, three, four, five hits in a game; one RBI in a game, or two RBI, or three runs scored, or any of this data for any season, or what his career batting average has been in one-run wins or one-run losses, or in any ballpark that he has ever played in, or against any team, or . . . take my word for it; if there is anything you want to know about Pete Rose, just ask Mr. Frank. When I met the man last summer, Pete Rose had played exactly 3000 games in his career. He had had no hits in a game 761 times, one hit 1,141 times, two hits 744 times, three hits 285 times, four hits 60 times and five hits nine times. (There are things you can do with this data; for example, figure out what are the chances that such a player would hit in 56 straight games. Since Rose had hit in 74.633% of his games, the chance that he would hit in 56 straight is .74633 to the 56th power, or .000 000 076 602. Since there are 2,945 56-game strings in 3000 games, the chance that he would hit in 56 straight at some point is .000 000 076 602 times 2,945, or .000 022 559, or less than one in 44,000. The chance that he would hit in 40 straight games, as he did, is much better, .0245, or about 1 in 40. This figure would be higher if you selected the most relevant data, which is what Rose hit in 1979, rather than using the entire career.)

Anyway, of those 3000 games, Rose's team had won 1,681, lost 1,314 and tied five. His lifetime average in one-run games, a brief addendum to the discussion concerning Carew, was .289, 21 points lower than his .310 career mark (.300 in one-run victories, .276 in one-run losses). He had almost 4000 at-bats in one-run games. His highest lifetime batting average against any team was .343 against Atlanta. And he had had 40 hitting streaks of 10 games or more, which Mr. Frank believed was one less than the record, 41, held by Musial. (17-14; 3-2)

### *16. Ray KNIGHT, Houston (17-13)*

I don't really buy the notion that the Knight trade was the one trade too many that did in the Reds. There were too many trades, but I think you've got to look at the disposal of the outfield before you start counting .275 hitters . . . Knight's hitting against lefthanders had to be a major disappointment to the Astros. He had always hit about 50 points better against lefthanders than right, but slipped to .273 against left-handed pitchers last year, and it was lefthanders who were beating the Astros (they had a better record against righthanders than LA or Atlanta). (16-12; 1-1)

### *17. Reggie SMITH, San Francisco (8-5)*

A great percentage player, like Morgan. Hits for a good average, but the average represents only 46% of his offensive value, as he walks a lot, hits for power and stole seven bases in seven attempts. You never know whether he's going to be healthy tomorrow, but he is some kind of a player when he's in there . . . still has all his power left-handed . . . If he's healthy should hit 40 homers in Japan. (7-4; 1-1)

### *18. Broderick PERKINS, San Diego (11-9)*

Doesn't have the power to stay around as a .270-hitting first baseman. (9-8; 2-1)

### *19. Dave KINGMAN, New York Mets (16-16)*

An appropriate successor to the throne of Throneberry. Marv, after he was sent down by the Mets in '63, played at Buffalo, where he had one double, no triples and 16 home runs. He hit .176 and fielded .984. If that's not a Dave Kingman year, I don't know what is . . . among Kingman's unique contributions to the ball club: Met shortstops and third basemen made 73 errors. An average figure was around 50 . . . retained the title of the worst defensive first baseman in baseball despite stiff competition from Dave Collins, Gary Gray, Reggie Smith and Al Oliver, with a defensive won-lost percentage of .28 (others were .32, .32, .33, .34, respectively).

It's a pity he got his average out of the ones; it made for such an interesting line. There has never before been a home-run champion who hit anything like .200. . . There have been 10 other HR champs in the century who hit under .250, but nine of those hit in the .240s, the exception being Gavvy Cravath in 1918, who hit .232. Cravath hit only 8 home runs, though, so that's not really a fair comparison. You always wonder how many weird records Kingman really set—over a third of his hits were home runs, which is not a record (38% of Maris' hits were homers in 1961), he averaged 2.12 bases per hit, which is probably not a record . . . what else? His batting average represents only 34% of his offensive value. (15-13; 1-3)

### *20. Dave HOSTETLER, Texas (8-7)*

Note that the seven lowest-rated first basemen are all American Leaguers. It could well be that the DH rule is creating a drain on the pool of players available for the position; first base is the left-most position on the defensive spectrum, and many of the players who are now designated would otherwise be first basemen.

I don't know what to think about Hostetler . . . I put together his age (26), his strikeouts, the fact that there is absolutely only one thing that he can do, the late-season slump, and I've got to look at him as a John Milner, a Pat Putnam. But I know he probably hits the ball as far as anybody in the game, and I know a lot of people like him. (7-6; 1-1)

### *21. Dave COLLINS, New York Yankees (11-12)*

Much better suited to Toronto than Yankee Stadium. . . . The only thing Collins can do like a first baseman is supposed to is throw. (10-12; 0-1)

### *22. Dave STAPLETON, Boston (13-15)*

Grounded into 24 double plays . . . One of the things that I do to evaluate first basemen defensively is to estimate the number of first-to-second-to-first (3-6-3) double plays. Boston had about 49, easily the highest total in the league, which is not at all surprising if you have ever seen Stapleton on that play. He received a lot of credit for improving the Sox defense all around last year because he cut down on the ground everybody else had to cover. I might be convinced that this low rating is wrong if somebody could convincingly demonstrate that he did save the Red Sox a significant number of runs. But what the hay, Eddie Murray and Cecil Cooper and Kent Hrbek and Keith Hernandez can field, too. I don't see a lot of teams winning the pennant with glove men at first. (12-14; 1-1)

### 23. *Willie UPSHAW, Toronto (11-13)*

I noticed in drawing up the ratings that almost all of the Toronto players rated lower than I expected them to. There are three reasons for this: One, that it is a hitter's park which inflates all of the stats a little (Upshaw hit .307 at home, .228 on the road); two, that the ratings are based on 1982 and 1981, and most of the people who had good years here still have to prove that they can settle in and do it year after year, a test which a lot of players fail; Upshaw is a case in point: remember before you criticize the rating that the man hit .171 in '81. The third reason is a generally poor collection of peripheral stats. In Upshaw's case, he was caught stealing 8 times in 16 tries and made 17 errors, five more than any other AL first baseman. His basic offensive stats are decent, but American League first basemen in '82 averaged .281 with 17 home runs and 79 RBI per 580 at-bats, so .263 with 21 and 75 doesn't draw a lot of attention. (10-11; 1-2)

### 24. *Gary GRAY, Seattle (7-9)*

Radical improvement in his strikeout/walk ratio, from 44-4 in '81 to 59-24 in '82. He's 30, but you'd have to figure that anybody who can hit .300 forty-seven straight times in the minor leagues can hit. If it was my ball club, I'd say let Bochte go and see what this guy can do. (7-7; 0-2)

### 25. *Dan MEYER, Oakland (7-12)*

One of the most curious decisions of 1982 was Billy Martin's reluctance to go with Kelvin Moore at first base. You've got a team out of the pennant race, a hole at first base, and a kid with dynamite qualifications, but Meyer kept playing. Am I missing something? (7-11; 0-1)

### 26. *Enos CABELL, Detroit (10-19)*

.261 average represents 73% of his offensive value. The normal figure is 53% in the American League. When Enos Cabell was hot early in the year, you'd ask Sparky Anderson about him and Sparky would say "Enos Cabell is a *we* ballplayer. You don't hear Enos Cabell saying 'I did this' and 'I did that.'" I think that's what drives me nuts about Sparky Anderson, that he's so full of brown stuff that it just doesn't seem like he has any words left over for a basic, fundamental understanding of the game. I want to look at a player on the basis of what, specifically, he can and cannot do to help you win a baseball game, but Sparky's so full of "winners" and "discipline" and "we ballplayers" and self-consciously asinine theories about baseball that he seems to have no concept of how it is, mechanically, that baseball games are won and lost. I mean, I would never say that it was not important to have a team with a good attitude, but Christ, Sparky, there are millions of people in this country who have good attitudes, but there are only about 200 who can play a major-league brand of baseball, so which are you going to take? Sparky is so focused on all that attitude stuff that he looks at an Enos Cabell and he doesn't even see that *the man can't play baseball*. This we ballplayer, Sparky, can't play first, can't play third, can't hit, can't run and can't throw. So who cares what his attitude is? (8-18; 1-2)

# SECOND BASEMEN

### 1. *Bobby GRICH, California (25-12)*

A typical Bobby Grich season. All the American League second basemen had on-base percentages within a normal range of .305 to .343 except Randolph (.369), Grich (.382) and two guys who were below .300. Eight AL second basemen had isolated power below .100 (one extra base per 10 at bats), and all were below .150 except Frank White (.171) and Grich (.188). Three AL second basemen turned more than 110 double plays: Whitaker (120), Bernazard (116) and Grich (111). Two AL second basemen made more than five and a half plays per game—Bernazard and Grich. His fielding average, .986, was the fifth best in the league. His team won the division; he has now played on six divisional champions. A lot of AL second basemen are close to him in one respect or another—but as a complete player, nobody else is on the same planet. (Offensive 17-8; Defensive 9-3)

### 2. *Joe MORGAN, San Francisco (21-12)*

Morgan has now played more games at second base than anyone except Eddie Collins. And to the end of his career, he remains the unknown great of our time. Throughout his career, Joe Morgan has been an unquestionably greater player than Yastrzemski or Rod Carew or Reggie, but his name draws blank stares from the public that has selected these men as idols. At the age of 38, all he does is hit .289 with power and speed, play a solid second base, draw 85 walks, and lead a mediocre team into contention until the last week of the season. But according to the national media, you'd think he retired five years ago.

For years and years, Joe Morgan was the best ballplayer in the National League. In 1972 he hit .292, had an on-base percentage of .414, hit 16 homers, stole 58 bases, fielded a league-leading .990 at a key defensive position and led the league in runs scored with 122. For this incredible performance—Bobby Grich with speed and another 30 points on his batting average—he finished fourth in the league's MVP voting. I will grant you that there were a lot of people having good years. So in 1973 Joe repeated his season and tagged on another 10 home runs and another 12 doubles and another nine stolen bases and 14 more double plays at second so he could lead the league in that, too. Again, he finished fourth in the MVP voting. So in 1974 he did it all again. He finished eighth in the MVP voting.

I have written that Amos Otis is the only player in baseball who can be evaluated in the nine basic areas of performance and come up with nine positives. But has there *ever* been a player who had so many double positives and triple positives as Morgan? For exceptional performance over a wide range of skills, I can't think of anybody who compares to him. Sure, Henry Aaron had twice as much power, but did he steal 60 bases a year and turn the double play? Or walk 120 times a year?

Yes, Morgan did win two MVP awards—after he towered over the league like Babe Ruth in a Babe Ruth league. In one season, he hit 27 home runs, averaged .320, drove in 111 runs, drew 114 walks, stole 60 bases, won a gold glove award at a key defensive position, led the league in the two most important offensive categories (on-base percentage and slugging percentage) and for good measure threw in league-leading totals in sacrifice flies, stolen-base percentage and fewest grounded-into-double-plays. Who the hell else are you going to give the award to?

And so, for a brief time, the public became dimly aware that Joe Morgan was a great ballplayer, which they quickly and happily forgot as soon as he was no longer the greatest player in the game. You hear every ten minutes about winning teams following Reggie around, with incessant and interminable and unending explanations about his taking the pressure off everybody else and hitting in the clutch and breeding a winning atmosphere. Reggie's teams in Oakland, Baltimore, New York and California have a combined record of 914 wins, 650 losses in the last ten years. Morgan's teams in Cincinnati, Houston and San Francisco have a record of 913 wins, 655 losses. Do you hear a word about winning teams following Joe Morgan around? Reggie and Grich won the division in California with a supporting cast of seven all-stars; Morgan and Jack Clark won 87 games and missed by two with a cast of seven Bozos. Which is the more impressive accomplishment? I'm not saying this to rip Rose or Schmidt or Bench or anybody else, but no player since Mantle in the mid-1950s has reached a peak of performance as high as Morgan's in the mid-seventies. It's a shame that the only effect of that has been to cast a shadow over the rest of his brilliant career. The three greatest second basemen ever are Hornsby, Gehringer and Joe Morgan. (16-6; 5-5)

### 3. *Lou WHITAKER, Detroit (22-16)*

Finally put it in gear last July after making no progress for three and a half years. Hit .246 through the first three months of the season, then .321, .304, .313 the last three and with a big increase in power. He had never been a late-season player before, so I would tend to interpret this as a real change in the level of his play . . . Note the uncanny similarity between his record in seasonal notation and Trammell's:

| | Years | AB | R | H | 2B | 3B | HR | RBI | SB | Avg |
|---|---|---|---|---|---|---|---|---|---|---|
| Whitaker | 4.22 | 548 | 81 | 148 | 19 | 7 | 6 | 59 | 13 | .271 |
| Trammel | 4.37 | 547 | 80 | 149 | 22 | 5 | 6 | 54 | 14 | .272 |

Trammell's late season splurge was even more dramatic than Lou's. (14-12; 8-4)

### 4. *Tony BERNAZARD, Chicago White Sox (22-17)*

Really like this kid a lot . . . Highest double-play percentage (double plays per game, adjusted for the number of runners on base) of any American League second baseman . . . scored 90 runs . . . hit only 1 home run in Comiskey, 10 on the road . . . stole 11 bases without being caught. How different Montreal's season might have been had they not made this trade. (15-12; 8-4)

### 5. *Frank WHITE, Kansas City (20-17)*

Isolated power since he has been in the majors, by two-year groups:

| | |
|---|---|
| 1973–74 | .067 |
| 1975–76 | .093 |
| 1977–78 | .110 |
| 1979–80 | .113 |
| 1981–82 | .153 |

I wouldn't guess you could find a whole lot of second baseman who have hit 45 doubles in a season, at least since 1940. (Decided to check that out. The last time any second baseman hit as many as 45 doubles in a season was 1936, when both Charlie Gehringer and Billy Herman hit over 50.)

Did you ever notice that players named "White" are almost always black, and players named "Black" are usually white? Why is that? The last White major leaguer who was actually white was Mike White, who played for Houston in the early sixties. Since then we've had Bill White, Roy White, Frank White and Jerry White, all of whom were black; Mike White probably would have been black except that his father played in the majors in the thirties and they didn't allow you to be black then. The Royals also had a Black on their roster, Bud, who of course is white; in fact, the Royals had to set some sort of record by having four colored people on their team, White, Black, Blue and Brown. Scott Brown is not any browner than anybody else, Vida is definitely not blue, nor for that matter is Darryl Motley. I suppose that it is the nature of names, as with Peacekeeping Missiles and Security Police, to disguise the truth more often than they reveal it. Horace Speed stole only four bases in his career, Vic Power was a singles hitter, Bill Goodenough was not good enough, and Joe Blong did not belong for long. (13-12; 7-5)

### 6. *Tom HERR, St. Louis (20-18)*

In the attempted first game of the NL play-offs—the game that, as Howard said, "proved not to be capable, meteorologically speaking, of resumption"—there was a beautiful illustration of why people overrate the stolen base so badly. The first inning went like this:

*Tom Herr . . . . . . . . . . single*
*caught stealing*

*Ken Oberkfell . . . popped to left*

*Lonnie Smith . . . . . . . . triple*
*ball got to the wall; Smith could have scored*

*Keith Hernandez . . . . . . Out 5-3*
*lined off Horner's chest; ran it down and threw him out*

The Cardinals committed three base-running mistakes in the inning and didn't score, the third being that Hernandez wasn't running down the line. Hernandez' failure to hustle down the line cost the Cardinals a run, and both Lasorda and Al Michaels pointed that out. Smith's failure to watch his third base coach cost the Cardinals the same run, and Lasorda pointed this out *four times*, once when it happened, again after the Cards were retired, again in the fourth when the Braves mounted a threat, and again when the rains came with the Cards trailing 1-0.

But Herr's attempt to steal a base cost the Cardinals *two runs and a win*—and not one word was said about it. Not only would Herr have scored on the triple, but with only one out Smith would easily have scored on the ground-out, giving the Cardinals a 2-1 win.

How many 2-run innings do you have to lose before the stolen base becomes a bad gamble? Damn few. People overestimate the value of the stolen-base gamble because they fail to make a reasonable accounting of the cost of a caught-stealing. It's an invisible loss; you don't really see the runs you don't get, whereas you do see it when it pays off. But I've noticed something about those big innings that win ball games. You hardly ever see anybody caught stealing in the middle of a three-run rally. (13-14; 7-4)

### 7. *Willie RANDOLPH, New York Yankees (20-19)*

A heck of an off year, hit .280, scored 85 runs for a sub-.500 team. He isn't the percentage base stealer that he was when he was younger, but he is still a championship-calibre ballplayer. (13-14; 7-5)

### 8. *Phil GARNER, Houston (19-18)*

His birthday is April 30; let's keep an eye out to see what he does that day this time . . . hit six home runs in the Astrodome, the most by any player since Cruz hit seven in 1978 . . . right-handed batter, but didn't hit lefties in '82. (14-12; 6-5)

### 9. *Jim GANTNER, Milwaukee (17-16)*

Seems to have a very pronounced tendency to hit some teams and not hit others. He hit a combined .526 (41 for 78) against Chicago, New York and Detroit, but .186 (19 for 102) against Kansas City, Boston and Cleveland. I haven't checked, but I'd bet nobody else had that radical a split—in fact, I find very few cases of any regular hitting .500 against even one team, let alone three. Robin Yount didn't hit as high as .400 against anybody, but also hit at least .250 against everybody. (10-12; 7-4)

### 10. *Manny TRILLO, Philadelphia (19-19)*

His acceptance of the end of his errorless streak should be recorded as one of the real class acts of 1982 . . . had the highest defensive won-lost percentage in the league in '82 (at second). Offensive season is unmistakably subpar, with 52 runs scored and 39 RBI in 410 outs. His offensive won-lost percentage was .383; DeJesus was .388. It's hard to win with bats like that in your lineup. The only other teams in the league with two regulars having offensive won-lost percentages below .400 were New York and Cincinnati, and they both finished last. (12-14; 8-4)

### 11. *Rich DAUER, Baltimore (19-19)*

I did a study several years ago in which I compared Mark Belanger's batting record when he was hitting second to his hitting when he was at the bottom of the order. The reason for doing this was to serve as a sort of test on Earl's books. Weaver would bat Belanger second, which is a silly decision on the surface of it, but a defensible decision if Weaver could, in fact, pick those days or those pitchers that Belanger was likely to hit.

He couldn't, or at least in that case he didn't; Belanger hit .170 batting second. Rich Dauer, a much better hitter than Belanger (obviously), now flip-flops from the top to the bottom of the order, and I decided to repeat the study. If, in fact, Weaver's famous books did allow him to pick the days when Dauer was likely to hit, then we should find that Dauer hit better when hitting second than when hitting eighth.

**Dauer's Record**

| | G | AB | R | H | 2B | 3B | HR | RBI | SB | Avg |
|---|---|---|---|---|---|---|---|---|---|---|
| Batting Second | 88 | 337 | 48 | 91 | 16 | 1 | 6 | 31 | 0 | .270 |
| Batting Eighth | 17 | 51 | 4 | 12 | 1 | 0 | 0 | 4 | 0 | .235 |
| Batting Ninth | 53 | 170 | 23 | 53 | 7 | 1 | 2 | 22 | 0 | .312 |

Dauer's batting average when batting second was, in fact, 24 points lower than his combined average when hitting eighth or ninth.

I'm not suggesting that Weaver wasn't a great manager; he was. I just thought I'd check that one item. (14-13; 5-6)

### 12. *Julio CRUZ, Seattle (19-20)*

Hit .302 and slugged over .500 against left-handed pitchers. Has always hit well against lefties—.270 in 1981, .341 in 1980. Very comparable to U.L. Washington—a switch hitter but all of the power and most of the hits coming right-handed. His low on-base percentage (.317) makes him a poor lead-off man, even though he is one of the best percentage base stealers ever to play the game. But he's a good second baseman, and he does make some offensive contributions. (12-15; 7-4)

### *13. Ron OESTER, Cincinnati (18-19)*

The government has a category of "discouraged workers" for people who have been unemployed so long that they have given up trying to find work. Maybe we should have a category of "discouraged ballplayers." Oester's got talent and I think he could help a good ball club. (13-13; 5-6)

### *14. Johnny RAY, Pittsburgh (15-16)*
### *Steve SAX, Los Angeles (15-16)*

Odd, isn't it . . . how are you supposed to pick one of them for Rookie of the Year? Their defensive stats were as close as their offensive. They both fielded .977; Ray turned 89 double plays in 162 games, Sax 83 in 149. Their range factors were 5.51 and 5.36 (edge to Ray). Sax drew a few more walks and ran a lot more, but Ray stole just about as successfully and hit with a little more power. Very little. Their minor league averages a year ago were .349 and .346. Ray did have an 8-1 edge in game-winning hits. But they are as close to being indistinguishable as any two candidates for the same award that I've ever seen. (Sax 12-11, 4-4; Ray 11-11, 5-4)

### *16. Damaso GARCIA, Toronto (16-18)*

The next three rankings—Garcia's #16, Hubbard's #17, Remy's #18—are ones that are definitely not going to please the home folks. Garcia will rank higher next year if he can repeat the kind of year that he just had; that 16-18 won-lost mark breaks down as 13-11 in '82, but 3-7 in '81. But I don't know what happened to Toronto's double-play combination last year. They dropped from 206 double plays in '80 to 146 last year with only an 11% drop-off in the number of opposition base runners. The double play was supposed to be the strong point of Garcia's game. (11-13; 5-5)

### *17. Glenn HUBBARD, Atlanta (18-21)*

Hit .248; all the other NL second basemen hit over .260 except Doug Flynn. Dropped down 20 sacrifice bunts (high in the league) and grounded into only five double plays, so his runs created would increase from 60 to 62 under the advanced version of the formula. (11-16; 7-5)

### *18. Jerry REMY, Boston (18-22)*

There are two people who always surprise me whenever I figure anything for them—runs created, approximate value, ratings. Sixto Lezcano always comes out looking a lot better than I think he will, and Jerry Remy always comes out looking a lot worse.

Why? For one thing, he has less power than anybody else in the league at any position. (Tim Foli is close.) So you say, from the standpoint of a Red Sox fan, that that's not his job, that his job is to get on base in front of the power hitters, which is fine except that he doesn't get on base all that much either. He has a .339 on-base percentage, which is way behind Grich and Randolph and pretty much indistinguishable from Bernazard (.340), Dauer (.340), Gantner (.339), Garcia (.339) or Whitaker (.343). Then he is supposed to be a good second baseman, but the first thing I look at is double plays, and he doesn't turn very many, and the second thing is range, and he doesn't make that many plays, either. So you've got a negative there with no identifiable positive to offset it, and he's got to rate behind those people. He's a quiet, respectable little drain on the Red Sox efforts. I think they'd win more games if they'd put Stapleton at second and try to find a first baseman who can hit. (12-16; 5-7)

### *19. Wally BACKMAN, New York Mets (6-6)*

Funny ballplayer, presents an odd and interesting problem for the Mets. The man can get on base, which is one of the most valuable skills in the game, but he plays second base about as well as Tip O'Neill. On the chart of the defensive spectrum, he has far more offensive ability than is needed to play regularly as a second baseman, but just can't handle the spot:

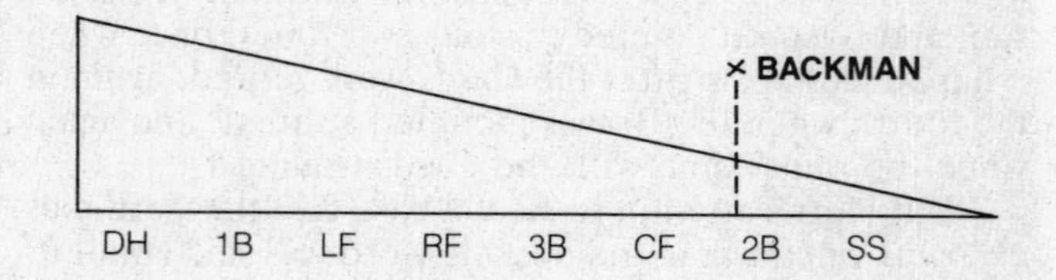


A shift to center field is out; he doesn't have the mobility or arm to run Mookie Wilson out of a job. Is his arm good enough for third? I don't know. Even if he has to be shifted to left field to get his bat in the lineup, the Mets had still better do it. His offensive won-lost percentage was .583, and it is reasonable to think he could get it over .600 in time. Players who get on base 39% of the time are hard to come by; you can't afford to kick one in the head just because he can't play second base. (6-3; 1-4)

### *20. Bump WILLS, Chicago (15-19)*

He had the same kind of year defensively that George Foster and Dan Ford had offensively. He couldn't live up to what was expected of him, came under fire for not doing what he was brought in to do, and just buckled under the pressure. (11-13; 4-6)

### *21. Davey LOPES, Oakland (13-17)*

On-base percentage only .305, not much power left, no range at all at second. Grounded into way too many double plays. He still hits enough against lefthanders to help somebody as a platoon player, maybe left fielder or DH. But as a regular, he is through. (9-12; 5-4)

### *22. Tim FLANNERY, San Diego (8-10)*

Sometimes in literature a hero forms a sort of bond, good or malignant, voluntary or involuntary, with some object or image (automobiles, freight trains, playing cards, locked doors), that are a part of everyone's life but which seem to haunt him and protrude inescapably into his fate. So it is with Dick Williams and second basemen. He has never, for one thing, stayed with the second baseman that he inherited. On every new managerial assignment, one of the first three things that he has done has been to change his second baseman. There is nothing, perhaps, so odd about this, and sometimes the exchange has gone smoothly enough. Mike Andrews settled in smoothly in Boston, Jerry Remy in California. Sometimes it has not been so smooth, as in this case . . . more on that later. But looking back over Williams' career, now: He was fired in Montreal because he became locked in a struggle with his players and his front office that came about in large part because of his irrational insistence that a .210 hitter with no power who is none too swift on the double play and who frankly did not belong on a major-league roster was, believe it or not, the best player on his team. I find it a wonderful instruction on the usefulness of emotional attachments in decision making that this man who is ordinarily as canny a judge of talent as there is could form a blind spot so large that it would hide from him such monstrous ineptitude.

Yet having been finally released from this struggle, having been eventually and deservedly fired because of it, and having been directly and deservedly rehired by another team because when not dealing with Rodney Scott he is a wonderful manager, what does he do? He attempts —no, he *demands*, insists, sits in his office and throws a temper tantrum when his attempt is thwarted—to take this problem to San Diego with him!

Earlier in his career, do you remember how he left Oakland? He left in a dispute over Mike Andrews, a second baseman. This put an end to one of his noble experiments. Having no real second baseman in Oakland, he spent about a month in 1973 using three or four of them and pinch-hitting for each one when his turn came to bat. He used 10 men at second in Oakland in 1973 and an average of 1.7 second basemen a game for the whole year. An unfortunate side effect was that Williams was so busy with this clever nonsense that he never seemed to recognize that one of those second basemen was a 22-year-old kid named Manny Trillo.

I am one of Dick Williams' biggest fans, but his conduct in the case of Tim Flannery is just bizarre, reprehensible, SICK. He had a young kid who was struggling to make a place for himself in the major leagues, and he did everything that he could to destroy that kid, shatter his confidence and tear him down. That is *not* what you hire a manager to do. And why did he do this? Because he was pouting. Because he wanted to bring his problem with him from Montreal, and Ballard Smith and Jack McKeon had the sense to tell him no, he couldn't. What I would have done, had I been Smith or McKeon, is lose my own temper and fire Williams. They handled it better than I would have; they stuck with him, and insisted that Williams stick with Flannery. Flannery might not make it—it is still an open question—but he deserves a chance. Rodney Scott has had quite enough chances, thank you. (6-7; 2-3)

### *23. John CASTINO, Minnesota (12-16)*

I've never been very high on him, but obviously he can expect a better season when he gets a year away from the back operation. (9-14; 2-3)

### *24. Mike RICHARDT, Texas (7-10)*

I like him, despite the rating. He was the American Association batting champion in 1981, so you have to think he's not as bad a hitter as he showed in '82, and he did the job in the field. (4-8; 3-2)

### *25. Larry MILBOURNE, Cleveland (8-13)*

Worst prediction of the 1982 season; Bill James, *Baseball Abstract*, for nominating Jack Perconte as a potential AL Rookie of the Year.

On the other hand, who looks worse here, me or Dave Garcia? Look at Perconte's record, broken down by parts of the season:

| | G | AB | R | H | 2B | 3B | HR | RBI | SB | Avg |
|---|---|---|---|---|---|---|---|---|---|---|
| First 28 Games | 24 | 75 | 10 | 21 | 2 | 2 | 0 | 7 | 2 | .280 |
| Next 20 Games | 11 | 32 | 2 | 3 | 0 | 0 | 0 | 1 | 1 | .094 |
| Next 94 Games | 47 | 84 | 12 | 19 | 1 | 1 | 0 | 6 | 4 | .226 |
| Final 20 Games | 11 | 28 | 3 | 9 | 1 | 1 | 0 | 1 | 2 | .321 |

Read it through with me: for the first month of the season he played regularly and he hit .280. Then he went through a little slump, 3 for 32, which is nothing compared to what Cal Ripken went through. Hell, I don't imagine there were five players in the league who didn't go through a 3-for-32 stretch sometime in the year. But for Garcia, that was all he needed to see; if he ain't going to hit for me I ain't going to play him. For three and a half months Perconte sat on the bench, until finally even Garcia realized that the Indians were just playing out the string.

Sat on the bench, for whom? For *Larry Milbourne*. For *Alan Bannister*. For a couple of past-30 journeymen utility players, players who have established beyond the furthest remove of doubt that they are *not* championship-quality ballplayers. What is the point? How can anyone be that blind?

Garcia took some heat early in the year for not playing Von Hayes regularly, but in the end he did give Hayes enough playing time (150 games, 527 at-bats) to see what he could do. Perconte doesn't have Hayes' kind of talent, but if you gave him 150 games he'd hit .260 or better, he'd draw 80 or 90 walks, he'd steal 30 or 40 bases with a good stolen-base percentage and he'd settle down and turn the double play better than any Indian second baseman in years. I just can't imagine why you wouldn't want to let him do that. (Milbourne 7-9; 2-3)

### *26. Doug FLYNN, Montreal (11-24)*

One of the ten nicest people in baseball, according to everybody I know who has dealt with him. (6-18; 6-5)

# THIRD BASEMEN

### 1. *Mike SCHMIDT, Philadelphia (25-9)*

Another player who has taken quite a bit of criticism for his clutch performances and did again last summer after a couple of years quiescence. The most meticulous and extensive of the studies that I did attempting to identify key games and record performances in them was a thorough breakdown of the Phillies' World Championship season in 1980. I identified what I regarded as the Phillies' 25 most important games by a complicated and cumbersome 8-factor weighting scale. There were four basic factors considered, with four other bonus considerations. The basic four were:

1. The position on the schedule (11 of the 25 games were played in September, 19 after the All-Star Game).
2. The quality of the opposition (18 of the 25 games were against better-than-.500 teams).
3. Whether it was in-division or out-of-division (15 of the 25 games were against Eastern division teams.)
4. Whether or not it was a close game (18 of the 25 were one-run games).

Bonus points were given:

1. If the Phillies were trying to snap a previous losing streak (14 of the 25 games followed a loss on the previous day; six of them were played with the Phillies carrying a losing streak of three or more);
2. If the team which eventually won was behind at some point (in 20 of the 25 games the loser blew a lead, several times a big lead);
3. If it was the rubber game of a series (6 of the 25 were);
4. If the team which had the combination of hits and walks which should ordinarily be most productive by the runs-created formula did not win (this happened in 10 of the 25 games).

To study each box score for the whole season and extract all of this data is a prohibitive amount of work; it took me two days to do one team/season, so it would take two months to figure for the entire major leagues. But it worked, or at least I am satisfied that it worked; looking at the 25 games selected, I had no question in my mind about whether or not they were the right 25 games. All of the games which should have been there, were; no games were included unless there were very good reasons for it.

There were two things that happened in those 25 games which were most interesting. The Phillies won 18 of the 25 games, which considering the calibre of the competition in those games is extraordinary. They were 11 games over .500 in these 25 key games against tough teams; they were only nine games over .500 (73-64) in the other 137 games. I think it is quite fair to say that that remarkable percentage presaged their victories over Houston and Kansas City in the fall.

The other thing that happened was that the three men who dominated the Phillies' 1980 season—Schmidt, McGraw and Carlton—leapt dramatically to the fore in the key games, while virtually everybody else dropped off. I wrote in an *Esquire* article in the spring of 1981 that the Phillies were what you would get if you took the Toronto Blue Jays and added Willie Mays, Sandy Koufax and Hoyt Wilhelm. I still think that was a fair summation of that team. (*Esquire* later published a letter from an outraged Phillies' fan who felt that I had maltreated Bake McBride, "One of the true unrecognized superstars of the game." A year later, Bake McBride was traded to the Cleveland Indians for Sid Monge, considerably damaging the reader's case.) I still think it was the worst 22-man championship team that I ever saw and the best 3-man combo that any team has had at least since World War II.

In these 25 key games:

Tug McGraw pitched in 14, won three, saved eight, pitched 25.2 innings, struck out 23 men and posted a 0.70 ERA.

Steve Carlton won six and lost two.

Mike Schmidt hit .367 with 11 home runs, 24 RBI, and an .886 slugging percentage.

These games accounted for only 15% of the Phillies' schedule against difficult opposition, but they accounted for three of McGraw's five wins, for 40% of his saves, for 25% of Carlton's wins, for 23% of Schmidt's home runs and for 20% of his RBI. Projected out over a 162 game schedule, the impact was that of a reliever who went 19-6 with 52 saves, a starter who went 39-13, and a third baseman who hit .367 with 71 home runs and 156 RBI.

Everyone else on the team, meanwhile, faded into the background. Rose hit only .212 in the key games, Luzinski .208, Maddox .230, Trillo .227, Boone .210, Bowa .226. The arguable exception was the maligned superstar, Bake McBride, who hit .368 in these games, but with only one home run and nine RBI, down a third from his normal production.

The great difficulty about clutch performance, it seems to me, is that it separates what a player *is* from what he *does*. A lot of people have the same trouble with fielding . . . This new guy has hit well for us, they will say, but he is a bad fielder, and he can't hit in the clutch. Get it? A subtle linguistic shift, from has done to is; batting is simply performance, clutch hitting is character. But I don't see it that way, perhaps because statistics are so clumsy at measuring character. In 1982 Mike Schmidt didn't hit well with men on base, and he didn't hit well in the thick of the pennant race. But in 1980, he hit *very* well in key games, and he might again in 1983. I don't see a conflict, any more than I see a conflict in the 1980 and '82 batting averages of Miguel Dilone or the 1980 and '82 earned run averages of Mike Norris. (21-4; 5-4)

### 2. *Buddy BELL, Texas (23-11)*

Quick now, what family has had the most hits in the major leagues? As I figure it, the top 12 are:

1. The Waners (Big Poison & Little Poison) .....5611
2. The Alous (Felipe, Matty and Jesus) .....5094
3. The DiMaggios (Dom, Joe & Vince) .....4853
4. The Delahantys (Jim, Joe, Ed, Frank & Tom) .....4211
5. The Cobbs (Ty and Un-Ty) .....4191
6. The Aarons (Hank & Tommy) .....3987
7. The Roses (Pete and Re-Pete) .....3869
8. The Musials (Stan and the Man) .....3630
9. The Sewells (Luke and Joe) .....3619
10. The Boyers (Ken, Clete and Cloyd) .....3559
11. The Sislers (George, Dick and Dave) .....3557
12. The Wagners (Honus and Butts) .....3489

The Bells, Buddy and Gus, are only 24 off the list with 3465 (alright, Rangers, I expect to see a press release on this in early May). Bump and Maury Wills are close enough to make the list in about three years, but we don't count Japan, and if Dale Berra is as good as he looks, the Berras will get there. Yaz Jr. wouldn't have to turn in too much of a career to put them on the list; Marc Sullivan, on the other hand, has his work cut out for him. Little Petie Rose might make the majors and help out if somebody doesn't strangle him first. (17-8; 7-2)

### *3. Doug DeCINCES, California (25-13)*

Combination of doubles and home runs gives him tremendous isolated power . . . continues to be the most consistent second-half hitter in baseball, with 1976-1982 totals of 47 home runs in the first three months of the season, 86 in the last three. The funny thing is that it isn't a short or gradual gathering of steam throughout the year, like Gene Richards has or Graig Nettles, but a sudden hits-the-switch hammering that begins like clockwork on July 1. His worst month is June; his best July. Since 1976 he has hit *at least* 43 points higher in July than in June in every season except 1981, when he hit .167 in early June and there was no July. The average gain has been about twice that:

| | | G | AB | R | H | 2B | 3B | HR | RBI | SB | Avg |
|---|---|---|---|---|---|---|---|---|---|---|---|
| June, | 1976-1982 | 137 | 471 | 48 | 101 | 20 | 5 | 11 | 71 | 5 | .214 |
| July, | 1976-1982 | 147 | 521 | 79 | 155 | 41 | 1 | 23 | 77 | 8 | .298 |

. . . 13 of his 32 home runs were against Minnesota or Seattle. Nobody else in the league hit 13 HR against two teams. (18-10; 6-4)

### *4. George BRETT, Kansas City (22-11)*

What has happened to George over the last two seasons is unusually simple to explain, and can be traced unmistakably in the records. It all began on October 10th, 1980, and no, that is not the date of Dickie Noles' knockdown pitch. That is the date on which, after the nation had just spent three days listening to Billy Martin explain how his pitchers had stopped George in 1980 by a steady diet of breaking balls, Goose Gossage delivered a 98-MPH fastball, and George Brett deposited it in the third deck. And it is overstating the case, but not by much, to say that that was the last fastball that George has seen.

Pitchers, basically, like to throw fastballs. Most of them are in the major leagues because they have strong arms and can throw hard. They are proud of the fact that they can throw hard. They like to. When a pitcher throws breaking stuff and changes speeds a lot, the hitters will sit in the dugout and scream at him, essentially, to fight like a man. Challenge the hitters, that's the spirit. Besides that, the fastball is easier to control than a breaking pitch, and it doesn't put as much strain on the arm.

I have known since 1976 that George Brett was basically a fastball hitter, and so, I suspect, has every pitcher in the American League. But there's knowing something, and then there's *knowing* it. Before 1980, the fact that Brett was a fastball hitter represented a challenge to the pitchers. It didn't dissuade most of them from throwing their fastballs, it simply caused them to try to throw harder. But when the Goose loaded up and threw him the best fastball that he had and George said Whoopee, that did it. Billy's bragging about getting George out with slop took on a whole new meaning. Throwing him a fastball was no longer regarded as a challenge, it was regarded as suicidal.

Before 1980, he didn't walk much; since then, because breaking pitches are harder to control, he walks quite a bit (71 times in '82). Because he is taking more pitches, he is also striking out a lot more (51 times in '82, about twice his pre-1981 average). Through 1980 he was an amazing clutch performer; now, with men on base he gets impatient and lunges at off-speed pitches. Whereas he used to hit 100 points better in Kansas City, he now does better on the road where the fences are easier to reach if a curve ball hangs.

But watch out; he is adjusting. I think there is a definite limit to how many curve balls you can show the man before he starts rocketing them all over the park, and I think we're pretty close to reaching that limit.

We'll see. There is more to the story than just that, of course; there's a Roger Maris Syndrome involved. I think that the irate locals who portrayed George's contract disaffection as an act of infantile temper were making a more profound point than they realized. George is a man whose masculine family—his father and his brothers—are everything to him. He is a bachelor. In the Herzog years, the Royals were a close team, with a warm, we're-all-in-this-together sort of atmosphere—exactly as the Cardinals are now. They're not that way any more; Howser is a fine manager, but he's just different. I think George misses that terribly. How does he feel when he sees Jamie Quirk, whom he's been with since the low minors, pushed out of the nest? Like it's time for him to go, too, I suspect. He wants the Royals to tell him that they love him, and instead they tell him it's a business. Sure, he's a spoiled kid, but we're not all too adult to sympathize with those feelings, are we? (18-7; 4-4)

### *5. Bill MADLOCK, Pittsburgh (20-10)*

Defense is degenerating to the point at which he may have to be moved . . . still has the third-highest lifetime batting average among major-league players and now trails Brett, .31633 to .31629. (17-5; 3-5)

### *6. Paul MOLITOR, Milwaukee (20-11)*

Started 48 double plays at third, the third-highest total ever. A lot of that is Gantner, of course, but a lot of it isn't. There is a very clear relationship between a third baseman's ability to go to his left (on his feet) and his DP total; good third basemen, like Schmidt and Nettles, start *a lot* more double plays than average defensive players. The two players who had more than 48 were Nettles and Harland Clift, a superb third baseman of the thirties. (In the MacMillan Encyclopedia, Butch Hobson is listed as having started 57 double plays in 1977, which is another Ron Fairly-type error. He actually started 27.) (17-10; 4-2)

### 7. *Toby HARRAH, Cleveland (23-14)*

The Toby-Harrah-for-the-All-Star-team controversy... how can the entire country get so confused about these things? Let's review the facts: Toby Harrah plays in the major leagues for roughly 40 years, during which he clearly and unmistakably establishes that he is *not* an All-Star. George Brett, over a period of several years, establishes beyond any shadow of a doubt that he *is* an All-Star. Toby Harrah has a hot streak early in the year, on the strength of which he carries a .336 batting average into the All-Star break with 17 home runs and 45 RBI, while George Brett was stumbling along barely over .300 with only 10 homers. Nevertheless, the nation's baseball fans elect George Brett to the All-Star team, which strikes me as an act of abundant good sense, because everybody in the country knows that George Brett is a better ballplayer than Toby Harrah.

But what comes of this? Why do we have to put up, every All-Star season, with these asinine editorials about why is this guy on the All-Star team when his numbers are only this when this guy isn't on the team when his numbers are this and this and that guy has done this. Was there one of you out there who really thought that Toby Harrah had become a .336 hitter? And if you didn't think that he was a .336 hitter, why did you think that he should have been on the All-Star team? Would you be happy if we scheduled an All-Mediocrities-Who-Had-Good-First-Halves Game? We could play it in Cleveland every year.

There is a debate that goes along with this every June and July about the "relevance" of this season's statistics and the "relevance" of career statistics to the question of who belongs in the All-Star Game. I can see how this would be a difficult issue to resolve, particularly if you haven't stopped to think about the subject for 35 seconds before joining into the debate. If you have, the resolution of the debate is absurdly obvious.

Q) What are baseball statistics? What do they mean?

A) Baseball statistics are valuable as evidence about the ability of baseball players.

Q) Why do we keep them?

A) We keep them to tell us how good a baseball player somebody is.

Q) Which statistics are relevant to the selection of an All-Star team?

A) *All statistics are relevant to the extent that they provide credible evidence about the abilities of the player involved.*

That's it. That's all you need to know to put an end to this whole stupid argument. If you're comparing an unknown quantity—a Kent Hrbek in 1982—to an old, once-great ballplayer—Carl Yastrzemski in 1982—then by all means, the seasonal statistics are relevant evidence. When you talk about career records, Carl Yastrzemski's 1967 season is clearly and obviously irrelevant, because no sensible person would use what happened in 1967 as evidence about what kind of a ballplayer somebody was in 1982. A sensible man, looking at the 1982 statistics of Kent Hrbek, could very possibly conclude that he was a better ballplayer than Yastrzemski. If Toby Harrah had been hitting .383 and George Brett .250, then that would have been credible evidence that Harrah had become the legitimate All-Star. But just because somebody goes on a hot streak early in the year...who cares? There is no reason to let it confuse you. (19-8; 5-5)

### 8. *Ron CEY, Los Angeles (20-13)*

Except for a .354 mark against the Mets, the three teams that he hit the best against were the Giants (.371), the Braves (.283) and the Padres (.281)—the three teams the Dodgers were trying to beat. Against San Francisco and Atlanta he hit .331 with nine homers and 25 RBI in 130 at-bats . . .

Cey won the Lou Gehrig Award in 1982. The qualifications for winning this Award are (pick one):

1) Getting hit in the head by a Rich Gossage fastball.
2) Playing major-league baseball for twelve years despite the fact that your knees are the height of a seven-year-old's.
3) Having your name drawn out of a hat by the appropriate committee; or
4) Putting up with the second-hand opinions of Frank Sinatra for six years without cracking under the strain.

Maybe this comment is fatuous and absurd, but it seems to me that to imply an equality between battling against Amyotrophic Lateral Sclerosis and any of the above is equally so. (15-10; 5-3)

### 9. *Ken OBERKFELL, St. Louis (19-14)*

Led league in fielding percentage, but .972 was the lowest league-leading percentage at third in six years.... On-Base percentage has gone down every season since he became a regular: .400, .380, .356, .346. He's a good ballplayer, but I'd like him a lot better if the numbers were going up. (14-10; 6-3)

### 10. *Carney LANSFORD, Boston (18-13)*

His year is just the reverse of Yastrzemski's: He hit below .300 in every month of the season except August, but pulled average to .301 with big month . . . grounded into a few too many double plays. I still don't think he's a great fielder, but he'll help Oakland. (16-9; 4-3)

### 11. *Darrell EVANS, San Francisco (18-13)*

One of my longtime favorites. His career batting average isn't good, but it represents only 41% of his offensive ability, plus he was the second-best defensive third baseman in the NL in the 1970s, though he never got credit for it... that's past; Tom O'Malley is a better defensive third baseman now. The Giants were 42-32 with O'Malley in the lineup, just 45-43 without him. (16-9; 2-4)

### *12. Bob HORNER, Atlanta (18-14)*

There were two numbers that really surprised me when I got the NL official stats, one of which was Horner's fielding percentage, .970. One less error and he would have led the league. But because of poor range his defensive won-lost percentage was still only .42, and the bad defense is the basic reason he doesn't rank higher. Also, his offensive stats are inflated by his home park. His career totals are now 97 home runs in Atlanta and 39 on the road. And he isn't helped by his injury history. (15-9; 3-5)

### *13. Art HOWE, Houston (17-13)*

Drew 15 intentional walks despite batting .232 with little power, which tells you a lot about the Astros . . . not as bad a hitter as 1982's .238 or as good as 1981's .296. Good third baseman; would have had a good career if he'd entered organized ball about six years earlier. Reggie's about the same age, but had three and a half years in the majors before Howe entered baseball. (12-10; 5-4)

### *14. Cal RIPKEN, Baltimore (12-9)*

Did you realize that Ripken and Benny Ayala have identical career totals of 28 home runs and 93 RBI? The amazing thing is that although Ayala is a 32-year old veteran who once played in the Mets outfield with Cleon Jones, he still has fewer career at-bats than the Rookie Ripper, 567-637. Ayala has a better batting average, too, .265 to .256.

People who see things to which the rest of the species is blind are called "mad" or "brilliant," "lunatics" or "geniuses," according to whether or not they are able to convince us that the things they see are real. Had any manager but Earl Weaver decided in the middle of the summer to make Cal Ripken Jr. his shortstop, I would have written the guy off as a nut case. I was talking to John Walsh, the editor of *Inside Sports*, in late July. "What's Weaver up to with Ripken?" he wondered. "What's the idea of putting him at short?"

"I'm damned if I know," I replied. "I sure don't see any percentage in it. But I'm sure Earl Weaver knows more about what he is doing than I do." A couple of weeks later the Orioles came to Kansas City and wiped out in a four-game series, during which Ripken looked as much like a major-league shortstop as he does like Leon Spinks. Tom Evans called me from Baltimore.

"Why is our 'genius' manager playing this oaf at shortstop?" he wanted to know.

"Don't have an answer for you," I told him. "It looks just as silly to me as it does to you. I don't think that there has ever been a good six foot-four inch, 200 pound shortstop."

But Earl Weaver saw something that the rest of us did not see, and no fair person, in the end, could say that the move didn't work. He was so sure that he saw something out there that when the Orioles lost five straight games, he refused to recant and return Ripken to third, and when they continued to stumble around he refused to give it up, and when they fell flat on their face with seven more losses in a row and nine out of 10, he still refused to crack. What other manager can you name who ever showed such a commitment to an invisible advantage? But when the Orioles picked themselves up and somehow, miraculously, got back in the race, Cal Ripken was still at shortstop.

The record? The Orioles' record when Cal Ripken was not in the lineup was 0-4. When he started the game at third base, the Orioles' record was 37-30 with one tie, a .552 percentage. When Ripken started at short; it was 55-36, a .604 percentage. Those figures do not prove that the switch to short improved the team, but they are inconsistent with the notion that the move weakened the team. The Orioles did allow more runs per game when Ripken was at short (4.26 per game, 308 total), than they did when he was at third (3.94 per game, 268 total). But their improved offense, from 4.29 runs per game to 5.22, much more than offset the difference.

Where did the offensive improvement come from? Again, I can't see it. It would have been one thing to move Ripken to short to get another bat in the lineup, but much of the time it was simply a matter of shifting Sakata from short to second, and Dauer from second to third, thus winding up with the same three players in the lineup but all three out of position. Gulliver and Rayford, the prospective new third basemen, hit a combined .182, although Gulliver did make an offensive contribution.

It is fair and accurate to point out that the DeCinces trade probably cost the Orioles the pennant. Dan Ford didn't do anything, and if the Orioles were going to play Ripken at short, they might as well have kept DeCinces at third. But Weaver didn't make that trade; reportedly, he didn't even like the trade. Indeed, that comment in one sense points out how unique and gutty Weaver's handling of the situation was, because most organizations, having made that kind of a commitment to Ripken at third, would rather die than switch him to short, effectively admitting that the first move was a mistake. Weaver didn't look at the move on the basis of how it reflected on what had been done before, and he didn't look at it on the basis of how well Ripken fits the image of a shortstop. He looked at it on the basis of how it would change the performance of the ball club. And he saw something the rest of us couldn't see. (10-8; 2-1)

### *15. Tim WALLACH, Montreal (16-14)*

Offensive stats about as close to Ripken's as they could get—28, 97, .268 against 28, 93, .264; 31 doubles and 3 triples against 32 and 5, not many stolen bases (3 and 6), fairly similar strikeout-to-walk totals, 89 runs scored against 90, 15 double play balls against 16. They're similar in size; Wallach is a couple of years older. And the defensive right-shift involving Wallach was probably as much a key to the Expos' season as the one involving Ripken was to the Orioles, although in this case it was done to accommodate another player . . . had defensive problems at third at first (at first at third? whatever . . .) but seemed to adapt pretty well by season's end. (12-11; 3-4)

*16. Luis SALAZAR, San Diego (19-14)*

Fielded only .938 but had the best complete defensive line of any NL third baseman. That's not all that strange when you think about it; NL third basemen fielded .951 as a group, so the difference between Salazar and an average third baseman in that regard is just one play in 77, between 5 and 6 errors over the season. The difference between Salazar and Oberkfell, the percentage leader, is just 14 plays. Salazar had more put-outs per game, more assists per game, more double plays per game. Salazar also played 18 games at shortstop, a fact which powerfully suggests that he must cover quite a bit of ground.

I'll teach you a trick for trying to get a line on what kind of a defensive player somebody out of the past was, somebody you didn't see play. If the player's position is at the right of the defensive spectrum (shortstop is the extreme right; second base and center field are nearest to it), the less he played at some other position, the better defensive player he probably was. Look at the current shortstops: Rick Burleson hasn't played a game at any other position since 1975 (one game at second then), Concepcion has about 99.9% of his playing time in the last ten years as SS, while Belanger went 14 years without playing an inning at any other position and Ozzie Smith has yet to do so. So if you look at the records out of the past, you'll see a player like Aparicio who never played a game at any position other than short while his contemporaries like McAuliffe and Hansen and Petrocelli and Menke were switched around a certain amount, and the record will tell you how good of a shortstop Aparicio was. Same thing with Marty Marion as opposed to Eddie Joost or Skeeter Newsome; or George McBride as compared to Ivy Olson or whoever.

On the left end of the spectrum, however, just the opposite rule applies; the great defensive first basemen like Vic Power and Wes Parker and George Scott were usually men who came from some other position and were continually shifted around to help plug gaps. In the middle of the spectrum, as at third base, a good defensive player will have a few games when he is shifted rightward; a poor defensive player will have games when he is shifted leftward. Mike Schmidt has played 17 games in his career at shortstop, six at second, only two at first; Brooks Robinson played second and short, never first; and Buddy Bell is used at short in emergencies, not at first. But with a player like Horner or Bench, if something goes funny in the middle of a game, they'll put in a defensive sub at third and move him to first base or left field.

Sure, it's not a perfect generalization. But if I was evaluating a third baseman out of the past, and I could know one of two things, his fielding percentage or how many games he played at shortstop, I would a lot rather know how many games he played at short . . . Ignore this rule when dealing with the San Francisco Giants. (14-13; 4-4)

*17. Graig NETTLES, New York Yankees (15-15)*

Zero percent chance of getting 3000 career hits. (11-11; 4-4)

*18. Wayne GROSS, Oakland (13-13)*

About as good as a player can be if he hits .235, which is Gross' career average, and doesn't run . . . my idea of an ideal #2 hitter. He gets on base a lot to set up the inning, he takes a lot of pitches, which allows the running game to take place naturally, and despite his speed he very rarely grounds into a double play (only 31 in his entire career, never more than eight in a season). I don't know why that is, really; Darrell Evans is the same. Murphy is a heckeva #2 hitter, too, of course, but Murphy has developed into a #3 or 4 hitter. (9-10; 3-4)

*19. Johnny BENCH, Cincinnati (10-11)*

Defensive won-lost percentage was .12; second lowest in the majors was .30. But offensive totals for the two rated seasons are 577 at-bats, 21 homers and a .275 average. If the management of Bench's decline is typical of what we can expect from the Reds in the future, it may be a long way back.(10-7; 0-4)

*20. Ryne SANDBERG, Chicago (11-13)*

Rating surprises me, as he seems to have a lot of positives. But I guess the positives are many but small; you combine a poor on-base percentage with no power at a position where there are a lot of hitters, and you don't get a high rating. (8-11; 2-3)

*21. Gary GAETTI, Minnesota (10-12)*

Only two American Leaguers were in double figures in sacrifice flies last year, Robin Yount (again?) with 10, and Gaetti with 13 . . . hit over his season's .230 average in July (.258), August (.245), and September (.232) . . . looks like he can play if he can hit .250, and I think he can. (7-10; 3-2)

*22. Hubie BROOKS, New York Mets (14-18)*

I mentioned in a team comment that the Mets have done a poor job of adapting to their ballpark. One of the things the Mets should do to adapt to the park better is forget all about developing this type of player, the one-dimensional singles-hitter. In a park like St. Louis or Cincinnati, a singles-hitter can be valuable because you've got a reasonable chance of putting four or five singles together. Ken Oberkfell is the same kind of player. But in a park like Shea, where the grass and the poor visibility cut averages by 10 or 15 points, it can't be done. The Pirates team batting average is only 11% higher than the Mets, but the chance of their getting four straight hits is 50% higher, five straight 67% higher. (11-13; 3-5)

*23. Aurelio RODRIGUEZ, Chicago White Sox (5-9)*

Of the three White Sox midsummer lineup changes, this is the only one that I really disagree with. Morrison isn't popular and he isn't a great ballplayer, but he can hit for power and he's not as bad defensively as all that. Would you—would anybody—go into a season saying that Aurelio Rodriguez was your third baseman? No, you wouldn't. There are too many things he can't do. So why go to him in the middle of a stretch run? It was an emotional overreaction to Morrison's very visible weaknesses. The White Sox were 28-22 (.560) with Morrison in the lineup, 59-53 (.527) without him. The White Sox just decided they would rather not see the games they were losing go sailing over the first baseman's head. They hit a slump and had to have somebody to blame it on. (4-5; 2-3)

### *24. Tom BROOKENS, Detroit (9-17)*

Looks competent enough at second to be a good utility player; doesn't hit anywhere near enough to be a regular third baseman . . . hits lefthanders well enough to serve as the right-handed part of a platoon arrangement. But I don't know if Sparky really understands that complicated stuff like platooning. (6-13; 4-3)

### *25. Garth IORG, Toronto (8-16)*

I know, I know . . . how can you rate a .285 hitter this low? He doesn't get on base enough to score any runs, he doesn't have enough power to drive in any runs, he doesn't save himself with the glove. He had only 12 walks, only one home run. And he has yet to prove that he is a legitimate .285 hitter . . . defensive won-lost percentage might be lowered unfairly due to platooning. But it would be a bad defensive record no matter what you did to it . . . Mullinicks, despite .244 average, would rate higher (I rated the man with more at-bats). The Blue Jays were 45-52 with Iorg in the starting lineup, 33-32 without him . . . hit .345 in day games, only .255 at night. (7-12; 1-4)

### *26. Manny CASTILLO, Seattle (6-14)*

A classic "bat-control" second hitter. He hit only .257, and his batting average represented 73% of his offensive value, as his peripheral stats were awful (included 2 stolen bases and 8 caught stealing). So why would anyone say "bat-control" as if these words were a magic wand, and jam an unproductive player right up the middle of your offense? (5-10; 2-3)

# SHORTSTOPS

### *1. Robin YOUNT, Milwaukee (30-14)*

I am reliably assured that Robin Young is not, in addition to his other virtues, a brilliant man, but he made the one most perceptive comment that I heard on television in the summer of 1982. When asked who he thought should vote for the All-Star Game, the players or the fans, he said, "I can't really answer that question because I don't know who the game is supposed to be for. I don't know if the game is supposed to be for the fans or if it is supposed to be for the players." You see the point? You know those people who run around saying that the players should elect the All-Star teams because look at this vote and look at that one and there are all kinds of people who don't deserve the honor who wind up in the starting lineup? Those people are making an assumption, without even realizing that they are doing it, that the purpose of the All-Star game is to honor the players, and therefore that the desire to honor the right people takes precedence over the desire to put in front of the fans the people that the fans want to see. Is the game basically an honor for the players, or is it basically an entertainment for the fans? The answer that you select to that question will tell you who ought to elect the teams. People simply leap over that question and construct their reasoning from beyond it; Yount sliced up the argument with a deftness that William Buckley should envy.

He also, so nearly as one can tell, did everything else right. I mentioned a year ago that in the years from 1950 to 1965, there was an implicit recognition of the defensive spectrum in the MVP. Choosing between a first baseman or outfielder who created 130 runs and a shortstop or catcher who created 110, the voters of that period would pick the player who played a key defensive position:

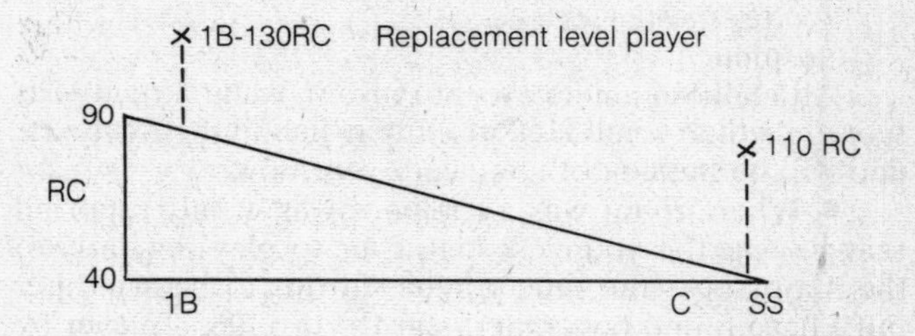


This makes sense to me, because the shortstop who creates 110 runs is further above the line representing a replacement-level ballplayer, which is to say that he would be harder to replace if you lost him, than would the first baseman. But after 1965, this is no longer true; after that the award has tended to go to the player with the best numbers, given some other qualifications.

Anyway, the selection of Yount in no way reverses this, because Yount, with the season he was having, would have been the obvious MVP even if he had been a left fielder. He created 142 runs, 12 more than anyone else in the league; he played for a championship team; he missed the batting championship by just one hit; and he was near the league lead in everything. The fact that he was a Gold Glove shortstop was just a bonus.

A few other notes:

- The last six MVPs to get into the World Series have all gone sort of hog-wild there. Their records are:

| | G | AB | R | H | 2B | 3B | HR | RBI | Batting Avg | Slugging Pct |
|---|---|---|---|---|---|---|---|---|---|---|
| 1976 Munson | 4 | 17 | 2 | 9 | 0 | 0 | 0 | 2 | .529 | .529 |
| 1976 Morgan | 4 | 15 | 3 | 5 | 1 | 1 | 1 | 2 | .333 | .733 |
| 1979 Stargell | 7 | 30 | 7 | 12 | 4 | 0 | 3 | 7 | .400 | .833 |
| 1980 Brett | 6 | 24 | 3 | 9 | 2 | 1 | 1 | 3 | .375 | .667 |
| 1980 Schmidt | 6 | 21 | 6 | 8 | 1 | 0 | 2 | 7 | .381 | .714 |
| 1982 Yount | 7 | 29 | 6 | 12 | 3 | 0 | 1 | 6 | .414 | .621 |
| Total | 34 | 136 | 27 | 55 | 11 | 2 | 8 | 27 | .404 | .691 |

Against the kind of pitching you're facing in a World Series, that's a pretty fair performance even for an MVP. I guess if they want to the announcers can stop saying that the Series will probably be dominated by some unheralded bit-player like Billy Martin or Gene Tenace.

• Speaking of clutch performances, Yount hit 7 of his 29 home runs against Baltimore, and averaged .352 with almost half of his home runs against the Brewer's three toughest opponents. The three teams against which he drove in the most runs were Baltimore (15), Detroit (14) and Boston (11). The seven home runs against Baltimore were as many as anyone in the league hit against any team and were matched only by Gorman Thomas (seven against Boston) and two players who hit seven against the Twins.

• Yount was born in September, 1955, so his "1982 Age" was 26. The all-time leaders in hits through age 26 are:

| | | |
|---|---|---|
| 1. | Ty Cobb | 1602 |
| 2. | Mel Ott | 1440 |
| 3. | Al Kaline | 1390 |
| 4. | Vada Pinson | 1381 |
| 5. | ROBIN YOUNT | 1363 |
| 6. | Freddie Lindstrom | 1347 |
| 7. | Rogers Hornsby | 1323 |
| 8. | Hank Aaron | 1309 |
| 9. | Jimmie Foxx | 1307 |
| 10. | Frankie Frisch | 1300 |

All Hall of Famers except Pinson. Yount already has more hits than some Hall of Famers had in their careers, and will be passing others every year now.

• When Yount was a rookie it was widely reported that he was the youngest man ever to play regularly in the majors. At the time I believed this to be accurate, but I have found now that it wasn't. In 1906, a player by the name of Johnny Lush played almost exactly as much as Yount did in 1974 (Yount, 107 games, 344 at bats; Lush, 106, 369). Lush was about three weeks younger than Yount. (18-9; 10-6)

### 2. *Dave CONCEPCION, Cincinnati (26-19)*

The senior nonpitcher on the National League's all-incumbency team (see Amos Otis):

| Pos | Longest Incumbent, Team | Who has been there since: |
|---|---|---|
| 1B | Garvey, Los Angeles | 1973 |
| 2B | Trillo, Philadelphia | 1979 |
| 3B | Schmidt, Philadelphia and Cey, Los Angeles | 1973 |
| SS | Concepcion, Cincinnati | 1970 |
| LF | Cruz, Houston | 1976 |
| CF | Maddox, Philadelphia | 1975 |
| RF | Parker, Pittsburgh | 1975 |
| C | Carter, Montreal | 1977 |
| RHP | Niekro, Atlanta | 1967 |
| LHP | Carlton, Philadelphia | 1972 |

(Offensive 17-11; Defensive 10-7)

### 3. *Dickie THON, Houston (15-11)*

Gentlemen, this is a *good* young ballplayer. I didn't realize that he would rate this high either, but one of the virtues of doing rating systems is that they force you to look at every phase of every player's game. What you have here is:

A) The second-best lead-off man in the National League;

B) The best-hitting shortstop in the National League;

C) A shortstop with a tremendous double-play rate despite playing for a team that was last in the league in hits allowed.

A shortstop with the fourth-best fielding percentage in the league.

A player who hit 31 doubles and 10 triples in less than 500 at-bats; and

One of the best percentage base stealers in the National League.

You never know, but I believe he will be the best shortstop in the National League in the 1980s. (11-6; 5-4)

### 4. *Alan TRAMMELL, Detroit (23-22)*

The only regular in the American League to hit 100 points better after the All-Star break (.310) than before (.205). He used to wear down as the season wore on, but that was probably related to his youth and slight build. There's a lot more pop in his bat now, with 34 doubles and 9 homers in 1982. I think he is ready to enter his prime, with a .300 season (1980) and a couple of Gold Gloves (1980, 1981) already behind him . . . hits far better in Detroit than on the road (.286, .301 in Detroit the last two years; .230, .216 on the road). (13-14; 11-7)

### 5. *Ozzie SMITH, St. Louis (23-22)*

The argument for Ozzie Smith as the National League's Most Valuable Player shine with a pristine logical clarity, unpolluted by evidence. The argument is that Ozzie saved the Cardinals . . . oh, I don't know, let's say 100 runs. He is an amazing shortstop to watch, and nobody can prove that he didn't.

I know that an awful lot of people are going to say that this rating is wrong. (Rating? It's an insult! Ozzie Smith below Dickie Thon? It's crazy.) Indeed, all up and down the list of shortstops, people are going to tell me that I have overrated all of the hitting shortstops—Smalley, Almon, Russell, Sakata—and underrated all of the light-hitting glove men (Smith, Foli, Griffin). But while the detailed, specific nature of offensive records enables us to estimate with great accuracy how many runs are produced by a hitter, they do not enable us to state with equal finality how many are prevented by a fielder. And that flexibility, that looseness, is what enables this difference of opinion to survive. So let us take a minute to examine the logical underpinnings of the ranking (which could, indeed, very possibly be wrong).

If Ozzie Smith saved the Cardinals 100 runs, 100 runs as opposed to what? As opposed to not having a shortstop? Then 100 runs seems reasonable; there'd be an awful lot of balls go rolling through that hole if there wasn't anybody there. A hundred runs as opposed to having me playing shortstop? Hey, 100 is conservative. By the time I got through kicking the ball around, it'd be 300.

But with saying that Ozzie is 100 runs better than another shortstop . . . well, you're going to have real trouble there. The St. Louis Cardinals allowed 609 runs in 1982, which was the lowest total in the National League. If you say that Ozzie was 100 runs better than an average shortstop, then you are saying that the Cardinals would have allowed 100 runs more than they did had they had an average shortstop.

Now, an average National League team in 1982 allowed 662 runs. The Cardinals, the best defensive team in the league, were only 53 runs better than that. You see the problem that you're beginning to run into? If Ozzie was 100 runs better than the average National League shortstop, but the team as a whole was only +53, then the rest of the team is −47. In other words, all of the rest of the Cardinals—Joaquin Andujar, Bruce Sutter, Keith Hernandez, the Gold Glove first baseman, all of them—are 47 runs worse than an average National League team. That strikes me as a difficult position to defend logically.

Well, how about 100 runs better than a *bad* shortstop? There is, as it happens, a National League team which allowed exactly 100 runs more than the Cardinals. That team had, by a fortunate coincidence, a very bad shortstop, the 36-year-old Larry Bowa. He had the lowest defensive won-lost percentage of any NL shortstop. If you take the position that Smith was 100 runs better than Bowa, then you must then argue that in all other respects, the Cardinals and Cubs are defensively equal. You must argue if the Cardinals had Larry Bowa at short, they would have allowed as many runs as the Cubs did. You've got Bump Wills up against Tommy Herr, Jody Davis against Darrell Porter, Bruce Sutter against Lee Smith. You've got Wrigley Field against Busch Stadium, you've got 94 home runs allowed by the Cardinals' staff against 125 allowed by the Cubs. Let's compare the defensive won-lost percentages of the regulars on the two teams:

| St. Louis | | Chicago | | Advantage | |
|---|---|---|---|---|---|
| Hernandez | .63 | Buckner | .62 | St. Louis | +.01 |
| Herr | .63 | Wills | .25 | St. Louis | +.38 |
| Oberkfell | .57 | Sandberg | .48 | St. Louis | +.09 |
| O. Smith | .77 | Bowa | .38 | St. Louis | +.39 |
| L. Smith | .53 | Moreland | .58 | Chicago | +.05 |
| McGee | .25 | Woods | .41 | Chicago | +.16 |
| Hendrick | .44 | Durham | .51 | Chicago | +.07 |
| Porter | .53 | Davis | .44 | St. Louis | +.09 |
| TOTAL | 4.35 | | 3.67 | St. Louis | +.72 |

Even without drawing the pitchers into it, it is obvious that the Cardinals' 100-run edge is created not by one advantage but by many.

In other ways, the notion that Smith was the most valuable player in the league is difficult to reconcile with the facts. Ozzie went to the bench with an injury on September 21, with the Cardinals in second place. He didn't get back in the lineup until the race was virtually over. I find that a most curious qualification for the MVP award. Ozzie missed 22 games altogether, and the Cardinals had a better record without him in the game than with him. I find that very curious for an MVP. The Cardinals pitching staff had a significantly better ERA when Ozzie was not in the lineup (2.75) than when he was (3.47). I certainly would not conclude from that that Smith's presence in the lineup was costing the Cardinals runs. But it's a lot easier for that to happen if Smith's defensive value was 2/10 of a run then it would be if it was 6/10.

Did the Cardinals' runs-allowed total drop by 100 runs when they acquired Smith? The Cardinals allowed 3.98 runs per game in 1981, 3.76 per game in 1982—an improvement of about 36 runs. Did the Padres runs allowed go up by 100 runs when they lost Smith? The Padres allowed 4.09 runs per game with Smith in 1981, 4.06 without him in '82. Where did the 100 runs go to?

The deal, you see, is this. For 100 years, baseball has been buried in a blizzard of records. On every season it has fallen, on every player, on every game and on every issue. And yet, people are so fond of talking about these large factors in the game that don't happen to show up in the records anywhere—clutch hitting, hitting behind base runners, saving runs with the glove. Can't you see how absurd it is? It's like saying that there were a bunch of elephants playing in the snow, but that they left without leaving any tracks. If there was an elephant in the snow, he's going to leave some tracks. If there's 100 runs out there, I can damn well find their tracks. Baseball has had thousands of shortstops, hundreds of thousands of games, over a hundred seasons—and a blizzard that fell over each of them. There are too many counts of too many things for there to be any dinosaurs living out there without a trace.

The defensive statistics clearly show that Smith is a superb defensive player. The highest defensive won-lost percentage among major league shortstops in 1982:

| | Pct | W-L |
|---|---|---|
| Smith, St. Louis | .77 | 7-2 |
| Foli, California | .61 | 6-4 |
| Thon, Houston | .60 | 5-3 |
| Concepcion, Cincinnati | .59 | 6-4 |
| Ramirez, Atlanta | .59 | 6-5 |
| T. Cruz, Seattle | .59 | 5-4 |

I think that by the time Smith retires, he may well have the best career defensive record of any shortstop in history. But how many runs a year are we talking about here?

I don't know. The method above credits Smith with a defensive value of 2½ games above. 500, which is to say that he is about 20 to 25 runs a year better than an average defensive shortstop. But where does that come from? I made it up. I decided, logically but still arbitrarily, to give shortstops a defensive assignment of 11 games a season; I decided, logically but arbitrarily, to give Smith 36 points for his range factor. It is possible that a more accurate result would be achieved by using 13 games and 38 points. This would improve the ranking of Smith, and in its turn of all the other glove men at the position.

But I had good reasons for choosing the numbers that I chose. Smith made 814 clean plays in 139 games; an average defensive shortstop would have handled 698 plays in the same number of games. He made 116 plays that an average shortstop would not have made. If we assumed that 80% of those plays had the value of a negative hit, and that all of the hits prevented by a shortstop would be singles (they would, you know) and that each hit prevented saves one-third to four-tenths of a run, then we could estimate that Smith saved the Cardinals 31 to 37 runs.

Perhaps I have not plugged the right numbers into the scheme. I do not know, exactly, how many runs Smith saved the Cardinals. But I have a hell of a lot better reason for thinking it was 25 or 35 runs than anybody has for thinking it was 100. (11-18; 12-4)

### *6. Roy SMALLEY, New York Yankees (15-14)*

Rated higher than Ozzie in the free agent rankings by Elias . . . The 1982 part of his rating totals 10 wins, 11 losses; Smith's totals are 14-10. So Smith is 3½ games better, or about 28-35 runs. With the bat, Smalley created 14 more runs in almost exactly the same number of outs, so Smith's defensive edge over Smalley is about 42 to 49 runs. I think that's a very generous estimate; I don't really think the number of runs is that large.

I don't see how the Yankees could convince themselves that Robertson is a major-league shortstop. There isn't anything of it in his record. If Nettles goes over the edge, shifting Smalley to third isn't going to solve anything . . . Smalley drove in 26 runs after September 1, tying Robin Yount for second in the league. (Eddie Murray had 28.) (11-9; 3-6)

### *7. Garry TEMPLETON, San Diego (20-21)*

Away from the artificial turf in St. Louis, he may have had his last good year. He's just a bad offensive player now. 82 strikeouts and 26 walks (granted, the 26 walks were a career high), .247 average, caught stealing 16 times in 43 tries, *19* double-play balls (fifth highest in the league) . . . if he doesn't hit for average he has no offensive positives. But, of course, he does give you that great effort . . . he'll be out of baseball in six years. (12-15; 8-6)

### *8. U.L. WASHINGTON, Kansas City (19-20)*

I'm not sure, but I think U.L. is in line to become my favorite player when Amos retires . . . has tremendous power against a lefthander: hit .323 against them and slugged .561. He's always been a lot better hitter as a RHB, so much so that you've got to seriously question whether the decision to make a switch hitter out of him at the AAA level was wise. A normal platoon differential is 32 points, with about .045 slugging. U.L. drops off way more against righthanders than a normal RHB would . . . homered in three different games in '82 against Tommy John . . . also rated higher than Ozzie in the Elias rankings . . . hit 64 points higher against Western division teams (.320) than Eastern (.264), the second largest East-West split in the league. (11-13; 8-7)

### *9. Bill ALMON, Chicago (16-17)*

Improves the Oakland infield immensely. . . . Randy Hendricks has observed that whenever a team goes to arbitration against a player, it seems like two times in three the guy has a bad year, and particularly so when the team uses a lot of negative stuff. Without doing any research to check it out, I tend to agree with him. I know in my own experience, the only arbitration case I've ever worked where the guy went on and had a good year was Sambito's. It makes sense; it fits my notion that almost everybody plays better when he feels that he is a part of something, rather than that he is on the spot to perform for somebody else's benefit. So you had the odd figure of the White Sox in '82, making noises about winning the pennant, but arbitrating everybody in sight and ripping at will. (9-10; 7-5)

### *10. Rafael RAMIREZ, Atlanta (21-24)*

One of the dozen or so real surprise years of 1982. In fact, I should make up a "Gosh, I never knew he was that good" All-Star team . . . catcher Bo Diaz, infield of Boggs, Whitaker, Sandberg and Ramirez, outfield of Gary Ward, Mookie Wilson and Larry Herndon, starting corps of Sutcliffe, Krukow, Lollar and Andujar, with Caudill in relief. . . . His 130 double plays were 29 more than anybody else in baseball, and the most by an NL shortstop since 1970. (11-17; 9-8)

### *11. Chris SPEIER, Montreal (20-23)*

Also rated higher than Ozzie in the Elias rankings . . . a real underrated player; he plays a good shortstop and has driven in 60 runs or more 4 times in his career . . . his .982 fielding percentage matched his career best, and just missed leading the league for the second time. No Giant has led the league in fielding percentage at any position since he and Von Joshua did it in '75 . . . having half of a double play combination is kind of like having half of a phone number. (10-15; 10-8)

### *12. Bill RUSSELL, Los Angeles (17-20)*

Is this a misprint? The '82 stats list Russell with 63 walks and only 30 strikeouts. He's never been better than even before, now he's better than 2-1? It would have been a lot better career if he'd made that switch about 10 years ago. . . . A reader (I don't remember who) once pointed out to me that Walter Alston always had a good glove man at first base, whether he could hit or not, and always had shortstops who were, at least by the standards expected of shortstops, more notable as offensive players than defensive. His first basemen were Hodges, Fairly, Parker and Garvey, two of whom could also hit but all four of whom were good gloves; his shortstops were Reese, Wills and Russell. . . . The better the opponent, the better Russell hit 'em in 1982. He hit .415 and .377 (overall 45/114, .395) against Atlanta and San Francisco, the two teams the Dodgers were trying to beat, and he hit .333 against the Cardinals. But he was below his season's average against everyone else, hit only .171 against Chicago, hit .222 against Cincinnati and .214 against New York, the teams you are supposed to grow fat on. (11-11; 7-8)

### *13. Dale BERRA, Pittsburgh (15-20)*

No whiz with the glove, but it looks like he's going to hit . . . hit .263 against righthanders, .263 against lefthanders. (10-13; 5-7)

### *14. Vance LAW, Chicago (8-10)*

Decided to rate both Chicago shortstops. . . . I like

Almon but I won't criticize the move. Law looks like the kind of player you'd want to get into the lineup . . . drove in 45 runs after the All-Star break. (5-7; 3-3)

*15. Len SAKATA, Baltimore (9-13)*

Hit better after he moved to second . . . maybe that's why Weaver made the move (he thought playing short was affecting Sakata's hitting). (7-8; 2-5)

*16. Tim FOLI, California (16-24)*

I was among the many people who described the Foli trade as a stupid move at the time that it was made. I don't know now whether I should apologize like a gentleman or confess my private opinion that it was a stupid move that happened to work out well, at least in the short run. I still can't see trading a good prospect for a backup shortstop as a percentage move, unless you have prearranged an injury. (7-17; 9-7)

*17. Johnnie LeMASTER, San Francisco (14-22)*

Winner of the John Gochnaur Award for 1982. (7-13; 7-9)

*18. Larry BOWA, Chicago (16-26)*

I was amused to notice what happened to his defensive statistics last summer after changing teams. After eight years of hearing that his range factor was unfairly lowered because he played beside Mike Schmidt, he was traded to another team. His defensive won-lost percentages: 1981, .38; 1982, .38.

It occurred to me last summer, though, that the things people think I have written and said about Larry Bowa are a lot more derogatory than the things I have actually written and said. I was trying to make a limited point, which was that he was given a couple of Gold Glove awards which he manifestly did not deserve, because he didn't cover enough ground to be a Gold Glove shortstop. People would argue with that and I would defend it, and they would point out something in his favor and I would point out three things against him, and eventually people thought I was saying that Bowa was a lousy ballplayer. He wasn't; he was one of the six or eight best shortstops of the 1970s. But he had no business winning the Gold Glove award with Ozzie Smith and Dave Concepcion in the league. (10-15; 7-10)

*19. Bucky DENT, Texas (11-18)*

The 11-18 breaks down as 6-6 for 1981, but 5-12 for 1982. He's only 31, and he might bounce back for another year or two. (5-12; 6-6)

*20. Todd CRUZ, Seattle (9-15)*

He had a lot of bad numbers . . . the worst strikeout-to-walk ratio in baseball (96 strikeouts and 12 walks), the worst stolen-base percentage in baseball among players with ten or more attempts (2 for 12; Charlie Moore was the same, actually), 18 double-play balls, a .248 on-base percentage. But he's a good shortstop and he'll hit the ball out of the park occasionally, so I think Lachemann did the smart thing in giving him a season to see how all the positives and negatives add up. Also, he had just a remarkable clutch season; he probably had as many really big hits as anybody in baseball except Jack Clark. He had five late-inning game-winning RBIs, and some other very big hits:

APRIL 18—With a man out and the bases loaded in the bottom of the ninth, he got the winning run home on a ground ball to deep short.

APRIL 20—Tied game with a fifth-inning double, scored winning run, drove in insurance run later.

APRIL 21—RBI double drove in winning run in the sixth.

APRIL 24—Seventh-inning home run broke a 2-2 tie; 3-2 was final.

APRIL 25—Hit a home run in the bottom of the 11th to win the game, 5-4.

APRIL 27—Another 11th-inning home run provided an insurance run.

MAY 6—His two-run single was one of the keys to Seattle's 5-run third in Gaylord's 300th.

He didn't go on at the same rate all season, obviously, but he had an awful lot to do with the Mariners starting the season on the right foot. But the holes in his game are so large that they will destroy him if he doesn't improve. His K/W ratio will either go to 4-1 or it will go to 20-1, because 8-1 is an unstable uncombination, and nobody stays at that level. (4-11; 5-4)

*21. Ron WASHINGTON, Minnesota (9-15)*

Faedo seems to have won the job late in the year. . . . Washington's .271 average is deceptive, as his strike zone judgment is nearly as bad as Cruz', and his .972 fielding percentage would be more impressive if he could turn the double play more than twice a week. These things should keep him around long enough to get a shot at pension, though. . . . Faedo is a decent prospect, grade B maybe. He's a lot better prospect than Andre Robertson, which (who knows?) may make him the Yankees' shortstop of the future. . . . Ron, by the way, was (despite being a rookie) the oldest "Washington" in the majors, a year and a half older than U.L., two and a half older than Claudell. (6-10; 3-5)

*22. Ivan DeJESUS, Philadelphia (17-29)*

I don't know what happened to him, either . . . hit only .187 against lefthanders . . . (8-21; 9-8)

*23. Mike FISCHLIN, Cleveland (6-11)*

The first player to imitate Rickey Henderson's batting style. He was getting on base with it, too—.268 batting average and 34 walks in half-time play. He's 27, and was about out of chances. (3-6; 2-6)

*24. Ron GARDENHIRE, New York Mets (8-15)*

Not an impressive rookie year . . . below average in batting, power, strikeout-and-walk frequency, poor stolen-base percentage, grounded into a few too many DP, defensively did not have a good fielding percentage, range factor or DP rate. The thing is he's not far off the pace in anything; in contrast to a Phil Garner who is just above the norm in everything, he's just below. But it does add up, and he's going to have to improve if he's going to stay around. As far as I know, though, Tigger made it through the year . . . (4-9; 4-6)

### *25. Alfred GRIFFIN, Toronto (16-31)*

Had a good defensive year, but he's just such an offensive millstone that I wouldn't want him around. He stops every ball that comes his way, and every rally, too . . . hits righthanders well enough to be used as a platoon player. (6-23; 9-9)

### *26. Glenn HOFFMAN, Boston (12-25)*

The Red Sox are *not* going to win the pennant with this guy at short. (5-17; 7-8)

### *27. Fred STANLEY, Oakland (5-18)*

One rating that nobody is going to argue about. (2-10; 2-9)

# LEFT FIELDERS

### *1. Dave WINFIELD, New York Yankees (22-10)*

Has averaged 13.7 assists per 162 outfield games (the norm is about 10.5). What I was very surprised to note while drawing up the lists of outfield assists per game was that, out of the 48 American League outfielders in 80 or more games in 1982, only two (Amos Otis and Reggie Jackson) had played more OF games in their careers than Winfield. Wow, that was fast . . . now has hit 17 HR in Yankee Stadium, 33 on the road in the last two years . . . a great ballplayer. (Offensive, 18-8; Defensive 4-2)

### *2. Rickey HENDERSON, Oakland (24-12)*

The number of runs that a lead-off man will score can be predicted quite accurately by use of a format that I first introduced in the 1979 *Baseball Abstract*, and have not mentioned since. I picked it up last summer in the middle of the record run, dusted it off and discovered that it still works.

What you do is, you figure the number of times the guy is likely to be on first, and you multiply that by .35. You figure how many times he is likely to be on second, and you multiply that by .55. To this you add .80 times the number of triples and 1.00 times the number of home runs the player has hit. The result gives the number of runs that he is likely to have scored, given a normal offense coming up behind him and normal clutch performance when he is on base, plus perhaps a little variation for the player's speed. The chart below runs through the projections for all American League lead-off men. Categories are:

A) Times on first (H + W − XBH − SB − CS)
B) Times on second (SB + 2B)
C) Times on third
D) Home runs
E) Projected runs scored (.35A + .55B + .8C + D)
F) Actual runs scored
G) Outs made (AB − H + CS)
H) Projected Runs Scored per 100 outs, which we will call "Lead-off Efficiency."

| Rank | Player | A 1st | B 2nd | C 3rd | D HR | E PRO | F Act | G Outs | H Effic |
|---|---|---|---|---|---|---|---|---|---|
| 1. | Rickey Henderson | 49 | 154 | 4 | 10 | 115 | 119 | 435 | 26.4 |
| 2. | Brian Downing | 191 | 39 | 2 | 28 | 118 | 109 | 449 | 26.3 |
| 3. | Paul Molitor | 167 | 67 | 8 | 19 | 121 | 136 | 474 | 25.5 |
| 4. | Rudy Law | 58 | 51 | 8 | 3 | 58 | 55 | 239 | 24.2 |
| 5. | Chet Lemon | 127 | 21 | 1 | 19 | 76 | 75 | 324 | 23.4 |
| 6. | Willie Wilson | 135 | 56 | 15 | 3 | 93 | 87 | 402 | 23.1 |
| 7. | Willie Randolph | 177 | 37 | 4 | 3 | 88.5 | 85 | 407 | 21.7 |
| 8. | Damaso Garcia | 92 | 86 | 3 | 5 | 87 | 89 | 432 | 20.1 |
| 9. | Julio Cruz | 96 | 68 | 5 | 8 | 83 | 83 | 429 | 19.3 |
| 10. | Jerry Remy | 183 | 38 | 3 | 0 | 87 | 89 | 467 | 18.7 |
| 11. | Al Brumbry | 147 | 30 | 4 | 5 | 76 | 77 | 420 | 18.1 |
| 12. | Bobby Mitchell | 131 | 19 | 6 | 2 | 63 | 48 | 350 | 18.0 |
| 13. | George Wright | 131 | 23 | 5 | 11 | 73.5 | 69 | 417 | 17.6 |
| 14. | Miguel Dilone | 58 | 45 | 3 | 3 | 50 | 50 | 295 | 17.1 |

All of the projections are fairly close to the player's actual runs scored, except for Paul Molitor's 121/136 split, for which the reason is obvious (initials are MVP), and Bobby Mitchell's 63-48 differential, for which an explanation can probably be found in Tom Brunansky's unique home run and RBI counts. Henderson had an expectation of 115 runs scored and actually scored 119.

OK, granting that the formula works—and it does—this gives us another tool with which to evaluate the impact of Rickey's running. Henderson ranks as the best lead-off man in the league, which is not news. But this system enables us to estimate how many runs Rickey would have scored had he not been a base stealer. Taking his 172 stolen base attempts out of the picture, we get:

| | | | | |
|---|---|---|---|---|
| Times on first | 49 + 172 = | 221 × | .35 = | 77.35 |
| Times on second | 154 − 130 = | 24 × | .55 = | 13.20 |
| Triples | = | 4 × | .80 = | 3.20 |
| Home Runs | = | 10 × | 1.00 = | 10.00 |
| Alternative Projected Runs | | | | 103.75 |
| Alternative Outs | | 435 − | 42 = | 393.00 |
| Alternative Efficiency | | | | 26.40 |

Henderson's lead-off efficiency, without any stolen base attempts, would have been exactly what it was anyway—26.4 runs per 100 outs. The only value resulting from his base stealing was that he was able to extend that high level of performance over a larger number of outs.

In an article for *Sports Illustrated* last summer, I credicted Rickey Henderson with creating about a dozen extra runs for the A's. This did not exactly generate a round of cheers from the Oakland fans, who were, I think it is not overstating the case, horrified. But actually, when I said that I was being *awfully* kind to Rickey Henderson. First of all, it's not a dozen runs—it's 11.3, by this method or by Pete Palmer's run-value estimates, which also use +.20 as the value of a stolen base and -.35 as the cost of a caught stealing. By the runs created method, Henderson's base stealing increased his runs contributed to the team by 11.12 runs.

| Without Stolen Bases | With Stolen Bases |
|---|---|
| $\frac{(143 + 116)(205)}{536 + 116}$ | $\frac{(143 + 116 - 42)(205 + .7(130))}{536 + 116 + 42}$ |
| 81.43 | 92.55 |

The difference between the two estimates, of course, is that a projection that you will score 115 runs is not the same as actually creating 115 runs. You also have to ask how many runs the guy is going to drive in, and you ain't going to drive in 115 runs with 205 total bases.

But. Henderson created 11.1 or 11.3 runs by his base stealing, but he also used up an extra 42 outs. That's 42 outs he took away from some Oakland batter. He didn't actually add even 11 runs to the Oakland total; he simply lifted some of those away from a teammate. The Oakland offense scored 4.27 runs per game, which translates to 6.64 runs per 42 outs. The actual increase in runs scored resulting from Henderson's base running: 4½ runs.

Four and a half goddamn runs, and they want to give him an MVP award for it. But is it even that? What about Dwayne Murphy's hitting 0 and 1 or 0 and 2 all year? What about closing up the hole on the right side 172 times? Rickey Henderson's stolen base attempts didn't mean anything to the Oakland A's—nothing at all. He's a great young ballplayer, but his selfish pursuit of the stolen-base record did not help the Oakland A's. It hurt them. (20-9; 40-3)

### 3. *Dusty BAKER, Los Angeles (21-12)*

Another in a class with Gary Matthews, Al Oliver . . . career offensive wins and losses are 102 and 64; Oliver at the same age was 108-60 . . . has 41 career game-winning RBI, behind only Clark, Murray and Hernandez. (19-8; 3-3)

### 4. *Tim RAINES, Montreal (21-12)*

By the lead-off formula given in the Henderson comment, Raines ranks as by far the best lead-off man in the National League. But the formula says he should have scored 111 runs, and he wasn't anywhere near that (he had 90; the -21 is easily the largest discrepancy of the season). This suggests two things—1) that the Expos lacked a decent #2 hitter, which it is pretty obvious they did, and 2) that all of the Montreal fans who wrote to me that Dawson wasn't hitting anything in the clutch probably weren't imagining it.

TRIVIA TIME—He came to the majors as an infielder, he was shifted to left field as a rookie, he had an outstanding rookie year in which he led the National League in stolen bases, he was then shifted back to second base, and he had a long and outstanding career in the major leagues as a second baseman. Who is he?

I'm not going to give you the answer, by the way. But I'll give you a hint: he is still active and at the major-league level in some phase of the game. (19-10; 3-2)

### 5. *Willie WILSON, Kansas City (21-13)*

I get asked a lot why Willie doesn't run as much as he used to. I can point to three reasons, or three and a hamstring. On a psychological level, when Willie first came up he drew a lot of flack about not really being a ballplayer, but just a runner. John Wathan used to call him "Herbie," meaning Herb Washington, the celebrated pinch-runner of the Oakland A's. Willie got it into his head that he wanted to be known as a ball player, not a runner. He accomplished this goal with yards to spare, becoming a batting champion and the best defensive outfielder in baseball. But the dependant clause was, not a runner.

Another factor in Willie's decreased effectiveness as a runner has been the departure of Steve Boros, generally recognized as the best base-running coach in baseball. Boros was with the Royals under Herzog, later was with Montreal when Tim Raines came up and now manages the A's. That, again, probably has decreased Willie's concentration on the running game.

One always tends to assume that the psychological factors are the dominant ones; it isn't always so. Perhaps the largest factor is that John Wathan was batting behind Willie until he cracked his ankle on July 5. Wathan will not take a pitch to allow Willie to steal; neither, for that matter, will Brett. Wilson on July 5 had 12 stolen bases, and I swear there must have been 20 times when he had second stolen and Wathan fouled the pitch off. *I stress that I am not criticizing John Wathan for this (see comments concerning Dwayne Murphy, page ).* Wathan is a fastball hitter, and I think the best thing he can do when he sees a fastball is to hit it. But Willie stole a lot more bases late in the season, when Washington was batting second.

The criticism of Wilson for not playing the last game of the season is so obviously unfair that I just can't understand why it goes on. The Royals had been engaged in a racking pennant race that ended on Saturday night. Wilson had been playing every day during that pennant race, playing his heart out, even though his legs were hurting him. In that last game George Brett didn't play, Amos Otis didn't play, Willie Aikens didn't play; Hal McRae and Frank White, who both had a chance to lead the league in doubles, passed it up and sat out the game. If Wilson had really ducked the game, that might have been one thing, although even so there is 75 years of precedence for it. But in view of the fact that nobody else was playing, what people are saying is that Wilson should have gone out there specifically to endanger his batting championship. What kind of sense does that make? Maybe he should have deliberately struck out the first two at bats so that when he came back to save it, he would really have shown them that he was true champion. He had earned a day off, and he took it. (17-11; 4-2)

### *6. Jim RICE, Boston (22-14)*

Led the AL in grounding into double plays, 29, only three less than the record . . . delivered only three sacrifice flies. . . . Rice has taken quite a bit of criticism over the years for not delivering in the clutch. A Red Sox fan by the name of Gary Waseleski keeps or has a friend who keeps scoresheets from every Sox game, and at my request he focused on Rice's production from the seventh inning on in games in which the score was from +1 (Red Sox one run ahead) to -2. In 79 at-bats in those circumstances, Rice hit .304, about his average, but had an excellent slugging percentage, .580 (.494 overall) and drove in 16 runs. When there were runners in scoring position in those games, he was 7 for 20 (.350) and had 15 total bases (.750) and 10 RBI. (18-11; 4-3)

### *7. Gary MATTHEWS, Philadelphia (21-13)*

Note the resemblance between his career record in seasonal notation (19 HR, 83 RBI, .288) and his 1982 record (19 HR, 83 RBI, .281) . . . A name-brand ballplayer. You know what you're getting before the season starts. I would compare Matthews to Al Oliver before all of the "unrecognized-superstar" stories started to appear about Oliver. Here's a comparison of their runs created and offensive wins and losses through age 31 (figured without stolen bases, caught stealing or park adjustments):

| | MATTHEWS | | | OLIVER | | |
|---|---|---|---|---|---|---|
| Age | RC | OWL% | OW-L | RC | OWL% | OW-L |
| 21 | 11 | .729 | 1-1 | 0 | .017 | 0-0 |
| 22 | 90 | .680 | 10-5 | 65 | .601 | 8-5 |
| 23 | 89 | .645 | 10-6 | 72 | .509 | 8-8 |
| 24 | 70 | .672 | 8-4 | 75 | .623 | 9-6 |
| 25 | 94 | .665 | 11-6 | 85 | .670 | 10-5 |
| 26 | 89 | .615 | 10-6 | 96 | .627 | 11-7 |
| 27 | 78 | .677 | 9-5 | 106 | .711 | 11-5 |
| 28 | 116 | .714 | 12-5 | 88 | .595 | 11-7 |
| 29 | 79 | .593 | 9-7 | 77 | .725 | 9-3 |
| 30 | 63 | .724 | 7-3 | 93 | .634 | 10-6 |
| 31 | 92 | .618 | 11-7 | 91 | .696 | 10-4 |
| | 871 | .643 | 99-55 | 849 | .634 | 97-56 |

He also has become an outstanding percentage base stealer, 21 of 25 last year, 47 of 56 over the last three years (83.9%). Rickey Henderson, I would repeat, has yet to have an 80% season. (18-10; 3-3)

### *8. Lonnie SMITH, St. Louis (17-10)*

You hear sometimes about tradition-rich positions, such as the Yankee's center fielder and catcher's slots and the Red Sox left field position. The St. Louis Cardinals' left field spot has a record that is a match for any. With a year off now and then, the Cardinals have had a Hall of Famer playing the position since 1927. The main men have been Chick Hafey, 1927-31; Joe Medwick, 1933-39; Stan Musial, a large share of the time from 1942 to 1963; and Lou Brock (election to follow), 1964-79. The Cardinals regular left fielder also hit .300 every year between 1921 and 1942, which if memory serves me is a record of its kind. Ten different men kept that streak alive: Austin McHenry, Joe Schultz, Jack Smith, Ray Blades, Hafey, Ernie Orsatti, Medwick, Ernie Koy, Johnny Hopp and Musial. Smith is the 16th Cardinal left fielder to hit .300 since 1900, and the list also includes such names as Jesse Burkett, Enos Slaughter and Bill White.

Smith's rating may be surprising to some of you. Winfield and Henderson rate ahead of him on the basis of being better ballplayers, the others on the basis of having had two good seasons in the last two years, while Smith has had one. As an MVP candidate, I can't see the argument for him at all. Sure, he's a good ballplayer, but is he better than Hendrick or Hernandez or Sutter or Andujar? Or is it only that one tends to assume that the straw that breaks the camel's back must be heavier than the other straws?

The Cardinals had a surprisingly poor record in games that Lonnie led off. They were 40-26 (.606) with Tom Herr leading off, 11-6 (.647) with Ozzie and 5-3 (.625) with Willie McGee, but basically a .500 team (36-35, .507) with Lonnie. It could be that he is more effective as a #2 hitter than as a lead-off man. (15-7; 2-3)

### *9. Gary WARD, Minnesota (19-12)*

What an astonishing season. There is nothing in his record that would suggest that he is capable of this kind of a season, never had a year half this good in the minors. You think it was a fluke? Fluke seasons are more rare in baseball than most people realize; if a player has a season this good once, usually he's 98% sure to have another season or two almost as good. But when you're talking about a 28-year-old player who comes out of nowhere, you've got to wonder . . . had 13 stolen bases in 14 attempts. (15-10; 4-2)

### *10. Steve KEMP, Chicago (20-14)*

What a good, hard-nosed player he is. He was traded to Comiskey, didn't hit at all there, but still went out and hit enough on the road to have a decent year.

An odd thing is that Kemp's and Luzinski's stats all along the board are extremely similar (18 and 19 homers, 98 and 102 RBI, .286 and .292, 89 walks apiece), but the way they put them together is exactly and emphatically opposite. Kemp hit way better on the road than he did in Chicago, Luzinski just the opposite; Luzinski hit lefthanders, Kemp hit righthanders *(see breakdowns on page for details)*; Luzinski hit 57 points better in night games, Kemp was 69 points better in day games; Luzinski hit better against the Western division teams, Kemp against the East. (17-11; 2-4)

### *11. Brian DOWNING, California (19-13)*

One of the many small things that Gene Mauch did right. Downing doesn't fit the image of a lead-off man at all, but he does get on base and he can get a rally started for you. When Burleson went out early in the year, Mauch didn't look around for somebody who looked like a lead-off man, but reviewed the candidates on the basis of what they could actually do . . . had his remarkable season without a hot streak or a slump. He hit above .260 and below .300 in every month of the season . . . fielded 1.000. (16-11; 2-3)

*12. John LOWENSTEIN, Baltimore (13-7)*

The most effective hitter, per plate appearance or per out, in baseball in 1982. His .419 on-base percentage was 35 points higher than Robin Yount's and 20 points higher than Rickey Henderson's. His .602 slugging percentage was 34 points higher than Yount's. And those are the two most important offensive statistics . . . Hit .372 and slugged over .700 against Western division teams last year (.276 and .466 against the East) . . . Doubt that he can turn in anything like the same production without Weaver picking the spots for him. (10-5; 3-2)

*13. Larry HERNDON, Detroit (19-14)*

Being rated here off the two best seasons of his life, and he still rates as the ninth-best left fielder in the league. Only three AL left fielders had a lower on-base percentage (Dilone, Sample and Oglivie, and Oglivie just barely), while as an RBI man he doesn't match up against Benji, Rice, Kemp or Winfield. He's not a hole, at least if he plays the way he did in his contract season; he could play a role on a championship team, but not a lead role. (16-11; 3-3)

*14. George FOSTER, New York (19-14)*

The Mets fans and press really earned this one. Foster didn't have a bad first half. He hit 10 homers, .283, 41 RBI at the All-Star break. You've got a bad hitter's park and nobody on base in front of you, how much better are you going to do? But to listen to the talk you'd have thought they wanted Steve Henderson back. They put so much pressure on him that he started trying to hit a home run every pitch, and then they found out what a slump is really like.

One friend of mine who is a Mets fan told me that he was amazed by what a good outfielder Foster was; another said you had to watch him every day to appreciate how bad he was. (16-11; 3-3)

*15. Jose CRUZ, Houston (20-16)*

Getting near replacement age (he turns 36 in August) . . . has had more hits for the Astros than anyone but Cedeno, Watson, or Wynn. (17-12; 4-3)

*16. Gene RICHARDS, San Diego (18-13)*

A distinctly subpar year; didn't do the things he usually does . . . Drew only 36 walks, was caught stealing 20 times. A good lead-off man when on his game. (16-10; 3-2)

*17. Mike EASLER, Pittsburgh (16-13)*

Reversed form and hit .328 against lefthanders.

*18. Ben OGLIVIE, Milwaukee (19-17)*

Can't rate any higher on the basis of a couple of sub-.250 seasons. Lefthanders, whom he hit so well in his first two seasons after getting out of the platoon cage, are giving him trouble (.218 against lefties in '81, .219 last year), and his strikeout-to-walk ratio is better than even against righthanders, but against lefties 2½-1 . . . also didn't hit well at night last year. He had a .292 average and a .615 slugging percentage in day games, but dropped to .222 and .378 slugging at night. (16-14; 3-3)

*19. Bruce BOCHTE, Seattle (14-12)*

I wrote an article for *Inside Sports* last summer of which the central thesis was that managers tend to select their lineups on the basis of images that they inherited with their first can of Desenex, and not on the basis of any logic or analysis or even reflection as to which combination of hitters will produce the most runs. Your lead-off man now, he's a speedy singles hitter, little guy most of the time; the guy batting second has to have good bat control, middle infielder if you've got one; and then in the middle of the lineup you've got the big slow guys. There are good reasons why these images have evolved, and thus a lineup selected on the basis of these images will be at least a reasonably well-ordered one probably 70% of the time.

Mike Hargrove is the classic counter-example; Bochte isn't too far behind. Bochte' on-base percentage last year was .382, which is outstanding. Despite the fact that he is a big fella, he does not have the kind of power that you would like a #3 or #4 hitter to have. His career high in home runs is 16, that in the Kingdome, and his advancement percentage (total bases divided by at-bats + wins) was .361, which is below average. The Mariners had several other players who could do at least as good a job at bringing people around. Cowens' advancement percentage was .439, Dave Henderson's was .397, Zisk's was .435; even Gary Gray and Todd Cruz had more total bases per plate appearance than Bochte.

Yet in spite of all this, the Mariners led off their offense with two players with terrible on-base percentages (Julio Cruz, .317, and Manny Castillo, .291); and had Bochte batting third. Why? Why start off the offense with two people who aren't getting on base, then bring somebody who is not particularly good at advancing base runners up behind them? Images: speed, bat control, big slow guy.

Let's evaluate Bruce Bochte as a potential lead-off man, by the formula introduced concerning Rickey Henderson:

$$.35(151+67-13-33) + .55(21+8) + .8(0) + 12 = 88.30$$

Bochte would have scored about 88 runs while using up 363 outs, or 24.3 runs per 100 outs. This would rank him as the third-best lead-off man in the league; Julio Cruz ranked ninth.

A key question here is to what extent Bochte's lack of speed would have reduced the number of runs that he scored. Most people, I suspect, would say that it would cost him a lot; I think it would cost him very, very few—

less than one per 100 outs, probably. He is 5 per 100 ahead of Cruz. I can't really prove that the number of runs that would be lost is that small; that's merely an opinion. The only slow lead-off man in the league was Brian Downing, who scored nine less runs than projected by the formula (109/118), but I think most of that was created by his not being used exclusively as a lead-off man. Well, I could prove that the loss isn't as large as five runs per 100 outs, because that's too large an elephant to be playing in the snow without leaving any tracks. This is one of the reasons we need to get hold of the scoresheets, with which we could easily untangle the mess. Anyway, my feeling is that 1) Bochte isn't any faster batting third than he would be batting lead-off, and 2) the largest single cost of a lack of speed is that it causes double plays, which Bochte grounds into in great profusion while batting third. (13-11, 1-1)

***20. Billy SAMPLE, Texas (13-11)***

I called him "Johnny" last year. Sorry . . . Some decent peripheral stats—10 stolen bases in 12 tries, only 4 double-play balls . . . could be a rare "reverse-platoon" player. He's a right-handed batter but the last two years he's hit better against righthanders than lefties. Maybe that's what the problem is. He hits as much as he should hit against righthanders, but instead of going up 30 points against lefties he drops off 30. (10-8; 3-3)

***21. Jeff LEONARD, San Francisco (8-6)***

Will the real Jeff Leonard please stand up? . . . has really changed his style as a hitter since his good rookie season in '79. He's hitting with a lot more power, but striking out more and not getting on base as much. (7-5; 1-1)

***22. Eddie MILNER, Cincinnati (8-7)***

Grade D prospect . . . 27 years old, has never hit .300 in the minors, no power, just fair base stealer. I think it says a lot about where the Reds are headed that in the early '70s they didn't have room to give a decent shot to George Foster for two or three years, and not to Hal McRae at all, but now they've got so few candidates for the work that they're giving long trials to Trevino and Milner. (6-6; 2-1)

***23. Keith MORELAND, Chicago Cubs (11-11)***

Will have to be a 90-RBI man to play . . . failed to steal a base in six tries. (10-10; 1-1)

***24. Barry BONNELL, Toronto (10-12)***

Record breaks down as 2-5 for '81, 8-7 for '82 . . . even as a .293 hitter, he is something less than a major offensive force. Hit .325 the first half of the season, .251 the second . . . he hits lefthanders well enough to be a good platoon player, but that's all. (9-10; 1-2)

***25. Miguel DILONE, Cleveland (9-14)***

The Indians seem to have more players who have one good year for them and then two or three bad ones than all the rest of the league combined. Look at the players who have given them one big year, just in the last three or four years—Dilone, Charboneau, Hassey, Thornton, Rick Wise, Monge. That's what you get when you collect other organizations' castoffs. Gabe Paul always thinks he's made a good trade because he can spot the talent that these players have, but eventually you're going to find out why the other organizations didn't want them. Who knows when Rick Sutcliffe's next good year will be? You wind up with four people having good years and four having bad ones, which translates to 81-81. (8-12; 1-2)

***26. ATLANTA LEFT FIELD (VACANT)***

Candidates are Royster, Harper, Linares, Porter, Whisenton and White, plus Murphy may wind up back in left with Butler in center.

# CENTER FIELDERS

***1. Andre DAWSON, Montreal (26-11)***

Had the highest power/speed number in the major leagues for the second straight year, 28.9 (23 homers and 39 stolen bases) . . . now has three straight .300 seasons, has established a 20% chance of getting 3000 career hits. Considering desire (seems excellent), diversity of talents (the man does everything; he's not going to be cut if his average slips 20 points) and injury history (none), that 20% chance is probably too low . . . 1983 NL MVP? (Offensive 21-7; Defensive 6-3)

***2. Dwayne MURPHY, Oakland (23-15)***

I agree with the rating; I think Murphy is clearly the best center fielder in the American League. I haven't got the wrong Murphy. One of the more intriguing questions in the Rickey Henderson saga is to what extent Henderson's running might have detracted from Murphy's hitting. Almost everyone would agree that it is easier to hit when you are even in the count than when you are behind. If you don't believe it, Pete Palmer has done an extensive pitch-by-pitch analysis of several years of World Series data which leaves little room for doubt; there is a large difference—about 30 points—between what a player hits even in the count and what he hits from behind.

The fans love to talk about Murphy's sacrificing a few points off his batting average to enable Henderson to get into scoring position, and I don't think there is any doubt that he did, but they usually talk about this in a way that presupposes that it is worthwhile for him to do so. I doubt very seriously that it is. I am convinced that, if he is taking pitches that he could hit in order to enable Henderson to run, then for the good of the team he should *cut it out*. Even if you assume that Henderson's base stealing increased the A's production by a dozen runs net (which, as I've said, is a tremendously generous estimate), it still is not at all clear that the A's are coming out ahead on the deal. Given the ratio between Murphy's total offensive output and his batting average, how much would the batting average have to increase in order to off-set the loss in runs resulting from the running game? You can find the number of hits that Murphy would have needed by solving for x in this equation, which represents Murphy's hitting as it is and would need to be:

$$\frac{(1.7230x)(1.7615x)}{637} - \frac{(130 \times 1.7230)(130 \times 1.7615)}{637} = 12$$

I will spare you the math, but Murphy's runs created total would have been 12 runs higher than it was had he hit only .259. And this makes the terribly unrealistic assumption, again favorable to the running game, that *all* of the value of Henderson's stolen bases would have been eliminated by Murphy's cutting down on the number of pitches that he took.

I also took the time to figure out what Murphy hit last year when he was hitting behind Henderson and when he wasn't. The breakdown looks like this:

| | G | AB | R | H | 2B | 3B | HR | RBI | SB | Avg |
|---|---|---|---|---|---|---|---|---|---|---|
| A | 111 | 413 | 64 | 97 | 11 | 1 | 21 | 77 | 22 | .235 |
| B | 40 | 130 | 20 | 33 | 5 | 0 | 6 | 17 | 4 | .254 |

The "A" line includes only games in which Henderson was batting lead-off and Murphy batting second; the "B" line includes all other games. (18-11; 6-3)

### 3. *Gorman THOMAS, Milwaukee (23-15)*

The best year-in, year-out power hitter in the American League. He and Dale Murphy are basically similar types of hitters, slugging center fielders, strike out a lot. Thomas has hit 60 homers and driven in 177 runs over the two years rated, .251 average; Murphy has hit 49 homers, 159 and .268, so you can see why Thomas would rate ahead of him. Besides, if you put Thomas in Atlanta he'd hit 50, 55 home runs in a good year. I don't think Thomas has ever had a season when he didn't hit more home runs on the road than at home, while Murphy has hit more home runs in Atlanta than on the road every year except 1981. (18-10; 5-5)

### 4. *Dale MURPHY, Atlanta (22-16)*

As you might have guessed, I don't think much of the MVP selection. I've always like Murphy; I just don't think he's the best player in the league. As a hitter, he doesn't stand out in the class of the MVP candidates:

| Player | Runs Created | Outs |
|---|---|---|
| Murphy | 114 | 441 |
| Thompson | 111 | 394 |
| Durham | 107 | 385 |
| Guerrero | 118 | 403 |
| Carter | 105 | 399 |
| L. Smith | 98 | 436 |
| Oliver | 124 | 415 |
| Schmidt | 113 | 377 |

Murphy created fewer runs per out expended than any other MVP candidate except Lonnie Smith, and also fewer than some other people (like Madlock, Lezcano).

But this is without adjusting for the fact that Murphy played in the second-best hitter's park in the league, where the runs that he creates are less valuable. He hit .310 with 24 home runs in Atlanta; .252 with 12 on the road. His park-adjusted offensive won-lost percentage is only .686, which on the list of the best figures in the league, isn't. He was not one of the ten best hitters in the league.

Defense? I don't know; the whole nation gets to see him on cable. What do you think? I didn't see him earn no Gold Glove. His defensive stats sure don't say Gold Glove. The argument that Murphy is the MVP because he carried the team early in the season, when they established themselves as contenders, would carry more weight if it were true. It isn't. In the 13-game explosion that started the Braves off winning, Murphy didn't get a hit in six games, hit .256 overall, drove in 12 runs. His only game-winning RBI in that stretch was a fifth-inning homer that provided the first run off a 5-0 game. He played pretty well in that stretch, but not as well as Rafael Ramirez or Rick Camp. And what about the *last* two weeks of the season, when the Braves struggled to nail it down and Murphy couldn't buy a hit? Aren't those games traditionally considered somewhat important?

My view of the MVP race, in short, is that there are very good reasons not to vote for each body, with two exceptions: Gary Carter and Pedro Guerrero. And I'd choose Carter. I know the Expos had a disappointing year, but we're picking the best player, not the best team. Is it fair to vote against Carter because Jim Fanning doesn't know which way is up in a pennant race? Some people wanted to give the award to Ozzie Smith because he played one of the two key defensive positions better than anyone else in the league, but there was a player who plays the other key defensive position better than anyone else in the league and on top of that hits better than Murphy. How can you *not* vote for him for the MVP? If the Expos were to trade Carter to Atlanta in exchange for Murphy, which team would that help and which one would it hurt? It's obvious, isn't it? (18-10; 5-5)

### 5. *Amos OTIS, Kansas City (20-14)*

Has been playing the same position for the same team longer than any other major league player at this moment, with the exception of a couple of pitchers. In fact, I wonder how many teams have ever had one center fielder for 13 straight years? I'd be surprised if the total was five, and amazed if it was 10. I made up all-incumbency teams last summer. The AL's was:

| POS | Longest Incumbent, Team | Who has been there since |
|---|---|---|
| 1B | Cecil Cooper, Milwaukee | 1977 |
| 2B | Frank White, Kansas City | 1975 |
| 3B | George Brett, Kansas City | 1974 |
| SS | Robin Yount, Milwaukee | 1974 |
| LF | Jim Rice, Boston | 1975 |
| CF | Amos Otis, Kansas City | 1970 |
| RF | Dwight Evans, Boston | 1973 |
| C | Jim Sundberg, Texas | 1974 |
| DH | Hal McRae, Kansas City | 1976 |
| RHP | Jim Palmer, Baltimore | 1969 |
| LHP | Paul Splittorff, Kansas City | 1971 |

From this we might safely conclude two things: 1) that if you want to stay put in the major leagues, it helps to be a great ballplayer; and 2) that Kansas City has by far the most stable personnel in the American League. (14-11; 6-3)

### 6. *Jerry MUMPHREY, New York Yankees (18-12)*

If the Yankees do move in the left field fence—a final decision had not been announced at this writing—I think it will cut about 20 points off Mumphrey's average. Mumphrey has hit very well in Yankee Stadium (.357 in '81, .321 in '82), and looking over my scoresheets from Yankee games I see an awful lot of s8 (singles in front of the left fielder) and 2B9 (double in the left-center gap) next to his name. I think if they pull in the fence they're going to pull in the fielder and trim Mumphrey's average. (15-7; 3-5)

### 7. *Rupe JONES, San Diego (19-14)*

Another exciting season for him, played like an MVP for half a season and then hurt himself. Grounded into only four double plays, but made up for that by being caught stealing 15 times. Trading for this guy is like speculating in the silver market. There's no denying that he's valuable, but you never know for sure what you're going to wind up with. (14-11; 5-3)

### 8. *Kirk GIBSON, Detroit (12-8)*

One more thing he has in common with Mickey Mantle: Mantle got hurt all the time, too. I can't believe he's thinking about pro football if he can't stay healthy enough to play baseball . . . plays it well when he's healthy, though. Big improvement in his K/W ratio last year, from 64-18 to 41-25. He would probably be the best center fielder in the league if he could turn in a 150-game campaign. (10-6; 2-2)

### 9. *Ken LANDREAUX, Los Angeles (18-15)*

Baseball statistics are fascinating, among other reasons, because they form crude but detailed imitations of realities that are in origin psychological or mental or physical or emotional or . . . who knows. If the people who believe in biorhythms were scientists rather than suckers and charlatans, they would find in baseball their perfect laboratory, where the ebbs and flows and highs and lows and double-highs and triple-whammies of thousands of players, date-of-birth known, have been recorded in unconscionable detail for decades. The psyche that is imitated in the month-by-month performance log of Ken Landreaux is . . . well, I don't know what it is, but it is certainly unique. Ken is not your basic .240-to-.320 range .280 hitter. He mixes up a fascinating collage of .390 months and .170 months. His good months are so good that if he could just stay within a hundred points of top form from beginning to end, he would be dropping bread crumbs on the road to Cooperstown.

| Month | G | AB | R | H | 2B | 3B | HR | RBI | SB | Avg |
|---|---|---|---|---|---|---|---|---|---|---|
| May 1979 | 26 | 105 | 15 | 35 | 5 | 1 | 3 | 21 | 0 | .333 |
| July 1979 | 28 | 106 | 14 | 37 | 6 | 1 | 1 | 16 | 5 | .349 |
| August 1979 | 28 | 104 | 19 | 43 | 4 | 3 | 4 | 21 | 2 | .413 |
| May 1980 | 26 | 99 | 5 | 38 | 4 | 0 | 1 | 13 | 0 | .384 |
| April 1982 | 21 | 83 | 18 | 29 | 3 | 1 | 0 | 6 | 8 | .349 |
| June 1982 | 24 | 83 | 16 | 30 | 9 | 4 | 1 | 17 | 9 | .362 |

Mixed up with these streaks, unfortunately, are months that Mark Belanger wouldn't sign for, like the .184 that he hit in June of '79 between the .333 and .349 months, and the .167 month that split April (.349) and June (.362) in '82, and the .178 and .192 months of 1980. And unless he switches on and off according to the calendar it must be assumed that the monthly figures do not precisely contain his hot streaks and his slumps, and thus that the full swings in his performance are even wider.

What is he? Moody? Lazy? Manic-depressive? Given to fits of depression and weeks of exhilaration? But I see every set of numbers as a puzzle, and some puzzles can be solved in too many ways.* (14-11; 4-4)

### 10. *Fred LYNN, California (16-13)*

Still has one of the largest platoon differentials around, 73 points last year. If you've got a lefthander in the bullpen you definitely want to get him up before the Carew-Lynn part of the lineup gets there. Carew had the largest platoon differential in the league last year, 114 points. Some people save the left-handed short man to face Reggie, but Reggie hits lefthanders good. (12-9; 5-3)

### 11. *Cesar CEDENO, Cincinnati (16-13)*

The amazing thing about Chief Bender's controversial radio interview last summer was that he only got one out of the three right. He was looking for people to pin the blame on without getting holes on his shirt, so he chose Cesar Cedeno, Jim Kern and Johnny Bench. Kern was a silly idea, because you've got your #3 reliever there with the best ERA on the staff, so who is going to believe he's the reason you're in last place? Bench was terrible at third, so we'll give Bender some credit there without arguing about whose stupid idea it was to put him at third. But Cedeno? That's ridiculous. Cedeno was the team's leading hitter at .289, with 35 doubles and 10 game-winning hits, both figures also leading the team, and he was sharing the outfield with a .221 hitter. The rest of the lineup was burgeoning with truly terrible ballplayers like Ale-

*This comment was written before Landreaux' mid-winter visit to the clinic. It is considerably more interesting now than it was when written.

jandro Trevino and Eddie Milner, Tom Seaver was getting the devil beat out of him regular as clockwork, and you're going to blame the season on the .289 hitter? Regardless of what kind of expectations they had for Cedeno, most intelligent people could figure out that Householder's failure to hit .230 had more to do with the Red's season than Cedeno's failure to hit .320. (13-10; 2-4)

### *12. Mookie WILSON, New York Mets (19-19)*

The Mets' best player in '82 . . . doesn't get on base enough to be a very good lead-off man, but who on the Mets is really good at anything? Hits for a pretty good average, pretty fair center fielder, steals some bases for you. (15-14; 4-5)

### *13. Chili DAVIS, San Francisco (13-12)*

The best young center fielder to come up since Andre Dawson. Very comparable to Dawson five years ago, in fact. Dawson (6′3″, 192 pounds) hit .350 at Denver in '75, then. 282 with 19 HR, 65 RBI as a rookie in '76. Davis (6′3″, 195 pounds) hit .350 at Phoenix in '81, then .261, 19 homers, 76 RBI in '82. Their age as rookies was about the same. Dawson had 21 stolen bases; Davis 24. Their strikeout-to-walk ratios were 2.7-1 and 2.6-1. (10-9; 3-3)

### *14. Rudy LAW, Chicago White Sox (7-5)*

The almost eerie thing about the White Sox' mid-season switch to the legal firm was that in both cases it was a switch from one player to another who had exactly the same strengths and the same weaknesses. If you rate Law and LeFlore excellent/good/fairly good/just fair/poor/very poor across a full spectrum of abilities, you get this:

| | LeFlore | Law I |
|---|---|---|
| Hitting for Average | Good | Good |
| Hitting for Power | Poor | Poor |
| Strike-Zone Judgment | Just Fair | Just Fair |
| Speed | Excellent | Excellent |
| Durability | Fairly Good | Unproven |
| Range Afield | Fairly Good | Fairly Good |
| Throwing Arm | Poor | Very Poor |
| Defensive Reliability | Poor | Just Fair |

In this case I can definitely see making the switch, because you've got a talented young kid with something to prove against an aging once-brilliant player with a big contract, a bad attitude and a problem. I'm not so sure about the other switch, but the point is that it is, again, a choice between nearly identical combinations of skills:

| | Almon | Law II |
|---|---|---|
| Hitting for Average | Good | Good |
| Hitting for Power | Poor | Poor |
| Strike-Zone Judgment | Just Fair | Just Fair |
| Speed | Fairly Good | Just Fair |
| Durability | Fairly Good | Unproven |
| Range Afield | Fairly Good | Fairly Good |
| Double-Play Skills | Just Fair | Poor |
| Defensive Reliability | Poor | Poor |

Pick any other shortstop or any other center fielder in the league and fill in a row for him and you'll see how odd this is, that the Sox had two such similar players at two positions.

An odd contrast between Ron LeFlore and my favorite center fielder, Amos Otis, occurred to me last summer. Their throwing arms, I think, are very similar. The odd thing is that Amos has a reputation for having a good throwing arm, and it was good when he was younger, but really it isn't all that good any more, pretty good on short throws but if he has to throw long the ball is not going to be where it is needed most of the time. LeFlore, on the other hand, has a reputation for having a very bad throwing arm, but he throws out a lot of people on the base paths, and if you watch him you will see him cut loose some decent throws. It's not a great arm, but . . . well, it's about like Amos's, mediocre to poor.

Why the difference? One play, but a play that a center fielder makes about a hundred times a year, I'd guess: runner on second, ball hit into shallow left-center or right-center. The center fielder can try to make the throw home, which is going to be too late or off-line or dropped by the catcher the huge majority of the time, or he can throw to second, concede the run and hold the runner at first. The difference is this: Amos will throw to second 90% of the time, throwing home only if the run is crucial. LeFlore will throw the ball home 90% of the time. LeFlore's try to throw home will get the runner—and thus get an assist for LeFlore—maybe 10 times a season. Another five or seven times a season LeFlore's throw will be so bad that he draws an error on it, hence his career .968 fielding percentage. Another 40 or 50 times a year, I would guess, the runner goes to second. Otis doesn't get the assists, doesn't get the errors, and keeps the runners on first. But also, he does not expose the weakness of his arm. LeFlore's continual attempts to make the very difficult throw home put the weakness of his arm on constant display and lead to his bad-arm reputation; Amos is making the much easier throw to second, which protects his reputation.

Who is doing what is better for the team? I don't know; I don't think you could figure it out without actual data on how many errors result on this play and how many runners advance to second. I would guess that it's fairly even, but not knowing any more than I do, I'd rather have the play made to second and keep the inning in control. (6-3; 1-2)

### *15. Al BUMBRY, Baltimore (17-20)*

The Orioles' offensive weak point (with the exception of Ford, who is assumed to be merely way off his game). Shelby probably will get the center fielder's job, but I doubt that he'll hit, which will provide another problem for the new manager. (13-15; 5-4)

### *16. Rick MANNING, Cleveland (17-20)*

Had a pretty good year, but as a general manager, I'd think you'd have to be extremely cautious about signing a player who hits .259, .234, .244, then goes for free agency and tacks another 30 points on his average . . . did all of his hitting on the road last year, but that hasn't been his pattern over a period of years, so I wouldn't conclude that the Cleveland park has been hurting his average much. (12-15; 5-5)

***17. Garry MADDOX, Philadelphia (13-15)***

Drew only 12 walks, scored only 39 runs. Some people feel that the Phillies would have been better off sticking with Dernier. I don't know about that, but they sure would have been better off if Dernier had kept playing the way he was early in the year. (10-11; 3-4)

***18. Dave HENDERSON, Seattle (10-11)***

Hit only .201 against the Western division teams, but .303 against the tough Eastern division. I made a list of the players who hit 40 points better against one division than another, of which 70% had the advantage against the West. (6-8; 4-3)

***19. Omar MORENO, Pittsburgh (19-24)***

Remember when Miguel Dilone and Omar Moreno were battling for the Pirate center fielder's job? Look at the chart of the worst lead-off men in baseball in '82:

| Rank | Player | Projected Runs | Actual Runs | Outs | Lead-off Efficiency |
|---|---|---|---|---|---|
| 22 | Al Bumbry | 76 | 77 | 420 | 18.1 |
| 23 | Bobby Mitchell | 63 | 48 | 350 | 18.0 |
| 24 | George Wright | 73.5 | 69 | 417 | 17.6 |
| 25 | Miguel Dilone | 50 | 50 | 295 | 17.1 |
| 26 | Omar Moreno | 83 | 82 | 513 | 16.2 |

I'm a big fan of Chuck Tanner's, but I still have trouble understanding why he didn't rest Moreno once in a while. He hit only .199 against lefthanders, and the Pirates face a lot of lefthanders. And they sure weren't beating them with Moreno in there. (14-19; 6-4)

***20. George WRIGHT, Texas (10-12)***

Would have been a rookie of the year candidate in most seasons . . . one of the better defensive center fielders in the American League. Made great strides as a hitter to finish with the same stats in the AL that he had a year ago in the Texas League (Texas League: 11 HR, 58 RBI, .260; AL: 11, 50, .264). (7-9; 3-3)

***21. Tony SCOTT, Houston (15-20)***

Plays hard, but not too well. (11-15; 4-5)

***22. Bobby MITCHELL, Minnesota (8-10)***

Had the highest defensive won-lost percentage of any AL center fielder. How good he really is I don't know, but one big reason for the rating is his .997 fielding percentage. I made fielding percentage the 30-point (second largest) consideration for outfielders, which was something of a compromise with what other people's opinions are. *I* don't think it's very important whether an outfielder makes one error a year or five, but fielding percentage is the most commonly cited defensive stat. I may change the formula later to make fielding average less of a factor. Mitchell's fielding stats are excellent across the board, and he would rate fairly well anyway. (5-9; 3-1)

***23. Willie McGEE, St. Louis (7-9)***

A poor man's Mookie Wilson...well, I suppose I should qualify that by saying that if Mookie Wilson was in St. Louis, he'd hit about 25 points higher, and he'd be a lot more valuable than he is in New York. I don't mean to prejudge McGee before giving him a chance to develop, because there's no point in doing that. If he can continue to show the power that he had in post-season play, if he can steal bases with the effectiveness that he had late in the season, if he can get on base more, if he can cut down on the misplays in the outfield, he can be a good ballplayer. But we can't evaluate a player on the basis of what he might do sometime later. McGee, given the .296 batting average and the exposure in post-season play, finished above Chili Davis in the voting for the NL Rookie of the Year, which I think is just bizarre. McGee had the worst strikeout-to-walk ratio in the league, the second-worst fielding percentage in the league, was a 67% base stealer, which has no value at all, and so the batting average represents 73% of his offensive value. (6-6; 1-3)

***24. Gary WOODS, Chicago Cubs (6-8)***

Mel Hall, rookie, looks like somebody prayed him up. Don't see how Hall could miss being a star, although sometimes they find a way. (4-6; 2-2)

***25. Rick MILLER, Boston (12-18)***

Reid Nichols overdue for more playing time...Nichols only batted 245 times and had *four* late-inning game-winning hits. This total is one less than Jim Rice, one more than anybody else on the team, and four more than Dwight Evans. (9-12; 4-5)

***26. Lloyd MOSEBY, Toronto (12-20)***

Great athlete, but he just can't hit. The man is blaspheming Rod Carew's batting stance. (9-18; 3-2)

**ADDENDUM TO COMMENTS ON CENTER FIELDERS**

I've been worrying about the public acceptance of the ratings, particularly among the center fielders, and I thought it would help make the reasons for some of the ratings clearer if we flipped the record of the hitter so that it represents the record of the pitchers facing him. There are 24 categories of a pitcher's record, but we'll trim it to 12 to keep the discussion in hand:

G IP W L Pct H R ER HR SO BB ERA

Four of these categories we can fill in simply by picking the numbers off the hitter's record. Those four are hits, strikeouts, walks and home runs. *Hits* become *hits allowed*, etc. I'll use all totals from 1981 and 1982, and for illustration I'll use Dwayne Murphy and Willie McGee:

| | G | IP | W | L | Pct | H | R | ER | HR | SO | BB | ERA |
|---|---|---|---|---|---|---|---|---|---|---|---|---|
| Murphy | | | | | | 228 | | | 42 | 213 | 167 | |
| McGee | | | | | | 125 | | | 4 | 58 | 12 | |

Innings pitched can be found by adding together all of the batter's outs. This means all his at-bats except hits, plus his sacrifice hits, sacrifice flies, caught stealing and grounded-into-double-plays. Since, because of errors, this actually creates a figure about ½ of 1% too high, we'll multiply it by .995 before dividing by three to get innings.

| | Murphy | McGee |
|---|---|---|
| At-Bats—Hits | 705 | 297 |
| Sac Hits | 20 | 2 |
| Sac Flies | 12 | 1 |
| Caught Stealing | 12 | 12 |
| Double-Play Balls | 14 | 9 |
| TOTAL OUTS | 763 | 321 |
| Technical Adjustment (× .995) | 759 | 319 |
| Divided by Three | 253 | 106.3 |
| Innings | 253 | 106.1 |

| | G | IP | W | L | Pct | H | R | ER | HR | SO | BB | ERA |
|---|---|---|---|---|---|---|---|---|---|---|---|---|
| Murphy | 39 | 253 | 11 | 18 | .379 | 228 | 142 | 126 | 42 | 213 | 167 | 4.48 |
| McGee | 15 | 106.1 | 6 | 6 | .500 | 125 | 51 | 45 | 4 | 58 | 12 | 3.81 |

You can see where we're heading already, because the pitcher facing Murphy has walked 167 men and been hammered for 42 home runs in 253 innings, and I think you can see intuitively that no pitcher who did those sorts of things would win any arbitration cases. The pitcher facing McGee, on the other hand; well, his hits/inning ratio isn't very good, but you can see from the pitcher's vantage that with an exceptional strikeout-to-walk ratio and never allowing any home runs, he's going to be alright.

For *runs* I will, of course, use runs created. If you're uncomfortable with the runs-created formula, then use the average of his runs-scored and runs driven in totals. This will give you about the same thing, but for those of you who want to keep the method simple, it will help. Since about 89% of runs are earned runs, we will multiply this by .89 for earned runs:

| | Murphy | McGee |
|---|---|---|
| 1981 Runs Created | 59 | |
| 1982 Runs Created | 83 | 51 |
| Total Runs | 142 | 51 |
| Earned Runs | 126 | 45 |

The "averaging" method would show Murphy with 132 earned runs and McGee with 44, so you can see that I am not choosing this option to hurt McGee's record; his actual runs and RBI counts would make the comparison worse.

| | G | IP | W | L | Pct | H | R | ER | HR | SO | BB | ERA |
|---|---|---|---|---|---|---|---|---|---|---|---|---|
| Murphy | | 253 | | | | 228 | 142 | 126 | 42 | 213 | 167 | 4.48 |
| McGee | | 106.1 | | | | 125 | 51 | 45 | 4 | 58 | 12 | 3.81 |

The win and loss records can be figured by asking the question, "How often would a pitcher who allowed this number of runs win, and how often lose, given normal offensive support?" The Pythagorean method will tell you that, but it would happen to be just the reverse of the park-adjusted offensive won-lost records, which are given in the chart of how the rankings are devised:

| | G | IP | W | L | Pct | H | R | ER | HR | SO | BB | ERA |
|---|---|---|---|---|---|---|---|---|---|---|---|---|
| Murphy | | 253 | 11 | 18 | .379 | 228 | 142 | 126 | 42 | 213 | 167 | 4.48 |
| McGee | | 106.1 | 6 | 6 | .500 | 125 | 51 | 45 | 4 | 58 | 12 | 3.81 |

For *games*, just so we have a complete line, we'll figure that the average number of innings per out that a man works is 11 minus his ERA, but with an upper limit of 40. This inning average would be 6.52 for the pitcher facing Murphy and 7.19 for the pitcher facing McGee:

| | G | IP | W | L | Pct | H | R | ER | HR | SO | BB | ERA |
|---|---|---|---|---|---|---|---|---|---|---|---|---|
| Murphy | 39 | 253 | 11 | 18 | .379 | 228 | 142 | 126 | 42 | 213 | 167 | 4.48 |
| McGee | 15 | 106.1 | 6 | 6 | .500 | 125 | 51 | 45 | 4 | 58 | 12 | 3.81 |

These "pitcher's records" for all 26 center fielders are given below.

| | G | IP | W | L | Pct | H | R | ER | HR | SO | BB | ERA |
|---|---|---|---|---|---|---|---|---|---|---|---|---|
| 1. Dawson | 40 | 247.2 | 5 | 21 | .192 | 302 | 187 | 166 | 47 | 146 | 69 | 6.03 |
| 2. Dwayne Murphy | 39 | 253 | 11 | 18 | .379 | 228 | 142 | 126 | 42 | 213 | 167 | 4.48 |
| 3. Thomas | 40 | 245.2 | 10 | 18 | .357 | 233 | 155 | 138 | 60 | 228 | 134 | 5.06 |
| 4. Dale Murphy | 40 | 245.2 | 10 | 18 | .357 | 259 | 162 | 144 | 49 | 206 | 137 | 5.20 |
| 5. Otis | 33 | 222 | 11 | 14 | .440 | 236 | 117 | 104 | 20 | 124 | 68 | 4.22 |
| 6. Mumphrey | 35 | 200.1 | 7 | 15 | .318 | 241 | 130 | 116 | 15 | 93 | 74 | 5.21 |
| 7. Jones | 31 | 218.1 | 11 | 14 | .440 | 219 | 109 | 97 | 16 | 156 | 105 | 4.00 |
| 8. Gibson | 24 | 139 | 6 | 10 | .375 | 169 | 90 | 80 | 17 | 105 | 43 | 5.18 |
| 9. Landreaux | 32 | 221.1 | 11 | 14 | .440 | 229 | 110 | 98 | 14 | 96 | 64 | 3,98 |
| 10. Lynn | 31 | 191.2 | 9 | 12 | .429 | 197 | 113 | 101 | 26 | 114 | 96 | 4.74 |
| 11. Cedeno | 30 | 207.1 | 10 | 13 | .435 | 225 | 105 | 93 | 13 | 72 | 65 | 4.04 |
| 12. Wilson | 34 | 245.1 | 14 | 15 | .483 | 267 | 115 | 102 | 8 | 161 | 52 | 3.74 |
| 13. Davis | 24 | 174.2 | 9 | 10 | .474 | 169 | 81 | 72 | 19 | 117 | 46 | 3.71 |
| 14. Law | 15 | 82.1 | 3 | 6 | .333 | 107 | 56 | 50 | 3 | 41 | 23 | 5.47 |
| 15. Bumbry | 33 | 250.2 | 15 | 13 | .536 | 254 | 106 | 94 | 6 | 128 | 95 | 3.38 |
| 16. Manning | 32 | 237 | 15 | 12 | .556 | 240 | 108 | 96 | 12 | 117 | 94 | 3.65 |
| 17. Maddox | 26 | 190 | 10 | 11 | .476 | 202 | 84 | 75 | 13 | 74 | 29 | 3.55 |
| 18. Henderson | 17 | 121.1 | 5 | 5 | .500 | 103 | 56 | 50 | 20 | 91 | 52 | 3.71 |
| 19. Moreno | 36 | 288.1 | 19 | 14 | .576 | 278 | 111 | 99 | 4 | 197 | 79 | 3.09 |

(continued)

| | G | IP | W | L | Pct | H | R | ER | HR | SO | BB | ERA |
|---|---|---|---|---|---|---|---|---|---|---|---|---|
| 20. Wright | 19 | 145 | 9 | 7 | .563 | 147 | 61 | 54 | 11 | 78 | 30 | 3.35 |
| 21. Scott | 28 | 227.2 | 15 | 11 | .577 | 216 | 79 | 70 | 5 | 110 | 35 | 2.77 |
| 22. Mitchell | 15 | 121.1 | 9 | 5 | .643 | 114 | 45 | 40 | 2 | 57 | 55 | 2.97 |
| 23. McGee | 15 | 106,1 | 6 | 6 | .500 | 125 | 51 | 45 | 4 | 58 | 12 | 3.81 |
| 24. Woods | 12 | 95.1 | 6 | 4 | .600 | 89 | 38 | 34 | 4 | 70 | 32 | 3.21 |
| 25. Miller | 25 | 187.1 | 12 | 9 | .571 | 196 | 81 | 72 | 6 | 77 | 68 | 3.46 |
| 26. Moseby | 29 | 233.2 | 18 | 9 | .667 | 203 | 86 | 77 | 18 | 192 | 57 | 2.97 |

# RIGHT FIELDERS

### 1. *Dwight EVANS, Boston (25-11)*

Has created more runs in the last two years than any other major league player...has career average of 13.3 assists per 162 games. (20-8; 5-3)

### 2. *Pedro GUERRERO, Los Angeles (22-10)*

The best offensive player in the National League. (19-7; 3-3)

### 3. *Jack CLARK, San Francisco (23-12)*

First of all, there is no such thing as a meaningless RBI which turns out later, after some runs are scored on this side and that, to be a game-winning RBI. All game-winning RBI put the team ahead, and any time you drive in a run which puts your team ahead, it's meaningful. When you put your team ahead and they *stay* ahead and win . . . well, that's not a meaningless RBI, no matter what the final score is.

There are, on the other hand, some GWRBI which are more meaningful than others. There are times when the GWRBI is a first-inning ground ball in a 7-5 game, which is not exactly the type of hit that the name suggests. You may remember that a year ago I commented that Clark had had more GWRBI than Mike Schmidt both years that the statistic had been kept. Well, last year Jack Clark tied for the league lead in GWs with Keith Hernandez of St. Louis, and the contrast between Clark's 21 game-winners and Hernandez' 21 "game-winners" could hardly be more extreme or extraordinary. Sixteen of Hernandez' game-winners came in the first three innings of the game, only five after that (three in the middle innings, two in the late innings, none in extra innings). By contrast:

| | Innings | | | |
|---|---|---|---|---|
| | 1-3 | 4-6 | 7-9 | X |
| Hernandez | 16 | 3 | 2 | 0 |
| Clark | 6 | 7 | 4 | 4 |

Hernandez had six "game-winning RBI" that were on fly balls or ground-outs, nine that were on singles and only six on extra base hits including two on home runs. By contrast.

| | Outs | Singles | XB-Hits | HR |
|---|---|---|---|---|
| Hernandez | 6 | 9 | 6 | ( 2) |
| Clark | 1 | 8 | 12 | (10) |

Clark hit *ten* game-winning home runs, which has got to be a record, including a pinch-hit grand slam, a three-run shot in the ninth and a couple of extra-inning blasts. In fact, *twice* Clark hit game-winning home runs in extra innings *in the Astrodome*, the toughest home-run park in the world.

In addition:

*Most of Hernandez' game-winning RBI were early in the season, while Clark had four in the first two months of the season, eight in the middle two months, and nine in August and September (KH: 8-6-7).*

*Most of Hernandez' game winning RBI were against sub-.500 teams, including seven against the Chicago Cubs, while over 60% of Clark's were against winning teams.*

*Two-thirds of Hernandez' game-winning hits were in games decided by two runs or more (14 of the 21), and almost half (nine) were in games decided by four runs or more. By contrast, the majority—12 of 21—of Clark's GWRBI won one-run games.*

I want to stress that I am not knocking Hernandez, but it is very clear that Clark really did have an unusual number of immense, game-reversing blows; while Hernandez very clearly did not. In no way should Keith's 21 be compared to Clark's. (19-8; 5-3)

### 4. *Sixto LEZCANO, San Diego (17-8)*

Had eight outfield double plays; only other outfielder in the league with more than four was Guerrero with six. Eight would be above average for a team . . . fourth-best career assists record of any established outfielder, 15.3 per 162 games. Like his idol, Clemente, Lezcano has been slow to gain acceptance as the ballplayer he is. His on-base percentage was near .400, and he adds a lot of doubles-and-triples power to his above-average home-run power, and he's the best defensive right fielder in the league. (14-5; 4-2)

### 5. *George HENDRICK, St. Louis (23-12)*

I did a once-a-week radio show last summer on KMOX in St. Louis, the flagship station of the Cardinals. A caller asked me to evaluate George Hendrick as a fielder, and I do not recall exactly what I first said about it. It wasn't very derogatory, but it was to the effect that I didn't regard him as a great outfielder. Two or three calls later, some nerdwit called up and demanded to know how I could criticize George Hendrick's fielding when I didn't even live in not only not St. Louis, but not a National League city.

To back up a minute, I had done the show a few times earlier with Bob Costas and Bob Burns, radio veterans, when another listener had called in with some twisted version of what one of us had said. What both of them did in that circumstance was to turn on the guy instantly. Costas would chew the caller out for about two minutes for dragging the level of the conversation down; Burns would just snap at him, but set the record straight. But I thought I'd be nice about it, which was my first mistake, and use the opportunity to get a little spirited debate going on the show, which was my second mistake. So, to be nice about it and give the show a little contrast in viewpoints, I said, "Well, if you live in St. Louis and see him play a lot, then I'll accept your word for it, but . . ." That was my third mistake.

For about three weeks after that, I felt like the new guy in the cellblock. That comment, of course, was intended to set a polite tone for the discussion that followed, and also to put an end-point to the discussion by making it clear that I didn't have a closed mind on the subject, and would be happy to learn what the Cardinal fans had to say. The third mistake, though, was to assume that I was dealing with an intelligent audience. There is an intelligent audience out there, but sometimes they call and sometimes they don't. There was another audience out there, which interpreted this deferential opening as a sign of weakness, and therefore as a signal to attack.

There are still several thousand baseball fans in St. Louis County who are convinced that Kenny Reitz was an outstanding third baseman and a productive hitter who was driven out of baseball by an establishment conspiracy. In Kansas City, their cousins still espouse the cause of Pete LaCock, and I am not making that up. These people, take my word for it, do not wish to be educated. The sole criterion of baseball expertise which these types recognize is, "How many Cardinal games did you see last year?" I was introduced to a good many of these people last May; another thing which I learned about them is that they don't really listen to the show, but it doesn't matter much. I received perhaps a dozen calls which could be recorded quite literally as "I wasn't listening to that show so I don't know what you said, but you sure shouldn't say something like that unless you see a lot of Cardinal games." It is also very important to these people to register their sentiment personally, even if those sentiments are not distinguishable from those of the last eight callers.

By the middle of the summer, of course, Hendrick had begun to play right field in the manner to which he has long been accustomed, and we were receiving calls every week about what a lackadaisical right fielder George is, and why doesn't somebody do something about it? I didn't say a word; just chuckled during the commercials. I'm not complaining; over the course of the summer, we received a lot of good calls, with thoughtful comments from intelligent people. I enjoyed talking to them. But if you ever hear me doing a radio call-in show, by all means, reader, call in. Because if you don't, the ignorant shall inherit the air waves. (17-9; 2-2)

### *6. Leon DURHAM, Chicago Cubs (20-13)*

He's a good one, and he's going to be a great one. He's already a .300 hitter, he's probably going to be a 30-30 man, and he might be a triple-crown candidate. (17-8; 3-5)

### *7. Chet LEMON, Detroit (16-10)*

Is hit by a pitch far more often than any other major-league player—15 times in 1982, 13 in '81, and 13 in 1979, all of those figures the highest in the majors. In 1980 he was second in the league with 12. His career total is 79 bruises; I can't find any AL record listed, but I suspect Don Baylor must be very close, with 133. This creates significant unrecognized value—an extra ten times a year that he's on base—and if this was somebody else I might be tempted to switch to the advanced version of the runs-created formula to form a more accurate RC estimate, hence ranking. But since it's Lemon, you've got to figure he makes an extra 20 or 25 base-running mistakes a year, which the records don't show, either. One of the things I will count if I can ever get access to the scoresheets is how many times each player is put out on the basepaths. Until then, on the basis of what I've seen, I'd have to assume that the leaders were Chet Lemon and Don Baylor. (13-9; 2-2)

### *8. Harold BAINES, Chicago White Sox (19-14)*

Wonder how many people realize that this guy drove in 100 runs last year? 105, in fact, which was the most of any major league right fielder. (Hendrick 104, Clark 103, Jackson 101, Guerrero 100). You know you've got a player when he drives in 100 runs and all you hear about him is what a graceful outfielder he is. He may develop into a player without a weakness. Has made a big improvement in his strikeout-to-walk ratio, is a good percentage base stealer, doesn't ground into many double plays. His fielding stats are not really good, though. (16-10; 3-4)

### *9. Reggie JACKSON, California (18-13)*

The lowest defensive won-lost percentage of any AL right fielder in '82, tied with Claudell Washington for major-league worst at .32 . . . Reversed his pattern last year and hit extremely well in front of large crowds:

| | G | AB | R | H | 2B | 3B | HR | RBI | SB | Avg |
|---|---|---|---|---|---|---|---|---|---|---|
| Under 40,000 | 126 | 435 | 71 | 111 | 13 | 0 | 28 | 79 | 3 | .255 |
| Over 40,000 | 27 | 95 | 21 | 35 | 4 | 1 | 11 | 22 | 1 | .368 |

This difference is so large that it pulls him fairly near even for the seven years 1976 to 1982. Which is certainly fine with me, because I'm sick of talking about it . . . I ran a shorter form of the "crucial game identification system" introduced in the comment on Mike Schmidt for the Yankees in 1980 to see what Reggie had done in the big games that year. His performance in crucial games in 1980 couldn't have been any closer to his overall performance than it was. In what I judged to be the 26 biggest games of that season, he hit .293 with 8 HRs and 17 RBI; his norms for any 26 games would have been .300 with 7 homers and 20 RBIs . . . . With the retirement of Perez,

Reggie has as many 100-RBI seasons (6) as any active player.

Jackson's defensive substitute, Bobby Clark, struck out 29 times and did not draw a walk in 90 at-bats. (16-9; 2-4)

### *10. Warren CROMARTIE, Montreal (17-12)*

After years of writing that Cromartie wasn't as good a ballplayer as a lot of people thought he was, I'm now going to have to reverse field and try to convince people that his 1982 season wasn't nearly as bad as it seemed. He cut his double-play grounders way down, was walking more and matched his career high in home runs. It's a fairly dramatic change of style and looks like a conscious attempt to broaden his base of talent. That's a tough thing to do in midcareer, and I wish him luck. There are contrasts and parallels between the pitcher's record that he would have had in 1978, when he hit .297, and last year:

| | G | IP | W | L | Pct | H | R | ER | HR | SO | BB | ERA |
|---|---|---|---|---|---|---|---|---|---|---|---|---|
| 1978 | 23 | 152 | 7 | 10 | .412 | 180 | 82 | 73 | 10 | 60 | 33 | 4.32 |
| 1982 | 19 | 128 | 6 | 9 | .400 | 126 | 69 | 61 | 14 | 60 | 69 | 4.29 |

The results are about the same, but the method is different. Note also that there isn't much change in his run and RBI counts. He isn't that bad an outfielder, either. (16-9; 2-2)

### *11. Ken GRIFFEY, New York Yankees (17-12)*

Hit .308 in August, .301 in September. I think he'll be back to .300 level in '83...(15-10; 2-2)

### *12. Tony ARMAS, Oakland (20-16)*

Only two dimensions to his game: can throw and hit home runs. Charlie Moore with power. (15-14; 5-2)

### *13. Terry PUHL, Houston (18-14)*

Hit only .184 against left-handed pitching. (14-11; 4-3)

### *14. Tom BRUNANSKY, Minnesota (11-7)*

Good outfielder, will probably walk 100 times a year... his batting average, home runs and RBI totals: on the road—.274, 10, 23; in Minnesota—.270, 10, 23. It's a good home-run park, but his strikeout-to-walk ratio deteriorated badly in coming home (46-42 on the road; 55-29 at home). This would usually indicate either a) poor visibility or b) home-run fever. In this case, since almost everyone else on the team saw the ball very well there, you'd have to assume it was b. And I don't think it's unfair to draw a connection between that and his off HR-to-RBI ratio; both indicate that he is susceptible to feeling the pressure to perform. But he *is*, after all, a rookie, and a damned good one... hit .302 and slugged .564 against left-handed pitching. (8-6; 3-1)

### *15. Al COWENS, Seattle (16-14)*

From *The Sporting News*, September 27, 1982, page 45: "Of the Mariners' three potential free agents (Cowens, Floyd Bannister, Bruce Bochte) those close to the club feel that Cowens is the most important one to re-sign." Those close to the club are bonkers. I'm not knocking Cowens but the two crucial differences between Cowens and Bannister are that Al is 4+ years older and that Bannister has been a valuable year-in, year-out player, while Cowens has turned in two good years in a nine year career... Seattle outfielders threw out 48 baserunners last year, high in the AL. Cowens led them with 14, with Henderson adding 11. (12-11; 4-3)

### *16. Lee LACY, Pittsburgh (11-9)*

His career makes very little sense—a modern Myril Hoag?—but the rating is not wrong. He's not a true right fielder, but he can hit. Over the two years rated he has batted 572 times, scored 97 runs, stolen 64 bases, averaged .295. If he *could* play right field, he'd rate in the top 10... Richie Hebner in right field? Is the system that dry? (9-7; 2-4)

### *17. Claudell WASHINGTON Atlanta (16-16)*

Struck out 107 times, fielded .950... I think he's one of three or four players in history to have a career of more than a thousand games, but have his best season at the age of 20. (14-12; 2-4)

### *18. Jerry MARTIN, Kansas City (13-13)*

Had a decent year, didn't hurt KC...he seems to throw extremely well to second base or third base, when his natural motion is to throw into his stride, but he doesn't throw real well to home or when the ball is hit in front of him, when he is throwing across his body... struck out 138 times, a Royals' record. (10-12; 2-2)

### *19. Larry PARRISH, Texas (13-14)*

Another trade that hurt both teams...I don't think I would ever make a trade like this, where you give up somebody who is the heart of your offense (Oliver) right at the end of spring training, because it seems to me that such a trade would just be psychologically devastating. I think that to win a pennant you have to do basically three things: get talent, deploy the talent correctly and build up group confidence to where the talent feels that it can win. The first two are the ones that I write about 99% of the time—who has talent, what talent, how it should be used—but I still recognize that the third element is really the tricky one. You can have all kinds of talent—indeed, the Rangers did have all kinds of talent—and still lose if the players don't feel that they can win. It seems to me that to take a team all through the process of getting ready for the season with a hitter like Al Oliver in the center of the lineup and then suddenly to tell the team that you're opening the season without that player, that you've traded him for two complete strangers with unimpressive records . . . well, that's suicide, isn't it? Isn't that a commercial for self-doubt?

Looking at it from the standpoint of Parrish, the trade doesn't look any brighter. Parrish was traded from the other league; he probably didn't know who his teammates were in his first game as a Ranger. He was moved to a brand-new defensive position, third base to right field.

He probably had never even seen the park that he would be playing in. He didn't know the pitchers that he was going to have to hit. He didn't know the manager that he would be playing for. He'd played all his life on artificial turf; now he was on grass.

To make the trade in midwinter is one thing; even so, I wouldn't do it, ask a man to come to a new league and adjust to a new defensive position at the same time. But at the end of spring training, when there is no time to learn anything, no time to adapt, no time to adjust psychologically and ease into your role with the new team? Maybe it's hindsight, but no way can I see it. (12-11; 1-3)

### *20. Von HAYES, Cleveland (11-12)*

Missed .400 by only 79 hits. Power will increase in Philly. (9-10; 2-2)

### *21. Dan FORD, Baltimore (14-17)*

A lower-case George Foster story. He was moving from a park where he'd always hit well to one that gave him fits (.203, .120 isolated power, 7 walks in Baltimore; .262, .148 isolated power, 16 walks on the road), had a disappointing first half (.250), began fighting himself and then really had a bad second half (.209). (11-13; 3-4)

### *22. Charlie MOORE, Milwaukee (10-12)*

I couldn't believe the ecstatic reviews of Moore's fielding during the play-off's—or, for that matter, all summer. The Associated Press, *The Sporting News* and *Sports Illustrated* all did stories about what a great outfielder he'd become. This guy's your basic bad ballplayer. Sure he can throw. So what? Everybody can do *something*. Dave Kingman can hit home runs. That's a hell of a lot more valuable. Besides, there were at least three places in post-season play where Moore's inexperienced outfield play could have cost the Brewers a run. Do you remember Don Baylor's triple in the first game of the play-offs, when Gorman Thomas kept fading back, fading back, but the ball hit the wall? The announcers said that Thomas misplayed the ball, but that assumes that Thomas should have been able to read the wind and the flight of the ball and tell that it would get to the fence. I think that's a very tough assumption. But what I kept wondering is, "Where's Charlie Moore? Where's Charlie Moore?" All Moore had to do was see that Thomas was going to the wall, and he should have known that if he *didn't* catch it, it would come off the wall. Thomas had to run the ball down himself. Fortunately, though, he was playing, and didn't have to listen to the announcers saying what a great outfielder Charlie Moore was. (7-11; 2-2)

### *23. Bob DERNIER, Philadelphia (7-8)*

Not a great prospect, but not too far away from being a pretty good lead-off man. (5-6; 2-2)

### *24. Ellis VALENTINE, New York Mets (10-13)*

Is starting to remind me of Downtown Ollie Brown. You remember Ollie, used to warm up by sort of casually lobbing the ball from the warning track to the third baseman, took two infielders and a bat boy to get it back to him. About 1976 somebody asked him if he still had that great arm; he said "Yeah, and I'd sure like to trade it for a great bat." Big guy, had some power and ran well, but his career just drifted away among inconsistent offense and too many strikeouts. I don't usually pay that much attention to Ks, but you've got to worry about a guy whose strikeout-to-walk ratio deteriorates year after year. Valentine drew only 5 walks in '82 . . . has 17.0 assists per 162 games, the second-best record in the game. Joel Youngblood has the best. (8-10; 2-3)

### *25. Jesse BARFIELD, Toronto (8-11)*

I like him, despite the rating; he has a good arm and power...the American League Leaders in home runs against left-handing pitching:

| | |
|---|---|
| Dave Winfield | 19 |
| Gorman Thomas | 15 |
| Jesse Barfield | 15 |
| Hal McRae | 14 |
| Reggie Jackson | 14 |

The Blue Jays do see more left-handed pitching than anybody else. (7-8; 2-2)

### *26. Paul HOUSEHOLDER, Cincinnati (8-12)*

He can't really be that bad. I think he'll be around, at least as a platoon player (*see breakdowns*) although he is supposed to be a switch hitter. He's a legitimate grade-C prospect, so I'd still rather have him than Eddie Milner. Walker is about the same; Redus is too odd a case to even make a guess at what he'll do. (5-10; 3-2)

# DESIGNATED HITTERS

### *1. Greg LUZINSKI, Chicago White Sox (18-9)*

Coming off first 100-RBI season since 1978; hit higher than career average for the first time since 1977. Would have been close to 100 RBI in '81, though, but for the strike, which makes him the only DH in the league to have delivered consistently for the last two seasons. White Sox designated hitters (who were 96% pure Luzinski-on-the-Hoof) also led the AL in on-base percentage (.389) and runs scored (96). (Won-lost records for Designated people are entirely offensive.)

### *2. Richie ZISK, Seattle (16-8)*

I am not very happy with this rating. I don't use RBI counts in deriving the ratings because they are too dependent on the offensive context in which the man hits. But in a case like this . . . well, it's got to bother you. There was an early-season note in the *Sporting News* that said he was 4-for-37 with runners in scoring position.

One way in which RBI totals could be used without being inconsistent with the premise that we are trying to isolate individual value from the team context would be to find the normal performance levels in RBI relative to other stats, and then establish parameters or limits to the deviation therefrom that can reasonably be explained by context. Simply put, when somebody in the middle of the lineup hits .311 with 16 homers but only 43 runs batted in, then .292 with 21 HRs and only 62 RBI, one knows intuitively that something is wrong. Lacking access to scoresheets, you can't document exactly what is amiss, you can't know how many times Richie Zisk batted with men on base, or how many times McRae did. However, in view of the fact that Kansas City's team on-base percentage was only 8½% higher than Seattle's, and that their runs-scored total was only 20% higher, we could safely assume that Hal McRae did not bat with 115% more runners on base than Zisk did. We could establish limits, then, on how much of an RBI difference we would ignore.

Perhaps we could begin to do this by looking at the ratios between total bases and RBI of all the league's designated hitters:

| | Total Bases | RBI | RBI/TB |
|---|---|---|---|
| 1. Thornton | 285 | 116 | .407 |
| 2. McRae | 332 | 133 | .401 |
| 3. Luzinski | 263 | 102 | .388 |
| 4. Yastrzemski | 198 | 72 | .364 |
| 5. Howell | 105 | 38 | .362 |
| 6. Baylor | 258 | 93 | .360 |
| 7. Singleton | 214 | 77 | .360 |
| 8. Gamble | 165 | 57 | .345 |
| 9. Nordhagen | 59 | 20 | .339 |
| 10. Burroughs | 144 | 48 | .333 |
| 11. L. Johnson | 116 | 38 | .328 |
| 12. Ivie | 116 | 38 | .328 |
| 13. R. Johnson | 98 | 32 | .327 |
| 14. Zisk | 240 | 62 | .258 |

In the basic runs-created formula, it is assumed that total bases represent "advancement." The complement, then, should be "on-base percentage." So we compare these figures to the on-base percentages of the teams for whom they toil:

| | Individual .RBI/TB | Team On-Base Percentage |
|---|---|---|
| Thornton | .407 | .343 |
| McRae | .401 | .340 |
| Luzinski | .388 | .340 |
| Yastrzemski | .364 | .342 |
| Howell | .362 | .337 |
| Baylor | .360 | .350 |
| Singleton | .360 | .344 |
| Gamble | .345 | .331 |
| Nordhagen | .339 | .317 |
| Burroughs | .333 | .309 |
| L. Johnson | .328 | .312 |
| Ivie | .328 | .326 |
| R. Johnson | .327 | .319 |
| Zisk | .258 | .313 |

There is an unmistakable correlation there:

The seven designated hitters who played for teams with on-base percentages of .340 or more all had RBI ratios of .360 or more.

The six designated hitters who played for teams with on-base percentages of .326 or less all had RBI ratios of .339 or less.

Oscar Gample straddled the fence, in both categories.

The RBI ratio averaged about 20 points higher than the team on-base percentage.

One might suggest, then, that if the player's RBI ratio ranges from the team on-base percentage to 40 points higher, that deviation might be explained by his offensive context. But above that range or below it, we could legitimately adjust the player's runs created to reflect the RBI column. It is a failure of the rating system used that it completely exculpates Zisk for his failure to drive in runs.

### 3. *Hal McRAE, Kansas City (18-10)*

A few random notes on a remarkable season . . .

- I wonder how many times you could find, in all of baseball history, when a 35-year old ballplayer, a fine hitter for many seasons, has set a new career high in RBI? Not many, I'd wager. Now I wonder how many times you could find when the hitter has set a new high in RBI *by 41*?
- This is just a thought (sheer unsupported speculation) but I wonder if John Wathan could have been stealing signs for him? Wathan was batting ahead of McRae in the early part of the season and stealing a lot of bases. John's a catcher and he's smart, probably will manage someday. And for about two-thirds of the season, McRae was just unbelievable with runners in scoring position. I watched and couldn't pick up anything, though.
- There was a note in the paper—in August—which said that McRae's batting average with runners in scoring position was .495. The smallest number of at-bats in which it is possible to hit .495 is 91.
- I have never seen a team defense Hal McRae correctly. McRae will hit the ball right down the base line, (either one) about once a game. Usually it's foul, but when it's not it's a double. Why take the chance? Guard the lines. Sure he'll hit the ball by you in the hole, but that's a single.
- McRae made a comment on a pregame show last spring that he liked to face a pitcher twice in a few days, as one often does in the American League. He said he thought he got a good reading on how the pitcher worked him that way.

This causes me to wonder if Hal McRae really did hit when he got a second quick look at the pitcher. Talk about a study getting *results*. This is Hal McRae's record when he was facing a pitcher for the second time within 17 days (which proved to be the maximum distance involved in those turnaround series, two week-ends apart):

| G | AB | R | H | 2B | 3B | HR | RBI | SB | Avg |
|---|---|---|---|---|---|---|---|---|---|
| 37 | 144 | 27 | 57 | 15 | 2 | 5 | 24 | 1 | .396 |

A late-season slump in these games drew him down from .455. McRae hit .281 in all games except these 37. Further, the pitchers he faced in these 37 games were significantly better than an average group of pitchers, as is reflected in McRae's record the first time he faced them:

| G | AB | R | H | 2B | 3B | HR | RBI | SB | Avg |
|---|---|---|---|---|---|---|---|---|---|
| 37 | 139 | 16 | 34 | 7 | 1 | 4 | 22 | 0 | .245 |

This gets me to wondering if there is a generalized "second-look" effect on performance, if batters in general or veteran hitters in particular tend to pick up their ears when they get a second shot at somebody they've just seen. Should a manager try to minimize those games in his pitching plans?

It also seems to me that this method might be used to shed light on the old issue about whether the pitcher or the batter has the advantage the first time they face each other. It has always seemed obvious to me that the pitcher should have the advantage. The pitcher starts the action; the batter reacts to what the pitcher does. It seems obvious that the more the batter has seen of the pitcher, the better prepared he is to react to him.

More research needed; back to the subject next year.

### 4. *Andre THORNTON, Cleveland (15-9)*

Hot weather hitter, destroys lefthanders... The Red Sox fans are convinced that the reason Jim Rice isn't hitting as well anymore is that there's nobody coming up behind him. I don't buy it, never have. Look at the year that Thornton had, and who'd he have coming up after him? Ron Hassey, Carmen Castillo and Chris Bando, among others. He tied for the league lead with 18 intentional walks. The difference is that Thornton won't swing at a pitch if it's not worth swinging at. He took 109 walks, but he had a big year.

### 5. *Ken SINGLETON, Baltimore (16-11)*

He still walks a lot, which has a certain value with Eddie Murray and John Lowenstein around, but basically his rating is rescued by the super first half in '81. It's not only a disappointing 1982 season we're talking about here, but now a 206-game span since the strike in which Singleton has hit .241 with less than half an RBI per game. He's 35, and it's clearly time for a redefinition of his work load. Still fairly effective against righthanders, but hit only .177 without a homer in 147 at-bats against lefthanders; hit .238 against lefties in 1981. Hits better on the road than in Baltimore.

### 6. *Oscar GAMBLE, New York (10-5)*

Has to be one of the five best career platoon players ever. He's never been close to 500 at-bats in a season, but he's getting near 200 career homers, and he walks and hits for a good average . . . only 34 AB against left-handers in '82, but hit them hard, too (.353 average, .676 slugging percentage, .476 on-base percentage) . . . 1982 slugging percentage was .522, and that was only the fourth best of his career. His .250 isolated power was exceeded by only four regulars in the league and was higher than, among many others, DeCinces, Parrish, McRae and Eddie Murray. Yankee designated hitters totaled 28 homers and 109 RBI.

### 7. *Jeff BURROUGHS, Oakland (11-6)*

Has a lifetime .300 mark as a pinch hitter (27 for 90). In the last three years has gone 20-for-58 as a pinch hitter (.345) with seven pinch-hit home runs... doesn't fit the image of a pinch hitter, who is supposed to be a free swinger. I've never really known what to think about that. If you're talking about a first-base-open, two-out situation, then I can see why you'd want a free swinger. But it seems to me that a lot of pinch-hit appearances come either a) at the start of an inning and the bottom of the order, which is when a walk is the most valuable, or b) with first base occupied (and possibly other bases as well), in which case the pressure is on the pitcher to throw a strike, and you would want a selective hitter, like Burroughs, to take advantage of that... A few notes on the subject from around the league. The four teams whose pinch hitters walked the *least* often were Milwaukee (one walk by a pinch hitter), Boston (three walks), Minnesota, and Kansas City, in that order. Note that three of those are very good teams, and should have enough talent to have a hitter on the bench. The pinch hitters for the four teams hit .232, .182, .190 and .164, respectively. Among them they hit 6 HR and drove in a run every 6.64 AB. The team whose pinch hitters walked the *most* often was California, whose pinch hitters also hit .338, with an excellent RBI ratio, (1/3.82 AB). Following them, in order, were Cleveland, Toronto, Oakland, Detroit and Baltimore. The pinch hitters for these five teams all hit above .200, hit 26 home runs among them and drove in a run every 5.22 at-bats. And note that three of these are rather bad teams.

### 8. *Don BAYLOR, California (15-14)*

Now a Yankee. Over the last six years his batting average in Yankee Stadium has been pretty good, .287. Still, there is no way in the world I would have signed him. His 1982 season was his best in three years, and it wasn't at all impressive. He had 98 RBI, but with 18 double-play balls he accounted for 478 outs, which means he had less than .2 RBI per out. McRae, Thornton, Luzinski, Gamble, Yaz and Burroughs were all comfortably over .2 RBI per out. He had 21 game-winning RBI and 8 late-inning game-winning RBI, which tied Amos Otis for the highest total in the league. In all other respects, though, he was the most average designated hitter in the league, with an on-base percentage of .333 (average for DHs, .341) and a .424 slugging percentage (.420 average). He'll be 34 in midsummer, and all he's going to do for the Yankees even if he has a good year is take playing time away from other people who are at least as good.

### 9. *Carl YASTRZEMSKI, Boston (12-11)*

Hit over .280 in April, May, June, July, September and October, but ruined his season with a dreadful August (.144, 0 homers and 5 RBI). Predictably, he batted more times in August than any other month... overall batting average was .309 in the other six months.

### *10. Somebody Named JOHNSON, Minnesota (4-3)*

What I want to know is just where the hell are all these Johnsons coming from? Is there a Johnson factory down there in the Sun Belt somewhere? In 1980 there were only four Johnsons playing in the majors—Cliff, John Henry, Lamar and Randy (John Henry is one Johnson), and Randy only batted 20 times. Last year we had at least five R. Johnsons alone—R. Johnson of Atlanta, R.R. Johnson and R.W. Johnson of Montreal, plus Randy Johnson of Minnesota (I think this is Randy I'm supposed to be writing about here) and Ron Johnson of Kansas City, with at least eleven total Johnsons around the majors. How are we supposed to keep track of all these people? Maybe we should start assigning them distinctive nicknames, Clicker and Turkey Shoot and stuff like that. Howard Johnson of Detroit, needless to say, is exempted from this requirement. And Drungo Larue Hazewood languishes in the minors. What a waste.

### *11. Mike IVIE, Detroit (5-5)*

A short sermon on the worth of raw talent in baseball: There are probably not ten players in baseball today who have as much natural talent at hitting a baseball as Mike Ivie.

Our topic for next Sunday: John Mayberry is one of those ten.

Our topic for the Sunday following: Pete Rose isn't.

### *12. Wayne NORDHAGEN, Toronto (5-6)*

Toronto designated hitters finished last in the league in home runs (8), runs batted in (56), runs scored (52) and batting average (.238). But what gets me is their base stealing stats, 7 successful steals in 23 tries. I figure the Toronto manager can make a probable gain of about a half-game this season simply by ordering the designated hitters to stop trying to steal.

### *13. Roy HOWELL, Milwaukee (7-9)*

Don Money would rate higher, but Howell had more playing time. A classic bass-ackwards platoon arrangement: Money played mostly against lefthanders, against whom he hit .269, but hit .308 in 104 at-bats against righthanders; Howell played against righthanders and hit .245 against them, but went 10 for 23 (.435) against southpaws. Wouldn't hold up over a full season, of course . . . or how about this: Try a little day/night platooning. Money hit .337 to Howell's .224 in day games, but Howell outhit Money .274 to .253 at night. Don't know if that would hold up or not. Better yet, why not release Howell and put Money on the bench and play Mark Brouhard? But then, I'm a known Brouhard fan. . .

### *14. Lamar JOHNSON, Texas (6-8)*

Has never hit as well while serving as DH as when he was in the field. Career records given below:

**AS DESIGNATED HITTER**

| YEAR | G | AB | R | H | 2B | 3B | HR | RBI | SB | Avg | Slugging Pct |
|---|---|---|---|---|---|---|---|---|---|---|---|
| 1974 | 3 | 7 | 0 | 1 | 0 | 0 | 0 | 0 | 0 | .143 | .143 |
| 1975 | 2 | 9 | 0 | 0 | 0 | 0 | 0 | 0 | 0 | .000 | .000 |
| 1976 | 35 | 110 | 13 | 30 | 5 | 1 | 2 | 11 | 4 | .273 | .391 |
| 1977 | 68 | 207 | 24 | 56 | 7 | 2 | 9 | 37 | 17 | .271 | .454 |
| 1978 | 36 | 139 | 15 | 42 | 7 | 0 | 0 | 17 | 8 | .302 | .353 |
| 1979 | 37 | 145 | 16 | 44 | 7 | 0 | 3 | 26 | 8 | .303 | .414 |
| 1980 | 66 | 253 | 25 | 70 | 11 | 3 | 4 | 39 | 19 | .277 | .391 |
| 1981 | 2 | 8 | 1 | 2 | 0 | 0 | 0 | 1 | 0 | .250 | .250 |
| 1982 | 77 | 265 | 29 | 67 | 9 | 0 | 5 | 31 | 27 | .253 | .343 |
| Total | 1326 | 1143 | 123 | 312 | 46 | 6 | 23 | 162 | 83 | .273 | .384 |

**NOT AS DESIGNATED HITTER**

| YEAR | G | AB | R | H | 2B | 3B | HR | RBI | SB | Avg | Slugging Pct |
|---|---|---|---|---|---|---|---|---|---|---|---|
| 1974 | 7 | 22 | 1 | 9 | 0 | 0 | 0 | 2 | 0 | .408 | .408 |
| 1975 | 6 | 21 | 2 | 6 | 3 | 0 | 1 | 1 | 1 | .286 | .571 |
| 1976 | 47 | 112 | 16 | 41 | 6 | 0 | 2 | 22 | 15 | .366 | .473 |
| 1977 | 50 | 167 | 28 | 57 | 5 | 3 | 0 | 28 | 7 | .341 | .569 |
| 1978 | 112 | 359 | 37 | 94 | 16 | 2 | 8 | 55 | 35 | .262 | .384 |
| 1979 | 96 | 334 | 44 | 104 | 22 | 1 | 9 | 48 | 33 | .311 | .464 |
| 1980 | 81 | 288 | 26 | 80 | 15 | 0 | 9 | 42 | 28 | .278 | .424 |
| 1981 | 39 | 126 | 9 | 35 | 7 | 0 | 1 | 14 | 5 | .278 | .357 |
| 1982 | 28 | 59 | 8 | 17 | 2 | 0 | 2 | 7 | 4 | .288 | .424 |
| Total | 466 | 1488 | 171 | 443 | 76 | 6 | 41 | 219 | 128 | .298 | .440 |

Besides having an average 25 points higher when he is in the field, he has homered 37% more often, doubled 27% more often and walked 18% more often when not DHing. His average has been lower as a DH in every season but one.

A man by the name of Harry Agens delivered a presentation on the effects of the DH rule at the SABR convention last summer in Baltimore. He found, among other things, that hardly anyone hits as well as a DH as he does as a fielder. My note from the occasion says that he found 70 players who had 100 or more at-bats both as a DH and as a non-DH, of whom only eight had hit better as a DH. Whether that is 100 career or season at-bats, whether we have eight who hit better or who hit significantly better . . . these things I can't tell you. He also reported that Jim Rice had hit 26 points higher when playing the field, Don Baylor 14 points higher, and Yaz over 30 points higher.

One can see a credible connection. Pinch hitting has long been known to be a drain on a player's batting average; it's hard to imagine that players in general could hit as well cold as they do hot. Hal McRae has been the most successful career designated hitter, and he has worked hard at keeping himself A) warm and loose and B) mentally in the game. It seems to me that the strategic implications of this difference, if it is real, could be fairly important.

## CATCHER

| | 1981 Pct | Offensive W–L | 1981 Pct | Defensive W–L | 1982 Pct | Offensive W–L | 1982 Pct | Defensive W–L | Total | .400 Chance |
|---|---|---|---|---|---|---|---|---|---|---|
| 1. Carter | .581 | 6-5 | .64 | 4-2 | .733 | 12-4 | .67 | 6-3 | 28-14 | .00043 |
| 2. Kennedy | .616 | 7-4 | .40 | 2-4 | .697 | 11-5 | .56 | 5-4 | 25-17 | .00824 |
| 3. Parrish | .476 | 5-5 | .55 | 3-3 | .642 | 9-5 | .61 | 5-3 | 22-16 | .01945 |
| 4. Diaz | .737 | 4-1 | .45 | 1-2 | .602 | 9-6 | .56 | 5-4 | 19-13 | .02088 |
| 5. Sundberg | .580 | 6-4 | .64 | 4-2 | .479 | 7-7 | .48 | 4-4 | (20-18) | .07835 |
| 6. Fisk | .509 | 5-5 | .47 | 3-3 | .543 | 8-6 | .57 | 5-3 | (20-18) | .07835 |
| 7. Pena | .559 | 3-3 | .59 | 2-2 | .559 | 8-6 | .48 | 4-4 | 17-15 | .09197 |
| 8. Ashby | .608 | 5-3 | .58 | 3-2 | .585 | 6-4 | .36 | 2-5 | 16-14 | .09706 |
| 9. Porter | .586 | 3-2 | .46 | 1-2 | .554 | 6-5 | .53 | 4-3 | 14-12 | .10819 |
| 10. May | .649 | 6-3 | .48 | 3-3 | .513 | 6-5 | .44 | 3-4 | (17-16) | .1211 |
| 11. Stearns | .530 | 4-4 | .51 | 2-2 | .618 | 6-4 | .45 | 2-3 | (15-14) | .13623 |
| 12. Dempsey | .412 | 3-5 | .57 | 3-3 | .459 | 5-5 | .60 | 5-3 | 16-16 | .1648 |
| 13. Scioscia | .526 | 4-4 | .54 | 3-3 | .359 | 4-7 | .55 | 4-4 | (16-17) | .20593 |
| 14. Simmons | .380 | 5-7 | .41 | 2-3 | .554 | 8-7 | .55 | 4-4 | 19-21 | .2089 |
| 15. Davis | .474 | 2-3 | .48 | 2-2 | .492 | 6-6 | .44 | 4-4 | 14-15 | .23412 |
| 16. Benedict | .501 | 5-4 | .56 | 3-3 | .328 | 4-8 | .55 | 4-3 | 16-18 | .25117 |
| 17. Whitt | .343 | 2-3 | .59 | 2-2 | .512 | 4-4 | .46 | 3-3 | 11-12 | .2869 |
| 18. Boone | .316 | 2-5 | .44 | 2-3 | .381 | 5-9 | .65 | 6-3 | (16-19) | .29974 |
| 19. Trevino | .406 | 2-2 | .48 | 1-2 | .390 | 4-6 | .52 | 4-3 | 11-13 | .3497 |
| 20. Wathan | .355 | 3-6 | .37 | 2-3 | .488 | 6-7 | .47 | 3-4 | (15-19) | .37261 |
| 21. Hassey | .282 | 2-4 | .59 | 2-1 | .474 | 5-5 | .47 | 3-3 | (11-14) | .4141 |
| 22. Heath | .375 | 3-6 | .54 | 3-2 | .412 | 4-6 | .44 | 3-3 | 13-17 | .42154 |
| 23. Sweet | | | | | .382 | 3-5 | .63 | 3-2 | 6- 7 | .4257 |
| 24. Cerone | .381 | 3-4 | .54 | 2-2 | .277 | 2-7 | .52 | 3-2 | 10-15 | .5753 |
| 25. Gedman | .564 | 3-3 | .39 | 2-2 | .320 | 3-5 | .29 | 1-4 | 9-14 | .6115 |
| 26. Laudner | .222 | 0-1, | .58 | 1-0 | .469 | 4-5 | .24 | 1-5 | 6-11 | .7362 |

## FIRST BASE

| | 1981 Pct | Offensive W–L | 1981 Pct | Defensive W–L | 1982 Pct | Offensive W–L | 1982 Pct | Defensive W–L | Total | .400 Chance |
|---|---|---|---|---|---|---|---|---|---|---|
| 1. Murray | .753 | 8-3 | .70 | 1-1 | .780 | 12-3 | .62 | 2-1 | 23- 8 | .00012 |
| 2. Hernandez | .744 | 9-3 | .70 | 1-1 | .670 | 11-5 | .63 | 2-1 | 23-10 | .00053 |
| 3. Oliver | .658 | 7-4 | X | | .779 | 12-4 | .34 | 1-2 | (21- 9) | .00085 |
| 4. Cooper | .725 | 8-3 | .53 | 1-1 | .702 | 13-5 | .59 | 2-1 | (23-11) | .00103 |
| 5. Thompson | .741 | 5-2 | .39 | 0-1 | .742 | 11-4 | .52 | 2-1 | 18- 8 | .00245 |
| 6. Buckner | .671 | 8-4 | .38 | 1-1 | .604 | 11-7 | .62 | 2-1 | 22-13 | .00526 |
| 7. Paciorek | .722 | 8-3 | X | | .660 | 7-3 | .47 | 1-1 | (15- 8) | .0127 |
| 8. Carew | .617 | 6-4 | .55 | 1-1 | .580 | 9-6 | .50 | 1-1 | 17-10 | .01337 |
| 9. Chambliss | .575 | 7-5 | .64 | 1-1 | .572 | 9-6 | .64 | 2-1 | 19-13 | .02088 |
| 10. Hrbek | .408 | 1-1 | .58 | 0-0 | .667 | 10-5 | .56 | 2-1 | 13- 7 | .0211 |
| 11. Garvey | .586 | 7-5 | .55 | 1-1 | .560 | 10-8 | .55 | 2-1 | 20-15 | .03005 |
| 12. Hargrove | .697 | 6-3 | .55 | 1-1 | .496 | 8-9 | .66 | 2-1 | (18-13) | .03199 |
| 13. Aikens | .679 | 7-3 | .43 | 1-1 | .600 | 8-5 | .45 | 1-1 | (16-11) | .03369 |
| 14. Driessen | .537 | 4-3 | .49 | 1-1 | .626 | 9-6 | .65 | 2-1 | 16-11 | .03369 |
| 15. Rose | .653 | 8-4 | .60 | 1-1 | .466 | 9-10 | .54 | 2-1 | 20-16 | .04264 |
| 16. Knight | .495 | 5-6 | X | | .619 | 11-6 | .46 | 1-1 | 17-13 | .04811 |
| 17. R. Smith | .431 | 0-1 | X | | .720 | 7-3 | .33 | 1-1 | 8- 5 | .0977 |
| 18. Perkins | .565 | 4-3 | .55 | 1-0 | .503 | 5-5 | .55 | 1-1 | 11- 9 | .1276 |
| 19. Kingman | .632 | 7-4 | .21 | 0-1 | .494 | 8-9 | .28 | 1-2 | 16-16 | .1648 |
| 20. Hostetler | .976 | 0-0 | X | | .516 | 7-6 | .40 | 1-1 | 8- 7 | .2131 |
| 21. Collins | .577 | 6-5 | X | | .370 | 4-7 | .32 | 0-1 | (11-12) | .2869 |
| 22. Stapleton | .528 | 5-5 | .39 | 0-0 | .412 | 7-9 | .56 | 1-1 | 13-15 | .30498 |
| 23. Upshaw | .243 | 1-3 | .60 | 0-0 | .512 | 9-8 | .40 | 1-2 | 11-13 | .3497 |
| 24. Gray | .504 | 3-3 | .41 | 0-1 | .467 | 4-4 | .32 | 0-1 | 7- 9 | .4729 |
| 25. Meyer | .388 | 3-4 | X | | .376 | 4-7 | .40 | 0-1 | 7-12 | .6916 |
| 26. Cabell | .368 | 4-8 | .42 | 0-1 | .318 | 4-10 | .42 | 1-1 | (10-19) | .78534 |

## SECOND BASE

| | 1981 Pct | Offensive W–L | 1981 Pct | Defensive W–L | 1982 Pct | Offensive W–L | 1982 Pct | Defensive W–L | Total | .400 Chance |
|---|---|---|---|---|---|---|---|---|---|---|
| 1. Grich | .762 | 8-2 | .71 | 4-1 | .599 | 9-6 | .67 | 5-2 | (25-12) | .00064 |
| 2. Morgan | .624 | 6-3 | .54 | 2-2 | .734 | 10-3 | .50 | 3-3 | (20-12) | .00841 |
| 3. Whitaker | .501 | 5-5 | .67 | 3-2 | .573 | 9-7 | .69 | 5-2 | 22-16 | .01945 |
| 4. Bernazard | .574 | 6-5 | .54 | 3-2 | .532 | 9-7 | .68 | 5-2 | (22-17) | .02802 |
| 5. White | .436 | 5-6 | .65 | 3-2 | .579 | 8-6 | .58 | 4-3 | 20-17 | .05865 |
| 6. Herr | .512 | 6-6 | .70 | 3-2 | .454 | 7-8 | .63 | 4-2 | 20-18 | .07835 |
| 7. Randolph | .437 | 5-6 | .65 | 3-2 | .512 | 8-8 | .51 | 4-3 | 20-19 | .10206 |
| 8. Garner | .415 | 4-5 | .49 | 2-2 | .586 | 10-7 | .54 | 4-3 | (19-18) | .10799 |
| 9. Gantner | .425 | 4-6 | .68 | 3-2 | .507 | 6-6 | .60 | 4-2 | 17-16 | .12110 |
| 10. Trillo | .565 | 6-4 | .57 | 3-2 | .383 | 6-10 | .65 | 5-2 | (19-19) | .13753 |
| 11. Dauer | .515 | 6-5 | .56 | 3-2 | .518 | 8-8 | .40 | 2-4 | 19-19 | .13753 |
| 12. J. Cruz | .492 | 5-6 | .63 | 3-2 | .423 | 7-9 | .52 | 4-3 | 19-20 | .17133 |
| 13. Oester | .581 | 6-4 | .51 | 3-2 | .436 | 7-9 | .41 | 2-4 | 18-19 | .18199 |
| 14. Sax | .397 | 2-2 | .57 | 1-0 | .527 | 10-9 | .47 | 3-4 | (15-16) | .21942 |
| 15. Ray | .375 | 1-2 | .54 | 1-0 | .502 | 10-9 | .48 | 4-4 | (15-16) | .21942 |
| 16. Garcia | .335 | 2-5 | .41 | 1-2 | .506 | 9-8 | .56 | 4-3 | 16-18 | .25117 |
| 17. Hubbard | .404 | 4-7 | .53 | 3-2 | .418 | 7-9 | .60 | 4-3 | 18-21 | .26534 |
| 18. Remy | .542 | 5-5 | .49 | 2-2 | .381 | 7-11 | .43 | 3-5 | (18-22) | .31149 |
| 19. Backman | .565 | 1-0 | .05 | 0-1 | .583 | 5-3 | .14 | 1-3 | ( 6- 6) | .3348 |
| 20. Wills | .386 | 5-7 | .70 | 3-2 | .521 | 6-6 | .25 | 1-4 | 15-19 | .37261 |
| 21. Lopes | .381 | 3-4 | .54 | 2-1 | .427 | 6-8 | .43 | 3-3 | (13-17) | .42154 |
| 22. Flannery | .457 | 1-1 | X | | .481 | 5-6 | .37 | 2-3 | 8-10 | .4366 |
| 23. Castino | .465 | 5-6 | X | | .346 | 4-8 | .46 | 2-3 | (12-16) | .44897 |
| 24. Richardt | | | | | .322 | 4-8 | .53 | 3-2 | 7-10 | .5523 |
| 25. Milbourne | .641 | 3-1 | .52 | 0-0 | .324 | 4-8 | .37 | 2-3 | ( 8-13) | .6504 |
| 26. Flynn | .266 | 3-7 | .51 | 3-2 | .199 | 3-11 | .53 | 3-3 | (11-24) | .88874 |

## THIRD BASE

| | 1981 Pct | Offensive W–L | 1981 Pct | Defensive W–L | 1982 Pct | Offensive W–L | 1982 Pct | Defensive W–L | Total | .400 Chance |
|---|---|---|---|---|---|---|---|---|---|---|
| 1. Schmidt | .862 | 9-1 | .58 | 2-2 | .773 | 12-3 | .52 | 3-2 | (25- 9) | .00008 |
| 2. Bell | .677 | 7-3 | .74 | 3-1 | .657 | 10-5 | .74 | 4-1 | (23-11) | .00103 |
| 3. DeCinces | .637 | 6-4 | .57 | 2-2 | .657 | 12-6 | .72 | 4-2 | (25-13) | .00117 |
| 4. Brett | .699 | 7-3 | .41 | 1-2 | .710 | 11-4 | .57 | 3-2 | 22-11 | .00177 |
| 5. Madlock | .791 | 6-1 | .47 | 1-2 | .715 | 11-4 | .39 | 2-3 | 20-10 | .00285 |
| 6. Molitor | .463 | 4-4 | X | | .670 | 13-6 | .61 | 4-2 | (20-11) | .00504 |
| 7. Harrah | .658 | 7-3 | .40 | 2-2 | .717 | 12-5 | .48 | 3-3 | (23-14) | .00532 |
| 8. Cey | .719 | 6-3 | .54 | 2-1 | .582 | 9-7 | .52 | 3-2 | 20-13 | .01340 |
| 9. Oberkfell | .591 | 7-4 | .66 | 3-1 | .528 | 7-6 | .57 | 3-2 | (19-14) | .03104 |
| 10. Lansford | .667 | 7-4 | .53 | 2-1 | .589 | 9-5 | .46 | 2-2 | (18-13) | .03199 |
| 11. Evans | .639 | 7-4 | .48 | 1-2 | .624 | 9-5 | .31 | 1-2 | 18-13 | .03199 |
| 12. Horner | .623 | 6-3 | .26 | 1-2 | .627 | 9-6 | .42 | 2-3 | 18-14 | .04627 |
| 13. Howe | .680 | 7-3 | .54 | 2-2 | .457 | 5-7 | .58 | 3-2 | 17-13 | .04811 |
| 14. Ripkin | .020 | 0-1 | X | | .589 | 10-7 | .69 | 2-1 | 12- 9 | .0848 |
| 15. Wallach | .407 | 2-4 | .37 | 0-1 | .602 | 10-7 | .45 | 3-3 | (16-14) | .09706 |
| 16. Salazar | .609 | 7-4 | .45 | 1-2 | .410 | 7-9 | .59 | 3-2 | 18-17 | .11431 |
| 17. Nettles | .543 | 5-5 | 59 | 2-2 | .461 | 6-6 | .47 | 2-2 | 15-15 | .17537 |
| 18. Gross | .462 | 4-4 | .40 | 1-2 | .489 | 5-6 | .58 | 2-2 | (13-13) | .19935 |
| 19. Bench | .722 | 4-1 | X | | .519 | 6-6 | .12 | 0-4 | 10-11 | .3085 |
| 20. Sandberg | .039 | 0-0 | X | | .442 | 8-11 | .48 | 2-3 | (11-13) | .3497 |
| 21. Gaetti | .203 | 0-1 | X | | .431 | 7-9 | .57 | 3-2 | 10-12 | .3756 |
| 22. Brooks | .644 | 6-4 | .33 | 1-2 | .380 | 5-9 | .30 | 2-3 | 14-18 | .39614 |
| 23. Rodriguez | .770 | 1-0 | .23 | 0-1 | .331 | 3-5 | .46 | 2-2 | ( 5- 9) | .7207 |
| 24. Brookens | .367 | 3-4 | .57 | 2-1 | .291 | 3-9 | .43 | 2-2 | ( 9-17) | .77446 |
| 25. Iorg | .250 | 2-5 | .31 | 0-1 | .411 | 5-7 | .32 | 1-3 | 8-16 | .8081 |
| 26. Castillo | | | | | .306 | 5-10 | .31 | 2-3 | ( 6-14) | .8744 |

## SHORTSTOP

| SHORTSTOP | 1981 Pct | Offensive W–L | 1981 Pct | Defensive W–L | 1982 Pct | Offensive W–L | 1982 Pct | Defensive W–L | Total | .400 Chance |
|---|---|---|---|---|---|---|---|---|---|---|
| 1. Yount | .570 | 6-5 | .80 | 5-1 | .791 | 13-4 | .58 | 5-5 | (30-14) | .000146 |
| 2. Concepcion | .641 | 8-4 | .58 | 4-3 | .538 | 9-7 | .59 | 6-4 | (26-19) | .011975 |
| 3. Thon | .580 | 2-1 | .08 | 0-1 | .610 | 9-5 | .60 | 5-3 | (15-11) | .05176 |
| 4. Trammell | .467 | 6-6 | .67 | 5-2 | .480 | 7-8 | .53 | 6-5 | (23-22) | .086452 |
| 5. Smith | .294 | 4-10 | .67 | 5-2 | .466 | 7-8 | .77 | 7-2 | 23-22 | .086452 |
| 6. Smalley | .657 | 3-2 | .30 | 1-2 | .557 | 8-7 | .36 | 2-4 | (15-14) | .13623 |
| 7. Templeton | .481 | 5-5 | .70 | 3-2 | .400 | 7-10 | .51 | 5-4 | 20-21 | .161428 |
| 8. Washington | .327 | 4-7 | .52 | 4-3 | .559 | 7-6 | .53 | 4-4 | 19-20 | .17133 |
| 9. Almon | .580 | 6-4 | .60 | 4-3 | .383 | 3-6 | .43 | 3-2 | 16-17 | .20593 |
| 10. Ramirez | .293 | 3-7 | .49 | 3-3 | .456 | 8-10 | .59 | 6-5 | (21-24) | .222286 |
| 11. Speier | .362 | 3-6 | .55 | 4-3 | .455 | 7-9 | .52 | 6-5 | 20-23 | .235632 |
| 12. Russell | .329 | 3-5 | .55 | 3-2 | .545 | 8-6 | .43 | 4-6 | (17-20) | .28190 |
| 13. Berra | .410 | 3-4 | .16 | 0-2 | .460 | 7-9 | .47 | 5-5 | 15-20 | .42725 |
| 14. V. Law | .032 | 0-2 | X | | .500 | 5-5 | .48 | 3-3 | 8-10 | .4366 |
| 15. Sakata | .437 | 2-3 | .33 | 1-2 | .464 | 5-5 | .34 | 1-3 | 9-13 | .5459 |
| 16. Foli | .307 | 3-7 | .49 | 3-3 | .256 | 4-10 | .61 | 6-4 | 16-24 | .55978 |
| 17. LeMaster | .348 | 3-7 | .42 | 3-4 | .416 | 4-6 | .41 | 4-5 | 14-22 | .61603 |
| 18. Bowa | .478 | 5-5 | .38 | 3-4 | .327 | 5-10 | .38 | 4-6 | (16-26) | .65537 |
| 19. Dent | .465 | 3-4 | .64 | 3-2 | .170 | 2-8 | .43 | 3-4 | 11-18 | .65736 |
| 20. T. Cruz | | | | | .271 | 4-11 | .59 | 5-4 | 9-15 | .6721 |
| 21. R. Washington | .267 | 1-2 | .56 | 1-1 | .393 | 5-8 | .31 | 2-4 | 9-15 | .6721 |
| 22. DeJesus | .187 | 2-11 | .56 | 4-3 | .388 | 6-10 | .46 | 5-5 | 17-29 | .713700 |
| 23. Fischlin | .225 | 0-1 | .17 | 0-1 | .420 | 3-5 | .32 | 2-5 | ( 6-11) | .7362 |
| 24. Gardenhire | .394 | 0-1 | .23 | 0-1 | .327 | 4-8 | .40 | 4-5 | 8-15 | .7626 |
| 25. Griffin | .173 | 2-11 | .46 | 3-4 | .252 | 4-12 | .56 | 6-5 | (16-31) | .836997 |
| 26. Hoffman | .248 | 2-5 | .50 | 3-2 | .204 | 3-12 | .43 | 4-6 | 12-25 | .866666 |
| 27. Stanley | .203 | 1-4 | .29 | 1-3 | .211 | 1-6 | .21 | 1-6 | ( 5-18) | .9809 |

## LEFT FIELD

| LEFT FIELD | 1981 Pct | Offensive W–L | 1981 Pct | Defensive W–L | 1982 Pct | Offensive W–L | 1982 Pct | Defensive W–L | Total | .400 Chance |
|---|---|---|---|---|---|---|---|---|---|---|
| 1. Winfield | .715 | 8-3 | .57 | 2-1 | .695 | 10-5 | .53 | 2-1 | 22-10 | .00095 |
| 2. R. Henderson | .737 | 9-3 | .72 | 2-1 | .618 | 11-6 | .52 | 2-2 | 24-12 | .00111 |
| 3. Baker | .700 | 8-3 | .52 | 1-1 | .682 | 11-5 | .39 | 2-2 | (21-12) | .00517 |
| 4. Raines | .783 | 7-2 | .50 | 1-1 | .601 | 11-8 | .56 | 2-1 | 21-12 | .00517 |
| 5. Wilson | .559 | 7-5 | .77 | 2-1 | .633 | 10-6 | .73 | 2-1 | 21-13 | .00846 |
| 6. Rice | .586 | 8-5 | .64 | 2-1 | .656 | 10-6 | .48 | 2-2 | 22-14 | .00846 |
| 7. Matthews | .733 | 7-3 | .36 | 1-1 | .632 | 11-7 | .38 | 2-2 | 21-13 | .00846 |
| 8. L. Smith | .707 | 4-1 | .48 | 0-1 | .662 | 11-6 | .53 | 2-2 | 17-10 | .01337 |
| 9. Ward | .483 | 4-5 | .51 | 1-1 | .659 | 11-5 | .72 | 3-1 | 19-12 | .01348 |
| 10. Kemp | .657 | 7-4 | .62 | 1-1 | .612 | 10-7 | .33 | 1-3 | (20-14) | .02045 |
| 11. Downing | .487 | 4-5 | .42 | 0-1 | .657 | 12-6 | .60 | 2-2 | (19-13) | .02088 |
| 12. Lowenstein | .520 | 3-3 | .35 | 1-1 | .813 | 7-2 | .50 | 2-1 | 13- 7 | .0211 |
| 13. Herndon | .620 | 6-4 | .49 | 1-1 | .587 | 10-7 | .58 | 2-2 | 19-14 | .03104 |
| 14. Foster | .766 | 8-3 | .59 | 2-1 | .479 | 8-8 | .45 | 1-2 | 19-14 | .03104 |
| 15. J. Cruz | .620 | 7-5 | .55 | 2-1 | .566 | 10-7 | .43 | 2-2 | (20-16) | .04264 |
| 16. Richards | .683 | 8-3 | .51 | 2-1 | .510 | 8-7 | .60 | 1-1 | (18-13) | .03199 |
| 17. Easler | .579 | 6-4 | .51 | 1-1 | .586 | 8-6 | .41 | 1-2 | 16-13 | .07097 |
| 18. Oglivie | .499 | 6-6 | .53 | 1-1 | .548 | 10-8 | .60 | 2-2 | 19-17 | .08264 |
| 19. Bochte | .501 | 5-5 | .48 | 0-0 | .588 | 8-6 | .44 | 1-1 | 14-12 | .10819 |
| 20. Sample | .596 | 4-3 | .59 | 1-1 | .524 | 6-5 | .45 | 2-2 | 13-11 | .1142 |
| 21. Leonard | .727 | 3-1 | X | | .561 | 4-4 | .35 | 1-1 | 8- 6 | .1501 |
| 22. Milner | .542 | 0-0 | X | | .499 | 6-6 | .54 | 2-1 | 8- 7 | .2131 |
| 23. Moreland | .473 | 3-3 | X | | .469 | 7-7 | .58 | 1-1 | 11-11 | .2280 |
| 24. Bonnell | .297 | 2-5 | X | | .548 | 7-5 | .45 | 1-2 | 10-12 | .3756 |
| 25. Dilone | .511 | 4-4 | .45 | 0-1 | .340 | 4-8 | .29 | 1-1 | 9-14 | .6115 |
| 26. Atlanta (Vacant) | | | | | | | | | | |

## CENTER FIELD

| | 1981 Pct | Offensive W–L | 1981 Pct | Defensive W–L | 1982 Pct | Offensive W–L | 1982 Pct | Defensive W–L | Total | .400 Chance |
|---|---|---|---|---|---|---|---|---|---|---|
| 1. Dawson | .792 | 9-2 | .67 | 3-1 | .696 | 12-5 | .58 | 3-2 | (26-11) | .00019 |
| 2. Murphy, Oak | .641 | 8-4 | .65 | 3-1 | .581 | 10-7 | .63 | 3-2 | (23-15) | .00842 |
| 3. Thomas | .663 | 7-4 | .43 | 2-2 | .620 | 11-6 | .51 | 3-3 | 23-15 | .00842 |
| 4. Murphy, Atl | .513 | 6-5 | .50 | 2-2 | .686 | 12-5 | .43 | 3-3 | (22-16) | .01945 |
| 5. Otis | .552 | 6-5 | .70 | 3-1 | .549 | 8-6 | .62 | 3-2 | 20-14 | .02045 |
| 6. Mumphrey | .631 | 6-3 | .46 | 1-2 | .677 | 9-4 | .48 | 2-3 | 18-12 | .02124 |
| 7. R. Jones | .511 | 6-6 | .63 | 3-1 | .647 | 8-5 | .55 | 2-2 | 19-14 | .03104 |
| 8. Gibson | .714 | 6-2 | .27 | 1-1 | .533 | 4-4 | .61 | 1-1 | 12- 8 | .0566 |
| 9. Landreaux | .499 | 6-6 | .58 | 2-2 | .610 | 8-5 | .49 | 2-2 | 18-15 | .06455 |
| 10. Lynn | .377 | 3-5 | .51 | 2-1 | .683 | 9-4 | .54 | 3-2 | (16-13) | .07097 |
| 11. Cedeno | .571 | 5-4 | .47 | 0-1 | .574 | 8-6 | .45 | 2-3 | 16-13 | .07097 |
| 12. Wilson | .498 | 5-5 | .45 | 1-2 | .521 | 10-9 | .51 | 3-3 | 19-19 | .13753 |
| 13. C. Davis | .099 | 0-0 | X | | .528 | 10-9 | .54 | 3-3 | 13-12 | .1536 |
| 14. Law | | | | | .642 | 6-3 | .26 | 1-2 | 7- 5 | .1582 |
| 15. Bumbry | .505 | 6-6 | .51 | 2-2 | .420 | 7-9 | .53 | 3-2 | (17-20) | .28190 |
| 16. Manning | .489 | 5-6 | .53 | 2-2 | .445 | 7-9 | .44 | 3-3 | 17-20 | .28190 |
| 17. Maddox | .413 | 4-5 | .44 | 1-2 | .524 | 6-6 | .47 | 2-2 | 13-15 | .30498 |
| 18. D. Henderson | .282 | 1-3 | .48 | 1-1 | .505 | 5-5 | .50 | 3-2 | 10-11 | .3085 |
| 19. Moreno | .520 | 7-6 | .67 | 3-1 | .332 | 7-13 | .46 | 3-3 | (19-24) | .339888 |
| 20. Wright | | | | | .447 | 7-9 | .52 | 3-3 | 10-12 | .3756 |
| 21. Scott | .469 | 6-6 | .59 | 2-2 | .333 | 5-9 | .37 | 2-3 | 15-20 | .42725 |
| 22. Mitchell | .039 | 0-0 | X | | .342 | 5-9 | .68 | 3-1 | 8-10 | .4366 |
| 23. McGee | | | | | .512 | 6-6 | .25 | 1-3 | 7- 9 | .4729 |
| 24. Woods | .301 | 1-2 | X | | .474 | 3-4 | .41 | 2-2 | 6- 8 | .5141 |
| 25. Miller | .543 | 5-4 | .42 | 2-2 | .331 | 4-8 | .33 | 2-3 | (12-18) | .56892 |
| 26. Moseby | .348 | 4-8 | X | | .342 | 5-10 | .51 | 3-2 | 12-20 | .67669 |

## RIGHT FIELD

| | 1981 Pct | Offensive W–L | 1981 Pct | Defensive W–L | 1982 Pct | Offensive W–L | 1982 Pct | Defensive W–L | Total | .400 Chance |
|---|---|---|---|---|---|---|---|---|---|---|
| 1. Evans | .763 | 8-3 | .72 | 2-1 | .716 | 12-5 | .52 | 3-2 | 25-11 | .00034 |
| 2. Guerrero | .676 | 7-3 | .38 | 1-1 | .780 | 12-4 | .49 | 2-2 | 22-10 | .00095 |
| 3. Clark | .684 | 8-3 | .60 | 2-1 | .695 | 11-5 | .60 | 3-2 | (23-12) | .00323 |
| 4. Lezcano | .625 | 4-2 | .46 | 1-1 | .752 | 10-3 | .69 | 3-1 | (17- 8) | .0042 |
| 5. Hendrick | .697 | 8-3 | X | | .617 | 9-6 | .44 | 2-2 | 19-11 | .00830 |
| 6. Durham | .602 | 6-4 | .42 | 1-3 | .714 | 11-4 | .51 | 2-2 | 20-13 | .01340 |
| 7. Lemon | .678 | 6-3 | X | | .563 | 7-6 | .58 | 2-2 | (16-10) | .02166 |
| 8. Baines | .635 | 5-3 | .42 | 1-1 | .589 | 11-7 | .47 | 2-3 | 19-14 | .03104 |
| 9. Jackson | .562 | 6-4 | .47 | 1-1 | .693 | 10-5 | .32 | 1-3 | 18-13 | .03199 |
| 10. Cromartie | .678 | 7-3 | X | | .574 | 9-6 | .57 | 2-2 | (17-12) | .03290 |
| 11. Griffey | .676 | 7-4 | X | | .541 | 8-6 | .54 | 2-2 | 17-12 | .03290 |
| 12. Armas | .616 | 8-5 | .73 | 2-1 | .453 | 7-9 | .64 | 3-1 | 20-16 | .04246 |
| 13. Puhl | .555 | 6-4 | .66 | 2-1 | .549 | 8-7 | .45 | 2-2 | 18-14 | .04627 |
| 14. Brunansky | .468 | 0-1 | .49 | 0-0 | .636 | 8-5 | .69 | 3-1 | 11- 7 | .0577 |
| 15. Cowens | .437 | 3-4 | .64 | 2-1 | .560 | 9-7 | .55 | 2-2 | 16-14 | .09076 |
| 16. Lacy | .559 | 3-3 | .44 | 1-1 | .624 | 6-4 | .33 | 1-3 | 11- 9 | .1276 |
| 17. Washington | .559 | 5-4 | .57 | 1-1 | .531 | 9-8 | .32 | 1-3 | 16-16 | .16480 |
| 18. Martin | .465 | 3-4 | X | | .482 | 7-8 | .52 | 2-2 | (13-13) | .19935 |
| 19. Parrish | .506 | 5-5 | X | | .534 | 7-6 | .34 | 1-3 | 13-14 | .25012 |
| 20. Hayes | .601 | 2-1 | .41 | 0-0 | .437 | 7-9 | .56 | 2-2 | 11-12 | .2869 |
| 21. Ford | .599 | 6-5 | .32 | 1-2 | .374 | 5-8 | .48 | 2-2 | 14-17 | .33991 |
| 22. Moore | .568 | 2-2 | X | | .363 | 5-9 | .62 | 2-2 | (10-12) | .3756 |
| 23. Dernier | .954 | 0-0 | X | | .436 | 5-6 | .48 | 2-2 | 7- 8 | .3902 |
| 24. Valentine | .326 | 3-5 | .58 | 1-1 | .518 | 5-5 | .45 | 1-2 | 10-13 | .4436 |
| 25. Barfield | .317 | 1-2 | X | | .470 | 6-6 | .40 | 2-2 | (8-11) | .5119 |
| 26. Householder | .660 | 1-1 | .55 | 1-0 | .284 | 4-9 | .55 | 2-2 | 8-12 | .5841 |

**DESIGNATED HITTER**

| | 1981 Pct | Offensive W–L | 1982 Pct | Offensive W–L | Total | .400 Chance |
|---|---|---|---|---|---|---|
| 1. Luzinski | .681 | 7-4 | .661 | 11-5 | 18- 9 | .00461 |
| 2. Zisk | .705 | 7-3 | .635 | 9-5 | 16- 8 | .0075 |
| 3. McRae | .533 | 6-5 | .714 | 12-5 | 18-10 | .00812 |
| 4. Thornton | .473 | 3-4 | .668 | 11-6 | (15- 9) | .0216 |
| 5. Singleton | .697 | 7-3 | .528 | 9-8 | 16-11 | .03369 |
| 6. Gamble | .613 | 4-2 | .718 | 6-3 | 10- 5 | .0338 |
| 7. Burroughs | .535 | 5-4 | .737 | 6-2 | 11- 6 | .0349 |
| 8. Baylor | .549 | 6-5 | .525 | 9-9 | 15-14 | .13623 |
| 9. Yastrzemski | .464 | 5-5 | .551 | 7-6 | 12-11 | .1635 |
| 10. R. Johnson | | | .514 | 4-3 | 4- 3 | .2897 |
| 11. Ivie | .412 | 1-1 | .479 | 4-4 | 5- 5 | .3670 |
| 12. Nordhagen | .639 | 4-2 | .322 | 2-3 | (5- 6) | .4672 |
| 13. Howell | .471 | 3-4 | .405 | 4-5 | 7- 9 | .4729 |
| 14. L. Johnson | .417 | 2-2 | .455 | 5-5 | (6- 8) | .5141 |

**1982 American League Value Approximations**

MILWAUKEE BREWERS: Yount 18, Molitor 15, Cooper 13, Thomas 13, Olgivie 12, Vuckovich 12, Simmons 11, Caldwell 11, Garner 10, Fingers 9, Slaton 8, Moore 8, Haas 8, McClure 7, Money 6, Bernard 4, Sutton 3, Lerch 3, Brouhard 2, Edwards 2, Howell 2, Romero 2, Medich 2, Yost 1, Augustine 1. Total 183.

BALTIMORE ORIOLES: Murray 14, Ripken 12, Palmer 11, T. Martinez 10, Lowenstein 10, D. Martinez 10, Bumbry 9, Dauer 9, Singleton 9, Flanagan 9, Roenicke 9, McGregor 8, Dempsey 7, Stewart 6, Stoddard 6, Davis 4, Sakata 4, Ford 4, Dwyer 3, Ayala 2, Gulliver 2, Nolan 2, Crow 1, Rayford 1, Shelby 1, Flinn 1, R. Grimsley 1. Total 165.

BOSTON RED SOX: Evans 14, Clear 12, Rice 12, Stanley 11, Remy 10, Lansford 10, Tudor 10, Eckersley 9, Yastrzemski 9, Boggs 9, Hoffman 8, Stapleton 7, Miller 7, Burgmeier 6, Torrez 5, Nichols 5, Allenson 4, Aponte 4, Rainey 3, Gedman 3, Perez 2, Denman 1, Ojeda 1, Hurst 1, Total 163.

DETROIT TIGERS: Whitaker 14, Parrish 13, Herndon 12, Trammell 11, Petry 11, Morris 11, Lemon 10, Wilcox 8, Tobik 7, Ujdur 6, Cabell 6, Brooks 5, Gibson 5, Wilson 5, Saucier 5, Wockenfuss 4, Underwood 4, Sosa 3, H. Johnson 3, Ivie 3, Pashnik 3, Lopez 2, Rucker 2, Turner 2, Leach 2, Hebner 2, Rozema 2, Laga 1, Jones 1, Fahey 1. Total 164.

NEW YORK YANKEES: Winfield 13, Smalley 12, Randolph 11, Mumphrey 11, Gossage 11, Griffey 9, Guidry 9, Righetti 8, Rawley 8, John 7, Gamble 7, Nettles 7, May 6, Frazier 6, Piniella 5, Morgan 5, Cerone 4, Collins 4, Wynegar 4, LaRoche 3, Mayberry 3, Dent 2, Mazzilli 2, Murcer 2, Robertson 1. Total 161.

CLEVELAND INDIANS: Harrah 13, Sutcliffe 12, Thornton 11, Hayes 11, Barker 10, Hargrove 9, Manning 8, Spillner 6, Bannister 6, Hassey 6, Whitson 5, Fischlin 5, Glynn 4, Brennan 4, Dilone 4, Milbourne 3, Sorensen 3, Waits 2, Denny 2, Anderson 2, Perconte 2, McBride 2, Dybzinski 2, Bando 2, Nahorodny 1. Total 135.

TORONTO BLUE JAYS: Garcia 13, Stieb 12, Clancy 11, Leal 10, Griffin 10, Upshaw 9, Murray 9, Barfield 7, McLaughlin 7, Bonnell 7, Moseby 7, Jackson 7, Iorg 6, Whitt 6, Martinez 5, Powell 4, Mullinicks 4, Gott 4, Woods 2, Nordhagen 2, Johnson 1, Mayberry 1, Petralli 1, Revering 1, Bombach 1, Garvin 1. Total 148.

CALIFORNIA ANGELS: DeCinces 15, Grich 13, Lynn 13, Downing 12, R. Jackson 12, Zahn 12, Carew 11, Forsch 9, Foli 9, Boone 9, Baylor 8, Kison 8, Sanchez 7, Witt 7, Renko 7, Goltz 4, Hassler 4, Aase 3, Corbett 3, Ron Jackson 3, John 2, Beniquez 2, Burleson 1, Clark 1, Ferguson 1, Wilfong 1, Mahler 1, Moreno 1. Total 179.

KANSAS CITY ROYALS: Brett 15, Quisenberry 14, Wilson 13, McRae 13, Gura 12, White 11, Aikens 9, Otis 9, Washington 9, Wathan 9, Blue 8, Martin 8, Armstrong 6, Splittorff 5, Leonard 4, Hood 3, Castro 3, Frost 2, Slaught 2, Pryor 2, May 2, Geronimo 2, Concepcion 2, Hammond 1, Quirk 1, Tufts 1, Black 1, Creel 1. Total 168.

CHICAGO WHITE SOX: Hoyt 12, Baines 11, Bernazard 11, Fisk 11, Luzinski 11, Kemp 10, Barojas 9, Lamp 9, Koosman 8, Dotson 8, R. Law 7, Paciorek 7, Hickey 6, Burns 6, V. Law 6, Almon 5, LeFlore 5, Rodriguez 3, Trout 3, Squires 2, Morrison 2, Walker 1, Hill 1, Hairston 1, Kern 1, Escarrega 1. Total 157.

SEATTLE MARINERS: Caudill 14, J. Cruz 11, Cowens 10, Bochte 10, Bannister 10, T. Cruz 9, Zisk 9, VandeBerg 9, Castillo 7, Henderson 7, Perry 7, Clark 6, Beattie 6, Stanton 5, Simpson 4, Sweet 4, Gray 3, Nelson 3, Moore 3, Stoddard 2, Essian 2, Bulling 2, Brown 2, Revering 1, Serna 1, Maler 1, Edler 1, Anderson 1. Total 150.

OAKLAND A's: Murphy 13, Henderson 12, Armas 10,

Underwood 10, Beard 8, Langford 8, Burroughs 7, Gross 6, Lopes 5, McCatty 4, Owchinko 4, Keough 4, Heath 4, Meyer 3, Newman 3, Stanley 3, Norris 3, Kingman 3, Davis 2, Johnson 2, Rudi 2, Hanna 1, Sexton 1, Phillips 1, Page 1, McKay 1, Klutts 1. Total 122.

TEXAS RANGERS: Bell 12, Sundberg 10, Wright 9, Hough 9, Darwin 8, Hostetler 7, Parrish 7, Matlack 7, Tanana 7, Schmidt 6, Richardt 5, Honeycutt 4, Sample 4, Grubb 4, Flynn 3, L. Johnson 3, Mirabella 3, Comer 3, Medich 2, Butcher 2, Mazzilli 2, B. Johnson 1, O'Brien 1, Stein 1, Wagner 1, Dent 1, Smithson 1. Total 123.

MINNESOTA TWINS: Ward 13, Hrbek 12, Brunansky 10, Castillo 10, R. Davis 9, Gaetti 9, Washington 7, Mitchell 7, Havens 7, Castino 5, Williams 5, O'Connor 4, Laudner 4, Feltner 3, Faedo 3, Viola 2, Vega 2, Johnson 2, Hatcher 2, Eisenreich 2, Butera 1, Engle 1, Wynegar 1, Boris 1, Little 1, Jackson 1, Bush 1, Erickson 1. Total 126.

**1982 National League Value Approximations**

ST. LOUIS CARDINALS: L. Smith 14, Sutter 13, Andujar 12, O. Smith 12, Herr 12, Hernandez 12, Hendrick 11, Oberkfell 9, Forsch 9, Porter 8, McGee 7, Bair 7, La Point 7, Mura 6, Stuper 5, Lahti 4, Kaat 4, Tenace 4, Ramsey 3, Iorg 3, Green 2, Martin 1, Rincon 1, Landrum 1, Gonzalez 1, Braun 1. Total 169.

PHILADELPHIA PHILLIES: Schmidt 15, Carlton 15, Diaz 13, Matthews 12, Krakow 10, Trillo 10, Rose 9, DeJesus 9, Christenson 8, R. Reed 8, Maddox 8, Ruthven 7, Monge 5, Dernier 5, Farmer 3, Vukovich 3, Gross 2, Lyle 2, McGraw 2, Bystrom 1, Virgil 1, Aguayo 1, Davis 1, Robinson 1. Total 151.

MONTREAL EXPOS: Carter 17, Rogers 16, Dawson 15, Oliver 12, Raines 11, Reardon 11, Speier 9, Wallach 9, Cromartie 9, Sanderson 8, Gullickson 8, Fryman 8, Lea 7, B. Smith 3, Burris 3, Palmer 3, Flynn 2, Youngblood 1, White 1, Norman 1, Mills 1, Gates 1, Francona 1. Total 157.

PITTSBURGH PIRATES:Thompson 14, Tekulve 13, Madlock 11, Pena 11, Moreno 10, Scurry 9, Robinson 9, Easler 9, Berra 9, Ray 9, Candelaria 8, Rhoden 8, Sarmiento 7, Lacy 6, McWilliams 5, Romo 4, Nicosia 2, Parker 2, Hebner 1, Morrison 1, Stargell 1, Robinson 1, Milner 1. Total 151.

CHICAGO CUBS: Durham 15, Buckner 13, Davis 9, Sandberg 9, Moreland 9, Jenkins 9, L. Smith 8, Tidrow 8, Bowa 8, Wills 7, Campbell 7, Martz 6, Hernandez 6, Noles 5, Proly 4, Bird 4, Johnstone 4, Woods 3, Ripley 2, Morales 2, Kennedy 2, Henderson 2, Hall 1, Thompson 1, Tabler 1, Filer 1. Total 146.

NEW YORK METS: Wilson 12, Kingman 9, Swan 8, Foster 8, Bailor 8, Allen 7, Gardenhire 6, Orosco 6, Falcone 6, Puleo 5, Valentine 5, Stearns 5, Brooks 5, Lynch 4, Zachry 4, Scott 4, Staub 3, Backman 3, Hodges 2, Rajsich 2, Youngblood 2, Jones 2, Leach 2, Holman 1, Veryzer 1, Jorgensen 1, Giles 1, Bochy 1, Ownbey 1, Diaz 1. Total 125.

ATLANTA BRAVES: Murphy 14, Ramirez 13, Horner 13, Garber 13, Chambliss 11, Washington 10, Hubbard 10, Niekro 10, Bedrosian 9, Camp 8, Mahler 7, Benedict 6, Walk 6, Royster 4, Butler 3, Whisenton 2, Harper 2, Linares 2, Pocoroba 2, Hrabosky 2, Perez 2, Diaz 1, Boggs 1, Hanna 1, Moore 1, Hausman 1, Cowley 1, Dayley 1, Watson 1. Total 157.

LOS ANGELES DODGERS: Guerrero 16, Valenzuela 14, Reuss 13, Garvey 11, Sax 10, Baker 10, Cey 10, Welch 10, Howe 9, Russell 9, Landreaux 9, Stewart 6, Niedenfuer 6, Scioscia 5, Forster 5, Monday 4, Yeager 2, Roenicke 2, Hooton 2, Beckwith 1, Belanger 1, Marshall 1, Orta 1, Thomas 1. Total 158.

SAN FRANCISCO GIANTS: Morgan 13, Clark 12, Davis 12, Minton 11, Lavelle 10, Evans 10, Laskey 9, Breining 8, Smith 7, Holland 7, LeMaster 6, Hammaker 6, Barr 5, Gale 5, O'Malley 5, May 5, Kuiper 4, Leonard 3, Wohlford 3, Brenly 3, Martin 3, Fowlkes 2, Bergman 2, Sularz 1, Summers 1, Venable 1. Total 154.

SAN DIEGO PADRES: Kennedy 13, Lezcano 13, DeLeon 11, Lollar 11, Jones 10, Templeton 9, Show 8, Lucas 8, Salazar 8, Richards 8, Montefusco 6, Eichelberger 5, Flannery 5, Dravecky 5, Chiffer 4, Curtis 4, Perkins 4, Welsh 3, Gwynn 3, Lefebvre 3, Wiggins 3, Bonilla 2, Hawkins 1, Pittman 1, Bevacqua 1. Total 149.

HOUSTON ASTROS: Niekro 13, Thon 11, Garner 11, Cruz 11, Ryan 11, Knight 10, Sutton 9, Puhl 8, Scott 6, Ashby 6, LaCoss 6, Smith 6, Ruhle 6, Howe 5, Moffitt 4, Knepper 4, LaCorte 2, Pujols 2, Heep 2, Walling 1, Reynolds 1, Garcia 1, Knicely 1, Roberge 1, Sambito 1, Doran 1. Total 140.

CINCINNATI REDS: Soto 12, Concepcion 11, Driessen 10, Cedeno 10, Berenyi 8, Milner 7, Oester 7, Trevino 6, Hume 6, Bench 6, Householder 6, Pastore 6, Shirley 6, Price 5, Leibrandt 4, Harris 3, Kern 3, Bittner 3, Walker 2, Vail 2, Krenchicki 2, Hayes 2, Seaver 1, Lesley 1, Van Gorder 1, O'Berry 1, Landestoy 1, Lawless 1. Total 133.

# Pitchers

## HOW THE PITCHERS ARE RATED

The pitchers are rated, as they were a year ago, by the number of runs that they have saved as opposed to a replacement level pitcher, a pitcher allowing one run per game more than the league average. A year ago, a pitcher's rating was based 70% on the number of runs that he allowed and 30% on his won-lost record in consideration of his offensive support. This year the weighting is 50-50. A year ago, as at the other positions, the players were rated on only one season; this time, they are rated on the last two seasons. This creates some very surprising ratings, such as those of Tim Lollar, Don Robinson and Bill Laskey, where a pitcher had a very good 1982 season merged with no 1981 or a bad 1981. I confess I have no particular reason for using two-year statistics; if you want to base it on 1982 alone, move Lollar and Robinson up about 40 notches. I just feel that if the guy is really that good, he'll get the rating he deserves next year, and if he isn't, why bother?

The mechanics of the ratings:

1) Figure the number of runs per nine innings the pitcher has allowed. Steve Carlton in 1982 allowed 3.470 runs per nine innings.
2) Adjust this for the park in which he pitches. Veteran's Stadium increases offensive production by a little over 3%.
   Carlton's average becomes 3.422.
3) Compare this to the replacement level.
   The NL average of runs per game was 4.088; the replacement level is 5.088. Carlton is 1.666 runs per nine innings better than the replacement-level pitcher.
4) Project this into the innings that he has pitched. 1.666 runs per nine innings are 54.73 runs per 295.2 innings.
5) Take the pitcher's offensive support average. Carlton's is 4.342 runs per start.
6) Using the Pythagorean method, answer this question: Given his offensive support, how many runs per game should the pitcher allow to achieve his won-lost record? This is done by the formula:

$$\frac{\text{Runs}^2}{x^2} = \frac{W}{L}$$

In Carlton's case:

$$\frac{4.342^2}{x^2} = \frac{23}{11}$$

$$x = 3.003$$

7) Park-adjust this figure.
   It becomes 2.961.
8) Compare it to the replacement level.
   Carlton won games with the consistency that would be expected of a pitcher who is 2.127 runs a game better than replacement level.
9) Multiply that by his number of decisions.
   2.127 runs a game for 34 games are 72.31 runs.
10) Form an average of the two figures.

$$\frac{54.73 + 72.31}{2} = 63.5 \text{ runs}$$

11) Add this to his 1981 figure.
    Carlton's 1981 runs-saved figure was 45.4.
    The total is 108.9.

Which is how I concluded that Carlton had saved his team 108.9 runs over the last two seasons.

### 1. *Steve CARLTON, Philadelphia (108.9)*

Hold: A –
DP Support: Below Average

Seems almost a cinch to become the #2 man on the all-time list of games started. He has 569; the all-time #2 man is Pud Galvin with 682. He sure looks like he's got more than three years left . . . His career won-lost marks, by three-year groups:

| | W | L | Pct |
|---|---|---|---|
| 1965-67 | 17 | 12 | .586 |
| 1968-70 | 40 | 41 | .494 |
| 1971-73 | 50 | 39 | .562 |
| 1974-76 | 51 | 34 | .600 |
| 1977-79 | 57 | 34 | .626 |
| 1980-82 | 60 | 24 | .714 |

This is without adjusting for the strike in '81 . . .

With respect to Carlton's latest Cy Young Award, the question of whether or not he deserves it resolves itself to a question of which is the meaningful statistic here, his won-lost record, which is Cy Young calibre, or his ERA, which isn't.

A careful game-by-game review of the seasons of the pitchers who were candidates for the award—Carlton, Rogers and Andujar—convinces me beyond a syllable of doubt that Carlton deserves the award. His won-lost record would be misleading if he picked up a lot of cheap victories, games when he didn't pitch that well but won. You know how many cheap victories he had? None. Zero, Zilch, didn't happen. The definition of a cheap victory that is employed here (see *Not of Any General Interest*) is brutal; pitchers would scream to high heaven if I started applying it generally. It designates a victory as "cheap" if a pitcher allows three earned runs in 6⅔ innings.

It is Carlton's ERA that is misleading. The reason is that Corrales has so much confidence in Carlton that he will leave him in the game much longer than anybody would leave in Rogers or Andujar. R & A between them had only three games in which they allowed more than four earned runs, and none in which they allowed more than five, because they are taken out of the game when they reach that level. Carlton had nine games in which he allowed more than four earned runs and four in which he allowed more than five. So he allows more runs when he loses. So what?

Cardinal and Expo fans will tell you about all of the times their man pitched great but didn't get a break. The fact is, though, that Carlton had *more* games in which he suffered from poor offensive support than either of the other two pitchers. Carlton was the victim of a shutout three times, R & A twice each. Carlton had 14 starts in which the Phillies scored two or less runs for him; Andujar had 12 and Rogers only 8. The other two did have more tough losses than Carlton, but the reason for that is simple. When the Cardinals didn't score for Andujar, he took a tough loss. When the Phillies didn't score for old Bucolic Buffalo, Buke hung a tough loss on the other guy. Think about this: There were four times this year when the Phillies scored only one run for Carlton. He pitched shutouts and won three of those games. He also won games 2-0, 2-0 and 2-1 giving him six victories with fewer than three runs of support. (Rogers had two, Andujar two. Steve Stone in 1980 had none). He beat the division champion Cardinals five times. That, ladies and gentlemen, is Cy Young pitching.

### 2. *Dave STIEB, Toronto (104.6)*

Hold: A
DP Support: Average

Clearly the best starting pitcher in the AL . . . with league-average offensive support, his record would likely have been about 19-12; with Milwaukee, about 22-9 . . . now has 3+ years in the majors; arm needs to hold up for three more years to get him to free agency . . . just missed being the toughest pitcher in the league to run on . . . was 6-7, 3.99 ERA on 3 days rest; 9-4, 2.45 on four.

### 3. *Fernando VALENZUELA, Los Angeles (101.5)*

Hold: B–
DP Support: Below Average

Smashed all pitchers' attendance records to smithereens, pitching in front of 1,602,526 fans. Mark Fidrych in '76 just nosed above 1,000,000. Fernando's average, 43,312 per start, was 2,800 above 1981. And 47,704 a start at home? Just amazing. . . . About 1.3 million of those 1.6 are attributable to the Dodgers; an estimated 285,300 to Fernando. Both figures are astonishing.

### 4. *Steve ROGERS, Montreal (92.5)*

Hold: B
DP Support: Average

Away from Montreal last year he was 13-1 with a 1.71 ERA. Hasn't had much of a home-road split in the past.

### 5. *Jack MORRIS, Detroit (88.1)*

Hold: B+
DP Support: Average

You notice that with 27 starts, 198 innings in '79 he was 17-7, 3.27 ERA, and with 25 starts, 198 innings in '81 he was 14-7, 3.05 ERA. But in '80, when he had 36 starts and 250 innings he was just 16-15, 4.18 ERA, and in '82, with 37 starts, 266 innings he was 17-16, 4.06. Over the four years he's 64-45, which is pretty good, but you've got to wonder if he wouldn't win as many games and lose fewer on a 5-man rotation.

### 6. *Joe NIEKRO, Houston (87.6)*

Hold: D+
DP Support: Average

A Philadelphia gentleman named Mark Lazarus has awakened from the dead long enough to do a thorough study of the number of errors committed in games started by each and every major league pitcher, and the fielders behind him at each position. He was kind enough to send me a copy, for which I am grateful. These sheets are capable of many types of analysis and would probably yield many secrets if you had time enough to search for them—for example, how different is the infield/outfield error ratio behind a sinker baller, Mike Caldwell type, from that behind a hard thrower? The impact that the pitcher has on the distribution of errors is probably very similar to the impact that he has on the distribution of hit balls, which is something I'd like to know.

Unfortunately, I don't have time to figure out stuff like that at the moment, so I'll take the moronic approach of just picking the extremes off the charts and passing them along to you. Fewer errors per game were committed behind Joe Niekro last year than behind any other major league starter, 0.46 per start, 0.37 per start if you don't count Niekro's own errors. The outfielders behind him did not make an error all year. Whenever you see a figure like this, credit Mark Lazarus.

Niekro didn't pitch nearly as well on an extra days rest (3.55 ERA) as he did on rotation (2.21) . . . He had nine starts on long rest . . .

### 7. *Nolan RYAN, Houston (78.0)*

Hold: D–
DP Support: Low

Led the NL in hit batsmen, 8 . . . excellent September record, 39-25 since 1971 . . . a better pitcher now than he's ever been. His .614 won-lost percentage over the last two years is easily the best two-year stretch of his career.

### 8. *Dan PETRY, Detroit (76.3)*

Hold: B+
DP Support: Above Average

Effective on short rest (2.88 ERA, 10 starts on 3 days' rest; 3.13 on 4 days' rest, but 4.42 on 5 days).

### *9. Jerry REUSS, Los Angeles (76.0)*

Hold: A–
DP Support: Average

Another note on the 5-man pitching rotations... Reuss had always been a poor September pitcher before joining the Dodgers, but has been a very good finisher since then . . . I don't know who the GM was, but I don't think I'd recommend him as a judge of pitching talent. The Cardinals, in less than one year in the early '70s, traded Jerry Reuss for Scipio Spinks and Lance Clemons, traded Mike Torrez for Bob Reynolds, and traded Steve Carlton for Rick Wise. Combining the three trades, they gave up 500 wins and still counting fast, and received 134.

### *10. Pete VUCKOVICH, Milwaukee (75.4)*

Hold: D
DP Support: Average

Demolished all the old records for mediocrity by a Cy Young Award winner. The worst ERA by a Cy Young winner used to be 3.23, by Steve Stone in 1980; Vuckovich's was 3.33. The worst strikeout-to-walk ratio used to be 1.31-1 by Bob Turley in 1958; Vuckovich wasn't even close to that (1.03-1). He allowed more hits per inning than any Cy Young winner ever by far (he allowed 9.40 per nine innings; no one else has been over nine), which combined with more than four walks per game gave him a total of 13.56 runners on per nine innings, almost two runners per game over the previous worst (11.65 by Steve Stone). He pitched only 223 innings, 22 less than any other starter to win Cy Young recognition in a full season; his 18 wins are the fewest ever, with the same qualifications.

I think it's just an incredibly bad selection. Dave Stieb pitched over 60 innings *more* than Vuckovich and pitched better. Including unearned runs Vuckovich allowed 3.86 runs a game—not close to Stieb's average of 3.62, Palmer's 3.37 or Dan Petry's 3.59. Sure, he went 18-6 (as if that were a Cy Young-type record) but that was obviously because of the Milwaukee offense. I think the lack of a legitimate Cy Young season in the AL disoriented the voters to where they couldn't make a selection on the basis of the established criteria, and they kind of made a blind stab at it, and punched Vuckovich.

### *11. Mario SOTO, Cincinnati (75.4)*

Hold: B–
DP Support: Very Low

I really think he should rate higher. His offensive support average is deceptive because of a few 9-2 and 10-1 victories, but he really did take a lot of tough losses.

### *12. Larry GURA, Kansas City (72.6)*

Hold: A
DP Support: Below Average

The toughest pitcher to run on in the American League last year... he has no leg kick... only AL pitcher to win two 1-0 games in '82. There were only 12 1-0 games in the league, and he won two of them.

Scoring games when he was pitching, I noticed that he gets very few ground balls in the early innings, but gets a lot in the late innings. Looking at his runs allowed by inning, I get this:

| Inning | Innings Pitched | Runs Allowed | Runs/9 Innings |
|---|---|---|---|
| First Three | 109 | 36 | 2.97 |
| Fourth & Fifth | 65.1 | 50 | 6.89 |
| Sixth and after | 73.2 | 38 | 4.64 |

The early innings figure is great; the late innings figure is pretty respectable, because a starter has a very high concentration of innings there in which he pitches the first part of the inning but not the last, and those run up his runs allowed-per-inning rate. It looks like what happens is that in the early innings they pop the ball up, and in the late innings they beat it into the ground, but he goes through that crisis period in the fourth and fifth innings when they hit the ball square around the park.

### *13. Don SUTTON, Los Angeles (70.9)*

Hold: C
DP Support: Average

If you were going to pick up a pitcher to help in the stretch run, you couldn't pick a better one than Don Sutton. Last September 1st, wondering who I should be watching for to close with a rush, I went through the *Guides* for the years 1971 to 1981, and figured the won-lost records in September of all the game's big-name pitchers. The best September pitcher in baseball, I concluded, was Don Sutton, the man the Brewers had just acquired the day before. Sutton certainly didn't do anything to hurt that record, posting a 4-1 record in September of '82. For the last 12 Septembers combined (including the tag end of the season, which sometimes runs into October), his record is 42 wins, 15 losses, a .737 percentage. Although he is a good pitcher wire to wire, he has accounted for 22% of his wins and only 13% of his losses in September, so he is way over his head late in the year. He was 5-1 in September of '71, 5-1 in '72, 7-0 in '74 (with the Dodgers in a pennant race), 5-1 in '76, 4-1 in '80, 4-2 in '81, 4-1 in '82. The only other top pitcher who has been in the same class in September has been Tom Seaver, but of course Seaver doesn't have as far to rise to get to that level.

Major league pitchers with the most consecutive seasons in double figures in wins:

1. Don Sutton........17
2. Steve Carlton.....16
3. Nolan Ryan .......12
4. Dennis Leonard... 8

### *14. Phil NIEKRO, Atlanta (70.7)*

Hold: C+
DP Support: Low

Received the best offensive support in the National League last year, 5.40 runs per game... was 14-1 with a 2.61 ERA away from County Stadium.... His 1982 season reclassified him from "probably will not" get into the

Hall of Fame to "probably will." He went from 89 Hall of Fame points to 110 to reach the level of 257 wins, and above 250 Hall of Fame selection becomes almost automatic. Another season like it would leave no question.

### *15. Joaquin ANDUJAR, St. Louis (68.1)*

Hold: B–
DP Support: Below Average

I worked on Joaquin's salary arbitration case three years ago. When you do an arbitration case you go through the player's whole career game by game, looking for anything—any patterns, any counts, any oddities—that might be of use to you in trying to convince Mr. Arbitrator (that is really what you call him, by the way). One of the things we found about Joaquin was that he had pitched very well when he was in rotation, on three or four or five days rest, but very poorly when he was being shuttled back and forth between bullpen and rotation. In particular, his control was excellent when he was in rotation, but bad when he was not.

So why didn't they leave him alone? Basically, because they didn't like him. The Astros couldn't resist the continual temptation to try to teach him a lesson, make him a little more normal. I asked David Hendricks, one of his agents, about him a year later. He said, "You know, Joaquin has really been a pleasure to deal with. You go to dinner with him, he'll pick up the check; likes to do things for you. He just goes nuts when he's not pitching." Herzog was smart enough to look at what he could do on the field without being blinded by the man's reputation as a head case.

I suppose I might offer a few comments on arbitration cases, while we're on the subject. I have worked in salary arbitration cases for four years now, first of all with the Hendricks Brothers of Houston, who represent Andujar, and later with other agents. A lot of the public, I think, has the idea that arbitration hearings are sort of bullshit sessions in which the agent tries to convince the arbitrator that Joaquin Andujar is Steve Carlton's brother, and the club tries to convince him that he is Juan Berenguer's niece. It's not really like that. The first and foremost rule of an arbitration proceeding is that you never, ever, say *anything* which can be shown to be false. To make any error, no matter how small—a typo—in the presentation of a case gives the other side the opportunity to call into question the accuracy of everything you have said. A serious error can provide a serious embarrassment in a $70,000 one-afternoon psychological war.

The limits of bending the truth, then, are severe. I prepared an exhibit a year ago showing that the average attendance in the games started by Steve Trout was consistently above the White Sox team average. Now, I don't really think that Steve Trout was an attendance draw. In my opinion that was just a coincidence. But for Randy Hendricks to take that data and argue that Steve Trout was a hometown boy and the son of a major-league star and . . . well, that doesn't bother my conscience at all. I am not required to spout off with my opinions.

The second rule of an arbitration case is that you don't start any arguments that you can't win. The White Sox in the Trout case argued that Trout was not in shape and ready to pitch after the strike; we introduced an exhibit detailing Trout's first eight appearances in the second half of that dread season. In those eight games, he walked only eight men in 47 innings and had a 3.06 ERA. We won the case.

But the key is, stick to the facts. A lot of arbitration cases that are lost are lost because the player himself is convinced that he is a grade-A player when he isn't. He wants a grade-A salary; to justify it you've got to argue that he is a grade-A player; to do that you've got to compare him to the people who are grade-A players. If he isn't up to that level, you can't hide it. You can hide it in your own case, but the club will rip you apart. Tell the truth. It's the only chance you've got.

### *16. Steve McCATTY, Oakland (65.6)*

Hold: D
DP Support: Below Average

Allowed 16 home runs in 129 innings, worse-than-even K/W ratio . . . record could easily have been a lot worse.

### *17. Milt WILCOX, Detroit (64.7)*

Hold: A–
DP Support: Above Average

Amazing, just amazing. The last 5 years he has averaged 12.4 wins a season, with a low of 12 and a high of 13, and 10.4 losses a season, with a low of 9 and a high of 12. His won-lost percentage in that period has stayed between .520 and .571; his innings pitched have stayed between 166 and 215 despite injuries, strikes, rain, sleet, hail and Sparky Anderson. I should make up an all-consistency team. There's no doubt who'd be on the mound.

### *18. Britt BURNS, Chicago (62.8)*

Hold: B
DP Support: Below Average

Quick starter, has 1.69 ERA for the last three Aprils.

### *19. Bob FORSCH, St. Louis (61.0)*

Hold: B–
DP Support: Above Average

Had his first career save in '82 . . . had a 1.75 ERA in September.

### *20. Jim PALMER, Baltimore (60.4)*

Hold: A–
DP Support: Below Average

Only active pitcher who has pitched more than one shutout in post-season play. . .

### 21. *Dennis ECKERSLEY, Boston (58.7)*

Hold: D
DP Support: Low

Poorest September record of any big-name pitcher in baseball, 18-21. . . . Another case in point of the law of competitive balance. Eckersley is one of the easiest pitchers in baseball to run on. His opposition stolen-base rates have been terrible; they were down a little last year, but mostly because of fewer attempts; Mr. Waseleski (see "Jim Rice") reports that when Eckersley was actually on the mound, opponents were 18 of 20 in attempts to steal second, 2 of 4 at third.

And why is he so easy to run on? Because he is a good pitcher, ultimately. He knows they are stealing on him, but he rationalizes . . . been doing it for years, won a lot of ballgames, that sort of thing. This guy has the material to be a Jim Palmer, but while a player like Palmer constantly changes, adjusts, adapts, and thus avoids being dragged to the center by the law of competitive balance, Eckersley uses the success he has had in the past as an excuse to keep on doing something poorly, and thus winds up as a .500 pitcher. And he won't adjust until he becomes a .400 pitcher.

### 22. *Vida BLUE, Kansas City (58.6)*

Hold: B+
DP Support: Low

Had a 2.43 ERA in Royals Stadium, 5.20 on the road. That may be the widest differential in baseball, other than Randy Jones. . . . You want to know something funny? *My wife* analyzed this trade better than I did at the time it was made. I was like an eight-year-old, calling up people saying, "Hey, did you hear? We got Vida Blue!" My wife kept saying, "I don't know, Bill; I've heard you point out so many times how people get burnt on trades by trading off prospects to get some old guy." "But honey, it's *Vida Blue*," I protested. . . . The Royals may not have gotten burnt, but I'd sure trade him back to get Atlee Hammaker, and looking a few years down the road. . .

### 23. *Ken FORSCH, California (57.2)*

Hold: C
DP Support: Below Average

Both Forsch brothers pushed past 100 wins last year, Bob to 108, Ken to 102. Ken is now 36, but he's in good shape and hasn't thrown that many innings . . . besides, on the Angels' staff, 36 is young.

### 24. *Dave RIGHETTI, New York Yankees (56.7)*

Hold: D
DP Support: Very Low

Still only 24. Probably the one Yankee who will be most helped by Billy's return.

### 25. *Ron GUIDRY, New York Yankees (56.2)*

Hold: A–
DP Support: Below Average

Who was the only pitcher to win 100 games with a better lifetime won-lost percentage than Guidry's .706? (1943 AL MVP, Spud Chandler) Guidry's six straight seasons of .600 ball are pretty impressive. I think Palmer's the only other active player who has done that.

### 26. *Bruce BERENYI, Cincinnati (55.7)*

Hold: F
DP Support: High

Made big strides last year; cut walks per game from 5.50 to 3.89, posted sharp 3.36 ERA . . . he was the worst-supported pitcher in baseball, at 2.59 runs per game; would have finished 15-12 with average offensive support, 17-10 with good support . . . also was fourth in the league in double-play-support average, odd for a power pitcher. . .

### 27. *Tommy JOHN, California (54.1)*

Hold: A–
DP Support: Very High

Was the #10 man in career wins (active pitchers) one year ago, and all 10 pitchers won at least a game last year, so the list is still surging upward. John passed Luis Tiant; he's now #9.

### 28. *Rick CAMP, Atlanta (53.0)*

Hold: D–
DP Support: Very High

A classic case study in how raw statistics can disguise a player's performance. His 11-13 record, 3.65 ERA, and poor hits-per-inning ratio belie a much more effective season. One of his most important advantages, his ability to get a double play when he needs it, is not, by a historical oversight, even hinted at in the traditional records. The Braves turned 33 double plays in his 21 starts, the highest DP-support average in baseball. The decision to make a starter of him was one of the major reasons for the Braves' big increase in double plays; no other Braves' starter was even close to that 1.57-per-start average.

That's a small thing. The first large thing is the park he plays in, and the impact that has on earned runs averages. Although Camp is ideally suited to the park—his ground balls are safe; anything hit in the air is dangerous—a 3.65 ERA in Atlanta is a very different thing from a 3.65 in another park. A 3.65 ERA in County Stadium, to be specific, is equivalent to 3.36 in a neutral park, 3.11 in San Diego or Houston.

The second big thing is his offensive support, which was miserable, and which saddled him with an 11-13 won-lost record. The Braves in 1982 scored nearly 5½ runs a game for Phil Niekro, over 5 for Bob Walk, over 4½ for Mahler. But for Camp, they scored a miserly 3.05 runs per game. With the offensive support given to Phil Niekro,

Camp's won-lost percentage would likely have been around .616 (15-9); with Mahler's, around .539 (13-11).

It's an odd case, of course: a misleading ERA, a misleading won-lost record. You look at those two numbers and they'll give you a pretty good idea of how well the guy has pitched 80% of the time. It's not an example of what usually happens, but is a clear example of what can happen.

***29. Luis LEAL, Toronto (52.6)***

Hold: D+
DP Support: Low

Pitched much better on three days rest than on the normal four. In 17 starts on three days rest his ERA was 3.39; in 15 starts on four it was 5.04. But Stieb and Clancy were both better on four, so I don't imagine they're going to set up their rotation to accommodate Luis.

***30. Bob WELCH, Los Angeles (52.2)***

Hold: B+
DP Support: Low

Did you ever notice that the lion's share of baseball players who develop famous drinking problems are pitchers? Make a list—Welch, Duren, Dalkowski, McDowell, Newcombe, Buck Newsome, Ellis Kinder, even on back to Howie Camnitz and Pete Alexander. How many other known problem drinkers can you name? Newcombe and Alexander stand out on the list because they were control pitchers; the others were hard throwers with control problems. Welch seems to be the only one who got ahold of the problem before it beat him. Of course, many other people have done that but they did it privately.

***31. Dennis MARTINEZ, Baltimore (51.0)***

Hold: D
DP Support: Average

Closes out a game as well as anybody in the league; allowed only seven runs in 28 innings from the eighth inning on. . . . Over the last two years is 18-4 in Baltimore, sub-.500 on the road.

***32. Len BARKER, Cleveland (49.3)***

Hold: D+
DP Support: Very Low

I commented a year ago that his DP support was the lowest of anybody's . . . it was again, last in the AL at .58 per start. . .

***33. Rick SUTCLIFFE, Cleveland (48.9)***

Hold: F
DP Support: Below Average

Was very effective in the early innings, allowing only 25 runs in the first three innings which is 2.78 per nine innings pitched . . . among the people leading the AL in ERA since 1960: Frank Baumann, Hank Aguirre, Dick Bosman, Diego Segui, Mark Fidrych, Rudy May, Rick Sutcliffe . . . you might say I'm not impressed.

***34. Mike CALDWELL, Milwaukee (48.2)***

Hold: A+
DP Support: Very High

Continues to beat the Yankees like a drum; last year 3-1, 2.38 ERA against them, now career mark of 12-3 against them. . . Geoff Zahn, one of the two most-similar pitchers in the league, was 3-1 with a 1.16 ERA against the Yanks . . . with 16 more wins he can set a record for pitchers named "Caldwell."

***35. Mike KRUKOW, Philadelphia (47.0)***

Hold: D–
DP Support: Average

Poor September kept him from having super stats.

***36. Floyd BANNISTER, Seattle (45.3)***

Hold: D+
DP Support: Low

Another of the logical consequences of free agency, it seems to me, is that you definitely don't want to rush a player to the majors before he is ready to help you. Bannister is really just coming into his own; he's only 27. He pitched seven games in the minors and was rushed to the majors by the Astros with just a sort of half-idea of how to pitch. If you've only got a player for six years you want to let him mature a little first, so you'll get six good years.

***37. Lamar HOYT, Chicago (44.7)***

Hold: D
DP Support: Average

19-15 record is not impressive in view of offensive support, five and a third runs a game. . . He was, however, the only AL pitcher to lose two 1-0 games in '82.

***38. Dennis LEONARD, Kansas City (43.6)***

Hold: C
DP Support: Average

Didn't pitch well in September this time, 1-3. If he and Gura had split their decisions in September the Royals would have won the division.

***39. Scott SANDERSON, Montreal (43.1)***

Hold: B–
DP Support: Very Low

Was 4-3, 1.88 ERA on five days rest; 5-7, 4.08 on four days (see Bill Gullickson).

***40. Dennis LAMP, Chicago White Sox (42.9)***

Hold: D+
DP Support: Above Average

Has done the tough starter-reliever job well for two seasons.

***41. Bill GULLICKSON, Montreal (42.9)***

Hold: B
DP Support: Low

Was the only National League pitcher to start 10 times on five days rest, and actually the extra days rest seemed to help him. He was 5-3 with a 2.75 ERA on five days rest, as opposed to 4-10, 4.27 on four days. I don't know why that is, but I do notice that most of the pitchers who pitch better on five days rest are youngsters, and Gullickson was only 23.

***42. John TUDOR, Boston (42.9)***

Hold: A
DP Support: Average

How many runners did he pick off first last year? I don't have the count, but I remember it was a bunch... Why don't they keep records of stuff like that? If you count balks but not runners picked off, then you're counting the negative but you're not counting the positive that goes along with it. Steve Carlton leads the league in balks above every year, but he picks so many people off base that it is obviously a good gamble. But the record books make it look like he is doing something wrong. Statistics aren't supposed to lie to you, they're supposed to be designed to tell you the truth.

***43. John CANDELARIA, Pittsburgh (42.7)***

Hold: A
DP Support: Above Average

What is odd about him is that he is such a flaky person but such a heady pitcher. The press always talks about what a screwball he is, but he's just a masterful pitcher—sets up the hitters, never beats himself... good hitter, like all the Pirate pitchers.

***44. Jim CLANCY, Toronto (42.5)***

Hold: A–
DP Support: Above Average

Does not pitch well in Toronto, at all—6.08 ERA at home in 1981, 4.79 last year (3.33, 2.85 on the road)... A difference like that should be respected, even if you have to hold him back a day to get him away from Toronto...

***45. Steve RENKO, California (42.1)***

Hold: B
DP Support: Below Average

In the last two seasons he has made 38 starts, pitched 258 innings with 19-10 won-lost mark... excellent spot starter.

***46. Doc MEDICH, Milwaukee (41.5)***

Hold: D+
DP Support: Above Average

Retired: practicing.

***47. Charlie HOUGH, Texas (41.1)***

Hold: D+
DP Support: Below Average

It took a remarkably long time, in retrospect, to make a starter out of him. In '77 he started once after the race was over, threw five innings of two-hit shutout ball. In '79 the Dodgers' pitching rotation disintegrated, and, after they had tried everyone else, they tried Charlie. Although his ERA as a starter was not good, he lasted at least five innings in 12 of his 14 starts, allowed two or less earned runs in seven, and the Dodgers won 10 of them. He made an important contribution to stabilizing the Dodgers' staff, which cut its team ERA from 4.26 at the All-Star break to a final 3.83.

Unimpressed, the Dodgers returned him to the bullpen, giving him only one start in 1980, just before getting rid of him. But with Texas, he got a start on July 29 and pitched a good (complete) game, giving Baltimore three runs and striking out eight. Impressed? Nope, back to the pen. On August 26, he made an emergency start when the league suggested that afternoon that Fergie should not start because of the cola incident. He pitched a shutout.

This, surely, would earn him a starting job? Not even another look. Not until over a year later, September 8, 1981. Hough started five times that September, won four of them and averaged eight innings a start with a 1.83 ERA.

So that's what it took to make people recognize Hough as a starter; 23 starts, a 12-6 record as a starter and 150 innings with a 3.66 ERA. Again, I am near a point which I may be in danger of driving into the ground, which is that people think so much in terms of images that they sometimes simply fail to see what a person is capable of doing. Hough's problem is that he doesn't *look* like a starting pitcher.

### *48. Mike WITT, California (41.0)*

Hold: B–
DP Support: Above Average

Big improvement in his OSB rate last year *(see Bob Boone)*...had 2.59 ERA in California, 4.50 on the road...still think he will be an outstanding pitcher...

### *49. Mike FLANAGAN, Baltimore (40.9)*

Hold: A–
DP Support: Above Average

Wonder if the new manager will have the patience to keep sticking him out there when he's in one of his famous slumps?...The Orioles' answer to Mike Torrez.

### *50. Scott McGREGOR, Baltimore (40.1)*

Hold: A–
DP Support: Average

Had a lot of trouble in the early innings, allowed 24 first-inning runs, 61 in the first three innings. Runs-allowed-per-nine-innings averages: first three: 5.40; middle three: 3.80; last three: 6.81. Most pitchers have a high figure for the last three.

### *51. Jim BEATTIE, Seattle (39.3)*

Hold: D–
DP Support: Average

Has improved his mechanics so much he looks like a whole different pitcher...One thing I watch when I see a game is to see if I can pick up any small things that a manager does which show an awareness of details. Rene Lachemann is in the class of managers, with Mauch, Weaver, Herzog, Howser, who do those little things just constantly, inning after inning. It makes his team very interesting to watch. One striking example was in an early September game that Beattie was pitching well against the Royals; he was behind but it was close. I'd been saying to Susie for about three innings "Wait until we get this guy into the seventh inning," because Beattie's ERA suddenly does a triple somersault in the seventh inning. But you know what happened? He didn't come out. He pitched a perfect sixth, had allowed only one run since the first and had the bottom of the order coming up—but he stayed in the dugout. I looked back at his record and found four more times that the same thing had happened—twice, in fact, he was lifted after six with a shutout going. So Lachemann, obviously, was aware that six innings was his limit. In fact, that was one of the biggest reasons for Beattie's 3.35 ERA. His manager got him out of the game before he got into trouble, not afterwards.

### *52. Rick MAHLER, Atlanta (39.0)*

Hold: B
DP Support: Above Average

Rafael Ramirez made 12 errors in the 33 games Mahler started. Ozzie Smith made 13 errors all year.

### *53. Bobby CASTILLO, Minnesota (38.8)*

Hold: A–
DP Support: Average

A completely unexpected year . . . may get out of the trivia class yet. You know that question, answers are Part A: Norm Sherry; Part B: Bobby Castillo.

### *54. Gaylord PERRY, Seattle (36.6)*

Hold: A–
DP Support: Above Average

A year ago, concerning Gaylord Perry, I commented on the fact that we have a basketful of pitchers around with 200, 250 or more career victories, whereas in 1968 there was only one active pitcher with 200 wins (Don Drysdale with 204), and the tenth man on the list of leading pitchers in career wins had the preposterously unprepossessing figure of 123. There are now around 30 active pitchers with more than 123 wins. Pitchers who were 35 years of age or older accounted for only 84 major league wins in 1967: in 1980, they accounted for 266. And one of the major sports stories of the 1983 season figures to be that a strikeout record which has stood untouched for over a half a century is going to be broken three times within about a month. Within a few years more and more pitchers will break 3500, and the record will break 4000 and head for five.

The question before the house is, Why has this happened? I developed an interesting theory. From the 1960s until now the offensive game has changed from being one in which the home run was suffocatingly predominant, toward a broader-based offense making much use of the running game. This change could well benefit an older pitcher. A young pitcher is likely to be a power pitcher, and a power pitcher is difficult to hit home runs off of, but usually fairly easy to run on. An older pitcher is more likely to be a control-type pitcher, and a control pitcher is difficult to run on but usually will give up more home runs. We have shifted toward an offense which a control-type pitcher, and thus an older pitcher, can deal with. Perry, for example, gives up many more home runs than he did in the early '70s, but has better control and is probably harder to run on.

Believe it? Don't; it won't hold water. All of the statements which comprise the argument are true, but there is one very major problem. The same thing—the same sudden (in historical terms), forceful shift toward older pitchers—has occurred once before in baseball. Oddly enough—unfortunately, for this clever argument—it occurred at exactly the moment when the opposite trends were in motion with regard to offensive types. Between 1917 and 1932, the number of home runs hit in the major leagues jumped around four-fold, while stolen bases declined by 60%. But in the same years, the number of wins posted by pitchers 35 or older increased from 7 (!) to about 150.

What is the true explanation? A more likely candidate is economics. Do you remember Waite Hoyt's quote, "Wives of ballplayers, when they teach their children their prayers, should instruct them to say: 'God bless mommy, God bless daddy, God bless Babe Ruth.' Babe has upped daddy's paycheck by 15 to 40 percent!" The common thread in the two periods 1917-1932 and 1967-1982 is a dramatic upsurge in player salaries. Suppose that you are Gaylord Perry, and for years and years you were one of the best pitchers in the game, and for this you were paid—oh, I don't know, $40,000 to $75,000 a year, I suppose, which is a good living wage but by the time the government takes its share it won't buy very much farm land, and then all of a sudden at age 40 people are throwing whole counties at you if you can just hang around and pitch .500 baseball for another year. Are you going to retire, or are you going to hang in there for as long as you can?

A related matter here is that I have always believed that many pitchers pass through a crisis about the age of 30 when they lose their good fastball, and that that causes many of them—far too many of them—simply to give up, walk away from the game, when if they would stay around and try to learn how to work with what they have left, they could become just as effective as they were. It was Curt Simmons, actually, who led me to this belief; Simmons went down to the minor leagues at the age of 30 and with a good career behind him to learn how to pitch all over again. He did it, and he came back to have a couple of fine, fine years with the Cardinals in '63 and '64. Jerry Koosman, Jerry Reuss, Luis Tiant, Jim Kaat . . . a large percentage of all pitchers who will put their heads down and bull their way through the crisis, it has always seemed to me, would come out of it better pitchers than they ever were. But most, like Drysdale, don't want to do it; either they walk away, or they try to keep pitching the way they have always pitched, getting gradually less effective until they are released at 33.

Anyway, this notion dove-tails nicely with the economic interpretation of the phenomenon . . . you don't walk away from the chance to earn five times as much as you were earning two years ago. But the economic incentive is not relevant unless it is, indeed, possible to make the transition.

### *55. Randy MARTZ, Chicago Cubs (36.2)*

Hold: B+
DP Support: Above Average

Ruined his stats with a June record of 0-3, 10.71 ERA. Pitched pretty well after August 1st, 7-3 . . . looks like he's going to mess up the Cubs' record of wasting every first-round draft pick. I think he is already the best player they've ever gotten with a #1 pick.

### *56. Burt HOOTON, Los Angeles (35.7)*

Hold: D–
DP Support: Average

Career 31-19 record in September, one of the best in baseball. . .

### *57. Ferguson JENKINS, Chicago Cubs (35.0)*

Hold: D
DP Support: Below Average

Jenkins? What's Ferguson Jenkins still doing around? Do you realize that Ron Santo retired in 1974? That's nine years ago. Billy Williams retired in 1976, seven years ago, Glenn Beckert in 1975, Don Kessinger in 1979, Jim Hickman in 1974, Randy Hundley in 1977, Bill Hands in 1975, Phil Regan in 1971. Ernie Banks gave it up in 1971. Ken Holtzman, two years Fergie's junior, quit four years ago, in 1979. Even the Cubbies who *replaced* that lot—Andy Thornton and Manny Trillo and Jerry Morales and Steve Stone and Rick Reuschel—are getting old and disappearing. You planning to bury Bull Durham and Ryne Sandberg too, Fergie?

A few notes . . . Don Zimmer remains the only manager to take Fergie out of the rotation . . . he should make the list of the top 10 in career starts with 33 more. He has 565; Tim Keefe is #10 with 595, but Steve Carlton will knock him off so Fergie will have to get Pete Alexander, a 598 . . . his 1982 comeback cut his distance to 300 wins from 3.3 years to 1.9, in terms of his established win level . . . has never pitched in a post-season game . . . was 8-3 in August and September. . . . Walt Campbell says that he wrote last spring that if Fergie Jenkins had an ERA lower than 4.00 in Wrigley Field he would eat a Shooty Babbit Baseball Card. Says it wasn't all that bad with a little mayo. . .

### *58. Larry CHRISTENSON, Philadelphia (34.2)*

Hold: B
DP Support: Average

Homered again last year; also stole a base. The thing is he's really not a good-hitting pitcher, unless he happens to reach the seats. He strikes out about half the time and his lifetime average is .154 . . . now 29; still looks 21.

### *59. Rick RHODEN, Pittsburgh (34.1)*

Hold: A–
DP Support: Average

In the NL value approximations, three pitchers got a point each for their value as hitters—Rhoden, Robinson, and Lollar. . .

### *60. Geoff ZAHN, California (33.7)*

Hold: A+
DP Support: Very High

Another player whose rating is a combination of one

bad year and one good one... I believe the ratio between his double-play support and stolen bases allowed is the best in baseball, 246-73 over the last six years . . . was 10-1 with 2.87 ERA in California; 8-7, 4.61 on the road. . .

### *61. Charlie LEA, Montreal (33.2)*

Hold: B+
DP Support: Below Average

Has made huge strides in the last couple of years. Doesn't seem to have the stuff of Sanderson or Gullickson, but seems likely to emerge into the Bob Forsch, Rick Reuschel class, and you sure need some of those.

### *62. Craig SWAN, New York Mets (33.0)*

Hold: D
DP Support: Above Average

His career record is 56-63, he's 16-18 over the last three years, and he's the Mets' top starter. You could say that staff needs work.

### *63. Tom SEAVER, Cincinnati (32.3)*

Hold: C+
DP Support: Below Average

I'm always kind of fascinated by strategies that go out of fashion. Remember Ted Lyons, the Sunday pitcher? Pitched every Sunday for the White Sox for several years; pitched great. In the period 1935 to 1950 there were a number of old but skilled pitchers who would start 20 to 25 times a year, not because they were injured, but just because it was felt that that was the way they could be most effective. They were, by and large, damned effective—Ted Lyons was from 1934 to '42, Grove from 1939 to '41, Red Ruffing pitched that way for a couple of years, Spud Chandler for a year, Freddie Fitzsimmons and Carl Hubbell for several years each. They were all at the tag ends of brilliant careers, and they weren't really strong enough to hitch up to the plow every fifth day, but they were effective at the level of 20 starts a year.

For some reason, the strategy fell out of favor about 1950, and I don't really understand why. I keep waiting for somebody to try to revive the idea. Tom Seaver last year was 3-2, 4.13 ERA when he was starting on long (five days) rest. He was 2-11 otherwise with an ERA over six. You've got a team going nowhere; you've got Soto and Berenyi to build the pitching around. Why not pitch Seaver once a week, see what he can do? Indeed, why not set Sunday aside for him? Maybe there's a good reason why the strategy went out of use, but I don't know what it is.

### *64. Rick LANGFORD, Oakland (32.2)*

Hold: A
DP Support: Low

Billy Martin's reported comment about Langford's being a seven-inning pitcher got me to wondering how well he had, in fact, pitched in the late innings. Here is his inning-by-inning breakdown in 1982:

| Inning | Innings | Runs | Runs per 9 Innings |
|---|---|---|---|
| 1st | 31 | 13 | 3.77 |
| 2nd | 31 | 7 | 2.03 |
| 3rd | 31 | 16 | 4.65 |
| 4th | 30 | 15 | 4.50 |
| 5th | 28⅓ | 22 | 6.99 |
| 6th | 26 | 9 | 3.12 |
| 7th | 24⅓ | 13 | 4.81 |
| 8th | 20⅓ | 9 | 3.98 |
| 9th | 11⅔ | 14 | 10.80 |

It would seem to be more accurate to say that he was an eight-inning pitcher in 1982, but this got me to wondering whether Langford's innings pattern was ever all that different, or if it was simply that the A's were so desperately thin in the bullpen that they stuck with him regardless of how well he was pitching. So I figured the same data for him (as a starter) for every year back to 1977. There is one immediate striking contrast: In 1981, Langford pitched into the ninth inning 14 times, and pitched 14 shutout ninth innings—the complete opposite of his ninth-inning troubles in 1982. A couple of charts summarizing his patterns:

| | 1977 | 1978 | 1979 | 1980 | 1981 | 1982 |
|---|---|---|---|---|---|---|
| First Six Innings | 4.82 | 3.87 | 4.01 | 3.82 | 3.79 | 4.16 |
| Seventh and After | 5.46 | 4.58 | 4.47 | 3.53 | 3.57 | 5.75 |

In case this is not as self-explanatory as I take it to be . . . in 1979 Rick Langford allowed 4.01 runs per nine innings pitched in the first six innings of the game, 4.47 per nine after that.

OK, something clearly seems to have happened when Billy Martin took over. In the first six innings of the game, Langford pitched only slightly better in 1980 and 1981 than he had in 1978 and 1979. But after the sixth, he was dramatically better. Confidence? Something Billy taught him? A statistical illusion created by the fact that he was getting to pitch the end of the inning as well as the beginning? That wouldn't account for his having a lower ERA after the seventh than before.

Whatever it was, it moved out last summer. His complete, six-year inning-by-inning summary presents a riddle:

| Inning | Innings | Runs | Runs per 9 Innings |
|---|---|---|---|
| 1st | 171 | 75 | 3.95 |
| 2nd | 170 | 69 | 3.65 |
| 3rd | 165.2 | 72 | 3.91 |
| 4th | 161.1 | 55 | 3.07 |
| 5th | 151 | 101 | 6.02 |
| 6th | 134 | 60 | 4.03 |
| 7th | 117 | 65 | 5.00 |
| 8th | 98 | 37 | 3.40 |
| 9th | 74 | 39 | 4.74 |
| Extra | 8.2 | 3 | 3.12 |

What's with the fifth inning? For one year you'd figure it was just a coincidence, but do coincidences get that large? His fourth-inning run averages are 2.25, 1.80, 2.03, 4.68, 2.24 and 4.50, while his fifth-inning averages jump to 12.49, 4.26, 6.39, 3.13, 3.86 and 6.99. The only thing I can think of is that you have to get through five to get a win, and if you start thinking about that too much it might mess you up.

***65. Larry McWILLIAMS, Pittsburgh (31.9)***

Hold: B+
DP Support: Below Average

A model of inconsistency.

***66. Bob SHIRLEY, Cincinnati (31.1)***

Hold: A–
DP Support: Average

Second-poorest offensive support in baseball last year, 2.65 runs per game. Still is cursed with that starter-relief split role. I still think he could help a team more as a starter.

***67. Brad HAVENS, Minnesota (30.9)***

Hold: C–
DP Support: Low

Another good-looking kid... Expect to see him among the American League leaders in strikeouts this year.

***68. Richard DOTSON, Chicago White Sox (30.6)***

Hold: D
DP Support: Low

I'm sure glad he isn't a relief pitcher (You know: "Dotson Saves")... Wonder if he'll change his name to Richard Nissan?... progress has been disappointing, but he's only 23 now, and who learns how to do *anything* before he is 23? Looks to me like he is likely to catch free agency (six years in the majors) just at the crest of his wave, and again, I think the Sox were very short-sighted to rush him to the majors at 20, spend four years teaching him how to pitch and then risk losing him in the market.

***69. Pete FALCONE, New York Mets (30.4)***

Hold: C+
DP Support: Below Average

Hey, I am not going to be shocked if this guy turns it around after all these years and becomes a pretty good pitcher. Stranger things have happened. Remember Mike Caldwell. Remember Joe Niekro. Remember Jerry Reuss. Remember Joe Quinn Andujar. It happens.

***70. Dave LaPOINT, St. Louis (30.1)***

Hold: F
DP Support: Very High

Odd combination: the easiest pitcher to run on in the National League, but gets very high double-play support, second highest in the league... if he's a ground-ball-type pitcher, he'd better learn to keep them on first.

***71. Bob KNEPPER, Houston (28.6)***

Hold: D–
DP Support: Average

Can pitch great at times, but you never know when the next time is going to come. Belongs with Cleveland.

***72. Jerry UJDUR, Detroit (28.4)***

Hold: D+
DP Support: Above Average

Gave up 29 homers in 178 innings. As a right-handed, HR-vulnerable pitcher, he is in the worst possible park. Looks good otherwise, though.

***73. Al WILLIAMS, Minnesota (28.3)***

Hold: D–
DP Support: Above Average

One of the 10 best human-interest stories in the game. You know what a human-interest story is; means the guy has done something other than play baseball. Lance Parrish is a human-interest story because he worked one time as a body-guard for Lois Lane or Sandre Dee or somebody.

***74. Doug BIRD, Chicago Cubs (25.8)***

Hold: B–
DP Support: Very Low

Received the lowest double-play support in the majors last year... Allowed almost as many home runs (26) as walks (30). I wonder if anybody has ever allowed more homers than walks in 200 innings or more? Probably, but I don't know who....

***75. Vern RUHLE, Houston (25.5)***

Hold: B+
DP Support: Above Average

Made 11 off-rotation starts in 1982, three more than anyone else in the league. Ordinarily you'd figure that was hurting his stats, but actually Ruhle pitched very well in the spot-starter role. It was when he was in the rotation that he had troubles.

***76. Bill LASKEY, San Francisco (25.0)***

Hold: C–
DP Support: Below Average

Pitched some good games and has great control; will rank as a good one if he can stay on course.

***77. Moose HAAS, Milwaukee (24.2)***

Hold: C+
DP Support: Average

Probably the smallest major leaguer ever called Moose. He's only 170 pounds . . . has gone 10-12, 11-11, 11-7, 11-8 . . . excellent strikeout-to-walk ratios.

***78. Mike TORREZ, Boston (23.0)***

Hold: C+
DP Support: Above Average

Does he have a comeback left? Who knows . . . pitched 40 innings with a 2.93 ERA in September. . .

***79. Dick RUTHVEN, Philadelphia (22.4)***

Hold: D–
DP Support: Below Average

Over the last three years is 23-10 in Veteran's Stadium, 17-18 on the road.

***80. John STUPER, St. Louis (20.6)***

Hold: A
DP Support: Average

Toughest pitcher to run on in the National League.

***81. John DENNY, Itinerant (20.2)***

Hold: B–
DP Support: Average

Corrales must have seen something in him that I never saw.

***82. Atlee HAMMAKER, San Francisco (18.4)***

Hold: D–
DP Support: Low

Had 3.43 ERA on five days rest (nine starts), 4.46 on four days . . . Super strikeout-to-walk ratio, 102 to 28 . . . give him 60-40 shot at emerging as Giants' best pitcher. know this: Rich Gale ain't going to do it.

***83. Paul SPLITTORFF, Kansas City (18.0)***

Hold: C+
DP Support: Average

About as effective as any pitcher in the league in the first two or three innings of a ballgame (an average of only 0.54 runs allowed in the first two innings.) But as the game wears on he is just a kind of time bomb out there; ERA if he starts the seventh is over 7.00.

***84. Mike NORRIS, Oakland (18.0)***

Hold: D+
DP Support: Above Average

The A's committed 38 errors behind him (32 infield), in 28 games, the worst error-support rate in baseball.

***85. Chuck RAINEY, Boston (17.6)***

Hold: D+
DP Support: Very High

ERA is unsightly, but lifetime won-lost mark is now 23-14.

***86. Tim LOLLAR, San Diego (17.0)***

Hold: A–
DP Support: Low

Obviously Williams' chosen pitcher. Williams would shift anybody else off-schedule to keep Lollar starting on four days rest. But you can't argue with his results.

***87. Dickie NOLES, Chicago Cubs (14.4)***

Hold: D
DP Support: Below Average

4.72 ERA over the final three months of the season.

***88. Jim GOTT, Toronto (14.2)***

Hold: C
DP Support: Below Average

Poorest offensive support in the American League.

***89. Frank PASTORE, Cincinnati (14.0)***

Hold: C+
DP Support: Above Average

The amazing thing about this division is that the last-place team, the Reds, had a far better starting rotation than the first place team, the Braves. That was all they had, but . . . Pastore's been a disappointment, but he's the Red's #5 starter, and with the Braves he'd be #3.

***90. Bob McCLURE, Milwaukee (14.0)***

Hold: A–
DP Support: Average

Best-supported starter in the American League, 5.96 runs per start.

***91. Frank TANANA, Texas (13.4)***

Hold: B+
DP Support: Low

Dismal offensive support made his year look worse than it was . . . 12-13 would be a better indication of how he pitched than 7-18.

Tanana was one of those pitchers they used to compare to Sandy Koufax at the same age. Remember those? It's so stupid. . . the whole point about Koufax is that he *became* a great pitcher. It's like comparing Robert Redford to Ronald Reagan at the same age.

Anyway, did you ever hear the saying that lefthanders don't find themselves until age 26? It's obviously a "magic" theory—there is a magic about turning 26—but people say it, so there must be people who believe it. Usually the people who believe it are 24-year old lefthanders going nowhere, but I'm afraid I took the issue more seriously than it warrants. I figured the complete career won-lost records for all left-handed pitchers born between 1920 and 1939. That group includes the man most responsible for the myth, Koufax, plus most of the auxiliary pitchers who are cited as supporting examples: Spahn, Gary Peters, Chris Short. On balance, though, there's nothing to it:

**ALL LEFT-HANDED PITCHERS BORN 1920-1939**

| Age | Won | Lost | Pct | 20 Wins |
|---|---|---|---|---|
| 16 | 1 | 1 | .500 | 0 |
| 17 | 1 | 6 | .143 | 0 |
| 18 | 5 | 3 | .625 | 0 |
| 19 | 50 | 52 | .440 | 0 |
| 20 | 82 | 94 | .466 | 0 |
| 21 | 157 | 156 | .502 | 0 |
| 22 | 207 | 276 | .429 | 0 |
| 23 | 322 | 287 | .529 | 2 |
| 24 | 531 | 523 | .504 | 5 |
| 25 | 617 | 627 | .496 | 2 |
| 26 | 721 | 711 | .503 | 3 |
| 27 | 796 | 743 | .517 | 7 |
| 28 | 724 | 703 | .507 | 4 |
| 29 | 667 | 687 | .493 | 4 |
| 30 | 627 | 601 | .511 | 3 |
| 31 | 403 | 444 | .476 | 1 |
| 32 | 337 | 336 | .501 | 4 |
| 33 | 337 | 279 | .547 | 2 |
| 34 | 282 | 238 | .542 | 2 |
| 35 | 200 | 161 | .554 | 2 |
| 36 | 144 | 122 | .541 | 2 |
| 37 | 94 | 75 | .556 | 2 |
| 38 | 62 | 63 | .496 | 1 |
| 39 | 38 | 34 | .528 | 1 |
| 40 | 24 | 19 | .558 | 1 |
| 41 | 26 | 22 | .542 | 0 |
| 42 | 29 | 13 | .690 | 1 |
| 43 | 11 | 16 | .407 | 0 |
| 44* | 7 | 16 | .304 | 0 |
| TOTAL | 7502 | 7308 | .507 | 49 |

*One pitcher from group still active.

Nothing too much happens to left-handed pitchers as a group at age 26. Their wins increase by 17%; their losses by 13%.

You didn't expect me to throw the chart away, did you? The week wasn't entirely wasted. There are a couple of points worth noting.

1) The left-handed pitchers, as a group, are a little bit over .500, and therefore righthanders as a group must be a little below .500.

2) The highest won-lost percentages for lefthanders—I suspect the same is true for righthanders—come after the age of 33. Although the number of wins posted from ages 34 to 37 is only 27% of the number posted from 24 to 27, the number of losses is only 23% as large, and thus the won-lost percentage is much higher. I take this to support my belief that pitchers who come through the "fastball crisis" about age 30 often come out on the other side as better pitchers than when they went in.

***92. Lary SORENSEN, Cleveland (12.0)***

Hold: A–
DP Support: High

The new Ernie Broglio.

***93. Charlie PULEO, New York Mets (10.9)***

Hold: F
DP Support: Above Average

Pitched very well on three days rest (3-1, 2.77 ERA), but was 0-6, 5.46 on four days and even worse (6.51 ERA) with five days rest. Bamberger obviously wasn't aware of that, because there were several times when it was his turn to pitch, but Bamberger held him back and used a spot starter.

***94. John MONTEFUSCO, San Diego (10.4)***

Hold: F
DP Support: Average

Assume that he is strictly a stop-gap move. He's not the type of pitcher that Williams like to work with at all, although he is throwing strikes now. Still gives you the stolen base.

***95. Mike MORGAN, New York Yankees (9.4)***

Hold: C
DP Support: High

Where the hell did the Yankees ever get the idea that this guy could pitch? In 1980 he was 6-9, 5.40 ERA at Ogden; in '81 8-7, 4.42 at Nashville. You think you're going to win a pennant with somebody like that?

***96. Steve MURA, St. Louis (8.9)***

Hold: F
DP Support: High

The Cardinals' Renie Martin.

*97. Don ROBINSON, Pittsburgh (8.7)*

Hold: B–
DP Support: Low

Was 5-8 with a 5.96 ERA in Pittsburgh; 10-5 with a 2.65 on the road.... Tied for the NL lead in home-runs allowed (26) and finished second in the league in walks (103). If he's going to have a successful career it would be a real good idea if he would cut out one or the other... had 2.93 ERA in six starts on long rest (five days)...

*98. Mike MOORE, Seattle (6.6)*

Hold: D–
DP Support: Low

See Floyd Bannister. As soon as this guy learns to pitch he's going to be a free agent anyway.

*99. Randy LERCH, Montreal (5.7)*

Hold: D–
DP Support: High

Will beat a bad team fairly consistently.

*100. Rick HONEYCUTT, Texas (3.9)*

Hold: A
DP Support: Very High

Had the highest double-play support in the league, 1.35 per start... The fielders certainly did not want for opportunities.

*101. Brian KINGMAN, Oakland (3.3)*

Hold: C
DP Support: Below Average

His lifetime won-lost percentage, after 66 decisions, is 13 points below Rod Carew's batting average.

*102. Chris WELSH, San Diego (3.1)*

Hold: A–
DP Support: High

While Williams was hammering on everybody else to throw strikes—San Diego's walks dropped from 3.76 per game to 3.10—Welsh's control slipped from 2.9 walks per game to over four.

*103. Rich GALE, San Francisco (2.9)*

Hold: D–
DP Support: Below Average

Is showing constant improvement in his K/W ratios—0.88-1 as a rookie in '78, 1.04-1 in '79, 1.24-1 in '80, 1.24-1 in '81, 1.26-1 in '82. At the rate he's going it'll be where it should be about when Kent Hrbek becomes a manager. The man cannot pitch, and it's only a matter of time until people stop saying, "But if only..." and face facts... I remember as a rookie I said I thought he would have a Gene Conley-type career, which doesn't seem too far off.

*104. Matt KEOUGH, Oakland (1.8)*

Hold: B
DP Support: Average

Name pronounced Key-ugh. He pitched pretty decent last year once he got past the third inning, but he gave up 83 runs in the first three innings, which was 7.89 per nine innings. He had nine starts in '82 in which he gave up five runs in the first three innings, and you sure can't win doing that.

*105. Bob WALK, Atlanta (-2.0)*

Hold: F
DP Support: Above Average

What a terrible name for a pitcher... season would have been a disaster with normal offensive support... second-easiest pitcher to run on in the National League.

*106. Juan EICHELBERGER, San Diego (-2.2)*

Hold: D
DP Support: Below Average

One last, permanent, on-the-record cheer for the outstanding scoring decision of 1982: Dave Nightingale's proud refusal to pretend that an obvious hit (the hit that ruined Eichelberger's no-hitter) was an error. We've had a couple of ha-ha no-hitters already. Where are we going to wind up? Looking over a list of "no-hitters" with our daughters, explaining, "That was a real one, there; and this one was fairly clean, only a couple of scratch hits that they called errors... that one, of course, that was the famous seven-error affair where the scorer kept waiting for that first really clean hit." We will still have to explain that Bob Forsch didn't really throw a no-hitter, but just had an official who turned a blind eye. But Mr. Nightingale's articulate defense of the position that the fan is entitled to an accurate record of the game kept another door down that alley from flying open.

*107. Renie MARTIN, San Francisco (-4.9)*

Hold: B–
DP Support: Below Average

The Giants' Steve Mura.

*108. Mike SCOTT, New York Mets (-7.2)*

Hold: B–
DP Support: Low

Received the worst defensive support in the league, 28 errors in 22 games. And deserved it . . . monthly ERAs:

2.81, 5.03, 7.11, 5.53, 5.52 and 9.00. Good consistency there after April.

***109. Frank VIOLA, Minnesota (-11.3)***

Hold: D
DP Support: Above Average

Pitched very well on the road but was 1-8, 6.25 ERA in the dome . . .

***110. Randy JONES, New York Mets (-14.8)***

Hold: B
DP Support: High

Had a 7.47 ERA in Shea Stadium last year, 2.37 on the road . . .

***111. Rick WAITS, Cleveland (-32.4)***

Hold: C
DP Support: Average

Didn't pitch well anywhere, anytime, against anyone.

**Best Offensive Support**

| *American League* Pitcher (W-L) | Runs per Game | *National League* Pitcher (W-L) | Runs per Game |
|---|---|---|---|
| McClure (12-7) | 5.96 | P. Niekro (17-4) | 5.40 |
| Leonard (10-6) | 5.90 | Walk (11-9) | 5.07 |
| Lerch (8-7) | 5.90 | Mura (12-11) | 4.87 |
| Torrez (9-9) | 5.74 | Martin (7-10) | 4.84 |
| McCatty (6-3) | 5.65 | D. Robinson (15-13) | 4.83 |

**Worst Offensive Support**

| *American League* Pitcher (W-L) | Runs per Game | *National League* Pitcher (W-L) | Runs per Game |
|---|---|---|---|
| Gott (5-10) | 3.16 | Berenyi (9-18) | 2.59 |
| Tanana (7-18) | 3.30 | Shirley (8-13) | 2.65 |
| Honeycutt (5-17) | 3.38 | Ruhle (9-13) | 3.00 |
| Moore (7-14) | 3.52 | Camp (11-13) | 3.05 |
| Kingman (4-12) | 3.65 | Gale (7-14) | 3.21 |

**Best Opposition-Stolen-Base Rate**

| *American League* Pitcher | OSB | *National League* Pitcher | OSB |
|---|---|---|---|
| Gura | 0.27 | Stuper | 0.38 |
| Stieb | 0.29 | Welsh | 0.40 |
| Zahn | 0.29 | Shirley | 0.45 |
| Clancy | 0.33 | Candelaria | 0.47 |
| John | 0.33 | Rhoden | 0.49 |

**Worst Opposition-Stolen-Base Rate**

| *American League* Pitcher | OSB | *National League* Pitcher | OSB |
|---|---|---|---|
| Vuckovich | 1.17 | LaPoint | 1.57 |
| Lerch | 1.10 | B. Walk | 1.44 |
| Medich | 1.03 | Knepper | 1.38 |
| Sutcliffe | 1.00 | Puleo | 1.33 |
| Williams | 1.00 | Berenyi | 1.32 |

**Highest Double-Play Support**

| *American League* Pitcher | D.P. Support | *National League* Pitcher | D.P. Support |
|---|---|---|---|
| Honeycutt | 1.35 | Camp | 1.57 |
| Sorensen | 1.30 | LaPoint | 1.48 |
| Caldwell | 1.26 | Mura | 1.17 |
| Lerch | 1.25 | Jones | 1.15 |
| Zahn | 1.21 | Berenyi | 1.15 |

**Lowest Double-Play Support**

| *American League* Pitcher | D.P. Support | *National League* Pitcher | D.P. Support |
|---|---|---|---|
| Barker | 0.58 | Bird | 0.48 |
| Denny | 0.67 | Scott | 0.55 |
| Bannister | 0.69 | Sanderson | 0.56 |
| Righetti | 0.74 | Soto | 0.59 |
| Blue | 0.74 | Gullickson | 0.62 |
| Leal | 0.74 | Lollar | 0.62 |

**Fastest Working Pitchers**

| *American League* Pitcher | Time | *National League* Pitcher | Time |
|---|---|---|---|
| Stieb | 2:19 | Carlton | 2:19 |
| Eckersley | 2:22 | Ruthven | 2:23 |
| Clancy | 2:25 | Berenyi | 2:25 |
| Castillo | 2:26 | Bird | 2:26 |
| John | 2:27 | J. Niekro | 2:27 |
| Havens | 2:27 | Candelaria | 2:27 |

**Slowest Working Pitchers**

| *American League* Pitcher | Time | *National League* Pitcher | Time |
|---|---|---|---|
| McCatty | 2:56 | Martin | 2:48 |
| Burns | 2:53 | Welch | 2:42 |
| Dotson | 2:52 | Walk | 2:43 |
| Norris | 2:52 | Gale | 2:42 |
| Lamp | 2:51 | Puleo | 2:42 |
| Barker | 2:48 | Hooton | 2:42 |

**Pitchers Drawing Largest Attendance**

| *American League* Pitcher | Att. | *National League* Pitcher | Att. |
|---|---|---|---|
| Forsch | 31,900 | Valenzuela | 43,300 |
| Zahn | 29,500 | Welch | 36,500 |
| Renko | 29,400 | Stewart | 35,600 |
| John | 28,300 | Hooten | 35,100 |
| Guidry | 28,200 | Reuss | 34,300 |

**Pitchers Drawing Least Attendance**

| *American League* Pitcher | Att. | *National League* Pitcher | Att. |
|---|---|---|---|
| Williams | 12,900 | Hammaker | 15,800 |
| Moore | 14,000 | Candelaria | 16,400 |
| O'Connor | 14,200 | Berenyi | 17,200 |
| Sutcliffe | 14,900 | Martz | 18,000 |
| Viola | 15,000 | Shirley | 18,400 |
| Castillo | 15,000 | | |

Section

# IV

# THE GAME

# RECORDS IN PROGRESS

Which active players are likely to get 3000 hits? 500 home runs? Which career records are likely to be broken? I have a method for dealing with these questions, a method called the *Favorite Toy*. The method looks at the player's records for the last three seasons, figures the level of performance that the player has established, assigns him a number of "years remaining" based on his age (or other considerations in some cases), and assesses the chance that he will reach the goal. I call this the Favorite Toy because I love to play around with it.

The five major league players most likely to get 3000 hits in their careers are, in order, Rod Carew, Al Oliver, Robin Yount, Bill Buckner and Willie Wilson. The full chart is given below:

**PLAYERS WHO HAVE ESTABLISHED AT LEAST A .01 CHANCE OF GETTING 3000 CAREER HITS**

| Player | 1982 Age | Established Hit Level | Career Hits | Chance of Getting 3000 Hits |
|---|---|---|---|---|
| 1. Rod Carew | 36 | 168.8 | 2772 | .93 |
| 2. Al Oliver | 35 | 201.8 | 2362 | .49 |
| 3. Robin Yount | 26 | 186.3 | 1363 | .46 |
| 4. Bill Buckner | 32 | 197.2 | 1789 | .28 |
| 5. Willie Wilson | 26 | 201.8 | 797 | .27 |
| 6. George Brett | 29 | 166.7 | 1532 | .25 |
| 7. Steve Garvey | 33 | 182.3 | 1968 | .24 |
| 8. Jim Rice | 29 | 177.1 | 1429 | .24 |
| 9. Eddie Murray | 26 | 173.5 | 997 | .23 |
| 10. Buddy Bell | 30 | 159.3 | 1642 | .20 |
| 11. Andre Dawson | 27 | 180.7 | 978 | .20 |
| 12. Rickey Henderson | 23 | 168.8 | 553 | .20 |
| 13. Keith Hernandez | 28 | 175.8 | 1155 | .19 |
| 14. Carney Lansford | 25 | 165.7 | 757 | .16 |
| 15. Cecil Cooper | 32 | 205.5 | 1436 | .13 |
| 16. Cesar Cedeno | 31 | 138.2 | 1801 | .12 |
| 17. Chris Chambliss | 32 | 155.3 | 1806 | .12 |
| 18. Gary Matthews | 31 | 167.0 | 1548 | .12 |
| 19. Ted Simmons | 32 | 138.5 | 1931 | .12 |

Others: Steve Kemp, Dave Winfield, 9%; Jack Clark, 8%; Dale Murphy, Claudell Washington, 7%; Harold Baines, Gary Carter, Dwight Evans, Greg Luzinski, 6%; Terry Puhl, Willie Randolph, Gene Richards, 5%; Dusty Baker, Bill Madlock, Tim Raines, Lou Whitaker, 4%; Omar Moreno, 3%; Leon Durham, Damaso Garcia, Larry Herndon, Jerry Remy, Steve Sax, Garry Templeton, 2%; and Alan Trammell, 1%.

The expectation from this list would be that six active players would get 3000 career hits. Those six will include Rod Carew, and might include...well, one of the two, Yount or Oliver, one of the next four, one of the next five, one of the following seven, and one of the longshots, Leon Durham or Bill Madlock or somebody. When I figured this list two years ago I also presented a list reconstructed from 10 years earlier (post-1970, pre-1971). The contrast between the two lists was that while in 1970 there had been an expectation that seven active players would get to 3000 career hits and in 1980 an expectation for six, in 1970 it was fairly clear who those players would be, while in 1980 it was not clear at all. In just the last two years there has been a surprising reclarification of the 3000 hit candidates. Carew's fine 1982 all but sewed it up for him; Oliver and Yount have come out of the pack to rank as men-most-likely-to.

Three players at this moment have established at least a 1% chance of getting 4000 career hits.

| Player | 1982 Age | Career Hits | Established Hit Level | 4000 Chance |
|---|---|---|---|---|
| Pete Rose | 41 | 3869 | 186.8 | .73 |
| Robin Yount | 26 | 1363 | 186.3 | .09 |
| Willie Wilson | 26 | 797 | 201.8 | .03 |

Rose has an estimated 42% chance of breaking Cobb's career hit record; Yount also has a 5% shot at that record. I should note that Yount's ranking here is not strictly a result of his superb 1982 season; he showed a 4% chance of getting 4000 career hits two years ago.

Seventeen players have established at least a 1% chance of hitting 500 career home runs.

| Player | 1982 Age | Career HR | Established HR Level | Chance of Hitting 500 |
|---|---|---|---|---|
| Reggie Jackson | 36 | 464 | 33.83 | .92 |
| Mike Schmidt | 32 | 349 | 41.00 | .80 |
| Eddie Murray | 26 | 165 | 32.33 | .31 |
| Bob Horner | 24 | 138 | 29.33 | .24 |
| Dave Kingman | 33 | 329 | 32.50 | .22 |
| Gorman Thomas | 31 | 197 | 36.33 | .15 |
| Jim Rice | 29 | 237 | 24.50 | .11 |
| Jason Thompson | 27 | 161 | 26.50 | .11 |
| Gary Carter | 28 | 171 | 27.33 | .10 |
| Jack Clark | 26 | 132 | 25.67 | .09 |
| Dave Winfield | 30 | 204 | 28.33 | .08 |
| Dwight Evans | 30 | 182 | 30.00 | .07 |
| Andre Dawson | 27 | 132 | 25.83 | .05 |
| Tony Armas | 28 | 111 | 30.83 | .03 |
| Lance Parrish | 26 | 102 | 25.00 | .03 |
| Greg Luzinski | 31 | 262 | 22.67 | .01 |
| Cal Ripken | 21 | 28 | 21.00 | .01 |

The expectation would be that three or four active players probably will crash the 500 barrier; it is 99.78% sure that some active player will reach that level.

I also presented this list two years ago, and while it looked pretty much the same then, it is worth noting who is gaining on it and who is losing. Up significantly are Eddie Murray (19% to 31%), Schmidt (67% to 80%), Jack Clark (2% to 9%) and Jason Thompson (1% to 11%). Down and in some cases out are Willie Stargell (54% to zero), Jim Rice (30% to 11%) and Johnny Bench (29% to off the list). John Mayberry and George Foster also dropped off the list, from much lower perches (.07 and .09).

The only active player who has established a really good shot at hitting 600 home runs in his career is Mike Schmidt (28% now; it was about the same two years ago). Four others have some shot at that level—Murray (12%), Horner (11%), Reggie (10%) and Dale Murphy (3%). It is about a 50-50 shot that some active player will hit 600 career home runs, assuming, of course, that no radical movement toward a livelier ball comes about.

This method, had it then existed, would have shown Hank Aaron as having a clear shot at Babe Ruth's career record from the time he was in his early twenties. In the 1960s, it would have shown several players as having a shot at the 714 total, including Mays, Robinson, Mantle and (for a moment) Maris. It would have shown the record as likely-to-fall or 50-50-to-fall from 1960 on.

It now lists Aaron's 755 total as safe, completely safe. No active player has established even the most remote chance of hitting 755 career home runs, as of this time. The only players listed with a shot at 700 are Schmidt (6%) and Murray (1%). Schmidt in order to get there would have to keep blasting 40-45 home runs a year until he is 40 years old. That's not likely.

But another record of the same vintage, Lou Brock's career stolen-base record, is doomed; it will be broken by some active player. The players who have established a shot at it are given in the chart below:

| Player | 1982 Age | Established SB Level | Career SB | Chances of 938 Career SB |
|---|---|---|---|---|
| Rickey Henderson | 23 | 109.67 | 319 | .79 |
| Tim Raines | 22 | 75.33 | 156 | .54 |
| Omar Moreno | 28 | 65.50 | 472 | .40 |
| Willie Wilson | 26 | 48.67 | 287 | .13 |
| Julio Cruz | 27 | 52.00 | 257 | .10 |
| Lonnie Smith | 26 | 50.00 | 128 | .02 |

The somewhat erratic nature of stolen-base totals, which fluctuate more than most categories from season to season, may cause this formula to overestimate the record chances of Henderson and Raines, but by the same token it underestimates the chances of others, like Lonnie Smith, Willie Wilson and Steve Sax. I have no hesitation about predicting that the career stolen-base record will be shattered by some player now active.

The difference between the relative invulnerability of Aaron's record and the complete vulnerability of Brock's can be shown in several other ways. With the possible exception of some 18- or 19-year old kid who may have hit a home run already, no major-league player at any age has hit as many home runs as Henry Aaron had at the same age. This has been true for several years; nobody is really close. Mike Schmidt has had a fine career and he has 349 career home runs. But Aaron at the same age had 442 home runs. Eddie Murray is a great young hitter, but his 165 home-run total is 54 behind Aaron's at the same age, and it is getting further behind every year. In addition, the best five-year home-run stretch of Aaron's career began when he was 35 years old, a powerful finishing kick that makes it extremely unlikely that anyone can haul him down from behind.

With Brock, on the other hand...well, *everybody* is ahead of his total at the same age. Henderson leads him 319-16; Brock didn't steal his 319th base until age 29. Moreno, Sax, Wilson, Raines—they're all years ahead of his pace. Ahead by smaller margins are a lot of other people, such as Cesar Cedeno and Julio Cruz. Sure, Brock had a finishing kick too, but it's not going to save him.

Another way of assessing the vulnerability of a record is to ask how many seasons of outstanding performance it represents. You can do this by looking at the league-leading totals of the last five years, at the top five totals for the last three years, or...whatever. This represents the "contemporary outstanding performance level"; if you divide it into the record, you get the number of outstanding seasons that would be required to break the record. I'm about 30 pages over budget already, so I can't get into the details, but if you do this for all categories, it becomes obvious just how soft Brock's career stolen-base record is. Aaron's home run record represents about 20 seasons worth of top-flight home-run hammering; Cobb's hit total is over 20 seasons worth, Crawford's triples total is over 20, Cy Young's victory total around 25. But Brock's 938 stolen bases, assuming an outstanding-performance level of just 80, are not even 12 seasons' worth. All of the other records are in the 18-22 years range except strikeouts, and that record is being cut to ribbons, too.

Any time performance levels in a given category rise to where the record represents less than 18 seasons of outstanding performance, the record becomes soft; less than 15, very soft. Almost all records become visibly soft 10 to 15 years before they are broken; most records which become soft will be broken. That is what is remarkable about Pete Rose's run at Ty Cobb's hit record. He is trying to pick off a record that shows no signs of being ripe.

# POWER/SPEED NUMBER

For good reasons and bad, in the public's mind a link has developed between power (home runs) and speed (stolen bases). For every combination of these two, there is a separate list. For Bobby Bonds, there was the 30/30 list and the elusive goal of 40/40; for Joe Morgan and Cesar Cedeno, there were 20/50 lists and 25/60 lists; for Lonnie Smith, the trick was to join stolen bases and RBI to make a 70/70 list, (although he came up just shy of 70 in both, making it a 65/65 list).

I jimmied together a way of dealing with tandem offense that makes sense to me. What we are measuring is not one or the other, but the combination of the two, the balance between them and also the level to which the balanced pair can be raised. That formula is:

$$\frac{2\,(HR \times SB)}{HR + SB}$$

If a player hits 30 home runs and steals 30 bases, this computes to 30.0; if 20 of each, 20.0, etc. As the two become imbalanced, the number diminishes; 20 and 31 is 29.97, 28 and 32 is 29.9, and so on. To complete the "so-ons" with other things which total up to 60, 25 and 35 make a PSN of 29.2, 20 and 40 make 26.7, 15 and 45 make 22.5, 10 and 50 make 16.7, 5 and 55 make 9.2 and 0 and 60 make zero.

Andre Dawson is the reigning power/speed combination in baseball today; Bobby Bonds and Willie Mays are the greatest ever. The charts below give 1) the 1982 leaders in Power Speed Number, 2) the leaders among active players ranked by career highs and 3) the all-time greatest power/speed seasons.

**1982 LEADERS**

| | HR | SB | PSN |
|---|---|---|---|
| 1. Andre Dawson | 23 | 39 | 28.9 |
| 2. Dale Murphy | 36 | 23 | 28.1 |
| 3. Dwayne Murphy | 27 | 26 | 26.5 |
| 4. Pedro Guerrero | 32 | 22 | 26.1 |
| 5. Paul Molitor | 19 | 41 | 26.0 |
| 6. Leon Durham | 22 | 28 | 24.6 |
| 7. C. Washington | 16 | 33 | 21.6 |
| 8. Chili Davis | 19 | 24 | 21.2 |
| 9. Toby Harrah | 25 | 17 | 20.2 |
| 10. Mike Schmidt | 35 | 14 | 20.0 |

**CAREER HIGHS**

| | HR | SB | PSN |
|---|---|---|---|
| 1. Joe Morgan, 1973 | 26 | 67 | 37.5 |
| 2. Cesar Cedeno, 1974 | 26 | 57 | 35.7 |
| 3. Dave Lopes, 1979 | 28 | 44 | 34.2 |
| 4. Mike Schmidt, 1975 | 38 | 29 | 32.9 |
| 5. Carl Yastrzemski, 1970 | 40 | 23 | 29.2 |
| 6. Andre Dawson, 1979 | 25 | 35 | 29.2 |
| 7. Don Baylor, 1975 | 25 | 32 | 28.1 |
| 8. Dale Murphy, 1982 | 36 | 23 | 28.1 |
| 9. Mitchell Page, 1977 | 21 | 42 | 28.0 |
| 10. Reggie Jackson, 1976 | 27 | 28 | 27.5 |

**ALL-TIME HIGHS**

| | HR | SB | PSN |
|---|---|---|---|
| 1. Bobby Bonds, 1973 | 39 | 43 | 40.9 |
| 2. Bobby Bonds, 1977 | 37 | 41 | 38.9 |
| 3. Ken Williams, 1922 | 39 | 37 | 38.0 |
| 4. Willie Mays, 1956 | 36 | 40 | 37.9 |
| 5. Joe Morgan, 1973 | 26 | 67 | 37.5 |
| 6. Bobby Bonds, 1969 | 32 | 45 | 37.4 |
| 7. Joe Morgan, 1976 | 27 | 60 | 37.2 |
| 8. Willie Mays, 1957 | 35 | 38 | 36.4 |
| 9. Hank Aaron, 1963 | 44 | 31 | 36.4 |
| 10. Bobby Bonds, 1978 | 31 | 43 | 36.0 |

The formula also works for career records. The highest career PSN ever was 447.1 by Willie Mays, which is an amazing accomplishment when you consider that Joe DiMaggio didn't hit 447 homers and George Case didn't steal 447 bases. A few years ago it appeared that someone would break that record, but all of the people who might have—Bonds, Cedeno, Schmidt—have taken another course or pulled up short, and it now does not appear that anyone will launch a serious threat on the figure before Andre Dawson, and Dawson is ten years away. The career leaders among active players and all-time are given below.

**Active**

| | HR | SB | PSN |
|---|---|---|---|
| 1. Joe Morgan | 246 | 663 | 358.9 |
| 2. Reggie Jackson | 464 | 216 | 294.8 |
| 3. Cesar Cedeno | 171 | 503 | 255.2 |
| 4. Carl Yastrzemski | 442 | 168 | 243.5 |
| 5. Amos Otis | 187 | 336 | 241.9 |
| 6. Don Baylor | 213 | 259 | 233.8 |
| 7. Mike Schmidt | 349 | 155 | 214.7 |
| 8. Reggie Smith | 314 | 137 | 190.8 |
| 9. Toby Harrah | 169 | 206 | 185.6 |
| 10. Dave Lopes | 110 | 446 | 176.5 |

**All-Time**

| | HR | SB | PSN |
|---|---|---|---|
| 1. Willie Mays | 660 | 338 | 447.1 |
| 2. Bobby Bonds | 332 | 461 | 386.0 |
| 3. Hank Aaron | 755 | 240 | 364.3 |
| 4. Joe Morgan | 246 | 663 | 358.9 |
| 5. Frank Robinson | 583 | 204 | 302.2 |
| 6. Reggie Jackson | 464 | 216 | 294.8 |
| 7. Vada Pinson | 256 | 305 | 278.4 |
| 8. Lou Brock | 149 | 938 | 257.2 |
| 9. Cesar Cedeno | 171 | 503 | 255.2 |
| 10. Jimmie Wynn | 291 | 225 | 253.8 |

# THE LAW OF COMPETITIVE BALANCE

Several years ago I undertook a series of studies which were designed to enable me to predict the movement of a team upward or downward in one year based on an analysis of several factors from the year before—a subject, it happens, which no longer interests me. I was attempting, by finding the answers to a series of relevant questions, to develop a sort of "technical analysis" of the season to come. Those questions included:

*What percentage of the time does a team improve in one season if its starting lineup in the previous season averages 25 years of age? Or 26, 27, 28,...33?*

*If a team improves in one season, what percentage of the time will they also improve in the next?*

*What is the average win total in the next season of teams which win 100 games in one season? Teams that win 70 games? 90?*

*Do teams which change managers usually improve?*

I eventually concluded, to complete the digression, that while there was knowledge to be gained by answering the questions, the subject was...how shall I say? Beyond the capacities of the research. A lot of fans feel that your ability to predict the pennant race is a test of your expertise as an analyst. My feeling is that nobody in the world can predict a pennant race, period, because the outcome is dependent on major variables of which no knowledge can exist at the time the prediction must be made. And to the very limited extent that a race is predictable, I think you'd have better luck with systematic fundamental analysis, as Pete Palmer has, than with the technical analysis that I was trying to develop.

But some of the answers to these questions remain interesting:

1) What I have since described as the Plexiglass Principle: If a team improves in one season, it will likely decline in the next.

2) Now called the Whirlpool Principle: All teams are drawn forcefully toward the center. Most of the teams which had winning records in 1982 will decline in 1983; most of the teams which had losing records in 1982 will improve in 1983.

Other studies later extended both of these principles to individuals. If a player's batting average improved in one season, I found, it would likely decline in the next, and vice versa. The players who hit for the highest averages in one season, I found, would reliably decline in the next season. Of those who hit for the lowest averages, most would not be playing regularly in the following season, but most of those who were playing regularly would raise their batting averages.

There was also an odd similarity in the percentages of improvement and decline, which we will call the 70/50 rule. About 70% of all teams which improve in one year will decline in the next; about 70% of the declines will then improve. Also, 70% of winning teams decline, and 70% of losing teams improve. The same percentages apply to players. In all cases, the amount of overall decline or improvement is about 50%; that is, teams which finish 20 games over .500 in Year I will finish an average about 10 games over in Year II, players who improved their batting averages by 30 points in Year I would decline by 15 points in Year II.*

Why does this happen?

These were not things that I had expected to find. Weaned on the notion of "momentum" since childhood, I had expected a team which won 83 games one year and 87 the next to continue to improve, to move on to 90; instead, they consistently relapsed. Half-expecting to find that the rich grow richer and the poor grow poorer, I found instead that the rich and the poor converged on a common target at an alarming rate of speed. Sporting teams behave over a period of years as if a powerful magnetic center was drawing on them, tugging them toward it, defying them to stay up or to stay down or to drift away from it.

Why does this happen, and how does it happen? The Law of Competitive Balance: There develop over time separate and unequal strategies adopted by winners and losers; the balance of those strategies favors the losers, and thus serves constantly to narrow the difference between the two. There develop (in all sports and in life in general—it is merely that the orderliness and detailed record-keeping of the games of life enables us to trace its effects more clearly in the sporting world) over-time (within a season, between seasons, within a game, between games) separate and unequal strategies which are adopted by winners and losers (and which logically *should* be adopted by winners and losers). The balance of those strategies always favors the team which is behind, and thus serves constantly to narrow the difference between the two (between the team which is behind in a game and the team which is ahead, between the team which has been strong and the team which has been weak).

The essence of that difference is in how the two teams view the need to make changes. If a team wins 96 games and its division, that team develops a self-satisfaction which colors all of the decisions that the team needs to face. The team looks over its roster and discovers, say, a 31-year

*For the sake of clarity, the 70/50 rule does not apply uniformly regardless of distance from .500, or regardless of previous movement. If you're talking about a team which is 40 games over .500 or a batter whose average improves 75 points, the chance of a decline is over 90%, while if you are talking about an 82-80 team or a player whose average is up 5 points, it is barely over 50%.

old shortstop coming off a .238 season. If the team had finished out of contention, there is little doubt that they would replace that player. As a bad team, what they would likely do is look for a kid with ability, somebody who might play the position for them for 10 or 12 years. As a near-miss contender, what they would do is look for a proven player who could help them get over the hump. But as a winner there is a tendency to say "Well, he's only 31, he's had some good years, and he's still doing the job on defense. We won the pennant with him last year." And thus the winning team, because they are winners, does not address the problem.

I did a little study to demonstrate that this really does happen. What I did was to take all of the teams since the 162-game schedule was adopted which have won 90 to 96 games (except in the strike-shortened 1972 season). About each of them I asked four things:

1) Did they win the pennant or division?
2) How many of the same eight regulars returned as regulars in the following season?
3) How many games did the team win in the following season?
4) Did the team win its league or division in the following season?

The 90-96 group was chosen because it contains both winners and nonwinners. Actually, the study covered 18 of the former and 40 of the losers. Those two groups of teams when compared in the first season were nearly identical in all categories of performance except "finish." The "winners" group averaged 92.3 wins, 714 runs scored and a .5705 won-lost percentage. The losers averaged 92.1 wins, 706 runs scored and a .5698 won-lost percentage. But in the following seasons:

1) The winners returned 81% of the same regulars to the starting lineup (116 of 144 players), the losers only 75% (241 of 320).
2) The won-lost percentages of both groups declined in the following seasons, but while the winners declined to an aggregate .536 won-lost percentage, the losers held up to .549.
3) Twelve of the 40 "losers" won the pennant or division in the following season, or 30%. Only three of the 18 "winners" did the same.

Exactly the effects that the Law of Competitive Balance would predict. It would predict many others which I haven't checked out. For example, if you studied the replacement rates for players hitting .220-.229, .230-.239, .240-.249 and .250-.259, you should find that a regular player who hits, let's say, .236, is more likely to be replaced if he plays on a team which wins 70 games than if he plays on a team which wins 80, is more likely to be replaced on a team which wins 80 games than on a team which wins 85, more likely on 85 than 90, and more likely on a team which wins 90 and the pennant than on a team which wins 90 and finishes second. Below 70...well, you might get into a range there where a .236 hitter is one of the team's stars.

In other sports more than in baseball this process of adaptation takes place inside the game. In a basketball game, if one team runs off a string of points which team calls time? Review the situation in your mind: Notre Dame leads Grunt State 33-28 with 8 minutes left in the first half. Suddenly, Grunt State rips off nine quick points; it is 37-33 with five left in the half. Who calls time out? Obviously, Notre Dame. What does the announcer say? "Only a four point lead in the first half, but Grunt State really has the momentum going for them now." But what actually happens, in your experience, when the teams come out of the meeting? Does Grunt State go into the half with a 10-point lead? Never happen. Notre Dame will come out and restore order 9½ times in 10.

Why? Because, who changes his strategy? Who runs in a substitute? The Notre Dame coach says "Hey, they're beating us bad on the boards and killing us on the outlet. John, you've got to get up over the back of that Moose; I put Wilson in to get back and head off the break." But what can the Grunt State coach do? He is frozen by his success. The operating dynamic in the situation is not the "momentum" that the announcer will be talking about; it is the Law of Competitive Balance.

A beautiful example of the Law of Competitive Balance occurs in football, with respect to what is called the Nickle Defense: The Nickle Defense involves the use of an extra—a fifth—defensive back, a move which makes it easier to move the ball on the ground (the line is short a man) but more difficult to throw a long pass. Most fans hate the thing; the call-in shows are full of it. "Why do they use that thing? How often do you see a team hold its opponent in check all game, get a lead late and go to that Nickle Defense and allow the other team to march right down the field and get back into the game." In a narrow sense, they're right—it does happen. A lot. But what people don't understand is that when a team gets behind, say 12 points behind in the middle of the fourth quarter, they become increasingly willing to gamble. They might have a long pass play in their book which they figure has maybe a 30% chance of being a long gainer, a 5% chance of being a touchdown, but a 15% chance of being intercepted. Now, in a close game you're not going to use that play except on 3rd and long; it helps your opponent more than it helps you. But if you're two touchdowns behind with time running out, you go to it. It doesn't make any difference if you lose by two touchdowns or three; a play that improves your chances of winning from 15% to 18% is worth running. If your chances of winning are 50%, a 30% gamble looks bad; if they are 15%, it looks great.

It is worth running, and it is worth defending against. If you don't use the Nickel Defense, you're giving them the 15% to 18% improvement; if you do, you're letting them march downfield on the ground.

What the fan is observing when he sees the late rally is not the effect of the Nickle Defense, at all; it is the effect of the Law of Competitive Balance. Teams which have been held in check all game are going to score late sometimes, regardless of what defense you use, because they gain a strategic advantage from being behind.

There is a very similar defensive maneuver that takes place in baseball—except, being baseball, it happens in a much more subtle way. You know the saying about guarding the lines in the late innings of a close game? Why do they do that?

To move the third baseman nearer the line decreases the chance that a ball will be hit safely down the line, but increases the chance that a ball will be hit between third and short. Thus it *increases* the chance of a single, but *decreases* the chance of a double. The move generally allows more singles than it prevents doubles, thus it *increases* the chance that the opposition will be able to put together a big inning. But, because it prevents the double which would put the runner in scoring position, it *decreases* the chance of allowing a single run. Announcers like to puzzle over why you guard the lines in the late innings when you don't early. You guard the lines in late innings when you wouldn't early for exactly the same reason that you bunt in the late innings or issue an intentional walk in the late innings. Baseball is a big-inning game; in the third inning, the key thing is not to give up those three- or four-run innings that will blow you out. But in the 8th inning, it doesn't matter whether you lose by one or three. The one-run inning becomes much more important, so you guard the line.

Plunging on into what is now a full-fledged digression...

I am convinced that the rule of thumb about guarding the lines in the late innings of a close game is on balance a good one. It has evolved through the Natural Selection of Strategies; it has stood the test of time. However, I am much less sure that it is a good one *in all parks*. It is very possible that there are parks, like Royals Stadium and Three Rivers and Busch, where the danger of a double down the line should *always* take precedence, from the first inning on, and it could well be that there are parks, like Dodger Stadium, where the grass slows the ball down to where it is never that grave of a threat, and in which, therefore, one should not guard the lines in the late innings. How long would it take you to come to that realization just by watching?

In the first stages of free agency, many people believed that free agency would enable the rich to grow richer while the poor grew poorer. Of course, just the opposite has happened—the standard deviation of wins has declined from 12.3 in 1978 to 11.6 in 1980 and 10.5 in 1982. Fourteen teams were within 5½ games of first place on September 15, 1982, and if that isn't a record it sure isn't a symptom of ailing competitive balance. George Foster said last year, and was widely quoted as saying, that we would never again see superteams like the 1975-76 Reds; with free agency, he said, nobody could afford them. What people are saying about free agency now, we should note, is *exactly the opposite* of what they originally said. Then they said it would *destroy* competitive balance; now, it is going to *enforce* competitive balance.

Why has that happened? For a lot of reasons, but what it comes down to is, the Law of. How many players have actually left weak teams to go join contenders? Damn few. A lot of the strong teams—the Dodgers, the Royals, the Reds—began by turning up their noses at free agency. They could afford to. The St. Louis Cardinals may have wanted Floyd Bannister, but when it comes right down to it, did they want him as much as the cities that didn't already *have* a World Champion? Of the four early big spenders in the free agent market, three—the Angels, Braves and Padres—were poor teams trying to buy championships. The more help you need, the more seriously you look at the options that can help you. The more fluid talent is (the more free is its movement from team to team), the greater competitive balance there will be.

Incidentally, this song about the rich getting richer and the poor getting poorer has been sung many times before. For example, when the roster limits were raised to 25 men, people said that this would enable the strong teams to stockpile talent and keep players who could play for other teams sitting on the Yankees' bench. But as the chart below shows, competitive balance in fact has grown steadily throughout the century, leading now to the virtual disappearance of the .650 baseball team:

| Years | Standard Deviation of Won-Lost Percentage | Percentage of Teams Finishing Within Ten Games of First Place |
|---|---|---|
| 1900-1904 | .102 | 33% |
| 1910-1914 | .100 | 18% |
| 1920-1924 | .087 | 34% |
| 1930-1934 | .098 | 30% |
| 1940-1944 | .094 | 24% |
| 1950-1954 | .103 | 32% |
| 1960-1964 | .087 | 32% |
| 1970-1974 | .069 | 41% |

Another place where the Law of Competitive Balance can be observed statistically is in World Series play, by breaking down the won/lost sequences. Who usually wins the second game of the World Series, the team which won the first game and thus leads 1-0, or the team which is behind 1-0? The team which has lost the first game of the series will win the second game 56% of the time (44-35 in 79 World Series). If the series is 2-1 after three games, who usually wins the fourth? Again, over half (52%, 33 of 63) have been won by the teams which were behind. If it is 3-2 after five games, who usually wins the sixth? The teams training 3-2 have won 62% of the time in those games, 28 of 45.

Why? Because they adjust. Who moved his infielders in a couple of steps after the first game of the 1982 Series? Look at the lineups for the first two games of the series:

| MILWAUKEE | | ST. LOUIS | |
|---|---|---|---|
| First | Second | First | Second |
| Molitor | Molitor | Herr | Herr |
| Yount | Yount | L. Smith | Oberkfell |
| Cooper | Cooper | Hernandez | Hernandez |
| Simmons | Simmons | Hendrick | Hendrick |
| Oglivie | Oglivie | Tenace | Porter |
| Thomas | Thomas | Porter | L. Smith |
| Howell | Howell | Green | Iorg |
| Moore | Moore | Oberkfell | McGee |
| Gantner | Gantner | O. Smith | O. Smith |

Granted, Milwaukee switched from a lefthander to a righthander, and granted, Herzog switches his lineup around a lot more than Kuenn. But I would bet dollars to pesos that if you checked, you would find that teams *losing* the first game of a World Series make far more lineup changes than teams *winning* the first game. You lose the first game, you start wondering, do we have enough power to win in this park? Could we take more advantage of the bunt with their third baseman? Is our first baseman ever going to come out of his slump? You win the first game, and you make excuses for the first baseman.

A team which *loses* a pennant by three games or less is much more likely to win the race in the following season than is a team which wins by three or less. Again, an observable fact, which the Law of Competitive Balance explains.

The Law of Competitive Balance also applies to individuals. Who experiments with a new batting stroke, a .300 hitter or a guy who is fighting to keep his job? Who tries to develop a new slider, an 18-game winner or a guy fighting to stay in the big leagues? The less talent you have, the more you are forced to learn, to adapt, to adjust. Among the ten best managers in baseball today, who was more than a marginal player? This process constantly diminishes the distance between the best players and the worst; it draws the George Bretts and Dennis Eckersleys down and it lifts the Brian Downings and the Charlie Houghs up.

And finally, it defines greatness. It is true in all sports, but it is more true in baseball than in others: Greatness in an athlete is self-defined. Great ballplayers in baseball are those who erect standards for themselves so that they redefine an 18-13 season as a failure and only a hard 20 as a success. Great ballplayers continue to experiment, continue to try things, continue to learn before they are on the road to oblivion. What does Pete Rose talk about when he talks about hitting? Adjustments: move up in the box, move back in the box; choke up on the bat, go down to the knob. He is talking about not letting them drag you down. He is talking about what you have to do to defy the Law of Competitive Balance.

# LEADERS IN ISOLATED POWER

Isolated power combines all extra-base power into one statistic and separates it from batting average. It is figured as simply slugging percentage minus batting average. The power statistic it competes with, under different names, is slugging percentage divided by batting average. Slugging percentage, without any adjustments, is a very meaningful stat in itself, but it is simply not a "power" category—Willie Wilson had about the same slugging percentage last year (.431) as Tony Armas (.433), and Carney Lansford (.444) about the same as Gary Gaetti (.443). You have to make an adjustment for batting average to focus on the "power" part of it. The difference between the two adjustments is shown below:

**POWER ACCORDING TO ISOLATED POWER**

| Rank | Player | Slugging Pct. | | Batting Avg. | | Power |
|---|---|---|---|---|---|---|
| 1. | Mike Schmidt | .547 | – | .280 | = | .267 |
| 2. | Dave Kingman | .432 | – | .204 | = | .228 |

**POWER ACCORDING TO BASES PER HIT:**

| Rank | Player | Slugging Pct. | | Batting Avg. | | Power |
|---|---|---|---|---|---|---|
| 1. | Dave Kingman | .432 | ÷ | .204 | = | 2.12 |
| 2. | Mike Schmidt | .547 | ÷ | .280 | = | 1.95 |

It has always seemed to me to be a little bit silly to say that Dave Kingman hits with more power than Mike Schmidt, when clearly he doesn't hit with more power than Mike Schmidt—he hits about the same number of homers but a third as many doubles and triples—to say this merely because he doesn't get as many hits.

The top and bottom men in 1982 isolated power are given below (minimum 400 plate appearances):

| | American League | | | | National League | | | |
|---|---|---|---|---|---|---|---|---|
| | Highest | | Lowest | | Highest | | Lowest | |
| **Catcher:** | | | | | | | | |
| | Parrish | .245 | Wathan | .058 | Carter | .217 | Trevino | .053 |
| | Simmons | .182 | Boone | .081 | Kennedy | .191 | Benedict | .057 |
| **First Basemen:** | | | | | | | | |
| | Murray | .233 | Cabell | .062 | Kingman | .228 | Rose | .067 |
| | Cooper | .215 | Hargrove | .067 | Thompson | .227 | Knight | .108 |
| **Second Basemen:** | | | | | | | | |
| | Grich | .188 | Remy | .044 | Garner | .149 | Trillo | .048 |
| | White | .171 | Richardt | .048 | Morgan | .149 | Herr | .054 |
| **Third Basemen:** | | | | | | | | |
| | DeCinces | .247 | Castillo | .079 | Schmidt | .267 | Brooks | .068 |
| | Gaetti | .213 | Iorg | .080 | Horner | .240 | Oberkfell | .081 |
| **Shortstop:** | | | | | | | | |
| | Yount | .247 | Foli | .056 | Berra | .123 | Bailor | .042 |
| | Ripken | .211 | Griffin | .073 | Thon | .121 | LeMaster | .050 |
| **Left Field:** | | | | | | | | |
| | Winfield | .280 | Dilone | .071 | Easler | .160 | Raines | .092 |
| | Ward | .230 | Wilson | .099 | Baker | .158 | Richards | .073 |
| **Center Field:** | | | | | | | | |
| | Thomas | .261 | Mitchell | .064 | Murphy | .226 | Scott | .054 |
| | Lynn | .218 | Miller | .071 | Dawson | .197 | Moreno | .070 |
| **Right Field:** | | | | | | | | |
| | Jackson | .257 | Moore | .106 | Guerrero | .232 | Householder | .115 |
| | Evans | .242 | Griffey | .130 | Durham | .209 | Puhl | .117 |
| **Designated Hitter:** | | | | | | | | |
| | McRae | .234 | Singleton | .130 | | | | |
| | Thornton | .211 | Yastrzemski | .156 | | | | |

Over 75% of the players on the "highest" list in isolated power played for .500 or better teams.

# WHAT DOES IT TAKE?

## DISCERNING THE DE FACTO STANDARDS OF THE HALL OF FAME

*This article is a reprint of an article from the 1980* Abstract, *an article attempting to find a way to take the records of players and deduce from them an effective definition of Hall of Fame standards. The 1980 Abstract only had a few hundred readers. The article is presented exactly as it was originally written, but a postscript is added to review some things that I might have said at the time.*

I used to write a lot about the Hall of Fame. I wrote about how they could design more equitable election systems. I wrote about why the different boards inevitably used different standards. I wrote about the statistical illusions that tend to reinforce the Senile Ballplayers Committee in their inevitable belief that the Boys I played with were the best ever. Nobody paid any attention. I made up charts that demonstrated the New York bias in the Hall of Fame's composition. No New Yorkers called in to resign. Eventually I gave it up. I dislike howling into the wind.

What never ceases to amaze me is the hold that this unremarkable institution has on the imagination of baseball fans. You go to a meeting of the Society for American Baseball Research, and every third word is Cooperstown. Every separate interest group scratches at the base of this one pedestal. The Committee on the Negro Leagues wants to get more old-time blacks into the Hall of Fame. The Committee on Stat Analysis wants to establish standards for election to the Hall of Fame. The Committee on the Minor Leagues feels unfulfilled until there exists a minor-league Hall of Fame. And everybody and his 14-year-old son wants to collar me and explain why Ross Barnes, Arky Vaughn, Johnny Mize and Bob Elliott belong in the Hall of Fame. I get sick of hearing about it. The Negro Leagues are fascinating, stat analysis will obviously hold my interest. The minor leagues are a delicious memory and even Ross Barnes might be interesting if you knew something about him. Why must all of these topics be submerged into a never-ending argument about who belongs in the Hall of Fame?

Men without voices rattle their cups, I suppose. And so, for three *Abstracts*, I have said hardly a word about the Hall of Fame—admirable restraint, I think, if I must say so myself. But it is a major subject of stat analysis, and one can't avoid it forever. The notion floats around that one can detect patterns among the random selections of the various committees, and in that way discern some sort of general standards for Hall of Fame selection. What I propose to do here is to try to get those standards down on paper, to make them add, and in that way to bring some hard evidence out about what it is that will make a record stand out when the memory of the man has cooled.

Understand, I am not in the least talking about what Hall of Fame standards *should be*. I am talking about what they *are*. *De facto* standards, inferred from a study of who has made it and who hasn't. If we can build a prediction formula that will take the records of Enos Slaughter, Chick Hafey, Gil Hodges and Ralph Kiner and tell us that from that group Hafey and Kiner are the Hall of Famers, then we will have, it seems to me, that much better of an understanding of what it takes to become a Hall of Famer. That understanding we can then apply to the records of contemporary players.

In some ways the system which results is far from being logical. The Hall of Fame prediction system (HOFPS) awards 8 points for each season that an outfielder hits .300, only 3 points for each season that he drives in 100 runs. As a statement of the relative value of hitting .300 and driving in 100 runs, this is asinine. But it is also what works. The fact is that Indian Bob Johnson, Del Ennis, Bob Elliott and Gil Hodges, who have around 30 100-RBI seasons among them, are not in the Hall of Fame, while a bunch of singles hitters who have had about the same number of .320 seasons are.

So then, the prediction system. Actually, I have two prediction systems, one for pitchers, one for outfielders. Both require 100 points. There are no partial or percentage qualifications; 100 points and you're in, 99 and you're out. I don't have anything for infielders or catchers; somebody who has the time is encouraged to try to develop something. Anyway, here's what I have:

### Pitchers

1. Count 3 points for each season of 15 or more wins.
2. Count 10 points for each season of 20 wins.
   a. 20-20 seasons (that is, seasons with both 20 wins and 20 losses) should be counted as 15-victory seasons.
   b. Seasons are not to be counted in more than one win category; that is, 20-victory seasons are not to be double-counted with the 15-victory seasons, nor 30-victory seasons as also 20-victory seasons.
3. Count 30-win seasons at one point per win recorded.
4. Career wins are not counted before 150. After 150, count one point per three wins until 235. For example, count 1 point for 153-155 career wins, 11 points for 183-185. Count one point for each win above 235.
5. Count 2 points for each World Series *start*.
6. Count 3 points for each World Series *win*.
   a. Total points awarded for World Series performances are not to exceed 30.
7. Count 5 points for each season leading the league in ERA.

8. Count 5 points for each season leading the league in strikeouts.
9. Count 1 point for each .010 the pitcher's career W/L Pct is above .500.

There are 36 pitchers from this century (not counting the Negro Leagues) who are in the Hall of Fame. There are 35 pitchers from this century who would be predicted to be in the Hall of Fame. There are 33 pitchers who are on both lists, thus the HOFPS makes three or five errors, depending on how you figure it. The two pitchers who are not in although they have 100 qualification points are Carl Mays, who has been informally blacklisted because he threw the pitch that killed Ray Chapman, and Hal Newhouser, whose records are (rightfully) discounted because they were posted with the aid of a war.

The three pitchers who are in although they lack 100 qualification points are Addie Joss, Pop Haines and Rube Marquard, who are in for reasons that I will be kind enough not to speculate on. I will add that not only do these pitchers not have 100 points, they're not close, either. These, unless I missed somebody, are the only five pitchers from this century for whom the system fails to make a correct In/Out decision:

| Pitcher (W-L) | Points Under Rule Number: 1 | 2 | 3 | 4 | 5 | 6 | 7 | 8 | 9 | Total | In-Out |
|---|---|---|---|---|---|---|---|---|---|---|---|
| Gomez (189-102) | 9 | 40 | 0 | 13 | 14 | 16 | 10 | 15 | 14 | 131 | In |
| Lemon (207-128) | 6 | 70 | 0 | 19 | 8 | 6 | 0 | 5 | 11 | 125 | In |
| Chesbro (199-127) | 6 | 40 | 41 | 14* | 0 | 0 | 0 | 0 | 11 | 112 | In |
| Rixey (266-251) | 12 | 40 | 0 | 59 | 0 | 0 | 0 | 0 | 1 | 112 | In |
| Walsh (194-130) | 9 | 30 | 39 | 14 | 4 | 6 | 10 | 10 | 9 | 131 | In |
| Dean (150-83) | 3 | 30 | 30 | 0 | 8 | 6 | 1 | 20 | 14 | 111 | In |
| Hoyt (237-182) | 8 | 20 | 0 | 30 | 22 | 8 | 5 | 0 | 6 | 109 | In |
| Pennock (241-162) | 18 | 20 | 0 | 34 | 10 | 15 | 0 | 0 | 9 | 106 | In |
| Waddell (184-141) | 12 | 30 | 0 | 12* | 0 | 0 | 10 | 35 | 6 | 105 | In |
| Lyons (260-230) | 9 | 30 | 0 | 55 | 0 | 0 | 5 | 0 | 3 | 102 | In |
| Bender (210-128) | 18 | 20 | 0 | 20 | 20 | 10 | 0 | 0 | 12 | 100 | In |
| Derringer (223-212) | 12 | 40 | 0 | 24 | 14 | 6 | 0 | 0 | 1 | 97 | Out |
| Reynolds (182-107) | 18 | 10 | 0 | 10 | 18 | 12 | 5 | 10 | 13 | 96 | Out |
| Drysdale (209-166) | 15 | 20 | 0 | 19 | 12 | 9 | 0 | 15 | 5 | 95 | Out |
| Bridges (194-138) | 6 | 30 | 0 | 14 | 10 | 12 | 0 | 10 | 8 | 94 | Out |
| Shawkey (198-150) | 12 | 40 | 0 | 16 | 10 | 3 | 5 | 0 | 6 | 92 | Out |
| Coombs (158-110) | 0 | 20 | 30 | 2 | 12 | 15 | 0 | 0 | 9 | 88 | Out |
| Walters (198-160) | 12 | 30 | 0 | 16 | 6 | 6 | 10 | 5 | 5 | 90 | Out |
| Cicotte (210-148) | 9 | 30 | 0 | 20 | 10 | 6 | 5 | 0 | 8 | 88 | Out |
| Warneke (193-121) | 15 | 30 | 0 | 14 | 6 | 6 | 5 | 0 | 11 | 87 | Out |
| Ferrell (193-128) | 3 | 60 | 0 | 14 | 0 | 0 | 0 | 0 | 10 | 87 | Out |
| Bunning (224-184) | 21 | 10 | 0 | 24 | 0 | 0 | 0 | 15 | 4 | 84 | Out |
| Burdette (203-144) | 18 | 20 | 0 | 17 | 12 | 12 | 5 | 0 | 8 | 92 | Out |
| Reulbach (185-104) | 12 | 30 | 0 | 11 | 10 | 6 | 0 | 0 | 14 | 83 | Out |

But also

| Pitcher (W-L) | 1 | 2 | 3 | 4 | 5 | 6 | 7 | 8 | 9 | Total | In-Out |
|---|---|---|---|---|---|---|---|---|---|---|---|
| Mays (208-126) | 6 | 50 | 0 | 19 | 14 | 9 | 0 | 0 | 12 | 110 | Out |
| Newhouser (207-150) | 9 | 40 | 0 | 19 | 6 | 6 | 10 | 10 | 8 | 108 | Out |
| Marquand (204-179) | 6 | 30 | 0 | 18 | 16 | 6 | 0 | 5 | 3 | 84 | In |
| Haines (210-158) | 5 | 30 | 0 | 20 | 8 | 9 | 0 | 0 | 7 | 79 | In |
| Joss (160-97) | 6 | 40 | 0 | 3 | 0 | 0 | 10 | 0 | 12 | 71 | In |

**Does not include pre-1900 accomplishments.*

Obviously, the first set of numbers that I tried did not draw that line there. At a glance it is not really obvious why Rube Waddell (184-141) is in the Hall of Fame but Lou Warneke (193-121) is not, or why Jack Chesbro (199-127) is in but Ed Reulbach (185-104) is not. Among the most pronounced patterns in the taste of Hall of Fame voters is that they are much impressed by pitchers who were starters on championship teams, thus the points awarded for World Series performance (the same is true among other players). But the key element in most cases is 20-victory seasons. Well, you've got a choice: you can get in by winning 20 games every year, or you can get there by winning 235 or more total.

Among active pitchers and recently retired pitchers, totals of note include:

| Pitcher | Points Under Rule Number: 1 | 2 | 3 | 4 | 5 | 6 | 7 | 8 | 9 | Total |
|---|---|---|---|---|---|---|---|---|---|---|
| Seaver | 18 | 50 | 0 | 28 | 8 | 3 | 25 | 15 | 13 | 160 |
| Palmer | 6 | 80 | 0 | 25 | 16 | 9 | 10 | 0 | 14 | 160 |
| Gibson | 15 | 50 | 0 | 44 | 18 | 12 | 5 | 5 | 9 | 158 |
| Perry | 24 | 50 | 0 | 72 | 0 | 0 | 0 | 0 | 6 | 152 |
| Jenkins | 9 | 70 | 0 | 40 | 0 | 0 | 0 | 5 | 17 | 131 |
| Marichal | 9 | 60 | 0 | 36 | 2 | 0 | 5 | 0 | 13 | 129 |
| Hunter | 6 | 50 | 0 | 24 | 18 | 15 | 5 | 0 | 7 | 125 |
| Kaat | 15 | 30 | 0 | 57 | 6 | 13 | 0 | 0 | 4 | 115 |
| Carlton | 15 | 40 | 0 | 25 | 2 | 0 | 5 | 10 | 8 | 105 |
| Tiant | 6 | 40 | 0 | 22 | 6 | 6 | 10 | 0 | 8 | 98 |
| Lolich | 18 | 20 | 0 | 22 | 6 | 9 | 0 | 5 | 3 | 83 |
| Sutton | 24 | 10 | 0 | 22 | 12 | 6 | 0 | 0 | 6 | 80 |
| P. Niekro | 21 | 20 | 0 | 22 | 0 | 0 | 5 | 5 | 3 | 76 |
| Ryan | 12 | 20 | 0 | 5 | 0 | 0 | 0 | 35 | 1 | 73 |
| Blue | 9 | 30 | 0 | 2 | 10 | 0 | 5 | 0 | 8 | 64 |
| Guidry | 6 | 10 | 0 | 0 | 4 | 6 | 10 | 0 | 25 | 61 |
| T. John | 6 | 20 | 0 | 14 | 6 | 3 | 0 | 0 | 7 | 56 |
| Richard | 9 | 10 | 0 | 0 | 0 | 0 |  | 10 | 9 | 43 |

It is appropriate for those two to tie for the top spot. I was going to apologize for Luis Tiant being shown as still needing a couple of points (6 wins would do it), because I thought he was an obvious in, but then I read that Bill Mead of SABR wrote an article in which he rated Tiant as a dark horse. I don't know how in the world he figured that. The contrast between his seat-of-the-pants analysis and the prediction formula is interesting; he has Ferguson Jenkins, with 7 20-victory seasons and 247 career wins, in the same class with Mickey Lolich, in "more than even chance." Jenkins may have to wait a few years, like Robin Roberts, but he will obviously go, while Lolich is very unlikely to make it unless Hall of Fame standards drop markedly.

It should be noted that while Vida Blue (64 points) and Ron Guidry (61 points) look about even, this is not really true; 25 of Guidry's points are "soft" points which could be lost unless he is able to maintain a .756 lifetime won-lost percentage, which no one ever has. If he goes 12-12 in 1980, he will end the year with 55 points, 6 less than he has now. Blue, on the other hand, has crossed the magic "150"-line above which career victory totals begin to help you, so if he goes 12-12 he will wind up the year with 67 points. If both were to go 21-10 and lead their leagues in ERA, Guidry would advance to 74 points and Blue would leap to 87.

The system for outfielders delivers about the same degree of accuracy. Somehow I have misplaced my count of the number of outfielders from this century who are in the Hall of Fame, but it is about the same, somewhere around 30. The system for outfielders makes, again, 5 errors. One of those, on Shoeless Joe Jackson, has nothing to do with statistics. Another, Richie Ashburn, probably will be changed within a few years; Ashburn is fully qualified and will eventually go. Two other players are figured as qualified but not in; both of them, interestingly enough, are players with impressive records, but records which are completely dwarfed by the company they keep. The names are Bobby Veach and Bob Meusel. One cannot think of Veach and Meusel without thinking about Crawford and Cobb and Ruth and Gehrig, and when you think about records like that, Veach and Meusel don't look so good. But they are, in fact, better than the records of many Hall of Famers. The fifth error is Harry Hooper, in for his defensive reputation, but far from being qualified as a hitter. And, again, I may have missed somebody:

**OUTFIELDERS**

1) Award 8 points for each season of hitting .300, 100 or more games, up to a limit of 60 points.
2) Award 15 points if the player has a lifetime batting average of .315 or better in 1000 games.
3) Award 3 points per 100-RBI season.
4) Award 8 points per 200-hit season.
5) a. Award 4 points for each season leading the league in stolen bases.
   b. Award 5 points/season leading in RBI
   c. Award 8 for leading in HR.
   d. Award 12 for leading in Batting.
6) Count 1 point per World Series game played, up to a limit of 18.
7) Add 10 points if the player has 3000 career hits.
8) Add 10 points if the player has 400 career home runs.

Points Under Rule Number:

| Player | 1 | 2 | 3 | 4 | 5a | 5b | 5c | 5d | 6 | 7 | 8 | Total | In-Out |
|---|---|---|---|---|---|---|---|---|---|---|---|---|---|
| Wheat | 60 | 15 | 6 | 24 | 0 | 0 | 0 | 12 | 12 | 0 | 0 | 129 | In |
| Wilson | 40 | 0 | 18 | 8 | 0 | 10 | 32 | 0 | 12 | 0 | 0 | 120 | In |
| Snider | 56 | 0 | 18 | 0 | 0 | 5 | 8 | 0 | 18 | 0 | 10 | 115 | In |
| Manush | 60 | 0 | 6 | 32 | 0 | 0 | 0 | 12 | 5 | 0 | 0 | 115 | In |
| Combs | 56 | 15 | 0 | 24 | 0 | 0 | 0 | 0 | 18 | 0 | 0 | 113 | In |
| Waner, L | 60 | 15 | 0 | 32 | 0 | 0 | 0 | 0 | 4 | 0 | 0 | 111 | In |
| Averill | 60 | 15 | 15 | 16 | 0 | 0 | 0 | 0 | 3 | 0 | 0 | 109 | In |
| Youngs | 56 | 15 | 3 | 16 | 0 | 0 | 0 | 0 | 18 | 0 | 0 | 108 | In |
| Rousch | 60 | 15 | 0 | 0 | 0 | 0 | 0 | 24 | 8 | 0 | 0 | 107 | In |
| Kaline | 60 | 0 | 9 | 8 | 0 | 0 | 0 | 12 | 7 | 10 | 0 | 106 | In |
| Kiner | 24 | 0 | 18 | 0 | 0 | 5 | 56 | 0 | 0 | 0 | 0 | 103 | In |
| Carey | 48 | 0 | 0 | 8 | 40 | 0 | 0 | 0 | 7 | 0 | 0 | 103 | In |
| Hafey | 48 | 15 | 9 | 0 | 0 | 0 | 0 | 12 | 18 | 0 | 0 | 102 | In |
| I. Meusel | 48 | 0 | 12 | 16 | 0 | 5 | 0 | 0 | 18 | 0 | 0 | 99 | Out |
| D. Walker | 60 | 0 | 6 | 0 | 0 | 0 | 8 | 12 | 12 | 0 | 0 | 98 | Out |
| Slaughter | 60 | 0 | 9 | 0 | 0 | 0 | 8 | 0 | 18 | 0 | 0 | 95 | Out |
| K. Williams | 60 | 15 | 6 | 0 | 0 | 5 | 8 | 0 | 0 | 0 | 0 | 94 | Out |
| Cramer | 60 | 0 | 0 | 24 | 0 | 0 | 0 | 0 | 9 | 0 | 0 | 93 | Out |
| Kuenn | 60 | 0 | 0 | 16 | 0 | 0 | 0 | 12 | 4 | 0 | 0 | 92 | Out |

There are 100 more players who just miss, but that's enough. I will leave the computation of the errors and the active outfielders for your idle moments, or mine.

Perhaps in future *Abstracts* a list of the active players who are charting Hall of Fame progression will be a regular feature. That, however, would require frequent updating of the system so as to continue to minimize errors. I have no idea how well the outfielder's system would adapt to other positions; I would guess very well at first and fairly well at third and second, but not very well at short and catcher. I haven't tried it.

Finally, I will offer my opinion with regard to the recurrent proposal that fixed statistical guidelines for Hall of Fame selection should be established. Explicit criteria, it is argued, would do two things: it would end the erosion of standards that has already brought into the Hall too many second-rate stars, and it would end the "injustices" of players like Freddie Lindstrom and Pop Haines being inducted while obviously better players wait outside.

In my opinion, this is not the way. Justice? One cannot do an injustice to a bunch of numbers. One can deal unfairly with a man, with a memory perhaps, but not with lines of statistics. Such injustices as there are here have nothing to do with statistics and will not be prevented by establishing statistical reference points.

The declining quality of Hall of Fame inductees, not to mention the fact that an increasing percentage of them are dead and forgotten, is caused by two things: 1) the system of multiple review boards, in which one takes up again the players who have already been passed over by the others, creates an inevitable downward spiral as the decisions of the latter reflect back on the standards of the former. 2) More importantly, fair judgments are prevented by favoritism, by passions, by PR campaigns and personal loyalties—all of the things which create the vortex of controversy which is both the strength and the liability of the institution. So long as people carry every grand and petty cause that they stumble over to bang on the door of Cooperstown, that door will continue to be battered. If you would save the institution, then consider in your judgments not only what is good for your favorite player, but what is good for the Hall itself.

But there is an even better reason not to have statistical standards, which is that there is no way in the world to evolve a set of standards which is as comprehensive, as complex, as fair or as open to improvement as is human judgment. I have spent all of my life, sad as it may sound, learning to understand baseball records. If I couldn't make up standards which are fair and comprehensive, who could? And I don't feel that I could. There are simply too many things in the game of baseball which are not measured, are poorly measured, are still in the process of being measured. You could state that Mark Belanger over his career has won as many games by his glove as Joe DiMaggio did by his bat, and while we might not agree, there is no way in hell that anybody could prove you wrong. Statistical analysis is simply one more way of understanding the game of baseball. It is not our place to stand in judgment of the others.

**POSTSCRIPT**

—On the chart of active pitchers, Tiant has moved over the line (now at 101), Lolich retired without getting really close, Sutton has put himself in with 121 and still counting. Phil Niekro is borderline but probably in (107), and Nolan Ryan is drawing very near to the Hall of Fame class (95). Vida Blue has made little progress in the last three years (64 then, 74 now), Ron Guidry even less (61 to 66). Tommy John has gotten into the serious fray with 88 points; one or two more good seasons would make him a good bet to get in.

—The crack about SABR meetings no longer seems justified; the 1982 SABR convention, at least, was not dominated by the subject.

—The article has been widely misunderstood, so apparently I should have made some things clear that I didn't. One small publication (by the way, I appreciate your sending me the copy and I apologize for not responding) wrote something like "James' purpose as I understand it was to show that there is a logic to the Hall of Fame voting, and therefore that although that logic is arbitrary and haphazard, the institution is consistent in its selections and thus does not violate its purpose with capricious selections." Not an exact quote; I'm going from memory, but anyway, no, that was not my purpose in writing the article. It would be more accurate to say that I wrote the article to show that although the Hall of Fame does have some consistent patterns in its voting, those patterns are so arbitrary and haphazard that when you analyze the voting as to its internal patterns you are struck by the confusion and the analytical numbness that those patterns reveal. But actually, it wasn't my purpose to demonstrate anything of the sort, on either side. It was my purpose simply to figure out what the standards were and not to write an editorial on the subject.

—Some people have argued that, since many people who go into the Hall of Fame do so 30 or 40 years after their careers are over, it is not realistic to assume that the same standards are going to hold over a period that long. It is thus, perhaps, more accurate to say that "If the same standards are applied to players of our generation as were applied to players of the 1920s and 1930s, Phil Niekro will go into the Hall of Fame" than to say that "Phil Niekro will go into the Hall of Fame." Well, I can't argue with that, but I thought at the time that it was too obvious to trifle with. Sure, Hall of Fame voting patterns will change over time and invalidate some of what is shown here. So what? End of subject.

—The nominations of Bob Gibson as an automatic selection and Juan Marichal as an inevitable but less immediate selection have been justified by the voting. The comment about Richie Ashburn, on the other hand, has not stood up so well, as Ashburn has faded in the voting in recent seasons.

# TEAM AGE ANALYSIS IN GRAPH FORM

The following diagrams make a visual representation of the "team age analysis" reported with the teams. The first bar represents the teams' young talent, the second their prime talent, the third past-prime, the fourth old. When you put these side by side, the difference in the age composition of, say, San Diego and Houston is unmistakeable:

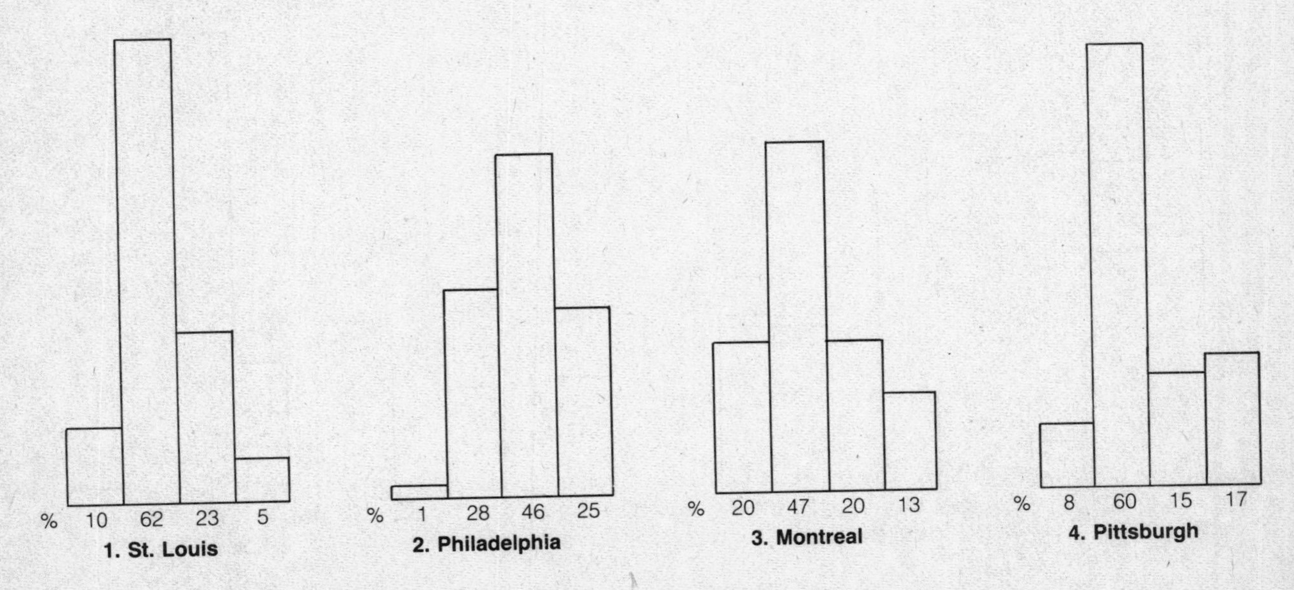

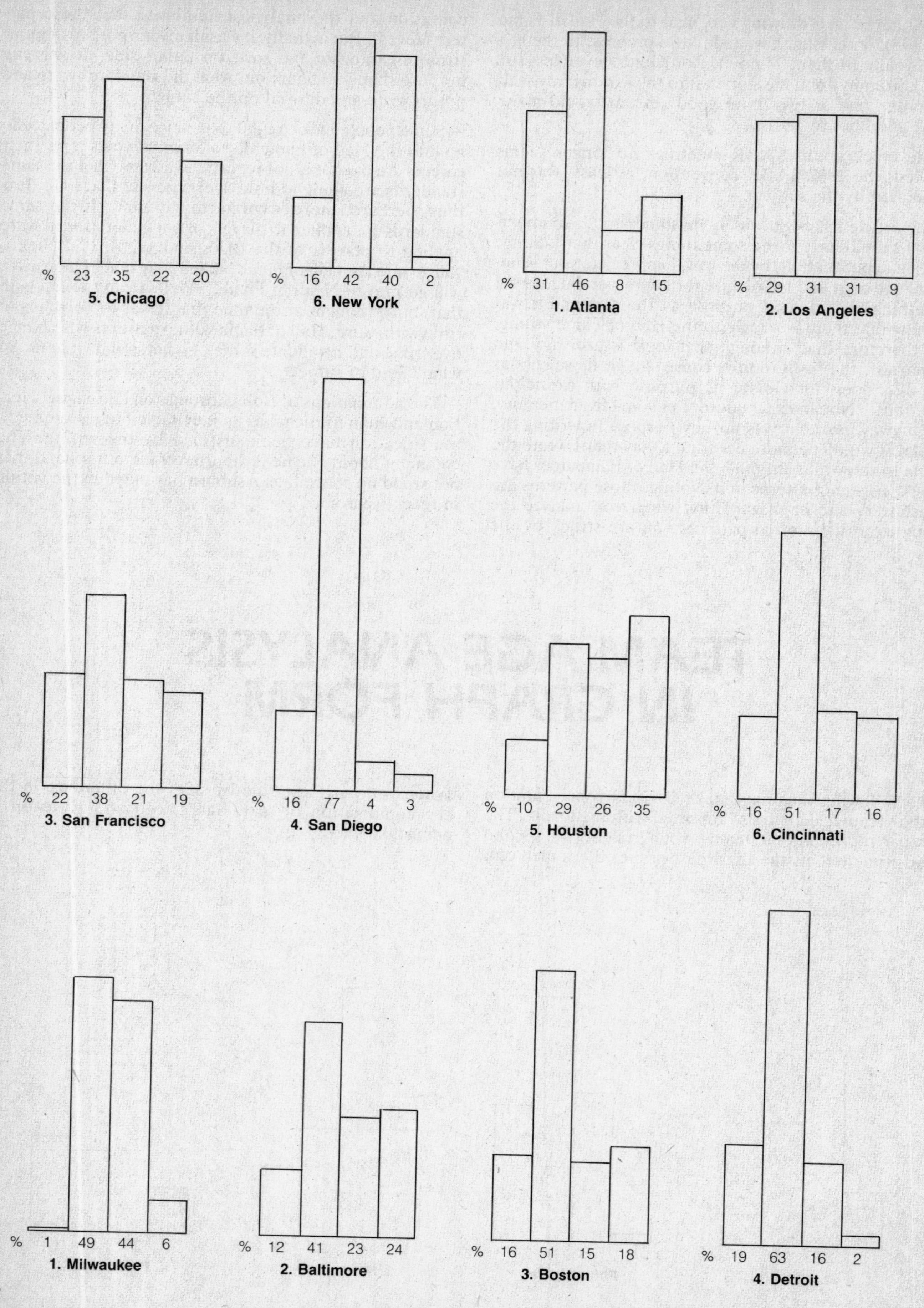

% 23 35 22 20
5. Chicago
% 16 42 40 2
6. New York
% 31 46 8 15
1. Atlanta
% 29 31 31 9
2. Los Angeles
% 22 38 21 19
3. San Francisco
% 16 77 4 3
4. San Diego
% 10 29 26 35
5. Houston
% 16 51 17 16
6. Cincinnati
% 1 49 44 6
1. Milwaukee
% 12 41 23 24
2. Baltimore
% 16 51 15 18
3. Boston
% 19 63 16 2
4. Detroit

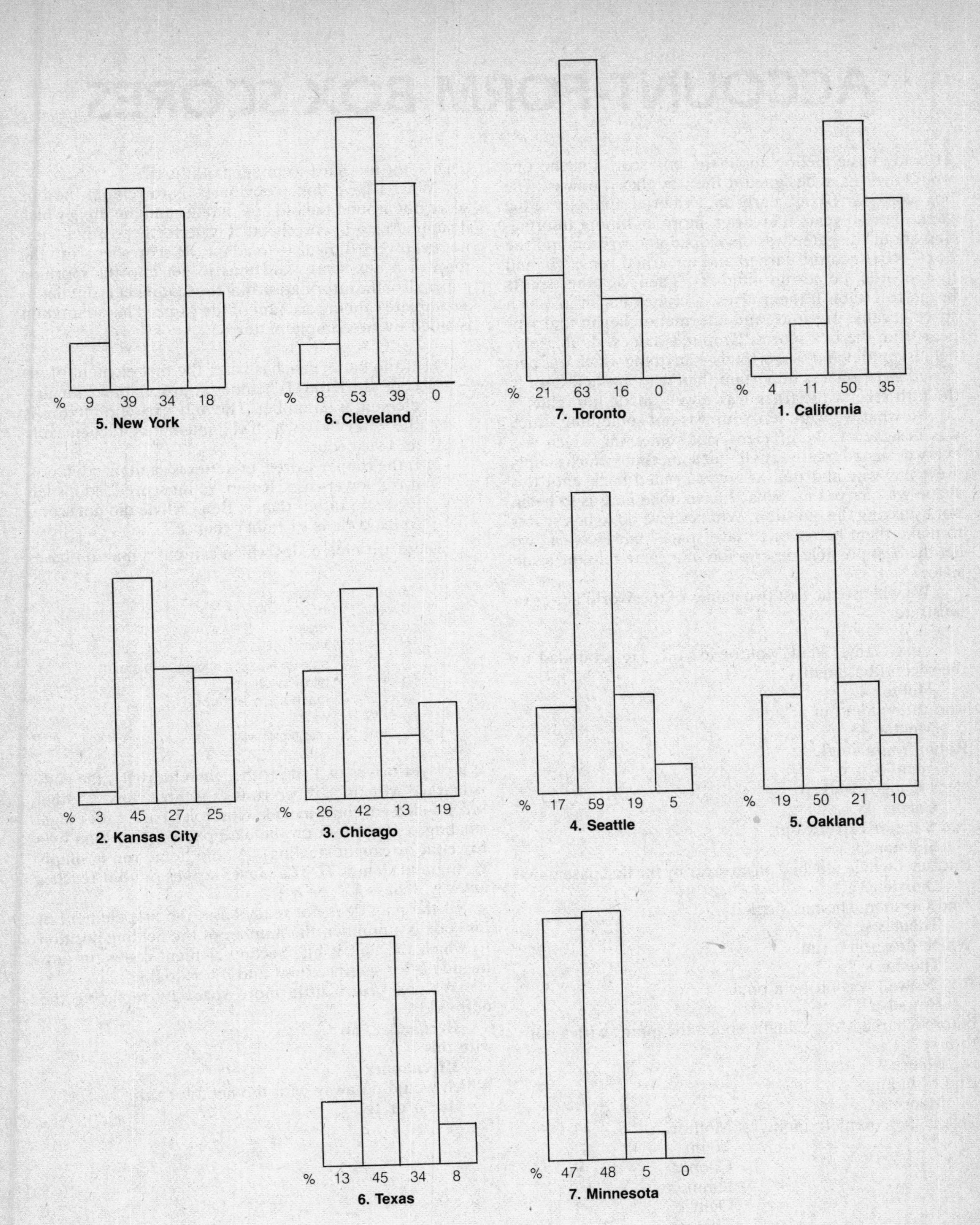
% 9 39 34 18
5. New York
% 8 53 39 0
6. Cleveland
% 21 63 16 0
7. Toronto
% 4 11 50 35
1. California
% 3 45 27 25
2. Kansas City
% 26 42 13 19
3. Chicago
% 17 59 19 5
4. Seattle
% 19 50 21 10
5. Oakland
% 13 45 34 8
6. Texas
% 47 48 5 0
7. Minnesota

# ACCOUNT-FORM BOX SCORES

It is my basic feeling about the box score that no one would ever have designed it the way that it now is. The box score started out, early on, as a brief summary of the game. For 40 years thereafter, more and more information about the game was developed and written into the box—RBI records, earned and unearned runs, win and lost records, home-run numbers. Then, as other sports began to establish themselves, a crunch began in which space became precious, and information began to disappear from the box scores. Umpire's names, double-play details, putout and assists totals—anything which was perceived as being less important than who finished third in the fifth race at the track was...well, made into glue.

So what we were left with was not something which was designed to be efficient, not something which was every designed, really, at all, but something which simply grew this way and that and was pruned back until this shape was arrived at. What I have done here is to begin not by asking the question, What can we do to box scores to make them better or to save space? but How can we get the best possible description of a game into the same space?

We will use the first two games of the World Series to illustrate.

First Game. Paul Molitor led off. He grounded to the second baseman,

**Molitor 4**

who threw him out at first.

**Molitor 43**

Robin Yount singled.

**Yount S**

Cecil Cooper walked.

**Cooper W**

Ted Simmons struck out.

**Simmons k**

But Ben Oglivie reached on an error by the first baseman.

**Oglivie e3**

And Gorman Thomas singled

**Thomas s**

Which drove in a run.

**Thomas s′**

Roy Howell was hit by a pitch

**Howell p**

before Charlie Moore finally ended the inning with a pop to first.

**Moore 3**

End of inning.

***Moore 3***

This is the complete inning:

| | |
|---|---|
| Molitor | 43 |
| Yount | S |
| Cooper | W |
| Simmons | k |
| Oglivie | e3 |
| Thomas | s′ |
| Howell | p |
| Moore | *3* |

That's not too hard to understand, is it?

What I have done, obviously, is to rebuild the box score not around the old box, but around the thing which it summarizes, a scoresheet. It is perfectly possible—it is not even very difficult—to adapt the scoresheet into the form of a box score, and thus to get into the morning paper all of the information that the score sheet contains—a complete running account of the game. This adaptation is aided by two simple patterns:

1) If the batter reaches base, the first element of his code is a letter. If he does not reach base, the first element is a number. The only exception to this is the letter "k," which is immediately recognizable as a strikeout.
2) If the runner scores, his letter is capitalized; if not, it is a lower-case. Robin Yount scored, so his letter was *S* rather than *s*; Ben Oglivie did not score, so his code is *e3* rather than *E3*.

There are nine codes which can put a man on base.

| | |
|---|---|
| s or S | single |
| d or D | double |
| t or T | triple |
| H | home run |
| f or F | safe on fielder's choice or forceout |
| p or P | hit by pitch |
| e or E | reached on an error |
| w or W | walk |
| i or I | intentional walk |

If a player drives in a run (other than himself), the code is marked with an ′; if two runs, ″; if three runs, */*. Other second-element codes include *s* for stolen base, *c* for caught stealing, *x* for putout on the base paths (other than by a forceout or caught stealing). A solo home run is simply *H*, a grand slam is *H!* If a player strikes out but reaches anyway, that is *k+* or *K+*.

If the man does not reach base, the first element of his code is a number, the number of the fielding position to which the ball is hit. Second-element codes on outs include *b* for sacrifice bunt and *p* for double play.

We can save a little more space by replacing the outmoded

**Hernandez, 1b**

with this:

**3Hernandez**

Which would do away with the need for this:

**Her'n'ez,1b**

See if there is anything in this account of the first 1982 World Series game that you can't follow:

| | | | | | | | | | | | |
|---|---|---|---|---|---|---|---|---|---|---|---|
| 5Molitor | 43 | s | s'x | S | s | s' | 4Herr | 63 | *6* | w | *9* |
| 6Yount | S | s | *53* | d" | s | *k* | 7LSmith | 53 | k | *k* | 9 |
| 3Cooper | W | 6 | 7 | *k* | *46* | | 3Hernandez | *43* | 43 | 31 | 43 |
| 2Simmons | k | *4* | H | s | 8 | | 9Hendrick | 8 | *31* | 43 | *3* |
| 7Oglivie | e3 | 43 | 43 | 3p | W | | 0Tenace | 3 | 13 | *k* | |
| 8Thomas | s' | 53 | *3–* | w | 53 | | 2Porter | d | 31 | s | |
| 0Howell | p | *43* | 3– | *9* | S' | | 8Green | *3* | *53* | 9 | |
| 9Moore | *3* | D | 63 | 7 | S | | 5Oberkfell | 43 | 43 | s | |
| 4Gantner | 3 | 36 | S | 63 | T" | | 6O Smith | 43 | 8 | 9 | |

Pitchers: St. Louis, Forsch (9992L) Kaat (xxx5) LaPoint (xxx27) Lahti (xxxx22). Milwaukee, Caldwell (w)

| | | | | | | | |
|---|---|---|---|---|---|---|---|
| Milwaukee | 200 | 112 | 004 ................................ | 10 | 17 | 0 | 10 |
| St. Louis | 000 | 000 | 000 ................................ | 0 | 3 | 1 | 4 |

T—2:30 A—53,723

The pitching summary means that Forsch faced all nine batters the first three times through the order and two batters the fourth time through. Kaat faced five batters after Forsch—he struck out Cooper and pitched the seventh— before giving way to LaPoint, who went one time through the order before yielding to Lahti.

OK, what does an ordinary box score tell you about Charlie Moore's game?

5 2 2 0
double-Moore

It tells you that he batted five times, hit a single and a double and scored two runs. That's it.

And what does the account-form box score tell you? It tells you that he batted in the first with the bases loaded and two out and popped to first. It tells you that he led off the fourth inning with a double and scored on Paul Molitor's single. It tells you that he grounded to short for the second out of the sixth inning. It tells you that he led off the eighth, facing Dave LaPoint, with a fly ball to left. It tells you that, with one on and two out, in the ninth, he singled and scored on Gantner's triple.

And does all of this extra information cost you extra space? Take a look at Game 2, with the account form and the traditional box score side by side:

| | | | | | | | | | | |
|---|---|---|---|---|---|---|---|---|---|---|
| 5Molitor | 53 | Ss | *k* | k | sc | 4Herr | 7 | D' | k | w |
| 6Yount | w | 4' | D | 7 | 63 | 5Oberkfell | 9 | s' | Ss | |
| 3Cooper | s | 6 | s' | d | *8* | oTenace | | | | *8* |
| 2Simmons | *3p* | H | 8 | i | | 5Ramsey | | | | |
| 7Oglivie | k | s | 6 | *63* | | 3Hernandez | *9* | 7 | 9 | w |
| 8Thomas | w | *54* | *k* | 2 | | 9Hendrick | k | 3 | W | F3 |
| 0Howell | F3 | k | k | k | | 2Porter | 43 | 43 | *1 | s |
| 9Moore | d' | 53 | 8 | s | | 7L Smith | *63* | *53* | *k* | w |
| 4Gantner | *8* | w | *6* | *3–* | | 0Iorg | s | 43 | | |
| | | | | | | 0Green | | | k | |
| | | | | | | 0Braun | | | | w'x |
| | | | | | | 8McGee | F3s | 6 | k | 6 |
| | | | | | | 6O Smith | 63 | *63* | ss | *s* |

*1—d"e7

Pitchers: St. Louis, Stuper (992) Kaat (xx3) Bair (xx43) Sutter (xxx63W). Milwaukee, Sutton (996) McClure (xx35L) Ladd (xxx4)

| | | | | | | | |
|---|---|---|---|---|---|---|---|
| Milwaukee | 012 | 010 | 000 ................................ | 4 | 10 | 1 | 8 |
| St. Louis | 002 | 002 | 01x ................................ | 5 | 8 | 0 | 7 |

T—2:54 A—53,723

| | ab | r | h | bi | | ab | r | h | bi |
|---|---|---|---|---|---|---|---|---|---|
| Molitor, 3b | 5 | 1 | 2 | 0 | Herr, 2b | 3 | 1 | 1 | 1 |
| Yount, ss | 4 | 1 | 1 | 1 | Oberkfell, 3b | 3 | 1 | 2 | 1 |
| Cooper, 1b | 5 | 0 | 3 | 1 | Tenace, ph | 1 | 0 | 0 | 0 |
| Simmons, c | 3 | 1 | 1 | 1 | Ramsey, 3b | 0 | 0 | 0 | 0 |
| Oglivie, lf | 4 | 0 | 1 | 0 | Hernandez, 1b | 3 | 2 | 0 | 0 |
| Thomas, cf | 3 | 0 | 0 | 0 | Porter, c | 4 | 0 | 2 | 2 |
| Howell, dh | 4 | 1 | 0 | 0 | L. Smith, lf | 3 | 0 | 0 | 0 |
| Moore, c | 4 | 0 | 2 | 1 | Iorg, dh | 2 | 0 | 1 | 0 |
| Gantner, 2b | 3 | 0 | 0 | 0 | Green, dh | 1 | 0 | 0 | 0 |
| | | | | | Braun, dh | 0 | 0 | 0 | 1 |
| | | | | | McGee, cf | 4 | 1 | 0 | 0 |
| | | | | | O. Smith, ss | 4 | 0 | 2 | 0 |
| | 35 | 4 | 10 | 4 | | 31 | 5 | 8 | 5 |

Milwaukee 012 010 000—4
St. Louis 002 002 01x—5

| Milwaukee | IP | H | R | ER | BB | SO |
|---|---|---|---|---|---|---|
| Sutton | 6 | 5 | 4 | 4 | 1 | 3 |
| McClure (L) | 1⅓ | 2 | 1 | 1 | 2 | 2 |
| Ladd | ⅔ | 1 | 0 | 0 | 2 | 0 |

| St. Louis | IP | H | R | ER | BB | SO |
|---|---|---|---|---|---|---|
| Stuper | 4* | 6 | 4 | 4 | 3 | 3 |
| Kaat | ⅔ | 1 | 0 | 0 | 0 | 0 |
| Bair | 2 | 1 | 0 | 0 | 0 | 3 |
| Sutter (W) | 2⅓ | 2 | 0 | 0 | 1 | 1 |

*Pitched to one batter in the fifth
Game-Winning RBI—Braun
E—Oglivie. DP—St. Louis 1. LOB—Milwaukee 8, St. Louis 7. 2B—Moore, Herr, Yount, Porter, Cooper. HR—Simmons. SB—Molitor, McGee, Oberkfell, O. Smith. T—2:54 A—53,723.

In the process of giving you all of this extra information, the account-form box score has reduced the space needed for a typical box by 30%. For most of us, of course . . . well, what difference does it make? But to the editors who have been in a "what-can-we-take-out-of-the-box-scores-next" bind for years, this would represent a savings of thousands of lines of type over the course of a season.

A couple of small points to clear up . . . a **1* (or *2, *3) is used when a 4-element code becomes necessary, and refers you to a note at the bottom. A *3–* means a ground ball to the first baseman; a *3* means a ball caught in the air by the first baseman.

To get a better idea of the "knowledge gain" that this would represent, let us consider a situation in which information about a subject 1) is hotly desired, and 2) is unavailable from any source other than the box scores. You're the manager of a baseball team, and in the game tomorrow you are facing a red-hot rookie who has made three starts in the major leagues and won them all, none of them complete games. Your scouts have not seen him; nobody on the team has faced him. In order to select your lineup, there are all kinds of things you'd like to know about him. Have the left-handed batters been having any better luck with him than the righthanders? Have the hitters been able to pull him? Does he get his outs on the ground (*43,63*) or in the air (*8,9*)? Which hitters have done the best against him? How has he pitched with men on base? Have they tried to run against him? Did those two stolen bases in his starts come when he was in the game and is that *two* for *two* or *two* for *six*? Did he start getting the ball up (fly ball outs) an inning or two before he was lifted? Did he have any control troubles early in the game?

A traditional box score will not tell you any of these things; an account-form box score explains them all.

Having this kind of information is important in my line of work. The aid that A–F box scores would give to a sabermetrician is incalculable. Of all of our greatest areas of ignorance, about half would simply melt away after a year's worth of this data became available. Who hit well in the clutch? How many times did a hitter bat with runners in scoring position? How many times in the late innings with men on? Which *pitchers* have a platoon advantage and which don't? Managerial strategy—in what situation will Tom Lasorda make a pitching change, and in what situation will Herzog make it? What are the differences in how they use their pinch hitters? The stolen base game . . . who runs a lot in good-percentage situations, and whose running game is situation unconscious? Over a period of years, we could build up a complete book on who hits who. How often does each hitter pull the ball? How often does he hit it on the ground? Such information would be immensely valuable in improving projections of how a player will do in changing parks.

And what would be lost? It would be harder to read. But would it? Is it inherently harder to understand 63 6 W 9 than it is 3100? Would the public accept it? Would the old farts of the nation cry "You've taken our box scores away from us!" with soporific letters to the editor about the beauty and simplicity of the old box scores and how ugly and confusing the new ones are? Would they refuse to understand them? And how many people are there who really want to know all that stuff?

I can't answer those questions. I can build a better box score, and I have. I can't force anybody to use it.

# TINKERING WITH THE RUNS FORMULA

My basic attitude toward several of the less-cited offensive statistics, such as the numbers of times hit by a pitch, sacrifice flies and sac bunts is that they are not worth messing with. Some people find this to be a less-than-satisfactory approach to the subject, an attitude downright pernicious for a statistician. One must understand that the great purpose of my work, simply stated, is to free baseball statistics from the cage of minutia in which they have so long been confined, and to sketch the outlines of a statistical method which can be used to pursue answers to larger questions. For that it is necessary that we state a player's offensive production in a form—runs—that can be related to the other issues, but it is also necessary that we then close that door and turn our attention to those other issues. Every hour that we spend on the first goal detracts from the second.

If, however, you do not take that tack . . .

There are two other problems with the attempts to include a broader spectrum of offensive stats into the runs-created formula: accuracy, and logical consistency. The runs-created formula as it is already is so accurate in predicting runs scored by teams and leagues that almost anything you do to it makes it less accurate. Despite the many other offensive statistics that there are, I have never found any way to include any of them in the formula and make it significantly more accurate.

And second, there is the question of whether or not we *should* be including them, even if we could. The reason that I prefer runs created to run and RBI counts is that runs and RBI are distorted to such an extent by the neighbors one has in the batting order that they are not truly reflections of the player's individual ability. The data I use—walks, hits, total bases—are truly individual accomplishments, things which can be done in any at-bat. Sacrifice hits, sacrifice flies, grounding into double plays—these, again, reflect unequal opportunities.

So that is my introduction to this next formula—it's not any more accurate, it creates logical problems, and it's a lot of trouble. But I do have a version of the runs-created formula which deals with HB, SH, SF, and GDP. Actually, I think it is a little bit more accurate than the simpler form; I believe it is. I wouldn't know for sure unless I spent about a week double-checking it, and I don't have a spare week. If anybody else wants to run some tests and let me know, I'd be grateful.

That formula is:

$$\frac{(H + W + HB - CS)(TB + .65(SB + SH + SF))}{AB + W + SH + SF + CS + HB + GDP}$$

H = Hits
W = Walks
HB = Hit by Pitch
CS = Caught Stealing
TB = Total Bases
SB = Stolen Bases
SH = Sacrifice Hits
SF = Sacrifice Flies
GDP = Grounded into Double Plays

We'll call this the advanced version of the formula.

The runs-created estimates for all 14 American League teams, with and without these adjustments, are given below:

**RUNS CREATED**

| TEAM | Stolen-Base Version | Advanced | Actual Runs |
|---|---|---|---|
| Milwaukee | 863 | 860 | 891 |
| California | 816 | 822 | 814 |
| Chicago | 776 | 776 | 786 |
| Kansas City | 817 | 810 | 784 |
| Baltimore | 787 | 784 | 774 |
| Boston | 763 | 757 | 753 |
| Detroit | 742 | 742 | 729 |
| New York | 716 | 713 | 709 |
| Oakland | 630 | 631 | 691 |
| Cleveland | 709 | 710 | 683 |
| Minnesota | 685 | 680 | 657 |
| Toronto | 651 | 653 | 651 |
| Seattle | 655 | 654 | 651 |
| Texas | 591 | 595 | 590 |

The adjustments to the formula reduce the gross error in the AL estimate from 236 to 226; in the NL, they reduce the gross error from 316 to 310.

This verison of the formula is derived by some reasonably simple adjustments to the stolen-base version of the formula. The initial parenthesis, which represent the number of runners on base, are increased by the addition of hit basemen. The second parenthesis, which gives credit for the advancement of baserunners, are now expanded to include .65 for each sacrifice hit and scoring fly ball. The credit for a stolen base is reduced from .7 to .65 because one of the benefits of a stolen base is that it helps to reduce double plays and we are now dealing with double plays separately.

The denominator of the formula represents the opportunities involved, or the setting in which the offense described above takes place. To this we now add HB, SH, and SF, and also GDP, as what each GDP does is to waste an opportunity. It also takes a runner off base, but I haven't found a way to deal with that which makes the formula work.

If these adjustments tend to make team and league runs-created estimates *slightly* more accurate, it is reasonable to think that they might make individual RC estimates for players *significantly* more accurate, as individual's tendencies to get hit by a pitch, drop down a bunt or ground into a Tinkers to Evers are much, much more pronounced than are team or league tendencies. But the adjustments are still small-time, unless you're talking about Ron Hunt. Not one time in 200 would the difference in an individual runs-created estimate change by five. And the change in runs created *per out* would be even smaller than that.

One of the most interesting things about this adaptation of the formula is its treatment of the sacrifice hit. Its handling is a logical extension of the way in which stolen bases are included. (If you can't argue that what you do is right, it is at least handy to have a precedent for it.) Anyway, several sabermetricians (separately) have concluded that the sacrifice bunt is not a very good play, that generally speaking you'll score more runs if you don't bunt much than you will if you do. These studies have been done in several different ways, and their conclusion on the most basic level is difficult to argue with. My problem with the studies is that they miss a key point, which is that most managers already know that, and thus don't use the bunt to try to *increase* their offensive production, but rather to try to *preserve* it through a weak spot in the batting order. Almost all bunts are laid down by poor hitters—65% of all bunts in the NL last year were laid down by hitters hitting less than .250. This knowledge changes the equation. If we know, for example, that on a given team a player's chance of scoring from second with one out is 42%, and his chance of scoring from first with nobody out is 40%, then we might be tempted to say that you shouldn't bunt because the lousy 2% gain in the chance of getting one run doesn't off-set your chance of losing a two-run inning or a big inning. But if a bad hitter is at the plate—the pitcher, say—then that 40% chance of scoring from first does not apply. The chance *in that situation* might be 25% or 20%, and then the percentages are far, far different. It seems obvious, but the people who have tried to refute the logic of a sac bunt too often haven't dealt with it. Managers don't bunt with the middle of their lineup.

What exactly *is* the point at which a hitter becomes somebody you would ask to bunt? Suppose that you have a player who, in 250 plate appearances, reaches base 100 times and has 100 total bases. This is a very good hitter we are talking about here, and we figure that he would create about 40 runs in those 250 PA:

$$\frac{(100)\,(100)}{250} = 40.000$$

If you ask him to bunt ten times, then the number of runs that he creates increases to 40.962:

$$\frac{(100)\,(100 + .65(10))}{250 + 10} = 40.962$$

He has created an extra run, but the crucial ratio between his runs created and his outs used has actually gotten worse. His runs created *per out* are:

Without Bunts: $\frac{40.000}{150} = .26666$

With Bunts: $\frac{40.962}{160} = .25601$

So, by the technical adjustments to the RC formula, you would not ask this man to bunt.

Suppose, however, that you look at a not-so-good hitter, a player who has the same on-base and advancement totals in 150 more plate appearances, or 400 total. Without bunting, he has created 25 runs:

$$\frac{(100)\,(100)}{400} = 25.000$$

If he bunts 10 times, his runs created are shown to increase by a similar amount:

$$\frac{(100)\,(100 + .65(10))}{400 + 10} = 25.976$$

There is a logical reason for the small difference in the number of runs resulting from ten sacrifice bunts, which I will not digress to explain. However, for this hitter, the number of runs that he creates *per out used* actually increases:

| Without Bunts: | With Bunts: |
|---|---|
| $\frac{25.000}{300} = .08333$ | $\frac{25.976}{310} = .08379$ |

This presents a fascinating brace of questions, which are:

1) What is the theoretical point at which a player should be asked to bunt, and
2) What is the empirical level at which players *are* asked to bunt.

Get it? You bunt with Doug Flynn; you don't bunt with Andre Dawson. Where is the line of demarcation? I would bet that if you studied the frequency with which various grades of hitters are asked to bunt, you would get a graph something like this:

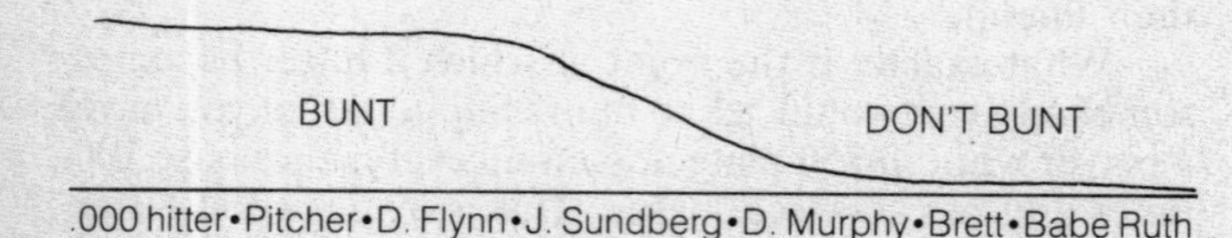


While the theoretical model would draw an absolute line:

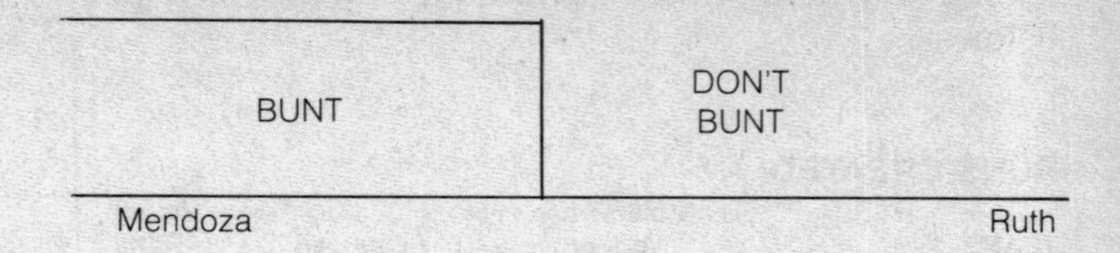


Well, actually, there would be a small grey area because different types of hitters at the same level of productivity would have different incremental changes from bunting.

Anyway, I would bet that when this research is done, we will find a very, very close resemblance between the two. We might have to fine-tune the formula a bit, change it to .75 sac hit instead of .65 or something, but basically I think we will find that major-league managers bunt with the people that they should bunt with.

The world needs more sabermetricians; I'm never going to get this all figured out by myself.

# NOT OF ANY GENERAL INTEREST

1. **Runs Created Formula**:

$$\frac{(\text{Hits} + \text{Walks} - \text{Caught Stealing}) \times (\text{Total Bases} + .7\ \text{Stolen Bases})}{\text{At Bats} + \text{Walks} + \text{Caught Stealing}}$$

2. **Isolated Power** is simply slugging percentage minus batting average.
3. **Defensive Efficiency Record** (DER)

To figure DER, you begin by making two estimates of the number of times that a team's defense has turned a batted ball into an out. The first is:

$$\text{PO} - \text{K} - \text{DP} - \text{A(c + of)}$$

This assumes that a batted ball has been turned into an out every time a putout is recorded unless (1) the putout was a strikeout, (2) two putouts were recorded on the same play, or (3) a runner has been thrown out on the bases.

$$\text{BFP} - \text{K} - \text{H} - \text{W} - \text{HBP} - 5/6\ \text{Errors}$$

This assumes that a batted ball has been turned into an out every time a batter faces the pitcher unless (1) the batter strikes out, (2) he hits safely, (3) he walks, (4) he is hit by the pitch, or (5) he reaches base on an error.

These two estimates are rarely identical, but I've been figuring them for years and I've never yet seen a case where they differed by more than 1%.

We then take the average of the two, which we call Plays Made (PM). DER is Plays Made divided by Plays Made plus Plays *Not* Made:

$$\frac{\text{PM}}{\text{PM} + \text{H} - \text{HR} + 5/6\ \text{Errors}}$$

I should also point out that while the differences derived may look small, they are anything but. DER is similar to the complement of batting average. The effect of having a DER which is .020 below the league average would be very similar to the effect of having a team batting average which is .017 to .018 below league, which is to say that it would wipe you out of a pennant race 99% of the time.

4. **The Favorite Toy.**

Category = Pigs (hits, walks, stolen bases, home runs, whatever)
Need Pigs = Number of Pigs needed to reach goal
Years Remaining = A number of years remaining to the player, assigned by his age by the formula: 24 − .6(age)
Established Pig Level = The number of Pigs per year that the player has shown the ability to gather.
Projected Remaining Pigs = Years remaining times established Pigs level
Chances of Reaching Goal:

$$\frac{\text{Need Pigs} - .5(\text{Projected Remaining Pigs})}{\text{Need Pigs}}$$

With, however, these limitations:

1) If a player is younger than 33, his chance of continuing to progress toward a goal cannot exceed .98 per season for a period of five years or less or .96 per season for a period longer than five years. For example, since Rickey Henderson is 6.21 years away from 1000 stolen bases, his chance of stealing 1000 cannot exceed $.96^{6.21}$. Since Robin Yount is 3.42 years away from 2000 hits, his chance of getting 2000 hits cannot exceed $.98^{3.42}$. If he is 33 or older, his chances can't exceed .92 per year for any period of years.

2) If a player's offensive won-lost percentage is below .500, his chance of continuing toward a goal cannot exceed .75 per season.

3) If a player's offensive won-lost percentage is above .500, and if he is within four years of the goal, then his chance of continuing to proceed to the goal can't be less

than .75 per season regardless of age. If his won-lost percentage is over .400, it cannot be less than .600 per season. For example, although Pete Rose was 41 years old in 1982, since his won-lost percentage is over .400, and he is only 1.73 years away from Ty Cobb's career hit record, his chance must be at least $.60^{1.73}$, or 41%. If the player's offensive won-lost percentage is above .600, his chance must be at least .80 per year if the goal is within four years.

5. **Value Approximation Method**.

The value approximation method has 13 rules for non-pitchers, 5 for pitchers. These are:

NONPITCHERS:

1) Award 1 point if the player has played at least 10 games, 2 if 50 or more, 3 if 100 or more, 4 if 130 or more.

2) Award 1 point if the player has hit .250 or more, 2 if .275 or more, 3 if .300 or more . . . 7 if .400 or more.

3) Award 1 point if the player's slugging percentage is above .300, 2 if above .400, 3 if above .500 . . . 6 if above .800.

4) Award 1 point if the player has a HR% (HR/AB) of 2.5 or more, 2 if 5.0 or more, 3 if 7.5 or more, 4 if 10.0 or more.

5) Award 1 point if the player walks 1 time for each 10 official at-bats, 2 if 2 times for each 10 AB, 3 if 3 times for each 10 AB.

6) Award 1 point if the player steals 20 bases, 2 if 50, 3 if 80.

7) Award 1 point if the player drives in 70 runs while slugging less than .400, 1 point if he drives in 100 while slugging less than .500, or 1 if he drives in 130 while slugging less than .600.

8) Award 1 point if the player's primary defensive position is second base, third base or center field, 2 if it is shortstop. For catchers, award 1 point if the player catches 10 games, 2 if he catches 80, 3 if he catches 150.

9) Award 1 point if the player's range factor is above the league average at his position. Catchers and first basemen have no range factors; first basemen get 1 point if they have 100 assists or more.

10) Award 1 point if the player's fielding average is above the league average at his position.

(On points 9 and 10, if you are figuring a player over the course of his career, you will probably wish to establish period norms for range factor and fielding range rather than trying to figure the league average in each separate year.)

11) Award 1 point to a shortstop or second baseman who participates in 90 or more double plays, two for 120 or more double plays and three for 150 or more double plays. Award 1 point to an outfielder who has 12 or more assists plus double plays. Award 1 to a catcher who is better than the league average in opposition stolen-base rate.

12) Award 1 point if the player has 200 hits. Award 1 point if the player leads the league in RBI.

13) Reduce all points awarded on rules 1 through 12 for players who have less than 500 at-bats and less than 550 at-bats plus walks. Reduce by the formula **at-bats/500** or **(at-bats plus walks)/550**, whichever is larger for the player.

When figuring *career* value approximations, ignore rules 7 through 12. For defensive players, instead assign a verbal description to the player's defensive ability, and read his AV for the season off the chart below.

**POSITION**

| Description | 1B | LF | RF | 3B | CF | 2B | C | SS |
|---|---|---|---|---|---|---|---|---|
| Outstanding | 2.50 | 3.00 | 3.00 | 3.00 | 4.00 | 4.50 | 5.00 | 5.00 |
| Excellent | 2.30 | 2.75 | 2.75 | 3.00 | 3.50 | 4.00 | 4.50 | 4.50 |
| Very Good | 2.10 | 2.50 | 2.75 | 2.75 | 3.25 | 3.50 | 4.00 | 4.00 |
| Good | 2.00 | 2.50 | 2.50 | 2.75 | 3.00 | 3.20 | 3.50 | 3.50 |
| Above Average | 1.80 | 2.25 | 2.50 | 2.50 | 3.00 | 3.00 | 3.25 | 3.25 |
| Solid | 1.50 | 2.00 | 2.25 | 2.50 | 2.50 | 3.00 | 3.00 | 3.00 |
| Average | 1.25 | 2.00 | 2.00 | 2.25 | 2.50 | 2.50 | 3.00 | 3.00 |
| Below Average | 1.00 | 1.76 | 1.75 | 2.00 | 2.00 | 2.25 | 2.50 | 2.50 |
| Poor | .075 | 1.50 | 1.50 | 1.75 | 1.75 | 2.00 | 2.25 | 2.25 |
| Bad | 0.40 | 1.40 | 1.25 | 1.50 | 1.50 | 2.00 | 2.00 | 2.00 |
| The Worst Ever | 0.00 | 0.50 | 0.75 | 1.00 | 1.00 | 1.50 | 2.00 | 2.00 |

PITCHERS

1) Award 1 point if the pitcher has pitched in 30 or more games, 2 if 55 or more games, 3 if 80 or more.

2) Award 1 point if the pitcher has pitched 40 innings, 2 if 90 innings, 3 if 140 . . . . 7 if 340 innings.

3) Figure for the pitcher his total of 2 (wins plus saves) minus losses. Award 1 point if the total is 6 or more, 2 if 14 or more, 3 if 24, 4 if 36, 5 if 50, 6 if 66, 7 if 84.

4) Award 1 point if the pitcher has won 18 or more games. Award 1 point if the pitcher led the league in ERA. Award 1 point if the pitcher led the league in saves.

5) Subtract the pitcher's ERA from the league ERA, and add 1.00. Multiply this by the number of decisions that the pitcher has had, and divide by 13. (What you are doing here is giving credit for a low ERA. This will result in a negative figure—a subtraction—if the pitcher's ERA is more than one run above league. A pitcher's AV cannot be reduced below zero.)

6. **Park Adjustment Factors**.

**AMERICAN LEAGUE**

| | | | |
|---|---|---|---|
| Milwaukee | .97223 | California | 1.01191 |
| Baltimore | .95498 | Kansas City | 1.00659 |
| Boston | 1.08061 | Chicago White Sox | .99574 |
| Detroit | 1.02711 | Seattle | 1.02921 |
| New York Yankees | .96879 | Oakland | .95179 |
| Toronto | 1.04754 | Texas | .92285 |
| Cleveland | .99617 | Minnesota | 1.01785 |

**NATIONAL LEAGUE**

| | | | |
|---|---|---|---|
| St. Louis | 1.00465 | Atlanta | 1.08770 |
| Philadelphia | 1.01407 | Los Angeles | .96939 |
| Montreal | .99340 | San Francisco | .96516 |
| Pittsburgh | 1.03921 | San Diego | .92776 |
| Chicago Cubs | 1.09466 | Houston | .92910 |
| New York Mets | .97908 | Cincinnati | 1.00724 |

7. **Cheap Victory**.

A cheap victory, for purposes of discussion, is a game in which the pitcher receives credit for a win despite having a game-ERA higher than 4.00, with the following exceptions:

1) A victory should not be labeled cheap on the basis of runs allowed in the late innings which do not endanger the lead. Ignore any runs allowed from the seventh inning on which do not enable the opposition to pull within four runs of a tie.

2) Before figuring the game-ERA, deduct one run for each run that the pitcher himself has driven in or scored.

8. **How The Defensive Ratings Are Derived**.

As I have explained, each defensive player's DW/L% (defensive won-lost percentage) is based on four considerations which differ from position to position. The maximum point levels are deliberately set at almost impossible levels, since for a player to attain those standards would indicate that he was performing at such a level that he should never lose, which is presumed to be as impossible for a fielder as it is for a hitter or a pitcher. In order to receive the maximum 40 points, a catcher must throw out every base runner who attempts to steal against him; a shortstop, to receive the maximum 20 points for fielding average, would have to field 1.000.

The explanation from that point consists of three charts. Chart I explains what the defensive factors considered are. Chart II sketches out the standards for performance evaluation. Chart III explains how these are combined at each position.

## CHART I

WHAT THINGS ARE CONSIDERED

*For Catchers*: The 40 point consideration is opposition stolen bases per game, divided by league opposition stolen bases per game. The 30 point consideration is the ERA of his staff when he is in the lineup, compared to the league ERA. The 20 point consideration is fielding average. The 10 point consideration is assists per game.

*For First Basemen*: The 40 point consideration is fielding average. The 30 point consideration is assists per game. The 20 point consideration is an estimate of the number of 3-6-3 double plays turned by the team, an estimate formed by taking the team's double-play total and subtracting all double plays involving a second baseman or outfielder. The 10 point consideration (E 5 & 6) is the number of errors turned by the team's third basemen and shortstops, the theory being that a good first baseman can prevent E 5 & 6 by picking out bad throws.

*For Second Basemen:* The 40 point consideration is double-play percentage (DP %), which is figured by taking the number of double plays turned by the player, dividing by the number of games played, and dividing that by the number of hits plus walks per game allowed by the team. This adjusts raw double-play rates for the number of men on base. The 30 point consideration is range factor, minus double plays per game (RF − DP/G); we don't want to give overlapping credit for the one skill. The 20 point consideration is fielding average. *The 10 point consideration for all players other than first basemen and catchers is the defensive efficiency record of the team for which the fielder plays.*

*For Third Basemen*: the 40 point consideration is range factor. The 30 point consideration is fielding percentage. The 20 point consideration is DP%.

*For Shortstops*: the 40 point consideration is RF − DP/G. The 30 point consideration is DP%. The 20 point consideration is fielding percentage.

*For Outfielders*: the 40 point consideration is range factor. The 30 point consideration is fielding percentage. The 20 point consideration is the player's career record of assists per 162 outfield games played. (While I am not going to take the space this year to document the statement, the notion that some outfielders have high assists totals because they have bad arms and a lot of people are running on them is sheer nonsense. It is certainly true that single season assists totals can be very misleading, but if assists records are looked at over a period of years, it is marvelously clear that outfielders who have good arms throw out many more runners than outfielders who have poor arms.)

## CHART II

WHAT THE STANDARDS ARE

The standards in this chart are derived from an extensive examination of the fielding records of major league leaders over the last ten years. The middle of each chart represents an average performance over that period; anything above 75% represents an unusual performance. It should be stressed that fielding statistics, like all others, change from decade to decade; these statistics, while they might be useful in evaluating fielders from other eras, were not designed for that purpose and in some cases would yield very misleading results if lifted out of their time.

To save space, each notch of the chart is not detailed; if you want to use it, some interpolation will be required.

## POSITION

| Standard | Catcher | First Base | Second Base | Third Base | Shortstop | Left and Right Field | Center |
|---|---|---|---|---|---|---|---|
| 40 | .00 | 1.0000(*2) | .0884 | 3.91 | 5.65 | 3.41 | 3.81 |
| 35 | .25 | .9994 | .0706 | 3.60 | 5.15 | 2.82 | 3.35 |
| 30 | .50 | .9973 | .0639 | 3.31 | 4.76 | 2.54 | 3.11 |
| 25 | .75 | .9950 | .0575 | 3.01 | 4.45 | 2.27 | 2.87 |
| 20 | 1.00 | .9928 | .0516 | 2.77 | 4.05 | 2.00 | 2.63 |
| 15 | 1.25 | .9906 | .0459 | 2.55 | 3.70 | 1.80 | 2.44 |
| 10 | 1.50 | .9878 | .0388 | 2.27 | 3.46 | 1.65 | 2.20 |
| 5 | 1.75 | .9846 | .0310 | 1.98 | 3.12 | 1.48 | 1.95 |
| 1 | 1.95 | .9790 | .0164 | 1.70 | 2.93 | 1.29 | 1.57 |
| | | | | | | | |
| 30 | −1.50 | 1.14 | 6.02 | 1.000 | .0760 | 1.000(*3) | 1.000(*4) |
| 25 | − .65 | .94 | 5.34 | .985 | .0642 | .998 | .996 |
| 20 | − .25 | .78 | 4.93 | .970 | .0575 | .990 | .991 |
| 15 | ± .00 | .63 | 4.53 | .955 | .0497 | .983 | .986 |
| 10 | + .25 | .46 | 4.16 | .940 | .0422 | .969 | .976 |
| 5 | + .65 | .31 | 3.65 | .925 | .0348 | .954 | .965 |
| 1 | +1.33 | .10 | 2.99 | .909 | .0302 | .938 | .955 |
| | | | | | | **ALL OUTFIELDERS** | |
| | | | | | | **Over 400 G** | **Under 400 G** |
| 20 | 1.000(*1) | 73 | 1.000 | .0227 | 1.000 | 16.2 | 22.4 |
| 15 | .994 | 48 | .990 | .0182 | .981 | 13.2 | 16.4 |
| 10 | .986 | 32 | .980 | .0141 | .966 | 10.4 | 10.6 |
| 5 | .997 | 15 | .970 | .0104 | .950 | 8.8 | 7.6 |
| 1 | .968 | 3 | .955 | .0057 | .931 | 4.7 | 1.5 |
| | | | | | | | |
| 10 | 1.02 | 29 | | | .727 | | |
| 7 | .70 | 44 | | | .706 | | |
| 5 | .52 | 53 | | | .694 | | |
| 3 | .34 | 63 | | | .682 | | |
| 1 | .05 | 72 | | | .663 | | |

*1: minimum 100 games played
*2: minimum .80 assists per game
*3: minimum 2.40 range factor
*4: minimum 3.00 range factor

## CHART III

HOW THESE ARE COMBINED

The player's scores on these four counts are added together and become, with the insertion of a decimal point, his defensive won-lost percentage. These percentages are multiplied by a number of "games" which differs according to the position. Per 162 games played, the defensive games assigned to each position are:

| 1B | LF | RF | 3B | CF | 2B | C | SS |
|---|---|---|---|---|---|---|---|
| 3 | 4 | 5 | 6 | 6 | 8 | 10 | 11 |

This yields a number of defensive wins and losses. These are added to the offensive wins and losses to obtain the player ratings used in Part III.